Why Do You Need This New Edition?

If you're wondering why you should buy this edition of *The Effective Reader*, here are 6 good reasons!

1. Review each chapter on-the-go with our new *Chapter Review Cards*. Easy to tear out and take with you wherever you need to study—on the bus, at your job, in the library—*Chapter Review Cards* boil each chapter down to the fundamentals, making them the perfect tool to check your comprehension or prepare for an exam.

2. Understand what you need to learn with *Learning Outcomes* at the beginning of each chapter. New Learning Outcomes begin each chapter to help you focus on the key skills you need to learn to understand and apply to become an effective reader.

3. Write about what you read with new *What Do You Think?* writing prompts. How can you raise awareness for environmental issues? Should colleges address the problem of binge drinking? In short, what do *you* think about today's issues? Throughout the book, new *What Do You Think?* questions challenge you to respond to today's issues as explored in our longer reading selections at the end of each chapter and in Part Two: Additional Readings.

4. Explore new topics in our many new readings. New topics include building good communication skills, developing good study skills, participating in your community, managing your finances, and many more! With over 25 percent of the readings and accompanying activities new to the edition, you will find topics that help you build new skills to master not only reading, but your life.

5. Master finding the main idea and its supporting details. The table of contents has been rearranged to teach these related topics in order—making it easier for you to learn these fundamental skills.

6. Take your reading online with our new *Connect to MyReadingLab* features. New *Connect to MyReadingLab* sections provide directions for accessing activities for additional practice on Pearson's MyReadingLab program.

Third Edition

The Effective Reader

D. J. Henry

Daytona State College

Longman

Boston   Columbus   Indianapolis   New York   San Francisco   Upper Saddle River
Amsterdam   Cape Town   Dubai   London   Madrid   Milan   Munich   Paris   Montreal   Toronto
Delhi   Mexico City   Sao Paulo   Sydney   Hong Kong   Seoul   Singapore   Taipei   Tokyo

Editor in Chief: Eric Stano
Senior Acquisitions Editor: Kate Edwards
Editorial Assistant: Lindsey Allen
Associate Development Editor: Erin Reilly
Senior Supplements Editor: Donna Campion
Marketing Manager: Tom DeMarco
Production Manager: Ellen MacElree
Project Coordination, Text Design, and Electronic Page Makeup: Nesbitt Graphics, Inc.
Cover Designer/ Manager: Wendy Ann Fredericks
Cover Photo: © Masterfile Corporation. All rights reserved.
Photo Researcher: Rona Tuccillo
Senior Manufacturing Buyer: Dennis J. Para
Printer and Binder: Quad/Graphics-Taunton
Cover Printer: Lehigh-Phoenix Color/Hagerstown

For permission to use copyrighted material, grateful acknowledgment is made to the copyright holders on pp. 751–753, which are hereby made part of this copyright page.

Library of Congress Cataloging-in-Publication Data

Henry, D. J. (Dorothy Jean)
  The effective reader / D.J. Henry. -- 3rd ed.
      p. cm.
  Includes index.
  ISBN 978-0-205-78088-4
  1. Reading (Higher education) 2. Critical thinking--Study and teaching
(Higher) 3. College readers. I. Title.
  LB2395.3.H48 2011
  428.4071'1--dc22
                            2010038328

Longman
is an imprint of

ISBN-0-205-78088-1

ISBN-13: 978-0-205-78088-4

ISBN-10: 0-205-82826-4

ISBN-13: 978-0-205-82826-5

Brief Contents

Detailed Contents

PART TWO

Additional Readings   607

Preface

Dear Colleagues:

The story of Annie Sullivan and Helen Keller is one of my favorite success stories. Annie patiently, lovingly tapped thousands of words into Helen's palm, knowing that Helen's stubborn rebellion would melt once the flame of knowledge was ignited. These two remarkable women and their teaching and learning relationship serve as reminders of two ideals: reading empowers an individual life, and our work as instructors is of great and urgent importance. Many of our students come to us needing to reinforce the basic skills that make effective reading and clear thinking possible. Too often they struggle with text structure and feel uncertain about their comprehension. However with solid instruction and guided practice, these students can discover the power and pleasure of reading. *The Effective Reader,* Third Edition, has been designed to address these challenges.

New to This Edition

The following changes have been made to *The Effective Reader*, Third Edition, to help students become effective readers and critical thinkers.

- **New order for the Main Ideas and Supporting Details Coverage.** Based on extensive feedback from instructors across the country, the order of presentation has been rearranged to bring the main ideas and supporting details coverage together, closer to the beginning of the book. The table of contents now progresses from Main Ideas to Implied Main Ideas, to Supporting Details—more in line with the way instructors nationwide present these topics. Of course, each chapter is still self-contained, allowing instructors to easily teach these important topics in any order they choose.

- **New chapter review cards.** New chapter review cards will make studying more accessible and efficient by distilling chapter content down to the fundamentals, helping students to quickly master the basics, to review their understanding on the go, or to prepare for upcoming exams. Because they're made of durable cardstock, students can keep these Review Cards for years to come and pull them out whenever they need a quick review.

- **New Learning Outcomes.** Each chapter now opens with learning outcomes keyed to Bloom's taxonomy. Learning outcomes help students to understand why they are learning the material and help them to set goals for their learning.

- **New "Connect to MyReadingLab" features.** New *Connect to MyReadingLab* sections offer specific activities tied to chapter content for use as lab activities or additional outside-of-class practice. Never search for an appropriate online activity again: *Connect to MyReadingLab* provides easy-to-follow click paths and descriptions of specific MyReadingLab activities and how they fit with chapter content.

- **More attention to the connection between reading and writing.** Part Two now opens with a 6-Step Reading/Writing Action Plan that encourages students to see reading as a chance to enter a conversation with the writer and helps students to see how the reading process and the writing process work together to help them participate in this conversation.

- **New "What Do You Think?" writing prompts.** Found at the end of longer reading selections throughout the book, our new "What Do You Think?" writing prompts challenge students to respond to the issues explored.

- **New Reading Level Indications in the Annotated Instructor's Edition.** The reading level of all selections within our Review and Mastery Tests, Additional Readings, and Combined Skills Tests are now indicated in the Annotated Instructor's Edition (levels are not indicated in the student edition).

- **New Longer Reading Selections.** In addition to eight new longer readings in Part Two, over 25 percent of the reading selections and accompanying pedagogy throughout the text have been revised, giving students new reading material that is lively, up to date, and thought-provoking.

- **New Design.** In addition to appearing more modern and mature, the new design visually clarifies the text's different features to help students navigate and find the content they are looking for with greater ease.

Guiding Principles

The Effective Reader, Third Edition, was written to develop in students the essential abilities that will enable them to become effective readers and critical thinkers.

Practice and Feedback

The best way *to learn* is *to do*. Thus, one of the primary aims of this text is to give students plentiful opportunities to practice, practice, practice! Every concept introduced in the book is accompanied by an **explanation** of the concept, an **example** with explanation of the example, and one or more **practice** exercises. Each chapter also contains **brief skill applications, four review tests, and four mastery tests.** Furthermore, a removable chapter review card is included for each chapter.

High-Interest Reading Selections

For many, enthusiasm for reading is stimulated by material that offers high-interest topics written in a fast-paced style. Every effort has been made to provide reading passages in examples, reviews, and tests that students will find lively and engaging. Topics are taken from issues arising out of popular culture and textbooks—some examples are gangs, movies, weight loss, sports figures, depression, interpersonal relationships, drug use, nutrition, inspirational and success stories, role models, stress management, and exercise—all written in active language using short, lively sentences. A special effort was made to include a variety of passages from textbooks across the curriculum.

Integration of the Reading Process and Reading Skills

Effective readers blend individual reading skills into a reading process such as SQ3R. Before reading, effective readers skim for new or key vocabulary or main ideas. They create study questions and make connections to their prior knowledge. During reading, effective readers check their comprehension. For example, they annotate the text. They notice thought patterns and the relationship between ideas. They read for the answers to the questions they created before reading. After reading, effective readers use outlines, concept maps, and summaries to review what they have read and deepen their understanding. Students are taught to integrate each skill into a reading process in Part One.

In Chapter 1, "A Reading System for Effective Readers," students are introduced to SQ3R. In every other Part One chapter, students actively apply SQ3R strategies in "Before Reading About" and "After Reading About" activities. "Before Reading About" activities are pre-reading exercises that appear at the beginning of each chapter. These activities guide the student to review important concepts studied in earlier chapters, build on prior knowledge, and preview upcoming material. "After Reading About" activities are review activities that appear after the review tests in each chapter. These activities guide the student to reflect upon his or her achievements and assume responsibility for learning. Since many students are visual learners, the "Before Reading About" and "After Reading About" activities are signaled with reading process icons.

Comprehensive Approach

The Effective Reader, Third Edition, offers several levels of learning. First, students are given an abundance of practice. They are able to focus on individual reading skills through a chapter-by-chapter workbook approach. In each chapter of Part One, Review Test 4 offers a multi-paragraph passage with items on all the skills taught up to that point. In addition, Chapter 1, "A Reading System for Effective Readers," teaches students how to apply their reading skills to the reading process before, during, and after reading by using SQ3R. Students also learn to apply all skills in combination in Part Two, "Additional Readings," and Part Three, "Combined-Skills Tests." The aim is to provide our students with varied and rich opportunities to learn and practice reading skills and to apply reading processes.

Textbook Structure

To help students become effective readers and critical thinkers, *The Effective Reader,* Third Edition, introduces the most important basic reading skills in Part One and then provides additional readings in Part Two, and combined-skills tests in Part Three.

Part One, Becoming an Effective Reader

Essential reading skills are introduced sequentially in Part One. Each chapter focuses on a particular skill.

- Chapter 1, "A Reading System for Effective Readers," guides students through the reading process. Stages of the SQ3R process are explained thoroughly, with ample opportunities for practice, review, and mastery. The aim is to show students how to apply the skills they acquire in each of the chapters before, during, and after reading.

- Chapter 2, "Vocabulary and Dictionary Skills," fosters vocabulary acquisition during reading by using a mnemonic technique: SAGE stands for **S**ynonyms, **A**ntonyms, **G**eneral context, and **E**xample. The chapter also develops language skills by demonstrating how to determine word meanings from prefixes, roots, and suffixes. Finally, the chapter offers instruction in dictionary skills.

- Chapter 3, "Stated Main Ideas," offers both verbal and visual strategies to enable students to see the building-block relationship among topics, main ideas, and supporting details and explains strategies to identify main ideas along with extensive practice in doing so. In addition, this chapter teaches students to identify the central idea of multi-paragraph passages.

- Chapter 4, "Implied Main Ideas and Implied Central Ideas," furthers students' understanding about the central idea of longer passages and the main idea by explaining unstated main ideas and unstated central ideas. The chapter offers extensive practice.

- Chapter 5, "Supporting Details," identifies the differences between major and minor details.

- Chapter 6, "Outlines and Concept Maps," reinforces the skills of locating main ideas and identifying major and minor supporting details. The chapter teaches the students the structure of a text by offering instruction and practice in the applications of outlines and concept maps.

- Chapter 7, "Transitions and Thought Patterns," introduces the fundamental thought patterns and the words that signal those patterns. Students are given numerous opportunities to practice identifying the signal words and their relationships to the thought patterns they establish. The chapter includes the time order, space order, listing, and classification patterns.

- Chapter 8, "More Thought Patterns," introduces more complex thought patterns and the words that signal those patterns. Just as in Chapter 7, students are given extensive practice opportunities. Chapter 8 introduces the comparison-and-contrast, cause-and-effect, generalization-and-example, and definition patterns.

- Chapter 9, "Fact and Opinion," explains the differences between fact and opinion and develops the higher-level thinking skills that enable students to separate fact from opinion through extensive practice.

- Chapter 10, "Tone and Purpose," continues the students' study of the importance of word choice and the author's purpose. Detailed instruction and extensive practice develop the students' ability to determine whether the author's purpose is to entertain, to inform, or to persuade.

- Chapter 11, "Inferences," carefully addresses the advanced skill of making inferences by dividing the necessary mental processes into units of activity. Students are taught the basic skills necessary to evaluate an author's purpose and choice of words.

- Chapter 12, "The Basics of Argument," teaches the fundamental logical thought process used to examine the author's claim and supports. Students learn to recognize the author's claim and to evaluate supports as adequate and relevant.

- Chapter 13, "Advanced Argument: Persuasive Techniques," offers extensive explanations and practice of several common biased arguments that use logical fallacies and propaganda techniques. The logical fallacies include personal attack, straw man, begging the question, either-or, false comparison, and false cause. The propaganda techniques covered are name-calling, testimonials, bandwagon, plain folks, card stacking, transfer, and glittering generalities.

Part Two, Additional Readings

Part Two is a collection of ten reading selections followed by skills questions designed to give students real reading opportunities and the opportunity to gauge their growth. This part begins with a key discussion about the relationship between reading and writing and offers a few pointers on basic writing skills. The readings, which include magazine articles and textbook excerpts, were chosen based on each one's likelihood to engage, encourage, and motivate readers. Each selection is followed by skills questions so that students can practice all the skills taught in Part One. The skills questions are followed by discussion and writing topics so that students can practice making connections among listening, speaking, reading, and writing.

Part Three, Combined-Skills Tests

Part Three is a set of ten reading passages and combined-skills tests. The purpose of this part is to offer students ample opportunities to apply reading skills and strategies and to become more familiar with standardized testing formats to help prepare them for exit exams, standardized reading tests, and future content course quizzes, tests, and exams.

Part Four, Reading Enrichment

Supplementary material is provided here for students to learn a process for reading informational graphics. Appendix A, "Reading Graphics in Textbooks," offers basic guidelines for reading and analyzing graphics, followed by specific examples and explanations of tables, line graphs, bar graphs, pie charts, diagrams, and pictograms.

Chapter Features

Each chapter in Part One has several important features that help students become effective readers.

Learning Outcomes: New to this edition, each chapter opens with learning outcomes to help students preview and assess their progress as they master chapter content.

"Before Reading About . . .": "Before Reading About . . ." activities appear at the beginning of Chapters 2–13 in Part One. These activities are pre-reading exercises based on SQ3R: they review important concepts studied in earlier chapters, build on prior knowledge, and preview the chapter. The purpose of "Before Reading About . . ." is to actively teach students to develop a reading process that applies individual reading skills as they study.

"After Reading About . . .": "After Reading About . . ." activities appear after Review Test 4 in Chapters 2–13 of Part One. Based on SQ3R, "After Reading About . . ." activities teach students to reflect on their achievements and assume responsibility for their own learning. These activities ask students reflective questions to check their comprehension of the skill taught in the chapter. Students learn to integrate individual reading skills into a reading process; they learn the value of reviewing material; and finally, students create a learning journal that enables them to see patterns in their behaviors and record their growth as readers.

Instruction, example, explanation, and practice: The chapter skill is broken down into components, and each component is introduced and explained. Instruction is followed by an example, an explanation of the example, and a practice. Each section has its own instruction, example, explanation, and practice exercises.

Textbook
Skills

Textbook Skills: In the last section in each chapter, students are shown the ways in which the skills they are learning apply to reading textbooks. These activities, signaled by the icon to the left, present material from a textbook reading and direct students to apply the chapter's skill to the passage or visual. In a concerted effort to prepare students to be effective readers in their content courses, activities that foster textbook skills across the curriculum are also carefully woven throughout the entire textbook. The Textbook Skills icon signals these activities.

Visual Vocabulary: The influence of technology and the media on reading is evident in the widespread use of graphics in newspapers, magazines, and textbooks. Throughout this textbook, visual vocabulary is presented as part of the reading process, and students interact with these visuals by completing captions or answering skill-based questions. The aim is to teach students to value photos, graphs, illustrations, and maps as important sources of information.

Applications: Brief applications give students a chance to apply each component of the reading skill as a strategy.

Review Tests: Each chapter has four Review Tests. Review Tests 1 through 3 are designed to give ample opportunity for practice with the specific skill taught in the chapter; Review Test 4 offers a multi-paragraph passage with combined-skills questions based on all the skills taught up to and including that particular chapter. Review Tests 3 and 4 also give "What Do You Think?" writing prompts so that teachers have the opportunity to guide students as they develop critical thinking skills.

Mastery Tests: Each chapter includes four Mastery Tests. Most of the Mastery Tests are based on excerpts from science, history, psychology, social science, and literature textbooks.

Chapter Review Cards: New to this edition, a chapter review card is included for each chapter. The chapter review card serves as a comprehensive check for the reading concepts being taught.

The Longman Teaching and Learning Package

The Effective Reader, Third Edition, is supported by a series of innovative teaching and learning supplements. Ask your Pearson sales representative for a copy, or download the content at **www.pearsonhighered.com/irc.** Your sales representative will provide you with the username and password to access these materials.

The **Annotated Instructor's Edition (AIE)** is a replica of the student text, with all answers included. ISBN 0-205-82826-4.

The **Instructor's Manual,** prepared by Mary Dubbé of Thomas Nelson Community College, features teaching strategies for each textbook chapter, plus additional readings that engage students with a variety of learning styles and encourage active learning through class, group, and independent practices. Each chapter includes an introduction designed to hook the students, reproducible handouts, and study-strategy cards. Also included are a ten-item quiz for each chapter and a summary of corresponding activities in the Companion Website. A supplemental section provides a sample syllabus, readability calculations for each reading in *The Effective Reader,* Third Edition, five book quizzes to encourage independent reading and the creation of book groups, sample THEA and Florida State Exit Exams, and a scaffolded book review form. ISBN 0-205-82828-0.

The **Lab Manual**, prepared by Mary Dubbé of Thomas Nelson Community College, is designed as a student workbook and provides a collection of 65 activities that provide additional practice, enrichment, and assessment for the skills presented in *The Effective Reader,* Third Edition. The activities for each chapter include practice exercises, one review test, and two mastery tests that mirror the design of *The Effective Reader,* Third Edition, and emphasize the reading skills and applications students need in order to succeed in college. The lab activities give students realistic practice, encourage them to use the strategies they have learned, and offer an opportunity for students to continue to build a base of general, background knowledge. This lab manual can be used to strengthen students' reading skills, to allow them to assess their own progress, and to measure their success and readiness for college level reading. The lab manual is available packaged with *The Effective Reader,* Third Edition, for an additional cost. ISBN 0-205-82827-2.

MyReadingLab is a website specifically created for developmental students that provides diagnostics, practice tests, and reporting on student reading skills and reading levels.

Acknowledgments

As I worked on the third edition of this reading series, I felt an overwhelming sense of gratitude and humility for the opportunity to serve the learning community as a textbook author. I would like to thank the entire Longman team for their dedication to providing the best possible materials to foster literacy. To every person, from the editorial team to the representatives in the field, all demonstrate a passion for students, teachers, and learning. It is a joy to be part of such a team. Special thanks are due to the following: Kate Edwards, Acquisitions Editor, and Erin Reilly, Developmental Editor, for their guidance and support; Kathy Smith with Nesbitt Graphics, Inc. for her tireless devotion to excellence; Ellen MacElree and the entire production team for their work ethic and gracious attitudes, including Genevieve Coyne. I would also like to thank Mary Dubbé for authoring the Lab Manual and the Instructor's Manual that supplement this reading series.

For nearly twenty-five years, I worked with the most amazing group of faculty from across the State of Florida as an item-writer, reviewer, or scorer of state-wide assessment exams for student learning and professional certification. The work that we accomplished together continues to inform me as a teacher, writer, and consultant. I owe a debt of gratitude to this group who sacrificed much for the good of our students.

I would also like to acknowledge two of my colleagues at Daytona Beach State College: Dustin Weeks, Librarian, and Sandra Offiah-Hawkins, reading professor. As Tennyson extols in "Ulysses," these are the "souls that have toiled, and wrought, and thought with me."

Finally, I would like to gratefully recognize the invaluable insights provided by the following colleagues and reviewers. I deeply appreciate their investment of time and energy: Julia Erben, Gulf Coast Community College; Sondra Grove, Portland Community College; Valerie Hennen, Gateway Technical School; Valerie Hicks, The Community College of Baltimore County; Martha Hofstetter, Delaware Technical & Community College; Debbie McCarty, MCC–Maple Woods; Vicki Raine, MCC Penn Valley; Frederia Whitlow Sampson, Albany Technical College; and Jacquelyn Warmsley, Tarrant County College.

D .J. Henry
Daytona Beach, Florida

PART ONE

Becoming an Effective Reader

A Reading System for Effective Readers

1

LEARNING OUTCOMES

After studying this chapter you should be able to do the following:

1. Define prior knowledge.
2. Discuss the three phases of the reading process.
3. Describe and illustrate SQ3R.
4. Explain your reading process.
5. Assess your comprehension of prior knowledge and the reading process.
6. Evaluate the importance of prior knowledge and SQ3R.
7. Activate prior knowledge and apply SQ3R to your reading process.
8. Develop textbook skills: Ask and answer questions before, during, and after reading.

Many people think that reading involves simply passing our eyes over words in the order that they appear on the page. But reading is much more than that. Once we understand the **reading process**, we can follow specific steps and apply strategies that will make us effective readers. The most important aspect of being an effective reader is being an active reader.

Reading is an active process during which you draw information from the text to create meaning. When you understand what you've read, you've achieved **comprehension** of the material.

> **Comprehension** is an understanding of what has been read.

Active reading means that you ask questions, find answers, and react to an author's ideas. Before we examine the reading process in detail, it is important to talk about the role of prior knowledge.

Prior Knowledge

We all have learned a large body of information throughout a lifetime of experience. This body of information is called **prior knowledge**.

Knowledge is gained from experience and stored in memory. Every day, our prior knowledge is expanded by what we experience. For example, a small child hears the word *hot* as her father blows on a spoonful of steaming soup. The hungry child grabs for the bowl and cries as some of the hot liquid spills on her hand. The child has learned and will remember the meaning of *hot*.

Prior knowledge is the large body of information that is learned throughout a lifetime of experience.

The following graphic illustrates specific ways to connect to prior knowledge in each phase of the reading process. Connecting to prior knowledge increases comprehension.

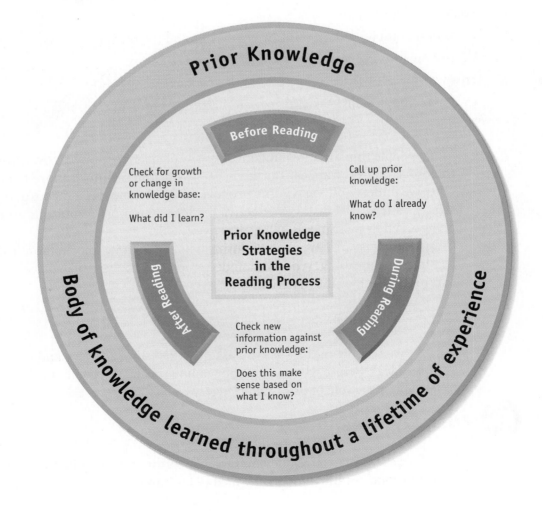

EXAMPLE Read the following paragraph. In the space provided, list any topics from the paragraph about which you already have prior knowledge.

Physical and Mental Fitness

Just as physical exercise builds up the body, mental exercise builds the mind. None of us expects to be able to suddenly run a marathon or lift heavy weights without training. And our bodies rarely take on that lean, toned look without physical effort. However, as we exercise our bodies, they become stronger and leaner. Likewise, as we exercise our minds through reading and writing, our mental abilities become stronger and more efficient.

_____

_____

EXPLANATION If you know about psychology and the issues linked to mental well-being, then this paragraph makes more sense to you than it would to someone who does not understand the complexity suggested by the expression "mental fitness." However, even if you do not know much about psychology, you may have helpful prior knowledge about some of the other ideas in the passage. For example, most of us have seen the effects of working out on the human body. Either we know someone who is dedicated to physical fitness, or we have that goal ourselves. We understand that physical fitness comes from hard work and commitment. People who stay in shape work out on a regular basis. Our prior knowledge about physical fitness helps us understand the kind of commitment we must make to our own mental fitness.

The more prior knowledge we have about a topic, the more likely we are to understand that topic. The more you know, the easier it is to learn. This is why effective readers build their knowledge base by reading often!

Active readers call up prior knowledge by using questions. The following practice will prepare you to use questions before you read. You will study this skill in more depth in the next section.

PRACTICE 1

Textbook
Skills

Read the following paragraph from a college health textbook. Then answer the questions that follow it.

Toxic Fumes: Cigarette Smoke

[1]Most of the compounds in cigarette smoke are gaseous, and many of them are toxic. [2]By far the most hazardous of these gases is carbon

monoxide, the same gas that is emitted from the exhaust pipe of a car. [3]The difference is that there are community or statewide standards to keep carbon monoxide auto emissions within a safe level, whereas no standards exist for cigarette smoke. [4]The amount of carbon monoxide that stays in a smoker's blood is related to activity levels. [5]During the day, carbon monoxide remains in the blood for two to four hours; during sleep, however, it remains for up to eight hours.

—Adapted from Pruitt & Stein, *Health Styles*, 2nd ed., p. 185.

1. What did you already know about carbon monoxide? That is, what was your prior knowledge? _____

_____

2. What did you already know about cigarette smoke? _____

_____

3. When you think of carbon monoxide, what do you think of? Describe ideas and experiences that come to mind. _____

_____

4. When you think of cigarette smoke, what do you think of? Describe ideas and experiences that come to mind. _____

_____

5. Was this an easy passage to understand? How does your prior knowledge affect your understanding of this passage? _____

_____

6. List any parts of the passage you had no prior knowledge of: _____

_____

 ## The Reading Process

Triggering prior knowledge is a reading skill that you as an active reader can turn into a reading strategy by using it as you read. **Reading** is best described as a process defined by three distinct phases. Each phase has its own thinking steps. SQ3R is a reading system that connects to prior knowledge and offers strategies for each phase of the reading process. The following graphic illustrates the phases of the reading process through SQ3R. Effective readers repeat or move among phases as needed to repair comprehension.

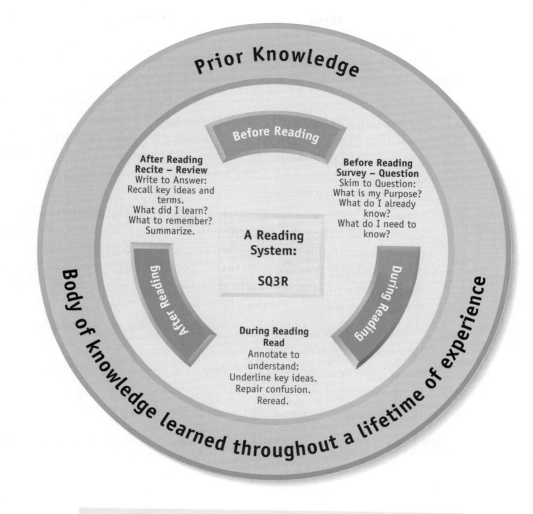

SQ3R stands for Survey, Question, Read, Recite, and Review.

Before Reading: Survey and Question

Survey

Quickly look over, or **skim,** the reading passage for clues about how it is organized and what it is going to talk about or teach you.

To skim effectively, look at *italic* and **bold** type and take note of titles, the introduction, and headings. Also look at pictures and graphs. Finally, read the first paragraph, summaries, and questions. Each of these clues provides important information.

Question

To aid in comprehension, ask questions before you read. The following list of prereading questions can be used in most reading situations:

- What is the passage about? The answer to this question will lead you to the main point the author is making. Sometimes the author will state the main idea in a topic sentence; other times the main idea will be implied. Chapter 3 gives in-depth instruction and practice on identifying and locating stated main ideas, and Chapter 4 teaches how to grasp main ideas that are not stated but only implied.

- How is the material organized? The answer to this question will help you identify and follow the thought pattern the author has used so that the ideas flow smoothly and logically. Chapters 7 and 8 offer detailed explanations about and practice with the following thought patterns: time, space, listing, classification, comparison and contrast, cause and effect, generalization and example, and definition and example.

- What do I already know about this idea? (What is my prior knowledge?)

- What is my purpose for reading?

- What is my reading plan? Do I need to read everything, or can I just skim for the information I need?

- What are the most important parts to remember?

EXAMPLE Before you read the following passage word for word, look over the passage and fill in the following information.

1. What is the passage about? _____

_____

2. What do I already know about this topic? _____

_____

3. What is my purpose for reading? That is, why am I reading this? What do I need to remember? _____

_____

_____

4. What ideas in the passage are in *italics* or in **bold** type? _____

_____

_____

The Problems of Designer Drugs

**Textbook
Skills**

Designer drugs are produced in chemical laboratories or made in homes and sold illegally. These drugs are easy to produce from available raw material. The drugs themselves were once technically legal because the law had to specify the exact chemical structure of an illegal drug. However, there is now a law in place that bans all chemical cousins of illegal drugs.

Collectively known as **club drugs**, these dangerous substances include *Ecstasy*, *Special K*, and *Rohypnol*. Although users may think of them as harmless, research has shown that club drugs can produce a range of unwanted effects. Some of these effects include hallucinations, paranoia, amnesia, and in some cases, death. Some club drugs work on the same brain mechanisms as alcohol and therefore can dangerously boost the effects of both substances. Because the drugs are odorless and tasteless, people can easily slip them into drinks. Some of them have been associated with sexual assaults and for that reason are referred to as *date rape drugs*.

—Adapted from Donatelle,
Health, 5th ed., pp. 181–182.

EXPLANATION

1. What is the passage about? The title of the passage gives us a clue: "The Problems of Designer Drugs." So does the first paragraph. By quickly looking at the terms in *italic* and **bold** print, you can see that this passage is about the dangers of designer drugs, also known as club drugs.

2. What do I already know about this topic? This answer will vary for each of you. Some of you may know someone who has used or been a victim of designer drugs; thus you already know a great deal that will help you understand the details in this passage. Others may not have any experience with illegal drugs. Yet most of you probably know someone who has struggled with alcoholism or misuse of legal drugs. So you can connect your experience to the information in the passage.

3. What is my purpose for reading? I need to know what is so dangerous about designer drugs.

4. What are the words in *italic* and **bold** type? *Designer drugs, club drugs, Ecstasy, Special K, Rohypnol,* and *date rape drugs.* Simply by writing the highlighted words in a list, you have begun to summarize the author's main point (for more on summarizing, see pages 610–611).

Before Reading

To support the connection between reading skills and the reading process, Chapters 2 to 13 begin with activities to do before reading the chapter, called **Before Reading About**. . . . These activities apply a variety of surveying and questioning strategies. Sometimes, the activity directs you to review skills taught in previous chapters to trigger your memory for prior knowledge and to help you consider the relationship between individual skills. Other times, the activity asks you to skim the chapter and create questions that you can answer as you read about the skill. For example, in Chapter 3, "Before Reading About Stated Main Ideas" asks you to create several questions based on the learning outcomes. (Every chapter begins with a list of the main topics in the chapter, called the Learning Outcomes.)

During Reading: Read and Annotate

After you have surveyed and asked questions about the text, it's time to read the entire passage.

Read

As you read, think about the importance of the information by continuing to ask questions:

- Does this new information agree with what I already knew?
- Do I need to change what I thought I knew?
- What is the significance of this information? Do I need to remember this?

In addition to asking questions while you read, acknowledge and resolve any confusion as it occurs.

- Create questions based on the headings, subheadings, and words in **bold** type and *italics*.
- Reread the parts you don't understand.
- Reread when your mind drifts during reading.
- Read ahead to see if the idea becomes clearer.

- Determine the meaning of words from the context.
- Look up new or difficult words.
- Think about ideas even when they differ from your own.

Annotate

Make the material your own. Make sure you understand it by repeating the information.

- Create a picture in your mind or on paper.
- Mark your text by underlining, circling, or otherwise highlighting topics, key terms, and main ideas. (See pages 608–609 for more information about how to annotate a text.)
- Restate the ideas in your own words.
- Write out answers to the questions you created based on the headings and subheadings.
- Write a summary of the section or passage.

EXAMPLE

A. Before you read the following passage from a college science textbook, survey the passage and answer the following questions.

1. What is the passage about? _____

_____

2. What do I already know about this passage? What is my prior knowledge?

_____

_____

3. What is important about this passage? What do I need to remember?

_____

_____

4. What words in **bold** type will help me remember what I need to know?

_____

B. Once you have surveyed the information, read the passage. During reading, monitor your understanding: (1) highlight key words and ideas; (2) answer questions based on the ideas in **bold** print.

Textbook
Skills

5. What new or difficult words do I need to look up?

_____

_____

6. What is color resemblance?

_____

7. What are some examples of color resemblance?

_____

8. What is countershading?

_____

9. What is an example of countershading?

_____

Hiding to Live: Animal Camouflage

¹Animals in danger of being hunted and killed have evolved ways to camouflage themselves. ²Perhaps the simplest type of camouflage is **color resemblance**, in which an animal's color matches the color of its background. ³Color resemblance is illustrated by green aphids that live on vegetation, gray-brown lizards inhabiting sandy areas, and black beetles that cling to the bark of trees.

⁴Another type of camouflage is **countershading**. ⁵Without markings, an object will reflect more light—and appear lighter—on its top surface than on its bottom surface. ⁶This difference makes an animal stand out against its background. ⁷Countershading, or the placement of darker markings on the top of the animal, reduces the reflection and allows the animal to blend into its background. ⁸For example, most fish are darkest on their top sides and consequently less visible when alive than when dead and floating belly up.

—Adapted from Maier, _Comparative Animal Behavior: An Evolutionary and Ecological Approach_, pp. 148–149.

EXPLANATION

A. Before Reading: Survey and Question

  1. What is the passage about? Types of camouflage used by animals

  2. What do I already know about this passage? What is my prior knowledge? Answers will vary.

  3. What is important about this passage? What do I need to remember? Wording will vary: the ways in which camouflaging helps an animal survive

  4. What words are in **bold** type? Color resemblance and countershading

B. During Reading: Read and Annotate

  5. What are the new or difficult words I need to look up? Answers will vary.

  6. What is color resemblance? A type of camouflage in which an animal's color matches the color of its background

7. What are some examples of color resemblance? <u>Green aphids, gray-brown lizards, and black beetles</u>

8. What is countershading? <u>Markings on the top of the animal that are darker than those on the bottom</u>

9. What is an example of countershading? <u>Most fish</u>

10. Identify any ideas you needed to reread to understand. <u>Answers will vary.</u>

After Reading: Recite and Review

Once you have read the entire selection, go back over the material to review and respond to it.

Recite

As part of your review, take time to think and write about what you have read.

- Connect new information to your prior knowledge about the topic.
- Form opinions about the material and the author.
- Record changes in your opinions based on the new information.
- Write about what you have read. What do you think about what you have read?

Review

- Summarize the most important parts (for more information about how to summarize, see pages 610–611).
- Revisit and answer the questions raised by headings and subheadings.
- Review new words and their meanings based on the way they were used in the passage.

PRACTICE 2

Now that you have learned about each of the three phases of the reading process, practice putting all three together. Think before, during, and after reading. Apply SQ3R to the following passage. Remember the steps:

- **Survey:** Look over the whole passage.
- **Question:** Ask questions about the content. Predict how the new information fits in with what you already know about the topic.

■ **Read:** Continue to question, look up new words, reread, and create pictures in your mind.

■ **Recite:** Restate the ideas in your own words. Take notes: Write out questions and answers, definitions of words, and new knowledge.

■ **Review:** Think about what you have read and written. Use writing to capture your opinions and feelings about what you have read.

Before Reading: Survey and Question

Skim the passage from a college history textbook, and answer the following questions:

1. What is this passage about? _____

_____

_____

2. What do I already know about this information? _____

_____

3. What do I need to remember? _____

_____

4. What ideas are in *italics* and **bold** type? _____

_____

Before you go on: Use the words you listed in item 4 to create questions. Write the questions in the boxes beside the textbook passage. You will write your answers in these same boxes during reading.

During Reading: Read and Annotate

Textbook
Skills

As you read, highlight key ideas and answer the questions you created from the ideas in **bold** and *italic* type.

5. _____

_____

_____

_____

_____

Age and Opinion in American Politics and Public Opinion

[1]Age group differences in politics and public opinion are sometimes referred to as the **generation gap**. [2]In many cases, older people seem to be more conservative than younger people. [3]For example, older people are less likely to be in favor of legalizing marijuana. [4]Younger people in general seem to

6. _____

_____

_____

_____

7. _____

_____

_____

8. _____

_____

_____

be less interested in politics than their elders. [5]For example, younger people are less likely to keep up with political news. [6]They are also less likely to vote.

[7]How can we explain this generation gap in politics and public opinion? [8]The generation gap may be a product of **generational effects.** [9]This term describes the effect of historical events on the views of the people who lived through them. [10]For example, the *Great Depression generation,* who grew up in the 1930s, may give greater support to Social Security because of this experience. [11]The *baby boomers* were born in the high-birthrate years following World War II (1946–1964); they lived through the civil rights movement, the Vietnam War, and changes in sexual morality. [12]These events may affect their views on many social issues.

—Adapted from Dye, *Politics in America,* 5th ed., pp. 148–149.

After Reading: Review

9. What other political and public opinion differences do you think may be

based on age differences? _____

_____

10. What are some of the historical events that could shape the views of

young people today? _____

_____

Applying the After Reading Step: "After Reading" Activities

To reinforce the connection between reading skills and the reading process, Chapters 2 to 13 include sections called **"After Reading About . . ."** as a final comprehension check before the Mastery Tests. After you have completed the review tests, you will be asked questions that focus your studies. Your written answers to these questions can become an important learning log or journal that tracks your increasing strengths.

Asking Questions and Recording Answers Before, During, and After Reading

A vast number of textbooks use titles, headings, **bold** print, and *italics* to organize ideas. An effective reader applies the questioning and reciting steps to these pieces of information. For example, before reading, notice titles and headings. Use titles and headings to create questions. Write these questions out. During or after reading, write out the answers to these questions. After reading, use the questions and answers as a review quiz.

EXAMPLE Before you read the following passage from a college communications textbook, skim the information and write out five questions based on the title and words in **bold** print. After you read, answer the questions you created before you read.

Three Ways to Organize Perception

[1]**Perception** is the process by which you become aware of objects, events, and, especially, people through your *senses*: sight, smell, taste, touch, and hearing. [2]Perception is an active, not passive, process. [3]Your perceptions result from what exists in the outside world and from your own experiences, desires, needs and wants, loves and hatreds. [4]Three interesting ways in which people organize their perceptions are by rules, by schemata, and by scripts.

Organization by Rules

[5]One often used rule is that of *proximity*, or physical closeness. [6]The **rule,** simply stated, says that things that are physically close together make up a *unit*. [7]Thus, using this rule, you would perceive people who are often together, or messages sent one right after the other, as units, as belonging together. [8]For example, when you see a person nod her head and at the same time say yes, you think of the two messages (the nod and the yes) as one unit.

Organization by Schemata

[9]Another way you organize material is by creating schemata. [10]**Schemata** are mental patterns or structures. [11]These *patterns of thought* help you sort out and make sense of the millions of items of information you come into contact with every day as well as those you already have in memory. [12]Schemata may thus be viewed as general ideas

about people, yourself, or social roles. [13]You develop schemata from your own experiences. [14]These experiences include actual as well as vicarious experience gained from television, reading, and hearsay. [15]For example, you may have developed schemata about college athletes, and this might include that they are strong and ambitious.

Organization by Scripts

[16]A **script** is really a type of schema. [17]Like a schema, a script is an organized body of information about some action, event, or procedure. [18]It's a general idea of how some event should play out or unfold; it's the rules governing the events and their sequence. [19]For example, you probably have a script for how you do laundry.

—Adapted from DeVito, *Essentials of Human Communication*, pp. 55–57
© 2002. Reproduced by permission of Pearson Education, Inc.

1. Question: _____

_____

Answer: _____

_____

2. Question: _____

_____

Answer: _____

_____

3. Question: _____

_____

Answer: _____

_____

4. Question: _____

_____

Answer: _____

_____

5. Question: _____

_____

Answer: _____

_____

EXPLANATION Compare your questions and answers to the ones given here.

1. Question: What are the three ways to organize perception?

Answer: Three interesting ways in which people organize their perceptions are by rules, by schemata, and by scripts. (Note that this sentence is the main idea of the passage.)

2. Question: What is perception, and what is an example of it?

Answer:

Definition: Perception is an active process by which you become aware of objects, events, and, especially, people through your *senses*: sight, smell, taste, touch, and hearing.

Example: Ways in which people organize their perceptions are by rules, by schemata, and by scripts

3. Question: What is proximity, and what is an example of it?

Answer:

Definition: Proximity means physical closeness.

Example: Words and gestures that follow closely such as nodding the head and saying yes are seen as one unit.

4. Question: What are schemata, and what is an example of them?

Answer:

Definition: Schemata are mental patterns or structures; patterns of thought.

Example: general ideas about what athletes are like

5. Question: What is a script, and what is an example of it?

Answer:

Definition: A script is a general idea of how some event should play out; the rules governing the events and their sequence.

Example: how one does laundry

The phrase "three ways" suggests a list. And the list includes special terms, definitions of the terms, and examples of the terms. Thus the questions about the passage were created based on the terms in **bold** print and their definitions and examples, and then the answers were stated using the same pattern. By writing out the questions and answers in this way, you create an excellent study outline for later review. Not all passages give as much detail as the one used in this example; therefore, you must adapt your questions to the information in the passage.

PRACTICE 3

Before you read the following passage from a college psychology textbook, skim the information and write out three questions based on the title and words in **bold** print. During reading, annotate the text. After you read, answer the questions you created before you read.

Textbook
Skills

Neurons

[1]Every thought you think, every emotion you feel, every sensation you experience, every decision you reach, every move you make—in short, all of human behavior—is rooted in a biological event. [2]The story begins where the action begins, in the smallest unit of the brain—the nerve cell, or neuron.

The Structure of the Neuron

[3]All of our thoughts, feelings, and behaviors can ultimately be traced to the activity of neurons—the specialized cells that conduct impulses through the nervous system. [4]Neurons perform several important tasks. [5]First, **afferent** (sensory) neurons relay messages from the sense organs and receptors—eyes, ears, nose, mouth, and skin—to the brain or spinal cord. [6]Second, **efferent** (motor) neurons convey signals from the central nervous system to the glands and the muscles, enabling the body to move. [7]And third, interneurons carry information between neurons in the brain and between neurons in the spinal cord.

[8]Although no two neurons are exactly alike, nearly all are made up of three important parts: the cell body, the dendrites, and the axon. [9]The **cell body**, or *soma*, contains the nucleus; the cell body carries out the metabolic, or life-sustaining, functions of a neuron. [10]Branching out from the cell body are the **dendrites**; they look much like the leafless branches of a tree (dendrite comes from the Greek word for "tree"). [11]The dendrites are the primary receivers of signals from other neurons, but the cell body can also receive signals directly. [12]Dendrites also do more than just receive signals from other neurons and relay them to the cell body.

[13]The **axon** is the slender, tail-like extension of the neuron that sprouts into many branches, each ending in a bulbous axon terminal. [14]Signals move from the axon terminals to the dendrites or cell bodies of other neurons and to muscles, glands, and other parts of the body.

—Adapted from Wood, et al., *Mastering the World of Psychology*,
Text from pp. 39–40 © 2008 Pearson Education, Inc.
Reproduced by permission of Pearson Education, Inc.

VISUAL VOCABULARY

The _____, the long slender projection of a neuron, conducts electrical impulses.

a. cell body
b. dendrites
c. axon

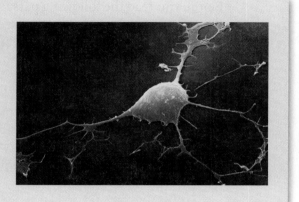

1. Question: _____

Answer: _____

_____

2. Question: _____

Answer: _____

_____

_____

_____

_____

3. Question: _____

Answer: _____

_____

APPLICATIONS

Textbook
Skills

Assume you have decided to major in hospitality management. The first reading assignment for the class gives you the opportunity to apply SQ3R. The following passage makes up the first two pages of a fifteen-page reading assignment from the textbook *Introduction to Hospitality Management*. Apply the full reading process to your reading of the passage. Follow the directions of each application: Before Reading, During Reading, and After Reading.

Application 1: Before Reading: Survey and Question.

Skim the passage; note headings and **bold** or *italic* type. Write a first response by answering the following: What do you already know? What are the key words and ideas? What do you need to learn? What is the most important idea?

_____

_____

_____

_____

Application 2: During Reading: Read and Annotate.

As you read, highlight key terms and ideas. Record questions or restate ideas in margin.

The Five Ages of Tourism

[1]The historical development of tourism has been divided into five distinct ages (or periods), four of which paralled the advent of a new means of transportation.
[2]Pre-Industrial Revolution (prior to 1840)
[3]The railway age
[4]The automobile age
[5]The jet aircraft age
[6]The cruise ship age

Pre-Industrial Revolution

[7]As early as 5,000 years ago, some ancient Egyptians sailed up and down the Nile River to visit and construct the pyramids. [8]Probably the first journey

ever made for the purposes of peace and tourism was made by Queen Hatshepsut to the Land of Punt (believed to be on the east coast of Africa) in 1480 B.C. [9]Descriptions of this tour have been recorded on the walls of the temple of Deir el-Bahri at Luxor. [10]These texts and bas-reliefs are among the world's rarest artworks and are universally admired for their wondrous beauty and artistic qualities. [11]The Colossi of Memnon at Thebes have on their pedestals the names of Greek tourists of the fifth century B.C. [12]The Phoenicians were among the first real travelers in any modern sense. [13]In both the Mediterranean and the Orient (now called Southeast Asia), travel was motivated by trade. [14]Later, the Roman Empire provided safe passage for travelers via a vast road system that stretched from Egypt to Britain. [15]Wealthy Romans traveled to Egypt and Greece, to baths, shrines, and seaside resorts. [16]The Romans were as curious as are today's tourists. [17]They visited the attractions of their time, trekking to Greek temples and places where Alexander the Great slept, Socrates lived, Ajax committed suicide, and Achilles was buried; the pyramids; the Sphinx; and the Valley of the Kings—just as today's tourists do. [18]The excavated ruins of the Roman town Pompeii, which was buried by the volcanic eruption of Mount Vesuvius, revealed some twenty-plus restaurants, taverns, and inns that tourists visit even today.

[19]The first Olympic Games for which we still have written records were held in 776 B.C. (though it is generally believed that the games had been going on for many years already). [20]Thus, sports has been a motivation for tourism for a long time.

[21]Medieval travel was mostly for religious or trade reasons. [22]People made pilgrimages to various shrines: Moslems to Mecca and Christians to Jerusalem and Rome. [23]The Crusades (which began in 1195 and lasted for the next two hundred years) stimulated a cultural exchange that was in part responsible for the Renaissance.

24Marco Polo (1254–1324) traveled the Silk Road, which was anything but a road as we know it, from Venice to Beijing. **25**He was the first European to journey all the way across Asia to Beijing, China, and his journey, which lasted twenty-four years, and the tales from it became the greatest travelogue.

26The journey was both difficult and dangerous (excerpts can be read at the several Marco Polo web sites). **27**One time, to make sure the Polo brothers would be given every assistance on their travels, Kublai Khan presented them with a golden tablet (or *paiza,* in Chinese, *gerege,* in Mongolian) a foot long and three inches wide inscribed with the words "By the strength of the eternal Heaven, holy be the Khan's name. **28**Let him that pays him not reverence be killed." **29**The golden tablet was a special VIP passport, authorizing the travelers to receive throughout the Great Khan's dominions such horses, lodging, food, and guides as they required. **30**This was an early form of passport.

—Walker, *Introduction to Hospitality Management,* 3rd ed., pp. 41–42.

Application 3: After Reading: Review and Recite

Now that you have read the passage, respond to what you have read. Use your questions and annotations to review and record ideas. In addition, take time to reflect about your reading process. Share your responses with a peer or small group of classmates.

A. State in a few sentences the most important ideas from the passage "The Five Ages of Tourism": _____

_____

_____

B. Describe the reading process you used to read this passage. Has your reading process changed? If so, how? If not, why not? _____

_____

_____

C. Make predictions. Based on the time it took you to read this passage, how much time do you think you need to read the entire fifteen-page assignment? What else do you expect to learn by completing the reading assignment? _____

_____

_____

REVIEW TEST 1

Score (number correct) _____ × 20 = _____%

Before Reading

Survey the following paragraph from a chapter summary of a college sociology textbook. Then, using the words in **bold** print, create at least five questions to guide your reading.

Textbook
Skills

Technology Is Linked to the Change
from One Type of Society to Another

[1]On their way to a postindustrial society, humans passed through four types of societies. [2]Each emerged from a social revolution. [3]And each revolution was linked to new technology. [4]First, the **domestication revolution** brought the pasturing of animals and the cultivation of plants. [5]Thus, **hunting** and **gathering societies** shifted into **pastoral** and **horticultural societies**. [6]Then the invention of the plow ushered in the **agricultural society**. [7]Machines that were powered by fuels brought about the **Industrial Revolution**. [8]And this revolution led to **industrial society**. [9]The computer chip ushered in a new type of society called **postindustrial** (or **information**) **society**. [10]Another new type of society, the **biotech society**, may be emerging.

—Adapted from Henslin, *Sociology: A Down to Earth Approach*,
Text from p. 174 © 2008 James M. Henslin. Reproduced
by permission of Pearson Education, Inc.

1. _____

2. _____

3. _____

VISUAL VOCABULARY

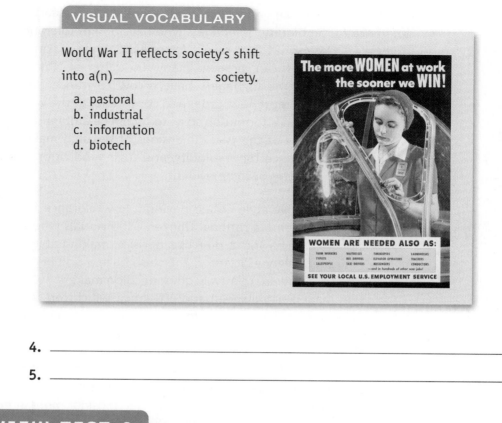

World War II reflects society's shift into a(n)——————— society.

a. pastoral
b. industrial
c. information
d. biotech

4. _____

5. _____

REVIEW TEST 2

Score (number correct) _____ × 25 = _____%

Using SQ3R, read the following passage from the college textbook *Introduction to Hospitality Management*. Then complete the study chart.

Decision-Making Styles

Textbook
Skills

[1]Decision makers differ in their way of thinking; some are rational and logical, whereas others are intuitive and creative. [2]Rational decision makers look at the information in order. [3]They organize the information and make sure it is logical and consistent. [4]Only after carefully studying all of the given options do they finally make the decision. [5]Intuitive thinkers, on the other hand, can look at information that is not necessarily in order. [6]They can make quick decisions based on their spontaneous creativity and intuition. [7]Although a careful analysis is still required, these types of people are comfortable looking at all solutions as a whole as opposed to studying each option separately.

[8]The second dimension in which people differ is each individual's **tolerance for ambiguity**. [9]Managers who have a high tolerance for ambiguity are lucky in that they save a lot of time while making a decision. [10]These individuals can process many thoughts at the same time. [11]Unfortunately, some managers have a low tolerance for ambiguity. [12]These individuals must have order and consistency in the way they organize and process the information so as to minimize ambiguity.

[13]Upon review of the two dimensions of decision making, ways of thinking and tolerance for ambiguity, and their subdivisions, four major decision-making styles become evident:

1. [14]The **directive style** entails having a low tolerance for ambiguity as well as being a rational thinker. [15]Individuals who fall into the category of having a directive decision-making style are usually logical and very efficient. [16]They also have a primary focus on the short run and are relatively quick decision makers. [17]Directive decision makers value speed and efficiency, which can cause them to be remiss in assessing all alternatives, such that decisions are often made with minimal information.

2. [18]Decision makers who have an **analytic style** of decision making have a large tolerance for ambiguity. [19]Compared to directive decision makers, these people require more information before making their decisions and, consequently, they consider more alternatives. [20]Individuals with an analytic style are careful decision makers, which gives them leeway to adapt or cope with unique situations.

3. [21]Decision makers who have a **conceptual style** of decision making look at numerous alternatives and are typically very broad in their outlook. [22]Their focus is on the long run of the decision made. [23]These individuals are typically creative and often find creative solutions to the problem with which they are dealing.

4. [24]Decision makers who work well with others are said to have a **behavioral style** of decision making. [25]This entails being receptive to suggestions and ideas from others as well as being concerned about the achievements of their employees. [26]They commonly communicate with their coworkers through meetings. [27]These individuals try to avoid conflict as often as possible, because acceptance by others is very important to them.

[28]At least one of these decision-making styles is always used by managers. [29]However, decision makers often combine two or more styles to

make a decision. [30]Most often a manager will have one dominant decision-making style and use one or more other styles as alternates. [31]Flexible individuals vary their decision-making styles according to each unique situation. [32]If the style is to consider riskier options (analytic style) or if the decision is made based on suggestions from subordinates (behavioral style), each style will eventually bring the decision maker to the optimal solution for the unique problem he or she is facing.

—Walker, *Introduction to Hospitality Management*, 3rd ed., pp. 565–567.

VISUAL VOCABULARY

The decision makers who have a(n) _____ style search out information in order to make a thoughtful decision.

a. directive
b. analytic
c. conceptual
d. behavioral

Study Chart for "Decision-Making Styles"

Style	Traits
1. _____	_____
	_____
	_____
	_____
	_____
2. _____	_____
	_____
	_____
	_____

3. _____   _____

_____   _____

_____

4. _____   _____

_____   _____

_____

_____

REVIEW TEST 3   Score (number correct) _____ × 10 = _____ %

Before, During, and After Reading

**Textbook
Skills**

A. Before you read, survey the following passage from a college health textbook, and then answer the questions given here.

1. What is the passage about? _____

_____

2. What are the ideas in *italics* or in **bold** print? _____

_____

3. What do I already know about this idea? _____

_____

4. What do I need to remember? _____

_____

_____

B. Read the passage. As you read, answer the questions in the left margin.

Aging: Physical Changes

[1]Although the **physiological** consequences of aging can differ in severity and timing, certain typical changes occur as a result of the aging process. [2]The changes that occur to skin and bones illustrate what can be expected.

5. What does **physiological** mean? _____

_____

_____

6. What are some of the effects of aging on the *skin?*

_____

_____

_____

_____

_____

7. What are some of the effects of aging on *bones?*

_____

_____

_____

8. What is *osteoporosis?*

_____

_____

_____

_____

Skin

³As a normal consequence of aging, the skin becomes thinner and loses elasticity. ⁴This loss occurs most in the outer surfaces. ⁵Fat deposits, which add to the soft lines and shape of the skin, diminish. ⁶Starting at age 30, lines develop on the forehead as a result of smiling, squinting, and other facial expressions. ⁷These lines become more obvious, with added "crow's feet" around the eyes, during the 40s. ⁸During a person's 50s and 60s, the skin begins to sag and lose color, leading to **pallor** in the 70s. ⁹Body fat in underlying layers of skin tends to shift away from limbs and into the trunk region of the body. ¹⁰Age spots become more numerous because of patches of excessive pigments under the skin.

Bones

¹¹Throughout the life span, bones are continually changing because of the accumulation and loss of minerals. ¹²By the third or fourth decade of life, mineral loss from bones becomes more prevalent than mineral accumulation. ¹³The result is weakness and porosity (diminishing density) of bony tissue. ¹⁴This loss of minerals, such as calcium, occurs in both sexes. ¹⁵However, it is much more common in females. ¹⁶Loss of calcium can lead to **osteoporosis,** a disease marked by low bone density and structural deterioration of bone tissue. ¹⁷These fragile, porous bones are prone to fracture. ¹⁸This condition, however, can occur at any age.

—Adapted from Donatelle, *Health: The Basics,*
5th ed., p. 387.

C. After reading, answer the following questions.

    9. In sentence 8, what does the term *pallor* refer to?

_____

10. What could a person do to minimize the impact of osteoporosis?

_____

VISUAL VOCABULARY

The best meaning of the word **melanin** as used in the caption below

is _____ .

  a. a vitamin
  b. a natural sunscreen
  c. dark skin color

 Melanin is a pigment that offers protection against UV rays for dark-skinned people. In contrast, fair-skinned people are much less protected and more susceptible to aging and diseases of the skin.

WHAT DO YOU THINK?

Do you think much about the aging process? Why or why not? In what ways do our choices affect the aging process? For example, in what ways do you think our diet or physical activity affects the aging process? Assume you are a counselor to a group of teenagers attending a summer camp, and this week's activities center on teaching youth about habits that foster life-long fitness and health. Write an article for a newsletter for the camp that explains the aging process on skin and bones along with healthy habits that promote healthy skin and bones throughout life.

Before reading: Survey the following passage from a college psychology textbook. Study the words in the Vocabulary Preview; then skim the passage, noting the words in **bold** print. Answer the Before Reading questions that follow the passage. Then read the passage and answer the After Reading question that follows.

Vocabulary Preview

debilitating (1): devastating
neurons (11): nerve cells
neurotransmitter (12): a substance that transmits or carries nerve impulses

Parkinson's Disease

1The connection between the brain and behavior is seen in the **debilitating** effects of Parkinson's disease, a brain disorder. **2**Parkinson's afflicts about half a million Americans from every slice of life—from celebrity Michael J. Fox to the lady next door.

3The physical effects are obvious. **4**The hands of people with Parkinson's disease shake; they may move slowly, *lethargically,* with a stooped posture and shuffling walk; their limbs often seem frozen in position and resist attempts to bend them. **5**Along with the physical effects, Parkinson's disease also takes an emotional and social toll.

6A piano tuner named John had to stop working because he developed Parkinson's disease. **7**He had difficulty controlling his movements, and his behavior changed as well. **8**He became so listless that he rarely left his house. **9**He missed meals. **10**And he started to contract various minor illnesses, which worsened his other symptoms.

11All these changes, physical and behavioral, were caused directly or indirectly by the death of certain **neurons** in John's brain. **12**In the brains of people with Parkinson's disease, cells that produce the **neurotransmitter** dopamine have died. **13**Dopamine plays a key role in the areas of the brain that are involved in planning movements. **14**When patients take a drug that helps produce dopamine, symptoms decrease, often for a long period of time.

15When John's neurons no longer produced enough dopamine, the working of his brain was affected, and his muscle control was impaired. **16**His shaky hands made it almost impossible for him to tune pianos, so John had to retire. **17**After he gave up the work he loved, he became depressed. **18**He began to think of himself as diseased. **19**As a consequence,

Textbook Skills

he lost interest in going out. [20]He stopped seeing many people, who in turn stopped seeing, and helping, him. [21]The events in his brain influenced his feelings about himself and his relationships with other people.

—Adapted from Kosslyn, *Psychology: The Brain, The Person, The World*, Text Excerpt from p. 52 © 2001 Allyn and Bacon. Reproduced by permission of Pearson Education, Inc.

Before Reading Questions

Complete the following sentence by filling in the blanks with the title of the passage and the words in the Vocabulary Preview:

The (**1**) _____ symptoms of (**2**) _____ are caused by the death of (**3**)_____ in the brain that produce the (**4**) _____ dopamine.

After Reading Question

5. What are the physical, emotional, and social effects of Parkinson's disease?

_____

_____

_____

WHAT DO YOU THINK?

Do you know someone who suffers from the debilitating effects of a disease? What diseases, other than Parkinson's disease, cause devastating effects? For example, what are the damaging physical effects of cancer, strokes, or heart disease? What are the emotional effects? Assume you want to do something to help those who are suffering from such a disease. Thus, you are volunteering with the local Rotary Club. This group is sponsoring a 5-mile run/walk to raise money for Mario Gomez, an electrician and father of four, suffering from a debilitating illness (such as Parkinson's disease, cancer, etc.). As a volunteer, you have been asked to write a letter that will go out to local businesses. In your letter, ask for participants and donations. Explain some of the emotional and physical effects of the disease from which Mario suffers. Also explain how the funds raised will benefit him.

After Reading About A Reading System for Effective Readers

Now that you have read and studied A Reading System for Effective Readers, take time to reflect on what you have learned before you begin the Mastery Tests. Think about your learning and performance by answering the following questions. Write your answers in your notebook.

- How has my knowledge base or prior knowledge about the reading process changed?

- Based on my studies, how do I think I will perform on the Mastery Test(s)? Why do I think my scores will be above average, average, or below average?

- Would I recommend this chapter to other students who want to learn more about the reading process? Why or why not?

Test your understanding of what you have learned about A Reading System for Effective Readers by completing the Chapter 1 Review Card in the insert near the end of the text.

CONNECT TO myreadinglab

To check your progress in meeting Chapter 1's learning outcomes, log in to www.myreadinglab.com, and try the following activities.

- The "Memorization and Concentration" section of MyReadingLab ties the use of prior knowledge to your ability to focus on and remember what you have read. To access this resource, click on the "Study Plan" tab. Then click on "Memorization and Concentration." Under the heading "Review Materials," choose option #3 "Model: Concentration and Memorization."

- The "Active Reading Strategies" section of MyReadingLab offers an overview, model, slide show, practices, and tests about the reading process. To access this resource, go to MyReadingLab.com. Click on the "Study Plan" tab. Then choose "Active Reading Strategies" from the menu.

- The "Reading Textbooks" section of MyReadingLab offers an overview, model, slide show, practices, and tests about the reading process and textbooks. For example, to learn about how to survey a textbook, click on

"Reading Textbooks." Then, under the heading "Review Materials," choose option #2 "Model: Reading Textbooks." To learn more about applying SQ3R to textbook reading, choose option #3 "Model: SQ3R."

To measure your mastery of the content of this chapter, complete the tests in the "Reading Textbooks" section and click on Gradebook to find your results.

Before you read, skim the following passage from a college humanities text-book. Also look over the blank chart labeled "Q and A Study Chart for 'The Beginnings of Culture.'" Write four questions in the "Question" column of the chart. **As you read**, annotate the text for details that answer your questions. **After you read**, record your answers in the "Answer" column of the chart. Use your own words.

The Beginnings of Culture

Textbook
Skills

[1]*Culture* can be defined as a way of living practiced by a group of people and passed on from one generation to the next. [2]It took thousands of years for cultures to develop into full-blown civilizations. [3]A civilization is distinct from a culture. [4]A *civilization* has the ability to organize itself thoroughly as a social, economic, and political entity by means, especially, of written language. [5]Written language did not come into being until about 3000 BCE, after human culture shifted from its hunter-gatherer origins to agriculture-based communities. [6]As cultures became more stable and permanent, they became capable of producing not only pottery but metal work, monumental architecture, and literature.

Mesopotamia

[7]In the Tigris and Euphrates valleys of the Fertile Crescent, a series of competing cultures arose. [8]First, in the late fourth century BCE, the Sumerians built monumental ziggurats dedicated to the gods and developed a system of writing. [9]They were succeeded by the Akkadians and Babylonians, the last of whom developed a code of law preserved in a carved stone monument. [10]The first epic poem to survive, the *Epic of Gilgamesh*, originated in these cultures. [11]Most cultures that arose in the Fertile Crescent were polytheistic (believing in many gods). [12]However, the Hebrew religion was monotheistic (believing in one god). [13]The written word was central to their culture and lives in their book of law, the *Torah*.

Egypt

[14]The predictable cycle of flood and sun, and with it the annual deluge of the Nile River valley, helped to create, in Egypt, a strong cultural belief in the stability and balance of all things. [15]Each night the sun god Re, with whom the Egyptian kings were strongly identified, descends into darkness only to rise again, as does the Nile, on a yearly basis. [16]Each person's soul or life force (the ka) was believed to follow this same cycle. [17]And as a result, most surviving Egyptian art and architecture is devoted to burial and the afterlife, the cycle of life, death, and rebirth.

China and India

[18]In the river valleys of China and India other civilizations arose. [19]In China, the Qin dynasty unified the country and built a Great Wall to protect it. [20]During the Shang dynasty, a philosophical and religious tradition arose that emphasized the balance of opposites embodied in the yin-yang symbol. [21]This tradition led to the development of the *Dao de jing* and Confucianism. [22]The *Dao de jing* (*The Way and Its Power*) is a book of 81 poems that aid the individual to let go of self through contemplation and to enter the flow of life. [23]Confucianism is a way of life based on self-discipline and proper relations among people. [24]In India, the Hindu religion developed, which also emphasizes the sacred rhythms of creation and destruction, birth, death, and rebirth.

—Adapted from Sayre, *Discovering the Humanities*, p. 32.

Q and A Study Chart for "The Beginnings of Culture"	
Questions (Before Reading)	Answers (After Reading)
1. _____	_____
_____	_____
_____	_____
_____	_____
2. _____	_____
_____	_____
_____	_____
_____	_____
3. _____	_____
_____	_____
_____	_____
_____	_____
4. _____	_____
_____	_____
_____	_____
_____	_____

Name _____ Section _____

Date _____ Score (number correct) _____ × 20 = _____ %

Read the following passage from a college science textbook. As you read, annotate the text. After you read, answer the questions in the box.

Textbook
Skills

Important and Unique Properties of Water

[1]Water has a number of unique properties related to its hydrogen bonds; three of these traits are high specific heat, high latent heat, and high viscosity.

1. What are the three traits of water? _____,

_____,

and _____

_____

2. What is **specific heat?**

_____

_____

_____

_____

3. What is **latent heat?**

_____

_____

_____

_____

4. What is **viscosity?**

_____

_____

_____

_____

[2]First, water has the property of high specific heat. [3]**Specific heat** is the number of calories necessary to raise one gram of water one degree Celsius. [4]The specific heat of water is defined as a value of 1, and other substances are given a value relative to water. [5]Water can store great amounts of heat energy with a small rise in temperature. [6]Because of the high specific heat of water, large quantities of heat energy must be removed before water can change from a liquid to a solid. [7]Conversely, large amounts of heat must be absorbed for ice to turn to water. [8]Collectively, the energy released or absorbed when water changes from one state to another is called **latent heat**.

[9]A third trait of water is high viscosity. [10]**Viscosity** is the resistance of a liquid to flow. [11]Because of the energy in hydrogen bonds, the viscosity of water is high. [12]Imagine liquid flowing through a glass tube. [13]The liquid behaves as if it lays in layers that flow over one another. [14]The rate of flow is greatest at the center; because of internal friction between layers, the flow decreases toward the side of the tube. [15]Viscosity is the source of frictional resistance to objects moving through water.

[16]Within all substances similar molecules are attracted to one another. [17]Water is no exception. [18]Molecules of water below the surface are surrounded by other molecules. [19]The forces of attraction are the same on all sides. [20]At the water's surface,

5. What is **surface tension?**

_____

_____

_____

_____

there is a different set of conditions. [21]Below the surface, molecules of water are strongly attracted to one another. [22]Above the water, air molecules and water molecules have a much weaker attraction to each other. [23]Therefore, molecules on the surface are drawn downward; thus the surface becomes taut like an inflated balloon. [24]This condition is called **surface tension,** and it is important in the lives of aquatic organisms.

[25]The surface of water is able to support small objects and animals, such as the water strider (Gerridae) and water spiders (_Dolomedes_ spp.) that run across the pond's surface. [26]To other small organisms, surface tension is a barrier, whether they wish to penetrate the water below or escape into the air above. [27]For some the surface tension is too great to break. [28]For others, it is a trap to avoid while skimming the surface to feed or to lay eggs. [29]If caught in the surface tension, a small insect may flounder on the surface. [30]Surface tension hinders the efforts of the nymphs of mayflies _(Ephemeroptera)_ and caddisflies _(Trichoptera)_ in their efforts to emerge from the water as winged adults. [31]Slowed down at the surface, these insects become easy prey for fish.

[32]Surface tension is associated with _capillary action,_ or capillarity—the rise and fall of liquids within narrow tubes. [33]Capillarity affects the movement of water in soil and the transport of water to all parts of plants.

—Adapted from Smith & Smith, _Elements of Ecology,_
4th ed., pp. 73–74.

Using SQ3R, read the following passage from a personal finance textbook.

Textbook
Skills

Advantages and Disadvantages of Credit

Background on Credit

¹Credit represents funds a creditor provides to a borrower that the borrower will repay in the future with interest. ²The funds borrowed are sometimes referred to as the principal, so we segment repayment of credit into interest and principal payments. ³Credit is frequently extended to borrowers as a loan with set terms such as the amount of credit provided and the maturity date when the credit will be repaid. ⁴For most types of loans, interest payments are made periodically (such as every quarter or year), and the principal payment is made at the maturity date, when the loan is to be terminated.

Advantages of Using Credit

⁵Individuals borrow funds when the dollar amount of their purchases exceeds the amount of their available cash. ⁶Many individuals use borrowed funds to purchase a home or car or to pay their tuition fees. ⁷In contrast, others use credit (such as a credit card) for convenience when making day-to-day purchases.

Disadvantages of Using Credit

⁸There can be a high cost to using credit. ⁹If you borrow too much money, you may have difficulty making your credit card payments. ¹⁰It is easier to obtain credit than to pay it back. ¹¹And having a credit line can tempt you to make impulse purchases that you cannot afford. ¹²College students are carrying credit cards in record numbers. ¹³Eighty-three percent of all students have at least one credit card, and the average credit card balance is $2,327. ¹⁴Many students make minimum payments on their credit cards while in school with the expectation that they will be able to pay off their balance once they graduate and are working full-time. ¹⁵Yet the accumulating interest fees catch many by surprise, and the debt can quickly become difficult to manage. ¹⁶Today's graduating students have an average of $20,402 in combined education loan and credit card balances. ¹⁷If you are unable to repay the credit you receive, you may not be able to obtain credit again or will have to pay a very high

interest rate to obtain it. [18]Your ability to save money will also be reduced if you have large credit payments. [19]If spending and credit card payments exceed your net cash flows, you will need to withdraw savings to cover the deficiency.

[20]Warren Buffett, a successful billionaire investor, recently offered financial advice to some students. [21]He told them that they will not make financial progress if they are borrowing money at 18 percent (a typical interest rate on credit cards). [22]In recent years, more than 1 million people in the United States have filed for bankruptcy each year. [23]A primary reason for these bankruptcies is that the individuals obtained more credit than they could repay. [24]Even if obtaining credit at a high interest rate does not cause personal bankruptcy, it limits the potential increase in personal wealth.

1. What is this passage about? _____

_____

Complete the following concept map with information from the passage.

Impact of Credit Payments on Saving

USE OF CREDIT

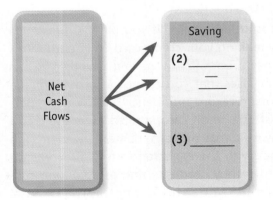

NO USE OF CREDIT

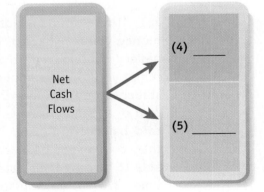

Name _____ Section _____

Date _____ Score (number correct) _____ × 10 = _____ %

A. Using SQ3R, read the following passage from a college psychology textbook. Answer the questions in the left margin.

Textbook
Skills

Mnemonic Devices

[1]**Mnemonic devices** are strategies that improve memory. [2]Mnemonics can easily double your recall and are well worth the effort of learning. [3]Mnemonic devices not only help you learn something in the first place, but should you forget it, you will be able to relearn it more effectively.

[4]Probably the single most effective mnemonic device is the use of **interactive images.** [5]Forming images of objects interacting will improve memory even without any effort to learn the material. [6]For example, if you want to learn someone's first name, visualize someone else you already know who has the same first name. [7]Then imagine that person interacting with your new acquaintance in some way. [8]You might envision them fighting or hugging.

[9]Another effective mnemonic device is the use of acronyms. [10]**Acronyms** are words made from the first letters of the important words in a phrase. [11]Acronyms can be pronounced. [12]One example is NOW, for the National Organization for Women. [13]**Initialisms** are simply the initial letters of words in a phrase that probably do not combine to make a word, such as DNA for deoxyribonucleic acid. [14]Initialisms may be easier to make up. [15]The idea of using both acronyms and initialisms is to create a single unit that can be "unpacked" as a set of cues for something more complicated.

—Adapted from Kosslyn, *Psychology: The Brain, the Person, the World,* Text excerpt from pp. 228–229 © 2001 Allyn and Bacon. Reproduced by permission of Pearson Education, Inc.

1. What are mnemonic devices?

_____

_____

_____

2. What are interactive images?

_____

_____

3. What are acronyms?

_____

_____

_____

4. What are initialisms?

_____

_____

_____

B. Using SQ3R, read the following paragraph taken from a college literature text-book.

Hyperbole and Understatement

Textbook
Skills

[1]Most of us, from time to time, emphasize a point with a statement containing an exaggeration: "Faster than greased lightning," "I've told him a thousand times." [2]We speak, then, not literal truth but use a figure of speech called **overstatement** or **hyperbole**. [3]Poets, too, being fond of emphasis, often exaggerate for effect. [4]Instances are Marvell's claim of a love that should grow "vaster than empires and more slow." [5]Another is John Burgon's description of Petra: "A rose-red city, half as old as time." [6]Overstatement can also be used for humor. [7]Take, for instance, the fat woman's boast (from a blues song): "Every time I shake, some skinny gal loses her home." [8]The opposite is **understatement**, which is a figure of speech that implies more than is said. [9]For example, Robert Frost's line "One could do worse than be a swinger of birches" uses understatement. [10]All through the poem, he has suggested that to swing on a birch tree is one of the most deeply satisfying activities in the world.

—Adapted from Kennedy & Gioia, *Literature*, 8th ed.,
p. 867.

5. What is this passage about? _____

_____

Complete the concept map with information from the paragraph.

Figure of Speech	Definition	Example
Overstatement or hyperbole	6. _____	7. _____
8. _____	9. _____	10. _____

Vocabulary and Dictionary Skills

2

LEARNING OUTCOMES

After studying this chapter you should be able to do the following:

1. Define vocabulary.
2. Classify context clues.
3. Describe how to comprehend new words as you read.
4. Assess your comprehension of context clues.
5. Analyze the meaning of a word based on word parts.
6. Use a glossary.
7. Read a dictionary.
8. Evaluate and explain the importance of what you have learned about vocabulary and dictionary skills.
9. Apply what you have learned about context clues and word parts to your reading process.

Before Reading About Vocabulary Skills

Chapter 1 taught you the importance of surveying material before you begin reading by skimming the information for **bold** or *italic* type. Throughout this textbook, key ideas are emphasized in bold or italic print where they appear in the passage; often they are also set apart visually in a box that gives the definition or examples of the term. Skim the chapter for key ideas in boxes that will help you understand vocabulary skills. Refer to these boxes and create at least six questions that you can answer as you read the chapter. Write your questions in the following spaces (record the page number for the key term in each question):

_____ (page _____)

_____ (page _____)

_____ (page _____)

_____ (page _____)

_____ (page _____)

Compare the questions you created with the following questions. Then write the ones that seem most helpful in your notebook, leaving enough space between each question to record the answers as you read and study the chapter.

What is vocabulary? (page 44) What is a context clue? (page 45) What are word parts? (page 56) What kind of information does a dictionary provide? (page 64) What is a glossary? (page 51) How will each of these skills help me develop my vocabulary? (pages 44 and 56)

 ## Words Are Building Blocks

Words are the building blocks of meaning. Have you ever watched a child with a set of building blocks such as Legos? Hundreds of separate pieces can be joined together to create buildings, planes, cars, or even spaceships. Words are like that, too. A word is the smallest unit of thought. Words properly joined create meaning.

> **Vocabulary** is all the words used or understood by a person.

How many words do you have in your **vocabulary**? If you are like most people, by the time you are 18 years old, you know about 60,000 words. During your college studies, you will most likely learn an additional 20,000 words. Each subject you study will have its own set of words. There are several ways to study vocabulary.

 ## Context Clues : A SAGE Approach

Effective readers interact with new words in a number of ways. One way is to use **context clues**. The meaning of a word is shaped by its context. The word _context_ means "surroundings." The meaning of a word is shaped by the words surrounding it—its context. Effective readers use context clues to learn new words.

A **context clue** is the information that surrounds a new word, and is used to understand its meaning.

There are four types of context clues:

- Synonyms
- Antonyms
- General context
- Examples

Notice that, put together, the first letter of each context clue spells the word SAGE. The word *sage* means "wise." Using context clues is a wise—a SAGE—reading strategy.

Synonyms

A **synonym** is a word that has the same or nearly the same meaning as another word. Many times, an author will place a synonym near a new or difficult word as a context clue to the word's meaning. Usually, a synonym is set off with a pair of commas, a pair of dashes, or a pair of parentheses before and after it.

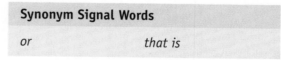

Synonym Signal Words	
or	*that is*

EXAMPLES   Each of the following sentences has a key word in **bold** type. In each sentence, underline the signal word or words and then circle the synonym for the word in **bold**.

1. At times, we pursue an activity as an end in itself, simply because it is enjoyable, not because of an attached award. We are pulled by **intrinsic motivation**, that is, internal incentives.

2. Other times, we act to gain a reward outside ourselves or to avoid some undesirable consequence. We are pulled by **extrinsic motivation** or external incentives.

EXPLANATIONS

1. The signal words **that is** clue the reader that the synonym for intrinsic motivation is **internal incentives**.

2. The signal word **or** clues the reader that the synonym for extrinsic motivation is **external incentives.**

VISUAL VOCABULARY

Exercise balls provide a better work-out because their _____ instability causes more of the body's muscles to respond.

a. extrinsic
b. intrinsic

PRACTICE 1

Textbook
Skills

Each of the following sentences from a college textbook contains a word that is a synonym for the word in **bold** type. Underline the signal words and circle the synonym in each sentence.

1. Directional terms allow medical workers to explain exactly where one body structure is in relation to another. For example, the forehead is **superior** to, that is above, the nose.

2. The navel is **inferior** to—or below—the breastbone.

3. The heart is **posterior** to (behind) the breastbone.

4. The breastbone is **anterior** to, or in front of, the spine.

—Marieb, *Essentials of Human Anatomy and Physiology,* 9th ed., p. 18.

VISUAL VOCABULARY

This image of the lungs is from the _____ view.

a. superior
b. anterior

Main stem bronchus
Bronchioles
Bronchi
Bronchial tree

Antonyms

An **antonym** is a word that has the opposite meaning of another word. Antonyms help you see the shade of a word's meaning by showing you what the original word is *not*. The following contrast words often act as signals that an antonym is being used.

Antonym Signal Words		
but	*instead*	*unlike*
however	*not*	*yet*
in contrast	*on the other hand*	

Sometimes antonyms can be found next to the new word. In those cases, commas, dashes, or parentheses set them off. At other times, antonyms are placed in other parts of the sentence to emphasize the contrast between the ideas.

EXAMPLES In each sentence, underline the signal word and circle the antonym for the word in **bold** type. In the blank, write the letter of the word that best defines the word in **bold**.

_____ **1.** During dinner, Anne Marie let out a long, loud burp that **mortified** her mother but amused her friends.

    a. embarrassed   c. silenced

    b. killed   d. delighted

_____ **2.** Suzanne's tone was surprisingly **flippant**, in contrast to her usual respectful manner.

a. polite

b. sassy

c. funny

d. loud

EXPLANATIONS

1. The signal word *but* clues the reader that the antonym is *amused*. The best definition of the word *mortified* is (a) *embarrassed*.

2. The signal words *in contrast* clue the reader that the antonym is *respectful*. The best definition of the word *flippant* is (b) *sassy*.

PRACTICE 2

In each sentence, underline the signal word and circle the antonym for the word in **bold** type. In the blank, write the letter of the word that best defines the word in **bold**.

_____ **1.** Please leave the kitchen **immaculate**, not filthy, when you finish your meal preparations.

a. messy

b. well-stocked

c. spotless

d. cool

_____ **2.** Maxine acted **smug** when instead she should have been humble.

a. joyful

b. depressed

c. calm

d. conceited

_____ **3.** At the beginning of Dickens's novel *A Christmas Carol,* the character Scrooge has a **mercenary** nature, but by the story's end, he has become a generous spirit.

a. carefree

b. angry

c. greedy

d. curious

General Context

Often you will find that the author has not provided either a synonym clue or an antonym clue. In that case, you will have to rely on the general context of the passage to figure out the meaning of the unfamiliar word. This requires you to read the entire sentence, or to read ahead for a few sentences, for information that will help you understand the new word.

Information about the word can be included in the passage in several ways. Sometimes a definition of the word may be provided. Vivid word pictures or descriptions of a situation can provide a sense of the word's meaning. Sometimes you may need to figure out the meaning of an unknown word by using logic and reasoning skills.

EXAMPLES In the blank, write the letter of the word that best defines the word in **bold** type.

_____ **1.** To ensure safety, written and road tests should be **mandatory** for everyone who seeks a driver's license for the first time; no exceptions should be allowed.
   a. optional
   b. difficult
   c. required
   d. debated

_____ **2.** Instead of being placed in adult prisons, where they often become more antisocial by mixing with hardened criminals, youth who have been convicted of crimes should be placed in programs that **rehabilitate** them.
   a. restore to useful life
   b. punish for good reason
   c. exhaust in order to break the spirit
   d. entertain

EXPLANATIONS

1. The best meaning of the word *mandatory* is (c) *required*. Clues from the sentence are the words *ensure* and *no exceptions should be allowed*.

2. The best meaning of the word *rehabilitate* is (a) *restore to useful life*. The passage suggests that placing young people in adult prisons just makes them tougher; the contrast word *instead* indicates that the word *rehabilitate* must mean something different.

PRACTICE 3

Each of the following sentences has a word in **bold** type. In the blank, write the letter of the word that best defines the word in **bold**.

_____ **1.** Jamie **speculated** about how much weight he wanted to gain during the three-month bodybuilding program he was beginning.
   a. knew
   b. wondered
   c. worried
   d. celebrated

_____   **2.** Losing weight too quickly—more than a pound or two a week—
can be **detrimental** to long-term weight control and good health.
   a. helpful   c. harmful
   b. odd   d. pleasing

_____   **3.** Many employers use yearly bonuses and raises as **incentives** to encourage work habits that go beyond expectations.
   a. dreams   c. barriers
   b. tricks   d. motivators

Examples

Many times an author will show the meaning of a new or difficult word by providing an example. Signal words indicate that an example is coming.

Example Signal Words
consists of   *for example*   *for instance*   *including*   *such as*

Colons and dashes can also indicate examples.

EXAMPLES   Using example clues, choose the correct meaning of the words
in **bold** type.

_____   **1.** The American presidency has suffered **infamous** events such as the
Watergate scandal of Richard Nixon and the impeachment of Bill
Clinton by the House of Representatives.
   a. exciting, little-known
   b. boring, well-known
   c. tarnishing, well-known
   d. frightening, little-known

_____   **2.** Some authors use **pseudonyms**; for example, famous American
author Mark Twain's real name was Samuel Clemens.
   a. typists   c. ghost writers
   b. mental tricks   d. pen names

EXPLANATIONS

1. The best meaning of the word *infamous* is (c) *tarnishing, well-known.*

2. The best meaning of the word *pseudonyms* is (d) *pen names.*

PRACTICE 4

Using example clues, choose the correct meaning of the word in **bold** type.

_____ **1.** Baseball figure Yogi Berra's humor was based on using **mala-propisms**; for instance, one of his most famous is "If you see a fork in the road, take it."

     a. misuses of words   c. social situations
     b. personal attacks   d. nature jokes

_____ **2. Rigorous** programs, such as boot camps and outward-bound programs, help develop character in the individuals who take part in them.

     a. required   c. difficult
     b. lengthy   d. abusive

Textbook
Skills

Textbook Skills: Using a Glossary

Each subject or content area, such as science, mathematics, or English, has its own specialized vocabulary. Therefore, some textbooks provide an extra section in the back of the book called a _glossary_ that alphabetically lists all the specialized terms with their definitions as they were used throughout the textbook. Other textbooks may provide short glossaries within each chapter; in these cases, the glossaries may appear in the margins or in highlighted boxes, listing the words in the order that they appear on the page. The meanings given in a glossary are limited to the way in which the word or term is used in that content area.

> A **glossary** is a list of selected terms with their definitions as used in a specific area of study.

Glossaries provide excellent opportunities to use strategies before and after reading. Before reading, skim the section for specialized terms (usually these words are in **bold** or _italic_ print). Checking the words and their meanings triggers prior knowledge or establishes meaning that will deepen your comprehension. In addition, you can create vocabulary review lists using glossary terms by paraphrasing or restating the definition in your own words. These vocabulary lists can be used after reading to review and test your recall of the material.

Textbook
Skills

EXAMPLE The following selection is from a college psychology textbook. Before reading, use the glossary to complete the vocabulary review list. Then read the passage. After reading, answer the questions.

Glossary

algorithm a set of steps that, if followed methodically, will guarantee the solution to a problem.

heuristic a rule of thumb that does not guarantee the correct answer to a problem but offers a likely shortcut to it.

representation a way of looking at a problem.

strategy an approach to solving a problem, determined by the type of representation used and the processing steps to be tried.

Algorithms and Heuristics:
Getting From Here to There

¹To solve a problem you need a **strategy,** an approach to solving a problem determined by the type of **representation** used and the processing steps to be tried. ²There are two types of strategies: algorithms and heuristics. ³Let's say you heard about a fantastic price being offered on a hit alternative music CD by an independent record store, but you don't know the name of the store. ⁴You could try to find it by calling every relevant listing in the yellow pages. ⁵This process involves using an **algorithm,** a set of steps that if followed methodically will guarantee the right answer. ⁶But you may not have time to call every store. ⁷Instead, you might guess that the record store is in a part of town where many students live. ⁸In this case, having reduced the list of candidates to those located near the campus, you might find the store after calling only a few. ⁹This process reflects use of a **heuristic,** a rule of thumb that does not guarantee the correct answer but offers a likely shortcut to it. ¹⁰One common heuristic is to divide a big problem into parts and solve them one at a time.

—Adapted from Kosslyn, *Psychology: The Brain, the Person, the World,* Text excerpt from p. 206 © 2001 Allyn and Bacon. Reproduced by permission of Pearson Education, Inc.

Before Reading

1. _____ an approach to solving a problem based on a way of looking at a problem and the steps taken to solve the problem

2. _____ a series of systematic steps that assures the right answer

3. heuristic _____

_____

After Reading

_____ 4. Which sentence uses most of the words listed in the glossary?

_____ 5. Which problem-solving strategy is described in the following example? Kimberly couldn't find the rice, but started in aisle 3 first, because she thought it might be with the pasta. Then she tried aisle 10, because she thought it might be with the international foods.

—Kosslyn & Rosenberg, p. 236.

a. algorithm   b. heuristic

EXPLANATION

1. A *strategy* is an approach to solving a problem based on a way of looking at a problem and the steps taken to solve the problem. Note that the paraphrase (restatement) of the definition for strategy draws on information given in the definition for *representation*.

2. *Algorithm* is a series of systematic steps that assures the right answer.

3. Compare your paraphrase of the definition for *heuristic* with the following: *use of prior knowledge or experience that is likely to lead to the solution more quickly.*

4. Sentence 1 uses most of the words listed in the glossary. Sentence 1 also states the main idea of the paragraph, the point the author is making.

5. Kimberly used (b), the heuristic approach. This approach is an experimental, trial-and-error approach in contrast to the algorithm, which approaches problem solving using proven formulas. The importance of glossaries is evident when you consider that this question about Kimberly came directly from the psychology textbook's chapter review. Textbook reviews and course tests often include questions about the key terms listed in glossaries.

PRACTICE 5

Textbook Skills

The following selection is from a college anatomy and physiology textbook. Before reading, use the glossary to complete your vocabulary review list. Then read the passage. After reading, answer the questions.

Energy

[1]In contrast to matter, energy is massless and does not take up space. [2]It can be measured only by its effects on matter. [3]Energy is commonly defined as the ability to do work or to put matter into motion. [4]When energy is actually doing work (moving objects), it is referred to as kinetic (kĭ-neh'tik) energy. [5]Kinetic energy is displayed in the constant movement of the tiniest particles of matter (atoms) as well as in larger objects, such as a bouncing ball. [6]When energy is inactive or stored (as in the batteries of an unused toy), it is called potential energy. [7]All forms of energy exhibit both kinetic and potential work capacities.

[8]Actually, energy is a physics topic, but it is difficult to separate matter and energy. [9]All living things are built of matter, and to grow and function they require a continuous supply of energy.

Glossary

energy the ability to do work

chemical energy energy form stored in chemical bonds that hold atoms together

electrical energy energy form resulting from the movement of charged particles

kinetic energy energy of motion

Glossary

mechanical energy energy form directly involved with putting matter into motion

potential energy stored energy

radiant energy energy of the electromagnetic spectrum, which includes heat, light, ultraviolet waves, infrared waves, and other forms

[10]Thus, matter is the substance, and energy is the mover of the substance. [11]Because this is so, it is worth taking a brief detour to introduce the forms of energy the body uses as it does its work.

Forms of Energy

- [12]**Chemical energy** is stored in the bonds of chemical substances. [13]When the bonds are broken, the (potential) stored energy is unleashed and becomes kinetic energy (energy in action). [14]For example, when gasoline molecules are broken apart in your automobile engine, the energy released powers your car. [15]In like manner, all body activities are "run" by the chemical energy harvested from the foods we eat.

- [16]**Electrical energy** results from the movement of charged particles. [17]In your house, electrical energy is the flow of electrons along the wiring. [18]In your body, an electrical current is generated when charged particles (called ions) move across cell membranes. [19]The nervous system uses electrical currents called nerve impulses to transmit messages from one part of the body to another.

- [20]**Mechanical energy** is energy directly involved in moving matter. [21]When you ride a bicycle, your legs provide the mechanical energy that moves the pedals. [22]We can take this example one step further back: As the muscles in your legs shorten, they pull on your bones, causing your limbs to move (so that you can pedal the bike).

- [23]**Radiant energy** travels in waves; that is, it is the energy of the electromagnetic spectrum, which includes X rays, infrared radiation (heat energy), visible light, radio, and ultraviolet waves. [24]Light energy, which stimulates the retinas of your eyes, is important in vision. [25]Ultraviolet waves cause sunburn, but they also stimulate our bodies to make vitamin D.

—Marieb, *Essentials of Human Anatomy and Physiology,* 9th ed., pp. 27–28.

Before Reading

Establish or activate prior knowledge. Use the glossary to fill in each blank with the appropriate word.

The ability to do work—**(1)** _____ takes on many forms. While there is the energy of motion, or **(2)** _____ energy, there is also **(3)** _____ or stored energy. In addition, there are four basic forms of energy. The movement of charged particles creates **(4)** _____ energy. Chemical bonds store **(5)** _____ energy. **(6)** _____ energy is directly involved with causing matter to move. And **(7)** _____ energy travels in many forms of waves.

After Reading

Recall and review information and test your comprehension by filling in the blanks with information from the passage.

_____ **8.** The muscles in the human body causing the limbs to move and legs pedaling a bicycle illustrate
      a. potential energy.   c. mechanical energy.
      b. electrical energy.   d. radiant energy.

_____ **9.** The human nervous system uses
      a. mechanical energy.   c. radiant energy.
      b. electrical energy.   d. chemical energy.

_____ **10.** What are the two work abilities exhibited by all forms of energy?
      a. kinetic and potential   c. radiant and chemical
      b. kinetic and mechanical   d. potential and electrical

VISUAL VOCABULARY

Fire is a form of _____ energy.

    a. chemical
    b. electrical
    c. mechanical
    d. radiant

Word Parts

Just as ideas are made up of words, words are also made up of smaller parts. *Word parts* can help you learn vocabulary more easily and quickly. In addition, knowing the meaning of the parts of words helps you understand a new word when you see it in context.

Many words are divided into the following three parts: *roots, prefixes,* and *suffixes.*

Root	The basic or main part of a word. Prefixes and suffixes are added to roots to make a new word.
	Example: *press* means "press."
Prefix	A group of letters with a specific meaning added to the beginning of a word (root) to make a new word.
	Example: ***com**press* means "press together."
Suffix	A group of letters with a specific meaning added to the end of a word (root) to make a new word.
	Example: *press**ure*** means "act of pressing."

Effective readers understand how the three word parts join together to make additional words. The following chart lists a few of the most common prefixes, roots, and suffixes in the English language. To improve your vocabulary, memorize these word parts.

	Commonly Used Word Parts	
Word Part:	**Meaning**	**Sample Word**
Prefix		
anti-	against	antisocial
de-	opposite	defrost
in-, im-	in, not	inside, impossible
pre-	before	predawn
sub-	under	subgroup
un-	not	unheard

Word Part:	Commonly Used Word Parts Meaning	Sample Word
Root		
cred	to believe	credible
dic-, dit-, dict-	to say	dictation
ducere-, duct-, duc-	to draw or lead	conduct
graph-, graf-	to write, draw	graph
mittere-, mit-, mis-, mise-	to put or send	remit
scribe-, script-	to write	scripture
stare-, stat-	to stand	stature
Suffix		
-able, -ible	can be done	capable
-ate	cause to be	graduate
-al	having traits of	practical
-er	comparative, one who	higher, controller
-ic	having the traits of	simplistic
-less	without	effortless
-ous, -eous, -ious	possessing qualities of	joyous
-y	characterized by	honestly

EXAMPLES   Look at the following root, prefix, and suffix. Make two new words by combining the word parts. The meaning of each part is in parentheses. You don't have to use all the parts to make a word.

Prefix:	*in-*	(not)
Root:	*vis*	(see)
Suffix:	*-ible*	(capable of)

1. _____   2. _____

EXPLANATIONS

1. The root and suffix combine to form the word *visible,* which means "capable of being seen," as in the following sentence: *Carmen's joy was visible in her smile.*

2. All three word parts combine to form the word *invisible,* which means "not capable of being seen," as in the following sentence: *Josie was so embarrassed that she wished she were invisible.*

PRACTICE 6

Identify the word parts for each of the following words. Circle prefixes and suffixes. Underline roots. Then use the chart "Commonly Used Word Parts" on pages 56–57 to write a definition of the meaning of each word based on its word parts.

1. incredulous _____

2. deductable _____

3. inscribable _____

4. submitter _____

Roots

The **root** is the basic or main part of a word. Many times a root combined with other word parts will create a whole family of closely related words. Even when the root word is joined with other word parts to form new words, the meaning of the root does not change. Knowing the commonly used roots will help you master many new and difficult words.

EXAMPLES The root *fact* means "make" or "do." Study the following words. Using the meaning of the root *fact* and the context of each sentence, put each word into the sentence that best fits its meaning. Use each word once.

Root	Meaning	Suffixes	Meaning	Example
fact	make, do	*-ion*	act	fact = make, do
		-oid	resembling a thing	faction factoid

1. In 2003, a writer for the *New York Times* was fired because he used _____, not the truth, in his stories.

2. A significant _____ of the population took to the streets in protest.

EXPLANATIONS Both words contain the root *fact* ("make" or "do"), and each word uses the meaning differently. The additional word parts—in this case, suffixes—created the different meanings. However, the meaning of the root word and the context of the sentence should have helped you choose the correct word for each sentence.

1. A *factoid* is a fact that has been made up or invented but is believed because it is in print. The *New York Times* writer was fired because he made up facts for his stories.

2. A *faction* is a group of people working together for a common cause against another group or the larger group. In this sentence, the faction has been formed to create a protest.

PRACTICE 7

Textbook
Skills

Study the word parts in the chart. Next, read the four sentences taken from college textbooks. Then, define the vocabulary words in **bold** print. Use information from the word chart and the general sense of the sentences. Write your definitions in the given spaces.

Prefix	Meaning	Root	Meaning	Suffix	Meaning
re-	back, again	*cadere/cis*	fall	*-er/-ist*	one who is or does
trans-	across	*mitt*	send	*-ism*	state or condition
		nuer	nerve	*-s*	plural

1. All our thoughts, feelings, and behavior can ultimately be traced to the activity of **neurons**.

—Wood et al, *Mastering the World of Psychology,* Text from pp. 39–40 © 2008 Pearson Education, Inc. Reproduced by permission of Pearson Education, Inc.

_____

2. Messages are transmitted between neurons by one or more of a large group of chemical substances known as **neurotransmitters**.

—Wood, Wood, & Boyd, *Mastering the World of Psychology,* 3rd ed., p. 42.

_____

3. According to one study, **recidivism** rates show that nearly 70% of young adults paroled from prison in 22 states during 1978 were rearrested for serious crimes one or more times within six years of their release.

—Schmalleger, *Criminal Justice Today,* 10th ed., pp. 472–473.

_____

4. Worse, still, observed the authors of the study, was the fact that 40% of **recidivists** would have been in prison at the time of readmission to prison if they had served the maximum term of their original sentence.

—Schmalleger, *Criminal Justice Today,* 10th ed., pp. 472–473.

_____

Prefixes

A **prefix** is a group of letters with a specific meaning added to the beginning of a word or root to make a new word. Though the basic meaning of a root is not changed, a prefix changes the meaning of the word as a whole. For example, the prefix *ex-* means "out of" or "from." When placed in front of the root *tract* (which means "pull" or "drag"), the word *extract* is formed. *Extract* means "pull or drag out." The same root *tract* joined with the prefix *con-* (which means "with" or "together") creates the word *contract*. A *contract* legally pulls people together to accomplish something.

The importance of prefixes can be seen in the family of words that comes from the root *ject*, which means "throw." Look over the following examples of prefixes and their meanings. Note the change in the meaning of the whole word based on the meaning of the prefix.

Prefix	Meaning	Root	Meaning	Example
e-	out of, from	*ject*	throw	*eject*
in-	in, into			*inject*
re-	back, again			*reject*

EXAMPLES   Using the meanings of the prefixes, root, and context clues, put each word into the sentence that best fits its meaning. Use each word once.

Prefix	Meaning	Root	Meaning
ex-	out of, from	*pel*	push, drive
pro-	forward, in favor of		

pel = push, drive	
expel	propel

1. The sorority threatened to _____ Danielle because she would not join in hazing new members.

2. Len Watson used his family's name and fortune to _____ him into a seat in the Senate.

EXPLANATIONS

1. The sorority wanted to "drive out" Danielle because she refused to conform.

2. Len used his family's success to push him forward into becoming a senator.

PRACTICE 8

Textbook
Skills

Study the word parts in the chart. Next, read the four sentences taken from a college textbook. Then, define the vocabulary words in **bold** print based on information from the word chart and the general sense of the sentences. Write your definitions in the given spaces.

Prefix	Meaning	Root	Meaning	Suffix	Meaning
intra-	within, inside			*-ive*	of, belonging to,
peri-	around, surrounding	*operis*	labor		quality of
pre-	before	*opus,*	work,		
post-	after				

1. Surgery encompasses three phases referred to as the **perioperative** period.

_____

2. The first phase, the **preoperative** phase, begins when the decision to have surgery is made and ends when the client is transferred to the operating table.

---

3. The second phase, the **intraoperative** phase, begins when the client is transferred to the operating table and ends when the client is admitted to the post-anesthesia care unit or recovery room.

---

4. The third phase, the **postoperative** phase, begins with the admission of the client to the recovery room and ends when healing is complete.

—Adapted from Berman, Snyder, Kozier, & Erb, *Kozier and Erb's Fundamentals of Nursing,* 8th ed., p. 940.

Suffixes

A **suffix** is a group of letters with a specific meaning added to the end of a word or root to make a new word. Though the basic meaning of a root does not change, a suffix can change the type of word and the way a word is used. Look at the following set of examples:

Root	Meaning	Suffix	Meaning	Word
psych	mind	*-ology*	study	*psychology*
		-ist	person	*psychologist*
		-ical	possessing or expressing a quality	*psychological*

EXAMPLES Using the meanings of the root, suffixes, and context clues, put each of the words in the box into the sentence that best fits its meaning. Use each word once.

Root	Meaning	Suffix	Meaning
tact	touch	*-ful*	full of
		-ile	of, like, related to, being
		-less	without
		-ly	in such a manner

tact = **touch**	
tactfully	tactile

1. Many blind people rely on their _____ sense to read braille.

2. I don't know how to tell you this _____, but your zipper is down.

EXPLANATIONS

1. Many blind people use the tips of their fingers to feel words written in braille; they are using their *tactile* sense, their sense of touch.

2. The speaker would like to have a gentle touch and deliver the embarrassing news about the zipper *tactfully*.

PRACTICE 9

Study the word parts in the chart. Next, read the four sentences taken from a college textbook. Then, define the vocabulary words in **bold** print based on information from the word chart and the general sense of the sentences. Write your definitions in the given spaces. Wording may vary.

Root	Meaning	Suffix	Meaning
socius	companion, ally, associate	*-al*	quality of
		-ist	one who
		-ology	study of
		-ity, -ty	quality, condition, state of

Textbook
Skills

1. Auguste Comte, the founder of sociology, stressed that the scientific method should be applied to the study of **society**.

   _____

2. **Sociology** only recently appeared on the human scene.

   _____

3. Sociology grew out of **social** upheaval.

   _____

4. Comte believed that **sociologists** would reform the entire society, making it a better place to live.

—Adapted from Henslin, *Sociology: Down to Earth Approach,* Text from pp. 8–9
© 2008 James M. Henslin. Reproduced by permission of Pearson Education, Inc.

 Reading the Dictionary

Experts believe that most English-speaking adults know and use between 25,000 and 50,000 words. That seems like a large number, yet the English language has over a million words. Effective readers use a dictionary to understand new or difficult words.

Most dictionaries provide the following information:

- Guide words (the words at the top of each page)
- Spelling (how the word and its different forms are spelled)
- Pronunciation (how to say the word)
- Part of speech (the function of the word)
- Definition (the meaning of the word)
- Synonyms (words that have similar meanings)
- Etymology (the history of the word)

All dictionaries have guide words at the top of each page. However, dictionaries differ from each other in the way they give other information about words. Some dictionaries give more information about the origin of the word; other dictionaries give long lists of synonyms. Each dictionary will explain how to use its resources in the first few pages of the book.

How to Read a Dictionary Entry

The following entry from *Merriam-Webster's Collegiate Dictionary,* 11th edition, will be used as an example for the discussions about the kinds of information a dictionary provides.

her·bi·cide \ˈ(h)ər-bə-ˌsīd\ *n* [L *herba* + ISV =*cide*] (1899) : an agent used to destroy or inhibit plant growth — **her·bi·cid·al** \ˌ(h)ər-bə-ˈsī-dᵊl*adj* — **her·bi·cid·al·ly** \-dᵊl-ē\ *adv*

—By permission. From *Merriam-Webster's Collegiate® Dictionary,* 11th Edition
© 2010 by Merriam Webster, Incorporated (www.Merriam-Webster.com).

Spelling and Syllables

The spelling of the main word is given first in **bold** type. The word is also divided into syllables. The word *herbicide* has three syllables: *her-bi-cide.* Spellings of words based on this word are given at the end of the entry. This listing is especially helpful when letters are dropped or added to create a new word. The word *herbicide* changes form and spelling to become *herbicidal,* which has four syllables, *her-bi-cid-al,* and *herbicidally,* which has five syllables, *her-bi-cid-al-ly.*

EXAMPLES   Use a dictionary to break the following words into syllables. Place a dot (·) between the syllables.

   1. intermit _____

   2. pedagogy _____

EXPLANATIONS

   1. *Intermit* has three syllables: *in-ter-mit.*

   2. *Pedagogy* has four syllables: *ped-a-go-gy.*

PRACTICE 10

Place a dot (·) between the syllables.

   1. scavenger _____

   2. tundra _____

Pronunciation symbols indicate the sounds of consonants and vowels. Dictionaries provide pronunciation keys so that you will understand the symbols used in the pronunciation guide to a word. Below is a sample pronunciation key.

Pronunciation Key

\ə**a**but \ᵊ\ kitt**en**, F table \ər**fur**ther \a**a**sh \ā**a**ce \ä\\ m**o**p, m**a**r
\au̇**ou**t \ch**ch**in \e**b**et \ē**ea**sy \g**g**o \i**h**it \ ī**i**ce \j**j**ob
\n\si**ng** \ō**g**o \ȯ\l**aw** \ȯi**b**oy \th**th**in \t̲h̲**th**e \ü\l**oo**t \u̇\f**oo**t
\y**y**et \zh\vi**s**ion, bei**ge** \k̲,ⁿ, œ, ᴌᴇ, ʸ\

Note that each letter and symbol is followed by a sample word. The sample word tells you how that letter and symbol sounds. For example, the long *a* sounds like *a* in *ace*. And the short *i* has the sound of the *i* in *hit*. The symbol that looks like an upside down *e* (ə) is called a schwa. The schwa has a sound like *uh*, as in *abut*.

Different dictionaries use different symbols in their pronunciation keys, so be sure to check the key of the dictionary you are using.

EXAMPLES Use the pronunciation key reprinted in this book to answer questions about the following words.

_____ **1.** con·sign (kən-'sīn)

The *i* in *consign* sounds like the *i* in
a. sit.
b. sigh.

_____ **2.** de·vi·ate('dē-vē-āt)

The *a* in *deviate* sounds like the *a* in
a. mat.
b. day.

PRACTICE 11

Using your dictionary, find and write in the pronunciation symbols and accent marks for each of the following words.

1. ouster _____

2. papyrus _____

Parts of Speech

Parts of speech indicate how a word functions in a sentence. Dictionary entries tell you what part of speech a word is—noun, verb, adjective, and so on. The part of speech is abbreviated and printed in italics. Your dictionary provides a full list of abbreviations. The following are the most common abbreviations for the parts of speech:

Parts of Speech			
adj	adjective	*n*	noun
adv	adverb	*prep*	preposition
conj	conjunction	*pron*	pronoun
interj	interjection	*v, vi, vt*	verb

Read again the sample dictionary entry for herbicide.

her·bi·cide \\'(h)ər-bə-ˌsīd\\ *n* [L *herba* + ISV =*cide*] (1899) : an agent used to destroy or inhibit plant growth — **her·bi·cid·al** \\, (h)ər-bə-'sī-dᵊl\\ *adj* — **her·bi·cid·al·ly** \\-dᵊl-ē\\ *adv*

—By permission. From *Merriam-Webster's Collegiate® Dictionary,* 11th Edition
© 2010 by Merriam-Webster, Incorporated (www.Merriam-Webster.com).

As the entry shows, the word *herbicide* is a noun. Two other forms of the word are identified as an adjective (*herbicidal*) and an adverb (*herbicidally*).

EXAMPLES   Use your dictionary to identify the parts of speech for each of the following words. A word may be used as more than one part of speech.

1. complement _____

2. before _____

3. fly _____

PRACTICE 12

Use your dictionary to identify the parts of speech for each of the following words. A word may be used as more than one part of speech.

1. graph _____

2. angle _____

3. degree _____

Definitions

Most words have more than one meaning. When there is more than one defin-ition, each meaning is numbered. Many times the dictionary will also provide examples of sentences in which the word is used.

EXAMPLES   Three definitions are given for the word *degree*. In the spaces pro-vided, write the number of the definition that best fits its meaning in each sentence.

1. A step or stage in a process

2. A unit of measurement for angles and curves

3. A title conferred on students by a college, university, or professional school upon completion of a program of study

_____ **A.** Joanne changed her physical fitness activities by degrees; she began with short 5-minute walks and built up to 30-minute walks every day of the week.

_____ **B.** John received his associate of arts degree from a community college and his bachelor of arts degree from a four-year university.

_____ **C.** If two triangles are similar, their corresponding angles have the same number of degrees.

PRACTICE 13

Here are two words, their definitions, and sentences using the words based on their various definitions. In the spaces provided, write the number of the definition that best fits each sentence. Note that one definition is not used.

A. factor: 1 something that brings about a result, ingredient; **2** one who acts or transacts the business of another; **3** a number that will divide into another number exactly

_____ **1.** The _factors_ of 10 are 1, 2, and 5.

_____ **2.** The doctor discovered that pollen was a _factor_ in Justine's sinus condition.

B. plot: 1 _n_ a small area of planted ground; **2** _n_ the plan or main story of a literary work; **3** _v_ to mark or note on as if on a map or chart

_____ **3.** I love to read a novel with a fast-paced _plot_.

_____ **4.** The graph of an equation is a drawing that _plots_ all its solutions.

_____ **5.** Grandmother worked in the vegetable _plot_ all morning.

Textbook Aids for Learning Content Words

Content Words

Many students think they should be able to pick up a textbook and simply read it. However, a textbook is written for a content or subject area, such as math, history, or English. Each content area has its own vocabulary. For example, a

Textbook
Skills

history textbook takes a different approach from that of a literature textbook. Different courses may use the same words, but the words often take on a new or different meaning in the context of the content area.

EXAMPLES The following sentences all use the word *parallel*. Write the letter of the course that would use the word in the context in which it appears.

_____ **1.** The brain appears to be a parallel processor, in which many different groups of neuron circuits work on different tasks at the same time.
    a. mathematics   c. history
    b. English   d. psychology

_____ **2.** Some writers use parallel structure of words and phrases for a balanced and smooth flow of ideas.
    a. mathematics   c. history
    b. English   d. psychology

_____ **3.** Parallel lines never intersect.
    a. mathematics   c. history
    b. English   d. psychology

EXPLANATIONS Use context clues to determine your answers.

1. The word *parallel* in this sentence is used in the study of the mind. So this term is used in a psychology class (d).

2. The word *parallel* in this sentence is used in an English class (b). Parallel structure refers to the repetition of words and phrases that are equal in their forms.

3. The word *parallel* in this sentence is used in a mathematics class (a). Parallel lines can run side by side without meeting.

Textbook Definitions

You do not always need to use the dictionary to find the meaning of a word. In fact, many textbooks contain words or word groups that you cannot find in a dictionary. The content word is usually typed in bold or italic print. The definition follows, and many times an example is given. Context clues are helpful.

EXAMPLES Read the following passage from a psychology textbook. Then answer the questions that follow it.

Textbook
Skills

Disconfirmation is a communication pattern in which you ignore a person's presence as well as that person's communications. You say, in effect, that the person and what she or he has to say aren't worth serious attention. Disconfirming responses often lead to loss of self-esteem. Note that disconfirmation is not the same as rejection. In **rejection**, you disagree with the person; you indicate your unwillingness to accept something the other person says or does. In disconfirming someone, however, you deny that person's significance; you claim that what this person says or does simply does not count.

—DeVito, *Interpersonal Communication Book,* p. 171 © 2009 by Pearson Education, Inc. Reproduced by permission of Pearson Education, Inc.

1. A communication pattern in which you ignore a person's presence as well as that person's communications is _____.

2. An unwillingness to accept something the other person says or does is

_____.

EXPLANATIONS The author knows that these words, or the specific uses of these words, may be new for many students, so the words are set in **bold** print and definitions are given.

1. disconfirmation   2. rejection

PRACTICE 14

Read each of the following textbook passages. Then write the definition for each of the words in **bold** print.

Textbook
Skills

1. To say that $x + 4 <$ (is less than) 10 and $x <$ (is less than) 6 are **equivalent** is to say that they have the same solution set. For example, the number 3 is a solution to $x + 4 < 10$. It is also a solution for $x < 6$. The number -2 is a solution of $x < 6$. It is also a solution of $x + 4 < 10$. Any solution of one is a solution of the other; they are equivalent.

—Bittinger/Beecher, *Introductory and Intermediate Algebra: Combined Approach,* Text excerpt from p. 143 © 2003 Pearson Education, Inc. Reproduced by permission of Pearson Education, Inc.

2. To borrow the useful terms of the English novelist E. M. Forster, characters may seem **flat** or round. A **flat** character has only one outstanding trait or feature: for example, the stock character of the mad scientist, with his lust for absolute power and his crazily gleaming eyes.

—Adapted from Kennedy & Gioia, *Literature*, 8th ed., p. 78.

_____

3. **Codependence** refers to a self-defeating relationship pattern in which a person is "addicted to the addict."

—Donatelle, *Access to Health*, 7th ed., p. 321.

_____

_____

Textbook Skills ## Visual Vocabulary

Textbooks often make information clearer by providing a visual image such as a graph, chart, or photograph. Take time to study these visual images and their captions to figure out how each one ties in to the information given in words.

EXAMPLES Study the following flow chart from a college psychology textbook. Then, use information from the flow chart to fill in the blanks in the paragraph that explains the flow chart in greater detail.

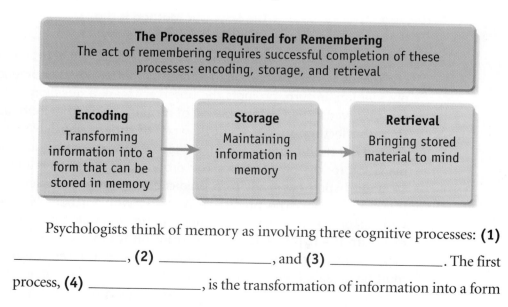

The Processes Required for Remembering
The act of remembering requires successful completion of these processes: encoding, storage, and retrieval

Encoding	Storage	Retrieval
Transforming information into a form that can be stored in memory	Maintaining information in memory	Bringing stored material to mind

Psychologists think of memory as involving three cognitive processes: **(1)** _____, **(2)** _____, and **(3)** _____. The first process, **(4)** _____, is the transformation of information into a form that can be stored. For example, if you witness a car crash, you might try to form a mental picture of it to enable yourself to remember it. The second process, **(5)** _____, involves keeping or maintaining information. For **(6)** _____ information to be stored, some physiological change must take place in the brain—a process called consolidation. The final process, **(7)** _____, occurs when information is brought to mind. To remember something, you must perform all three processes—**(8)** _____ the information, **(9)** _____ it, and then **(10)** _____ it.

> —Wood et al, *Mastering the World of Psychology,* Text from p. 178 © 2008 Pearson Education, Inc. Reproduced by permission of Pearson Education, Inc.

EXPLANATIONS The flow chart contains all the information you needed to fill in the blanks in the paragraph. As you compare your answers to the following, note the change in suffixes based on how certain words are used in context: (1) encoding; (2) storage; (3) retrieval; (4) encoding; (5) storage; (6) encoded; (7) retrieval; (8) encode; (9) store; and (10) retrieve.

PRACTICE 15

Read the following paragraph from a college biology textbook. Then, using information from the paragraph, fill in the flow chart to illustrate the ideas in the paragraph.

The Scientific Method Is the Basis for Scientific Inquiry

[1]The scientific method proceeds step-by-step. [2]It begins when someone makes an **observation** of an interesting pattern or phenomenon. [3]The observation, in turn, prompts the observer to ask a **question** about what was observed. [4]Then, after a period of contemplation (that perhaps also includes reflecting on the scientific work of others who have considered related questions), the person proposes an answer to the question, an explanation for the observation. [5]This proposed explanation is a **hypothesis**. [6]A good hypothesis leads to a **prediction**, typically expressed in "if . . . then" language. [7]The prediction is tested with further observations or with **experiments**. [8]These experiments produce results that either support or refute the hypothesis, and a **conclusion** is drawn about it. [9]A single experiment is never an adequate basis for a conclusion; the experiment must be repeated not only by the original experimenter but also by others.

> –Audesirk, Audesirk, & Byers, *Life on Earth,* 5th ed., p. 3.

The Scientific Method

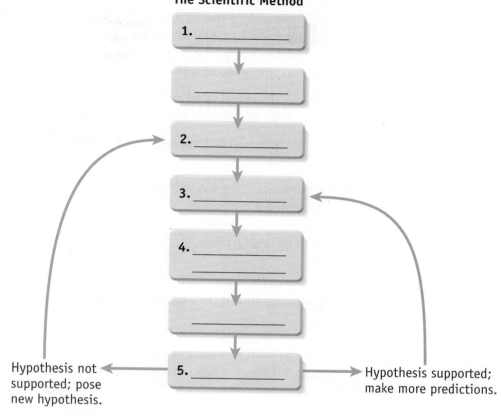

Hypothesis not supported; pose new hypothesis.

Hypothesis supported; make more predictions.

APPLICATIONS

Application 1: Synonyms and Antonyms

A. **(1–3.)** The following paragraph uses synonyms as context clues for three words. Underline the signal words and circle the synonym given for each of the words in **bold** type.

Liquidity

Liquidity refers to your ability to cover any short-term cash **deficiencies** or shortages. Some people rely on a credit card as a source of liquidity rather than keeping liquid investments. Many credit cards provide short-term or **temporary** free financing from the time you make purchases until the date when your payment is due. If you have **insufficient funds**—that is, not enough money to pay the entire credit card balance

Textbook Skills

when the bill is due—you may pay only a portion of your balance. You can then finance the rest of the payment. The interest rate is commonly quite high, ranging from 8 to 20 percent.

—Madura, *Personal Finance Update*, Text Excerpt from p. 160 © 2006 Pearson Education, Inc. Reproduced by permission of Pearson Education, Inc.

B. In the sentence, underline the signal word and circle the antonym for the word in **bold** type. In the blank, write the letter of the best definition for the word in **bold**.

4. A **hypothesis** is not a factual statement: it is a tentative idea that might explain a set of facts or actions.

_____ **5.** The best definition for **hypothesis** is
a. an educated guess.
b. a well-thought-out lie.
c. a set of facts or actions.

Application 2: Context Clues

Read the following paragraph, and then answer the questions.

Empathy

Textbook
Skills

¹To **empathize** with someone is to feel as that person feels. ²When you feel empathy for another, you're able to experience what the other is experiencing from that person's point of view. ³**Empathy** is not a lack of concern, but neither does it mean that you agree with what the other person says or does. ⁴You never lose your own identity or your own attitudes or beliefs. ⁵To **sympathize**, on the other hand, is to feel for the individual—to feel sorry for the person, for example.

—DeVito, *Messages: Building Interpersonal Communication Skills*, Text from p. 221 © 2004. Reproduced by permission of Pearson Education, Inc.

_____ **1.** The synonym for **empathize** in sentence 1 is
a. think.
b. feel.
c. agree.

_____ **2.** The antonym for **empathy** in sentence 3 is
a. agreement.   c. concern.
b. feeling.   d. lack of concern.

3. What example of **sympathize** is given in sentence 5? Fill in the blank:

Sympathize means to feel _____ for another person.

Application 3: Word Parts

Study the chart of word parts and their meanings. Below the chart are three words made from the word parts in the chart. Answer the questions in sections A and B based on this chart.

Prefix	Meaning	Root	Meaning	Suffix	Meaning
bi-	two	*ocul*	eye	*-ar*	relating to, being
mono-	one	*primus*	leader, of first rank	*-ate*	quality, state

binocular	monocular	primate

A. Fill in the blanks to match each word to its definition.

1. _____ means "two-eyed."

2. _____ means "any of an order of mammals that includes humans, apes, and monkeys."

3. _____ means "one-eyed."

B. (**4–6.**) Using word meanings and context clues, put each word into the sentence that best fits its meaning. Use each word once.

binocular	monocular	primates

Textbook Skills

Depth Perception

Depth perception requires that we perceive the distance of objects in the environment from us and from each other. We do so by means of two kinds of cues: binocular and monocular. _____ cues arise from the fact that the visual fields of both eyes overlap. Only animals that have eyes on the front of the head (such as _____, cats, and some birds) can obtain binocular cues. Animals that have eyes on the sides of their heads (such as rabbits and fish) can obtain only

_____ cues.

—Carlson/Buskist, *Psychology: Science of Behavior,* Text Excerpt from p. 217
© 1997. Reproduced by permission of Pearson Education, Inc.

Application 4: Dictionary Skills

To expand your vocabulary, use a Dictionary Log. Before you read, identify one or two new or difficult words to add to your working vocabulary. Look up the words in a dictionary and record key information to remember. Then read. After reading, create a sentence using the word. Do this to expand your prior knowledge. A log like this is an excellent vocabulary building technique.

Read the following series of sentences. Use your dictionary to complete the following log based on words used in the sentences.

An **acrimonious** dispute about money divided the family. **Caustic** words spoken in anger left deep emotional wounds. An **arbitrator** had to be brought in to settle the dispute. Even once the money issue was **equitably** decided, certain family members could not forgive or forget the hurt.

		A Dictionary Log	
Word	**Part of Speech**	**Pronunciation and Syllables**	**Definition**
1. acrimonious	adj	\ˌa-krə–ˈmō-nē-əs\	biting, sharp in feelings, language, or manner
Use in new sentence: _____			
2. caustic	_____	_____	_____
Use in new sentence: _____			
3. arbitrator	_____	_____	_____ _____ _____
Use in new sentence: _____			
4. equitably	_____	_____	fairly, rightfully
Use in new sentence: _____			

REVIEW TEST 1   Score (number correct) _____ × 10 = _____ %

Context Clues

A. Use context clues. Select the letter of the best meaning for each word in **bold** type. Then identify the context clue you used.

_____ **1.** Manny's attendance **dwindled**, until he finally stopped coming altogether.
a. lessened   c. enhanced
b. improved   d. ended

_____ **2.** The context clue used for the word *dwindled* in sentence 1:
a. synonym   c. general context
b. antonym   d. example

_____ **3.** Researchers have learned to control or eliminate many **blights** such as smallpox and the bubonic plague.
a. barriers   c. diseases
b. tests   d. mysteries

_____ **4.** The context clue used for the word *blights* in sentence 3:
a. synonym   c. general context
b. antonym   d. example

B. Using context clues, write the definition for each word in **bold** type. Choose definitions from the box. Use each definition once.

complicated	environment	range
disagreement	illnesses	smooth-talking

5. Few singers can boast of a musical **repertoire** like that of Elvis Presley, who easily mastered gospel, ballads, and rock and roll.

_____

6. In a democratic society, individuals who disagree with government are allowed to voice their **dissent** by writing, speaking, and even marching in the streets.

_____

7. Washing hands with warm, sudsy water is an important step in the fight against **infirmities** caused by unseen germs.

_____

8. Con artists cheat countless numbers of us with their **glib** promises and high-pressure sales tactics.

_____

9. The handmade lacework on the tablecloth has a beautiful and **intricate** design of roses and scallops.

_____

10. Central Florida alligators enjoy a **habitat** of spring-fed waterways, sandy beaches with fallen logs, and shallow wetlands for hunting and nesting.

_____

REVIEW TEST 2   Score (number correct) _____ × 10 = _____%

Dictionary and Glossary Skills

Textbook Skills

A. Look over the following entry from *Merriam-Webster's Collegiate Dictionary* 11th edition. Then mark the numbered items **T** if it is true or **F** if it is false based on the entry.

> **my·o·pia** \mī-'ō-pē-ə\ *n* [NL, fr. GK *myōpia,* fr. *myōp-, myōps*] (ca.1752)
> **1:** a condition in which the visual images come to a focus in front of the retina of the eye resulting esp. in defective vision of distant objects
> **2:** a lack of foresight or discernment: a narrow view of something — **my·o·pic** \ -'ō-pik, -'ä*adj* — **my·o·pi·cal·ly** \ -pi-k(ə-)lē\ *adv*

—By permission. From *Merriam-Webster's Collegiate® Dictionary,* 11th Edition © 2010 by Merriam-Webster, Incorporated (www.Merriam-Webster.com).

_____ **1.** The entry gives three forms of the word *myopia.*

_____ **2.** *Myopia* can be a way of thinking about a topic.

_____ **3.** *Myopia* has three syllables.

_____ **4.** The *y* in *myopia* sounds like the *y* in *yard*.

_____ **5.** *Myopic* is a noun.

B. Look over the following list of words from the glossary of the college textbook *Access to Health*. Based on the definition of each word and the context of each sentence, label each statement **T** if it is true or **F** if it is false.

Textbook
Skills

> **Glossary**
>
> **Adjustment** The attempt to cope with a given situation.
> **Strain** The wear-and-tear sustained by the body and mind in adjusting to or resisting a stressor.
> **Stress** Mental and physical responses to change.
> **Stressor** A physical, social, or psychological event or condition that requires adjustment.

_____ **6.** **Stress** is usually the result of an internal state of emotional tension that occurs in response to the various demands of living.

_____ **7.** An angry parent is an example of a **stressor**.

_____ **8.** Adjustments are used as a last resort in response to **stress**.

_____ **9.** **Strain** is always a physical problem.

_____ **10.** Binge eating may be an unhealthy adjustment to the **stress** caused by low self-esteem.

REVIEW TEST 3

Score (number correct) _____ × 20 = _____%

Read the following passage from a college business textbook. Answer the questions that follow.

What Goes Up Continues to Go Up

[1]The sign in front of a Florida Shell gasoline station summed it up nicely: The "prices" for the three grades of gasoline sold at the station were listed as "An arm," "A leg," and "Your firstborn." [2]While the sign no doubt led to a few smiles from motorists, its sentiments were far from a laughing matter. [3]Indeed, in mid 2004 retail gasoline prices in the

Textbook
Skills

United States were at an all-time high, exceeding $2 per gallon in most places. [4]But while gasoline prices have often **fluctuated** up and down, the upward price spiral in 2004 left consumers, government officials, and business leaders struggling to find answers.

[5]What made this gas crisis unusual was that it was the result of an unusual **confluence** of supply, demand, and global forces. [6]In the past, for instance, gas prices generally increased only when the supply was reduced. [7]For example, an Arab **embargo** on petroleum exports to the United States in 1971 led to major price jumps. [8]But these higher prices spurred new exploration, and as new oil fields came online, prices eventually dropped again. [9]Subsequent supply disruptions due to political problems in Venezuela, Nigeria, and Iraq have also contributed to reduced supplies and hence higher prices at different times.

[10]But the circumstances underlying the 2004 increases were much more complex. [11]First of all, the supply of domestically produced gasoline in the United States has dropped steadily since 1972. [12]This has been due to the facts that domestic oil fields have been nearly exhausted at the same time that new sources were being identified in many other parts of the world. [13]Hence, global supplies have been increasing at a rate that has more than offset the declines in domestic production. [14]As a result, the United States has been relying more and more on foreign producers.

[15]Second, demand for gasoline in the United States has continued to rise. [16]A growing population, the increased popularity of gas-guzzling SUVs and other big vehicles, and strong demand for other products (plastics, for instance) that require petroleum as a raw material have all contributed to increased demand. [17]For example, in 2002 the United States consumed 7,191 million barrels of oil. [18]This total was greater than the combined **consumption** of Germany, Russia, China, and Japan. [19]As prices escalated, fears grew that there could be major economic damage. [20]In the words of one expert, "Higher energy costs flow into every nook and cranny of the economy."

[21]The final piece of the puzzle, surprisingly enough, was a surging global economy. [22]As nation after nation started to recover from the global downturn that had led economic growth, the demand for oil and gasoline also surged. [23]More people were buying cars, petroleum refiners worked around the clock to meet the **unprecedented** demand for gasoline. [24]China, in particular, has become a major consumer of petroleum.

[25]So, rather than weak supplies, it was strong global demand that was propelling the price increases that swept the country. [26]And these price increases were leading to a wide array of consequences. [27]For one

thing, automobile manufacturers stepped up their commitment to making more fuel-efficient cars. ²⁸Refiners posted record profits. ²⁹And even local police officers were kept busy combating a surge in gasoline theft.

³⁰While short-term oil and gas prices occupied the thoughts of consumers in 2004, government officials began to worry about the bigger picture. ³¹The surging global demand for gasoline has been forcing experts to face a stark reality: The global supply of petroleum will soon peak and then slowly begin to decline. ³²While no one can pinpoint when this will happen, virtually all the experts agree that it will happen well before the middle of this century.

—Adapted from Griffin & Ebert, *Business,*
8th ed., pp. 3–4.

_____ **1.** The best meaning of **fluctuated** in sentence 4 is
     a. occurred.
     b. resulted.
     c. stabilized.
     d. varied.

_____ **2.** The best meaning of **confluence** in sentence 5 is
     a. union.
     b. confusion.
     c. separation.
     d. conflict.

_____ **3.** The best meaning of **embargo** in sentence 7 is
     a. price.
     b. allowance.
     c. ban.
     d. trade.

_____ **4.** The best meaning of **consumption** in sentence 18 is
     a. use.
     b. stockpile.
     c. eating.
     d. cost.

_____ **5.** The best meaning of **unprecedented** in sentence 23 is
     a. expected.
     b. matchless.
     c. surprising.
     d. ordinary.

WHAT DO YOU THINK?

Is our dependence on petroleum a problem? Why or why not? How can we in the United States reduce our dependence on petroleum? For example, what could government, businesses, and individuals do to reduce our consumption of petroleum? Assume you are a concerned citizen, and write a letter to your senator or to the editor of your local newspaper about our consumption of petroleum. You may want to focus on one aspect of the problem and offer at least one solution.

REVIEW TEST 4

Score (number correct) _____ × 10 = _____%

Vocabulary Skills

Textbook
Skills

Before Reading: Survey the following passage from a college geography textbook. Answer the Before Reading questions that follow the passage. **After reading:** Check the answers you gave before reading to make sure they are accurate. Then, respond to the "What Do You Think" prompt to discuss and write about what you have read.

Vocabulary Preview

metallic (sentence 16): made of, containing metal
radius (sentence 16): a straight line extending from the center of a circle to its edge or from the center of a sphere to its surface
latitude (sentence 22): an imaginary line joining points on Earth's surface that are all of equal distance north or south of the equator
microorganisms (sentence 25): a tiny organism such as a virus or bacteria that can only be seen under a microscope

Earth's Physical Systems

¹Geographers study natural processes in terms of four systems: the atmosphere, the hydrosphere, the lithosphere, and the biosphere, which encompasses all of Earth's living organisms. ²The **atmosphere** is a thin layer of gases surrounding Earth to an altitude of less than 480 kilometers (300 miles). ³Pure, dry air in the lower atmosphere contains about 78 percent nitrogen and 21 percent oxygen by volume. ⁴It also includes about 0.9 percent argon (an inert gas) and 0.38 percent carbon dioxide. ⁵Air is a mass of gas molecules held to Earth by gravity creating pressure. ⁶Variations in air pressure from one place to another cause winds to blow, as well as create storms, and control **precipitation** or rainfall patterns. ⁷The **hydrosphere** is the water realm of Earth's surface. ⁸Water can exist as a vapor, liquid, or ice, such as the oceans, surface waters on land (lakes, streams, and rivers), groundwater in soil and rock, water vapor in the atmosphere, and ice in glaciers. ⁹Over 97 percent of the world's water is in the oceans in liquid form. ¹⁰The oceans sustain a large quantity and variety of marine life in the form of both plants and animals. ¹¹Seawater supplies water vapor to the atmosphere, which returns to Earth's surface

as rainfall and snowfall. [12]These are the most important sources of fresh water, which is essential for the survival of plants and animals. [13]Water changes temperature very slowly, so oceans also moderate seasonal extremes of temperature over much of Earth's surface. [14]Oceans also provide humans with food and a surface for transportation.

[15]The **lithosphere** is the solid Earth, composed of rocks and **sediments**—such as clay, silt, pebbles, or sand—overlying them. [16]Earth's core is a dense, **metallic** sphere about 3,500 kilometers (2,200 miles) in **radius**. [17]Surrounding the core is a **mantle** (or layer) about 2,900 kilometers (1,800 miles) thick. [18]A thin, brittle outer shell, the crust is 8 to 40 kilometers (5 to 25 miles) thick. [19]The lithosphere consists of Earth's crust and a portion of upper mantle directly below the crust, extending down to about 70 kilometers (45 miles). [20]Powerful forces deep within Earth bend and break the crust to form mountain chains and shape the crust to form continents and ocean basins. [21]The shape of Earth's crust influences climate. [22]If the surface of Earth were completely smooth, then temperature, winds, and precipitation would form orderly bands at each **latitude**.

[23]The **biosphere** consists of all living organisms on Earth. [24]The atmosphere, lithosphere, and hydrosphere function together to create the environment of the biosphere, which extends from the depths of the oceans through the lower layers of atmosphere. [25]On the land surface, the biosphere includes giant redwood trees, which can extend up to 110 meters (360 feet), as well as the **microorganisms** that live many meters down in the soil, in deep caves, or in rock fractures.

[26]These four spheres of the natural environment interact in many ways. [27]Plants and animals live on the surface of the lithosphere, where they obtain food and shelter. [28]The hydrosphere provides water to drink and physical support for aquatic life. [29]Most life forms depend on breathing air, and birds and people also rely on air for transportation.[30]All life forms depend on inputs of solar energy.

[31]Humans also interact with each of these four spheres. [32]We waste away and die if we are without water. [33]We pant if oxygen levels are reduced in the atmosphere, and we cough if the atmosphere contains pollutants. [34]We need heat, but excessive heat or cold is dangerous. [35]We rely on a stable lithosphere for building materials and fuel for energy. [36]We derive our food from the rest of the biosphere.

—Bergman & Renwick, *Introduction to Geography:
People, Places, and Environment*, 4th ed., p. 19.

Before Reading

A. Use context clues to answer the following questions.

_____ **1.** In sentence 6, the word **precipitation** means
   a. storm.
   b. air pressure.
   c. rainfall.
   d. gas.

_____ **2.** Identify the context clue used for the word **precipitation** in sentence 6.
   a. synonym
   b. antonym
   c. general context
   d. example

_____ **3.** In sentence 15, the word **sediments** means
   a. layers.
   b. rocks.
   c. sands.
   d. deposits.

_____ **4.** Identify the context clue used for the word **sediments** in sentence 15.
   a. synonym
   b. antonym
   c. general context
   d. example

_____ **5.** In sentence 17, the word **mantle** means
   a. garment.
   b. layer.
   c. core.
   d. metal.

_____ **6.** Identify the context clue used for the word **mantle** in sentence 17.
   a. synonym
   b. antonym
   c. general context
   d. example

B. Study the following word chart. Then match the word to its definition.

Root	Meaning
atmos	vapor, breath
bio	life
hydra	water
lilth	stone
sphaera	globe, ball

_____ **7.** atmosphere

_____ **8.** biosphere

_____ **9.** hydrosphere

_____ **10.** lithosphere

a. the part of Earth that is water

b. The solid outer layer of the Earth

c. the area of the Earth that is inhabited by living things

d. gases surrounding the Earth

VISUAL VOCABULARY

The Grand Canyon in Arizona represents Earth's

_____ .

   a. atmosphere.
   b. hydrosphere.
   c. lithosphere.

WHAT DO YOU THINK?

Climate change, global warming, and pollution are growing concerns, and experts believe that human behavior has an impact on Earth's four systems. For example, the use of fossil fuels pollutes the atmosphere. Assume you are taking a college course in geography, and your class is involved in service learning. Your service learning project is to raise awareness about the need for individuals to protect the environment. Write a report about the health of Earth's four systems in your local community. For example, what is the state of the hydrosphere where you live? Are the lakes, rivers, or ocean near you clean and healthy, or polluted? Assume your report counts as 10% of your final grade, but also write your report as a letter to the editor of the local newspaper.

After Reading About Vocabulary and Dictionary Skills

The reading system you learned in Chapter 1 is an excellent study system that will help you comprehend and retain large sections of information, such as this textbook chapter about vocabulary skills. Now that you have studied the chapter, take time to reflect on what you have learned before you begin the Mastery Tests. Stop and think about your learning and performance by answering the following questions. Write your answers in your notebook.

- How has my knowledge base or prior knowledge about vocabulary and dictionary skills changed?

- Based on my studies, how do I think I will perform on the Mastery Test(s)? Why do I think my scores will be above average, average, or below average?

- Would I recommend this chapter to other students who want to learn more about Vocabulary and Dictionary Skills? Why or why not?

Test your understanding of what you have learned about Vocabulary and Dictionary Skills by completing the Chapter 2 Review Card near the end of the text.

CONNECT TO PEARSON **myreadinglab**

The check your progress in meeting Chapter 2's learning outcomes, log in to www.myreadinglab.com, and try the following activities.

- The "Vocabulary" section of MyReadingLab offers several tools which can help to accomplish this goal, including the dictionary, vocabulary in context, synonyms and antonyms, and prefixes and suffixes. To access this resource, click on the "Study Plan" tab. Then click on "Vocabulary." Then click on the following links as needed:
  - "Overview"
  - "Model"
  - "Word Elements I: Root Words, Prefixes, and Suffixes (Flash Animation)"
  - "Compound Words (Flash Animation)"
  - "Word Elements II: Root Words, Prefixes, and Suffixes (Flash Animation)"
  - "Word Origins (Flash Animation)"
  - "Practice"
  - "Tests"

- The "Other Resources" section of MyReadingLab offers an overview of vocabulary and dictionary skills, along with an audio dictionary, activities, exercises and quizzes, spelling activities, and flashcards. To access resources for these skills, go to the "Other Resources" on the Home page of MyReadingLab. Click on the link labeled "Vocabulary Website." Under "select your level," choose the link labeled "Intermediate." Click on the following as needed: "Dictionary," "Context Clues," "Synonyms," "Antonyms," "Prefixes," "Roots," "Suffixes," and "Flashcards."

- To measure your mastery of the content in this chapter, complete the tests in the "Vocabulary" section and click on Gradebook to find your results.

A. Look over the following entry from *Merriam-Webster's Collegiate Dictionary,* 11th edition. Then mark each item **T** if it is true or **F** if it is false, based on the entry.

> ¹**myr·i·ad** \\'mir-ē-əd\\ *n* [GK *myriad-, myrias,* fr. *myrioi* countless, ten thousand] (1555) **1** : ten thousand **2** : a great number ⟨a ~ of ideas⟩
> ²**myriad** *adj* (1765) **1** : INNUMERABLE ⟨those ~ problems⟩; also : both numerous and diverse ⟨~ topics⟩ **2** : having innumerable aspects or elements ⟨the ~ activity of the new land—Meridel Le Sueur⟩

—By permission. From *Merriam-Webster's Collegiate® Dictionary,* 11th Edition © 2010 by Merriam-Webster, Incorporated (www.Merriam-Webster.com).

_____ **1.** The noun *myriad* comes from a Greek word meaning "ten thousand."

_____ **2.** The word *myriad* can be used as a noun or as an adjective.

_____ **3.** The word *myriad* has four syllables.

_____ **4.** The *i* in *myriad* sounds like the *i* in *sigh*.

B. Look over the following list of words from the glossary of an ecology textbook. Based on the definition of each word and the context of each sentence, label each statement **T** if it is true or **F** if it is false.

> **Glossary**
>
> **Alluvial** A water-carved canyon
> **Arroyo** Related to material deposited by running water
> **Playa** A natural, low water basin
> **Topography** The physical structure of the landscape

_____ **5.** The **topography** of a desert is made up of lush vegetation.

_____ **6.** **Playas** can receive water that rushes down a hill.

_____ **7.** After a violent storm, **alluvial** fans carved in the soil stretch across the desert.

VISUAL VOCABULARY

This _____ is located along the coastal shoreline of the Kuril Islands, Russia.

   a. alluvial fan
   b. arroyo
   c. playa

C. Look over the following list of words from the glossary of an English hand-book. Based on the definition of each word and the context of each sentence, label each statement **T** if it is true or **F** if it is false.

Textbook Skills

> **Glossary of Usage and Terms**
>
> **Annotation**   A brief note you write about a text while reading it by making marks such as underlining, circling, and highlighting. Notes can be words, phrases, questions, or statements.
> **Paraphrase**   A restatement in your own words of the author's ideas and structure. A paraphrase closely follows the original source, pulls in many details, and may be as long as the original text.
> **Summary**   A condensed version of a text in which you explain the author's meaning fairly and accurately in your own words. A summary focuses on the author's main idea and is shorter than the original text.

_____ **8. Annotations** are written directly on the pages of a textbook.

_____ **9.** A **summary** is longer than a **paraphrase.**

_____ **10. Paraphrasing** is an effective reading and writing skill when the order of the author's ideas is important for emphasis.

Read the following passage, adapted from a college mathematics textbook. Use context clues and the graphs to write the definitions for each word in **bold** type. Choose definitions from the box. One answer will be used twice.

Integers and the Real World

Textbook
Skills

[1]A **set** is a collection of objects. [2]For our purposes, we will most often be considering sets of numbers. [3]The set of **natural numbers** are those numbers to the right of zero. [4]The **whole numbers** are the natural numbers with 0 included. [5]We can represent these two sets of numbers on a visual called a **number line**.

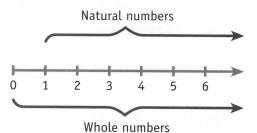

[6]We create a new set of numbers called *integers* by starting with the whole numbers, 0, 1, 2, 3, and so on. [7]For each natural number 1, 2, 3, and so on, we obtain a new number to the left of the zero on the number line: [8]For the number 1, there will be an opposite number –1 (negative 1); for the number 2, there will be an opposite number –2 (negative 2); and so on. [9]We call these new numbers to the left of zero **negative integers**. [10]The natural numbers are also called **positive integers**. [11]The set of **integers** equals { . . . –5, –4, –3, –2, –1, 0, 1, 2, 3, 4, 5 . . . }.

[12]Integers relate to many real-world problems and situations. [13]The following example will help you get ready to turn problem situations that use integers into mathematical language.

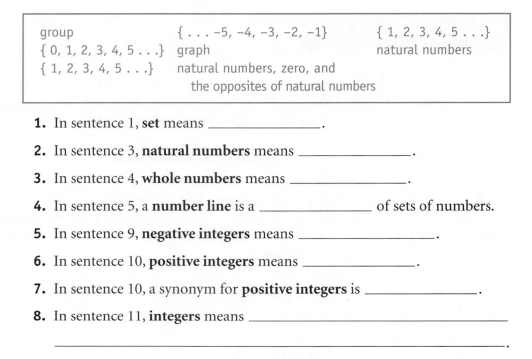

group	{ . . . −5, −4, −3, −2, −1}	{ 1, 2, 3, 4, 5 . . .}
{ 0, 1, 2, 3, 4, 5 . . .}	graph	natural numbers
{ 1, 2, 3, 4, 5 . . .}	natural numbers, zero, and	
	the opposites of natural numbers	

1. In sentence 1, **set** means _____.

2. In sentence 3, **natural numbers** means _____.

3. In sentence 4, **whole numbers** means _____.

4. In sentence 5, a **number line** is a _____ of sets of numbers.

5. In sentence 9, **negative integers** means _____.

6. In sentence 10, **positive integers** means _____.

7. In sentence 10, a synonym for **positive integers** is _____.

8. In sentence 11, **integers** means _____

_____.

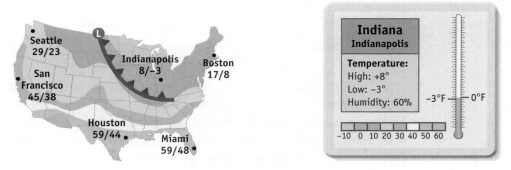

—Text and figure from Bittinger/Beecher, *Introductory and Intermediate Algebra: Combined Approach*, Text Excerpt and Figure from p. 13 © 2003 Pearson Education, Inc. Reproduced by permission of Pearson Education, Inc.

9–10. Use the temperature map to answer the following questions.

9. The low temperature in Indianapolis is 3 degrees below zero. Which integer corresponds to this situation? _____

10. The high temperature in Indianapolis is 8 degrees above zero. Which integer corresponds to this situation? _____

A. Read the following passage, adapted from a college psychology textbook. Use context clues to write the definition for each word in **bold** type. Choose definitions from the box. You will not use all of the definitions.

Textbook
Skills

Personality Types and Traits

¹It has long been clear that people differ in personality. ²The earliest known reason given for these individual differences is the humoral theory. ³This **premise** was first put forth by the Greek physician Galen in the second century. ⁴He based his beliefs on the then-current medical beliefs that had **originated** with the ancient Greeks. ⁵The body was thought to contain four humors, or fluids: yellow bile, black bile, phlegm, and blood. ⁶People were classified according to the disposition caused by the **predominance** or power of one of those humors in the body. ⁷Choleric people, who had an excess of yellow bile, were bad-tempered and **irritable**. ⁸Melancholic people, who had an excess of black bile, had gloomy and pessimistic natures. ⁹Phlegmatic people, whose bodies had large amounts of phlegm, were sluggish, calm, and unexcitable. ¹⁰Sanguine people had a **preponderance** of blood, which made them cheerful and passionate.

—Adapted from Carlson/Buskist, *Psychology: Science of Behavior*,
Text Excerpt from p. 449 © 1997. Reproduced by
permission of Pearson Education, Inc.

begun	great amount	offered
easily angered	idea	stopped
good-natured	influence	weakness

1. In sentence 3, **premise** means _____.

2. In sentence 4, **originated** means _____.

3. In sentence 6, **predominance** means _____.

4. In sentence 7, **irritable** means _____.

5. In sentence 10, **preponderance** means _____.

B. Read the following passage, adapted from a college health textbook. Use context clues and word parts to write the definition for each word in **bold** type. Choose definitions from the box. Use each definition once.

Textbook
Skills

The Pathogens: Routes of Transmission

¹**Pathogens** enter the body in several ways. ²They may be **transmitted** by direct contact between infected persons, such as by kissing, or by indirect contact such as by touching the object an infected person has had contact with. ³The hands are probably the greatest source of infectious disease transmission. ⁴You may also **autoinoculate** yourself, or transmit a pathogen from one part of your body to another. ⁵For example, you may touch a sore on your lip that is teeming with viral herpes and then transmit the virus to your eye when you scratch your itchy eyelid.

⁶Pathogens are also transmitted by airborne contact; you can breathe in air that carries a particular pathogen. ⁷Pathogens are also passed through foodborne infection if you eat something **contaminated** by **microorganisms**.

—Donatelle, *Health,* 5th ed., p. 348.

Prefix	Meaning	Root	Meaning	Suffix	Meaning
auto-	self	*mit*	send	*-ate*	make, do, cause
con-	with	*ocul*	eye, bud	*-gen*	cause
in-	into	*organ*	work	*-ism*	being
micro-	small	*path*	disease		
trans-	across	*tamin*	spoil		

germs	poisoned	to infect another
life forms too small to be seen by the naked eye	spread	part of one's body

6. In sentence 1, **pathogens** means _____.

7. In sentence 2, **transmitted** means _____.

8. In sentence 4, **autoinoculate** means _____.

9. In sentence 7, **contaminated** means _____.

10. In sentence 7, **microorganisms** means _____

_____.

Vocabulary Skills

A. Using the information in the chart and the context of each sentence, select the word that best fits the meaning of the sentence. Use each word once.

Prefix	Meaning	Root	Meaning	Suffix	Meaning
carni-	flesh	ent	intestines	-al	possessing or expressing a quality
dys-	bad, impaired	function	perform	-ery	state, condition
omni-	all	nocturn	night	-ous	possessing the qualities of
		vor	devour, feed		

| dysentery | nocturnal | dysfunctional | carnivorous | omnivores |

1. Some birds such as eagles and ospreys are _____, with diets consisting of fish and small animals.

2. Julia is suffering with _____ because of water she drank in the jungle.

3. Just like a bat, my son Chip is a _____ creature who prefers to sleep during the day.

4. Most _____ have two types of teeth: sharp, tearing teeth for eating meat and flat, grinding teeth for eating plants.

5. If I don't get enough sleep, I become completely _____.

B. Using the information from the chart and the context of each sentence, select the word that best fits the meaning of the sentence. Use each word once.

Prefix	Meaning	Root	Meaning	Suffix	Meaning
e-	out of, from	ject	throw	-ile	capability
pro-	forward, in favor of	pellere	to drive	-ion	action, state

ejection	ejects	projectile	projects	propel

6. Because mother _____ her fears into action, she taught all of us the Heimlich maneuver as a safety precaution.

7. The Heimlich maneuver is an emergency procedure that _____ foreign objects from a choking victim's airway.

8. The maneuver causes the _____ of the foreign object by forcing quick bursts of air up from the abdomen.

9. Sometimes a strong burst of air turns the object that is blocking the air passage into a _____ as it shoots out of the victim's mouth.

10. Place a clenched fist and hands together just below the sternum; use inward and upward thrusts to _____ the object from the air passage.

Stated Main Ideas

3

LEARNING OUTCOMES

After studying this chapter you should be able to do the following:

1. Identify the following: traits of a main idea, the topic of a paragraph, a topic sentence.
2. Distinguish the movement of ideas from general to specific.
3. Define the following terms: *central idea* and *thesis statement*.
4. Locate the stated main idea in a paragraph or longer passage.
5. Assess your comprehension of locating stated main ideas.
6. Evaluate the importance of locating stated main ideas.
7. Apply stated main ideas to improve comprehension.

Before Reading About Stated Main Ideas

Effective use of the reading process relies on developing questions about the material that will guide you as you read. Using the learning outcomes above, create at least five questions that you can answer as you study the chapter. Write your questions in the following spaces:

_____ (page _____)

_____ (page _____)

_____ (page _____)

_____ (page _____)

_____ (page _____)

Compare the questions you created based on the learning outcomes with the following questions. Then write the ones that seem the most helpful in your notebook, leaving enough space between each question to record the answers as you read and study the chapter.

What are the traits of a main idea? (p. 96) What is the difference between a topic and a topic sentence? (p. 102) How is the flow of ideas related to the placement of topic sentences? (p. 108) What is the central idea? (p. 117) What is the difference between the central idea and a topic sentence? (p. 117)

The Traits of a Main Idea

> A **main idea** is the author's controlling point about the topic. It usually includes the topic and the author's attitude or opinion about the topic, or the author's approach to the topic.

To identify the main idea, ask yourself two questions:

- Who or what is the paragraph about? The answer is the *topic*. The topic can be stated in just a few words.
- What is the author's controlling point about the topic? The answer is the *main idea*. The main idea is stated in one sentence.

Consider these questions as you read the following paragraph from a health textbook.

Textbook
Skills

The Cool-Down Period

The cool-down period is an important part of an exercise workout for several reasons. The cool-down involves reducing the intensity of exercise to allow the body to recover from the workout. During vigorous exercise such as jogging, a lot of blood is pumped to the legs, and there may not be enough to supply the heart and brain; failure to cool down properly may result in dizziness, fainting, and, in rare instances, a heart attack. By gradually reducing the level of physical activity, blood flow is directed back to the heart and brain.

—Adapted from Pruitt & Stein, *Health Styles*, 2nd ed., p. 169.

- Who or what is the paragraph about? The topic of the paragraph is "the cool-down period of an exercise workout."
- What is the author's controlling point about the topic? The controlling point is that it "is an important part." Putting topic and controlling point together, the main idea is "The cool-down period is an important part of an exercise workout for several reasons."

To better understand the traits of a main idea, compare a passage to a well-planned house of ideas. The *topic* or general subject matter is the roof. The roof covers all the rooms of the house. The *main idea* is the frame of the house, and the supporting details are the different rooms. The following diagram shows the relationship of the ideas:

Topic: Cool-down period

Main Idea (stated in a topic sentence):

The cool-down period is an important part of an exercise workout for several reasons.

Supporting   Details:

Cool-down allows the body to recover from the workout.	No cool-down may result in dizziness, fainting, and, in rare instances, a heart attack.	Cool-down directs blood flow back to the heart and brain.

Each of the supporting details explains why the cool-down period is an important part of an exercise workout.

Identifying the Topic of a Paragraph

When you ask the question "Who or what is the paragraph about?" you must be sure that your answer is neither too general nor too specific. A general subject needs specific ideas to support or explain it. However, no single paragraph can discuss all the specific ideas linked to a general idea. So an author narrows the general subject to a topic that needs a specific set of ideas to support it. For example, the very general subject "music" can be narrowed to "hip-hop music." And the specific details related to hip-hop music might include the different rappers, ranging from Eminem to Ludacris to Akon. In fact, a piece of writing dealing with the general topic "music" will include a very different set of specific ideas than the narrower topic of "hip-hop music." The more general category of music might include classical music and country music, for example. Or it might include symphonies, marching bands, and barber shop quartets.

Often an author shows the relationship between the topic and the specific details by repeating the topic throughout the paragraph as new pieces of information about the topic are introduced. To identify the topic, an effective reader often skims the material for this recurring idea. Skimming for the topic allows you to grasp the relationship among a general subject, the topic, and specific details.

EXAMPLE Skim the following paragraph. Circle the topic as it recurs throughout the paragraph. Answer the question that follows.

A Sincere Apology

[1]A sincere apology is a powerful human experience. [2]A sincere apology is a peace offering that honors the importance of the wronged one's feelings. [3]It defuses anger and fosters healing. [4]A genuine apology offers closure to a painful past and openness to a future built on forgiveness and empathy. [5]A genuine "I'm sorry" accepts the blame for wrongdoing and the painful results. [6]Consider the following example: as a child, Debra suffered greatly because of her abusive, alcoholic father. [7]At the age of 17, she left her father's house, and they had no contact for many years. [8]On her thirty-fifth birthday, Debra received a letter from her father, offering her a long, emotional apology. [9]Their relationship began healing that day. [10]To be brave and wise enough to apologize sincerely is to accept a lesson from life and a unique peace based on self-respect.

_____ Which of the following best states the topic?
   a. apologizing
   b. a sincere apology
   c. the importance of the wronged one's feelings

EXPLANATION "Apologizing" is too general, for it could cover insincere apologies, how to apologize, or what to do if someone will not accept an apology. "The importance of the wronged one's feelings" is too narrow. This idea is a supporting detail, just one of the reasons an apology is so powerful. The topic of this paragraph is (b), _a sincere apology_. You should have circled the following phrases: "sincere apology" (sentence 1), "sincere apology" (sentence 2), "genuine apology" (sentence 4), "genuine 'I'm sorry'" (sentence 5), and "apologize sincerely" (sentence 10). Note that the author used the synonym "genuine" to vary the wording of the topic. Note that the title of the paragraph also stated the topic. Authors often use titles to relay the topic of the material.

PRACTICE 1

Skim each of the following paragraphs and circle the topic as it recurs throughout the paragraph. Then, identify the idea that correctly states the topic. (Hint: one idea is too general to be the topic; another idea is too specific.)

_____ **1.**   [1]Many myths exist about the causes of acne. [2]Chocolate and greasy foods are often blamed, but foods seem to have little effect on the development and course of acne in most people. [3]Another common myth is that dirty skin causes acne; however, blackheads and other acne lesions are not caused by dirt. [4]Finally, stress does not cause acne.

—Adapted from National Institute of Arthritis and Musculoskeletal and Skin Diseases, "Questions and Answers about Acne."

    a. dirty skin

    b. causes of acne

    c. myths about what causes acne

_____ **2.**   [1]Playing rigorous sports in the heat can lead to several types of heat injuries. [2]The first type of heat-related illness is dehydration, which is a lack of body fluids. [3]The second type is heat exhaustion. [4]Heat exhaustion has numerous effects, including nausea, dizziness, weakness, headache, pale and moist skin, heavy perspiration, normal or low body temperature, weak pulse, dilated pupils, disorientation, and fainting spells. [5]A third type of heat injury is heat stroke. [6]Heat stroke can lead to headaches, dizziness, confusion, and hot dry skin, possibly leading to vascular collapse, coma, and death. [7]Each of these heat injuries can be prevented.

—Adapted from National Institute of Arthritis and Musculoskeletal and Skin Diseases, "Childhood Sports Injuries and Their Prevention."

    a. types of heat injuries

    b. injuries

    c. heatstroke

_____ **3.**   [1]Older people benefit from volunteer work in several ways. [2]First, being a volunteer improves the overall quality of an older person's life; it gives meaning and purpose to their lives. [3]Second, older persons who volunteer have fewer medical problems than other people their age who are not as active. [4]Older persons stay physically active when they volunteer; thus they do not suffer as often from heart disease and diabetes. [5]Finally, volunteer work helps keep the brain active, and an active brain helps protect the memory as people age.

—Adapted from Administration on Aging, "Older Volunteers Leading the Way."

    a. volunteer work

    b. benefits of volunteer work for older people

    c. fewer medical problems

Textbook
Skills

—— 4. ¹The barriers to women's advancement to top positions in the workforce are often very subtle, giving rise to the phrase *glass ceiling*. ²In explaining "why women aren't getting to the top," one observer argues that "at senior management levels, competence is assumed. ³What you are looking for is someone who fits, someone who gets along, someone you trust. ⁴Now that's subtle stuff. ⁵How does a group of men feel that a woman is going to fit in? ⁶I think it's very hard." ⁷Or as a woman bank executive says, "The men just don't feel comfortable." ⁸There are many explanations for the glass ceiling, all controversial. ⁹For example, some say that women choose staff assignments rather than fast-track, operating-head assignments. ¹⁰Others claim that women are cautious and unaggressive in corporate politics. ¹¹Finally, some believe that women have lower expectations about peak earnings and positions, and these expectations become self-fulfilling.

—Dye, *Politics in America*, 5th ed., p. 589.

a. working women
b. women's low expectations about earnings
c. the glass ceiling for women

VISUAL VOCABULARY

A "glass ceiling" is

—— an invisible barrier preventing women from rising to the highest positions in the workforce.

—— the sexual harassment a woman faces on the job.

—— a popular architectural design for large office complexes.

Textbook
Skills

5.   [1]Intellectual blocks involve obstacles to knowledge. [2]You may find yourself unable to solve a problem for two reasons. [3]First, you may be blocked because you lack information. [4]Second, you may be blocked because you have incorrect or incomplete information. [5]When you buy a car, for example, you can be blocked by being unaware of various cars' performance ratings, repair records, or safety features. [6]Or you may be blocked because you have only one-sided information—the information given by the salesperson. [7]Or maybe you simply don't know enough about cars to buy one with confidence.

—Adapted from Di Yanni and Hoy, *The Scribner Handbook for Writers*, 3rd ed., p. 65.

a. intellectual blocks
b. incorrect information
c. problem solving

Identifying a Topic Sentence

Most paragraphs have three parts:

- A topic (the general idea or subject)
- A main idea (the controlling point the author is making about the topic, often stated in a topic sentence)
- Supporting details (the specific ideas to support the main idea)

Think again of the house of ideas that a writer builds. Remember, the main idea *frames* the specific ideas. Think of all the different rooms in a house: the kitchen, bedroom, bathroom, living room. Each room is a different part of the house. The frame determines the space for each room and the flow of traffic between rooms. Similarly, the main idea determines how much detail is given and how one detail flows into the next. The main idea of a paragraph is usually stated in a single sentence called the **topic sentence**. The topic sentence—the stated main idea—is unique in two ways.

First, the topic sentence contains two types of information: the topic and the author's controlling point, which restricts or qualifies the topic. At times, the controlling point may be expressed as the author's opinion using biased words. (For more information on biased words see Chapter 9, "Fact and Opinion.") For example, in the topic sentence "A sincere apology is a powerful human experience," the biased words "sincere" and "powerful" limit and control the topic "apology."

Other times, the controlling point may express the author's thought pattern, the way in which the thoughts are going to be organized. (For more information on words that indicate thought patterns, see Chapters 7 and 8.) For example, the topic sentence, "Playing rigorous sports in the heat can lead to several types of heat injuries," uses the phrase "several types" to reveal that the author will control the topic by classifying or dividing the topic into types.

Often, an author will use both biased words and a thought pattern to qualify or limit the topic. For example, the topic sentence, "Older people benefit from volunteer work in several ways," combines the biased word "benefit" and the phrase "several ways" to indicate a list of positive examples and explanations will follow.

These qualifiers—words that convey the author's bias or thought pattern—helped you correctly identify the topic in the previous section. An important difference between the topic and the topic sentence is that the topic sentence states the author's main idea in a complete sentence.

> A **topic sentence** is a single sentence that states the topic and words that qualify the topic by revealing the author's opinion about the topic or the author's approach to the topic.

The second unique trait of the topic sentence is its scope: the topic sentence is a general statement that all the other sentences in the paragraph explain or support. A topic sentence states an author's opinion or thought process, which must be explained further with specific supporting details. For example, in the paragraph about the cool-down period after a workout, the topic and the author's controlling point about the topic are stated in the first sentence. Each of the other sentences in the paragraph gives a different reason to explain why the cool-down period is an important part of an exercise workout:

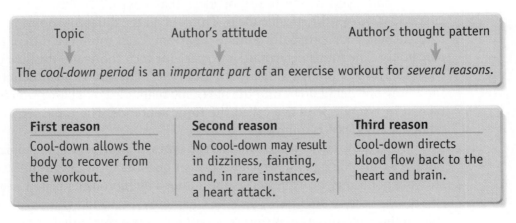

Topic	Author's attitude	Author's thought pattern

The *cool-down period* is an *important part* of an exercise workout for *several reasons.*

First reason	**Second reason**	**Third reason**
Cool-down allows the body to recover from the workout.	No cool-down may result in dizziness, fainting, and, in rare instances, a heart attack.	Cool-down directs blood flow back to the heart and brain.

> **Supporting details** are specific ideas that *develop*, *explain*, or *support* the main idea.

The supporting details of a paragraph are framed by the main idea, and all work together to explain or support the author's view of the topic. As an effective reader, you will see that every paragraph has a topic, a main idea, and supporting details. It is much easier to tell the difference between these three parts of a passage once you understand how each part works. A topic, as the general subject of the paragraph, can be expressed in a word or phrase. The main idea contains both the topic and the author's controlling point about the topic and can be stated in one sentence called the topic sentence. The supporting details are all the sentences that state reasons and explanations for the main idea. To locate the topic sentence of a paragraph ask yourself two questions:

- Which sentence contains qualifiers that reveal the author's controlling point—that is, the author's attitude about the topic or approach to the topic?
- Do all the specific details in the passage support this statement?

EXAMPLE

A. The following group of ideas presents a topic, a main idea, and two supporting details from an article posted on a popular website that offers health information. Circle the topic and underline the author's controlling point. Then answer the questions.

a. Chronic Fatigue Syndrome (CFS) is marked by extreme fatigue that has lasted at least six months; is not the result of ongoing effort; is not substantially relieved by rest; and causes a substantial drop in daily activities.

b. Despite an intensive, nearly 20-year search, the cause of CFS remains unknown.

c. Much of the ongoing research into a cause has centered on the roles that the immune, endocrine, and nervous systems may play in CFS.

d. CFS is not caused by depression, although the two illnesses often coexist.

—United States Department of Health and Human Services. "Risk Factors for CFS." Centers for Disease Control and Prevention. 7 June 2010. http://www.cdc.gov/cfs/cfsbasicfacts.htm#riskfactors.

_____ **1.** Which of the following best states the topic?
   a. symptoms of CFS   c. definition of CFS
   b. causes of CFS

_____ **2.** Which sentence is the stated main idea?

B. Read the following paragraph. Circle the topic and underline the author's controlling point. Then answer the questions.

In Love with Sodas

[1]According to *Beverage Digest*, in 2009, the U.S. carbonated soft drink market totaled 9.4 billion cases. [2]Not surprisingly, the U.S. consumes the most sodas per person of any place in the world. [3]The American love for sodas alarms many health experts. [4]Research shows that drinking too many sodas can cause a wide range of health concerns. [5]For example, according to the Center for Science in the Public Interest, sodas are the single biggest source of calories in the American diet. [6]An average serving of 12 ounces of a soda contains 155 calories, 35 to 38 milligrams of caffeine, and around 40 grams of sugar. [7]Sodas provide about 7 percent of calories in most adult diets. [8]And teenagers get 15 percent of their total calories from sodas. [9]No wonder the number of obese people in America is growing. [10]Alarmingly, animal studies reveal that phosphorus, a common ingredient in soda, can deplete bones of calcium. [11]And two recent human studies suggest that girls who drink more soda are more prone to broken bones. [12]This finding supports the fear that drinking too many sodas may lead to osteoporosis later in life. [13]Finally, according to the Academy for General Dentistry, the acids in sodas are harmful to teeth. [14]Exposing teeth to sodas, even for a short period of time, causes dental erosion. [15]And long-term exposure can lead to significant enamel loss.

1. What is the topic of the paragraph? _____

2. Which sentence is the topic sentence that states the main idea? _____

VISUAL VOCABULARY

Osteoporosis causes a weakness and softness of _____, making them more prone to fracture.

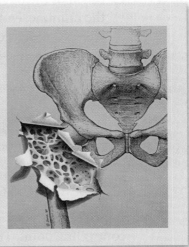

EXPLANATIONS

A. **1.** Item (b) "causes of CFS" is the best statement of the topic. Three of the four sentences refer to causes of CFS. Note that the topic is stated with just a few words—a phrase, not a complete sentence.

2. The main idea is best stated by item (b) "Despite an intensive nearly 20 year search, the cause of CFS remains unknown." This sentence is the only statement that is broad enough to be relevant to all the other ideas. For example, item (a) introduces the general topic "CFS" by stating a definition of CFS based on its major symptom. Items (c) and (d) are supporting details that offer two views about the causes of CFS.

B. **1.** The word "soda" occurs 13 times within 15 sentences. When you ask *Who or what is this paragraph about?* the recurring word "soda" becomes the obvious answer. However, another idea is also repeated or referenced in almost every sentence: "health problem." So the best statement of the topic would include both ideas as in "The Health Risks of Drinking Too Many Sodas."

2. The topic sentence of the paragraph is sentence 4. "Research shows that drinking too many sodas can cause a wide range of health concerns." The first three sentences introduce the topic and its importance. Sentences 5 through 15 explain the possible health problems caused by drinking too many sodas.

PRACTICE 2

A. Each of the following groups of ideas contains a topic, a main idea, and two supporting details. In each group, first identify the topic. Then identify the stated main idea. (Hint: circle the topic and underline the author's controlling point in each group.)

Group 1

a. A successful sales approach is sincere, optimistic, and confident.
b. Use a sincere smile and an optimistic attitude to attract a potential customer.
c. Look your customer directly in the eye and speak confidently and clearly at an easy-to-listen-to pace.

_____   **1.** Which of the following best states the topic?
        a. successful sales approach
        b. sales
        c. optimism

_____   **2.** Which sentence is the stated main idea?

Group 2

a. Malcolm X was a controversial African American activist during the civil rights era.

b. Malcolm X, born Malcolm Little, changed his name to protest bigotry.

c. Malcolm X, the son of a Baptist minister, became a member of the Black Muslim organization.

_____ **3.** Which of the following best states the topic?
   a. Malcolm X
   b. bigotry
   c. civil rights era

_____ **4.** Which sentence is the stated main idea?

Group 3

a. The collapse sinkhole is a common type of sinkhole in Florida.

b. It forms with little warning and leaves a deep, steep-sided hole.

c. Collapse sinkholes occur because of the weakening of the rock of the aquifer by erosion.

VISUAL VOCABULARY

The aquifer is _____.
   a. a naturally occurring deep well of water.
   b. a body of porous sediment or rock, consisting of sand, shell, or limestone, that allows water to move underground.

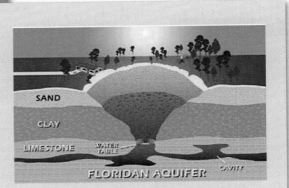

SAND

CLAY

LIMESTONE   WATER TABLE

FLORIDAN AQUIFER   CAVITY

Sinkholes form in a natural process of dissolving and eroding limestone that makes up the aquifer system.

Source: "Low Ground Waters Can Lead to Sinkholes." *Streamlines*, Fall 2000. Used by permission of the St. Johns River Water Management District. State of Florida.

_____ **5.** Which of the following best states the topic?
    a. deep, steep hole
    b. sinkholes
    c. a collapse sinkhole

_____ **6.** Which sentence is the stated main idea?

B. Read the following passage from a college textbook. Then answer the questions that follow.

Textbook
Skills

Tattoos

[1]Tattoos are made by using a needle to deposit pigment in the dermis. [2]Tattooing is an ancient practice believed to have originated around 10,000 years ago. [3]These days, tattoos are symbols of club membership for some men (street gangs, the military, fraternities); other people view them as symbols of individuality. [4]In recent years, more women have acquired tattoos as a means of expression and for cosmetic purposes; permanent eyeliner and tattooed liplines now account for over 125,000 tattoos a year.

[5]But what if a tattoo becomes unfashionable or the pigment migrates? [6]Tattoo removal has been and still is a pain—both physically and financially. [7]Until recently, once you had one, you were stuck with it, because attempts at removal—dermabrasion, cryosurgery (freezing), or applying caustic chemicals—left nasty scars. [8]Using new laser-based technologies, dermatologists have no problem destroying the black or blue pigments in tattoos applied a generation ago, but newer, multicolored tattoos pose a larger problem. [9]The multitude of pigments in tattoos today require several different lasers to be used over seven to nine treatments spaced about a month apart, each costing $75 to $150. [10]The cost in pain is roughly equal to getting tattooed in the first place. [11]Nonetheless, tattoo removal across the United States is skyrocketing.

[12]Tattoos present some other risks. [13]The FDA has some regulations concerning the composition of tattoo pigments, but their safety is not well established. [14]Indeed, studies of dyes collected from tattooing studios have been found to contain cancer-causing agents that could be activated during tattoo removal. [15]Statutory regulations vary widely (from none to complete prohibition) from state to state. [16]Still, in each case, needles are used and bleeding occurs, and practitioners' competence varies significantly. [17]If the practitioner does not adhere to strict sterile procedures, tattooing can spread infections. [18]The risk of hepatitis C

infection (a chronic liver infection) is 15 times higher in people who have been tattooed than in those who have not. [19]So if you're thinking about getting a tattoo, look into it carefully, and weigh your alternatives.

—Marieb, *Essentials of Human Anatomy & Physiology,*
9th ed., p. 113.

_____ **7.** The topic of paragraph 1 is
   a. tattoos.   b. the risks of tattoos.   c. the origins of tattoos.

_____ **8.** Which sentence is the topic sentence of paragraph 1 (sentences 1–4)?

_____ **9.** The topic of paragraph 2 (sentences 5–11) is
   a. the risks of tattoos.   b. tattoo removal.   c. the cost of tattoos.

_____ **10.** Which sentence is the topic sentence of paragraph 2 (sentences 5–11)?

_____ **11.** The topic of paragraph 3 (sentences 12–19) is
   a. the risks of tattoos.   b. tattoo dyes.   c. tattoo regulations.

_____ **12.** Which sentence is the topic sentence of paragraph 3 (sentences 12–19)?

The Flow of Ideas and Placement of Topic Sentences

So far, many of the paragraphs you have worked with in this textbook have placed the topic sentence/main idea as the first sentence in the paragraph. The three parts of a paragraph have flowed from general to specific ideas: the topic, the main idea stated in a topic sentence, and the supporting details. However, not all paragraphs put the main idea first. In fact, a topic sentence can be placed at the **beginning** of a paragraph, **within** a paragraph, or at the **end** of a paragraph. The placement of the topic sentence controls the flow of ideas. In a sense, when a writer builds a house of ideas, the floor plan—the flow of ideas—changes based on the location of the topic sentence. One of the first things an effective reader looks for is the location of the topic sentence.

Topic Sentence at the Beginning of a Paragraph

Remember that the topic sentence is the one sentence that is general enough to include all the ideas in the paragraph. So a topic sentence that begins a paragraph signals a move from general ideas to specific ideas. This flow from general to specific, in which an author begins with a general statement and moves to specific reasons and supports, is also known as deductive reasoning. Articles in encyclopedias and news stories in magazines and newspapers typically use the deductive flow of ideas. The chart below shows this flow from general to specific ideas.

Main idea: topic sentence
Supporting detail
Supporting detail
Supporting detail
Supporting detail

EXAMPLE Read the following paragraph, and identify its topic sentence. Remember to ask, "Does this sentence cover all the ideas in the paragraph?"

The Painful, Pesky Fire Ant

[1]Fire ants are painful and destructive pests. [2]The fire ant earned its name because of its venom. [3]The insect uses a wasplike stinger to inject the venom, which causes a painful burning sensation and leaves tiny, itching pustules. [4]The ants will swarm over anyone or anything that disturbs their nests. [5]In addition to causing pain, fire ants damage many crops by eating the plants and by protecting other insects that damage crops. [6]Fire ants are attracted to soybeans, eggplant, corn, okra, strawberries, and potatoes.

Topic sentence: _____

VISUAL VOCABULARY

Swarm can be used as a verb and as a noun. Write a definition for each use. Use your dictionary if you want to.

_____

Verb: _____

Noun: _____

_____

EXPLANATION   The topic sentence of this paragraph is sentence 1: "Fire ants are painful and destructive pests." All the other sentences explain the ways in which fire ants are painful and destructive. Notice how the passage first presents the general idea of fire ants as "painful and destructive." Next the details focus on the pain they cause, and then on the harm they do.

Topic Sentence Within a Paragraph

Topic sentences within a paragraph can be near the beginning or in the middle of the paragraph.

Near the Beginning

A paragraph does not always start with the topic sentence. Instead, it may begin with a sentence or two that give a general overview of the topic. These introductory sentences are used to get the reader interested in the topic. They also lead the reader to the topic sentence. Sometimes introductory sentences tell how the ideas in one paragraph tie in to the ideas of earlier paragraphs. At other times, the introductory sentences give background information about the topic.

The flow of ideas remains deductive as it moves from general ideas (the introduction) and main idea (topic sentence) to specific ideas (supporting details). Human interest stories and editorials in magazines and newspapers, as well as academic papers, often rely on this flow of ideas. The following diagram shows this flow from general to specific ideas:

Introductory sentence
Main idea: topic sentence
Supporting detail
Supporting detail
Supporting detail

EXAMPLE   Read the following paragraph, and identify its topic sentence. Remember to ask, "Does this sentence cover all the ideas in the passage?"

Ice Cream Myths

¹Ice cream reigns as a rich, delicious treat enjoyed by the majority of Americans. ²Many myths exist about the origin of this well-loved

concoction of sugar and ice. [3]The three most common myths involve an explorer and two members of royalty. [4]One popular legend has the famous explorer Marco Polo bringing water ices from China to Italy. [5]Another myth claims that Catherine de Medici of Florence took her sorbetto recipes with her when she married Henry II and became queen of France in 1533. [6]The third popular myth credits Charles I of England with a formula for "frozen milk" he bought from a French chef in the 17th century.

Topic sentence: _____

EXPLANATION   Sentence 3 is the topic sentence of this paragraph. Sentence 1 offers a simple but true background statement about the topic. The purpose of this sentence is to get the reader's attention. Sentence 2 introduces the topic "myths about the origin of ice cream." Sentences 4–6 are the supporting details that discuss the three myths.

In the Middle

At times, an author begins a paragraph with a few attention-grabbing details. These details are placed first to stir the reader's interest in the topic. The flow of ideas no longer follows the deductive pattern of thinking because the material now moves from specific ideas (supporting details) to a general idea (the topic sentence) to specific ideas (additional supporting details). Creative essays and special interest stories that strive to excite reader interest often employ this approach. Television news stories frequently begin with shocking details to hook the viewer and prevent channel surfing. The following diagram shows this flow of ideas:

Supporting detail
Supporting detail
Main idea: topic sentence
Supporting detail
Supporting detail

EXAMPLE   Read the following paragraph, and identify its topic sentence. Remember to ask, "Does this sentence cover all the ideas in the passage?"

Calculating Life

¹What if we could predict how long we might live? ²What if we could know for sure that certain behaviors could lengthen our lives? ³Shorten our lives? ⁴Would we choose a healthful lifestyle—giving up smoking, overeating, stressing out? ⁵Of course, none of us can with certainty predict the length of a life. ⁶Life is too unpredictable and full of events outside our control, such as those accidents that are bound to occur. ⁷However, the more scientists learn about our bodies, the more we understand the strong connection between our lifestyles and our longevity. ⁸A special online longevity calculator offers us estimation about how long we will live. ⁹Tom Peris, M.D., developed the calculator based on a formula based on lifestyle factors. ¹⁰We input information about our good and bad habits. ¹¹We input how often we exercise, drink alcohol, smoke, eat healthfully, and handle stress. ¹²Naturally, the calculator can't take into account genetic factors. ¹³Still, it offers powerful motivation for improvement. ¹⁴The calculator shows that we can take control of factors that affect how long we will live. ¹⁵And we can use the calculator to track our improvement. ¹⁶Try it out! ¹⁷If you are under 50, use the longevity calculator at LivingTo100.com. ¹⁸If you are over 50, use the calculator at eons.com.

—McCafferty, "How Long Will You Live?"
USAWEEKEND. 2 March 2007. pp. 6–8.

Topic sentence: _____

EXPLANATION   Sentences 1 through 4 are a series of questions that act to introduce the general topic of the desire to live for a long time. These questions are meant to engage the reader's interest. Sentences 5 through 7 narrow the topic to focus on the connection between lifestyles and longevity. The author's purpose is to direct the reader to the online longevity calculator so that the reader can learn more about his or her lifestyle and longevity connection. Sentence 8 states this main idea. Sentences 9 through 18 explain how the reader can use the calculator.

Topic Sentence at the End of a Paragraph

Sometimes an author waits until the end of the paragraph to state the topic sentence and main idea. This approach can be very effective, for it allows the details to build up to the main idea. The pattern is sometimes called climactic order.

The flow of ideas is known as inductive, as the author's thoughts move from specific (supporting details) to general (the topic sentence). Inductive reasoning is often used in math and science to generate hypotheses and theories, and to discover relationships between details. In addition, inductive reasoning is often used in argument (for more about argument, see Chapters 12 and 13). Politicians and advertisers use this approach to convince people to agree with their ideas or to buy their products. If a politician begins with a general statement such as "Taxes must be raised," the audience may strongly disagree. Then they may not listen to the specific reasons about why taxes must be raised. However, if the politician begins with the details and leads up to the main idea, people are more likely to listen. For example, people are more likely to agree that roads need to be repaired. Once they hear the specific details, they may then agree to raise taxes. Inductive reasoning is the process of arriving at a general understanding based on specific details. The following diagram shows the ideas moving from specific to general.

Supporting detail
Supporting detail
Supporting detail
Supporting detail
Main idea: topic sentence

EXAMPLE Read the following paragraph, and identify its topic sentence. Remember to ask, "Does this sentence cover all the ideas in the passage?"

A Personal Journey

[1]Every summer, my mother and I journeyed from our home in Florida to the farm in Mississippi on which she was raised. [2]However, the summer of my twenty-second year, we began our trip from Alabama instead of Florida. [3]The entire Mississippi clan had traveled over to witness my graduation from Judson College. [4]As a first-generation college graduate, I just knew I knew more than any of them, especially my mother. [5]Relief, joy, and a sense of freedom flooded me as Mother suggested I drive her car and she ride with Aunt Kaye. [6]Every so often, I purposefully lagged behind the caravan, lit up a cigarette, and smoked as I pleased—no matter that smoking was absolutely forbidden in Mother's car. [7]The cross-breeze from the rolled-down windows and my flicking the butts out the front window guaranteed she

would never know. [8]Late that evening, as we unloaded the back seat, we both came upon a startling discovery at the same time: a deep burn hole the size of a knuckle. [9]One of the butts had blown back in and lodged in the back seat. [10]Silence loomed. [11]Then Mother said, "People are more important than things; I will not let this ruin this special time for us." [12]In a blink, I traveled from pride to shame to redemption. [13]Mother's one moment of mercy taught me more than four years of college.

Topic sentence: _____

EXPLANATION Sentences 1 through 11 tell the story of the author's journey to her mother's birthplace. The details of the story show the author's immaturity. In sentence 12, the author makes a statement that connects the physical trip and her journey of personal growth. Sentence 13 is the topic sentence. It clearly states the point the author is making, and it sums up the lesson of the story. Starting the passage with the details of the author's journey makes the idea much more interesting. Ending the passage with the main idea is very powerful.

Topic Sentence at the Beginning and the End of a Paragraph

A paragraph may start and end by stating one main idea in two different sentences. Even though these two sentences state the same idea, they usually word the idea in different ways. A topic sentence presents the main idea at the beginning of the paragraph. Then, at the end of the paragraph, the main idea is stated again, this time using different words. This flow of ideas is based on the age-old advice given to writers to "tell the reader what you are going to say; say it; then tell the reader what you said." Many essays written by college students rely on this presentation of ideas. The following diagram shows this flow of ideas:

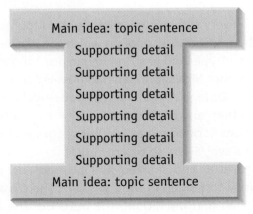

Main idea: topic sentence
Supporting detail
Supporting detail
Supporting detail
Supporting detail
Supporting detail
Supporting detail
Main idea: topic sentence

EXAMPLE Read the following paragraph, and identify its topic sentences. Remember to ask, "Do these sentences cover all the ideas in the passage?"

[1]Using art as a form of therapy calls for a level of concentration that allows a person to relieve the pain of mental or emotional stress. [2]Art therapy is not limited to painting or drawing but can include dance, photography, music, writing, or any other art form. [3]The main goal of art therapy is healing through self-expression. [4]It allows a person to use visual means to explore feelings and emotions, to make the unseen seen, to discover how the mind works. [5]Art therapy does not require artistic ability, nor does it demand high artistic products. [6]Indeed, art therapy focuses on the process, not the product. [7]Art is therapy; art heals.

Topic sentences: _____

EXPLANATION Sentences 1 and 7 both state the main idea of the passage: Art therapy is healing. Notice how the wording changes at the end of the passage. Repeating the main idea makes the point much stronger and more likely to be remembered.

PRACTICE 3

Read the following paragraphs, and identify the topic sentence(s). Remember to ask, "Do these sentences cover all the ideas in the paragraph?"

Believe in Tomorrow

[1]If you had one wish, what would it be? [2]Would you wish for fame or for fortune? [3]The organization known as Believe in Tomorrow strives to grant the wishes and improve the quality of the lives of thousands of critically ill children and their families. [4]Just what are the wishes of these children? [5]One little girl in 1982 had just one wish as she faced a life-threatening illness: a pair of green roller skates. [6]Brian Morrison met that wish, and his simple act of compassion was the beginning of the Grant-a-Wish foundation. [7]That foundation is now named Believe in Tomorrow National Children's Foundation. [8]The foundation serves over 38,000 children each year and offers services that help ease pain, reduce loneliness, and bring joy over the course of their treatment. [9]Services include hospital housing for families, emotional support and networking, pain management, and once-in-a-lifetime adventures. [10]Each program is designed to inspire children and their families to focus on the promise of the future.

1. Topic sentence: _____

How to Prepare for a Natural Disaster

[1]Do you live in an area prone to tornados, flooding, hurricanes, fires, or earthquakes? [2]The best way to survive a natural disaster is to prepare for one. [3]The following steps offer an organized way to prepare for a natural disaster. [4]First, store a supply of disaster necessities. [5]Store water, non-perishable food items such as canned goods and packaged food that doesn't require cooking, and a survival-first aid kit of flashlights, radios, new batteries, extra clothing, and an emergency supply of your important medications. [6]Next, prepare your family and home. [7]Identify safe spots in your home. [8]Post a list of emergency contact numbers including the fire department, local hospital, your doctor, family members, and neighbors. [9]Protect your pets by creating disaster kits for them as well. [10]Third, prepare your car. [11]Keep your car well-maintained and ready to go. [12]Stock your car with emergency items such as a flashlight and first aid kit. [13]Fourth, make sure you have insurance and emergency funds. [14]Check your insurance policy to be sure you are covered for the types of disasters likely to occur in your area. [15]For example, in some areas, flood and wind insurance is extra. [16]Also make sure you have some spare money available in case of an emergency. [17]By following these few, simple steps, you will be better able to deal with a natural disaster.

2. Topic sentences: _____

You've Got Spam: How to "Can" Unwanted E-Mail

[1]Do you receive lots of junk e-mail messages from people you don't know? [2]It's no surprise if you do. [3]As more people use e-mail, marketers are increasingly using e-mail messages to pitch their products and services. [4]Some consumers find unsolicited commercial e-mail, also known as spam, annoying and time consuming; others have lost money to bogus offers that arrived in their e-mail in-box. [5]An e-mail spammer buys a list of e-mail addresses from a list broker, who compiles it by "harvesting" addresses from the Internet. [6]Following are five simple suggestions to help reduce the amount of spam you receive. [7]First, try not to display your e-mail address in public. [8]This includes newsgroup postings, chat rooms, websites, or in an online service's membership directory. [9]Second, check the privacy policy when you submit your address to a website. [10]Third, read and understand the entire form before you send personal information through a website. [11]Fourth, use two e-mail addresses: one for personal messages

and one for newsgroups and chat rooms. ¹²Finally, use an e-mail filter; your e-mail account may provide a tool to block potential spam.

—Adapted from Federal Trade Commission, "You've Got
Spam: How to 'Can' Unwanted E-Mail."

3. Topic sentence: _____

One Harmless Lie

¹Fourteen-year-old Laura Cantrell thought she was being a good friend when she lied for 15-year-old Rebecca Anderson. ²Rebecca told Laura that her parents were trying to control her life because they wouldn't let her date Sam Larson, who was 27 years old. ³Rebecca begged Laura to help her come up with a way to get out of the house so she could be with Sam one more time, just to tell him good-bye. ⁴So Laura covered for her by telling Rebecca's parents that Rebecca was spending the night with her. ⁵That night, Rebecca ran away from home. ⁶By the time the truth was discovered, Rebecca and Sam had vanished without a trace. ⁷Laura felt shocked, horrified, and betrayed. ⁸Laura's parents were ashamed of their daughter's part in Rebecca's disappearance. ⁹And Mr. and Mrs. Anderson struggled with grief, guilt, and fear. ¹⁰A lie that seems harmless can have devastating results.

4. Topic sentence: _____

The Central Idea and the Thesis Statement

Just as a single paragraph has a main idea, longer passages made up of two or more paragraphs also have a main idea. You encounter these longer passages in articles, essays, and textbooks. In longer passages, the main idea is called the **central idea**. Often the author will state the central idea in a single sentence called the **thesis statement**.

> The **central idea** is the main idea of a passage made up of two or more paragraphs.
> The **thesis statement** is a sentence that states the topic and the author's controlling point about the topic for a passage of two or more paragraphs.

You find the central idea of longer passages the same way you locate the main idea or topic sentence of a paragraph. The thesis statement is the one sentence that is general enough to include all the ideas in the passage.

EXAMPLE Read the following passage from a college communications textbook, and identify the thesis statement, which states the central idea.

Supportive Responses

Textbook
Skills

¹Listening stops when you feel threatened. ²No one likes to be proven wrong in front of others, criticized, or ignored. ³Defensive individuals are usually more concerned with protecting their self-concept and saving face than promoting communication. ⁴The more defensive a person becomes, the less able he is to perceive his partner's motives, values, and emotions.

⁵Your goal is to create situations that foster open communication in a supportive climate. ⁶Supportive responses are based on several behaviors that encourage problem solving and build healthy relationships. ⁷First, be aware of the use of "I" and "you." ⁸Instead of saying, "You're never around when I need you," a supportive response says, "I felt frustrated and needed your help." ⁹Second, focus on solving problems instead of placing blame. ¹⁰Third, show empathy instead of indifference. ¹¹And finally, be open-minded to the views of others instead of asserting your own view as the only or correct one.

—Adapted from Brownell, *Listening: Attitudes, Principles, and Skills*, p. 284 © 2002 by Pearson Education, Inc. Reproduced by permission of Pearson Education, Inc.

Thesis statement: _____

EXPLANATION The first four sentences introduce the need to know about the topic "supportive responses." These sentences are designed to hook the reader's interest in the topic. Sentence 5 is a link between the need to know and the author's central idea, which is stated in the next sentence. Sentence 6 is the central idea of the passage. It is the only sentence general enough to include most of the details in the passage. Note that sentence 6 includes the topic "supportive responses" and the author's controlling point about the topic; they are "behaviors that encourage problem solving and build healthy relationships." Sentences 7 through 11 are supporting details that list the supportive responses.

PRACTICE 4

Read the following passage from a college writing handbook, and identify the thesis statement, which states the central idea.

Creative Thinking: Shifting Attention

1Sometimes in writing you come to a dead end or run out of ideas because you focus too sharply on a single aspect of your topic. **2**As you think about what you are going to write, thoughtfully shifting attention away from the chief element of your topic can lead you to additional ideas. **3**For example, in writing a paper about the effects of excessive drinking, you may be concentrating on an individual drinker. **4**Shifting your focus to the effects of alcohol on the drinker's family and friends will stimulate further thought and additional ideas. **5**So will a different kind of shift, one to a consideration of the broader social effects of alcoholism. **6**You might find yourself refocusing your paper; you may even revise your initial purpose, point, and emphasis.

7The following example shows how a shift of attention can lead to the solution of a problem.

8As a man is driving home from work, his car comes to a halt. **9**Lifting up the hood, he notices that he has a broken fan belt. **10**His solution? **11**He takes off his necktie and ties it tightly in the fan belt position. **12**He drives a quarter of a mile to the nearest service station and replaces his fan belt. **13**With the money he saved on a towing charge, he buys a new tie.

—Adapted from Di Yanni & Hoy, *The Scribner Handbook for Writers*, 3rd ed., pp. 59–60.

Thesis statement: _____

Topics, Main Ideas, and Central Ideas in Textbooks

Textbooks identify topics in the title of each chapter. An excellent study strategy is to read a textbook's table of contents, a listing of all the chapters' titles, which are the general topics covered in the textbook. In addition to providing topics in chapter titles, textbooks also identify topics within each chapter. Other publications, such as newspapers and magazines, also use titles and headings to point out topics.

Textbook authors often state the topic of a passage or paragraph in a heading. For example, titles of graphs often help readers identify the main idea of the graph by stating the topic. Identifying the topic in a heading makes it easier to find the main idea and supporting details.

EXAMPLE Assume you are enrolled in a college level business course. Your professor has assigned Chapter 9 in your business textbook to read before your next class. Your professor has also stressed the importance of psychologist Abraham Maslow. Complete the following activities as if you were preparing for class.

A. Skim the table of contents for Chapter 9. Answer the question.

         1. "Maslow's Hierarchy of Needs" is a model that explains
           a. the importance of satisfaction and morale.
           b. motivation in the workplace.
           c. strategies for enhancing job satisfaction and motivation.
           d. managerial styles and leadership.

B. Read the textbook passage and study the graphic about "Maslow's Hierarchy of Needs." Answer the questions that follow.

Maslow's Hierarchy of Needs Model

[1]Psychologist Abraham Maslow's hierarchy of human needs model proposed that people have several different needs that they attempt to satisfy in their work. [2]He classified these needs into five basic types. [3]He also suggested that they be arranged in the hierarchy of importance. [4]According to Maslow, needs are hierarchical because lower-level needs must be met before a person will try to satisfy higher level needs.

[5]Once a set of needs has been satisfied, it ceases to motivate behavior. [6]This is the sense in which the hierarchical nature of lower- and higher-level needs affects employee motivation and satisfaction. [7]For example, if you feel secure in your job, a new pension plan will probably be

less important to you than the chance to make new friends and join an informal network among your coworkers.

[8]If, however, a lower-level need suddenly becomes unfulfilled, most people immediately refocus on that lower level. [9]Suppose, for example, you are seeking to meet your self-esteem needs by working as a divisional manager at a major company. [10]You learn that your division and, consequently, your job may be eliminated. [11]Then, you might very well find the promise of job security at a new firm as motivating as a promotion once would have been at your old company.

[12]Maslow's theory recognizes that because different people have different needs, they are motivated by different things. [13]Unfortunately, it provides few specific guidelines for action in the workplace. [14]Furthermore, research has found that the hierarchy varies widely, not only for different people but also across different cultures.

Maslow's Hierarchy of Needs

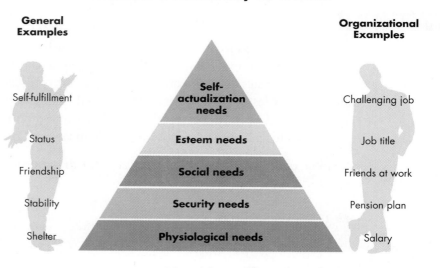

General Examples

Self-fulfillment
Status
Friendship
Stability
Shelter

Self-actualization needs
Esteem needs
Social needs
Security needs
Physiological needs

Organizational Examples

Challenging job
Job title
Friends at work
Pension plan
Salary

—Adapted from Griffin & Ebert, *Business,* 8th ed., pp. 244–245, and Maslow et al, *Motivation and Personality,* 3rd ed.

_____ **2.** The topic of this passage is
    a. Maslow's Hierarchy of Needs.
    b. Abraham Maslow.
    c. work satisfaction.
    d. Maslow's hierarchy of needs in the workplace.

_____ **3.** The central idea of the passage is stated in
    a. sentence 1.   c. sentence 8.
    b. sentence 5.   d. sentence 12.

      4. The best synonym for the word **Hierarchy** in the title of the graphic "Maslow's Hierarchy of Needs" is

a. list.   c. levels.

b. group.   d. demands.

EXPLANATIONS

A. 1. "Maslow's Hierarchy of Needs" is a model that explains (b) "motivation in the workplace."

B. 2. The topic of this passage is (d) "Maslow's Hierarchy of Needs in the Workplace."

   3. The central idea of the passage is stated in (a) sentence 1.

   4. The best synonym for the word **Hierarchy** in the title of the graphic "Maslow's Hierarchy of Needs" is (c) "levels."

PRACTICE 5

Assume you are enrolled in a college-level criminal justice course. Your professor has assigned Chapter 15 as a reading assignment on which you will be quizzed during your next class meeting. As you review your class notes, you notice that your professor has repeatedly stressed the following two topics: "Categories of children in the system" and "Court jurisdiction over young offenders." Complete the following activities as if you were preparing for the quiz.

A. Skim the table of contents for Chapter 15. Answer the question.

_____ 1. "Categories of Children in the Juvenile Justice System" is a subtopic of
   a. Juvenile Justice throughout History.
   b. The Legal Environment.
   c. The Juvenile Justice Process Today.
   d. The Post-Juvenile Court Era.

B. Read the following passage and study the graphic from the textbook *Criminal Justice Today*. Answer the questions that follow.

Categories of Children in the Juvenile Justice System

[1]By the time of the Great Depression, most states had expanded juvenile statutes to include the following six categories of children. [2]These categories are still used today in most jurisdictions to describe the variety of children subject to juvenile court jurisdiction.

- [3]**Delinquent children** are those who violate the criminal law. [4]If they were adults, the word criminal would be applied to them.
- [5]**Undisciplined children** are said to be beyond parental control, as evidenced by their refusal to obey legitimate authorities, such as school officials and teachers. [6]They need state protection.
- [7]**Dependent children** typically have no parents or guardians to care for them. [8]Their parents are deceased, they were placed for adoption, or they were abandoned in violation of the law.
- [9]**Neglected children** are those who do not receive proper care from their parents or guardians. [10]They may suffer from malnutrition or may not be provided with adequate shelter.
- [11]**Abused children** are those who suffer physical abuse at the hands of their custodians. [12]This category was later expanded to include emotional and sexual abuse.
- [13]**Status offender** is a special category that embraces children who violate laws written only for them. [14]In some states, status offenders are referred to as persons in need of supervision (PINS).

[15]**Status offenses** include behavior such as truancy, vagrancy, running away from home, and incorrigibility. [16]The youthful "status" of juveniles is a necessary element in such offenses. [17]Adults, for example, may "run away from home" and not violate any law. [18]Runaway children, however, are subject to apprehension and juvenile court processing because state laws require that they be subject to parental control.

[19]Status offenses were a natural outgrowth of juvenile court philosophy. [20]As a consequence, however, juveniles in need of help often faced procedural dispositions that treated them as though they were delinquent. [21]Rather than lowering the rate of juvenile incarceration, the juvenile court movement led to its increase. [22]Critics of the juvenile court movement quickly focused on the abandonment of due process rights, especially in the case of status offenders, as a major source of problems. [23]Detention and incarceration, they argued, were inappropriate options here because children had not committed crimes.

Limit of Juvenile Court Jurisdiction Over Young Offenders, By State

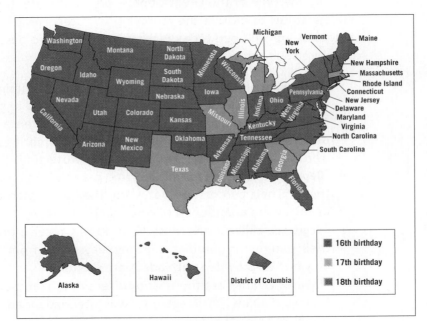

—Schmalleger, *Criminal Justice Today,*
10th ed., p. 562.

_____ **2.** The topic of this passage is
    a. juveniles.
    b. the legal system.
    c. legal classification of juveniles.
    d. juvenile offenses.

_____ **3.** The central idea of the passage is stated in
    a. sentence 1.
    b. sentence 2.
    c. sentence 15.
    d. sentence 22.

_____ **4.** The best synonym for the word **Jurisdiction** in the title of the graphic "Limit of Juvenile Court Jurisdiction Over Young Offenders, By State" is

a. area.

b. authority.

c. ruling.

d. official.

APPLICATIONS

Application 1: Identifying Topics

Read the following paragraphs. Circle the topic as it recurs in each paragraph. Then answer the question that follows each paragraph.

[1]Dipping and chewing tobacco has several harmful results. [2]Dipping and chewing can cause your gums to pull away from your teeth in the place where the tobacco is held. [3]The gums do not grow back. [4]In addition, the sugar in the tobacco may cause decay in exposed tooth roots. [5]Leathery white patches, called leukoplakia, and red sores are common in the mouths of dippers and chewers and can turn into cancer.

—National Institute of Dental and Craniofacial Research, "Welcome to Spit Tobacco: A Guide for Quitting."

_____ **1.** Which of the following best states the topic?

a. tobacco

b. dipping and chewing tobacco

c. leathery white patches called leukoplakia

[1]Pollution, sun, rain, and salt air can cause serious damage to your car's finish. [2]Waxing your car a few times a year will provide it with much-needed protection. [3]Occasional waxing not only keeps your car looking good but also extends its life and maintains the car's resale value. [4]Although you should be sure to wax your car at least twice a year, feel free to wax any time the finish looks dull or water fails to bead on its surface. [5]When you wax, wash and dry your car first to avoid grinding dirt into the finish, and wax in the shade for best results.

_____ **2.** Which of the following best states the topic?

a. water beading up

b. waxing your car

c. waxing your car in the shade

Application 2: Topics and the Main Idea

Read the following paragraph. Then answer the questions that follow it.

What Creates a Childhood Bully?

[1]The typical childhood bully is not the independent leader his peers think he is. [2]The bully is actually the product of his surroundings. [3]A bully thrives in a social climate that favors one group over another, where the "I am better than you" attitude is allowed to thrive. [4]This climate arises out of an intolerance toward anyone who is different and derives its power from the bystanders who say nothing while the bully torments his victim. [5]Most often the bully is simply a kid who needs to be accepted and liked by his peers.

_____ **1.** What is the topic of the paragraph?
   a. a bully
   b. a childhood bully
   c. a kid who needs to be accepted and liked by his peers

_____ **2.** Which sentence states the author's main idea?
   a. sentence 1   c. sentence 4
   b. sentence 2

Application 3: Topics, Main Ideas, and Supporting Details

Each of the following groups of ideas has a topic, one main idea, and two supporting details. In each group, first identify the topic. Then identify the stated main idea. (Hint: circle the topic and underline the author's controlling point in each group.)

Group 1

   A. _American Idol_'s faithful fans vote each week and ultimately choose their favorite performer as the winner.
   B. Even the judges—Simon Cowell, Randy Jackson, Kara DioGuardi, and Ellen DeGeneres—have a strong fan base.
   C. The television show _American Idol_ is a smash hit based on challenging competition, popular judges, and audience interaction.

_____ **1.** Which of the following best states the topic?
   a. the judges of _American Idol_
   b. the audience wins with _American Idol_
   c. _American Idol_ the smash hit

_____ **2.** Which sentence is the stated main idea?

Group 2

A. Sit up straight, pull your shoulders down to form a gentle V, and with your mouth closed, breathe deeply, pushing air in and out with your abdomen.

B. Take a break from your computer by standing up, lacing your fingers behind your back, bending forward, and pulling your hands up behind you as far as you can.

C. Two simple stretches can help you relieve workday stress.

_____ **3.** Which of the following best states the topic?
   a. two stretches
   b. workday stress
   c. a gentle V

_____ **4.** Which sentence is the stated main idea?

Group 3

A. Home safety is a simple matter of common sense.

B. Use slip-proof mats in showers and tubs, and use rubberized mats to secure scatter rugs to the floor so they won't slip.

C. Keep clutter picked up and train pets to stay out from under your feet to avoid stumbling or tripping.

_____ **5.** Which of the following best states the topic?
   a. safety
   b. eliminating clutter
   c. safety in the home

_____ **6.** Which sentence is the stated main idea?

Application 4: Location of Topic Sentences

Read the following paragraph from a college health textbook and identify its topic sentence or sentences. Remember to ask, "Does this sentence (Do these sentences) cover all the ideas in the passage?"

Sharing Feelings

Textbook Skills

[1]Although men tend to talk about intimate issues with women more often than with men, women still complain that men do not communicate enough about what is really on their minds. [2]This conflict is the result of the contrast in communication styles that comes from the different socializing processes experienced by women and men. [3]Throughout their lives, females are encouraged to share their thoughts and feelings with others. [4]In contrast, males receive strong messages to withhold their feelings. [5]The classic example of this training in very

young males is the familiar saying, "big boys don't cry." [6]Males learn very early that certain emotions are not to be shared. [7]The result is that they are more information-focused and businesslike in discussions with females than females are. [8]Such differences in communication styles contribute to misunderstandings and conflict between the sexes.

—Adapted from Donatelle, *Access to Health*, 7th ed., p. 136.

Topic sentence(s): _____

REVIEW TEST 1   Score (number correct) _____ × 20 = _____%

Topics, Main Ideas, and Supporting Details

A. Each of the following groups of ideas includes one topic, one main idea, and two supporting details. In each group, first identify the topic. Then identify the stated main idea. (Hint: circle the topic and underline the author's controlling point in each group.)

Group 1

A. Procrastination has two possible causes.
B. Many people may procrastinate because they have a fear of failure, and if they don't begin a task or project, they can't fail at it.
C. Others may procrastinate out of laziness; these careless workers have not yet developed a strong work ethic.

_____ **1.** Which of the following best states the topic?
    a. laziness   c. a strong work ethic
    b. procrastination

_____ **2.** Which sentence best states the main idea?

Group 2

A. A snake can control its body temperature in two ways.
B. First, a snake can darken its skin to absorb higher levels of solar heat; once its body reaches a suitable temperature, the snake can lighten its skin color.
C. A snake also spreads and flattens its body as it lies at a right angle to the sun's rays to expose more of its body and raise its temperature; to reduce its body temperature, a snake lies parallel to the sun's rays or moves into the shade.

—Adapted from Smith & Smith,
Elements of Ecology, 4th ed., p. 11-A.

_____ **3.** Which of the following best states the topic?

    a. body temperature   c. a snake's body temperature

    b. snakes

_____ **4.** Which sentence best states the main idea?

B. Read the paragraph. Then answer the question.

> [1]First Monday, Mississippi's largest flea market, and one of the nation's oldest, is a long-standing success that offers something for everybody. [2]Established in 1893, this open market was originally located on Ripley's downtown court square, but it is now stationed south of the city limits across from the county fairgrounds. [3]First Monday sits on over 50 acres and offers hundreds of booths that house vendors and assorted items for sale. [4]The variety of goods ranges from unique and hard-to-find items to new and used products, antiques, crafts, and much more, including pets. [5]First Monday is open the Saturday and Sunday preceding the first Monday of each month, and buyers travel hundreds of miles to trade there. [6]Admission is free, and the grounds provide dining facilities, electrical hookups, showers, a laundry room, table rental, cable TV hookup, and early-morning church services.

_____ **5.** Which sentence states the main idea of the paragraph?

    a. sentence 1   c. sentence 5

    b. sentence 2   d. sentence 6

REVIEW TEST 2

Score (number correct) _____ × 25 = _____%

Topics, Main Ideas, and Supporting Details

Read the following passage from a college geography textbook. Answer the questions that follow.

Textbook
Skills

**Grouping Humans by Culture,
Race, Ethnicity, and Identity**

[1]When we define human groups, we must be sure that we know and agree on exactly what the criteria of inclusion are and whom the group includes. [2]Unclear or vague references to groups may cause misunderstanding or even insults.

Culture groups   [3]The definition of a culture may include a great number of characteristics or just a few. [4]For example, all social scientists agree that language is an important attribute of human behavior. [5]Two people who share a language share something very important. [6]If, however, those two people hold different religious beliefs, feel patriotism for two different countries, and eat different diets, social scientists may insist that although those two people share one attribute of culture, they do not share one culture. [7]The great number of English speakers who presently live around the world share few attributes other than language, so we would not say that they all share one common culture. [8]If, however, two people do share a language, religious beliefs, political affiliation, and dietary preferences, then social scientists would agree that those two people share a culture.

[9]A subculture is a smaller bundle of attributes shared among a smaller group within a larger, more generalized culture group. [10]For example, Italian Americans, Chinese Americans, and African Americans share subsets of cultural attributes within the larger American culture. [11]Sometimes even one single attribute—shared loyalty for a sports team, for example—can bind individuals so strongly that that single attribute is termed a subculture.

[12]Ultimately, cultural affiliation may be a matter of the feelings or the preferences of the individuals. [13]Two people may share so many cultural attributes that observers insist that they share a culture, yet they may hate each other. [14]They may even kill each other because, to them, their differences are crucial. [15]Each day's newspaper proves this statement. [16]Psychologist Sigmund Freud (1856–1939) described what he called "the narcissism of the minor differences," pointing out that the most vicious and irreconcilable quarrels often arise between peoples who are to most outward appearances nearly identical. [17]Our study of political geography in Chapter 11 cites examples of countries, which outsiders regarded as homogeneous, that have nevertheless broken out in civil war. [18]Outsiders did not see the cultural fault lines within the countries. [19]In other cases, people whom observers would describe as very different from each other feel strong bonds. [20]What they share is more important to them than their differences. [21]We must always investigate people's feelings in order to understand their loyalties and their animosities. [22]People carry multiple identities. [23]For example, a middle-class, Baptist, Republican, disabled, black mother of West Indian ancestry and U.S. citizenship may feel many allegiances, and at different times she may allow any one of her identities

to determine her behavior. [24]This flexibility may either facilitate or hinder interaction with others.

[25]Many people may feel a sense of community with others of their own "race," but the concept of race remains ambiguous.

Ethnic groups   [26]The concept of an ethnic group is frequently confused with the concept of a cultural group. [27]The word ethnic comes from the Greek for "people," and the definition of an ethnic group may depend upon almost any attribute of biology, culture, allegiance, or historic background. [28]The word has historically been used in a pejorative sense: Its meanings have included "alien," "pagan," and often "primitive." [29]Some social scientists nevertheless define ethnic groups and study the groups' characteristics or attributes. [30]Ethnomusicology, for example, is the study of ethnic groups' music, and ethnobotany is the study of ethnic groups' knowledge of the uses of plants. [31]The migrations of people are sometimes described as migrations of ethnic groups.

[32]**Ethnocentrism** is the term given to the tendency to judge other cultures by the standards and practices of one's own, and usually to judge them unfavorably. [33]Practices in other cultures that may seem strange to us, however, may in fact be sensible and rational. [34]Conversely, some aspects of our own culture may seem strange or even offensive to others. [35]Most Americans, for example, assume that a man should have one wife and a woman one husband at a time, but any number of spouses are allowed in a series. [36]This would shock many people. [37]Americans, in turn, may be shocked to learn that Tibetans assume that a woman is married to all sibling brothers at once. [38]This is called fraternal polyandry. [39]Through thousands of years, fraternal polyandry has made possible sustainable population increases and prevented the fragmentation of landholdings in Tibet's poor mountain valleys. [40]The social ramifications of fraternal polyandry confound most Americans. [41]An American might ask how to identify the father of any given child. [42]To a Tibetan, however, it makes no difference, and a Tibetan might consider the question prurient.

[43]Any geography book will contain examples of ways of life that contrast with your own. [44]None is necessarily "right" or the best for everybody. [45]All people have to overcome the initial assumption that "different from" the way they do things themselves is "worse than" their way: people everywhere also can learn to appreciate and respect the integrity of other people's behaviors. [46]Shrewd people even learn from others whenever they can.

—Bergman & Renwick, *Introduction to Geography: People, Places, and Environment,* 4th ed., pp. 226–227.

_____ **1.** What is the topic of the passage?
   a. human groups
   b. ethnocentrism
   c. grouping humans by culture, race, ethnicity, and identity
   d. cultural and ethnic groups

_____ **2.** Which sentence states the main idea of paragraph 2 (sentences 3–8)?
   a. sentence 3   c. sentence 7
   b. sentence 4   d. sentence 8

_____ **3.** Sentence 9 states a
   a. main idea.   b. supporting detail.

_____ **4.** Which sentence states the central idea of the passage?
   a. sentence 1   c. sentence 32
   b. sentence 26   d. sentence 45

REVIEW TEST 3   Score (number correct) _____ × 25 = _____%

Topics, Main Ideas, and Supporting Details

Read the following passage from a college anatomy and physiology textbook. Answer the questions that follow.

Textbook
Skills

Skin Cancer

[1]Numerous types of neoplasms (tumors) arise in the skin. [2]Most skin neoplasms are benign and do not spread (metastasize) to other body areas. [3](A wart caused by a virus is one such example.) [4]However, some skin neoplasms are malignant, or cancerous, and they tend to invade other body areas. [5]Indeed, skin cancer is the single most common type of cancer in humans. [6]One in five Americans now develops skin cancer at some point in his or her life. [7]The most important risk factor is overexposure to ultraviolet radiation in sunlight. [8]Frequent irritation of the skin by infections, chemicals, or physical trauma also seems to be a predisposing factor.

Basal Cell Carcinoma [9]Basal cell carcinoma (kar'/sĭno'/mah) is the least malignant and most common skin cancer. [10]Cells of the stratum basale, altered so that they cannot form keratin, no longer honor the boundary between epidermis and dermis. [11]They proliferate, invading the dermis and subcutaneous tissue. [12]The cancer lesions occur most often on sun ex- posed areas of the face and appear as shiny, dome-shaped nodules that later develop a central ulcer with a "pearly" beaded edge. [13]Basal cell carcinoma is relatively slow-growing, and metastasis seldom occurs be- fore it is noticed. [14]Full cure is the rule in 99 percent of cases in which the lesion is removed surgically.

Squamous Cell Carcinoma [15]Squamous cell carcinoma arises from the cells of the stratum spinosum. [16]The lesion appears as a scaly, reddened papule (small, rounded elevation) that gradually forms a shallow ulcer with a firm, raised border. [17]This variety of skin cancer appears most often on the scalp, ears, dorsum of the hands, and lower lip. [18]It grows rapidly and metastasizes to adjacent lymph nodes if not removed. [19]This epidermal cancer is also be- lieved to be sun-induced. [20]If it is caught early and removed surgically or by radiation therapy, the chance of complete cure is good.

Malignant Melanoma [21]Malignant melanoma (mel"ah-no'mah) is a cancer of melanocytes. [22]It accounts for only about 5 percent of skin can- cers, but its incidence is increasing rapidly and it is often deadly. [23]Melanoma can begin wherever there is pigment; most such cancers ap- pear spontaneously, but some develop from pigmented moles. [24]It arises from accumulated DNA damage in a skin cell and usually appears as a spreading brown to black patch that metastasizes rapidly to surrounding lymph and blood vessels. [25]The chance for survival is about 50 percent, and early detection helps. [26]The American Cancer Society suggests that people who sunbathe frequently or attend tanning parlors examine their skin periodically for new moles or pigmented spots and apply the **ABCD rule** for recognizing melanoma:

A. **Asymmetry.** [27]The two sides of the pigmented spot or mole do not match.
B. **Border irregularity.** [28]The borders of the lesion are not smooth but exhibit indentations.
C. **Color**. [29]The pigmented spot contains areas of different colors (blacks, browns, tans, and sometimes blues and reds).
D. **Diameter**. [30]The spot is larger than 6 millimeters (mm) in diameter (the size of a pencil eraser).

[31]Some experts have found that adding an **E**, for *elevation* above the skin surface, improves diagnosis. [32]The usual therapy for malignant melanoma is wide surgical excision along with immunotherapy.

—Marieb, *Essentials of Human Anatomy & Physiology,*
9th ed., pp. 125–126.

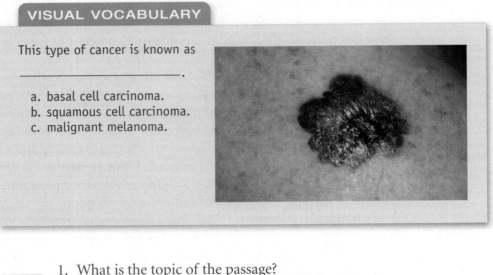

VISUAL VOCABULARY

This type of cancer is known as

_____.

a. basal cell carcinoma.
b. squamous cell carcinoma.
c. malignant melanoma.

_____ 1. What is the topic of the passage?
    a. cancer   c. skin cancer
    b. causes of skin cancer   d. three types of skin cancer

_____ 2. Which sentence states the main idea of paragraph 2 (sentences 9–14)?
    a. sentence 9   c. sentence 12
    b. sentence 10   d. sentence 14

_____ 3. Sentence 20 states a
    a. main idea.   b. supporting detail.

_____ 4. Which sentence states the central idea of the passage?
    a. sentence 1   c. sentence 5
    b. sentence 4   d. sentence 26

WHAT DO YOU THINK?

According to the passage, what is the most important risk factor that causes skin cancer? What are some of the other factors? What steps should be taken to avoid the risks of developing skin cancer? Assume you are involved in a service learning project for a college health class. Your class has agreed to speak to youth groups at local community centers and churches. Your goal is to educate youth about the risks of developing skin cancer and the steps they can take to protect themselves. Write a draft of the speech you will give. In addition, create a PowerPoint presentation to make your points vivid and clear. Consider working with a peer or small group of classmates.

REVIEW TEST 4

Score (number correct) _____ × 10 = _____%

Topics and Main Ideas

Before reading: Survey the following passage adapted from the college text-book *Psychology and Life*. Skim the passage, noting the words in bold print. Answer the Before Reading questions that follow the passage. Then read the passage. Next, answer the After Reading questions. Use the discussion and writing topics as activities to do after reading.

Vocabulary Preview

consistent (1): constant, regular
appreciation (6): admiration, enjoyment, understanding
philosophy (6): viewpoint, way of life
deteriorated (14): declined
maturation (21): growth

What Is Learning?

Textbook
Skills

¹Learning is a process that results in a relatively **consistent** change in behavior or behavior potential and is based on experience. ²The three critical parts of this definition deserve careful study.

A Change in Behavior or Behavior Potential

³It is obvious that learning has taken place when you are able to demonstrate the results, such as when you drive a car or use a microwave oven. ⁴You can't directly observe learning itself, but learning is **apparent** from improvements in your performance. ⁵Often, however, your performance doesn't show everything that you have learned. ⁶Sometimes, too, you have **acquired** general attitudes, such as an **appreciation** of modern art or an understanding of Eastern **philosophy**, that may not be apparent

in your measurable actions. [7]In such cases, you have achieved a potential for behavior change. [8]You have learned attitudes and values that can influence the kinds of books you read or the way you spend your leisure time. [9]This is an example of learning performance distinction; it is the difference between what has been learned and what is expressed, or performed, in **overt** behavior.

A Relatively Consistent Change

[10]To qualify as learned, a change in behavior or behavior potential must be relatively consistent over different occasions. [11]Thus once you learn to swim, you will probably always be able to do so. [12]Note that consistent changes are not always permanent changes. [13]You may, for example, have become quite a consistent dart thrower when you practiced every day. [14]If you gave up the sport, however, your skills might have **deteriorated** toward their original level. [15]But if you have learned once to be a championship dart thrower, it ought to be easier for you to learn a second time. [16]Something has been "saved" from your prior experience. [17]In that sense, the change may be permanent.

A Process Based on Experience

[18]Learning can take place only through experience. [19]Experience includes taking in information and making responses that affect the environment. [20]Learning is made up of a response affected by the lessons of memory. [21]Learned behavior does not include changes that come about because of physical **maturation**, nor does it simply rely on brain development as the organism ages. [22]Some learning requires a combination of experience and **maturity**. [23]For example, think about the timetable that controls when an infant is ready to crawl, stand, walk, run, and be toilet trained. [24]No amount of training or practice will produce those behaviors before the child is mature enough to be ready to learn.

—Adapted from Gerrig/Zimbardo, *Psychology and Life*, Text Excerpt from p. 181 © 2002. Reproduced by permission of Pearson Education, Inc.

Before Reading

Vocabulary in Context

_____ **1.** The word **apparent** in sentence 4 means
   a. unseen.
   b. obvious.
   c. reinforced.
   d. encouraged.

_____ **2.** The word **acquired** in sentence 6 means
    a. rated.   c. rejected.
    b. overcome.   d. gained.

_____ **3.** The word **overt** in sentence 9 means
    a. hidden.   c. visible.
    b. wise.   d. concerned.

_____ **4.** The word **maturity** in sentence 22 means
    a. fully developed.   c. passion.
    b. understanding.   d. inexperience.

Topics and Main Ideas

_____ **5.** What is the topic of the passage?
    a. demonstrating results   c. consistent change
    b. learning   d. change in behavior

After Reading

_____ **6.** Which sentence states the central idea of the passage?
    a. sentence 1   c. sentence 10
    b. sentence 3   d. sentence 24

_____ **7.** What is the topic of the third paragraph (sentences 10–17)?
    a. a change in behavior or behavior potential
    b. a relatively consistent change in behavior or behavior potential
    c. permanent changes in behavior potential
    d. prior experiences of behavior change

_____ **8.** Which sentence states the main idea of the third paragraph?
    a. sentence 10   c. sentence 12
    b. sentence 11   d. sentence 16

9–10. Label each of the following two sentences from the fourth paragraph (sentences 18–24). Use **A** if it states the main idea or **B** if it supplies a supporting detail.

_____ **9.** Learning can take place only through experience.

_____ **10.** Learning is made up of a response affected by the lessons of memory.

WHAT DO YOU THINK?

Have you or someone you know experienced a change in behavior or behavior potential because of a lesson learned? Assume you are applying for a scholarship to continue your education. The application calls for you to write a short essay that explains the value of learning. Describe an important lesson that has changed your or another person's behavior or behavioral potential.

After Reading About Stated Main Ideas

A crucial step in the reading process occurs during the after reading phase when you take time to reflect on what you have learned. Before you move on to the Mastery Tests on stated main ideas, take time to reflect on your learning and performance by answering the following questions. Write your answers in your notebook.

- How has my knowledge base or prior knowledge about stated main ideas changed?
- Based on my studies, how do I think I will perform on the Mastery Test(s)? Why do I think my scores will be above average, average, or below average?
- Would I recommend this chapter to other students who want to learn more about stated main ideas? Why or why not?

Test your understanding of what you have learned about stated main ideas by completing the Chapter 3 Review Card in the insert near the end of the text.

CONNECT TO myreadinglab

To check your progress in meeting Chapter 3's learning outcomes, log in to www.MyReadingLab.com, and try the following activities.

- The "Main Idea" section of MyReadingLab provides review materials, practice activities, and tests about topics and main ideas. To access this resource, click on the "Study Plan" tab. Then click on "Main Idea." Then click on the following links as needed: "Overview," "Model," "Practice," and "Tests."

To measure your mastery of the content in this chapter, complete the tests in the "Main Ideas" section and click on Gradebook to find your result.

A. Skim each of the following paragraphs and circle the topic as it recurs through-out the paragraph. Then, identify the idea that correctly states the topic. (Hint: one idea is too general to be the topic; another idea is too specific.)

_____ **1.** [1]Did you know that May is Foot Health Awareness Month? [2]The foot is often the most ignored part of our bodies. [3]Yet with its 28 bones, 33 joints, and 19 muscles, the foot deserves year-round pampering. [4]Good foot care begins with shoes that fit properly. [5]Ill-fitting shoes cause many problems, including poor circulation, injury due to lack of proper support, corns, bunions, and calluses. [6]Good foot care also entails keeping the feet clean. [7]Plantar warts are caused by a virus that enters the foot through an open sore or cut. [8]The best activity for the feet is walking. [9]Walking stimulates circulation and keeps the feet strong and limber.

    a. feet
    b. Foot Health Awareness Month
    c. proper foot care

_____ **2.** [1]"Hispanic" is a widely used term for a person of Spanish-language heritage living in the United States. [2]The term was first coined by the government for census-taking purposes. [3]Hispanic, from the Latin word for "Spain," refers generally to all Spanish-speaking peoples. [4]The term emphasizes the common factor of a shared language among groups that may have little else in common. [5]Hispanic can be used in referring to Spain and its history and culture. [6]A native of Spain residing in the United States is a Hispanic. [7]Hispanics are persons of Cuban, Mexican, Puerto Rican, South or Central-American, or other Spanish culture or origin, regardless of race. [8]The federal government considers race and Hispanic origin to be two separate and distinct concepts. [9]Hispanic Americans may be any race. [10]According to the 2000 U.S. Census, Hispanics of all races represent 13.3 percent of the U.S. population, which is about 37.4 million individuals. [11]The Census Bureau projects that by the year 2040 there will be 87.5 million Hispanic individuals, making up 22.3 percent of the population. [12]Though they share many aspects of a common heritage such as language and emphasis on extended family, Hispanic cultures vary greatly by country of origin. [13]Therefore, the broad term "Hispanic" is not an appropriate title for such a diverse people.

—Adapted from United States Centers for Disease Control. "Hispanic or Latino Populations." Office of Minority Health. 15 August 2007. http://www.cdc.gov/omh/Populations/HL/HL.htm.

    a. the origin of the term "Hispanic"
    b. Latin Americans
    c. the limitations of the term "Hispanic"

B. Read the following group of ideas from a college psychology textbook. Answer the questions that follow.

a. Basic emotions can combine to produce more complex and subtle ones.
b. For example, joy and acceptance, which are closely related, can combine to produce love; joy and fear, which are not closely related, can join to produce guilt.
c. When distant emotions mix, a person typically feels conflicted.

_____ **3.** Statement (a) is
    a. the main idea.   b. a supporting detail.

_____ **4.** Statement (b) is
    a. the main idea.   b. a supporting detail.

_____ **5.** Statement (c) is
    a. the main idea.   b. a supporting detail.

VISUAL VOCABULARY

What emotion does Plutchik's palette suggest will be the result of mixing fear and surprise?

_____

—From Robert Plutchik, Emotion, © 1980. Published by Allyn & Bacon, Boston, MA. Copyright © 1980 by Pearson Education. Adapted by permission of the publisher.

Plutchik's "Emotional Palette"

Plutchik proposed a set of emotions that can be combined to form other emotions, much as primary colors can be mixed to create other colors.

Name _____ Section_____

Date _____ Score (number correct) _____ × 25 = _____ %

Identify the topic sentence of each of the following paragraphs from college textbooks.

A. Paragraph from a college psychology textbook

Textbook Skills

Types of Personality Tests

[1]Think of all the ways in which you differ from your best friend. [2]Psychologists use personality tests to identify the different traits that characterize an individual. [3]They think about what sets one person apart from another; they want to know what distinguishes people in one group from another. [4]For example, certain traits seem to separate shy people from outgoing people. [5]Two beliefs are basic to these attempts to understand and describe human personality. [6]The first is that personal traits of individuals give logic to their behavior. [7]The second belief is that those traits can be measured. [8]Personality tests that represent these two beliefs are known as either *objective* or *projective*.

—Gerrig/Zimbardo, *Psychology and Life*, Text Excerpt from p. 460 © 2002. Reproduced by permission of Pearson Education, Inc.

Topic sentence(s): _____

B. Paragraph from a college health textbook

Textbook Skills

Determining What Triggers an Eating Disorder

[1]Before you can change a behavior, you must first determine what causes it. [2]Many people have found it helpful to keep a chart of their eating patterns: when they feel like eating, the amount of time they spend eating, where they are when they decide to eat, other activities they engage in during the meal (watching television or reading), whether they eat alone or with others, what and how much they consume, and how they felt before they took their first bite. [3]If you keep a detailed daily log of eating triggers for at least a week, you will discover useful clues about what in your environment or emotional makeup causes you to want food. [4]Typically, these dietary triggers center on problems in everyday living rather than on real hunger pangs. [5]Many people find that they eat when stressed or when they have problems in their relationships. [6]For

other people, the same circumstances diminish their appetite, causing them to lose weight.

—Adapted from Donatelle, *Health: the Basics*, 5th ed., p. 270.

Topic sentence(s): _____

C. Paragraph from a college accounting textbook

Cash Advances

Textbook
Skills

[1]Many credit cards allow cash advances at automated teller machines (ATMs). [2]Since a cash advance represents credit extended by the sponsoring financial institution, interest is charged on this transaction. [3]A transaction fee of 1 to 2 percent of the advance may also be charged. [4]Credit card companies also provide checks that you can use to make purchases that cannot be made by credit card. [5]The interest rate applied to cash advances is often higher than the interest rate charged on credit extended for specific credit card purchases. [6]The interest rate is applied at the time of the cash advance; the grace period that applies to purchases with a credit card does not apply to cash advances. [7]So, although cash advances are convenient, they can also be extremely costly.

—Madura, *Personal Finance Update*, Text Excerpt from p. 196 © 2006 Pearson
Education, Inc. Reproduced by permission of Pearson Education, Inc.

Topic sentence(s): _____

D. Paragraph from a college education textbook

Textbook
Skills

[1]Building expectations for student success means encouraging students to see that success can be reached through their own efforts. [2]Helping students realize that they control their fortunes in school by the amount of time and effort they are willing to put into their work is an important task. [3]This control principle can be impressed on students by having them keep track of the time they spend on a unit or project. [4]In addition, students can be shown how to evaluate their work using criteria developed by the teacher or the class. [5]Making students aware of their progress through the use of charts and graphs helps them see that they have control over their achievement. [6]They realize that the grades they receive are not given by the teacher but rather are the result of their own efforts.

—Wilen, Ishler, Hutchison, & Kindsvatter, *Dynamics of
Effective Teaching*, 4th ed., p. 41.

Topic sentence(s): _____

Read the passage. Then answer the questions that follow it.

Textbook
Skills

Tone in a Poem

[1]In old Western movies, when one hombre taunts another, it is customary for the second to drawl, "Smile when you say that, pardner" or "Mister, I don't like your tone of voice." [2]Sometimes in reading a poem, although we can neither see a face nor hear a voice, we can infer the poet's attitude from other evidence.

[3]Like tone of voice, tone in literature often conveys an attitude toward the person addressed. [4]Like the manner of a person, the manner of a poem may be friendly or belligerent toward its reader. [5]Again like tone of voice, the tone of a poem may tell us how the speaker feels about himself or herself: cocksure or humble, sad or glad. [6]But usually when we ask, "What is the tone of a poem?" we mean "What attitude does the poet take toward a theme or subject?" [7]Is the poet being affectionate, hostile, earnest, playful, sarcastic, or what? [8]We may never be able to know, of course, the poet's personal feelings. [9]All we need know is how to feel when we read the poem.

[10]Strictly speaking, tone isn't an attitude; it is whatever in the poem makes an attitude clear to us: the choice of certain words instead of others, the picking out of certain details. [11]In A. E. Houseman's "Loveliest of Trees," for example, the poet communicates his admiration for a cherry tree's beauty by singling out for attention its white blossoms; had he wanted to show his dislike for the tree, he might have concentrated on its broken branches, birdlime, or snails. [12]To perceive the tone of a poem correctly, we need to read the poem carefully, paying attention to whatever suggestions we find in it.

—Kennedy & Gioia, *Literature: An Introduction
to Fiction, Poetry, and Drama*, 8th ed., p. 757.

_____ **1.** What is the topic of the passage?
   a. old Western movies
   b. the tone of a poem
   c. tone
   d. A. E. Houseman's "Loveliest of Trees"

_____ **2.** Which sentence or sentences state the central idea of the passage?
  a. sentences 1 and 8
  b. sentence 2
  c. sentence 9
  d. sentence 11

_____ **3.** Which sentence states the main idea of the second paragraph?
  a. sentence 3
  b. sentence 5
  c. sentence 8
  d. sentence 9

_____ **4.** Which sentence or sentences state the main idea of the third paragraph?
  a. sentences 10 and 12
  b. sentence 10
  c. sentence 11
  d. sentence 12

VISUAL VOCABULARY

The tone or attitude of the parent portrayed in this photo is_____.

  a. compassionate.
  b. angry.
  c. joyful.

A. Each of the following groups of ideas includes one topic, one main idea, and two supporting details. In each group, first identify the topic. Then identify the stated main idea. (Hint: circle the topic and underline the author's controlling point in each group.)

Group 1

A. Gardening has emotional and physical benefits.

B. Pulling weeds, raking, digging, and planting while gardening strengthen all of the major muscle groups.

C. The sense of accomplishment and the enjoyment of beautiful surroundings bring many gardeners emotional satisfaction.

_____ **1.** Which of the following best states the topic?
a. pulling weeds
b. emotional satisfaction
c. gardening

_____ **2.** Which sentence best states the main idea?

Group 2

A. Also, surprise a child with an unexpected reward, such as a day trip to a special place, for a job well done.

B. Positive reinforcement teaches children the satisfaction and reward of good behavior.

C. One way to offer positive reinforcement is to give sincere praise when it is well deserved; children need to hear statements like "I'm proud of you" or "The way you mow and trim makes the yard look neat and healthy."

_____ **3.** Which of the following best states the topic?
a. parenting
b. positive reinforcement
c. good behavior

_____ **4.** Which sentence best states the main idea?

B. Read the following paragraph. Then identify the sentence (or sentences) that state(s) the main idea.

[1]Parents, educators, and students all have their own opinions about what should be taught in public schools. [2]The debate seems to be most heated when discussing elementary education. [3]Everyone seems to agree that reading, writing, and arithmetic are as important as ever, but agreement

seems to end there. [4]However, real-world needs should play a major role in early education. [5]For example, keyboard skills are basic and necessary. [6]Students who can master basic typing skills will be much more successful in school and on the job. [7]Research and writing can be accomplished at higher levels of proficiency when students know how to use the Internet and word processing programs. [8]Many jobs require personal computers, and the retail industry relies on complicated keypads to enter orders and track stock. [9]Public elementary schools should examine real-world needs when considering what to teach their students.

5. Topic sentence(s): _____

Implied Main Ideas and Implied Central Ideas

4

After studying this chapter you should be able to do the following:

1. Define the term *implied main idea*.
2. Analyze supporting details to identify and state topic of a passage.
3. Determine an implied main idea of a passage based on the topic, supporting details, and thought patterns of the passage.
4. Create a topic sentence that states the implied main idea of a paragraph.
5. Determine the implied central idea of a longer passage.
6. Create a thesis statement that states the implied central idea of a passage.
7. Evaluate the importance of stating implied main ideas.

Before Reading About Implied Main Ideas and Implied Central Ideas

Take a moment to study the learning outcomes. Underline key words that refer to ideas you have already studied in previous chapters. Each of these key words represents a great deal of knowledge upon which you will build as you learn about implied main ideas and implied central ideas. Now, circle terms that you need to know more about. Finally, identify your learning goals by completing the following chart:

What I Know and What I Need to Learn About Implied Main Ideas	
What I already know that will help me master implied main ideas	
What I need to learn to master implied main ideas	

After you study this chapter, compare the information you record in this chart to the information you record as you complete the Chapter Review Card, located near the end of this textbook.

 ## What Is an Implied Main Idea?

As you learned in Chapter 3, sometimes authors state the main idea of a paragraph in a topic sentence. However, other paragraphs do not include a stated main idea. Even though the main idea is not stated in a single sentence, the paragraph still has a main idea. In these cases, the details clearly suggest or imply the author's main idea.

> An **implied main idea** is a main idea that is not stated directly, but is strongly suggested by the supporting details in the passage.

When the main idea is not stated, you must figure out the author's controlling point about a topic. One approach is to study the facts, examples, descriptions, and explanations given—the supporting details. Another approach is to identify the author's thought pattern. An effective reader often uses both approaches. Learning how to develop a main idea based on the supporting details and thought patterns will help you develop several skills. You will learn how to study information, value the meaning of supporting details, appreciate the relationship between ideas, and use your own words to express an implied main idea.

Many different types of reading material use implied main ideas. For example, many paragraphs in college textbooks do not provide a topic sentence. In these passages, the author uses supporting details to imply the main idea. In addition, you will often need to formulate the implied main idea when you read literature. Short stories, novels, poems, and plays rely heavily on vivid details to suggest the author's point. The following short story is taken from a college literature textbook. Read the story, asking yourself, "What is the main idea?"

Independence

Written by Chuang Tzu and Translated by Herbert Giles

[1]Chuang Tzu was one day fishing, when the Prince of Ch'u sent two high officials to interview him, saying that his highness would be glad of Chuang Tzu's assistance in the administration of his government. [2]The latter quietly fished on, and without looking round, replied, "I have heard that in the State of Ch'u there is a sacred tortoise, which has been dead for three thousand years, and which the prince keeps packed up in a box on the altar in his ancestral shrine. [3]Now do you think that tortoise would

rather be dead and have its remains thus honored, or be alive and wagging its tail in the mud?" [4]The two officials answered that no doubt it would rather be alive and wagging its tail in the mud; whereupon Chuang Tzu cried out, "Begone! I too elect to remain wagging my tail in the mud."

> —Chuang Tzu, "Independence." Translated by Herbert Giles. Reprinted in Kennedy, X. J. & Dana Gioia. *Literature: An Introduction to Fiction, Poetry, and Drama*, 8th ed., pp. 6–7.

Did you notice that every sentence in this paragraph is a supporting detail? No single sentence covers all the other ideas. To figure out the implied main idea, ask the following questions.

Questions for finding the implied main idea:

1. What is the topic, or subject, of the paragraph?
2. What are the major supporting details?
3. Based on the details about the topic, what point or main idea is the author trying to get across?

Apply these three questions to the passage above by writing your responses to each question in the following blanks.

1. What is the topic of the story? _____

The title of the story gives us a strong clue that the topic is about independence. But each detail in the story also supports this topic.

2. What are the major supporting details?

   a. _____

   b. _____

   c. _____

   d. _____

3. What is the main idea the author is trying to get across? _____

_____

In order to formulate this main idea statement, you had to consider each of the details. For example, the author uses a vivid contrast between a dead tortoise which has an "honored" place on the Prince's "ancestral shrine" and a live tortoise "wagging its tail." In addition, the author has the two officials agree that the tortoise would have been better off alive and living freely. The tortoise serves as an example of independence, and helps the reader understand the significance of Chuang Tzu's choice. He did not value power or public honor as much as he valued his own freedom to live simply.

Asking and answering these questions allows you to think about the impact of each detail and how the details fit together to support the author's controlling point. Searching for an implied main idea is like a treasure hunt. You must carefully read the clues provided by the author. This kind of careful reading is a skill that improves dramatically with practice. The following examples and practices are designed to strengthen this important skill.

Using Supporting Details and Thought Patterns to Determine Implied Main Ideas

Remember that the main idea of a paragraph is like a frame of a house. Just as a frame includes all the rooms, a main idea must cover all the details in a paragraph. Therefore, the implied main idea will be general enough to cover all the details, but it will not be so broad that it becomes an overgeneralization or a sweeping statement that suggests details not given; nor can it be so narrow that some of the given details are not covered. Instead, the implied main idea must cover *all* the details given.

The skill of identifying a stated main idea will also help you grasp the implied main idea. You learned in Chapter 3 that the stated main idea (the topic sentence) has two parts. A main idea is made up of the topic and the author's controlling point about the topic. One trait of the controlling point is the author's opinion or bias. A second trait is the author's thought pattern. Consider, for example, the topic sentence "Older people benefit from volunteer work for several reasons." "Older people" and "volunteer work" make up the topic. "Benefit" states the opinion, and "several reasons" states the thought pattern. When you read material that implies the main idea, you should mentally create a topic sentence based on the details in the material.

EXAMPLE Read the following details from a paragraph in a college textbook for criminal justice. Circle the topic as it recurs throughout the details. Underline bias or opinion words and transition words. Then choose a statement that best states the author's controlling point about the topic.

- The American frontier was a vast and wild place until late in the nineteenth century.
- The backwoods areas of the frontier proved a natural haven for outlaws and bandits.

- For example, Henry Berry Lowery, a famous outlaw of the Carolinas, the James Gang, and many lesser-known desperadoes felt at home in the frontier's swamps and forests.
- Only the boldest of settlers tried to police the frontier.
- In the late eighteenth century, citizen posses and vigilante groups were often the only law available to settlers on the American frontier.
- Several popular frontier figures of the nineteenth century took it upon themselves to enforce the law on the books as well as the standards of common decency.
- For example, Judge Roy Bean, "Wild Bill" Hickok, Bat Masterson, Wyatt Earp, and Pat Garrett policed the frontier, sometimes in a semiofficial role.

—Adapted from Schmalleger, *Criminal Justice Today: An Introductory Text for the 21st Century,* 10th ed., p. 155.

_____ Which statement best expresses the implied main idea?
  a. The American frontier was a dangerous place.
  b. Bold settlers and citizens enforced the law on the American frontier.
  c. By the late nineteenth century, the vast and wild American frontier was policed by bold settlers, citizens, and popular figures who enforced the law.
  d. The American frontier was home to outlaws, bandits, and desperadoes.

VISUAL VOCABULARY

A group of _____ hold court on a captured criminal in this sketching from the 19th century.

  a. desperadoes
  b. vigilantes

EXPLANATION Two topics recur throughout these details. The most frequently recurring topic is the *American frontier*. The other topic appears less often, and in several forms such as *police* and *law*. Several bias words characterize the lack of law or the need for law on the American frontier. These words include *wild, haven, outlaw, bandit, swamps, forests, desperadoes,* and *vigilantes.* A few other biased words characterize the people who worked to bring law to the frontier. These words include *boldest, citizen posse, popular figures, standards of common decency,* and *semiofficial.* Two transitions give us the time frame about the American frontier and its law: *until the late nineteenth century* and *in the late eighteenth century.* The only statement that covers all these details is item (c). Item (a) states a general idea, and items (b) and (d) restate supporting details.

PRACTICE 1

Read the following groups of supporting details. Circle the topic as it recurs throughout the list of details. Underline transition words to help you locate the major details. Also underline biased words to determine the author's opinion. Then select the sentence that best expresses the implied main idea.

Group 1

Textbook
Skills

- Egypt's pyramids are the oldest existing buildings in the world.
- These ancient tombs are also among the world's largest structures.
- The largest pyramid stands taller than a 40-story building and covers an area greater than that of ten football fields.
- More than 80 pyramids still exist, and their once-smooth limestone surfaces hide secret passageways and rooms.
- The pyramids of ancient Egypt served a vital purpose: to protect the pharaohs' bodies after death.
- Each pyramid held not only the pharaoh's preserved body but also all the goods he would need in his life after death.

—Adapted from Sporre, Dennis J., *The Creative Impulse,* 6th, p. 45 © 2003. Printed and Electronically reproduced by permission of Pearson Education, Inc., Upper Saddle River, New Jersey.

_____ **1.** Which sentence best states the implied main idea?
   a. Pyramids are large, ancient buildings.
   b. Pyramids are massive structures with several distinctive traits.
   c. Pyramids are tombs that were built for the pharaohs.
   d. Pyramids are remarkable.

Group 2

- Cognitive therapy helps a person deal with negative or painful thoughts and behaviors.
- This therapy, a psychological treatment, was developed by a medical doctor, Aaron T. Beck, in the 1970s.
- First, a person seeks to change thinking patterns such as assumptions and core beliefs.
- Changes in feelings and actions will follow.
- To aid change, a person learns how to replace harmful thoughts and behaviors with positive coping tactics.
- Some of these tactics may include anger management and relaxation training.

_____ **2.** Which sentence best states the implied main idea?
   a. Cognitive therapy is a psychological treatment.
   b. Cognitive therapy is a psychological treatment that helps a person replace negative or painful thoughts and behaviors with positive coping skills.
   c. Cognitive therapy was developed by Aaron T. Beck, M.D., in the 1970s.
   d. Cognitive therapy focuses on negative or painful thoughts and behaviors.

Determining the Implied Main Ideas of Paragraphs

So far, you have learned to recognize the implied main idea by studying the specific details in a group of sentences. In this next step, the sentences will form a paragraph, but the skill of recognizing the implied main idea is exactly the same. The implied main idea of paragraphs must not be too broad or too narrow, so study the supporting details and look for thought patterns that suggest the main idea.

EXAMPLE Read the following paragraph from a college business textbook. Circle the topic as it recurs throughout the paragraph. Underline transition words to help you locate the major details. Also underline biased words to determine the author's opinion. Then select the sentence that best expresses the implied main idea.

Levels of Management

[1]**Top managers** are responsible for the overall performance and effectiveness of a firm. [2]Common titles for top managers are *president, vice president, treasurer, chief executive officer* (CEO), and *chief financial officer* (CFO). [3]They set general policies, plan strategies, approve all major decisions. [4]They also represent the company in dealing with other firms and government officials. [5]Just below the ranks of top managers is another group of managers called **middle managers**. [6]Middle managers go by titles such as *plant manager, operations manager,* and *division manager*. [7]In general, middle managers carry out the strategies, policies, and decisions made by top managers. [8]**First-line managers** have titles such as *supervisor, office manager,* and *group leader*. [9]First-line managers spend most of their time working with and supervising the employees who report to them.

—Adapted from Griffin & Ebert,
Business, 8th ed., pp. 165–166.

_____ The best statement of the implied main idea is:
a. Top managers have the most responsibility and receive the highest pay.
b. Managers are known by a variety of titles.
c. Management of a firm or company can be divided into three levels of managers.

EXPLANATION Clues to the implied main idea are found in both the title and the supporting details of this paragraph. The word *management* appears in the title, and the frequently recurring word *managers* appears in most sentences of the paragraph. Note the relationship between the words *management* and *managers*. In addition, the author uses specific words to quality three specific levels of managers: *top, middle,* and *first-line*. Thus, the best statement of the implied main idea is item (c). Item (a) states a supporting detail, and it includes the idea of "the highest pay," which is not mentioned in any of the details. Item (b) remains too general or vague for a main idea statement.

PRACTICE 2

Read the following paragraphs. In each paragraph, circle the topic as it recurs throughout the paragraph. Underline transition words to help you locate the major details. Also underline the biased words to determine the author's opinion. Then select the sentence that best expresses the implied main idea for each.

Overcoming Writer's Block

[1]Countless numbers of college students in first-year composition classes face writer's block. [2]One way to overcome writer's block is to read. [3]Beginning writers may not have enough information or prior knowledge about a topic to generate a paper. [4]Therefore, reading about a topic gives the writer information and ideas on which to draw. [5]Another way to overcome this problem is through discussion. [6]Talking to peers, teachers, and others about ideas and beliefs helps novice writers clarify their own understandings so that they can more easily share them on paper. [7]A third way to overcome writer's block is to brainstorm. [8]Brainstorming is just a way to focus thoughts through listing, freewriting, or making concept maps. [9]Brainstorming also allows a writer to discover what to say without worrying about how to say it. [10]Finally, writer's block can be reduced by the wise use of time management skills. [11]Beginning writers need to understand that writing is an outgrowth of thinking, and thinking takes time. [12]Often writer's block is the result of too much stress and too little time; therefore, to avoid this problem, writers should begin the assignment days before it is due.

_____ **1.** Which sentence best states the implied main idea?
  a. Writer's block is a problem for many first-year college students.
  b. Reading is an excellent way to overcome writer's block.
  c. Beginning writers can overcome writer's block in several ways.
  d. The writing process should be broken into three phases: prewriting, writing, and revising.

Green Tea: The Miracle Drink

[1]Green tea has been used for thousands of years in Asia as both a beverage and an herbal medicine. [2]This herbal tea contains catechin, which is a type of tannin that acts as an astringent. [3]Research suggests that men and women in Japan who drink five to six cups of green tea each day have much lower rates of cancer than people who do not. [4]Green tea is also thought to lower cholesterol and blood sugar, control high blood pressure, stop tooth decay, and fight viruses. [5]Green tea has even been credited with the power to slow down the aging process.

_____ **2.** Which sentence best states the implied main idea?
- a. Green tea is an ancient herbal drink.
- b. Green tea has caught the attention of medical researchers.
- c. Green tea lowers cholesterol and blood sugar and controls high blood pressure.
- d. Green tea, an ancient Asian herbal drink, is thought to have many health benefits.

One Handsome Young Man

[1]At 6-foot-4, Van stood taller than most young men. [2]The Florida sun tanned his skin to a deep bronze and bleached his dark brown hair to varying shades of sandy blond. [3]Endowed with the high cheekbones of his Indian ancestors, sapphire eyes, and a luminous smile, he drew attention. [4]He moved like an athlete at ease in his own skin. [5]In neighborhood orange wars, Van could throw an orange farther and more accurately than any of us. [6]In fact, he could outrun, outswim, outhunt, outfish, outdo all of us, and still we loved him. [7]Guys felt proud to be his friend; girls clamored to be his sweetheart. [8]Even now, 30 years later, at our high school reunion, Van looms larger than life to those of us he left behind: an unaging memory, a tragic loss.

_____ **3.** Which sentence best states the implied main idea?
- a. Van was a handsome, talented, well-liked young man who died young and is still missed.
- b. Van was a tall, good-looking young man.
- c. Van is a tragic figure.
- d. Van is still missed by his high school friends.

Stating the Implied Main Idea Based on the Supporting Details

You have developed the skill of figuring out main ideas that are not directly stated. This ability to reason from specific details to main ideas will serve you well throughout college. One further step will also prove helpful in your reading and studying: the ability to state the implied main idea in your own words. You must learn to summarize the most important details into a one-sentence statement; in other words, you must create a topic sentence. To formulate this one-sentence summary, find the topic, determine the author's opinion by examining the biased words, and use the thought pattern to locate the major details. Then combine these ideas into a single sentence. The summary sentence includes the topic and the author's controlling point, just like a topic sentence. The statement you come up with must not be too narrow, for it must cover all the details given. On the other hand, it must not be too broad or go beyond the supporting details.

Remember that a main idea is always written as a complete sentence.

EXAMPLE Read the list of specific ideas that follows. Circle the topic as it recurs throughout each group of details. Underline words that reveal thought patterns and bias to discover the controlling point. Then write a sentence that best states the implied main idea.

- Ranked number one on the Forbes list as the most powerful celebrity, Angeline Jolie made $27 million in 2009. She also grabbed headlines for her off-screen roles as mother and humanitarian.

- Ranked number two as a power figure is Oprah Winfrey. She slipped from last year's rank of number 1 due to the eroding viewership of her television show; however, Winfrey still made the most money, earning $275 million in one year.

- Number three on the list, Madonna toured the world with her Hard Candy album tour. She also adopted a son, divorced her husband, and earned $110 million.

- At number four, Beyoncé earned $84 million. She released a double album, starred in two films, and performed at both the Oscars and a presidential inaugural ball.

- Rounding out the top five on the 2009 Forbes list of the most powerful celebrities is Tiger Woods. He made $110 million through endorsements and designing golf courses even though an injury kept him from playing golf for 8 months.

1. Implied main idea: _____

_____

_____

EXPLANATION To formulate an implied main idea statement, you must learn to summarize the important details into a one-sentence summary. The topic is the "Forbes list of most powerful celebrities." The transition phrases include *ranked number one, ranked number two, number three, at number four, rounding out the top five.* To properly formulate a topic sentence, you should have noted that the details were organized as a list of celebrities from all walks of life. The details of their earnings provided the basis of their ranking on the list. The implied main idea could be expressed as follows: "The 2009 Forbes list of most influential celebrities is a diverse group ranked by their earnings and public interest in them."

EXAMPLE Read the following paragraph. Circle the topic as it recurs throughout the paragraph. Underline words that reveal thought patterns and bias to discover the controlling point. Then write a sentence that best states the implied main idea. Remember: not too narrow, not too broad—find that perfect fit!

Make It Right in the Lower Ninth Ward, New Orleans

[1]In 2005, Hurricane Katrina destroyed more than 4,000 homes in New Orleans' Lower Ninth Ward. [2]In 2007, Brad Pitt founded Make It Right to build 150 homes for families living in the Lower 9th Ward when the storm hit. [3]Importantly, Make It Right homes are storm resistant. [4]Make It Right homes include pervious concrete, escape hatches and attic windows, increased durability (able to withstand 160 mph winds), raised elevations, and hurricane window fabric. [5]Additionally, Make It Right homes are energy efficient. [6]Energy efficient features include metal roofs, hyper-insulation, solar panels, and Energy Star appliances. [7]Make It Right homes also use eco-friendly landscape designs. [8]Make It Right landscapes use native plants, rain gardens, edible gardens, roof-top gardens, xeric plantings, and street trees. [9]Finally, Make It Right homes are affordable. [10]Returning residents pay Make It Right what they're able—usually about $75,000. [11]And Make It Right loans them the rest. [12]The cost of a single Make It Right home is in the $150,000 range; a double about $200,000. [13]The repayment policy varies. [14]For some, the loan is free, if the recipient

agrees to live in the house for five to 20 years. [15]By the beginning of 2010, 15 Make It Right homes had been completed. [16]And another 19 homes were under construction—making it right for dozens of families who survived Hurricane Katrina.

2. Implied main idea: ______________________________

____

____

____

VISUAL VOCABULARY

In Make It Right landscapes, pervious concrete allows storm water to filter through the pavement where it can be reabsorbed by deep-rooted plants.

The best synonym for **pervious** is ______________.

a. transparent.
b. porous.
c. soaked.

EXPLANATION To formulate an implied main idea statement, you must learn to state the most important details of the paragraph in one sentence. Keep in mind that using your own words to formulate an implied main idea means that everyone's answer will be slightly different. The following sentence is one way to word the main idea of the paragraph: "In the years after Hurricane Katrina, Brad Pitt established the Make It Right foundation to build 150 storm resistant, energy efficient, affordable homes so families could return to the Lower Ninth Ward of New Orleans." The frequent use of the phrase *Make It Right* clearly makes it the topic of the paragraph. Notice, the signal words *Importantly* (sentence 3), *Additionally* (sentence 5), and *Finally* (sentence 9) point out the most important details that explain the topic.

PRACTICE 3

A. Read each group of supporting details. Circle the topic as it recurs throughout each group of details. Underline words that reveal thought patterns and bias to discover the controlling point. Then write a sentence that best states the implied main idea. After writing, check the sentence by asking if all the major details support it.

Group 1

- Recent DNA testing has proved several people on death row innocent of the crimes for which they were sentenced to death.
- The cost to taxpayers for death penalty appeals is staggeringly high.
- Many people believe that the death penalty is morally wrong and a form of legalized homicide.
- Many also believe that the death penalty does not deter crime.
- Finally, many believe that the death penalty unfairly targets the poor and the African American population.

1. **Implied main idea:** _____

_____

Group 2

- Narcotics used to control postsurgery pain cause side effects and don't always provide relief .
- A new technique is to drip a local anesthetic directly into the wound for two to five days while healing begins.
- One version, the ON-Q system, slowly drips the drug from a balloonlike ball into a tiny catheter inserted near the stitches, where it oozes out.
- The direct dose of pain medicine avoids the grogginess and other body-wide effects of narcotics.

—Boen, "On-Q System: A New Method of Pain Relief," *The News-Sentinel*, 24 April 2009, 1Lt.

2. **Implied main idea:** _____

_____

_____

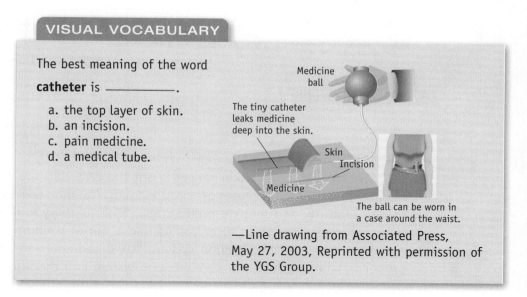

VISUAL VOCABULARY

The best meaning of the word

catheter is ───────.

    a. the top layer of skin.
    b. an incision.
    c. pain medicine.
    d. a medical tube.

Medicine ball

The tiny catheter leaks medicine deep into the skin.

Skin
Incision

Medicine

The ball can be worn in a case around the waist.

—Line drawing from Associated Press, May 27, 2003, Reprinted with permission of the YGS Group.

B. Read the following paragraphs. Circle the topic as it recurs throughout each paragraph. Underline words that reveal thought patterns and bias to discover the controlling point. Then write a sentence that states the implied main idea.

Slave Quilts: The Maps to Freedom

[1]Some historians believe that a number of African Americans escaped slavery through a network of supporters called the Underground Railroad. [2]In order for the Underground Railroad to work effectively, it was necessary to relay information to those attempting to make the trip to freedom. [3]Direct communication, however, was not an option. [4]Any overt signal would be quickly discovered. [5]In order to overcome this problem, the principals involved created a system based on designs sewn into quilts that could be conspicuously displayed in appropriate places. [6]Like any good system of subterfuge, the quilts appeared as commonplace items to the adversaries of fugitive slaves. [7]However, to those in flight, the quilts were an encouraging symbol that advised them of the who, what, when, and how of their journey to freedom. [8]Many of the symbols sewn into the patterns are obvious in their meanings, such as the monkey wrench, which denoted that it was time to gather the tools required to make the journey, or sailboats, which indicated the availability of boats for the crossing of crucial bodies of water. [9]Other symbols were more cryptic, such as the star pattern, which had several variations but whose purpose was to point to the North Star. [10]The Drunkard's Path pattern

served to remind those on the run to move east to west (in much the way a drunken man staggers) during their journey.

—Adapted from Weadon, "Follow the Drinking Gourd."

3. Implied main idea: _____

_____

Indoor Tanning: The Risks of Ultraviolet Rays

[1]The serious risk of skin cancer is not the only damage caused by tanning. [2]First, tanning causes premature aging. [3]Tanning causes the skin to lose elasticity and wrinkle prematurely. [4]This leathery look may not show up until many years after you've had a tan or sunburn. [5]Second, tanning suppresses the immune system. [6]UV-B radiation may suppress proper functioning of the body's immune system and the skin's natural defenses, leaving you more vulnerable to diseases, including skin cancer. [7]Third, tanning causes eye damage. [8]Exposure to UV radiation can cause irreversible damage to the eyes. [9]Fourth, tanning may develop an allergic reaction. [10]Some people who are especially sensitive to UV radiation may develop an itchy red rash and other adverse effects. [11]Advocates of tanning devices sometimes argue that using these devices is less dangerous than sun tanning because the intensity of UV radiation and the time spent tanning can be controlled. [12]But there is no evidence to support these claims. [13]In fact, sunlamps may be more dangerous than the sun because they can be used at the same high intensity every day of the year—unlike the sun whose intensity varies with the time of day, the season, and cloud cover.

—Adapted from FDA Consumer Health Information. U.S. Food and Drug Administration. Nov. 2009. http://www.fda.gov/downloads/ForConsumers/ConsumerUpdates/UCM190664.pdf.

4. Implied main idea: _____

_____

The Implied Central Idea

Just as a single paragraph can have an implied main idea, longer passages made up of two or more paragraphs can also have an implied main idea. You encounter these longer passages in articles, essays, and textbooks. As you learned in Chapter 3, the stated main idea or central idea of these longer passages is called the *thesis statement*. When the main idea of several paragraphs is implied, it is called the **implied central idea**. You use the same skills to formulate the implied central idea of a longer passage that you use to formulate the implied main idea of a paragraph.

> **The implied central idea** is the main idea suggested by the details of a passage made up of two or more paragraphs.

Annotating the text is a helpful tool in determining the implied central idea. Just as you did to grasp the implied main idea for paragraphs, circle the topic. Underline the signal words for thought patterns. Remember, transition words introduce supporting details. An author often pairs a transition word with a major supporting detail. Consider the following examples: *the first reason*, *a second cause*, *the final effect*, *another similarity*, an *additional difference*, and so on. When you see phrases such as these, your one-sentence summary may include the following kinds of phrases: *several effects*, *a few differences*, and so on.

A longer passage often contains paragraphs with stated main ideas. The stated main idea of a paragraph is a one-sentence summary of that paragraph and can be used as part of your summary of the implied central idea.

EXAMPLE Read the following passage from a college psychology textbook. Annotate the text. Then select the sentence that summarizes its central idea.

Textbook
Skills

Chunking

¹A chunk is a meaningful unit of information. ²A chunk can be a single letter or number, a group of letters or other items, or even a group of words or an entire sentence. ³For example, the sequence 1-9-8-4 consists of four digits, each of which is a chunk when they are remembered separately. ⁴However, if you see the digits as a year or the title of George Orwell's novel *1984*, they constitute only one chunk, leaving you much more capacity for other chunks of information.

⁵See how many chunks you can find in this sequence of 20 numbers: 19411917186518211776. ⁶You can answer "20" if you see the sequence as a list of unrelated digits or "5" if you break down the sequence into the dates of major wars in U.S. history. ⁷If you do the latter, it's easy for you to recall all the digits in the proper sequence after one quick glance. ⁸It

would be impossible for you to remember them from a short exposure if you saw them as 20 unrelated items.

—Gerrig/Zimbardo, *Psychology and Life*, Text Excerpt from p. 225 © 2002.
Reproduced by permission of Pearson Education, Inc.

_____   The sentence that best summarizes the central idea is:
  a. A chunk is a small part of a larger set of information.
  b. Chunking is a strategy that increases memory by organizing large pieces of information into smaller units of thought.
  c. Chunking is an excellent method of memorizing important dates in history.
  d. Chunking is helpful.

EXPLANATION This passage demonstrates the challenge of grasping the implied central idea. The thought pattern used in the first three sentences is definition. Sentences 1 and 2 introduce and define the term "chunk," and the transition *or* is used to add details to the definition. Sentence 3 introduces an example by using the signal phrase *for example*. Interestingly, the transition *however* adds a minor supporting detail to the example in sentence 4. Sentences 5 through 8 explain the process of chunking using an example. The author has mixed patterns (definition and process) to describe a memory strategy called "chunking." The sentence that best summarizes these details and thought patterns is (b) *Chunking is a strategy that increases memory by organizing large pieces of information into smaller units of thought*. This sentence presents a definition of the term and indicates that a process is going to be discussed. Sentences *a* and *c* are too narrow; sentence *d* is too broad.

PRACTICE 4

Read the following passage. Annotate the text. Then select the sentence that summarizes its central idea.

The Three Phases of Lyme Disease

[1]The first stage of Lyme disease shows up three to 30 days after a person is bitten by an infected tick. [2]During this phase, a red-rimmed circular spot or spots emerge, often described as a "bull's-eye" rash. [3]The centers of these expanding spots become pale, and the infected person experiences exhaustion, headaches, a fever, and joint and muscle pains.

⁴The second stage of Lyme disease can develop within weeks or take months to appear. ⁵One symptom is Bell's palsy, which causes one side of the face to droop and the eye on that side to stay opened. ⁶In addition, nerve problems can occur, the heart can become inflamed, and the rash seen in stage one can return.

⁷The third stage of Lyme disease, which can occur within weeks or take years to develop, is arthritis, the painful swelling of joints.

⁸Of course, not all cases of Lyme disease exhibit all these symptoms. ⁹Some cases may have only one or two of these signs.

_____ The sentence that best summarizes the central idea is
   a. Lyme disease can have long-term consequences.
   b. Lyme disease affects different people in different ways.
   c. Lyme disease can attack the nerves and heart.
   d. Lyme disease, a serious illness caused by a tick bite, occurs in three stages.

EXAMPLE   Read the following passage from a college history textbook. Annotate the text. Write a sentence that summarizes the central idea of the passage.

Textbook
Skills

Why It's Called *Brown* v. *Board of Education of Topeka, Kansas*

¹Seven-year-old Linda Brown of Topeka, Kansas, lived close to a good public school, but it was reserved for whites. ²So every day she had to cross railroad tracks in a nearby switching yard on her way to catch a run-down school bus that would take her across town to a school reserved for African American students. ³Her father, Oliver Brown, concerned for her safety and the quality of her education, became increasingly frustrated with his youngster's having to travel far from home to get an education.

⁴"The issue came up, and it was decided that Reverend Brown's daughter would be the goat, so to speak," recalled a member of the Topeka NAACP. ⁵"He put forth his daughter to test the validity of the law, and we had to raise the money."

⁶The NAACP continued to gather cases from around the nation. ⁷The Supreme Court first agreed to hear *Brown and Briggs* v. *Elliot* (South Carolina) in 1952. ⁸Two days before they were to be heard, the Court issued a postponement and added *Davis* v. *Prince Edward County* (Virginia) to its docket. ⁹Just a few weeks later, the Court added *Bolling* v. *Sharpe* from the District of Columbia and *Gebhart* v. *Belton*

(Delaware). [10]According to U.S. Supreme Court Justice Tom Clark of Texas, the Court "consolidated them and made Brown the first so that the whole question would not smack of being purely a Southern one." [11]Thus the case came to be known as *Brown* v. *Board of Education of Topeka, Kansas.*

—O'Connor & Sabato, *American Government: Continuity and Change,* 2000 ed., p. 190.

Implied central idea: _____

_____

_____

_____

EXPLANATION This passage shows the importance of a title or heading. Turn the heading into the question: *Why is it called* "Brown *v.* Board of Education of Topeka, Kansas"? Reading to find the answer to this question helps you decide what to annotate as you read. The opening two paragraphs use a narrative to give the history of this landmark court case. It is safe to infer that the events in this case are similar to the events in other cases. The problem of racial discrimination was widespread. Instead of underlining the time order transition words, an effective reader might write in the margin the phrase "racial discrimination." This label summarizes the point of the narrative. The third paragraph begins with a topic sentence about bringing in other cases to join *Brown.* The supporting details (the additional cases) that follow are joined by time and addition words. All these details lead up to the final sentence, which restates the title. The transition word *thus* reinforces that this court case was the result of a widespread fight against racial discrimination.

The wording of answers will vary. One possible answer is "The Supreme Court Case *Brown* v. *Board of Education of Topeka, Kansas* was actually four cases brought from different areas of the nation to challenge discrimination against African Americans in public education." This sentence covers all the supporting details but does not go beyond the information given in the passage. For example, this was a landmark case that could be considered the most important civil rights case of the twentieth century. The effect of the ruling dramatically changed our society. However, these details are not included in the passage; thus the thesis statement does not mention them.

PRACTICE 5

Read the following passage from a college communications textbook. Annotate the text. Write a sentence that summarizes the central idea.

Unspoken Messages

Textbook Skills

1Bob leaves his apartment at 8:15 A.M. and stops at the corner drugstore for breakfast. **2**Before he can speak, the counterman says, "The usual?" **3**Bob nods yes. **4**While he savors his Danish, a fat man pushes onto the adjoining stool and overflows into his space. **5**Bob scowls and the man pulls himself in as much as he can. **6**Bob has sent two messages without speaking a syllable.

7George is talking to Charley's wife at a party. **8**Their conversation is entirely trivial, yet Charley glares at them suspiciously. **9**Their physical proximity and the movements of their eyes reveal that they are powerfully attracted to each other.

10Jose Ybarra and Sir Edmund Jones are at the same party, and it is important for them to establish a cordial relationship for business reasons. **11**Each is trying to be warm and friendly, yet they will part with mutual distrust, and their business transaction will probably fall through.

12Jose, in Latin fashion, moved closer and closer to Sir Edmund as they spoke, and this movement was miscommunicated as pushiness to Sir Edmund, who kept backing away from this intimacy, which was miscommunicated to Jose as coldness. **13**The silent languages of Latin and English cultures are more difficult to learn than their spoken languages.

—DeVito, *Messages: Building Interpersonal Communication Skills,* Text from p. 139 © 2004. Reproduced by permission of Pearson Education, Inc.

Implied central idea: _____

_____

Textbook Skills

Graphics as Details That Imply a Main Idea

Textbook authors often use pictures, drawings, or graphs to make the relationship between the main idea and supporting details clear.

EXAMPLE Study the following figure from a health textbook. State the main idea suggested by the details in a sentence.

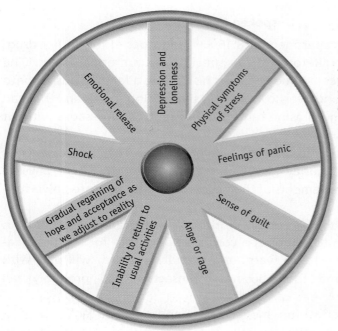

◄ Stages of Grief

—Image reprinted from Donatelle, Rebecca J.; Davis, Lorraine G., *Access to Health*, 7th, p. 545 © 2002. Printed and Electronically reproduced by permission of Pearson Education, Upper Saddle River, New Jersey.

Implied main idea: _____

_____

EXPLANATION This diagram is a circle graph. Circles often suggest a cycle or process. The caption tells us that each spoke is labeled with a different stage of grief. Each of the nine spokes that radiate from the center of the circle represents a stage of grief. The labels identify each stage. Therefore, by counting the number of spokes and using the caption, we can formulate a possible statement for the main idea: "Grief has nine stages." Since the main idea statement is a summary of the author's main point, it is not necessary to name each stage. Simply stating the number of stages indicates that a list of supporting details is given.

PRACTICE 6

Study the following figure from a health textbook. Put the main idea suggested by the details into a sentence.

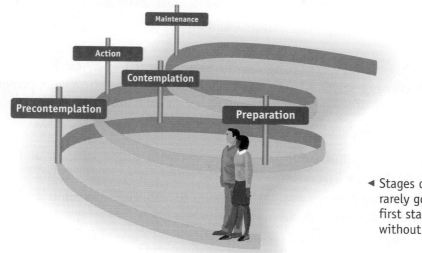

◄ Stages of change: People rarely go directly from the first stage to the last without relapsing.

—Figure 12.5 from *Changing for Good* by James O. Prochaska, John Norcross and Carlo C. Diclemente. Copyright © 1994 by James O. Prochaska, John Norcross, and Carlo C. Diclemente. Reprinted by permission of HarperCollins Publishers, Inc.

Implied main idea: _____

_____

_____

 ## A Final Note About Experience and Perspective

As you have worked through this chapter, hopefully you have had some lively discussions about the possible answers for activities that asked for implied main ideas to be stated. Often a set of details will suggest many things to many people. Determining main ideas requires that the reader bring personal understandings and experience to the task. Thus people with different perspectives may disagree about what the details suggest. Another complex aspect of determining main ideas is that authors may choose to give a collection of details because the idea suggested is difficult to sum up in one sentence. The author intends several meanings to coexist. The important point to remember is that the main idea you formulate should be strongly supported by the details in the paragraph or longer passage.

APPLICATIONS

Application 1: Using Supporting Details to Determine Implied Main Ideas

A. Read each group of supporting details. Annotate the text by circling the topic and underlining key words of support and transition. In the spaces provided, write the letter of the best implied main idea for each group.

1. Supporting details:

- A category 1 hurricane has winds of 74 to 95 miles per hour and causes some damage to trees, shrubbery, and unanchored mobile homes.
- A category 5 hurricane has winds up to 155 miles per hour and causes extreme damage to homes and buildings and can blow away small structures.
- During a major hurricane, storm surges can cause the sea to flow inland for several miles.
- A category 1 hurricane brings surges of 4 to 5 feet; a category 5 hurricane causes surges of 18 feet or more.
- Heavy rainfall also causes dangerous flooding.
- Floodwaters cause most of the deaths associated with hurricanes.

_____ Implied main idea:
  a. Hurricanes are powerful storms.
  b. People should evacuate when threatened by a hurricane.
  c. Hurricanes pose several threats.
  d. Hurricanes are driven by powerful winds.

2. Supporting details:

- Some experts believe that compulsive gambling is often linked to divorce.
- This type of gambling has also been tied to cases of neglected or abused children.
- Compulsive gambling also often leads to the gambler's loss of employment and income.
- Finally, gambling disorders may be a factor in some cases of homelessness.

_____ Implied main idea:
  a. Compulsive gambling is a disease.
  b. Compulsive gambling leads to economic problems for the gambler.
  c. Compulsive gambling is linked to child abuse.
  d. Compulsive gambling may have several devastating consequences.

B. Read the following paragraph. Annotate the text by circling the topic and underlining key words of support and transition. In the spaces provided, write the letter of the best implied main idea for the paragraph.

Genetically Modified Foods to Fight Malnutrition

[1]Malnutrition is an urgent concern in Third World countries. [2]In these countries, many poor people rely on a single crop such as rice as the main staple of their diet. [3]However, rice does not have all the necessary nutrients to prevent malnutrition. [4]Thus scientists wanted to find a way to alter the genetic makeup of rice to improve its nutritional value. [5]For example, blindness due to a lack of vitamin A is a common problem in Third World countries. [6]Swiss researchers have created a strain of "golden" rice. [7]Golden rice contains an unusually high content of beta-carotene (vitamin A).

_____ **3.** Which sentence best states the implied main idea?
  a. Beta-carotene prevents blindness.
  b. Genetically modified foods such as golden rice may help fight malnutrition in Third World countries.
  c. Scientists are developing genetically modified foods.
  d. Golden rice is a genetically modified food that has added vitamin A.

Application 2: Creating a Topic Sentence from Supporting Details

A. Read each group of supporting details. Annotate the text by circling the topic and underlining key words of support and transition. In the spaces provided, use your own words to write the implied main idea for each group.

Textbook
Skills

1. Supporting details from a college algebra textbook:

- The first step for solving problems is to *familiarize* yourself with the problem situation.

- You can try several approaches to become familiar with a problem.

- For example, read the problem out loud as if you were explaining it to someone else.

- Make and label a drawing with the information in the problem.
- Also, find needed information by looking up formulas or definitions.
- Once you have familiarized yourself with the problem, the second step for solving problems is to *translate* the problem to an equation.
- The third step is to *solve* the equation.
- The fourth step is to *check* the answer in the original problem.
- And, finally, the fifth step is to *state* the answer to the problem clearly.
- In summary, familiarize, translate, solve, check, and state.

—Adapted from Bittinger/Beecher, *Introductory and Intermediate Algebra: Combined Approach*, Text Excerpt from p. 127 © 2003 Pearson Education, Inc. Reproduced by permission of Pearson Education, Inc.

Implied main idea: _____

_____

Textbook Skills

2. Supporting details from a college history textbook:

- During the Revolutionary War, women had to take over the management of countless farms, shops, and businesses.
- Women also became involved in other day-to-day matters that men had normally managed.
- Their experiences made the women and their families more aware of their abilities.
- At the same time, women made significant contributions to the war effort.
- And their efforts made them aware of their importance.

—Adapted from Garraty/Carnes, *American Nation Single Volume Edition*, Text Excerpt from p. 130 © 2000 Pearson Education, Inc. Reproduced by permission of Pearson Education, Inc.

Implied main idea: _____

_____

B. Read the following paragraph from a college history textbook. Annotate the text. In the space provided, write a sentence that states the implied main idea for the paragraph.

Textbook
Skills

Thomas Jefferson

[1]Thomas Jefferson was in some ways a typical, pleasure-loving southern planter. [2]However, he had in him something of the Spartan. [3]He grew tobacco but did not smoke, and he rarely ate meat or drank alcohol. [4]Unlike most planters, he never hunted or gambled. [5]Yet he was a fine horseman and enjoyed dancing, music, and other social interests. [6]His practical interests ranged enormously: from architecture and geology to natural history and scientific farming. [7]Yet he displayed little interest in managing men. [8]Controversy dismayed him, and he tended to avoid it by assigning to some thicker-skinned associate the task of attacking his enemies. [9]Nevertheless, he wanted to have a say in shaping the future of the country. [10]And once engaged, he fought stubbornly and at times deviously to get and hold power. [11]He became the fourth President of the United States and held the office for two terms.

—Adapted from Garraty/Carnes, *American Nation Single Volume Edition,* Text Excerpt from p. 170 © 2000 Pearson Education, Inc. Reproduced by permission of Pearson Education, Inc.

3. Implied main idea: _____

_____

Application 3: Implied Central Idea

Read the following passages from a college science textbook. Annotate the text. Answer the questions that follow each passage.

Crying: A Stress Management Method?

[1]Researchers have asked why people cry and how crying might help with stress. [2]Although the eyes of all mammals are moisturized and soothed by tears, only human beings shed tears in response to emotional stress. [3]Yet we know little about this uniquely human behavior. [4]One theory suggests that tears help relieve stress by ridding the body of potentially harmful stress-induced chemicals. [5]One finding is that emotionally induced tears have a higher protein content than tears produced in response to eye irritation, such as those caused by an onion.

[6]Other interesting evidence includes a report that people with stress-related illnesses cry less than their healthy peers. [7]Reports based on experience are that people feel better "after a good cry." [8]It has been documented that men cry less often than women. [9]In America, two triggers of crying episodes are most common. [10]One involves personal

relationships, such as arguments, and the second trigger is movie or television scenes. [11]Thus a primary crying time in this country is between seven and ten in the evening, when people are likely to be with others and/or watching television. [12]So when one is feeling stressed, crying is thought by some to be beneficial.

—Adapted from McGuigan, *Encyclopedia of Stress*, p. 61.

_____ **1.** Which is the best statement of the implied central idea?
   a. Crying may be used primarily as a method of stress management.
   b. Crying most frequently occurs in the evening.
   c. Crying has physical benefits.
   d. The human act of crying has prompted research into its causes and its role as a stress management method.

Humor: A Stress Management Method?

[1]Stress has been cited as a contributing cause of depression, anxiety, and other psychological problems. [2]Several studies indicate that a sense of humor helps in dealing with the stresses of life. [3]It mitigates depression, and laughter can overcome the fear of death itself.

[4]Laughter has been likened to "stationary jogging." [5]It relieves tension while exercising heart, lungs, and muscles. [6]Laughter increases heart rate and blood pressure. [7]Circulation of blood is thus improved. [8]Better circulation increases the amount of oxygen and other metabolic and nutritional components that are carried to various parts of the body. [9]It can help relieve pain through the release of endorphins into the bloodstream. [10]Laughter's most profound effects may occur on the immune system. [11]Natural killer cells that destroy viruses and tumors apparently increase during a state of mirth.

[12]The science of laughter is thought of as a legitimate field of study. [13]Studies indicate that humor can be helpful in treating various problems due to stress. [14]It can be incorporated into groups as a learned interaction.

—Adapted from McGuigan, *Encyclopedia of Stress*, pp. 107–108.

2. Implied central idea: _____

_____

_____

REVIEW TEST 1

Score (number correct) _____ × 25 = _____ %

Implied Main Ideas

A. Read each group of supporting details. Annotate the list. Then choose the sentence that best expresses the implied main idea for each group.

1. Supporting details:

- Birthrates fell for teens overall throughout the 1990s and for unmarried teens starting in the mid-1990s.
- However, the number of births to teenagers that are unmarried continued to rise.
- The number of unmarried teenage mothers rose from 14 percent in 1940 to 67 percent in 1990 and to 79 percent in 2000.
- This is because very few teens are marrying today, and the birthrate for married teens has dropped substantially.

—Adapted from National Center for Health Statistics,
"New CDC Report Tracks Trends in Teen Births."

_____ **Implied main idea:**
   a. Although birthrates fell for teenagers during the 1990s, the proportional number of births to unmarried teens continued to rise.
   b. The birthrate for married teenagers has dropped significantly.
   c. Teenage marriage and parenthood are on the rise.
   d. Birthrates for teenagers have fallen in recent years.

2. Supporting details:

- Maria focused all her attention on the television set even when she was flipping through the channels.
- By the time her husband Jesse entered the room, one of the shows had caught her attention.
- Jesse tried to talk to Maria about an issue that had come up at work.
- Jesse felt anxious and needed to talk.
- Although Maria nodded at everything Jesse said, her eyes never left the television set.
- In addition, she offered no comments, nor did she ask any questions.
- Jesse finally fell silent, then sighed deeply, and quietly left the room.

_____ **Implied main idea:**
   a. Jesse and Maria are not happily married.
   b. Maria's lack of attention discouraged her husband at a time when he needed her support.
   c. Maria and Jesse do not listen to each other.
   d. Jesse's rude behavior of interrupting Maria's television show led to the couple's lack of communication.

B. Study the following chart, and examine the details given. In the space provided, write the letter of the sentence that best states the implied main idea of the chart.

3. Supporting details:

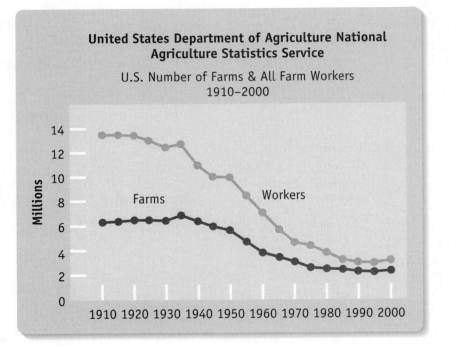

United States Department of Agriculture National Agriculture Statistics Service

U.S. Number of Farms & All Farm Workers 1910–2000

_____ **Implied main idea:**
   a. Fewer people were farmworkers in 2000 than in 1910.
   b. The numbers of farms declined from a little over 6 million farms in 1910 to only 2 million in 2000.
   c. The numbers of farms and farmworkers steadily declined from 1910 to 2000.
   d. Millions of people have fled farm life for jobs in towns and cities.

C. Read the following paragraph. Annotate the text. In the space provided, write the letter of the best statement of the implied main idea.

Textbook Skills

Most people think "Anything worth doing is worth doing well." In contrast, perfectionists think, "Anything worth doing is worth doing perfectly." Nothing less than perfection will do. "Procrastinating perfectionists" find the task so daunting that they wait until too late to prepare. They excuse themselves by thinking they could have done wonderfully, if only they had not procrastinated. "Tedious perfectionists" hone each step of preparation in great detail, but run out of time. For example, while preparing to deliver a speech, this perfectionist will gather volumes of material, write detailed outlines, but never practice delivering the speech.

—Adapted from Kelly,
Communication @ Work, p. 70.

_____ **4.** The best statement of the implied main idea is
   a. Don't aim for perfection; aim to do a very good job.
   b. Perfection is an excuse.
   c. Two types of perfectionists have unrealistic expectations.
   d. Perfectionists are failures.

REVIEW TEST 2   Score (number correct) _____ × 25 = _____ %

Implied Main Ideas and Implied Central Ideas

A. Read each group of supporting ideas. Annotate the lists. Then use your own words to write the best statement of the implied main idea for each group.

Group 1

Oil Pollution

- Used engine oil can end up in waterways.
- Coral reefs and mangroves are more likely to be damaged by oil pollution than are sandy beaches or sea-grass beds.
- Oil-covered fur or feathers do not provide the needed insulation for marine mammals and diving birds in cold water.
- When an animal cleans itself, it also swallows oil.

- Fish exposed to oil pollution such as tanker spills may develop liver disease and reproductive and growth problems.
- Oil pollution occurs through major oil spills, runoff from city and industrial wastes, and exhaust particles from automobiles.

1. Implied main idea: _____

_____

Group 2

A Few Duties for June for Florida Gardeners

- In June, Florida gardeners fertilize blackberries and blueberries.
- They also plant the herbs that thrive in heat, such as basil, chives, and lemongrass.
- Florida gardeners know that June is a good month to spread thick layers of mulch in flowerbeds to smother quickly growing weeds.
- With June come the early days of the hurricane season, so Florida gardeners also take notice of weak or rotting trees or limbs that need pruning.

2. Implied main idea: _____

_____

Group 3

"Do Not Call" Registry to Block Telemarketing Calls.

- Since July 2003, the Federal Trade Commission (FTC) has been registering consumers for the free online "do not call" registry.
- Telemarketers and other sellers have access to the registry.
- They will be required to check their call lists against the national "do not call" registry at least once every 90 days.
- The "do not call" registry accepts home phone numbers and cell phone numbers.
- Violators are subject to a fine of up to $11,000 per violation.

—Federal Trade Commission, "The 'Do Not Call' Registry."

3. Implied main idea: _____

_____

_____

B. Read the following poem, and then write a sentence that states the implied central idea.

Batteries and Bottled Water

by Dustin Weeks

I'm making a list of the things I need
To ride out the storm:
Candles and cans of tuna,
A deck of cards,
Tape for the windows,
Or better yet sheets of plywood
Securely screwed.

I'm still making my list
As the wind begins to rise.
How long will half a jar of peanut butter last
In desperate hours?
I decide to drink the milk
Before it's too late and
A white frown trickles down my chin.

I decide I am good at making lists
While watching the water rising from under the door.
Right here I listed the wet/dry vac,
Just after the chain saw
And before the first aid kit.
The TV says it pays to be prepared
And they will let me know in the event of an actual emergency.

I have almost completed my list
When the roof lifts off
Like a giant Japanese kite
And the list is torn from my hands.
I watch it whipped higher and higher
Into the raging sky
A bottleless message urging evacuation.

4. Implied central idea: _____

_____

_____

REVIEW TEST 3   Score (number correct) _____ × 20 = _____ %

Read the following passage from a college science textbook. Answer the questions that follow.

Textbook
Skills

Smoking—A Life and Breath Decision

[1]About 440,000 people in the United States die of smoking-related diseases each year. [2]These diseases include lung cancer, emphysema, chronic bronchitis, heart disease, stroke, and other forms of cancer.

[3]In smokers, microscopic smoke particles build up in the alveoli over the years until the lungs of a heavy smoker are literally blackened. [4]Adhering to the particles are about 200 different toxic substances. [5]Of these, more than a dozen are known or probable carcinogens (cancer-causing substances). [6]The longer the delicate tissues of the lungs are exposed to the carcinogens on the trapped particles, the greater the chance that cancer will develop.

[7]Some smokers will develop chronic bronchitis, a persistent lung infection. [8]Bronchitis is characterized by coughing, swelling of the lining of the respiratory tract, an increase in mucous production, and a decrease in the number and activity of cilia. [9]The result is a decrease in air flow to the alveoli. [10]Emphysema develops when toxic substances in cigarette smoke lead to brittle and ruptured alveoli. [11]The loss of the alveoli, where gas exchange occurs, deprives all body tissues of oxygen. [12]In an individual with emphysema, breathing becomes increasingly labored and loss of breath may ultimately be fatal.

[13]Carbon monoxide is present at high levels in cigarette smoke. [14]Carbon monoxide binds to red blood cells in place of oxygen. [15]This binding reduces the blood's oxygen-carrying capacity and thereby increases the work the heart must do. [16]Chronic bronchitis and emphysema compound this problem, making smokers twice as likely as nonsmokers to suffer a heart attack. [17]Smoking also causes atherosclerosis. [18]As a result, smokers are 70% more likely than nonsmokers to die of heart disease. [19]The carbon monoxide in cigarette smoke may also contribute to the reproductive problems of women who smoke during pregnancy. [20]These problems include infertility, miscarriage, lower birth weight of their babies, and, for their children, more learning and behavioral problems.

[21]Children whose parents smoke are more likely to contract bronchitis, pneumonia, ear infections, coughs, and colds. [22]Their lung

capacity is often decreased, and they are more likely to develop asthma and allergies as well. [23]For children with asthma, the number and severity of asthma attacks are increased by secondhand smoke. [24]Among adults, nonsmoking spouses of smokers face a 30% higher risk of both heart attack and lung cancer than do spouses of nonsmokers. [25]A recent study links even relatively infrequent exposure to secondhand smoke with atherosclerosis. [26]Government agencies report that secondhand smoke is responsible for an estimated 3,000 lung cancer deaths and at least 35,000 deaths from heart disease in nonsmokers in the United States each year. [27]For smokers who quit, however, healing begins immediately and the chances of heart attack, lung cancer, and numerous other smoking-related illnesses gradually diminish.

—Adapted from Audesirk, Audesirk,
& Byers, *Life on Earth*, 5th ed., p. 389.

_____ **1.** Which sentence best states the implied main idea of the second paragraph (sentences 3–6)?
   a. Tobacco smoke has a dramatic impact on the human respiratory tract.
   b. Tobacco smoke contains hundreds of toxic chemicals.
   c. Tobacco smoke can cause lung cancer.
   d. Tobacco smoke is deadly.

_____ **2.** Which sentence best states the implied main idea of the third paragraph (sentences 7–12)?
   a. Smoking causes chronic bronchitis.
   b. Smoking causes emphysema.
   c. Tobacco smoke harms the cilia and the alveoli of the lungs.
   d. Tobacco smoke can cause serious respiratory problems and may lead to death.

_____ **3.** Which sentence best states the implied main idea of the fourth paragraph (sentences 13–20)?
   a. Tobacco smoke contains carbon monoxide.
   b. The carbon monoxide in tobacco smoke causes heart disease.
   c. The carbon monoxide in tobacco smoke is linked to heart problems and contributes to reproductive problems in women who smoke.
   d. The carbon monoxide in tobacco smoke restricts the body's ability to absorb oxygen.

_____ **4.** Which sentence best states the implied main idea of the fifth paragraph (sentences 21–27)?
   a. Children are harmed by breathing secondhand smoke.
   b. Breathing secondhand smoke poses health hazards for both children and adults.
   c. Secondhand smoke causes health problems for adults.
   d. The harmful effects of smoking can be reversed.

_____ **5.** Which sentence best states the central idea of the passage?
   a. Smoking tobacco and breathing secondhand smoke lead to serious health problems and even death.
   b. The harmful effects of smoking are irreversible.
   c. Tobacco smoke has a dramatic impact on the human respiratory system.
   d. Quitting smoking saves lives.

WHAT DO YOU THINK?

Given the proven health risks, why do you think so many people choose to smoke? Assume you are taking a college health course, and your professor has assigned a paper worth 10 percent of your final grade. You are to write a paper about an avoidable health hazard. You have chosen to write about the dangers of smoking tobacco. In your paper, call for smokers to stop smoking, give them reasons to stop, and suggest a method to help them stop.

REVIEW TEST 4

Score (number correct) _____ × 10 = _____%

Implied Main Ideas and Implied Central Ideas

Before you read, skim the following passage from a college social science textbook. Answer the Before Reading questions. Read the passage and annotate the text. Then answer the After Reading questions.

Textbook
Skills

Two Types of Language: Denotation and Connotation

¹Consider a word such as *death*. ²To a doctor, this word might mean the point at which the heart stops beating. ³This is a denotative meaning, a rather **objective** description of an event. ⁴To a mother whose son has

just died, however, the word means much more. [5]It recalls the son's youth, his ambitions, his family, his illness, and so on. [6]To her, the word is emotional, subjective, and highly personal. [7]These emotional, subjective, and personal associations are the word's connotative meaning. [8]The **denotation** of a word is its objective definition; the **connotation** is its subjective or emotional meaning.

[9]Now consider a simple nod of the head in answer to the question, "Do you agree?" [10]This gesture is largely denotative and simply says yes. [11]What about a wink, a smile, or an overly rapid speech rate? [12]These nonverbal expressions are more connotative; they express your feelings rather than objective information.

[13]The denotative meaning of a message is general or **universal**; most people would agree with the denotative meanings and would give similar definitions. [14]Connotative meanings, however, are extremely personal, and few people would agree on the precise connotative meaning of a word or nonverbal behavior.

[15]"Snarl words" and "purr words" may further clarify the distinction between denotative and connotative meaning. [16]Snarl words are highly negative ("She's an idiot," "He's a pig," "They're a bunch of losers"). [17]Sexist, racist, and heterosexist language and hate speech provide lots of other examples. [18]Purr words are highly positive ("She's a real sweetheart," "He's a dream," "They're the greatest"). [19]Although they may sometimes seem to have denotative meaning and refer to the "real world," snarl and purr words are actually connotative in meaning. [20]They don't describe people or events, but rather, they reveal the speaker's feelings about these people or events.

—Adapted from DeVito, *Interpersonal Communication Book*, p. 162 © 2009 by Pearson Education, Inc. Reproduced by permission of Pearson Education, Inc.

Before Reading

Vocabulary in Context

_____ **1.** The best definition of the word **objective** in sentence 3 is
    a. personal.   c. honest.
    b. factual.   d. biased.

_____ **2.** The best meaning of the word **universal** in sentence 13 is
    a. lofty.   c. common to many people.
    b. narrow.   d. exact.

Thought Patterns

_____ **3.** What is the thought pattern suggested by the title of the passage?
   a. cause and effect   c. spatial order
   b. classification   d. comparison

After Reading

Main Ideas

_____ **4.** Which sentence is the topic sentence for the last paragraph (sentences 15–20)?
   a. sentence 15   c. sentence 18
   b. sentence 16   d. sentence 19

Supporting Details

_____ **5.** Based on the passage, a simple nod of the head
   a. is the only way to communicate agreement with an idea or person.
   b. can have many different meanings.
   c. is largely denotative and simply says yes.
   d. carries connotative meanings.

_____ **6.** Based on the passage, "snarl words" and "purr words"
   a. describe people or events.
   b. communicate denotative meanings.
   c. reveal the speaker's feelings about people or events.
   d. are highly positive.

Concept Maps and Charts

7. Complete the concept map with information from the passage.

Two Types of Language	
Denotation	**Connotation**
Objective descriptions	_____ associations
Nod of the head	Wink, smile, rapid rate of speech
Universal meanings	Extremely personal meanings
	Snarl and purr words

Implied Main Ideas and Implied Central Ideas

_____ **8.** Which sentence best states the implied main idea of the second paragraph (sentences 9–12)?
   a. Nonverbal language can also have denotative or connotative meanings.
   b. A nod of the head is an example of denotative language.
   c. A wink is an example of connotative language.
   d. Nonverbal language is powerful.

_____ **9.** Which sentence best states the implied main idea of the third paragraph (sentences 13–14)?
   a. Most people agree with denotative meanings.
   b. Most people disagree over connotative meanings.
   c. Denotative meanings are more widely agreed on than connotative meanings.
   d. Denotative and connotative meanings are very similar.

_____ **10.** Which sentence best states the implied central idea of the passage?
   a. Language has the ability to communicate many meanings.
   b. Verbal and nonverbal language express both denotation and connotation.
   c. Gestures are part of nonverbal language that can express both denotation and connotation.
   d. Racist language is an example of connotative meaning.

WHAT DO YOU THINK?

Which type of meaning do you think is more powerful: denotative or connotative? When are we most likely to rely on the denotative meanings of words? When are we most likely to rely on connotative meanings of words? Assume you are a reporter for your college newspaper. You are writing an article about the issue of cheating in college. Write a paragraph that uses the denotative meanings of words to discuss how widespread the problem is and to explain why students might cheat. After you have written your paragraph, revise it to use connotative meanings to make your point. Share your work with a peer or small group of classmates. Discuss how the use of connotative and denotative meanings affected your writing.

After Reading About Implied Main Ideas and Implied Central Ideas

Before you move on to the Mastery Tests on implied main ideas and implied central ideas, take time to reflect on your learning and performance by answering the following questions. Write your answers in your notebook.

- What did I learn about implied main ideas and implied central ideas?
- What do I need to remember about implied main ideas and implied central ideas?
- How has my knowledge base or prior knowledge about implied ideas changed?
- How has my knowledge base or prior knowledge about implied main ideas changed?
- Based on my studies, how do I think I will perform on the Mastery Test(s)? Why do I think my scores will be above average, average, or below average?
- Would I recommend this chapter to other students who want to learn more about implied main ideas? Why or why not?

Test your understanding of what you have learned about implied main ideas and implied central ideas by completing the Chapter 4 Review Card in the insert near the end of the text.

CONNECT TO **myreadinglab**

To check your progress in meeting Chapter 4's learning outcomes, log in to **myreadinglab.com,** and try the following activities.

- The "Main Idea" section of MyReadingLab provides review materials, practice activities, and tests about topics and main ideas. To access this resource, click on the "Study Plan" tab. Then click on "Main Idea." Then click on the following links as needed: "Overview," "Model," "Practice," and "Tests."

- To measure your mastery of the content in this chapter, complete the tests in the "Main Idea" section and click on Gradebook to find your results.

A. Read and annotate the following paragraphs. In the spaces provided, use your own words to write the best statement of the main idea for each.

[1]Kickboxing as an aerobic exercise uses a bouncing base move. [2]Added to the base move are a variety of self-defense moves such as punches, kicks, and knee strikes. [3]Some cardio-kickboxing classes may also include sparring routines. [4]In addition, some kickboxing classes may incorporate traditional exercises, such as jumping jacks, leg lifts, push-ups, and abdominal crunches.

1. Implied main idea: _____

_____

_____

[1]Lassie, one of the most famous animals ever on television, became a beloved symbol of loyalty and courage. [2]The popular sitcom *Friends* featured Marcel the monkey, who came to be regarded by the character Ross as a friend as much as a pet. [3]Another successful sitcom, *Married with Children*, had a dog named Buck—the sole trapping of normality in that dysfunctional family. [4]And who can forget the Taco Bell Chihuahua, who helped sell countless tacos?

2. Implied main idea: _____

_____

[1]Mohandas Gandhi was a 20th-century leader of the Indian Nationalist movement. [2]Mahatma, or "great soul," was the name by which he became known later in his life. [3]His use of nonviolent confrontation, or civil disobedience, won freedom for his own people and influenced leaders around the world. [4]Gandhi believed in hard work and humility; he spun his own thread and wove the material for his clothes. [5]Gandhi fought for the rights of the imprisoned and impoverished.

3. Implied main idea: _____

_____

B. Read and annotate the following passage from a college health textbook. Write the central idea in the space provided.

Textbook
Skills

Water: The Essential Nutrient

¹Without water, you could live only about one week. ²About 65 to 70 percent of your body weight is made up of water in the form of blood, saliva, urine, cellular fluids, and digestive enzymes. ³In all these various forms, water helps transport nutrients, remove wastes, and control body temperature.

⁴Water carries nutrients along the digestive path and to the cells. ⁵First, it does this by liquefying food and moving it through the stomach, small intestine, and large intestine. ⁶When the food is absorbed into the blood, water plays an important role by regulating the amount of nutrients on both sides of the cell wall.

⁷Water needs vary, depending on the climate and a person's activity level. ⁸In a cold climate, the demand by the body for water is less than in a warm climate. ⁹An active person's demand for water is much greater than an inactive person's demand. ¹⁰Also, more water is needed at higher altitudes than at lower altitudes.

¹¹There are many ways to get liquid from your diet. ¹²The most obvious source is a glass of water. ¹³Most experts agree that six to eight glasses of water per day provide an adequate supply to an average adult. ¹⁴Other healthy beverages are skim or low-fat milk and fruit juices. ¹⁵In addition, many fruits and vegetables are excellent sources of water.

—Adapted from Pruitt & Stein, *Health Styles: Decisions for Living Well*, 2nd ed., p. 107.

4. Implied central idea: _____

_____

Read and annotate the following paragraphs. In the spaces provided, write the letter of the sentence that best states the implied main idea for each paragraph.

Paragraph from a college history textbook

Textbook Skills

Growth of National Feelings

[1]Most modern revolutions have been prompted by strong national feelings, and most have resulted in independence. [2]In the case of the American Revolution, the desire to be free came before any national feeling. [3]The colonies did not enter into a political union because they felt an overwhelming desire to bring all Americans under one rule. [4]Instead they united as the only hope of winning a war against Great Britain. [5]The fact that the colonies chose to stay together after the war shows how much national feeling had developed during the war.

—Adapted from Garraty/Carnes, *American Nation Single Volume Edition,* Text Excerpt from p. 130 © 2000 Pearson Education, Inc. Reproduced by permission of Pearson Education, Inc.

_____ 1. Which sentence best states the implied main idea?
   a. One result of the American Revolution was the growth of national feelings.
   b. Most wars are caused by national feelings.
   c. The American Revolution was caused by a need for independence.
   d. The fact that the colonies stayed united after the Revolutionary War was a miracle.

Paragraph from a college mass media textbook

Textbook Skills

The Vital Role of Magazines

[1]Magazines began in colonial America as a forum for the essay. [2]Since then, magazines have helped develop the nation's social awareness. [3]By 1900, an educated middle class used magazines as the tool for social protest. [4]Today, consumer magazines and literary journals make up the bulk of magazine publishing. [5]In the future, magazines will continue to change to provide vital voices to national discussions about political and social issues.

—Adapted from Folkerts, Jean, and Stephen Lacy. *The Media in Your Life: An Introduction to Mass Communication,* 2nd ed., p. 141. Published by Allyn and Bacon, Boston, MA. Copyright © 2001, 1998 by Pearson Education, Inc.

_____ **2.** Which sentence best states the implied main idea?
a. Magazines are a unique American product.
b. Magazines were an important part of colonial America.
c. Magazines have provided many important services.
d. Magazines have been and will remain an important forum for American voices.

Paragraph from a college algebra textbook

Three Ways to Study

Textbook Skills

[1]During systematic study, you begin studying on November 1 for an exam scheduled on November 15, and you continue to study every day until the day of the test. [2]During intense study, you wait until November 14 to begin studying, and you cram all day and through the night. [3]Which of these methods would produce a better result on an exam? [4]Research shows that students who are successful use a third system that combines the first two. [5]They study systematically well ahead of the test, but they also do intense study the day before the test. [6]This works so long as they don't stay up all night.

—Adapted from Bittinger/Beecher, *Introductory and Intermediate Algebra: Combined Approach*, Text Excerpt from p. 805 © 2003 Pearson Education, Inc. Reproduced by permission of Pearson Education, Inc.

_____ **3.** Which sentence best states the implied main idea?
a. Systematic study requires that a student begin studying weeks before a test.
b. Intense study drives a student to "cram" the day before the test.
c. The most effective study system combines systematic and intense study sessions.
d. There are two basic ways to study for an exam: systematic and intense.

Read and annotate the following paragraphs. In the spaces provided, use your own words to state the implied main idea.

Poem reprinted in a college literature textbook

To See a World in a Grain of Sand

by William Blake (1803)

Textbook
Skills

To see a world in a grain of sand
And a heaven in a wild flower,
Hold infinity in the palm of your hand
And eternity in an hour.

1. **Implied main idea:** _____

_____

Paragraph from a college social science textbook

Textbook
Skills

Audience Demand in Movie Markets

[1]In the early days, movies catered to the family audience. [2]From the era of the nickelodeon to the age of Panavision, mothers, fathers, and children flocked to neighborhood movie houses and to the theater palaces in the cities. [3]After the advent of television, as couples settled down to raise children in the suburbs, the movies became less attractive. [4]For parents, going to a movie meant paying for a babysitter, tickets, and transportation. [5]So, many chose to stay home and watch television. [6]Slowly, the audience changed. [7]From the late 1960s until the late 1990s, the 17-year-old was the most reliable moviegoer. [8]Now, aging baby boomers far outnumber teenagers in the United States and present a viable group for studios to target.

—Adapted from Folkerts, Jean, and Stephen Lacy. *The Media in Your Life: An Introduction to Mass Communication*, 2nd ed., p. 166. Published by Allyn and Bacon, Boston, MA. Copyright © 2001, 1998 by Pearson Education, Inc.

2. **Implied main idea:** _____

_____

Paragraph from a college history textbook

America Isolated

[1]America was isolated from Europe by 3,000 miles of ocean or, as a poet put it, "nine hundred leagues of roaring seas." [2]The crossing took anywhere from a few weeks to several months, depending on wind and weather. [3]No one undertook an ocean voyage lightly, and few who made the westward crossing ever thought seriously of returning. [4]The modern mind can scarcely grasp the awful isolation that enveloped settlers. [5]One had to build a new life or perish—if not of hunger, then of loneliness.

—Adapted from Garraty/Carnes, *American Nation Single Volume Edition,* Text Excerpt from p. 38 © 2000 Pearson Education, Inc. Reproduced by permission of Pearson Education, Inc.

Textbook Skills

3. Implied main idea: _____

_____

Visual graphic or concept map from a college communications textbook

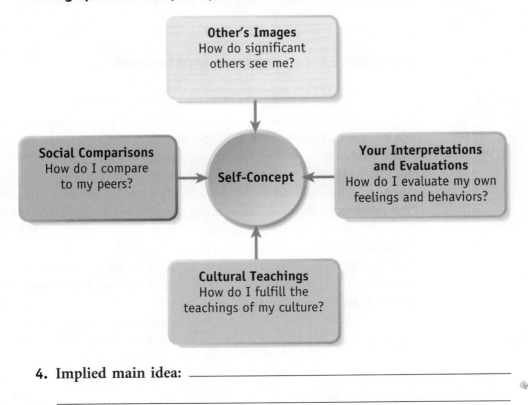

4. Implied main idea: _____

_____

_____

—Adapted from DeVito, *Interpersonal Communication Book,* p. 57 © 2009 by Pearson Education, Inc. Reproduced by permission of Pearson Education, Inc.

Read the following passage from college sociology textbook. Answer the questions that follow.

Textbook
Skills

Managing Diversity in the Workplace

[1]Times have changed. The San Jose, California, electronic phone book lists ten times more Nguyens than Joneses. [2]More than half of U.S. workers are minorities, immigrants, and women. [3]Diversity in the workplace is much more than skin color. [4]Diversity includes ethnicity, gender, age, religion, social class, and sexual orientation.

[5]In our growing global context of life, diversity is increasing. [6]In the past, the idea was for people to join the "melting pot," to give up their distinctive traits and become like the dominant group. [7]Today, with the successes of the civil rights and women's movements, people are more likely to prize their distinctive traits. [8]Realizing that assimilation (being absorbed into the dominant culture) is probably not the wave of the future, most large companies have "diversity training." [9]They hold lectures and workshops so that employees can learn to work with colleagues of diverse cultures and racial-ethnic backgrounds.

[10]Consider the case of Coors Brewery. [11]Coors went into a financial tailspin after one of the Coors brothers gave a racially charged speech in the 1980s. [12]Today, Coors offers diversity workshops, has sponsored a gay dance, and has paid for a corporate-wide mammography program. [13]In 2004, Coors opposed an amendment to the Colorado constitution that would ban the marriage of homosexuals. [14]The company has even had rabbis certify its suds as kosher. [15]Its proud new slogan: "Coors cares." [16]Now, that's quite a change.

[17]What Coors cares about, of course, is the bottom line. [18]It's the same with other corporations.

[19]Blatant racism and sexism once made no difference to profitability. [20]Today, they do. [21]To promote profitability, companies must promote diversity—or at least pretend to. [22]The sincerity of corporate leaders is not what's important; diversity in the workplace is.

[23]Diversity training has the potential to build bridges. [24]However, managers who are chosen to participate can resent it, thinking that it is punishment for some unmentioned insensitivity on their part. [25]Some directors of these programs are so incompetent that they create antagonisms

193

and reinforce stereotypes. [26]For example, the leaders of a diversity training session at the U.S. Department of Transportation had women grope men as the men ran by. [27]They encouraged blacks and whites to insult one another and to call each other names. [28]The intention may have been good (understanding the other through role reversal and getting hostilities "out in the open"), but the approach was moronic. [29]Instead of healing, such behaviors wound and leave scars.

—Adapted from Henslin, Sociology: *A Down to Earth Approach,*
Text from pp. 192–193 © 2008 James M. Henslin. Reproduced by
permission of Pearson Education, Inc.

_____ 1. Which sentence best states the implied main idea of the second paragraph (sentences 5–9)?
   a. Because of increased diversity of the workforce, diversity training in the workplace is becoming more popular.
   b. Diversity has occurred because of increased civil rights for minorities.
   c. Businesses are more diverse today than in the past.
   d. Assimilation no longer occurs.

_____ 2. Which sentence best states the implied main idea of the third paragraph (sentences 10–16)?
   a. Coors Brewery was a racist company at one time.
   b. Coors Brewery only changed to make money.
   c. Coors Brewery is a good example of a company that changed to meet the demands of diversity in the workplace and community.
   d. Coors Brewery produces kosher beer in honor of diversity.

_____ 3. Which sentence best states the implied main idea of the sixth paragraph (sentences 23–29)?
   a. Some managers resent diversity training.
   b. Incompetent managers create problems.
   c. Diversity training gets hostilities out in the open.
   d. Diversity training can backfire.

_____ 4. Which sentence best states the implied central idea of the passage?
   a. Diversity in the workplace is growing.
   b. Managing diversity in the workplace is good for business.
   c. Society has changed dramatically.
   d. Diversity in the workplace goes beyond skin color.

Supporting Details

5

After studying this chapter you should be able to do the following:

1. Define the terms *major and minor supporting details* and *summary*.
2. Create questions to locate supporting details.
3. Distinguish between major and minor supporting details.
4. Complete a simple chart that outlines the topic, main idea, and supporting details of a passage.
5. Create a summary of a passage.
6. Evaluate the importance of supporting details.

Before Reading About Supporting Details

In Chapters 3 and 4, you learned several important ideas that will help you as you work through this chapter. Use the following questions to call up your prior knowledge about supporting details.

What is a main idea? (page 96.) _____

_____

What are the three parts of most paragraphs? (page 101.) _____,

_____, and _____.

Define supporting details. (page 102.) _____

_____

What are the different possible locations of topic sentences? (pages 108–117.)

_____

_____

What is a central idea? (page 117.) _____

_____

 ## Questions for Locating Supporting Details

To locate supporting details, an effective reader turns the main idea into a question by asking one of the following reporter's questions: *who, what, when, where, why,* or *how.* The answer to this question will yield a specific set of supporting details. For example, the question *why* is often answered by listing and explaining reasons or causes. The question *how* is answered by explaining a process. The answer to the question *when* is based on time order. An author strives to answer some or all of these questions with the details in the paragraph. You may want to try out several of the reporter's questions as you turn the main idea into a question. Experiment to discover which question is best answered by the details.

> **Supporting details** explain, develop, and illustrate the main idea.

Take, for example, the topic "dog bites." An author might choose to write about a few of the reasons a dog might bite someone. The main idea of such a paragraph may read as follows:

Main idea: In certain situations, a dog's natural aggression will make it more likely to bite.

Using the word *when* turns the main idea into the following question: "When is a dog likely to bite?" Read the following paragraph for the answers to this question.

A Dog's Natural Aggression

[1]In certain situations, a dog's natural aggression will make it more likely to bite. [2]For example, a dog may react aggressively if its personal space is invaded. [3]Therefore, a dog that is sleeping, eating, or nurturing its puppies may very well react with violence to defend itself, its food, or its offspring. [4]Aggression may also occur when a dog has been fenced in or tethered outside. [5]In these cases, the dog may feel easily frustrated or threatened and thus feel the urge to protect itself or its territory by biting. [6]A final situation that arouses the dog's animal aggression occurs when a person runs away in fear from a dog. [7]A dog's natural desire is to pursue prey; therefore, running past or away from a dog will almost always incite the animal to give chase and perhaps bite.

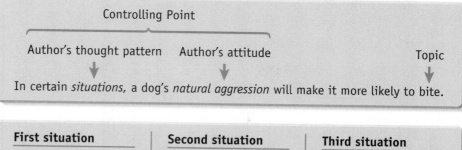

First situation	Second situation	Third situation
A dog may react aggressively if its personal space is invaded.	Aggression may also occur when a dog has been fenced in or tethered outside.	Animal aggression occurs when a person runs away in fear from a dog.

The supporting details for this main idea answer the question "when?" by listing the situations that are likely to arouse a dog's aggression and lead to biting. Then the paragraph discusses why the dog behaves this way.

Note the relationship between the author's controlling point and the supporting details.

Notice also that the details about situations directly explain the main idea. However, additional supporting details were given in the paragraph that are not listed. Each of the main supporting details needed further explanation. This paragraph shows us that there are two kinds of supporting details: details that explain the main idea and details that explain other details.

EXAMPLE   Read the paragraph. Turn the topic sentence into a question using one of the reporter's questions (Who? What? When? Where? Why? How?). Write the question in the space provided. Fill in the graph with the answers to the question you have created.

The Healthful Traits of Olive Oil

[1]Olive oil has several traits that benefit our health. [2]First, olive oil is a monounsaturated fat. [3]Monounsaturated fats lower blood cholesterol levels; they keep arteries free of blockages, and they reduce the chances of heart attacks and strokes. [4]Second, olive oil contains antioxidants. [5]Just like rust on a car, oxidation damages our cells. [6]Antioxidants help prevent oxidation. [7]They also may help increase immune function; thus they may decrease risk of infection and cancer. [8]Third, olive oil also has polyphenols. [9]Polyphenols also strengthen the immune system and protect the body from infection. [10]They have been linked to preventing cancer and heart disease.

Question based on topic sentence: _____

_____

Topic sentence: Olive oil has several traits that benefit our health.

First trait/benefit   **Second trait/benefit**   **Third trait/benefit**

(**1**) _____   (**2**) _____   (**3**) _____

_____   _____   _____

_____   _____   _____

_____   _____   _____

_____

EXPLANATION Using the reporter's question *What?*, you should have turned the topic sentence into the following question: *What are the several traits of olive oil that benefit our health?* The answer to this question yields the supporting details. Compare your answers to the following: (1) Monounsaturated fats, (2) Antioxidants, and (3) Polyphenols.

PRACTICE 1

Read the paragraph. Turn the topic sentence into a question using one of the reporter's questions (Who? What? When? Where? Why? How?). Write the question in the space provided. Fill in the graph with the answers to the question you have created.

Halitosis

[1]Halitosis, more commonly known as bad breath, occurs due to several specific circumstances. [2]As certain foods are digested, they result in bad breath. [3]Foods such as garlic and onions are absorbed into the bloodstream, carried to the lungs and expelled as bad breath through the mouth. [4]When dry mouth occurs and the flow of saliva decreases, bad breath occurs because saliva cleanses the mouth. [5]When oral hygiene is poor, bad breath is the result. [6]Improper brushing and flossing leaves food particles in the mouth. [7]In these instances, bacteria grows and creates sulfur compounds that also result in bad breath. [8]Finally, bad breath occurs when a medical disorder is present. [9]Bad breath may be a warning sign of infections of the sinuses or respiratory tract, liver or kidney problems, and diabetes.

Question based on topic sentence: _____

Topic sentence: Halitosis, more commonly known as bad breath, occurs due to several specific circumstances.

First circumstance	Second circumstance	Third circumstance	Fourth circumstance
(**1**) _____ _____	(**2**) When dry mouth occurs	(**3**) _____ _____	(**4**) When a medical disorder is present

Major and Minor Details

A supporting detail will always be one of two types:

> A **major detail** directly explains, develops, or illustrates the *main idea*.
> A **minor detail** explains, develops, or illustrates a *major detail*.

A **major detail** is directly tied to the main idea. Without the major details, the author's main idea would not be clear because the major details are the principal points the author is making about the topic.

In contrast, a **minor detail** explains a major detail. The minor details could be left out, and the main idea would still be clear. Thus minor details are not as important as major details. Minor details are used to add interest and to give further descriptions, examples, testimonies, analysis, illustrations, and reasons for the major details. To better understand the flow of ideas, study the following diagram:

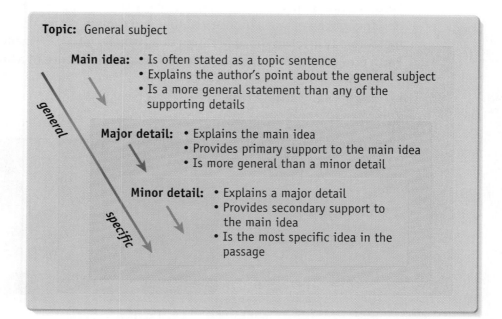

Topic: General subject

    Main idea: • Is often stated as a topic sentence
                  • Explains the author's point about the general subject
                  • Is a more general statement than any of the supporting details

general

        Major detail: • Explains the main idea
                      • Provides primary support to the main idea
                      • Is more general than a minor detail

            Minor detail: • Explains a major detail
                          • Provides secondary support to the main idea
specific   • Is the most specific idea in the passage

As ideas move from general to specific details, the author often uses signal words to introduce a new detail. These signal words—such as *first*, *second*, *next*, *in addition*, or *finally*—can help you identify major and minor details.

EXAMPLE   See if you can tell the difference between major and minor supporting details. Read the following paragraph from a college science textbook. Then complete the outline with the major and minor details from the paragraph.

What Is Earth Science?

Textbook Skills

[1]**Earth science** is the name for all the sciences that collectively seek to understand Earth and its neighbors in space. [2]Earth science includes geology, oceanography, meteorology, and astronomy. [3]First, **geology** literally means "study of Earth" and is divided into two broad areas—physical and historical. [4]*Physical geology* examines the materials comprising the Earth and the many processes that operate beneath and upon its surfaces. [5]In contrast to physical geology, the aim of *historical geology* is to understand the origin of Earth and the development of the planet through its 4.5-billion-year history. [6]Another Earth science is oceanography. [7]**Oceanography** includes all the study of the composition and movement of sea water, as well as coastal processes, seafloor topography, and marine life. [8]Oceanography is actually not a separate and distinct science. [9]Rather, it involves the application of all sciences in the study of the ocean. [10]A third Earth science is meteorology. [11]**Meteorology** is the study of the atmosphere and the processes that produce weather and climate. [12]Like oceanography, meteorology involves the application of all other sciences. [13]Finally, because Earth is related to all the other objects in space, the science of **astronomy** is

VISUAL VOCABULARY

Doppler radar is a tool used by _____ to monitor storms.

   a. oceanographers
   b. astronomers
   c. meteorologists

very useful. [14]Astronomy is the study of the universe. [15]Indeed, Earth is subject to the same physical laws that govern the many other objects populating the great expanses of space.

—Adapted from Lutgens & Tarbuck, *Foundations of Earth Science*, 5th ed., pp. 2–3.

Outline of "What Is Earth Science?"

Stated main idea: **Earth science** is the name for all the sciences that collectively seek to understand Earth and its neighbors in space.

A. _____

_____

    1. *Physical geology* examines the materials comprising the Earth and the many processes that operate beneath and upon its surfaces.

    2. _____

_____

_____

B. _____

    1. Oceanography includes all the study of the composition and movement of sea water, as well as coastal processes, seafloor topography, and marine life.

    2. _____

    3. Rather, it involves the application of all sciences in the study of the ocean.

C. _____

    1. _____

_____

    2. Like oceanography, meteorology involves the application of all other sciences.

D. _____

_____

    1. Astronomy is the study of the universe.

    2. _____

_____

EXPLANATION Every detail in the paragraph gives additional information that explains and supports the main idea or topic sentence. The topic sentence states a broad definition of Earth science. The author amplifies this definition by offering major and minor details about each of the four sciences that make up Earth science. Thus, the major details are sentences 3, 6, 10, and 13. Note that each of these major details is signaled by a transition: *First* (sentence 3), *Another* (sentence 6), *A third* (sentence 10), and *Finally* (sentence 13). Each of these major details is explained with minor supporting details. For example, the major detail "geology" is further defined by being divided into two subgroups. Thus, sentences 4 and 5 offer minor details about these two subtopics of geology: physical geology and historical geology. The other minor details in this paragraph are sentences 7, 8, 11, 12, 14, and 15. Note that some of these minor details are also introduced with transitions: *In contrast* (sentence 5), *Like* (sentence 12), and *Indeed* (sentence 15).

PRACTICE 2

Read the following passage from a popular online site for health information. Then identify the major and minor details by completing the outline that follows it.

What Is Insomnia?

[1]Insomnia (in-SOM-ne-ah) is a common condition in which you have trouble falling or staying asleep. [2]This condition can range from mild to severe, depending on how often it occurs and the type of insomnia it is.

[3]Insomnia can be chronic (ongoing) or acute (short-term). [4]Chronic insomnia means having symptoms at least 3 nights a week for more than a month. [5]Acute insomnia lasts for less time. [6]Some people who have insomnia may have trouble falling asleep. [7]Other people may fall asleep easily but wake up too soon. [8]Others may have trouble with both falling asleep and staying asleep. [9]As a result, insomnia may cause you to get too little sleep or have poor-quality sleep. [10]You may not feel refreshed when you wake up.

[11]There are two types of insomnia. [12]The most common type is called secondary or comorbid insomnia. [13]This type of insomnia is a symptom or side effect of some other problem. [14]More than 8 out of 10 people who have insomnia are believed to have secondary insomnia. [15]Certain medical conditions, medicines, sleep disorders, and substances can cause secondary insomnia. [16]In contrast, primary insomnia isn't due to a medical problem, medicines, or other substances. [17]It is its own disorder. [18]A number of life changes can trigger primary insomnia, including long-lasting stress and emotional upset.

[19]Finally, if you have insomnia, you may experience a variety of symptoms. [20]Insomnia can cause excessive daytime sleepiness and a lack

of energy. [21]It also can make you feel anxious, depressed, or irritable. [22]You may have trouble focusing on tasks, paying attention, learning, and remembering. [23]This can prevent you from doing your best at work or school. [24]Insomnia also can cause other serious problems. [25]For example, you may feel drowsy while driving, which could lead to an accident.

—U.S. Department of Health and Human Services and National Institutes of Health. "What Is Insomnia?" *Disease and Conditions Index.* March 2009. 7 June 2010. http://www.nhlbi.nih.gov/health/dci/Diseases/inso/inso_whatis.html.

Stated main idea: This condition can range from mild to severe, depending on how often it occurs and the type of insomnia it is.

A. _____

   1. Chronic insomnia means having symptoms at least 3 nights a week for more than a month.

   2. _____

   3. Some people who have insomnia may have trouble falling asleep.

   4. Other people may fall asleep easily but wake up too soon.

   5. Others may have trouble with both falling asleep and staying asleep.

      a. _____

         _____

      b. You may not feel refreshed when you wake up.

B. _____

   1. _____

      a. This type of insomnia is a symptom or side effect of some other problem.

      b. More than 8 out of 10 people who have insomnia are believed to have secondary insomnia.

      c. _____

         _____

   2. _____

         _____

      a. It is its own disorder.

      b. _____

         _____

C. _____

1. Insomnia can cause excessive daytime sleepiness and a lack of energy.

2. It also can make you feel anxious, depressed, or irritable.

3. You may have trouble focusing on tasks, paying attention, learning, and remembering.

4. This can prevent you from doing your best at work or school.

5. Insomnia also can cause other serious problems.

6. _____

Creating a Summary from Annotations

Reading for main ideas and major supporting details is an excellent study technique. After you finish reading, an effective strategy to deepen your understanding and provide study notes for review is to write down main ideas and major supporting details in a summary. (For more reading strategies see Chapter 1.) A **summary** condenses a paragraph or passage to only its primary points by restating the main idea, major supporting details, and important examples. Often you will want to paraphrase, that is, restate the ideas in your own words. Other times, you may need to use the exact language of the text to ensure accuracy. For example, scientific or medical terms have precise meanings that must be memorized; thus your summaries of these types of ideas would include the original language of the text.

Drafting a Summary: Stated Main Ideas

The length of a summary will vary, depending on the length of the original text.

> A **summary** is a brief, clear restatement of the most important points of a paragraph or passage.

For example, a paragraph can be summarized in one sentence or a few sentences. A passage of several paragraphs can be reduced to one paragraph, and a much longer selection such as a chapter in a textbook may require a summary of a page or two.

To create a summary after reading, you can **annotate**, or mark, your text during reading. For example, as you read, circle the main idea and underline the major supporting details and important examples. To learn more about annotating a text, see pages 608–609 in Part Two.

EXAMPLE   Read the following paragraph from a college accounting textbook. Circle the main idea, and underline the major supporting details. Then complete the summary.

Textbook
Skills

Liquid Assets

[1]**Liquid assets** are financial assets that can be easily sold without a loss in value. [2]They are especially useful for covering upcoming expenses. [3]Some of the more common liquid assets are cash, checking accounts, and savings accounts. [4]Cash is handy to cover small purchases, while a checking account is convenient for large purchases. [5]Savings accounts are desirable because they pay interest on the money that is deposited. [6]For example, if your savings account offers an interest rate of 4 percent, you earn annual interest of $4 for every $100 deposited in your account.

—Madura, *Personal Finance Update*, Text Excerpt from p. 40 © 2006 Pearson Education Inc. Reproduced by permission of Pearson Education, Inc.

Summary: Liquid assets are _____

_____

For example, three types are _____

_____

EXPLANATION   The main idea about the topic "liquid assets" is stated in the first sentence, which is the topic sentence of the paragraph: "Liquid assets are financial assets that can be easily sold without a loss in value." The paragraph goes on to list the following examples: cash, checking accounts, and savings accounts. To create a summary of the information, combine the main idea and major supporting details. Compare your summary to the following: Liquid assets are financial assets that can be easily sold without a loss in value. For example, three types are cash, checking accounts, and savings accounts.

PRACTICE 3

Read the following paragraph from a college health textbook. Circle the main idea, and underline the major supporting details. Complete the summary by filling in the blanks with information from the passage.

Textbook
Skills

The Body's Response to Stress

[1]Whenever we are surprised by a sudden stressor, such as someone swerving into our lane of traffic, the adrenal glands jump into action.

[2]These two almond-shaped glands sitting atop the kidneys secrete adrenaline and other hormones into the bloodstream. [3]As a result, the heart speeds up, breathing rate increases, blood pressure elevates, and the flow of blood to the muscles increases. [4]This sudden burst of energy and strength is believed to provide the extra edge that has helped generations of humans survive during adversity. [5]This response is believed to be one of our most basic, innate survival instincts. [6]Known as the **fight or flight response**, this physiological reaction prepares the body to combat a real or perceived threat. [7]It is a point at which our bodies go on the alert to either fight or escape.

—Donatelle, *Health: the Basics*, 5th ed., p. 54.

Summary: The **fight or flight response** is a _____ reaction that prepares the body to combat a real or perceived threat. For example, someone swerving into our lane of traffic triggers the _____ glands to speed up the _____, increase _____ rate, elevate blood pressure, and increase the flow of blood to the _____.

Creating a Summary: Implied Main Ideas

At times, a textbook author may choose to imply a main idea instead of directly stating it. As you learned in Chapter 4, you can use supporting details to create a topic sentence or thesis statement when the main idea or central point is implied. Annotating your text will also help you create a summary for passages with an implied main idea.

First, identify the topic of the passage. Underline recurring words or phrases. Locate each heading or major supporting detail in the passage. (Remember, minor details explain or support major details. Thus, to create a summary, you can ignore these minor details.) Assign a number or letter to each of the headings or major details you identified. Next, for each piece of information you have marked, ask the question "What controlling point or opinion about the topic does this detail reveal?" Often, a main heading can be turned into a question that will help you determine the implied main idea. Then, write a brief answer to each question in the margin next to the detail you marked. After you finish reading, create a topic sentence or thesis statement for the passage. Use only a few brief sentences to create the entire summary.

EXAMPLE Read the following passage taken from a college education text-book. As you read, complete the following steps. Then create a summary of the passage in the space provided after the passage.

Step 1: Annotate the text. Underline the recurring key terms or phrases and label the major supporting details with a number or letter.

Step 2: Turn the main heading into a question to determine the implied main idea. If needed, turn major details into questions that reveal the author's controlling point.

Step 3: Answer each question in your own words.

Step 4: Create a thesis statement based on the main heading and/or supporting details.

Step 5: Write a summary that combines the thesis statement and the major supporting details in one or a few brief sentences.

Textbook
Skills

Intelligence

[1]Intelligence has yet to be completely defined. [2]One view is that intelligence is the ability to learn. [3]As David Wechsler, the developer of the most widely used intelligence scales for children and adults, said: "Intelligence, operationally defined, is the aggregate or global capacity to act purposefully, to think rationally, and to deal effectively with the environment." [4]Other views on intelligence include the following:

- [5]It is *adaptive*. [6]It involves modifying and adjusting one's behavior to accomplish new tasks successfully.
- [7]It is related to *learning ability*. [8]Intelligent people learn information more quickly and easily than less intelligent people.
- [9]It involves the *use of prior knowledge* to analyze and understand new situations effectively.
- [10]It involves the complex interaction and coordination of *many different thinking and reasoning processes*.
- [11]It is *culture-specific*. [12]What is "intelligent" behavior in one culture is not necessarily intelligent behavior in another culture.

—Parkay and Stanford, *Becoming a Teacher*, p. 300 © 1995 by Pearson Education, Inc. Reproduced by permission of Pearson Education, Inc.

Summary: _____

_____

_____

_____

EXPLANATION In this passage, the heading of the passage gives a great clue about the implied main idea. Think about the following question based on the heading, "What is intelligence?" To answer this question, you have to number the major supporting details. The italic print and bullets make locating and numbering these details quite easy. All the supporting details describe intelligence as a mental ability. However, the author states that intelligence is hard to define and offers various views of intelligence. These various views indicate that intelligence is a complex mental ability. So, very quickly you can answer the question based on the heading: "Intelligence is a complex mental ability." This answer states the central point of the passage. By using your own words to combine the thesis statement and the major supporting details, you create your summary.

PRACTICE 4

Read the following passage from the National Safety Council's website *Teen Driver*. As you read, annotate the text. Then create a summary of the passage in the space provided after the passage.

Teen Drivers at Risk

[1]Teen drivers are at risk. [2]Every day—more than 10 young drivers ages 15–20 are killed in crashes and another 745 are injured. [3]About 25% of crashes killing young drivers involve alcohol. [4]39% of young male drivers and 26% of young female drivers were speeding at the time of their fatal crash. [5]Although young drivers only represent 6% of all licensed drivers, they are the drivers in 16% of all traffic crashes.

[6]Risk-taking behavior puts teen drivers at risk. [7]Most Americans typically learn to drive during the teen years, when the brain is not fully mature yet. [8]Recent research is beginning to give us insight why many teens have difficulty regulating risk-taking behavior:

- [9]The area of the brain that weighs consequences, suppresses impulses and organizes thoughts does not fully mature until about age 25.

- [10]Hormones are more active in teens, which influence the brain's neurochemicals that regulate excitability and mood. [11]The result can be thrill-seeking behavior and experiences that create intense feelings.

[12]Infotainment technologies also put teen drivers at risk. [13]Infotainment technologies include a wide array of devices that enable drivers to perform tasks unrelated to driving and place young drivers at risk, such as making telephone calls, watching videos, managing e-mail, sending and reading instant messages, and selecting and listening to music. [14]Even commonly accepted devices in vehicles, such as a car radio, are changing substantially with satellite radio and MP3 music players, like the iPod. [15]As of 2007, approximately 70% of new cars will include a capability to connect to iPods. [16]All of these systems have the potential to distract drivers, but cell phones have attracted the most attention.

—Teen Driver National Safety Council. Jan. 2009
http://www.teendriver.nsc.org/#behavior.

Summary: _____

_____

_____

Textbook
Skills

Textbook Skills: Chapter-End Questions in a Textbook

Textbooks often provide questions at the end of a chapter or section to help you identify and remember the most important points. In addition, the answers to questions at the end of a section summarize its main idea and major supporting details. Often, to deepen learning, the chapter-end questions will ask you to give some examples of minor details. As you read, annotate your text by marking content words, main ideas, and major supporting details. These key ideas will help you answer the chapter-end questions. Some students look at the chapter-end questions before they read as a guide to what is most important. These students use chapter-end questions before, during, and after reading.

EXAMPLE Read the following section from the college textbook *Introduction to Mass Communication*, 12th ed. Turn the heading into a question. Annotate the text as you read by underlining main ideas, circling content words, and underlining their definitions. Then, answer the questions.

What Communication Means

[1]Each of us communicates with another person by directing a message to one or more of the person's senses—sight, sound, touch, taste, or smell. [2]This is known as *interpersonal communication,* in contrast to *intrapersonal communication,* in which one "talks to oneself." [3]When we smile, we communicate a desire for friendliness; the tone in which we say "good morning" can indicate feelings all the way from surliness to warm pleasure; and the words we choose in speaking or writing convey a message we want to "put across" to the other person. [4]The more effectively we select and deliver these words, the better the communication.

[5]In today's complex society, one-to-one communication frequently is inadequate. [6]To be effective, our important messages must reach numerous people at one time. [7]The next step is *group communication,* such as when a homeowner couple invite their neighbors for coffee in order to propose a neighborhood improvement plan. [8]If the sponsoring couple convinces a local television news program to air a story about the project, thousands of people learn about it. [9]This is *mass communication.*

[10]The success of the message, in all phases of communication, depends on the *frame of reference,* that is, the life experience and mind-set of both the sender and receiver of the message. [11]The more these frames of reference overlap, the more likely there will be understanding and possible acceptance of the message. [12]One-to-one communication has heavy overlap when people are close friends or agree wholeheartedly on the subject of interpersonal discussion. [13]As the size of the receiving audience grows, these attributes decline. [14]So does the degree of interpersonal success.

[15]For example, a news story about plans by Congress to increase unemployment benefits raises hope in the mind of a person who fears being laid off a job; the same dispatch may disturb a struggling entrepreneur who sees in it the possibility of higher taxes.

[16]Similarly, when a presidential candidate appears on a national TV talk show he reaches millions of voters, vastly more than he could through handshaking tours. [17]His use of mass communication may be a comparative failure, however, if he is unable to project over the air the same feeling of sincerity and ability that he displays through a handshake and a smile in personal contacts.

[18]The art of mass communication, then, is much more difficult than that of face-to-face discussion.[19] The communicator who is addressing thousands of different personalities simultaneously cannot adjust

an appeal to meet their individual reactions. [20]An approach that convinces one part of the audience may alienate another part. [21]The successful mass communicator is one who finds the right method of expression to establish empathy with the largest possible number of individuals in the audience. [22]Psychological research and knowledge of communication theory help the speaker to "push the right buttons."

—Agee, et al, *Introduction to Mass Communications*, pp. 64–65 © 1997.
Reproduced by permission of Pearson Education, Inc.

1. What is interpersonal communication? _____

_____

_____

2. What is intrapersonal communication? _____

_____

3. When does group communication occur? _____

_____

4. When does mass communication occur? _____

_____

5. How and why does "frame of reference" affect communication? _____

_____

_____

_____

EXPLANATION To answer these questions, you should have circled the following terms and underlined their definitions: *interpersonal communication, intrapersonal communication, group communication, mass communication,* and *frame of reference.* Compare your answers to the chapter-end questions with the following:

1. What is interpersonal communication? Interpersonal communication is directing a message to one or more of another person's senses—sight, sound, touch, taste, or smell.

2. What is intrapersonal communication? <u>Intrapersonal communication occurs when one talks to oneself.</u>

3. When does group communication occur? <u>Group communication occurs when a message must reach numerous people at one time.</u>

4. When does mass communication occur? <u>Mass communication occurs when a message must reach thousands of people.</u>

5. How and why does "frame of reference" affect communication? <u>Frame of reference is made up of the life experiences and mind-sets of the people communicating. Understanding and accepting a message is more likely if the message is based on a shared frame of reference.</u>

PRACTICE 5

Read the following section from the college textbook *Introduction to Mass Communication*, 12th ed. Annotate the text as you read by underlining the main ideas, circling the content words, and underlining their definitions. Then answer the questions.

The Language Used to Research Communication

[1]Researchers identify four basic elements in the communication process. [2]To be precise in their findings, they use specialized terms to describe them. [3]These elements are:

[4]The *communicator*, called the *encoder*.

[5]The *message*. The words, pictures, or sounds comprising the message are called *codes or symbols*.

[6]The *channel*. In mass communication, this is one of the media, such as newspapers, magazines, radio, or television.

[7]The *audience*. A person in the audience is known as a *decoder*.

[8]The communicator understands the characteristics of the channel to be used and studies the varying comprehension levels of the groups of people comprising the total audience. [9]The message is molded to the requirements of each channel—pictures on television against only words on radio, for example— and to the characteristics of the audience being sought.

[10]Before a message enters our mass communication system, it must be approved by someone of authority within the medium. [11]These men and women, known to researchers as *gatekeepers*, include the responsible editor on a newspaper or magazine staff, the news editor of a radio or television station, and an advertising director or the equivalent for commercial messages. [12]These people judge the messages for public interest,

effectiveness, taste, and legality. [13]Since more candidates for publication exist than limited newspaper space and air time can absorb, news stories and entertainment offerings must be weighed against others in the same category—certainly not an exact science. [14]The lack of such gatekeepers in most computer communication services, such as online databases and the Internet, differentiates them from traditional mass media.

[15]Exerting pressure on the gatekeepers, in attempts to influence their decisions as to what will or won't be published, are organizations and individuals known to researchers as *regulators*. [16]These include public pressure groups, government agencies, advertisers, consumers, courts, and legislatures. [17]Such pressures, sometimes applied publicly and sometimes behind the scenes, do affect media content and performance.

—Agee, et al, *Introduction to Mass Communications*, pp. 65–66 © 1997.
Reproduced by permission of Pearson Education, Inc.

1. Who is the encoder? _____

2. What makes up the message? _____

_____

3. Who is the decoder? _____

4. Who are gatekeepers and what is their role? _____

_____

5. Who are regulators and what is their role? _____

_____

_____

APPLICATIONS

Application 1: Main Ideas, Major Supporting Details, and Minor Supporting Details

Read the following paragraph from a government website. Answer the questions.

Mother's Drinking Puts Baby at Risk

[1]Mothers who drank alcohol heavily during pregnancy gave birth to children who had damage to the nerves in the arms and legs, according to a study by researchers at the National Institute of Child Health and

Human Development. ²The study was conducted in partnership with researchers at the University of Chile. ³Adults who drink excessive amounts of alcohol can experience peripheral neuropathy; this is a condition that occurs when nerves involved in carrying messages between the central nervous system (the brain and spinal cord) and the rest of the body are damaged. ⁴This can lead to tingling sensations, numbness, pain, or weakness. ⁵"Heavy drinking" is defined as having four standard drinks per day (one standard drink is equivalent to one can of beer, one glass of wine, or one mixed drink).⁶The children exposed to alcohol before they were born faced significant problems in conducting a message through the nerves—both at one month and at one year of age. ⁷The alcohol-exposed children did not show any improvement in nerve function by the time they reached their first birthday. ⁸The study suggests that heavy alcohol consumption by the mother may cause permanent nerve damage to her child.

—Adapted from "New Study Finds Babies Born to Mothers Who Drink Alcohol Heavily May Suffer Permanent Nerve Damage." NIH News. National Institute of Health. 8 March 2004. 1 Jan 2010.

_____ **1.** Sentence 1 is a
    a. main idea.   c. minor supporting detail.
    b. major supporting detail.

_____ **2.** Sentence 5 is a
    a. main idea.   c. minor supporting detail.
    b. major supporting detail.

_____ **3.** Sentence 8 is a
    a. main idea.   c. minor supporting detail.
    b. major supporting detail.

Application 2: Using the Main Idea and Supporting Details to Summarize

Read the following passage from a college science textbook. Annotate the passage by circling the main idea and underlining the major supporting details. Then complete the summary with information from the passage.

Textbook
Skills

Body Movements

¹Generally speaking, body movement occurs when muscles contract across joints. ²The type of movement depends on the mobility of the joint and on where the muscle is located in relation to the joint. ³The most

obvious examples of the action of muscles on bones are the movements that occur at the joints of the limbs. [4]However, less freely movable bones are also tugged into motion by the muscles, such as the vertebrae's movements when the torso is bent to the side.

[5]Body movements are described as five common types. [6]First, **flexion** is a movement, generally in the sagittal plane, that decreases the angle of the joint and brings two bones closer together. [7]Flexion is typical of hinge joints (bending the knee or elbow), but it is also common at ball-and-socket joints (for example, bending forward at the hip). [8]Second, **extension** is the opposite of flexion, so it is a movement that increases the angle, or the distance, between two bones or parts of the body (straightening the knee or elbow). [9]If extension is greater than 180° (as when you tip your head or your torso posteriorly so that your chin points toward the ceiling), it is hyperextension. [10]Third, **rotation** is movement of a bone around its longitudinal axis. [11]Rotation is a common movement of ball-and-socket joints and describes the movement of the atlas around the dens of the axis (as in shaking your head "no"). [12]Fourth, **abduction** is moving a limb away (generally on the frontal plane) from the midline, or median plane, of the body. [13]The terminology also applies to the fanning movement of the fingers or toes when they are spread apart. [14]Fifth, **adduction** is the opposite of abduction, so it is the movement of a limb toward the body midline. [15]Sixth, **circumduction** is a combination of flexion, extension, abduction, and adduction commonly seen in ball-and-socket joints such as the shoulder. [16]The proximal end of the limb is stationary, and its distal end moves in a circle. [17]The limb as a whole outlines a cone.

—Adapted from Marieb, *Essentials of Human Anatomy and Physiology*, 9th ed., p. 199.

VISUAL VOCABULARY

This shoulder exercise required

_____ and

_____ movements.

a. flexion
b. extension
c. abduction
d. adduction

Summary: Body movements are described as (**1**) _____ common types: (**2**) _____ decreases the angle of the joint and brings two bones (**3**) _____ together; (**4**) _____ increases the angle, or the (**5**) _____, between two bones or parts of the body; (**6**) _____ is movement of a bone around its longitudinal axis; (**7**) _____ moves a limb (**8**) _____ from the midline of the body; adduction moves a limb (**9**) _____ the body midline; (**10**) _____ combines flexion, extension, abduction, and adduction.

REVIEW TEST 1   Score (number correct) _____ × 20 = _____%

Main Ideas, Major and Minor Supporting Details

Read the following passage from a college sociology textbook. Then answer the questions that follow.

Textbook
Skills

The Functionalist Perspective of Health:
The Sick Role

[1]Functionalists begin with an obvious point: If society is to function well, its people need to be healthy enough to perform their normal roles. [2]This means that societies must set up ways to control sickness. [3]One way they do this is to develop a system of medical care. [4]Another way is to make rules that help keep too many people from "being sick."

[5]**Elements of the Sick Role exist.** [6]Talcott Parsons, the functionalist who first analyzed the sick role, pointed out that it has four elements— you are not held responsible for being sick, you are exempt from normal responsibilities, you don't like the role, and you will get competent help so you can return to your routines. [7]People who seek approved help are given sympathy and encouragement; those who do not are given the cold shoulder. [8]People who don't get competent help are considered responsible for being sick, are refused the right to claim sympathy from others, and are denied permission to be excused from their normal routines. [9]They are considered to be wrongfully claiming the sick role.

[10]**Ambiguity exists in the Sick Role.** [11]Instead of a fever of 102°F, suppose that the thermometer registers 99.5°F. [12]Do you then "become"

sick—or not? [13]That is, do you decide to claim the sick role? [14]Because most instances of illness are not as clear-cut as, say, a limb fracture, decisions to claim the sick role often are based more on social considerations than on physical conditions. [15]Let's also suppose that you are facing a midterm, you are unprepared for it, and you are allowed to make up the test if you are ill. [16]The more you think about the test, the worse you are likely to feel—which makes the need to claim the sick role seem more legitimate. [17]Now assume that the thermometer still shows 99.5°, but you have no test and your friends are coming over to take you out to celebrate your twenty-first birthday. [18]You are not likely to play the sick role. [19]Note that in both cases your physical condition is the same.

[20]**Gatekeepers to the Sick Role exist.** [21]For children, parents are the primary gatekeepers to the sick role. [22]That is, parents decide whether children's symptoms are sufficient to legitimize their claim that they are sick. [23]Before parents call the school to excuse a child from class, they decide whether the child is faking or has genuine symptoms. [24]If they determine that the symptoms are real, then they decide if the symptoms are serious enough to keep the child home from school, or even severe enough to take the child to a doctor. [25]For adults, the gatekeepers to the sick role are physicians. [26]Adults can bypass the gatekeeper for short periods, but employers will eventually insist on a "doctor's excuse." [27]This can come in such forms as a "doctor's appointment" or insurance forms signed by the doctor. [28]In some instances, company doctors will examine the claims of their workers' private physicians. [29]In sociological terms, these are ways of getting permission to play the sick role.

[30]**Gender Differences exist in the Sick Role.** [31]Women are more willing than men to claim the sick role when they don't feel well. [32]They go to doctors more frequently than men, and they are hospitalized more often than men (Statistical Abstract 2007:Tables 156, 166). [33]Apparently, the sick role does not match the macho image that most boys and men try to project. [34]Most men try to follow the cultural ideal that they should be strong, keep pain to themselves, and "tough it out." [35]The woman's model, in contrast, is more likely to involve sharing feelings and seeking help from others, characteristics that are compatible with the sick role.

—Adapted from Henslin, *Sociology: A Down to Earth Approach*, Text from pp. 559–560
© 2008 James M. Henslin. Reproduced by permission of Pearson Education, Inc.

_____ **1.** Sentence 6 is a
    a. main idea.   c. minor supporting detail.
    b. major supporting detail.

_____ **2.** Sentence 7 is a
    a. main idea.
    b. major supporting detail.
    c. minor supporting detail.

_____ **3.** Sentence 10 is a
    a. main idea.
    b. major supporting detail.
    c. minor supporting detail.

_____ **4.** Sentence 16 is a
    a. main idea.
    b. major supporting detail.
    c. minor supporting detail.

_____ **5.** The central idea is stated in
    a. sentence 1.
    b. sentence 2.
    c. sentence 3.
    d. sentence 4.

REVIEW TEST 2

Score (number correct) _____ × 25 = _____%

Main Ideas, Major and Minor Supporting Details

Read the following passage from a college literature textbook. Answer the questions.

Textbook
Skills

Psychological Criticism

¹Modern psychology has had a vast effect on both literature and literary criticism. ²Sigmund Freud's theories of psychoanalysis changed our ideas about human behavior. ³His work explored wish-fulfillment, sexuality, the unconscious, and repression. ⁴He also showed how language and symbols reflect unconscious fears or desires. ⁵According to Freud, he learned a great deal about psychology from the study of literature. ⁶Reading classical literature was as important as his clinical studies to the development of his ideas. ⁷Some of Freud's most important writings could be seen as literary criticism. ⁸One of the most famous examples of his work is his analysis of Sophocles' Oedipus. ⁹(Written in the 5th century B.C.E., the play *Oedipus* depicts the rise and fall of the hero Oedipus the King; Oedipus unwittingly kills his father and marries his mother.) ¹⁰Freud believed that great literature truthfully reflects life.

¹¹Psychological criticism is a varied category. ¹²However, it often takes three approaches. ¹³First, it looks into the creative process of the artist. ¹⁴What is the nature of literary genius? ¹⁵How does it relate to normal mental functions? ¹⁶The second major area for this type of

criticism is the psychological study of a particular artist. [17]Most modern literary biographies rely on psychology to understand their subject's motivations and behavior. [18]One recent book stands as an example of this approach. [19]In her book *Anne Sexton: A Biography,* Diane Middlebrook actually used tapes of the poet's sessions with her psychiatrist as material for her study of the poet. [20]The third common area of psychological criticism is the analysis of fictional characters. [21]Freud's study of Oedipus is the model for this approach. [22]Freud tried to bring modern insights about human behavior into the study of how fictional people act.

—Adapted from Kennedy & Gioia, *Literature: An Introduction to Fiction, Poetry, and Drama,* 3rd Compact Ed., p. 1477.

_____ **1.** Which sentence is the thesis statement that states the topic and the author's controlling point about the topic?
    a. sentence 1   c. sentence 3
    b. sentence 2

_____ **2.** In the second paragraph, sentence 12 serves as a _____ for the paragraph.
    a. main idea   c. minor supporting detail
    b. major supporting detail

_____ **3.** In the second paragraph, sentence 16 serves as a _____ for the paragraph.
    a. main idea   c. minor supporting detail
    b. major supporting detail

_____ **4.** Sentence 19 is a
    a. main idea.   c. minor supporting detail.
    b. major supporting detail.

REVIEW TEST 3

Score (number correct) _____ × 20 = _____ %

Main Ideas and Supporting Details

Read the following passage from a college business textbook. Answer the questions that follow.

Textbook
Skills

Capitalism: Competing in a Free Market

[1]Competition doesn't suddenly disappear from your life when you finish the marathon, quit the football team, or refuse to play another game of Rock Band. [2]You can't even go out for fast food without running

into competition: McDonald's competes with Burger King, Coca Cola competes with PepsiCo. [3]Whether you're ordering a chicken sandwich or working in the back flipping burgers, those companies' competitive relationships shape your fast food experience by affecting how much customers pay for their meals, how much the burger-flipper is paid, which items are on the menu, what the quality of the food is, and many other details. [4]If you live in a capitalistic economy—an economic system in which the means to produce goods and services are owned by private interests—you can't avoid competition.

[5]So the United States is a capitalist economy, right? [6]Well, not exactly. [7]It's more of a mixed market economy. [8]This just means that the United States borrows elements from different economic systems, like capitalism or socialism, to create an ideal system. [9]In both capitalistic and mixed market economies, competition plays a very big role.

[10]For example, let's say you decide to open a business installing swimming pools. [11]You'll get the materials you need, hire employees, and prepare advertising. [12]In return, any profits you make belong to you. [13]But can you charge as much as you want to install a new pool? [14]Of course not. [15]If your prices are too high, nobody will buy your product. [16]If your prices are too low, you won't earn a profit. [17]In a capitalistic economy, the types of goods and services produced, the prices charged, and the amount of income received are all determined through the operation of the free market.

[18]Of course, the free market doesn't mean that everything is free of cost. [19]In this case, the word free refers to people's freedom to choose what they buy and sell. [20]For example, when you buy a DVD, you voluntarily exchange your money for a copy of the latest Oscar-winning film; no one is forcing you to buy that particular movie from that particular store. [21]An employee voluntarily exchanges his or her time and labor for money. [22]In return, a company voluntarily exchanges money for employees' time and labor. [23]Both parties take part in an exchange because they have something to gain. [24]If they didn't expect to gain, they wouldn't agree to the exchange.

[25]Think about that swimming pool company you started in the last section. [26]You're competing with other swimming pool builders for customers and money in order to make your business a financial success. [27]But how, exactly, do you measure success? [28]Is a company successful if it earns a profit for six months, one year, or maybe I 0 years?

[29]Often, if people see profits early on for a new company, they may call the company a success. [30]However, focusing on short-term profitability

doesn't give you the big picture. [31]Today, a better measure of success is sustainability. [32]In 1987, the World Commission on Environment and Development defined sustainable development as meeting "the needs of the present without compromising the ability of future generations to meet their own needs."

[33]What does that mean exactly? [34]**Sustainability** is the capacity for an organization to create profit for its shareholders today while making sure that its business interests are also in the best interests of the environment and other stakeholders for the future. [35]Stakeholders are all people who have an interest in an organization. [36]This may include employees, suppliers, and the community. [37]Shareholders are the people who actually own a company and directly benefit from its profits. [38]The good news about a sustainable business is that it stands an excellent chance of beating out the competition, being more successful tomorrow, and remaining successful for generations.

—Adapted from Van Syckle & Tietje, *Anybody's Business*, pp. 56–57.

_____ 1. The central idea or thesis statement is
      a. sentence 1.   c. sentence 6.
      b. sentence 2.   d. sentence 9.

_____ 2. Sentence 10 is a
      a. main idea.   c. minor supporting detail.
      b. major supporting detail.

VISUAL VOCABULARY

Striking and locked-out grocery workers rally outside a Pavilions supermarket in the Hollywood section of Los Angeles. These

_____ want better health insurance and wages for new union employees.

a. shareholders
b. stakeholders

_____ 3. Sentence 18 is a
   a. main idea.
   b. major supporting detail.
   c. minor supporting detail.

_____ 4. Sentence 34 is a
   a. main idea.
   b. major supporting detail.
   c. minor supporting detail.

_____ 5. Sentence 37 is a
   a. main idea.
   b. major supporting detail.
   c. minor supporting detail.

WHAT DO YOU THINK?

Do you think competition in the marketplace is good for customers? Is capitalism good for businesses? Why or why not? Assume you are taking a college business class, and that you are studying to become a business owner. An upcoming exam in your business class gives you an opportunity to test your understanding. Write a short-answer response of one to two paragraphs for the following essay exam question: "Describe why and how companies compete in a capitalist economy, and how a focus on sustainability keeps them competitive."

REVIEW TEST 4

Score (number correct) _____ × 10 = _____%

Main Ideas, Major and Minor Supporting Details

Before you read the following passage from a college sociology textbook, skim the material and answer the Before Reading questions. Read the passage. Then answer the After Reading questions.

Vocabulary Preview

subtly (2) indirectly
cohesion (3) unity
autonomy (5) independence, self-reliance
regulation (8) control
enmeshed (9) entangled, tangled

Textbook
Skills

Family Cohesion

[1]From the moment you were born, you have been learning how to handle distance or closeness within your family system. [2]You were taught

directly or **subtly** how to be connected to, or separated from, other family members. [3]**Cohesion** occurs on two levels. [4]First, cohesion deals with the levels of emotional bonding between family members. [5]In addition, cohesion considers the amount of **autonomy** a person achieves within the family system. [6]In other words, every family attempts to deal with the level of closeness that is encouraged or discouraged.

[7]Although different terms are used, cohesion has been identified by scholars from various fields as central to the understanding of family life. [8]Family researchers Kantor and Lehr (1976) view "distance **regulation**" as a major family function. [9]Family therapist Minuchin et al. (1967) talks about "**enmeshed** and disengaged" families. [10]Sociologists Hess and Handel (1959) describe the family's need to "establish a pattern of separateness and connectedness." [11]There are four levels of cohesion ranging from extremely low cohesion to extremely high cohesion. [12]These levels are as follows:

[13]**Disengaged:** Family members maintain extreme separateness and little family belonging or loyalty.

[14]**Separated:** Family members are emotionally independent with some joint involvement and belonging.

[15]**Connected:** Family members strive for emotional closeness, loyalty, and joint involvement with some individuality.

[16]**Enmeshed:** Family members are extremely close and loyal, and they express almost no individuality (Carnes, 1989).

[17]It is through communication that family members are able to develop and maintain or change their patterns of cohesion. [18]A father may decide that it is inappropriate to continue the physical closeness he has experienced with his daughter now that she has become a teenager, and he may limit his touching or playful roughhousing. [19]These nonverbal messages may be confusing or hurtful to his daughter. [20]She may become angry, find new ways of being close, develop more outside friendships, or attempt to force her father back into the old patterns. [21]A husband may demand more intimacy from his wife as he ages. [22]He asks for more serious conversation, makes more sexual advances, or shares more of his feelings. [23]His wife may ignore this new behavior or engage in more intimate behaviors herself.

[24]Families with extremely high cohesion are often referred to as "enmeshed." [25]Members are so closely bonded and over-involved that individuals experience little autonomy or fulfillment of personal needs and goals. [26]Family members appear fused or joined so tightly that personal

identities do not develop appropriately. ²⁷Enmeshed persons do not experience life as individuals, as indicated by the following example:

> ²⁸*My mother and I are the same person.* ²⁹*She was always protective of me, knew everything about me, told me how to act, and how to answer questions.* ³⁰*None of this was done in a bad way or had **detrimental** effects, but the reality is that she was and still is somewhat overbearing.* ³¹*If someone asked me a question, I typically answered, "Please direct all questions to my mother.* ³²*She knows what to say."*

³³"Disengaged" refers to families at the other end of the continuum in which members experience very little closeness or family **solidarity**, yet each member has high autonomy and individuality. ³⁴There is a strong sense of emotional separation or divorce. ³⁵Members experience little or no sense of connectedness to each other.

³⁶As you examine cohesion in families, you may want to look at factors such as "emotional bonding, independence, boundaries, time, space, friends, decision making, and interests and recreation" (Olson, Sprenkle, & Russell, p. 6). ³⁷Families do not remain permanently at one point on the cohesion scale. ³⁸Members do not come together and stay the same, as is evident from the previous examples. ³⁹Because there are widely varying cultural norms, what seems balanced for one family may be quite distant for another. ⁴⁰For example, Latino families may find balanced cohesion at a point that is too close for families with a Northern European background.

—Adapted from Galvin, Kathleen M., and Bernard J. Brommel. *Family Communication: Cohesion and Change*, 5th ed. Pp. 31–32. Published by Allyn and Bacon, Boston, MA. Copyright © 2000 by Pearson Education, Inc.

Before Reading

Vocabulary in Context

_____ **1.** In sentence 30 of the passage, the word **detrimental** means
  a. helpful.　　　　　　　c. long lasting.
  b. injurious.　　　　　　d. short term.

_____ **2.** In sentence 33 of the passage, the word **solidarity** means
  a. disengagement.　　　 c. understanding.
  b. independence.　　　　d. unity.

After Reading

Main Ideas

_____ **3.** Which of the following best states the topic and the author's controlling point about the topic?
a. levels of family cohesion
b. causes of family cohesion
c. ways to achieve family cohesion
d. dangers of family cohesion

_____ **4.** Which sentence is the thesis statement for the passage?
a. sentence 1
b. sentence 6
c. sentence 11
d. sentence 40

Supporting Details

_____ **5.** Sentences 13 through 16 are
a. major supporting details.
b. minor supporting details.

_____ **6.** Sentences 28 through 32 are
a. major supporting details.
b. minor supporting details.

7–10. Complete the summary notes with information from the passage. The four levels of family cohesion, which range from extremely low to high, include the following: _____ (family members are separate with little loyalty or sense of belonging), _____ (family members are independent with some involvement and sense of belonging), _____ (family members work to remain close, loyal, and involved, with some individuality), and _____ (members are extremely close, loyal, with almost no individuality).

WHAT DO YOU THINK?

How would you describe most American families in terms of family cohesion? Does family cohesion differ among cultures? Why or why not? Assume you are taking a college sociology course. Your professor has assigned a one-page report about family cohesion. In your own words, define family cohesion and its four levels. Give examples based on your observations of everyday life.

After Reading About Supporting Details

Before you move on to the Mastery Tests on supporting details, take time to reflect on your learning and performance by answering the following questions. Write your answers in your notebook.

- How has my knowledge base or prior knowledge about supporting details changed?

- Based on my studies, how do I think I will perform on the Mastery Test(s)? Why do I think my scores will be above average, average, or below average?

- Would I recommend this chapter to other students who want to learn more about supporting details? Why or why not?

Test your understanding of what you have learned about supporting details by completing the Chapter 5 Review Card in the insert near the end of the text.

CONNECT TO myreadinglab

To check your progress in meeting Chapter 5's learning outcomes, log in to **myreadinglab.com**, and try the following activities.

- The "Supporting Details" section of MyReadingLab offers more information about supporting details. You will find an overview, model, review materials, practice activities, and tests. To access this resource, click on the "Study Plan" tab. Then click on "Supporting Details." Then click on the following links as needed: "Overview," "Model," "Practice," and "Tests."

- The "Outlining and Summarizing" section of MyReadingLab gives an overview about memory and active reading. This section also provides a model for summarizing. You will find practice activities and tests. To access this resource, click on the "Study Plan" tab. Then click on "Outlining and Summarizing." Then click on the following links as needed: "Overview," "Model: Summarizing," "Practice," and "Tests."

- To measure your mastery of the content of this chapter, complete the tests in the "Supporting Details" section and click on Gradebook to find your results.

Read the following paragraph from a college literature textbook and answer the questions.

Textbook
Skills

Character in Fiction

¹A character is presumably an imagined person who inhabits a story. ²However, that simple definition may admit to a few exceptions. ³In George Stewart's novel *Storm,* the central character is the wind; in Richard Adams's *Watership Down,* the main characters are rabbits. ⁴But usually we recognize, in the main characters of a story, human personalities that become familiar to us. ⁵If the story seems "true to life," we generally find that its characters act in a reasonably consistent manner, and that the author has provided them with motivation. ⁶The author gives the characters sufficient reason to behave as they do. ⁷Should a character behave in a sudden and unexpected way, we trust that he had a reason, and sooner or later we will discover it. ⁸Characters may seem flat or round, depending on whether a writer sketches or sculpts them.

⁹A **flat** character has only one outstanding trait or feature, or at most a few distinguishing marks. ¹⁰For example, one familiar stock character is the mad scientist, with his lust for absolute power and his crazily gleaming eyes. ¹¹Flat characters, however, need not be stock characters. ¹²For instance, in all of literature there is probably only one Tiny Tim, though his functions in *A Christmas Carol* are mainly to invoke blessings and to remind others of their Christian duties. ¹³Some writers try to distinguish the flat ones by giving each a single odd physical feature or mannerism—a nervous twitch, a piercing gaze, an obsessive fondness for oysters. ¹⁴**Round** characters, however, present us with more facets—that is, their authors portray them in greater depth and in more generous detail. ¹⁵Such a round character may appear to us only as he appears to the other characters in the story. ¹⁶If their views of him differ, we will see him from more than one side. ¹⁷In other stories, we enter a character's mind and come to know him through his own thoughts, feelings, and perceptions. ¹⁸By the time we finish reading Katherine Mansfield's "Miss Brill," we are well acquainted with the central character and find her amply three-dimensional.

¹⁹Flat characters tend to stay the same throughout a story, but round characters often change—learn or become enlightened, grow or deteriorate. ²⁰In William Faulkner's "Barn Burning," the boy Sarty Snopes,

driven to defy his proud and violent father, becomes at the story's end more knowing and more mature. [21](Some critics call a fixed character **static**; a changing one, **dynamic**.) [22]This is not to damn a flat character as an inferior work of art. [23]In most fiction—even the greatest—minor characters tend to be flat instead of round. [24]Why? [25]Rounding them would cost time and space; and so enlarged, they might only distract us from the main characters.

—Adapted from Kennedy & Gioia, *Literature: An Introduction to Fiction, Poetry, and Drama*, 3rd Compact Ed., p. 61.

_____ **1.** Which sentence is the thesis sentence that states the topic and the author's controlling point about the topic?
   a. sentence 1
   b. sentence 2
   c. sentence 8

_____ **2.** Sentence 9 is a _____ of the paragraph.
   a. main idea
   b. major supporting detail
   c. minor supporting detail

_____ **3.** Sentence 19 is a _____ of the paragraph.
   a. main idea
   b. major supporting detail
   c. minor supporting detail

_____ **4.** Sentence 20 is a _____ of the paragraph.
   a. main idea
   b. major supporting detail
   c. minor supporting detail

_____ **5.** Sentence 21 is a _____ of the paragraph.
   a. main idea
   b. major supporting detail
   c. minor supporting detail

Read the following passage from a college humanities textbook. Then answer the questions and complete the summary.

Textbook
Skills

Displaying Emotions

¹Facial expressions that convey emotions are largely shared across cultures. ²However, questions have remained about facial expressions and emotions. ³How widespread or common are emotional facial expressions? ⁴Are these expressions accurately recognized by others? ⁵Research in New Guinea, Brazil, Chile, Argentina, Japan, and the United States speaks to these questions. ⁶According to the research, people are highly accurate in recognizing the meaning of facial expressions. ⁷This research has yielded some additional interesting conclusions.

- ⁸Apparently some emotions are "universal": enjoyment, sadness, anger, disgust, surprise, and fear (Ekman, Sorenson, & Friesen, 1969).

- ⁹Joy and surprise are consistently recognized, but interest and shame are the least often identified (Izard, 1979).

- ¹⁰Sadness is more identifiable in collectivist cultures (Matsumoto, 1989). ¹¹A comparison was made of Japanese and Americans regarding emotion recognition. ¹²Americans were better at identifying anger, disgust, fear, and sadness. ¹³Both groups recognized happiness and surprise. ¹⁴The Japanese have difficulty identifying negative emotions. ¹⁵Expressing such emotions is socially less desirable in Japan than in the United States (Smith & Bond, 1994, p. 61).

- ¹⁶Friesen (1972, cited in Smith & Bond, 1994) offered an unpublished but often discussed study. ¹⁷The study compared Japanese and American students' reactions as they watched two films. ¹⁸One was a short film about body mutilation, and the other was an emotionally neutral film. ¹⁹At first Japanese and American students alike showed disgust while they watched the film. ²⁰But when a "scientist" in a white coat (an apparent authority figure) was present, the Japanese displayed a slightly *smiling* expression.

²¹Emotions are expressed with similar expressions across cultures. ²²However, social correctness varies. ²³The ways, timing, and exchanges of

emotional expression vary greatly from culture to culture. [24]What is appropriate in one country may appear uncouth in another.

—Adapted from Kelly, *Communication@ Work,* pp. 127–128.

_____ **1.** Sentence 7 is a
   a. main idea.
   b. major supporting detail.
   c. minor supporting detail.

_____ **2.** Sentence 8 is a
   a. main idea.
   b. major supporting detail.
   c. minor supporting detail.

_____ **3.** Sentence 13 is a
   a. main idea.
   b. major supporting detail.
   c. minor supporting detail.

4–5. Complete the summary with information from the passage.

Research in New Guinea, Brazil, Chile, Argentina, Japan, and the United States has yielded several interesting conclusions about _____ that convey emotions. Emotions are expressed with similar expressions across cultures. In addition, people are highly accurate in recognizing the meaning of facial expressions. However, the social _____ of facial expressions of emotions varies from culture to culture.

Read the following passage from a college communications textbook. Then complete the summary.

Textbook
Skills

Touch Communication

[1]Touch communication (known technically as **haptics**) is perhaps the most primitive form of communication. [2]Touch develops before the other senses; even in the womb the child is stimulated by touch. [3]Soon after birth the child is fondled, caressed, patted, and stroked. [4]In turn, the child explores its world through touch and quickly learns to communicate a variety of meanings through touch. [5]Nonverbal researchers have identified the major meanings of touch:

- [6]**Positive emotion:** Touch may communicate such positive feelings as support, appreciation, inclusion, sexual interest or intent, and affection.
- [7]**Playfulness:** Touch often speaks of our intention to play. [8]This kind of touch can be either affectionate or aggressive.
- [9]**Control:** Touch may also direct the behaviors, attitudes, or feelings of the other person. [10]In attention-getting, for example, you touch the person to gain his or her attention. [11]This kind of touch says "look at me" or "look over here."
- [12]**Ritual:** Ritualistic touching centers on greetings and departures. [13]For example, shaking hands to say "hello" or "goodbye" or hugging, kissing, or putting your arm around another's shoulder when greeting or saying farewell are rituals.
- [14]**Task-relatedness:** Task-related touching occurs while you're performing some function. [15]Removing a speck of dust from another person's face or helping someone out of a car are two examples.

[16]Different cultures will view these types of touching differently. [17]For example, some task-related touching is viewed as acceptable in much of the United States. [18]However, this same touch would be viewed negatively in some cultures. [19]Among Koreans, for example, it's considered rude for a store owner to touch a customer while handing back change. [20]It's considered too intimate a gesture. [21]Members of other cultures, expecting some touching, may consider the Korean's behavior cold and insulting.

—Adapted from DeVito, *Messages: Building Interpersonal Communication Skills*, Text from pp. 152–153 © 2004. Reproduced by permission of Pearson Education, Inc.

VISUAL VOCABULARY

The people in this picture

illustrate ———————

touch.

   a. playful
   b. task-related
   c. ritualistic

1–5. Complete the summary with information from the paragraph.

Researchers of touch communication, which is also known as

(**1**) ———————, have identified several major meanings of

touch. Touch can convey positive emotion, (**2**) ———————,

(**3**) ———————, (**4**) ———————, and task-relatedness.

Different (**5**) ——————— view these types of touch differently.

Read the following news release published by the Federal Trade Commission. Answer the questions, and complete the summary.

Cigars: No Such Thing As a Safe Smoke

[1]Since 2000, cigar packages and ads have been required to warn smokers about the serious health risks of cigar smoking. [2]Whether you buy Coronas or Churchills, Panatelas, Robustos, Lonsdales, or any other kind of cigar, you will see five new federally mandated health warnings. [3]The messages should sound familiar: Cigarette companies have been required to give similar health warnings since the mid-1960's and smokeless tobacco manufacturers since the mid-1980's.

[4]The warnings came about as a result of a report by the National Cancer Institute detailing the health risks of cigar smoking. [5]Specifically, cigar smoking can cause cancers of the mouth, esophagus, pharynx, larynx, and lungs. [6]For smokers who inhale, the health risks increase dramatically. [7]Cigar smoking also can cause heart disease and emphysema.

SURGEON GENERAL WARNING:	Cigar Smoking Can Cause Cancers Of The Mouth And Throat, Even If You Do Not Inhale.
SURGEON GENERAL WARNING:	Cigar Smoking Can Cause Lung Cancer And Heart Disease.
SURGEON GENERAL WARNING:	Tobacco Use Increases The Risk Of Infertility, Stillbirth And Low Birth Weight.
SURGEON GENERAL WARNING:	Cigars Are Not A Safe Alternative To Cigarettes.
SURGEON GENERAL WARNING:	Tobacco Smoke Increases The Risk Of Lung Cancer And Heart Disease, Even In Nonsmokers.

[8]The warnings, which cigar companies are required to rotate, are shown on the previous page.

[9]Cigar companies must display these warnings clearly and prominently on packages, in print ads, on audio and video ads, on the Internet, and on point-of-purchase displays. [10]The point, say federal consumer protection and health officials, is to make sure that companies disclose the health risks of cigar smoking and that consumers understand that there's no such thing as a safe smoke.

—Adapted from "Cigars: No Such Thing As a Safe Smoke."
Federal Trade Commission. June 2000. 1 Jan 2010
http://www.ftc.gov/bcp/conline/pubs/alerts/cigaralrt.htm

_____ **1.** Sentence 1 is a
    a. main idea.   c. minor supporting detail.
    b. major supporting detail.

_____ **2.** Sentence 3 is a
    a. main idea.   c. minor supporting detail.
    b. major supporting detail.

_____ **3.** Sentence 10 is a
    a. main idea.   c. minor supporting detail.
    b. major supporting detail.

4–5. Complete the summary.

Cigar packages and advertisements are required _____

_____

Cigar smoking can cause _____

_____

_____

Outlines and Concept Maps

6

LEARNING OUTCOMES

After studying this chapter you should be able to do the following:

1. Define the terms *outline* and *concept map*.
2. Create an outline.
3. Create a concept map.
4. Evaluate the importance of outlines and concept maps.
5. Apply outlines and concept maps to passages to improve comprehension.

Before Reading About Outlines and Concept Maps

In Chapter 5, you learned several important ideas that will help you use outlines and concept maps effectively. To review, reread the diagram about the flow of ideas on page 199 in Chapter 5. Next, skim this chapter for key ideas in boxes about outlines, concept maps, and the table of contents in a textbook. Refer to the diagrams and boxes and create at least three questions that you can answer as you read the chapter. Write your questions in the following spaces (record the page number for the key term in each question):

_____

_____? (page _____)

_____

_____? (page _____)

_____

_____? (page _____)

Compare the questions you created with the following questions. Then write the ones that seem most helpful in your notebook, leaving enough space between each question to record the answers you find as you read and study the chapter.

How does an outline show the relationship among the main idea, major supporting details, and minor supporting details? Where are main ideas used in an outline, concept map, and table of contents? Where are major supporting details used in an outline, concept map, and table of contents? Where are minor supporting details used in an outline, concept map, and table of contents? What is the difference between a formal outline and an informal outline?

Outlines

An outline shows how a paragraph moves from a general idea to specific supporting details; thus it helps you make sense of the ways ideas relate to one another. An effective reader uses an outline to see the main idea, major supporting details, and minor supporting details.

> An **outline** shows the relationship among the main idea, major supporting details, and minor supporting details.

An author often uses signal words or phrases such as *a few causes, a number of reasons, several steps,* or *several kinds of* to introduce a main idea; in addition, an author often uses signal words such as *first, second, furthermore, moreover, next,* or *finally* to indicate that a supporting detail is coming. You will learn more about signal words, also called transitions, and their relationship to ideas in Chapters 7 and 8.

Outlines can be formal or informal. A **formal** or **traditional outline** uses Roman numerals to indicate the main idea, capital letters to indicate the major details, and Arabic numbers to indicate minor details. A formal outline is particularly useful for studying complex reading material. Sometimes, you may choose to use an **informal outline** and record only the main ideas and the major supporting details. Because these outlines are informal, their format may vary according to each student's notetaking style. Elements may or may not be capitalized. One person might label the main idea with the number 1 and the major supporting details with letters *a, b, c, d,* and so on. Another person might not label the main idea at all and label each major supporting detail with letters or numbers.

EXAMPLE   Read the following paragraph from a college geography textbook. Fill in the details to complete the outline. Then answer the questions that follow it.

Textbook
Skills

Two Natural Processes That Shape Earth's Landforms

[1]Geographers studying the shape of Earth's surface—its topography—recognize that it includes many features that seem to have distinctive characteristics. [2]Elements of Earth's surface that have such identifiable form—its mountains, valleys, hills, and depressions—are called **landforms**.

³Landforms are built through a combination of endogenic and exogenic processes. ⁴First, **endogenic** processes are forces that cause movements beneath or at Earth's surface, such as mountain building and earthquakes. ⁵These internal mechanisms move portions of Earth's surface horizontally and vertically. ⁶Endogenic forces raise some parts and lower others. ⁷Second, **exogenic** processes are forces from the atmosphere aided by gravity. ⁸Even as endogenic forces are building Earth's features, these features are simultaneously attacked by exogenic processes, which are forces of erosion, such as running water, wind, and chemical action. ⁹Endogenic and exogenic forces continually move and shape Earth's crust. ¹⁰Endogenic processes form rocks and move them to produce mountain ranges, ocean basins, and other topographic features. ¹¹As these rocks become exposed, exogenic activities go to work. ¹²They erode materials, move them down hill slopes, and deposit them in lakes, oceans, and other low-lying areas.

—Adapted from Bergman & Renwick, *Introduction to Geography: People, Places, and Environment*, 4th ed., pp. 96–97.

VISUAL VOCABULARY

The devastation caused by the high winds and heavy flooding in the greater New Orleans area due to Hurricane Katrina, August 30, 2005, is an example of

_____ forces.

a. endogenic
b. exogenic

Outline

Main Idea: _____

_____

A. Elements of Earth's surface that have such identifiable form—its mountains, valleys, hills, and depressions—are called **landforms**.

B. _____

_____

C. _____

Questions

1. What word or phrase in the title signals the major details in the paragraph?

_____

_____ **2.** Sentence 12 is a
     a. main idea.   c. minor supporting detail.
     b. major supporting detail.

3–5. How does the author signal each major supporting detail?

Major detail 1: _____

Major detail 2: _____

Major detail 3: _____

_____ **6.** The outline used in this activity is an example of
     a. an informal outline.   b. a formal outline.

EXPLANATION The main idea of this passage is located in two places: near the beginning (sentence 3) and in the middle (sentence 9). Although these two sentences differ in wording, they state the same main idea. The reason for stating the main idea twice might be due to the way the author organized the details. Sentences 1 through 8 introduce and define the terms *landform*, *endogenic forces*, and *exogenic forces*. Then, sentences 9 through 12 summarize how these two forces work together to affect landforms. The author previews each of the major details in the title by using the words "two natural processes" and "landforms." All three major details are signaled for the reader by the use of bold print. However, two major details are also introduced with the signal words "First" in sentence 4 and "Second" in sentence 7. Sentence 12 is a minor supporting detail that illustrates "exogenic forces," the third major supporting detail. This outline is an example of an informal outline that includes only the main idea and the major supporting details.

Notice how an outline of the main idea and major supporting details—without the minor details—condenses the material into a summary of the author's primary points.

A formal outline of the information looks like the following:

Stated Main Idea: Endogenic and exogenic forces continually move and shape Earth's crust.

    I. Elements of Earth's surface that have such identifiable form—its mountains, valleys, hills, and depressions—are called landforms.

II. Endogenic processes are forces that cause movements beneath or at Earth's surface, such as mountain building and earthquakes.

    A. These internal mechanisms move portions of Earth's surface horizontally and vertically.

    B. Endogenic forces raise some parts and lower others.

III. Exogenic processes are forces from the atmosphere aided by gravity.

    A. Even as endogenic forces are building Earth's features, these features are simultaneously attacked by exogenic processes, which are forces of erosion, such as running water, wind, and chemical action.

IV. Endogenic and exogenic forces continually move and shape Earth's crust.

    A. Endogenic processes form rocks and move them to produce mountain ranges, ocean basins, and other topographic features.

    B. As these rocks become exposed, exogenic activities go to work.

    C. They erode materials, move them down hill slopes, and deposit them in lakes, oceans, and other low-lying areas.

Note that in a formal outline of one paragraph, the first major supporting detail is labeled with the Roman numeral I, and the minor supporting details are labeled A and B. This pattern continues: the second and third major supporting details are labeled Roman numerals II and III, and each of the minor supporting details is labeled A, B, C, and so on.

PRACTICE 1

Read the following paragraph from a college communications textbook. Then answer the questions that follow it.

Textbook
Skills

Eye Contact

[1]You use eye contact to serve several important functions. [2]First, you can use eye contact to monitor feedback. [3]For example, when you talk with someone, you look at the person intently as if to say, "Well, what do you think?" or "React to what I have just said." [4]You also look at speakers to let them know you are listening. [5]Another important use of eye contact is to gain the attention and interest of your listeners. [6]When someone fails to pay the attention you want, you may increase your eye contact, hoping your focus on this person will increase attention. [7]When making an especially important point, maintaining close eye contact with your listeners may prevent them from giving attention to anything but what you are saying. [8]A third important function of eye contact is control of the conversation.

[9]Eye movements inform the other person that the channel of communication is open and that she or he should now speak. [10]A clear example of controlling the conversation occurs in the college classroom, where the instructor asks a question and then locks eyes with a student. [11]Without any verbal message, it is known that the student should answer the question.

—Adapted from DeVito, *Interpersonal Communication Book*, p. 187 © 2009 by Pearson Education, Inc. Reproduced by permission of Pearson Education, Inc.

1–5. Complete the following outline.

Stated main idea: You use eye contact to serve several important functions.

    I. _____

      A. _____

      B. Eye contact also lets speakers know you are listening.

    II. _____

      _____

      A. Increased eye contact will increase attention.

      B. Close eye contact prevents listeners from giving attention to anything but what you are saying.

    III. _____

      A. Eye movements inform the other person that the channel of communication is open.

      B. _____

      _____

6. What word or phrase in the topic sentence signals that a list of details will follow? _____

_____ **7.** Sentence 3, "For example, when you talk with someone, you look at the person intently as if to say, 'Well, what do you think?' or 'React to what I have just said,'" is a
a. major supporting detail. b. minor supporting detail.

8–10. What word or phrase introduces the first, second, and third major detail?

Major detail 1: _____

Major detail 2: _____

Major detail 3: _____

Concept Maps

An outline is one way to see the details that support a main idea. Another way to see details is through the use of a concept map. A **concept map** is a diagram that shows the flow of ideas from the main idea to the supporting details. Think of what you already know about a map. Someone can tell you how to get somewhere, but it is much easier to understand the directions if you can see how each road connects to the other by studying a map. Likewise, a concept map shows how ideas connect to one another.

> A **concept map** is a diagram that shows the flow of ideas from the main idea to the supporting details.

To make a concept map, an effective reader places the main idea in a box or circle as a heading and then places the major supporting details in boxes or circles beneath the main idea. Often arrows or lines are used to show the flow of ideas.

EXAMPLE Read the following paragraph. Then complete the concept map by filling in the four major supporting details from the paragraph.

A Brief History of Armor

[1]From the earliest civilizations to current times, humans have used armor to protect themselves from injury. [2]The earliest armor was most likely a shield made of wood and animal hide used to deflect rocks and spears during the Neolithic era. [3]Eventually, the Greeks fashioned a set of armor that consisted of a large round shield, a bronze helmet, and shin guards. [4]Later, body armor advanced with the development of scale armor, made of metal plates that overlap each other and chain mail, made up of thousands of iron rings that interlocked to form an entire suit. [5]Currently, armor is still used to protect soldiers in combat, but its use has been expanded to include athletes and workers. [6]Modern soldiers still use helmets and now have flak jackets or bullet proof vests made of Kevlar. [7]In addition, athletes use helmets, pads, and shin guards to protect themselves as they compete in various sports such as football and baseball. [8]Similarly, construction workers don hard hats and boots with reinforced steel toes to protect themselves from on-the-job injuries.

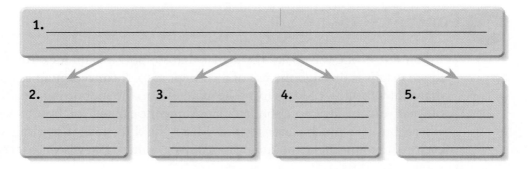

EXPLANATION Compare your answers to the following: (1) From the earliest civilizations to current times, humans have used armor to protect themselves from injury; (2) earliest, a shield; (3) Eventually, helmets; (4) later, body armor; (5) Currently, soldiers, athletes, workers. Note that the main idea is in the top box. The phrase "From the earliest civilizations to current times" in the topic sentence indicates that the major details follow a time order. The signal words "earliest," "eventually," "later," and "currently" indicate the major supporting details. As you can see, a concept map presents ideas in a highly visual manner, making it easy for the reader to grasp the author's primary points. This particular concept map includes only the major supporting details. However, mapping can include the minor supporting details as well. Look at the concept map below that follows the flow of ideas for the third major supporting detail, "Currently, armor is still used . . . " Concept maps, like outlines, can show all three levels of thought: the main idea, the major supporting details, and the minor supporting details.

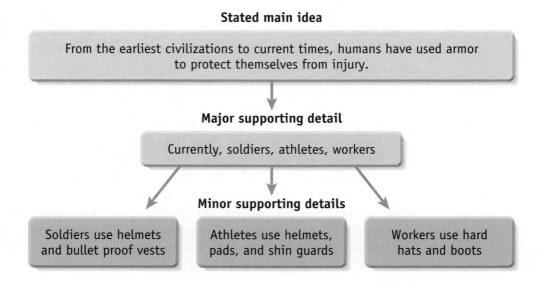

PRACTICE 2

Read the following paragraphs. Fill in the concept maps with the missing information from each paragraph.

Paragraph A

Keeping a Personal Journal

[1]Many people find that keeping a personal journal has several benefits. [2]The first benefit of a personal journal is the opportunity the act of writing gives to vent emotions in private; instead of allowing them to build up over time and then explode, writing acts as a release. [3]The second benefit of keeping a journal is the level of self-reflection it demands; the act of putting experiences and emotions into words forces one to think about what is and what is not important enough to record. [4]Another benefit is the personal historical record the writer compiles over time; instead of fading away, memories are in a lasting record that can be revisited at any time.

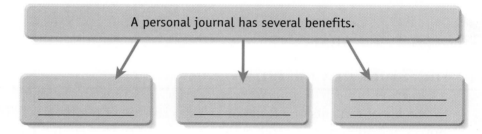

A personal journal has several benefits.

Paragraph B from a College English Handbook

Textbook
Skills

Syllogism: A Type of Argument

[1]A syllogism is an argument arranged in three parts: a major premise, a minor premise, and a conclusion. [2]First, a major premise or idea stipulates a general principle. [3]One example of a major premise is "that all spiders have eight legs." [4]Next, a minor premise reflects a specific instance. [5]For example, "the creature crawling across your desk has six legs" is a minor premise. [6]Finally, a conclusion is the idea that follows logically from the major and minor premises. [7]For example, your conclusion "that the creature crawling across your desk is not a spider" is logical, for it can be supported by the evidence.

—Adapted from DiYanni and Hoy, *The Scribner Handbook for Writers*, 3rd ed., p. 69.

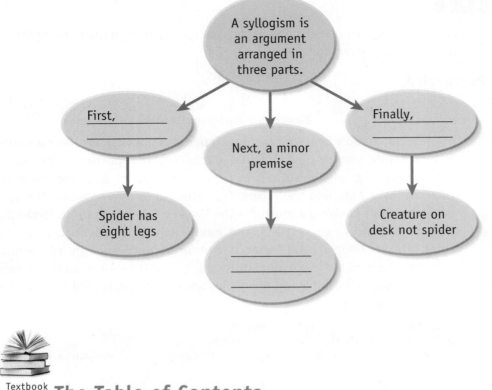

The Table of Contents

The table of contents of a textbook is a special kind of outline that is based on topics and subtopics. A **topic** is the *general subject,* so a **subtopic** is a *smaller part* of the topic. The general subject of the textbook is stated in the textbook's title. For example, the title *Health in America: A Multicultural Perspective* tells us that the book is about health concerns from the view of different cultures.

Textbooks divide the general subject into smaller sections or subtopics. These subtopics form the chapters of the textbook. Because a textbook looks deeply into the general subject, a large amount of information is found in each chapter. Thus, a chapter is further divided into smaller parts or subtopics, and each subtopic is labeled with a heading.

The table of contents lists the general subjects and subtopics of each chapter. Most textbooks provide a brief table of contents that divides the textbook into sections and lists the chapter titles for each section. A separate detailed table of contents may also be provided that lists the subtopics for each chapter. An effective reader examines the table of contents of a textbook to understand how the author has organized the information and where specific information can be found.

EXAMPLE   Survey, or look over, the following brief table of contents from the college textbook *Business* by Griffin and Ebert. Then answer the questions.

1. What is the general topic of this textbook? _____

_____

2. How many chapters did the author use to divide Part 1 ? _____

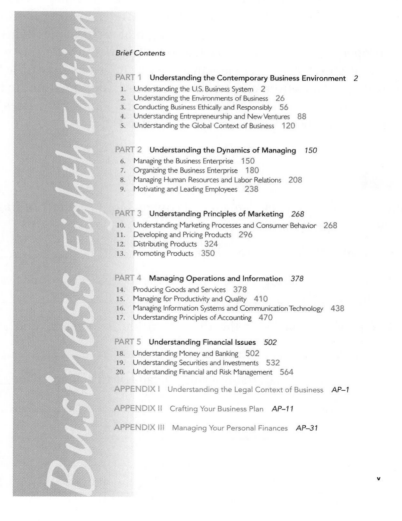

Brief Contents

PART 1   **Understanding the Contemporary Business Environment**   *2*
1.   Understanding the U.S. Business System   2
2.   Understanding the Environments of Business   26
3.   Conducting Business Ethically and Responsibly   56
4.   Understanding Entrepreneurship and New Ventures   88
5.   Understanding the Global Context of Business   120

PART 2   **Understanding the Dynamics of Managing**   *150*
6.   Managing the Business Enterprise   150
7.   Organizing the Business Enterprise   180
8.   Managing Human Resources and Labor Relations   208
9.   Motivating and Leading Employees   238

PART 3   **Understanding Principles of Marketing**   *268*
10.   Understanding Marketing Processes and Consumer Behavior   268
11.   Developing and Pricing Products   296
12.   Distributing Products   324
13.   Promoting Products   350

PART 4   **Managing Operations and Information**   *378*
14.   Producing Goods and Services   378
15.   Managing for Productivity and Quality   410
16.   Managing Information Systems and Communication Technology   438
17.   Understanding Principles of Accounting   470

PART 5   **Understanding Financial Issues**   *502*
18.   Understanding Money and Banking   502
19.   Understanding Securities and Investments   532
20.   Understanding Financial and Risk Management   564

APPENDIX I   Understanding the Legal Context of Business   *AP–1*

APPENDIX II   Crafting Your Business Plan   *AP–11*

APPENDIX III   Managing Your Personal Finances   *AP–31*

v

3. What is the topic of Part 1? _____

What is the approximate length of Chapter 2? _____ pages

4. Create two questions based on two of the chapter titles.

_____

_____

EXPLANATION The general topic of this textbook is stated as its title: *Business*. The author divided the textbook into parts and then divided Part 1 into five chapters. The topic of Part 1 is "Understanding the Contemporary Business Environment." Knowing the length of each chapter helps you set aside the proper amount of time needed to read and study. In this textbook, each chapter is about 30 pages in length. One way to get set a purpose for reading is to create questions from chapter titles. Compare your questions to the following: "What is the U.S. business system?"(Chapter 1) and "How does one conduct business ethically and responsibly?" (Chapter 3).

PRACTICE 3

Study the following detailed table of contents for Chapter 1 of *Business*, 8th ed. Answer the questions that follow.

1. What is the topic of the chapter? _____

2. How many subtopics are listed for the section "Economic Systems Around the World"? _____

3. On what page does the discussion about demand and supply begin?

_____

4. What are the major supporting details of this chapter? _____

_____

_____

_____

_____

_____

Contents

APPLICATIONS

Application 1: Major Supporting Details and Outlines

Read the following paragraph from a college health textbook.

Textbook
Skills

Spirituality

[1]Spirituality refers to the ability to develop spiritual nature to its
fullest potential and fosters three convictions: faith, hope, and love.

[2]Faith is the belief that helps us realize our purpose in life. [3]Hope is the belief that allows us to look confidently and courageously to the future. [4]And love involves accepting, affirming, and respecting self and others regardless of who they are. [5]Love also encompasses caring for and cherishing our environment.

—Adapted from Donatelle, *Access to Health*, 7th ed., p. 43.

1–4. Outline the paragraph by filling in the blanks.

Stated main idea: _____

_____

    a. _____

    b. _____

    c. _____

_____ **5.** This is an example of
      a. an informal outline.
      b. a formal outline.

Application 2: Major Details, Minor Supporting Details, and Outlines
Read the following paragraph from a college communications textbook.

Textbook Skills

Organizing Information: Schemata

[1]One important way you organize information is by creating *schemata*. [2]You build mental structures that help you organize the millions of items of information you come into contact with every day as well as those you already have in memory. [3](*Schemata* is the plural of *schema*.) [4]Thus, **schemata** may be viewed as general ideas about people, yourself, or social roles. [5]You develop schemata from your own experience. [6]Your experiences may be firsthand, or they may be from television, reading, and hearsay. [7]You might have a schema for college athletes, for example, and this might include that they're strong, ambitious, academically weak, and self-centered. [8]In contrast, another person who has had a different experience may have a schema that includes college athletes who are giving and successful students.

—Adapted from DeVito, *Interpersonal Communication Book*,
p. 92 © 2009 by Pearson Education, Inc. Reproduced
by permission of Pearson Education, Inc.

1–4. Outline the paragraph by filling in the blanks.

Stated main idea: _____

_____

A. Mental structures organize information.

B. _____

C. _____

    1. Experiences may be firsthand.

    2. _____

    3. One schema of college athletes might be that they're strong, ambitious, academically weak, and self-centered.

    4. Another schema might include college athletes who are giving and successful students.

_____   **5.** Sentence 6 is a
        a. major supporting detail.
        b. minor supporting detail.

Application 3: Concept Maps and Signal Words

Read the following paragraph. Then complete the concept map with the missing information from the paragraph.

Famous Dominican Americans

[1]During the last half of the twentieth century, many Dominican Americans immigrated to the United States due to civil war and economic depression in the Dominican Republic. [2]These new Americans combined talent and hard work to become famous for their contributions to American culture. [3]For example, Julia Alvarez is the daughter of immigrants from the Dominican Republic. [4]Although she was born in New York City, her parents returned to the Dominican Republic when she was three years old and did not come back until she was ten. [5]She evolved from knowing very little English into a world-renowned literary author. [6]Her work such as *In the Time of the Butterflies* has won her numerous awards and critical acclaim. [7]Another famous Dominican American is Oscar de La Renta, who has received world- wide recognition

for his fashion designs. [8]He left the Dominican Republic when he was 18 years old to study painting in Madrid, Spain, where he quickly became interested in clothing design. [9]He built a billion-dollar industry that includes high fashion, ready-to-wear clothing, accessories, and home décor. [10]Also born in the Dominican Republic, Mary Jo Fernandez stormed the tennis world by becoming one the best doubles players, winning two gold medals in the 1992 and 1996 Summer Olympics. [11]In addition, she garnered nineteen career titles, two of which were Grand Slam events. [12]By her retirement, she had thrilled fans and earned millions. [13]Perhaps one of the best known Dominican American sports figures is the legendary baseball player Sammy Sosa. [14]He made sports history in 1998 when he beat Roger Maris's record of sixty-one home runs in a single season. [15]At one point, he signed a contract that earned him $72 million.

—Adapted from Novas, *Everything You Need to Know About Latino History*, pp. 226–227.

> Several Dominican Americans have become famous for their contributions to American culture.

Application 4: Annotations and Summary

Read the following paragraph from a college political science textbook. Annotate the paragraph by circling the main idea and underlining the example. Complete the summary by filling in the blanks with information from the paragraph.

Textbook
Skills

Federalism

[1]**Federalism** is a way of organizing a nation so that two or more levels of government have formal authority over the same area and people. [2]It is a system of shared power between units of government. [3]For example, the state of California has formal authority over those who live there.

⁴However, the national government can also pass laws and put policies into place that affect those who live in the state. ⁵We are subject to the formal authority of both the state and the national governments.

—Adapted from Edwards, Wattenberg, & Lineberry, *Government in America: People, Politics, and Policy*, 5th ed., p. 55.

Summary:

Federalism is _____

_____

for example, _____

_____

REVIEW TEST 1

Score (number correct) _____ × 10 = _____%

Main Ideas, Major and Minor Supporting Details, and Outlines

A. **(1–5)** Read the paragraph. Then, complete the outline of the paragraph by giving the main idea and inserting the missing major and minor details.

Types of Strength Training

¹Building muscle mass has several advantages and can be accomplished through a variety of strength-training activities. ²First, well-defined muscles give the body a pleasing aesthetic quality. ³Second, muscle mass increases the body's metabolism, burning more calories than fat, thus making weight control by dieting less of an issue. ⁴In addition, strength training builds bone mass, which helps protect against fractures, "shrinking," and osteoporosis. ⁵Several types of strength-training exercises bring effective results. ⁶One of the most common methods is lifting weights using either free weights or machines. ⁷A second method is the use of resistance bands, which are rubberized strips or cables of varying tensions. ⁸A third method consists of doing exercises that bear the body's weight, such as push-ups and pull-ups.

Stated main idea: _____

_____

I.   Muscle mass

   A. _____

   B. _____

      _____

   C. In addition, strength training builds bone mass, which helps protect against fractures, "shrinking," and osteoporosis.

II.   _____

   A. One of the most common methods is lifting weights using either free weights or machines.

   B. A second method is the use of resistance bands, which are rubberized strips or cables of varying tensions.

   C. _____

      _____

B. **(6–10.)** Read the following paragraph. Then complete the outline with major and minor details from the paragraph.

To Drink or Not to Drink: The Question of Wine

[1]The research offers conflicting information on whether or not wine is actually good for you. [2]Some research shows that one or two glasses of wine a day may have several benefits. [3]For example, some studies indicate that drinking wine is good for the heart. [4]It lowers the overall level of cholesterol. [5]In women, it also protects against the hardening and thickening of blood vessels. [6]Furthermore, moderate wine consumption seems to reduce the risk of developing macular degeneration. [7]This condition causes the loss of central vision in older people. [8]It is believed that some of the natural agents in wine may prevent bleeding in tiny blood vessels in the eyes. [9]In addition, ongoing studies on aging indicate that moderate use of wine greatly decreases the risk of dementia. [10]However, research also shows that drinking wine does carry some risks. [11]For example, several large-scale studies have shown that one drink per day raises the risk of breast cancer by 10 percent. [12]In addition, drinking even small amounts of alcohol in the early weeks of pregnancy has been linked with fetal alcohol syndrome.

—Adapted from Loyd Wollstadt, MD, University of Illinois College of Medicine at Rockford, "Research Shows Potential Benefits, Risks of Wine."

Stated main idea: The research offers conflicting information on whether or not wine is actually good for you.

I. _____

_____

   A. _____

     1. It lowers the overall level of cholesterol.

     2. In women, it also protects against the hardening and thickening of blood vessels.

   B. _____

_____

     1. This condition causes the loss of central vision in older people.

     2. It is believed that some of the natural agents in wine may prevent bleeding in tiny blood vessels in the eyes.

   C. _____

_____

II. _____

   A. For example, several large-scale studies have shown that one drink per day raises the risk of breast cancer by 10 percent.

   B. In addition, drinking even small amounts of alcohol in the early weeks of pregnancy has been linked with fetal alcohol syndrome.

REVIEW TEST 2

Score (number correct) _____ × 10 = _____%

Main Ideas, Supporting Details, Signal Words, and Concept Maps

A. Read the following paragraph from a college health textbook.

Textbook
Skills

Risks for Depression

[1]Most experts believe that major depressive disorders are caused by several factors. [2]One factor is biology. [3]Biological theories suggest that chemical and genetic processes are the main reasons for depression. [4]Another factor is known as learned behavior. [5]Learning theories suggest that people develop flawed behaviors, and these behaviors make them

prone to depression. ⁶Finally, cognitive or thinking factors play a role in depression. ⁷Cognitive theories suggest that illogical behaviors and beliefs cause people to use poor coping behaviors.

—Adapted from Donatelle, *Access to Health*, 7th ed., p. 47.

Fill in the concept map with the main idea and the missing major supporting details from the paragraph.

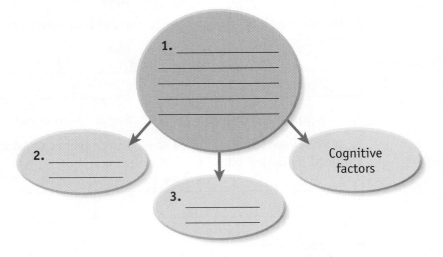

4. What signal word or phrase introduces the third major supporting detail?

_____

B. Read the following paragraph from a college political science textbook.

Textbook
Skills

Traditional Democratic Theory

¹Democracy depends on a number of key values. ²The first value is equality in voting. ³The ideal of "one person, one vote" is basic to democracy. ⁴Another principle of a self-ruling people is effective participation. ⁵Citizens must be able to express their desires and wishes during the decision-making process. ⁶A third value is enlightened understanding. ⁷A self-governing society must be a marketplace of ideas with a free press and free speech. ⁸Fourth, citizens must control the agenda. ⁹Citizens should have the collective right to control the government's policy agenda. ¹⁰Finally, inclusion is key. ¹¹The government must include, and extend rights to, all who are subject to its laws.

—Adapted from Edwards, Wattenberg, & Lineberry, *Government in America: People, Politics, and Policy*, 5th ed., p. 10.

Fill in the concept map with the main idea and major supporting details from the paragraph.

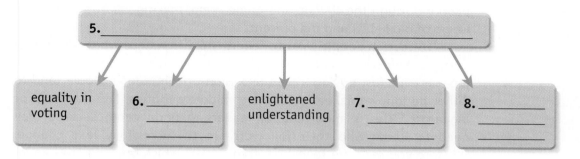

5. _____

equality in voting

6. _____

enlightened understanding

7. _____

8. _____

9. What word or phrase in the topic sentence indicates that a list of supporting details will follow? _____

10. What word or phrase introduces the second major supporting detail?

_____

REVIEW TEST 3   Score (number correct) _____ × 10 = _____%

Read the following passage from a college business textbook. Then complete the informal outline with details from the passage.

Textbook Skills

Helping Others Accept Change

[1]So, you know the power of change, but how does change happen? [2]And what can good leaders do to make others feel comfortable with change? [3]Often, people won't accept change until they understand how they can benefit from it. [4]According to communications scholar Everett Rogers, people go through a five-step process when assessing their reaction to something new:

[5]Step 1: **Know**: You're aware of the change and basically understand it.

[6]Step 2: **Persuade**: Once you learn more about the change, you form an attitude about whether or not you like it.

[7]Step 3: **Decide**: You actively decide to accept or reject the change.

[8]Step 4: **Implement**: You experience the change.

[9]Step 5: **Confirm**: After you experience the change, you evaluate your decision to adopt it.

[10]The leader's role in this process is to motivate and guide people throughout. [11]Leaders need to get people to see and understand their vision for the future—what they see as "better." [12]They also have to walk people through the change and guide them, making it safe for them to let go of old habits and the present.

[13]Although people tend to follow these five steps when faced with change, their reactions also vary. [14]Whether they're settling into a new job—or even just buying a new television or computer—people tend to either be innovators, early adopters, middle adopters, late adopters, or laggards. [15]This is important for leaders to understand, because they need to know who their followers are to successfully lead change. [16]Before you read the following, try to guess which one you are—an innovator? [17]Early, middle, or late adopter? [18]A laggard?

[19]**Innovators**: We all have friends who are always the first to buy the newest gadget. [20]Then, there are those who take it a step farther and actually play a part in developing the next big thing. [21]Maybe they beta-test software no one else has heard of, or use Apple's iPhone software developers' kit to create a new app. [22]These are the innovators. [23]Generally the first 5 to 10 percent of adopters, innovators are quick to embrace change and seek new ways to take advantage of existing technology. [24]Leaders do not have to convince innovators that change is necessary. [25]In fact, innovators actively seek to be the change themselves.

[26]**Early Adopters**: Early adopters make up 10 to 15 percent of the public and look to the innovators to help figure out whether they want to adopt the innovation or change. [27]For example, if early adopters see that the innovators are pleased with the change or a new purchase, they are more likely to adopt that change or go out and buy the new item themselves. [28]In terms of leadership, this is the group in which many leaders reside. [29]This group is highly regarded for being more cautious than innovators, while also being open to quickly embrace change.

[30]**Middle Adopters**: Approximately 30 percent of people fall into the category of middle adopter. [31]Middle adopters may not be as distrustful of change compared to late adopters or laggards, but they still avoid risk. [32]They are less likely to accept change, simply because they are not looking for change as eagerly as innovators and early adopters are. [33]However, if an innovation or change has positively benefited the first two groups, the middle adopters will likely adopt it. [34]Once something new reaches the middle adopter, it's likely no longer considered new and will have become the status quo. [35]In terms of leading change, if leaders can get middle adopters to accept and embrace change, they are well on their way to success.

36Late Adopters: Late adopters represent another large portion of society, approximately 30 percent, who follow the middle adopters. **37**Late adopters are reluctant to change, but they generally decide to change so they don't miss out on the next big thing. **38**Because they are risk-averse, late adopters will only take the plunge once they know the water is safe. **39**They hang on to the existing way of doing things out of loyalty for what they have or the fear of trying something different. **40**Leaders trying to create change will therefore have to work harder to get late adopters to accept and embrace change.

41Laggards: Laggards, about 20 percent of society, are most resistant to change. **42**These are the people who may prefer their VCRs because they don't understand how a DVD player works. **43**Laggards may be isolated from society. **44**When this happens, they have fewer social connections, which can prevent them from seeing the benefit of an innovation or change. **45**In business, leaders must be aware of the risks laggards pose. **46**For example, fear of upsetting the status quo may prevent laggards from investing in newer, better technology, thus, making the company less competitive.

—Van Syckle & Tietje, *Anybody's Business*, pp. 142–143.

VISUAL VOCABULARY

A synonym for **laggard** is

_____.

a. trail blazer.
b. straggler.
c. user.

LAGGING NEVER LEADS
People who 'rest on their oars' now and then
make slow progress
toward better things ahead

Stated Main Idea: _____

_____

I. Five-Step Process in Reaction to Something New

   A. _____

   B. _____

   C. _____

   D. _____

   E. _____

II. _____

   A. _____

   B. Early Adopters

   C. _____

   D. Late Adopters

   E. _____

WHAT DO YOU THINK?

Are you a leader? Are you comfortable with change? What kind of an adopter are you? If you have identified yourself as a leader, then you are also likely to be in one of the groups that is more comfortable with change. If you are slower to come around to change, what do you think a good leader could do to bring you around? Assume you are applying for a job in a management position for a local company that is looking for someone who can learn new technology and lead others to accept change. In your cover letter, describe how you would help an employee under your supervision accept change. Feel free to use your adoption of a piece of technology as an example of your willingness to accept change and your ability to lead others.

REVIEW TEST 4   Score (number correct) _____ × 10 = _____%

Supporting Details and Outlines

Before you read the following passage, skim the material and answer the Before Reading questions. Read the passage. Then answer the After Reading questions.

Vocabulary Preview

prevalence (4): frequency of occurrence

adolescence (5): teenage years

surveyed (9): studied, questioned

symptoms (16): warning signs

compulsiveness (24): urgent desire or driven behavior

deviant (24): abnormal, strange

Binge Drinking

[1]Despite laws in every state that make it illegal for anyone under the age of 21 to purchase or possess alcohol, young people report that alcohol is easy to obtain and that many high school and college students drink with one goal in mind—to get drunk. [2]Binge drinking is defined as consuming five or more drinks in a row for boys and four or more in a row for girls. [3]The alarming aspects of binge drinking cannot be overlooked or underestimated.

[4]One troubling aspect of binge drinking is its **prevalence** among youth and college students. [5]Often starting as young as age 13, these drinkers tend to increase bingeing during **adolescence**. [6]The behavior peaks in young adulthood, which includes the ages from 18 to 22. [7]Then this **perilous** conduct slowly decreases. [8]According to a 1997 national study, among 12- to 20-year-olds, fifteen percent were binge drinkers. [9]A 1995 study found that nearly half of all college students **surveyed** drank four or five drinks in one sitting within a two-week period. [10]In addition, students who live in fraternity and sorority houses are the heaviest drinkers. [11]Over 80 percent of them reported that they take part in binge drinking.

[12]Binge drinking is risky behavior that has serious **consequences**. [13]The most grave effect is **alcohol poisoning**, which is an **acute** physical reaction to an overdose of the alcohol. [14]During bingeing, the brain is deprived of oxygen. [15]This lack of oxygen eventually causes the brain to shut down the heart and lungs. [16]Alcohol poisoning has several **symptoms**. [17]They include vomiting and unconsciousness. [18]In addition, the skin becomes cold, clammy, pale or bluish in color. [19]Breathing becomes slow or irregular.

[20]Binge drinking brings about other disturbing behaviors or effects as well. [21]In schools with high binge drinking rates, binge drinkers are likely to insult, **humiliate**, push, or hit their peers. [22]Frequent binge drinkers were eight times more likely than nonbinge drinkers to miss a class, fall behind in schoolwork, get hurt or injured, and damage property. [23]Binge drinking during college may be linked with mental health disorders. [24]These disorders include **compulsiveness**, depression or anxiety, or early **deviant** behavior. [25]Alarmingly, nearly one out of every five teenagers has experienced "blackout" spells. [26]During these spells, they could not remember what happened the previous evening because of heavy binge drinking. [27]Finally, many who are frequent binge drinkers also drink and drive.

—Adapted from U.S. Department of Human and Health Services,
"Binge Drinking in Adolescents and College Students."

BEFORE READING
Vocabulary in Context

_____   **1.** In sentence 7 of the passage, the word **perilous** means
      a. adventurous.   c. fun-loving.
      b. dangerous.   d. disgusting.

_____   **2.** In sentence 13 of the passage, the word **acute** means
      a. unavoidable.   c. invisible.
      b. short-term.   d. severe.

AFTER READING
Main Ideas

_____   **3.** Which sentence states the central idea of the passage?
      a. sentence 1   c. sentence 3
      b. sentence 2   d. sentence 4

_____   **4.** Which sentence is the topic sentence of the fourth paragraph?
      a. sentence 20   c. sentence 26
      b. sentence 21   d. sentence 27

Supporting Details

5–7. Complete the summary with information from the passage.

Alcohol poisoning is _____.

Symptoms include vomiting; _____; cold, clammy, pale

or bluish skin; slow or irregular _____.

8–10. Complete the following informal outline of the fourth paragraph by filling in the blanks.

Stated main idea: Binge drinking brings about other disturbing behaviors or effects.

A. _____

B. Binge drinkers are more likely to do poorly in school, get hurt, cause damage.

C. _____

D. Binge drinkers may have blackout spells.

E. _____

WHAT DO YOU THINK?

Why is binge drinking so prevalent among youth and college students? Why do you think binge drinking is related to mental disorders? Should colleges address the problem of binge drinking? If so, how? Write a letter to a college or school newspaper explaining the dangers of binge drinking. Include real-life examples if you know of any.

 ## After Reading About Outlines and Concept Maps

Before you move on to the Mastery Tests on outlines and concept maps, take time to reflect on your learning and performance by answering the following questions. Write your answers in your notebook.

- How has my knowledge base or prior knowledge about outlines and concept maps changed?

- Based on my studies, how do I think I will perform on the Mastery Test(s)? Why do I think my scores will be above average, average, or below average?

- Would I recommend this chapter to other students who want to learn more about outlines and concept maps? Why or why not?

Test your understanding on what you have learned about outlines and concept maps by completing the Chapter 6 Review Card in the insert near the end of the text.

CONNECT TO **PEARSON myreadinglab**

To check your progress in meeting Chapter 6's learning outcomes, log in to www.myreadinglab.com, and try the following activities:

- The "Outlining and Summarizing" section of MyReadingLab gives an overview about memory and active reading. This section also provides a model for outlining and a model for mapping. You will also find practice activities and tests. To access this resource, click on the "Study Plan" tab. Then click on "Outlining and Summarizing." Then click on the following links as needed: "Overview," "Model: Outlining," "Model: Mapping," "Practice," and "Tests."

- To measure your mastery of the content in this chapter, complete the tests in the "Outlining and Summarizing" section and click on Gradebook to find your results.

Read the following passage from a college textbook about gender and communication. Complete the activities that follow with information from the passage.

Textbook
Skills

Self-Concept

[1]**Self-concept** is comprised of everything one thinks and knows about oneself. [2]It is the relatively stable set of views one attributes to oneself. [3]As a personal assessment of yourself, your self-concept can be summed up by what you think of yourself in relationship to others. [4]Your self-concept didn't form overnight. [5]Like your gender identity, your self-concept developed in early childhood. [6]And, once established, self-concept is fairly resistant to change. [7]The first day you said "I," or "me," you recognized yourself as separate from your surroundings. [8]You distinguished yourself from others around you. [9]The idea *self-concept* is sometimes broken into two components: *self-image* and *self-esteem*.

Self-Image and Self-Esteem

[10]**Self-image** is the sort of person you believe yourself to be. [11]Self-image is made up of physical and emotional descriptions of the self and the roles you play. [12]**Self-esteem** is a measure of the value you place on the images you have of yourself. [13]Self-esteem includes your attitudes and feelings about yourself including how well you like and value yourself. [14]It is your judgment of how you are doing in life (your perceived self) compared to how you think you should be doing (your ideal self).

[15]According to researcher Chris Mruk, self-esteem is composed of five dimensions:

- [16]*competence* (your beliefs about your ability to be effective),
- [17]*worthiness* (your beliefs about the extent to which others value you),
- [18]*cognition* (your beliefs about your character and personality),
- [19]*affect* (how you evaluate yourself and the feelings generated by this evaluation), and
- [20]*stability* or change (which greatly affects your communication with others).

[21]A number of social forces come together to help create and feed your self-concept. [22]First, the image people have of you guides what they expect of you, how they relate to you, and how they interact with you. [23]Second, as you learn about and understand their images, your

self-concept affects the way you think about yourself. [24]For example, if people who are important to you have a positive image of you, they are apt to make you feel accepted, valued, worthwhile, loved, and significant. [25]If, on the other hand, they have a negative image of you, more than likely they will contribute to your feeling small, worthless, unloved, or insignificant. [26]Whatever its nature, you never stop receiving information about yourself.

—Adapted from Gamble & Gamble, *The Gender Communication Connection*, pp. 43–44.

1–5. Complete the concept map by filling in the main idea and the missing major and minor supporting details. ————————————————.

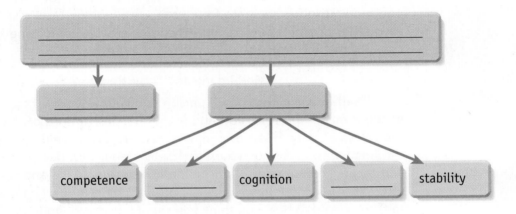

A. Read the following paragraph from a college algebra textbook.

Textbook
Skills

Applications of Slope: Rates of Change

[1]Slope has many real-world applications. [2]For example, numbers like 2%, 3%, and 6% are often used to represent the **grade** of a road, a measure of how steep a road on a hill or mountain is. [3]For example, a 3% grade means that for every horizontal distance of 100 feet, the road rises 3 feet. [4]The concept of grade also occurs in skiing or snowboarding, where a 4% grade is considered very tame but a 40% grade is considered extremely steep. [5]And in cardiology, a physician may change the grade of a treadmill to measure its effect on heartbeat. [6]Architects and carpenters use slope when designing and building stairs, ramps, or roof pitches. [7]Another application occurs in hydrology. [8]When a river flows, the strength or force of the river depends on how far the river falls vertically compared to how far it flows horizontally.

—Bittinger/Beecher, *Introductory and Intermediate Algebra: Combined Approach*,
Text Excerpt from p. 210 © 2003 Pearson Education, Inc. Reproduced
by permission of Pearson Education, Inc.

_____ **1.** Which sentence states the main idea of the paragraph?
    a. sentence 1   c. sentence 3
    b. sentence 2   d. sentence 8

_____ **2.** In general, the major details of this paragraph are
    a. facts that describe the causes of a slope.
    b. ways to measure a slope.
    c. definitions of slopes and grades.
    d. examples of slopes and grades in everyday situations.

_____ **3.** Numbers expressed in percentages are used to
    a. measure heartbeat.
    b. measure the distance of a road.
    c. represent the grade of a road.
    d. represent the force of a river.

_____ **4.** How many major details does the author give in this paragraph?
    a. two   c. four
    b. three   d. five

_____ **5.** The first major detail is signaled by the word or phrase
    a. first.   c. one.
    b. for example.   d. often.

VISUAL VOCABULARY

Which word or phrase best completes the following sentence?

The ski slope of the Headwall on Mount Washington in New Hampshire has an 80% grade, making it among the

_____ skiable terrains in North America.

    a. most tame
    b. safest
    c. steepest
    d. most interesting

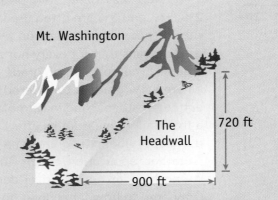

—Bittinger/Beecher, *Introductory and Intermediate Algebra: Combined Approach,* Figure p. 210. Copyright © 2003 Pearson Education, Inc. Reprinted by permission of Pearson Education, Inc.

Read the following passage. Then complete the form that follows.

Work Addiction

Textbook
Skills

[1]Work addiction is a serious problem for two reasons: lack of understanding about the addiction and the effects of the addiction on the addicts and those around them.

[2]First, in order to understand work addiction, we need to understand the concept of healthy work and how it differs from work addiction. [3]Healthy work provides a sense of identity, helps develop our strengths, and is a means of satisfaction, accomplishment, and mastery of problems. [4]Healthy workers may work for long hours. [5]Although they have occasional projects that keep them away from friends, family, and personal interests for short periods, they generally maintain balance in their lives and are in full control of their schedules. [6]Healthy work does not consume the worker. [7]In contrast, work addiction is the compulsive use of work to fulfill needs of intimacy, power, and success. [8]It is characterized by obsession, rigidity, fear, anxiety, low self-esteem, isolation, and the need to be perfect. [9]Work addiction is more than being unable to relax when not doing something thought of as "productive." [10]It is the pursuit of the "work persona," an image that work addicts wish to project onto others.

[11]In addition to understanding the basic traits of work addiction, we must also understand the dangerous effects it has on individuals and those around them. [12]One area that is deeply affected is family life. [13]Work addiction is a major source of marital problems and family breakups. [14]In fact, most work addicts come from homes that were alcoholic, rigid, violent, or otherwise unhealthy. [15]In addition to harming the family, work addiction takes a toll on people's emotional and physical health. [16]They may become emotionally crippled. [17]They lose the ability to connect with other people. [18]They are often riddled with guilt and fear; they fear failure, and they fear their shortcomings will be discovered. [19]Work addicts may also suffer several physical effects. [20]For example, because they are unable to relax and play, they often suffer from chronic fatigue syndrome. [21]Work addicts suffer as well from digestive problems, and they often report feeling pressure in the chest, difficulty breathing, dizziness, and lightheadedness.

—Adapted from Donatelle, *Access to Health*, 7th ed., p. 318.

_____ **1.** In the overall passage, sentence 2 is a
    a. thesis statement.   c. minor supporting detail.
    b. major supporting detail.

_____ **2.** How many major supporting details support the thesis statement in this passage?
    a. two   c. four
    b. three   d. five

_____ **3.** What word or phrase signals the first major supporting detail?
    a. first   c. for example
    b. one   d. during

_____ **4.** What word or phrase signals the second major supporting detail?
    a. and   c. in addition
    b. next   d. also

_____ **5.** In general, the supporting details of the second paragraph
    a. explain the differences between healthy work and work addiction.
    b. offer ways to cope with work addiction.
    c. explain the term _work persona_.
    d. list situations in which workers become addicted to their work.

_____ **6.** Overall, the supporting details of the third paragraph
    a. list the physical effects of work addiction.
    b. list the emotional effects of work addiction.
    c. explain the causes of work addiction.
    d. explain the emotional and physical effects of work addiction.

7–10. Complete the concept map with supporting details from the second paragraph.

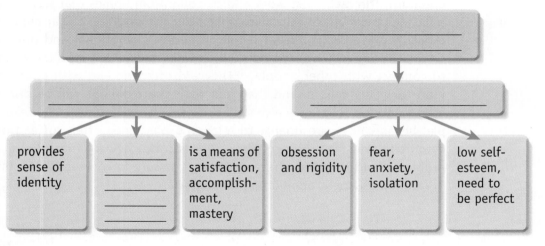

Read the following passage from a college textbook for a course in criminal justice. Then complete the outline that follows.

Textbook
Skills

Types of Evidence

[1]The crux of the criminal trial is the presentation of evidence. [2]First, the state is given the opportunity to present evidence intended to prove the defendant's guilt. [3]After prosecutors have rested their case, the defense is afforded the opportunity to provide evidence favorable to the defendant.

[4]Evidence can be either direct or circumstantial. [5]Direct evidence, if believed, proves a fact without requiring the judge or jury to draw inferences. [6]For example, direct evidence may consist of the information contained in a photograph or a videotape. [7]It might also consist of testimonial evidence provided by a witness on the stand. [8]A straightforward statement by a witness ("I saw him do it!") is a form of direct evidence.

[9]Circumstantial evidence is indirect. [10]It requires the judge or jury to make inferences and to draw conclusions. [11]At a murder trial, for example, a person who heard gunshots and moments later saw someone run by with a smoking gun in hand might testify to those facts. [12]Even without an eyewitness to the actual homicide, the jury might conclude that the person seen with the gun was the one who pulled the trigger and committed the crime. [13]Circumstantial evidence is sufficient to produce a conviction in a criminal trial. [14]In fact, some prosecuting attorneys prefer to work entirely with circumstantial evidence, weaving a tapestry of the criminal act into their arguments to the jury.

[15]Real evidence, which may be either direct or circumstantial, consists of physical material, traces of physical activity. [16]Weapons, tire tracks, ransom notes, and fingerprints all fall into the category of real evidence. [17]Real evidence, sometimes called physical evidence, is introduced at the trial by means of exhibits. [18]Exhibits are objects or displays that, after having been formally accepted as evidence by the judge, may be shown to members of the jury. [19]Documentary evidence, one type of real evidence, includes written evidence like business records, journals, written confessions, and letters. [20]Documentary evidence can extend beyond paper and ink to include stored computer data and video and audio recordings.

—Schmalleger, *Criminal Justice Today: An Introductory Text for the 21st Century*, 10th ed., p. 367.

Stated Main Idea: _____

    I. _____

        A. _____

        B. Photograph

        C. Video

        D. Statement by a witness

    II. _____

        A. _____

        B. Is sufficient to produce a conviction in a criminal trial

    III. _____

        A. May be either direct or circumstantial, consists of _____

            _____

            1. Weapons

            2. Tire tracks

            3. Ransom notes

            4. _____

        B. Is introduced at the trial by means of exhibits

        C. _____

            1. Business records, journals, written confessions, and letters

            2. _____

Transitions and Thought Patterns

7

LEARNING OUTCOMES

After studying this chapter you should be able to do the following:

1. Define the terms *transitions* and *thought patterns*.
2. Determine the relationships of ideas within a sentence.
3. Determine the relationships of ideas between sentences.
4. Recognize the following thought patterns and their signal words: *time order*, *space order*, *listing*, *classification*.
5. Determine the thought pattern used to organize a passage.
6. Evaluate the importance of transitions and thought patterns.
7. Use transitions and thought patterns to improve comprehension of the author's main idea.

Before Reading About Transitions and Thought Patterns

Using the reporter's questions (Who? What? When? Where? Why? and How?), refer to the learning outcomes and create at least three questions that you can answer as you study the chapter. Write your questions in the following spaces:

_____?

_____?

_____?

Now take a few minutes to skim the chapter for ideas and terms that you have studied in previous chapters. List those ideas in the following spaces:

_____

_____

Compare the questions you created based on the learning outcomes with the following questions. Then write the ones that seem the most helpful in your notebook, leaving enough space between each question to record the answers as you read and study the chapter.

What are transitions? What are thought patterns? What is the relationship between transition words and thought patterns? How do thought patterns use transition words?

On page 279, the terms main idea, supporting details, and outlines are discussed in relationship to transitions and thought patterns. Consider the following study questions based on these ideas: How can transitions help me understand the author's main idea? How can transitions help me create an outline?

Transition Words: Relationships Within a Sentence

Read the following set of ideas. Which word makes the relationship within the second sentence clear?

> In 1998, Major League Baseball player Mark McGwire broke the single-season home run record by hitting 70 home runs. In 2010, McGwire cast doubt on his record _____ he admitted to taking steroids during his record-breaking season.
>
> a. when   b. for example   c. however

The word that makes the relationship between the two ideas clear in the second sentence is (a) *when*. Mark McGwire's record of hitting 70 home runs was quite a feat, even for a natural and talented athlete like McGwire. His accomplishment was tarnished the moment he admitted to using performance enhancing drugs. Until he admitted drug use, his record stood as evidence of his natural ability. Thus the transition *when* best expresses the relationship between ideas in the second sentence.

Transitions are key pattern words and phrases that signal the logical relationships within and between sentences. **Transitions** help you make sense of an author's idea in two basic ways. First, transitions join ideas within a sentence.

> **Transitions** are words and phrases that signal thought patterns by showing the logical relationships within a sentence and between sentences.
>
> A **thought pattern** (or **pattern of organization**) is established by using transitions to show the logical relationship between ideas in a paragraph or passage.

Second, transitions establish **thought patterns** so readers can understand the logical flow of ideas between sentences.

Read the following sentence. Which word makes the relationship of ideas within the sentence clear?

Fernando deserves to be recognized for his public service _____

he has worked faithfully for twenty years with the Boy Scouts and the

youth soccer league.

a. before   b. in addition   c. because

All three of these choices are transitions; however, the word that best clarifies the relationship of ideas within this sentence is (c) *because*. Fernando's work with youth is the reason he deserves to be recognized. The relationship is one of cause and effect. Transition (a) *before* reveals time order, and transition (b) *in addition* indicates that the author is adding to the first idea. In the next section, you will learn more about these transitions and thought patterns. First, it is helpful to see how transitions serve a vital function in building ideas within a sentence.

EXAMPLE Complete the following with a transition that shows the relationship of ideas within each sentence. Fill in each blank with a word from the box. Use each word once.

also	as a result	inside	such as

1. Not only does academic cheating rob the cheating student of knowledge,

   it can _____ severely damage that student's reputation.

2. One kind of effective foot warmer is a soft, lightweight insole that generates its own heat with exposure to air and can be slipped _____ a shoe or boot.

3. Travis eliminated unhealthy eating habits, diligently worked out at the gym three times a week, and walked vigorously for 30 minutes every day;

   _____, after six months he attained his ideal weight.

4. Olivia invests in a variety of financial assets _____ stocks, bonds, and real estate.

EXPLANATION

1. The topic of this sentence is cheating. The author makes two points about cheating. *Also* indicates the addition of the second point.

2. The topic of this sentence is one kind of foot warmer. The author is describing its traits. One trait is where it is used; it is placed *inside* the shoe or boot.

3. This sentence brings two topics or ideas together. The first part of the sentence deals with Travis' healthy lifestyle (this topic is suggested by the list of details). The topic of the second part of the sentence is "ideal weight." The second idea is the result of the first. The correct answer is *as a result*.

4. The topic of this sentence is the variety of Olivia's assets. The phrase *such as* indicates that a list of examples follows.

Note that to determine the correct transition for each of the sentences, you had to rely upon context clues to first determine the relationship of ideas. Understanding relationships and thought patterns is closely related to a clear understanding of vocabulary.

PRACTICE 1

Textbook
Skills

Study the following list of scientific terms from a college textbook. Complete each item with a transition that shows the relationship of ideas within each sentence. Fill in each blank with a word from the box. Use each word once.

as	or	when	while

1. *Predation* occurs _____ members of one species, a *predator*, hunt, capture, kill, and consume members of another species, the *prey*.

2. In *parasitism*, one organism, the *parasite*, depends on another, the *host*, for food or some other benefit _____ doing the host harm.

3. In *mutualism*, species benefit from one another _____ they interact.

4. Mutualism and parasitism occur between organisms that live in close physical contact _____ *symbiosis*.

—Adapted from Withgott & Brennan, *Essential Environment: The Science Behind the Stories,* 3rd ed., p. 95.

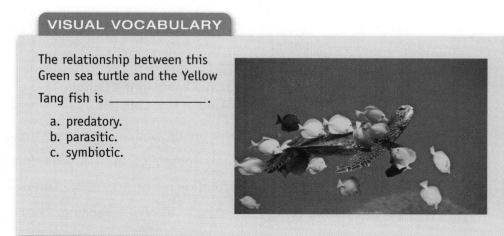

VISUAL VOCABULARY

The relationship between this Green sea turtle and the Yellow Tang fish is _____.

a. predatory.
b. parasitic.
c. symbiotic.

Transitions express a variety of relationships between ideas. You must therefore look carefully at the meaning of each transitional word or phrase. Some transition words have similar meanings. For example, *also*, *too*, and *furthermore* all signal the relationship of addition or listing. Sometimes a single word can serve as two different types of transitions, depending on how it is used. For example, the word *since* can reveal time order, or it can signal a cause. Notice the difference in the following two sentences.

> *Since* I began working, I have saved several thousand dollars.
>
> *Since* you are familiar with the assignment, Janice, please lead the group discussion.

The relationship between the ideas in the first sentence is based on time order. The relationship between the ideas in the second sentence is based on cause and effect.

Effective readers look for transition words, study their meaning in context, and use them as keys to unlock the author's thought patterns.

PRACTICE 2

Read the following paragraph from a government website. Fill in each blank with a transition that shows the relationship between ideas. Choose your answers from the words in the box. Use each word once.

although	as well as	for example	than	until
and	besides	such as	then	while

A Call to Action: Changing the Culture of Drinking at U.S. Colleges

(1) _____ the damage and injuries that occur during spring break each year, the only consequences of college drinking that usually come to the public's attention are occasional student deaths from alcohol overuse, **(2)** _____ alcohol poisoning. They prompt a brief flurry of media attention; **(3)** _____, the topic disappears **(4)** _____ the next incident. In fact, the consequences of college drinking are much more than occasional; **(5)** _____, at least 1,400 college student deaths a year are linked to alcohol. In addition, high-risk drinking results in serious injuries and assaults, **(6)** _____ other health and academic problems. Alcohol is a major factor in damage to college property. The relative lack of headlines about college drinking denies the facts. The consequences of excessive college drinking are more widespread and destructive **(7)** _____ most people realize. **(8)** _____ only isolated incidents tend to make news, many school presidents conclude that these pervasive, **(9)** _____ less obvious, problems are occurring on their campuses at the same time. It is a persistent and costly problem, **(10)** _____ it affects nearly all residential colleges, college communities, and college students, whether they drink or not.

—Adapted from "A Call to Action: Changing the Culture of Drinking at U.S. Colleges." *College Drinking: Changing the Culture*. National Institute on Alcohol Abuse and Alcoholism. 11 July 2007. 12 Jan. 2010. http://www.collegedrinkingprevention.gov/_usercontrols/printpage.aspx.

Thought Patterns: Relationships Between Sentences

Not only do transitions reveal the relationships of ideas *within* a sentence, they also show the relationship *between* sentences. Read the following sentences and choose the word that best states the relationship between the sentences.

Resistance training, such as weightlifting, offers several benefits.

_____, it tones the muscles and increases bone density.

    a. As a result   b. However   c. For example

The transition that best states the relationship between these sentences is (c) *For example*. The first sentence is a generalization. It contains a topic and a controlling point about the topic. The topic is "resistance training"; the point is "several benefits." The second sentence offers an example as a supporting detail for the general point. Transition (a) *As a result* signals cause and effect. And (b) *However* indicates a contrast. In this chapter and Chapter 8, you will study the ways in which authors use these and other thought patterns in paragraphs and longer passages. First, it is important to learn to find the relationship between sentences.

EXAMPLE Complete the following with transitions that make the relationship between the sentences clear. Fill in each blank with a word from the box. Use each word once.

after	above	furthermore

1. Simon Cowell became well known in the United States as a judge on the

popular TV show *American Idol*. _____ eight seasons on the show, Cowell left *American Idol* to star on the American version of *X-factor*.

2. A frustrated father talking to his son said, "You are going to make several major changes. You will come home at a decent hour. You will keep your room orderly. You will speak respectfully to your mother and me.

_____, you will get a job."

3. Airplanes offer two storage places for carry-on luggage. Small bags can be placed under the seat in front of a passenger. Larger bags must be stored in

compartments located _____ the seat.

EXPLANATION

1. The relationship between the sentences is based on time. The words "eight seasons" serve as a clue that the correct transition is *after*.

2. The father states a list of behaviors he expects from his son. The word *furthermore* signals an additional behavior that is expected.

3. The first sentence establishes the relationship between these sentences as space order with the use of the word "places." The correct transition is *above*.

PRACTICE 3

Complete the following with transitions. Fill in each blank with a word from the box. Use each word once.

as a result	before	during	in contrast	when

Kaleigh learned that equipment makes a significant difference in the success and enjoyment of a sport or exercise when she traded her old bike in for a new comfort bike. Her old bike was equipped with aerodynamic handle bars, a hard, narrow seat, and no shock absorbers. **(1)** _____, she endured bumpy, uncomfortable rides that left her sore, and she dreaded cycling as an activity. **(2)** _____, her comfort bike is equipped with upright handle bars, a plush gel seat, and state of the art shock absorbers. Now Kaleigh loves long-distance cycling. Every morning long **(3)** _____ most people are up, Kaleigh already has on her helmet, pads, and gloves. **(4)** _____ she first begins a ride, she considers how long the ride will be so that she can set a pace and conserve her energy. **(5)** _____ the ride, Kaleigh varies her pace to maximize her workout. After a long ride, Kaleigh feels a sense of satisfaction and strength.

PRACTICE 4

Complete the following paragraph by inserting transitions. Fill in each blank with a word from the box. Use each word once.

and	however	when
during	thus	

Confucius

The name Confucius is the latinized form of the Chinese characters, K'ung Foo-tsze, meaning, "The master, K'ung." The bearer of this name was born of an ancient and distinguished family in the district of Tsow, in the present province of Shen-tung, China, B.C. 551. His father was a soldier of reputation and governor of Tsow, but not a man of wealth. Confucius married at nineteen, **(1)** _____, in his early manhood held a minor office; but within a few years he became a public teacher, and soon attracted numerous disciples. Rising in reputation, he was invited to the court of Chow. **(2)** _____ this time, he investigated the traditional ceremonies and maxims of the ruling dynasty; and in the following year visited another state where he studied ancient music. **(3)** _____ he was nearly fifty, in the year 500 B.C., he again took office, becoming, in turn, chief magistrate of the town of Chung-too, Assistant-Superintendent of Works to the Ruler of Loo, and finally Minister of Crime. In spite of almost miraculous efficiency, he lost the support of his ruler in 496 B.C.; and until his death in 478 B.C., he wandered from state to state, sometimes well-treated, sometimes enduring severe hardships, always saddened by the refusal of the turbulent potentates to be guided by his beneficent counsels. No sooner was he dead, **(4)** _____, than his wisdom was recognized by peasant and emperor alike; admiration rose to veneration, veneration to worship. **(5)** _____, sacrifices were offered to him, temples built in his honor, and a cult established which has lasted almost two thousand years.

> —Adapted from *The Sayings of Confucius*. Vol. XLIV, Part 1. The Harvard Classics. New York: P.F. Collier & Son, 1909–14; Bartleby.com, 2001. www.bartleby.com/44/1/. 15 August 2007.

You will recall that a paragraph is made up of a group of ideas. Major details support the main idea, and minor details support the major details. Transitions make the relationship between these three levels of ideas clear, smooth, and easy to follow.

Before beginning to write, an author must ask, "What thought pattern best expresses these ideas?" or "How should these ideas be organized so that the reader can follow and understand my point?" A **thought pattern** (also called a **pattern of organization**) allows the author to arrange the supporting details in a clear and smooth flow by using transition words.

> **Thought patterns** (or **patterns of organization**) are signalled by using transitions to show the logical relationship between ideas in a paragraph, passage, or textbook chapter.

As you learned in Chapter 3, a main idea is made up of a topic and the author's controlling point about the topic. One way an author controls the topic is by using a specific thought pattern. Read the following paragraph. Identify the topic sentence by circling the topic and underlining the controlling point.

The Traits of Olfaction

The sense of smell, also known as olfaction, has two interesting traits. First, people have difficulty describing odors in words. Second, odors have a powerful ability to call to mind old memories and feelings, even many years after an event.

—Carlson/Buskist, *Psychology: Science of Behavior*, Text Excerpt from p. 191 © 1997. Reproduced by permission of Pearson Education, Inc.

The topic is the "sense of smell" and the controlling point is the phrase "two interesting traits." The word "interesting" states the author's opinion. The words "two traits" state the author's thought pattern. The author's controlling point limits the supporting details to listing and describing two interesting traits of smell. The transition words *first* and *second* signal each of the supporting details. Authors often introduce supporting details with transition words based on the controlling point. Creating an outline using transition words is an excellent way to grasp an author's thought pattern.

EXAMPLE Read the following paragraph. Complete the informal outline, then answer the question.

The Landscape of Taste

Moving from front to back, the surface of the tongue is differentially sensitive to taste. The front or tip is most sensitive to sweet and salty substances. Next, the sides are most sensitive to sour substances. Finally, the back of the tongue, the back of the throat, and the soft palate overhanging the back of the tongue are sensitive to bitter substances.

—Carlson/Buskist, *Psychology: Science of Behavior*, Text Excerpt from p. 190 © 1997. Reproduced by permission of Pearson Education, Inc.

Topic sentence: _____

_____

a. _____

b. _____

c. _____

_____

_____ What is the author's thought pattern?
   a. time order   b. space order

EXPLANATION   Compare your outline to the following:

Topic sentence: Moving from front to back, the surface of the tongue is differentially sensitive to taste.

   a. The front or tip is most sensitive to sweet and salty substances.

   b. Next, the sides are most sensitive to sour substances.

   c. Finally, the back of the tongue, the back of the throat, and the soft palate overhanging the back of the tongue are sensitive to bitter substances.

The topic is "the surface of the tongue." The thought pattern is expressed in the words "moving from front to back" and "differentially sensitive." The transitions clearly carry out the thought pattern by beginning with the *front* of the tongue, next the *sides*, and finally the *back* of the tongue. In this paragraph, the transitions establish the (b) space order thought pattern.

PRACTICE 5

Read the following paragraph. Then complete the informal outline.

Textbook
Skills

Taste Versus Flavor

Taste is different from flavor. On the one hand, taste is the simple ability to sense four sensations: sourness, sweetness, saltiness, and bitterness. On the other hand, the flavor of a food includes its odor as well as its taste. For example, you have probably noticed that the flavors of foods are diminished when you have a head cold. Mucus makes it difficult for odor-laden air to reach your receptors for the sense of smell.

—Carlson/Buskist, *Psychology: Science of Behavior*, Text Excerpt from p. 189 © 1997.
Reproduced by permission of Pearson Education, Inc.

Topic sentence: _____

a. _____

_____

b. _____

   1. _____

_____

   2. Mucus makes it difficult for odor-laden air to reach your receptors for the sense of smell.

Note how the headings for the paragraphs you just read show the close connection between the topic and the author's thought pattern used to present the main idea and organize the supporting details. For example, the title "The Landscape of Taste" uses the word "landscape" to clue the reader to the space order thought pattern. An excellent activity to do before reading is to read the heading and skim ahead for transition words to get the gist of the author's thought pattern.

In this chapter, we discuss four common thought patterns and the transition words and phrases used to signal each:

- The time order pattern
- The space order pattern
- The listing pattern
- The classification pattern

Some additional common thought patterns are covered in Chapter 8.

The Time Order Pattern

The **time order** thought pattern generally shows a chain of events. The actions or events are listed in the order in which they occur. This is called *chronological order*. Two types of chronological order are narration and process. An author will use narration to tell about the important events in the life of a famous person or a significant event in history. Narration is also used to organize a piece of fiction. The second type of chronological order is process. Process is used to give directions to a task in time order. In summary, there are two basic uses of time order: (1) narration: a chain of events and (2) process: steps, stages, or directions.

Narration: A Chain of Events

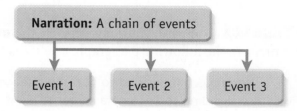

Transitions of **time** signal that the writer is describing *when* things occurred and *in what order.* The writer presents an event and then shows when each of the additional details or events flowed from the first event. Thus the details follow a logical order based on time.

> John Wilkes Booth, who led a very prominent life as an actor in the years before he assassinated Abraham Lincoln, ultimately died a traitor's death.

Notice that this sentence lays out three events. The transition words *before* and *ultimately* tell the order in which the events occurred.

Transitions Used in the Time Order Pattern for Narration				
after	during	later	previously	ultimately
afterward	eventually	meanwhile	second	until
as	finally	next	since	when
before	first	now	soon	while
currently	last	often	then	

EXAMPLE Determine the logical order of the following sentences. Write **1** by the sentence that should come first, **2** by the sentence that should come second, **3** by the sentence that should come third, and **4** by the sentence that should come last. (Hint: Circle the time transition words.)

_____ Eventually, his passion for learning earned him a master's degree and a doctorate.

_____ During those early years as a teacher, he found that the more he learned, the more excited he was about teaching, and he loved studying under the guidance of professional teachers.

_____ His first notions of wanting only a four-year bachelor's degree were quickly dispelled.

_____ When Corbin decided to become a teacher, he had no idea that he was also deciding to become a career student.

EXPLANATION Compare your answers to the sentences arranged in the proper order in the following paragraph. The transitions are in **bold** print.

> [1]**When** Corbin decided to become a teacher, he had no idea that he was also deciding to become a career student. [2]His **first** notions of wanting only a four-year bachelor's degree were quickly dispelled. [3]**During** those early years as a teacher, he found that the more he learned, the more excited he was about teaching, and he loved studying under the guidance of professional teachers. [4]**Eventually**, his passion for learning earned him a master's degree and a doctorate.

PRACTICE 6

Determine the logical order for the following sentences. Write **1** by the sentence that should come first, **2** by the sentence that should come second, **3** by the sentence that should come third, **4** by the sentence that should come fourth, and **5** by the sentence that should come fifth. (Hint: Circle the time transition words.)

Battling Emotional Eating

_____ Clara constantly struggles with the cycle of emotional eating.

_____ At the first sign of a stressor, she resists the urge to eat the foods that bring her comfort, such as fast-food hamburgers and fries, cookies, ice cream, or anything else high in fat and carbohydrates.

_____ Eventually, she gains enough unwanted weight to shock her into self-control.

_____ Then she begins to eat a balanced diet and lose the weight—until the next stressful time.

_____ As the stress stretches into days, she finds her resolve weakened and heads for the junk food.

Process: Steps, Stages, or Directions

The time order thought pattern for steps, stages, or directions shows actions that can be repeated at any time with similar results. This pattern is used to give steps or directions for completing a task.

> **Process:** Steps, stages, or directions
>
> **Step 1**
>
> **Step 2**
>
> **Step 3**

Read the following topic sentences. Underline the words that signal process time order.

1. Follow five simple steps to develop and deepen your friendships.

2. Procrastination recurs in a cycle of self destruction.

3. Grief moves through several stages.

Sentence 1 uses the word *steps* to introduce directions for the reader to follow. Sentence 2 signals that procrastination occurs as part of a pattern of self-destruction with the word *cycle*. Sentence 3 uses the process signal word *stages* to convey the time order of grief. In paragraphs that developed these topic sentences, transitions of time order would likely signal the supporting details.

Transitions Used in the Time Order Pattern for Process				
after	during	later	previously	ultimately
afterward	eventually	meanwhile	second	until
as	finally	next	since	when
before	first	now	soon	while
currently	last	often	then	

EXAMPLE The following paragraph from a college ecology textbook uses the time order pattern for process to organize its ideas. Complete the concept map that follows it by giving the missing details in their proper order. (Hint: Circle the time order transition words.)

Textbook
Skills

Earth as a System: The Rock Cycle

¹Earth is a system. ²This means that our planet consists of many interacting parts that form a complex whole. ³Nowhere is this idea better

illustrated than when we examine the rock cycle. [4]To begin, magma is molten material that forms inside the Earth. [5]Eventually magma cools and solidifies. [6]This process is called **crystallization**. [7]It may occur either beneath the surface or, following a volcanic eruption, at the surface. [8]The resulting rocks are called **igneous rocks**. [9]As igneous rocks are exposed at the surface, they will undergo weathering, in which the day-in and day-out influences of the atmosphere slowly disintegrate and decompose rocks. [10]Then, the materials that result are often moved downslope by gravity before being picked up and transported by any of a number of erosional agents, such as running water, glaciers, wind, or waves. [11]Eventually, these particles and dissolved substances, called **sediment**, are deposited. [12]Although most sediment ultimately comes to rest in the ocean, other sites of deposition include river floodplains, desert basins, swamps, and sand dunes. [13]Next, the sediments undergo **lithification**, a term meaning "conversion into rock." [14]Sediment is usually lithified into **sedimentary rock** when compacted by the weight of overlying layers or when cemented as percolating groundwater fills the pores with mineral matter. [15]When the resulting sedimentary rock is buried deep within Earth and involved in the dynamics of mountain building or intruded by a mass of magma, it will be subjected to great pressures and/or intense heat. [16]This phase is called **metamorphism**. [17]The sedimentary rock will react to the changing environment and turn into the third rock type, **metamorphic rock**. [18]Finally, if metamorphic rock is subjected to still higher temperatures, it will melt, creating magma, which will eventually crystallize into igneous rock, starting the cycle all over again.

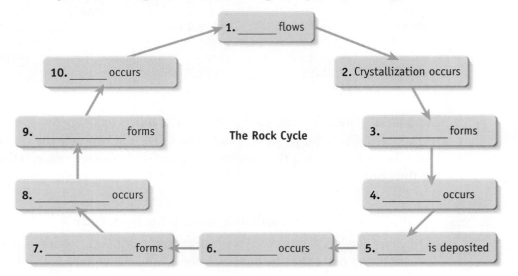

The Rock Cycle

1. _____ flows

2. Crystallization occurs

3. _____ forms

4. _____ occurs

5. _____ is deposited

6. _____ occurs

7. _____ forms

8. _____ occurs

9. _____ forms

10. _____ occurs

VISUAL VOCABULARY

The Devil's Tower in Wyoming is an

example of _____ rock.

    a. igneous
    b. sedimentary
    c. metamorphic

EXPLANATION Compare your answers to the following: (1) Magma flows; (2) Crystallization occurs; (3) Igneous rock forms; (4) Weathering occurs; (5) Sediment is deposited; (6) Lithification occurs; (7) Sedimentary rock forms; (8) Metamorphism occurs; (9) Metamorphic rock forms; (10) Melting occurs; and the cycle begins again (1) Magma flows.

PRACTICE 7

The following paragraph uses the time order pattern for process to organize its ideas. Complete the list of steps that follows it by giving the missing details in their proper order. (Hint: Circle the time order transition words.)

How to Change Your Car's Oil

¹First, warm up your car's engine. ²Next, before getting under your car, turn off the engine, block the wheels, and set the parking brake. ³Third, remove the drain plug on the bottom of the engine's oil pan, and allow the used oil to drain from your car into a drip pan. ⁴Fourth, tightly replace the drain plug. ⁵Fifth, carefully add the new engine oil. ⁶Do not overfill. ⁷Sixth, with the parking brake still set, and in a well-ventilated area, start the car, and allow the engine to run for a few minutes. ⁸Seventh, turn off the engine and check the oil level. ⁹Also check around the oil filter and drain plug for leaks. ¹⁰Eighth, so you know when to change your oil next, write down the date, mileage, grade, and brand of the motor oil you installed. ¹¹Next, carefully pour the used oil from the

drip pan into a suitable recycling container. [12]Finally, protect the environment and conserve resources by taking your used oil to the nearest public used-oil collection center, such as a service station or lube center. [13]Also look for the "oil drop." [14]This is a petroleum industry symbol indicating that used oil is collected for recycling or reuse.

—U.S. Environmental Protection Agency, "Collecting Used Oil for Recycling/Reuse."

How to Change Your Car's Oil

Step 1: _____.

Step 2: _____.

Step 3: Remove the drain plug on the bottom of the engine's oil pan, and drain oil into a drip pan.

Step 4: _____.

Step 5: Add the new engine oil.

Step 6: Start the car, and run the engine for a few minutes.

Step 7: Turn off the engine, check the oil level, and check the oil filter and drain plug for leaks.

Step 8: _____.

Step 9: Pour the used oil from the drip pan into a suitable recycling container.

Step 10: _____.

PRACTICE 8

The following passage uses time order to describe a Mexican American tradition. Complete the following passage by inserting transitions. Fill in each blank with a word from the box. Use each word once.

| after | finally | next | then | when |
| before | first | second | third | while |

How to Make Your Own Cascarones

The egg is the perfect symbol of renewal, befitting spring. **(1)** _____ Easter comes, Latinos add a new twist to Easter—egg decorating and hunting—the Mexican cascaron (eggshell). Mexican

American families take care to drain and clean whole eggshells at least a month **(2)** _____Easter, in order to create *cascarones*. *Cascarones,* filled with confetti and sealed with brightly colored tissue paper "hats," are meant to be cracked on people's heads. Creating your own *cascarones* takes some advance planning. How many *cascarones* you end up with depends on how many eggs your household regularly uses and how soon you start saving the emptied eggshells. Follow these steps:

(3) _____ save your eggshells. Starting at least a month in advance, every time you use an egg, it should be carefully broken from the narrow end, leaving as much of the oval eggshell intact as possible. (Since these eggs are not for decoration but for play, the use of an egg blower, which removes the yolk through a pinhole, is not necessary.) A hole approximately 1/2 inch in diameter is large enough to remove the egg's liq-uid contents as well as to insert confetti later. **(4)** _____, clean the eggshells. Prepare a soap bath for the empty shells. Swish through the soapy water and allow them to soak for a few minutes. Rinse well. **(5)** _____they are clean, let them air dry, and store them in egg cartons. **(6)** _____, decorate your eggshells. On the Saturday before Easter (Holy Saturday), your family can decorate the eggs as you would regular eggs—with PAAS Easter egg dye, glitter, paint, etc. Be very careful not to crack the delicate shells (it's a good idea to have a few extra on hand, just in case). **(7)** _____, fill your eggshells. To fill the eggs, use pre-made confetti or make your own confetti by cutting bits of colored construction paper (the second option is the traditional one). Fill half full. **(8)** _____ seal the eggshells. For egg covers, use brightly colored tissue paper. Cut out circles big enough to cover the open end of the egg. Apply glue around the rim of the egg and attach the tissue top so that it seals the opening without breaking. The seal should leave the egg with a small, flat top. Families can work in teams. One group can color and decorate the shells, **(9)** _____ the other group prepares the confetti and egg covers. **(10)** _____, enjoy! Remember, the purpose of making them is to break them on someone's head. Have fun.

—Adapted from Menard, *The Latino Holiday Book*, pp. 12, 15–16.

The Space Order Pattern

The **space order pattern** allows authors to describe a person, place, or thing based on its location or the way it is arranged in space. In the space order pattern, also known as spatial order, the writer often uses descriptive details to help readers create vivid mental pictures of what the writer is describing. An author may choose to describe an object from top to bottom, from bottom to top, from right to left, from left to right, from near to far, from far to near, from inside to outside, or from outside to inside.

Space Order: Descriptive Details

Descriptive detail 1 → Descriptive detail 2 → Descriptive detail 3

Transition words of **space order** signal that the details follow a logical order based on two elements: (1) how the object, place, or person is arranged in space, and (2) the starting point from which the author chooses to begin the description.

Transition Words Used in the Space Order Pattern

above	at the side	beneath	close to	here	nearby	right
across	at the top	beside	down	in	next to	there
adjacent	back	beyond	far away	inside	on	under
around	behind	by	farther	left	outside	underneath
at the bottom	below	center	front	middle	over	within

EXAMPLE Study the following paragraph from a college anatomy and physiology textbook. Choose a word from the box to fill in each blank with a signal word that shows the relationship between ideas. Use each word once.

| away from | erect | in | on | side |
| between | forward | left | right | sides |

Textbook Skills

The Language of Anatomy

Anatomy and physiology is the study of the structures and functions of the human body. To accurately describe body parts and positions, we must have an initial reference point and use directional terms. To avoid confusion, it always assumed that the body is (**1**) _____ the standard position called the anatomical position. In the **anatomical position**, the body is (**2**) _____ with the feet parallel and the arms hanging at the (**3**) _____ with palms facing (**4**) _____ and the thumbs pointing (**5**) _____ the body. **Directional terms** allow us to explain exactly where one body structure is in relation to another. For example, we can describe the relationship (**6**) _____ the ears and the nose informally by saying, "The ears are located (**7**) _____ each (**8**) _____ of the head to the (**9**) _____ and (**10**) _____ of the nose." Using anatomical terminology, this shortens to "The ears are lateral to the nose." Anatomical terms save a good deal of description and, once learned, are much clearer.

—Adapted from Marieb, *Essentials of Human Anatomy and Physiology,* 9th ed., p. 15.

EXPLANATION Compare your answers to the following: (1) in, (2) erect, (3) sides, (4) forward, (5) away from, (6) between, (7) on, (8) side, (9) right, and (10) left.

PRACTICE 9

Study the following paragraph from a college anatomy and physiology textbook. Choose a word from the box to fill in each blank with a signal word that shows the relationship between ideas. Use each word once.

above	at the level	internal	lengthwise	planes
along	front	into	middle	through

Textbook
Skills

Body Planes and Sections

When preparing to look at the **(1)** _____ structures of the body, medical students make a section, or cut. When the section is made **(2)** _____ the body wall or an organ, it is made **(3)** _____ an imaginary line called a plane. Because the body is three-dimensional, we can refer to three types of planes or sections that lie at right angles to one another.

A sagittal (saj'i-tal) section is a cut along the **(4)** _____, or longitudinal, plane of the body, dividing the body **(5)** _____ right and left parts. If the cut is down the median or **(6)** _____ plane of the body and the right and left parts are equal in size, it is called a median, or midsagittal, section.

A frontal section is a cut along a lengthwise plane that divides the body or an organ into anterior or **(7)** _____ and posterior or back parts. It is also called a coronal (ko-ro' nal) section.

A transverse section is a cut along a horizontal plane, dividing the body or organ into superior or **(8)** _____ and inferior or below parts. It is also called a cross section.

Sectioning a body or one of its organs along different **(9)** _____ often results in very different views. For example, a transverse section of the body trunk **(10)** _____ of the kidneys would show kidney structure in cross section very nicely; a frontal section of the body trunk would show a different view of kidney anatomy; and a midsagittal section would miss the kidneys completely.

—Adapted from Marieb, *Essentials of Human Anatomy and Physiology*, 9th ed., p. 17.

VISUAL VOCABULARY

This image shows the _____ view of the nerve supply of the upper body. The surface anatomy of the body is semi-transparent and tinted red.

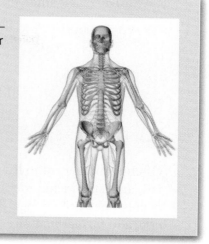

   a. median
   b. anterior
   c. transverse

—From Marieb, Essentials of Human Anatomy and Physiology, 9th ed.

PRACTICE 10

The following paragraph uses space order to discuss satellites in space. Complete the paragraph by inserting transitions. Fill in each blank with a word from the box. Use each word once.

above	from	high	into	over

Engineers design satellites to support instruments flown in space. Satellites must be light enough to be carried **(1)** _____ space on rockets, yet strong enough to withstand the forces of launching. Earth-observing satellites observe our planet **(2)** _____ paths called orbits, many of which are greater than 400 miles **(3)** _____ the ground. That distance is at least as far as Washington, D.C. to Boston, Massachusetts. Satellites are so **(4)** _____ above Earth and travel so quickly that, in the right orbit, a satellite can pass **(5)** _____ every part of Earth once every few days. Such orbits allow satellites to study and take pictures of all of Earth's features:

land, plant life, oceans, clouds, and polar ice. Some satellites, such as those used for weather forecasting, are placed in fixed orbits to look at Earth continuously.

—Adapted from United States, *Our Mission to Planet Earth: A Guide to Teaching Earth System Science.* NASA. March 1994. 14 Jan 2010. http://kids.earth.nasa.gov/guide/earth_system.pdf.

The Listing Pattern

Often authors want to list a series or set of reasons, details, or points. These details are listed in an order that the author has chosen. Changing the order of the details does not change their meaning. Transitions of addition, such as *and, also,* and *furthermore,* are generally used to indicate a *listing pattern.*

Listing pattern
Idea 1
Idea 2
Idea 3

Weightlifting builds *and* tones muscles; it *also* builds bone density.

Notice that in this statement, two words signal the addition of ideas: *and* and *also.* Transitions of addition signal that the writer is using a second idea along with the first one. The writer presents an idea and then adds other ideas to deepen or clarify the first idea.

Addition Transitions Used in the Listing Pattern				
also	final	for one thing	last of all	second
and	finally	furthermore	moreover	third
another	first	in addition	next	
besides	first of all	last	one	

EXAMPLE Refer to the box of addition transitions used in the listing pattern. Complete the following paragraph with transitions that show the appropriate relationship between sentences.

Preventing Childhood Obesity: A Community Checklist

Today, more than 12.5 million children—17 percent of children and adolescents ages 2 to 19—are overweight. Communities can hold events and create places that help kids stay active and encourage healthy eating habits. **(1)** _____, a community can help kids stay active. **(2)** _____, community leaders can work with schools to increase physical activity. **(3)** _____, a community can create and maintain community recreation areas, **(4)** _____ city planners can increase the "walkability" of the community. **(5)** _____, a community can encourage healthy eating habits. **(6)** _____ supporting the places people can get healthy food they can afford, community members can **(7)** _____ work with grocery stores and businesses to limit displays and ads of junk foods and candy aimed at children. **(8)** _____, faith-based community organizations can help promote healthy eating habits. Churches or other place of worship can encourage members of the congregation to bring healthier meal options such as more fruits and vegetables to functions. **(9)** _____, they can eliminate junk food in children's worship and fellowship programs. **(10)** _____, a community can promote healthy choices. Businesses, schools, and parents can create community groups to address childhood overweight and obesity.

—Adapted from Office of the Surgeon General, "Childhood Obesity Prevention: Community Checklist." U. S. Department of Health and Human Services. 13 Jan. 2010. http://www.surgeongeneral.gov/obesityprevention/pledges/community.html.

EXPLANATION Compare your answers to the following: (1) First, (2) For one thing, (3) In addition, (4) and, (5) Next, (6) Besides, (7) also, (8) Furthermore, (9) Moreover, and (10) Finally.

This paragraph begins with a general idea that is then followed by three major supporting details. Not only is each major detail introduced with transition to show addition, but also many of the minor supporting details are also signaled by transitions that show addition.

PRACTICE 11

The following paragraph uses the listing thought pattern. Finish the outline that follows it by listing the major supporting details in their proper order. (Hint: Circle the addition transition words.)

The Value of Artifacts

[1]Artifacts reveal much about the people who made them and the time period in which they were made. [2]Studying artifacts is important for several reasons. [3]First, artifacts tell a story. [4]By thinking about the purpose and need of the particular object, we can learn about the nature of the humans who created the object. [5]Studying the great pyramids teaches us to appreciate the human drive and sacrifice that went into building such mammoth structures. [6]Second, artifacts connect us to the people who used them. [7]By thinking about the ways in which the objects were used, we begin to understand more about the people who used them. [8]Consider children's lunchboxes popular from 1950 to 1980. [9]These lunchboxes, decorated with images from popular children's television shows, reflect the profound influence television has had on young children. [10]Finally, artifacts reflect and cause change. [11]Think of a typewriter and a computer. [12]Both are used for many of the same purposes; both reflect the change of their times, and both caused great change as well.

—Adapted from Lubar & Kendrick, "Looking at Artifacts, Thinking About History."
Artifact & Analysis. Smithsonian Center for Education and Museum Studies. 7 June
2010 http://www.smithsonianeducation.org/idealabs/ap/essays/looking.htm

The Value of Artifacts

Studying artifacts is important for several reasons.

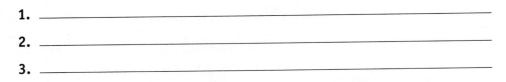

1. _____

2. _____

3. _____

PRACTICE 12

Determine the logical order of the following sentences. Write **1** by the sentence that should come first, **2** by the sentence that should come second, **3** by the sentence that should come third, and so on. (Circle the classification listing words.)

Avoiding Ageism

Textbook
Skills

_____ Third, avoid implying that relationships are no longer important. Older people continue to be interested in relationships.

_____ To avoid ageism, be on guard against the following:

_____ Ageism signifies discrimination against the old.

_____ Next, don't assume you have to refresh an older person's memory each time you see the person.

_____ Finally, don't speak in abnormally high volume; don't maintain an overly close physical distance.

_____ First, avoid talking down to a person because he or she is older. Older people are not slow; most people remain mentally alert well into old age.

—Adapted from DeVito, _Essentials of Human Communication_, pp. 93–94
© 2002. Reproduced by permission of Pearson Education, Inc.

The Classification Pattern

Authors use the **classification pattern** to sort ideas into smaller groups and describe the traits of each group. Each smaller group, called a _subgroup_, is based on shared traits or characteristics. The author lists each subgroup and describes its traits.

Because groups and subgroups are listed, transitions of addition are used in this thought pattern. These transitions are coupled with words that indicate classes or groups. Examples of classification signal words are _first type_, _second kind_, and _another group_.

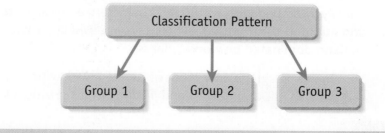

Transitions Used in the Classification Pattern		
another (group, kind, type)	first (group, categories, kind, type)	order
characteristics	second (group, class, kind, type)	traits

EXAMPLE Determine the logical order for the following sentences. Write **1** by the sentence that should come first, **2** by the sentence that should come second, **3** by the sentence that should come third, and **4** by the sentence that should come last. (Hint: Circle the classification transition words.)

Types of Wetlands

_____ Another type of wetland is the marsh, which is frequently or continually swamped with water; it is characterized by soft-stemmed vegetation adapted to saturated soil conditions.

_____ One type of wetland is a bog, one of North America's most distinctive wetlands; it is characterized by spongy peat deposits, acidic waters, and a floor covered by a thick carpet of sphagnum moss.

_____ Finally, a swamp is a type of wetland dominated by woody plants.

_____ *Wetlands* is a general term that includes several types of vital links between water and land.

—Adapted from U.S. Environmental Protection Agency, "America's Wetlands."

EXPLANATION Compare your answers to the sentences arranged in the proper order in the following paragraph. The transition words are in bold print.

Types of Wetlands

    [1]*Wetlands* is a general term that includes several types of vital links between water and land. [2]**One type** of wetland is a bog, one of North America's most distinctive wetlands; it is characterized by spongy peat deposits, acidic waters, and a floor covered by a thick carpet of sphagnum moss. [3]**Another type** of wetland is the marsh, which is frequently or continually swamped with water; it is characterized by soft-stemmed vegetation adapted to saturated soil conditions. [4]**Finally**, a swamp is a **type** of wetland dominated by woody plants.

    In this paragraph, transitions of addition work with the classification signal words. In this case, *another* and *finally* convey the order of the types listed.

PRACTICE 13

The following paragraph uses the classification thought pattern. Fill in the outline that follows by giving the missing details in their proper order. (Hint: Circle the classification transition words.)

Types of Volcanic Eruptions

[1]During an episode of activity, a volcano commonly displays a distinctive pattern or type of behavior. [2]One type of eruption is a Vesuvian eruption; during this type of eruption, great quantities of ash-laden gas are violently discharged. [3]These gases form a cauliflower-shaped cloud high above the volcano. [4]A second kind of eruption is the Strombolian. [5]In a Strombolian-type eruption, huge clots of molten lava burst from the summit crater to form luminous arcs through the sky. [6]The lava collects on the flanks of the cone, and then lava clots combine to stream down the slopes in fiery rivulets. [7]Another kind of eruption is the Vulcanian type. [8]In this eruption, a dense cloud of ash-laden gas explodes from the crater and rises high above the peak. [9]Steaming ash forms a whitish cloud near the upper level of the cone. [10]A fourth kind of eruption is a Peléan or Nuée Ardente (glowing cloud) eruption. [11]A large amount of gas, dust, ash, and incandescent lava fragments are blown out of a central crater, fall back, and form tongue-like glowing avalanches. [12]These avalanches move down slope at speeds as great as 100 miles per hour.

—Adapted from U.S. Geological Survey, "Types of Volcanic Eruptions."

Types of Volcanic Eruptions

1. _____

2. _____

3. _____

4. _____

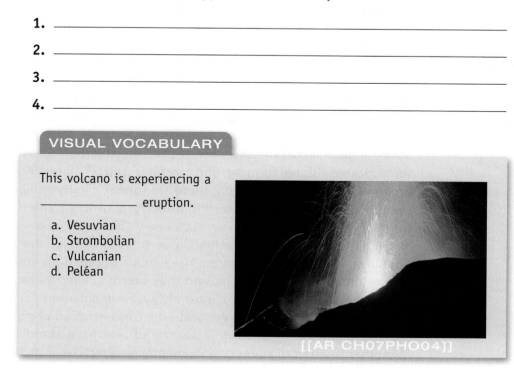

VISUAL VOCABULARY

This volcano is experiencing a _____ eruption.

a. Vesuvian
b. Strombolian
c. Vulcanian
d. Peléan

[[AR CH07PHO04]]

PRACTICE 14

The following paragraph uses the classification thought pattern. Complete the concept map by giving the missing details in their proper order. (Hint: Circle the classification transition words.)

Textbook
Skills

Types of Societies

[1]Several types of societies emerged in Latin America and the Caribbean prior to the European Conquest of the sixteenth century. [2]The first group, bands, are small-scale and highly mobile societies, typically numbering several dozen households related through kinship ties. [3]Bands gather edible wild plants, as well as occasionally hunt game. [4]Members have an equal right to the resources in their territories. [5]And there is an absence of political and coercive power, and of institutional-ized political offices and leadership. [6]For the greater part of history, most human societies were organized into bands. [7]At the moment of the European Conquest, some bands or foraging societies were present in northern Mexico, but more were in Amazonia, southern Chile, and southern Argentina. [8]The second type, tribes, are larger and are often less mobile. [9]Tribes are typically comprised of distinct groups, whose members claim a kinship to each other. [10]Tribes tend to cultivate plants and raise livestock. [11]Tribes display formal political positions and clearly recognizable political leaders, whose major role is to mediate disputes. [12]Many tribal groups still exist in Latin America, especially in Amazonia. [13]Another type of society is the chiefdoms. [14]Chiefdoms are much larger societies. [15]Sometimes chiefdoms number in the hundreds or thousands of households. [16]This society has control over wider, larger landscapes. [17]Higher population densities mean that the chiefdom develops more sophisticated fishing, farming, and ranching skills. [18]There is political and economic inequality. [19]Typically, there are formal, clearly named political positions and hereditary leadership or political offices ("chiefs"). [20]And, for the first time, coercive power surfaces. [21]Chiefdoms were widespread in Latin America and the Caribbean at the moment of the European Conquest. [22]Finally, states often have huge populations divided into many culturally distinct groups, and they exercise rule over much larger, far-flung territories. [23]States almost always have emerged through con-flict and warfare; they display an extreme concentration of political and coercive power; they are highly structured and have standing armies. [24]Another key trait of states is monumental architecture. [25]These building

programs showed the state's ability to wrench labor from large segments of the population.

—Adapted from Sanabria, *The Anthropology of Latin America and the Caribbean*, pp. 50–52.

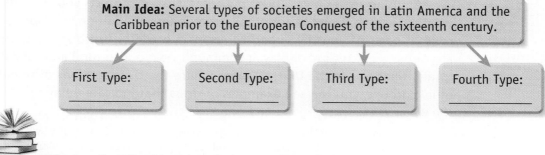

Main Idea: Several types of societies emerged in Latin America and the Caribbean prior to the European Conquest of the sixteenth century.

First Type: _____

Second Type: _____

Third Type: _____

Fourth Type: _____

Textbook Skills

Thought Patterns in Textbooks

Textbook authors often use transitions to make relationships between ideas clear and easy to understand. However, often an author will use more than one type of transition. For example, classification combines words that indicate addition and types. Sometimes addition and time words are used in the same paragraph or passage for a specific purpose. Furthermore, authors may mix thought patterns in the same paragraph or passage. Finally, be aware that relationships between ideas still exist even when transition words are not explicitly stated. The effective reader looks for the author's primary thought pattern.

EXAMPLE Read the following paragraphs from college textbooks. Circle the transitions or signal words used in each paragraph. Then identify the primary thought pattern used in the paragraph.

A.

Textbook Skills

A Dangerous Diet

Depriving the body of food for prolonged periods forces it to make adjustments to prevent the shutdown of organs. The body depletes its energy reserves to obtain the necessary fuels. The body first turns to protein tissue in order to maintain its supply of glucose. As this occurs, weight is lost rapidly because protein contains only half as many calories per pound as fat. At the same time, significant water stores are lost. Over time, the body begins to run out of liver tissue, heart muscle, blood, and so on, as these readily available substances are burned to supply energy.

—Adapted from Donatelle, *Health: the Basics*, 5th ed., p. 271.

_____ The primary thought pattern of the paragraph is
a. time order.
b. classification.

B.

Textbook
Skills

Clothing

Clothing serves a variety of purposes. First, it protects you from the weather and, in sports like football, from injury. In addition, it helps you conceal parts of your body and so serves a modesty function. Clothing also serves as a cultural display. It communicates your cultural and subcultural affiliations. In the United States, where there are so many different ethnic groups, you can see examples of dress that indicate what country the wearers are from.

—Adapted from DeVito, *Interpersonal Communication Book*, p. 204 © 2009 by Pearson Education, Inc. Reproduced by permission of Pearson Education, Inc.

_____ The primary thought pattern of the paragraph is
a. time order.
b. listing.

C.

Textbook
Skills

Types of Interest Groups

Whether they are lobbying politicians or appealing to the public, interest groups are everywhere in the American political system. As with other aspects of American politics and policymaking, political scientists loosely categorize interest groups into clusters. Among the most important clusters are those that deal with economic issues, environmental concerns, equality issues, and the interests of consumers. A study of these four distinct types of interest groups will give you a good picture of the American interest group system.

—Adapted from Edwards, Wattenberg, & Lineberry, *Government in America: People, Politics, and Policy,* 5th ed., p. 253.

_____ The primary thought pattern of the paragraph is
a. time order.   b. classification.

PRACTICE 15

Read the following paragraph from a college communications textbook. Circle the transitions or signal words used in the paragraph. Then identify the primary thought pattern used.

Culture Shock

Textbook
Skills

Culture shock refers to the psychological reaction you experience when you're in a culture very different from your own. Anthropologist Kalervo Oberg, who first used the term, notes that it occurs in stages. Stage one is the honeymoon. At first you experience fascination with the new culture and its people. This stage is characterized by cordiality and friendship in these early and superficial relationships. Stage two is the crisis. Here the differences between your own culture and the new one create problems. This is the stage at which you experience the actual shock of a new culture. Stage three is the recovery. During this period, you gain the skills necessary to function. You learn the language and ways of the new culture. Stage four is the adjustment. At this final stage, you adjust to and come to enjoy the new culture and experiences. You may still experience periodic difficulties and strains, but on the whole, the experience is pleasant.

—Adapted from DeVito, *Interpersonal Communication Book*, p. 59 © 2009 by Pearson Education, Inc. Reproduced by permission of Pearson Education, Inc.

_____The primary thought pattern of the paragraph is
    a. time order.
    b. classification.

APPLICATIONS

Application 1: Identifying Transitions

Fill in each blank with one of the words from the box. Use each word once.

another	finally	furthermore	next

1. Research has shown that cancers of the lip, tongue, mouth, throat, larynx, lung, and esophagus are connected to cigar smoking. _____, facts strongly suggest a link between cigar smoking and cancer of the pancreas.

—National Cancer Institute, "Questions and Answers About Cigar Smoking and Cancer."

2. Some of the television shows that have become classic favorites focus on relationships. One such show was *I Love Lucy*, which was based on the

marriage of Lucy and Ricky and their friendship with Ethel and Fred; _____ more recent example is *How I Met Your Mother*, which is based on the friendships among a group of friends.

3. Arturo's morning routine rarely varies: immediately after he wakes up, he makes his coffee. _____, he fetches the newspaper, feeds the animals, and wakes up the children. _____, he reads the paper while he drinks his coffee.

Application 2: Identifying Transitions

Fill in each blank with one of the words from the box. Use each word once.

afterward	currently	eventually	previously

1. Rebecca and Sean drove 120 miles round trip to see John Mayer in concert. _____, they agreed that the trip had been well worth the time, cost, and effort.

2. Juan came to the United States without money, family, or friends. He found a job, worked hard, and saved his money. _____, he bought a home and brought his family from Mexico to live with him.

3. In the United States, more than 550,000 people have died as a result of AIDS since the epidemic began in 1981. Experts believe that nationwide, over one million people _____ live with HIV, the virus that causes AIDS.

4. George finally went to a dealer's lot and bought a new car that had never been owned before—a red convertible Mustang. _____, he had bought only used cars.

Application 3: Identifying Thought Patterns

Identify the thought pattern suggested by each of the following topic sentences.

_____ **1.** Alcoholics Anonymous recommends the following 12-step recovery process to overcome addiction.
  a. time order
  b. classification

_____ **2.** Psychologists often discuss personality by types.
a. time order   b. classification

_____ **3.** Breaking a bad habit is a multistep process.
a. time order   b. listing

_____ **4.** Health care costs are soaring for several reasons.
a. space order   b. listing

_____ **5.** A health spa offers several types of services aimed at rejuvenating the body and the spirit.
a. space order   b. classification

_____ **6.** Five points need to be made about the Marshall Plan.
a. classification   b. listing

_____ **7.** Hearing involves three stages.
a. time order   b. classification

_____ **8.** Columbus set sail toward the West in search of new trade routes.
a. time order   b. space order

_____ **9.** The United States has three branches of government.
a. time order   b. classification

_____ **10.** Several forms of psychological stress affect a person's well-being.
a. space order   b. classification

REVIEW TEST 1   Score (number correct) _____ × 10 = _____%

Transition Words and Thought Patterns

Match each of the thought patterns to the appropriate group of transition words. Thought patterns will be used more than once.

a. time order
b. space order
c. listing
d. classification

_____ **1.** one type, several kinds, another group

_____ **2.** first, second, third, fourth

_____ **3.** before, after, while, during

_____ **4.** behind, below, above, over

_____ **5.** currently, eventually, previously

_____ **6.** furthermore, moreover, besides

_____ **7.** characteristics, traits, order

_____ **8.** beneath, nearby, within

_____ **9.** here, there

_____ **10.** and, also, for one thing

REVIEW TEST 2   Score (number correct) _____ × 10 = _____%

Transition Words

Select a transition word for each of the blanks. Then identify the type of transition you chose.

A. Pilates develops a strong and supple spine by extending the space _____ each vertebra.

_____ **1.** The best transition word for the sentence is
a. between. c. before.
b. after.

_____ **2.** The relationship between the ideas is one of
a. classification. b. space order.

B. Proper posture is a matter of correctly positioning your body; place the joints between your big and second toes under your knees; pull your abdominals

_____ your spine, relax your shoulders down, and lengthen your body through the crown of your head.

_____ **3.** The best transition word for the sentence is
a. toward. c. one.
b. eventually.

_____ **4.** The relationship between the ideas is one of
a. space order. b. addition.

C. The best course of action to take _____ one has made a mistake is to admit it, learn from it, and avoid making it again.

_____ **5.** The best transition word for the sentence is
a. when. c. since.
b. before.

_____ **6.** The relationship between the ideas is one of
  a. listing.   b. time order.

D. A character in a work of fiction is often studied on the basis of two groups of traits. The first group identifies whether the character is dynamic and changes

or is static and stays the same. The _____ identifies whether the character is round and fully developed or remains flat with only one main personality feature.

_____ **7.** The best transition word or phrase for the sentence above is
  a. additional part.   c. later time.
  b. second group.

_____ **8.** The relationship between the ideas is one of
  a. classification.   b. time order.

E. A monarch butterfly has four stages in its life cycle. The first stage begins

_____ a female monarch mates and lays eggs on leaves. The second stage occurs when a tiny larva hatches and begins to eat its eggshell and the leaves of the plant. The larva changes into the pupa or chrysalis, the third major stage of the monarch's life cycle. The final stage involves the adult monarch emerging from its chrysalis to dry its wings.

VISUAL VOCABULARY

This insect is in what stage of its life

cycle? _____

  a. egg
  b. larva
  c. chrysalis

_____ **9.** The best transition word for the sentence is
  a. before.   c. as.
  b. and.

_____ **10.** The relationship between the ideas is one of
  a. time order.   b. addition.

REVIEW TEST 3

Score (number correct) _____ × 25 = _____%

Transitions and Thought Patterns

Textbook
Skills

Read the following passage from a college psychology textbook.

Where Are You in the Career Development Process?

[1]Have you ever wondered what type of work you are best suited for? [2]If so, you may want to begin your quest for an answer by looking at two models of career development, the process of choosing and adjusting to a particular career. [3]Recommendations about what you might do to enhance your search for the ideal career can be derived from both. [4]Ultimately, though, the degree to which you are satisfied with your career may depend on how you integrate your work into your life as a whole.

Holland's Personality Types

[5]The work of John Holland has been very influential in shaping psychologists' ideas about personality and career. [6]Holland proposes six basic personality types: realistic, investigative, artistic, social, enterprising, and conventional. [7]His research shows that each of the six types is associated with work preferences. [8]First, realistic types are aggressive, masculine, and physically strong, often with low verbal or interpersonal skills. [9]The work preferences of this type include mechanical activities and tool use. [10]They often choose jobs such as mechanic, electrician, or surveyor. [11]Second, investigative types are oriented toward thinking (particularly abstract thinking), organizing, and planning. [12]They are often low in social skills. [13]Their work preferences include ambiguous, challenging tasks. [14]They often choose to become a scientist or engineer. [15]Third, artistic types are asocial. [16]They prefer unstructured, highly individual activity; often they become artists. [17]Fourth, the social types are extraverted, people-oriented, sociable, and need attention; additionally, they avoid intellectual activity and dislike highly ordered activity. [18]The social type likes

working with people in service jobs like nursing and education. [19]Fifth, the enterprising type is highly verbal and dominating; they enjoy organizing and directing others. [20]They are persuasive and strong leaders. [21]They often choose a career in sales. [22]Finally, the conventional type prefers structured activities and subordinate roles; likes clear guidelines; accurate and precise. [23]They may choose an occupation such as bookkeeping or filing.

[24]As Holland's theory predicts, people whose personality matches their job are also more likely to be satisfied with their work. [25]Thus, a personality assessment may help you make an appropriate occupational choice and give you confidence about the decision.

Super's Career Development Stages

[26]Psychologist Donald Super proposed that career development happens in stages that begin in infancy. [27]First comes the growth stage (from birth to 14 years), in which you learn about your abilities and interests. [28]Next is the exploratory stage, roughly between the ages of 15 and 24. [29]According to Super, there's a lot of trial and error in this stage, so job changes happen frequently. [30]Next is the establishment stage (also called the stabilization stage), from 25 to 45. [31]This stage begins with learning how things work in your career, the culture of your organization, and progression through the early steps of the career ladder. [32]Sometimes, additional formal training is required during this stage. [33]Setting goals is also important in this stage. [34]You must decide how far you want to go and how you intend to get there. [35]Mentoring by an experienced co-worker often helps you negotiate this stage successfully. [36]Once an individual has become well established in a career, she or he enters the maintenance phase (age 45 through retirement), in which the goal is to protect and maintain the gains made in earlier years. [37]Of course, in today's rapidly changing economy, people are often required to change careers. [38]Thus, an individual may reenter the exploratory stage at any time. [39]As with most stage theories, the ages associated with Super's stages of career development are less important than the sequence of the stages.

—Adapted from Wood, et al, *Mastering the World of Psychology*, Text from p. 275 © 2008 Pearson Education, Inc. Reproduced by permission of Pearson Education, Inc.

_____ **1.** The thought pattern of the second paragraph (sentences 5–23) is
   a. process. c. narration.
   b. classification. d. space order.

_____ **2.** The thought pattern of the third paragraph (sentences 26–39) is
   a. process. c. narration.
   b. classification. d. space order.

_____ **3.** The relationship of ideas within sentence 17 is
  a. time order.   c. space order.
  b. addition.

_____ **4.** The relationship of ideas between sentences 27 and 28 is
  a. time order.   c. space order.
  b. addition.

VISUAL VOCABULARY

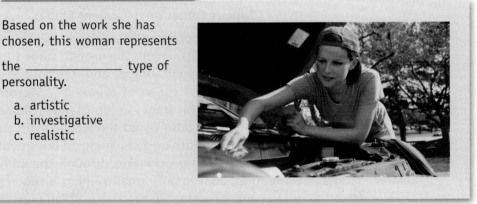

Based on the work she has chosen, this woman represents the _____ type of personality.

  a. artistic
  b. investigative
  c. realistic

WHAT DO YOU THINK?

Based on the information in the passage, what is your personality type? What stage of career development are you currently in? Assume you are applying for a scholarship from a local civic group such as the Rotary Club. Write a brief essay that describes your career goals based on your personality type and your current stage of career development.

REVIEW TEST 4

Score (number correct) _____ × 10 = _____%

Transition Words and Thought Patterns

The following essay is from a college social science textbook. Before you read, skim the passage and answer the Before Reading questions. Read the essay. Then answer the After Reading questions.

Textbook
Skills

The Early History of Human Motivation

[1]In your imagination, **transport** yourself back 100,000 years to the banks of the local river in your area. [2]Your tribe spent most of the day traveling up and down the river's banks hunting and fishing and gathering grubs, fruits, and other edibles. [3]However, not everyone worked equally hard. [4]Some individuals produced a lot of food for the tribe, while others produced none at all. [5]You may have **reflected** to yourself, "Some people in our tribe are not motivated," or "I wish everybody in our tribe were as motivated as I am." [6]In other words, you invented the concept of motivation to account for these differences in behavior. [7]The point of this imaginary scene is that humans have probably been thinking about their own and others' motivation for a long time, certainly before the beginning of psychology in 1879.

[8]Two bumper stickers from a much later time read: "If it feels good, do it" _____ "If it's no fun, why do it?" [9]Are these **edicts** accurate descriptions of human conduct? [10]If so, are we merely pursuers of pleasure and avoiders of pain? [11]Some early philosophers believe that we are. [12]The study of human motivation has a long history.

[13]Nearly 2,400 years ago, Greek philosophers were already discussing motivation under a principle known as hedonism. [14]Hedonism is the pursuit of pleasure and the avoidance of pain. [15]Although today the term often refers to sensory pleasures derived from food, drink, and sex, for philosophers this term meant striving for the greater good. [16]The phrase "the pursuit of happiness" from the Declaration of Independence most likely means a striving for the greater good. [17]It is doubtful that the signers of the Declaration meant for people to stop working and party all the time. [18]While it is true that sensory pleasure might be attained from spending your tuition money to pay for nightly partying, a hedonically greater benefit would result if that money were used to pay for your tuition and subsequent education.

[19]One of the first proponents of hedonism was the famous Greek philosopher Socrates (470–399 B.C.), who claimed a person should follow a course of action for which pleasure exceeds pain. [20]Further, Socrates claimed that the only reason a person would not do so is because he lacks complete knowledge of the pleasure or pain that can result. [21]For Democritus (460–370 B.C), it was both natural and good for people to follow this course. [22]However, he could not identify what was pleasurable or painful apart from a person's behavior. [23]Something was pleasurable if an individual strived for it, and something was painful if an individual avoided it. [24]But what was pleasurable or painful could differ for each

individual. [25]No matter what these things were, pleasure was to be pursued, and pain was to be avoided.

[26]One might get the idea that Socrates and Democritus meant that we should "eat, drink, and be merry as if there is no tomorrow." [27]On the contrary, they felt that our pursuits should be followed in moderation. [28]They believed that moderation would lead to greater pleasure in the long run. [29]This idea was developed further a century later by Epicurus (341–271 B.C.). [30]He believed that pleasure and pain average out. [31]Thus, we might give up certain intense pleasures if subsequent pain of greater degree is a result. [32]For instance, an individual might drink alcohol in moderation to avoid the painful aftereffects of drinking too much. [33]Likewise, moderation may require experiencing pain prior to pleasure. [34]A person may endure immediate pain because longer-lasting pleasure may result. [35]For example, a student may give up the short-term benefit of earning money at an unskilled job to earn a college degree; her hope is that the college degree will lead to more meaningful and fruitful employment later.

—Adapted from Deckers, Lambert, *Motivation: Biological, Psychological, and Environmental*, pp. 22–23. Published by Allyn and Bacon, Boston, MA. Copyright © 2001 by Pearson Education.

BEFORE READING
Vocabulary in Context

_____ **1.** The word **transport** in sentence 1 means
    a. delight.   c. carry.
    b. convey.   d. pass.

_____ **2.** The word **reflected** in sentence 5 means
    a. thought.   c. fumed.
    b. counted.   d. planned.

_____ **3.** The word **edicts** in sentence 9 means
    a. actions.   c. stickers.
    b. steps.   d. statements.

AFTER READING
Concept Maps

4. Finish the concept map by filling in the missing idea with information from the passage.

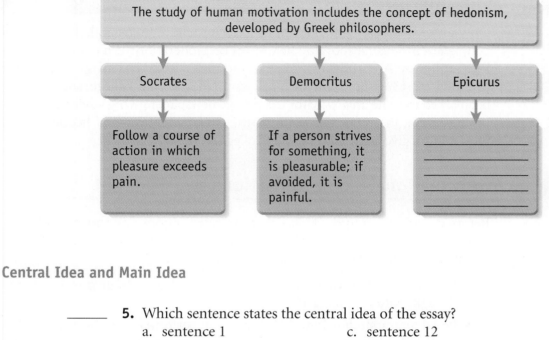

The study of human motivation includes the concept of hedonism, developed by Greek philosophers.

Socrates

Democritus

Epicurus

Follow a course of action in which pleasure exceeds pain.

If a person strives for something, it is pleasurable; if avoided, it is painful.

_____
_____
_____
_____
_____

Central Idea and Main Idea

_____ **5.** Which sentence states the central idea of the essay?
a. sentence 1   c. sentence 12
b. sentence 6   d. sentence 13

Supporting Details

_____ **6.** What type of supporting detail is sentence 35?
a. major supporting detail   b. minor supporting detail

Transitions and Thought Patterns

_____ **7.** The word **while** in sentence 4 is a transition that shows
a. time order.   b. comparison and contrast.

_____ **8.** What thought pattern is suggested by sentence 12?
a. time order   b. space order

_____ **9.** What is the relationship between sentence 19 and sentence 20?
a. time order   b. addition

_____ **10.** Which is the best transition for the blank in sentence 8?
a. and   c. first
b. a type of   d. finally

WHAT DO YOU THINK?

Do you see evidence of hedonism in today's society? In general, do you think people are motivated more by hedonism or moderation? What about on college campuses? Are students more likely to make decisions based on hedonism or moderation? Assume you are a peer counselor at your college, and you have been asked to write an article for the college newspaper giving advice to incoming freshman. In one or two paragraphs, using the concepts of hedonism and moderation, give advice to first-year college students.

After Reading About Transitions and Thought Patterns

Before you move on to the Mastery Tests on transitions and thought patterns, take time to reflect on your learning and performance by answering the following questions. Write your answers in your notebook.

- How has my knowledge base or prior knowledge about transitions and thought patterns changed?

- Based on my studies, how do I think I will perform on the Mastery Test(s)? Why do I think my scores will be above average, average, or below average?

- Would I recommend this chapter to other students who want to learn more about transitions and thought patterns? Why or why not?

Test your understanding of what you have learned about thought patterns by completing the Chapter 7 Review Card in the insert near the end of the textbook.

CONNECT TO **myreadinglab**

To check your progress in meeting Chapter 7's learning outcomes, log in to **www.myreadinglab.com**, and try the following activities.

- The "Patterns of Organization" section of MyReadingLab gives additional information about transitions and patterns of organization. The section provides a model, practices, activities, and tests. To access this resource, click on the "Study Plan" tab. Then click on "Patterns of Organization." Then click on the following links as needed: "Overview," "Model," "Signal Words (Flash Animation)," "Other Patterns of Organization (Flash Animation)," "Practice," and "Tests."

- To measure your mastery of the content in this chapter, complete the tests in the "Patterns of Organization" section and click on Gradebook to find your results.

A. The following items are from a college math textbook. Fill in the blanks with the correct transition word from the box. Use each word once.

before	during	in	then	when

1–2. Reading and highlighting a section of your textbook _____ your instructor lectures on it allows you to maximize your learning and understanding _____ the lecture.

3–4. Try to keep one section ahead of your syllabus. _____ you study ahead of your lectures, you can _____ concentrate on what is being explained in them instead of trying to write everything down.

5. Highlight key points _____ your textbook as you study.

—Adapted from Bittinger & Beecher, *Introductory and Intermediate Algebra*, 2nd ed., p. 43.

B. Read the following paragraph from a college communications textbook. Fill in each blank with the correct transition word from the box. Use each word once.

frequently	immediate	past	then	when

Gunnysacking

A gunnysack is a large bag, usually made of burlap. As a conflict strategy, gunnysacking refers to the practice of storing up grievances to unload them at another time. The (**6**) _____ occasion may be relatively simple (or so it may seem at first), such as someone's coming home late without calling. Instead of arguing about this, the gunnysacker unloads all (**7**) _____ grievances: the birthday

Textbook Skills

315

you forgot two years ago, the time you arrived late for dinner last month, and the hotel reservations you forgot to make. As you probably know from experience, gunnysacking leads to more gunnysacking. (8) _____ one person gunnysacks, the other person often does so as well. (9) _____ two people end up dumping their stored up grievances on one another. (10) _____, the original problem never gets addressed. Instead, resentment and hostility build up.

—Adapted from DeVito, *Essentials of Human Communication*, p. 177 © 2002.
Reproduced by permission of Pearson Education, Inc.

A. Fill in each blank with the correct transition word from the box. Use each word once.

another	during	in	occasionally	often

1. Although it doesn't happen frequently, American society has _____ been gripped by fear, and its responses have not done credit to the nature of freedom.

2. The Red Scare, the hunt for communist traitors living in America, is one example of a fear that occurred following World War I. _____ this time, hundreds of innocent immigrants were rounded up, imprisoned, and deported, for no reason other than fear of their allegedly radical ideas.

3. Even though the great fears of the first Red Scare were unfounded, the conflict between the United States and its allies and the Soviet Union and its allies, known as the Cold War, unleashed _____ Red Scare in the late 1940s and early 1950s.

4. The hunt for alleged traitors started during World War II and was furthered by congressional committees. These committees _____ abused their powers and harassed people who did not share their political views.

5. In February 1950, Senator Joseph McCarthy of Wisconsin began a witch hunt for so-called traitors; he claimed that communists were working _____ the State Department. For four years, he used his power improperly as he led a senate investigation. He and his aides made wild accusations, browbeat witnesses, ruined reputations, and threw mud at harmless people. Moreover, even the president of the United States was afraid to stand up to him.

—Adapted from U.S. Department of State,
"Censure of Senator Joseph McCarthy."

B. Read the following paragraph from a college social science textbook. Fill in each blank with the correct transition from the box. Then answer the question that follows it.

finally	one	second	third

Textbook
Skills

Relax and Listen

¹Learning to relax is among the best ways to improve concentration during listening. ²A variety of physical and mental exercises will help you sustain attention as you listen. ³**(6)** _____ activity is relaxing your muscles. ⁴Tighten a single muscle group such as your neck, your lower arm, or your foot for five or six seconds, and then completely relax it. ⁵Begin at the extremities of your body and work inward. ⁶You will realize that you were experiencing muscle stress as normal. ⁷**(7)** A _____ exercise is imagery. ⁸To relax before the listening session, vividly recall a positive experience; relive all of the sights, smells, and sounds. ⁹Your mind will relax as it focuses on these memories. ¹⁰This effect can also be reached through fantasy by calling up imaginary events or images. ¹¹A **(8)** _____ exercise is mental rehearsal, trying out in your mind various solutions to a stressful problem; when athletes have rehearsed mentally and see themselves winning, they have gone on to be highly successful. ¹²**(9)** _____, deep breathing clears your mind and enables you to relax; this technique is helpful for any stressful listening event.

—Adapted from Brownell, *Listening: Attitudes, Principles, and Skills*,
p. 88 © 2002 by Pearson Education, Inc. Reproduced
by permission of Pearson Education, Inc.

_____ **10.** The thought pattern of the paragraph is
  a. time order.   b. listing.

Name _____ Section _____

Date _____ Score (number correct) _____ × 10 = _____%

A. Read the following paragraph from a college mathematics textbook.

Textbook
Skills

A Five-Step Strategy for Solving Problems

[1]Many students fear solving mathematical problems so much that their thinking freezes with anxiety. [2]A five-step strategy can be very helpful in solving problems. [3]First, familiarize yourself with the problem situation; read it out loud or make and label a drawing, and assign a letter or variable to the unknown. [4]Second, translate the problem into an equation; use mathematical expressions and symbols and the letter or variable. [5]Third, solve the equation. [6]_____, check the answer in the original wording of the problem. [7]Finally, clearly state the answer to the problem with the appropriate units, such as dollars and cents or inches.

—Adapted from Bittinger/Beecher, *Introductory and Intermediate Algebra: Combined Approach*, Text Excerpt from p. 387 © 2003 Pearson Education, Inc. Reproduced by permission of Pearson Education, Inc.

_____ **1.** The transition word that best fits the blank in sentence 6 is
   a. First.
   b. Third.
   c. Next.

_____ **2.** The thought pattern used in the paragraph is
   a. classification.   b. time order.

3–8. Fill in the concept map with the topic sentence and major supporting details from the passage.

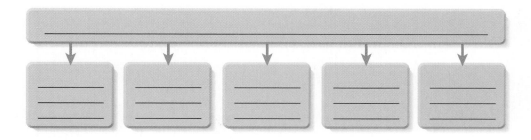

B. Read the following paragraph from a college English textbook.

Textbook
Skills

Learning the Stories Behind Words

¹Learning the roots of words will surely help you build your vocabulary. ²Another way is to learn the stories associated with some words. ³Many words have interesting stories connected with people, places, and myths, and most dictionaries include at least some information about words that came from mythology as well as those connected with people and places. ⁴_____, knowing the stories related to the words will help you remember their meanings and develop your vocabulary. ⁵One good example is the phrase *Achilles' heel*. ⁶If you know that the Greek hero Achilles was invulnerable except for one weak spot, his heel, you will know that *Achilles' heel* is a phrase meaning a small but important weakness.

—Adapted from DiYanni & Hoy, *The Scribner Handbook for Writers*, 3rd ed., p. 496.

_____ **9.** In this paragraph, the author
    a. lists a reason and example for learning the stories about words.
    b. explains step by step how to add words to your vocabulary.

_____ **10.** The transition word that best fits the blank in sentence 4 is
    a. First.
    b. Another.
    c. Furthermore.

Read the following passage from a college textbook about the environment. Fill in each blank with a transition from the box. Use each transition once. Then complete the concept map with information from the passage.

first	fourth type	one example	second type	third type

Textbook
Skills

Toxicants Come in Different Types

Toxicants can be classified based on their particular effects on health. **(1)** _____ are carcinogens, the best known. These are chemicals or types of radiation that cause cancer. In cancer, malignant cells grow uncontrollably, creating tumors, damaging the body's functioning, and often leading to death. In our society today, the greatest number of cancer cases is thought to result from carcinogens contained in cigarette smoke. Carcinogens can be difficult to identify because there may be a long lag time between exposure to the agent and the detectable onset of cancer.

Mutagens, a **(2)** _____, are chemicals that cause mutations in the DNA of organisms. Although most mutations have little or no effect, some can lead to severe problems, including cancer and other disorders. If mutations occur in an individual's sperm or egg cells, then the individual's offspring suffer the effects.

The **(3)** _____ of chemicals that cause harm to the unborn are called teratogens. Teratogens that affect the development of human embryos in the womb can cause birth defects. **(4)** _____ involves the drug thalidomide, developed in the 1950s as a sleeping pill and to prevent nausea during pregnancy. Tragically, the drug turned out to be a powerful teratogen, and caused birth defects in thousands of babies. Thalidomide was banned in the 1960s once scientists recognized this connection.

The (5) _____ of chemical toxicants, neurotoxins, assaults the nervous system. Neurotoxins include various heavy metals such as lead, mercury, and cadmium, as well as pesticides and some chemical weapons developed for use in war. A famous case of neurotoxin poisoning occurred in Japan, where a chemical factory dumped mercury waste into Minamata Bay between the 1930s and 1960s. Thousands of people there ate fish contaminated with the mercury and soon began suffering from slurred speech, loss of muscle control, sudden fits of laughter, and in some cases death. The company and the government eventually paid out about $5,000 in compensation to each poisoned resident.

—Adapted from Withgott & Brennan, *Essential Environment: The Science Behind the Stories*, 3rd ed., p. 218.

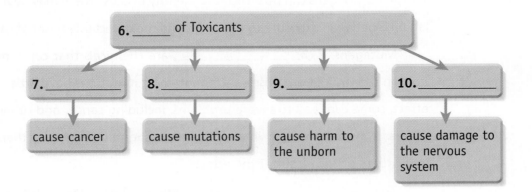

More Thought Patterns

LEARNING OUTCOMES

After studying this chapter you should be able to do the following:

1. Recognize the following relationships or thought patterns: *comparison, contrast, cause, effect, generalization and example, definition and example.*
2. Determine the relationships of ideas within a sentence.
3. Determine the relationships of ideas between sentences.
4. Determine the thought pattern used to organize a passage.
5. Evaluate the importance of transitions and thought patterns.
6. Use thought patterns to comprehend the author's main idea.

Before Reading About More Thought Patterns

In Chapter 7, you learned several important ideas that will help you as you work through this chapter. Use the following questions to call up your prior knowledge about transitions and thought patterns.

What are transitions? (Refer to page 272.) _____

_____

_____

What are thought patterns? (Refer to page 272.) _____

_____

_____

What is important to know about mixed thought patterns? Give an example from Chapter 7. (Refer to page 301.) _____

_____

_____

_____

You have learned that transitions and thought patterns show the relationships of ideas within sentences as well as between sentences and paragraphs, and you studied four common types: time order, space order, listing, and classification. In this chapter, we will explore some other common thought patterns:

- The comparison-and-contrast pattern
- The cause-and-effect pattern
- The generalization-and-example pattern
- The definition-and-example pattern

The Comparison-and-Contrast Pattern

Many ideas become clearer when they are thought of in relation to one another. For example, comparing the prices different grocery stores charge makes us smarter shoppers. Likewise, noting the difference between loving and selfish behavior helps us choose partners in life. The comparison-and-contrast pattern enables us to see these relationships. This section discusses both comparison and contrast, starting with comparison. The discussion then turns to the important and effective comparison-and-contrast pattern, in which these two basic ways of organizing ideas are combined when writing an explanation, a description, or an analysis.

Comparison

Comparison points out the ways in which two or more ideas are alike. Sample signal words are *similar, like*, and *just as*.

Words and Phrases of Comparison

alike	in a similar fashion	just as	resemble	similarly
as	in a similar manner	just like	same	
as well as	in like manner	like	similar	
equally	in the same way	likewise	similarity	

Here are some examples:

Just as we relate to others based on their personality traits, we tend to interact with our personal computers based on their performance.

Writing, **like** farming, follows a cycle of planting, growing, and reaping.

African and European artists use many of the **same** subjects in their art.

Each of these sentences has two topics that are similar in some way. The similarity is the author's main point. For example, the first sentence compares human personality traits to the way a personal computer performs. The comparison is introduced by the phrase *just as*. The second sentence compares the writing process to the farming process using the signal word *like*. And the third sentence compares the subjects African artists choose to the subjects European artists choose for their art.

When comparison is used to organize an entire paragraph, the pattern looks like the following chart.

Comparison Pattern		
Idea 1		**Idea 2**
Idea 1	*like*	Idea 2
Idea 1	*like*	Idea 2
Idea 1	*like*	Idea 2

EXAMPLE Determine a logical order for the following four sentences. Write **1** by the sentence that should come first, **2** by the sentence that should come second, **3** by the sentence that should come third, and **4** by the sentence that should come last. Then use the information to fill in the chart.

_____ Humans and mice both have about 30,000 genes.

_____ The genetic similarities between humans and mice support the use of mice in scientific research.

_____ Another important similarity is that 90 percent of genes linked to diseases are identical in the human and the mouse.

_____ In addition, 99 percent of the 30,000 genes in humans and mice are the same.

Genetic Similarities between Humans and Mice	
Humans	**Mice**
1. _____	1. _____
2. _____	2. _____
_____	_____
3. _____	3. _____
_____	_____

EXPLANATION Here are the sentences arranged in proper order. The organization and transition words are in bold type.

> The genetic **similarities** between humans and mice support the use of mice in scientific research. Humans and mice **both** have about 30,000 genes. **In addition**, 99 percent of the 30,000 genes in humans and mice are the same. **Another** important **similarity** is that 90 percent of genes linked to diseases are **identical** in the human and the mouse.

The addition signal words *in addition* and *another* provided important context clues for understanding the proper order of ideas. Compare your completed chart to the completed chart that follows.

Genetic Similarities between Humans and Mice	
Humans	**Mice**
1. have 30,000 genes	1. have 30,000 genes
2. share 99 percent of genes with mice	2. share 99 percent of genes with humans
3. have 90 percent of genes linked to diseases	3. have 90 percent of genes linked to diseases

PRACTICE 1

Complete the following ideas with a transition that shows comparison. Use each expression only once.

1. Physical fatigue affects the body; _____, mental stress affects the mind.

2. Jealousy destroys a relationship _____ thoroughly as a wildfire consumes a forest.

3. Compulsive gambling is an addiction _____ in some ways to drug addiction.

4. The toddler and the teenager often behave _____.

5. In her poem "Because I Could Not Stop for Death," Emily Dickinson writes that death _____ a gentleman.

PRACTICE 2

Read the following paragraph. Complete the ideas with transitions from the box that show comparisons. Use each word once.

both	likewise	similarities
in the same way	similar	

The Similarities between Christianity and Islam

Two of the most influential religions, Christianity and Islam, actually share many **(1)** _____. Both religions are monotheistic, worshipping one God, and the God of both religions is an all-powerful and all-knowing being. **(2)** _____ Islam and Christianity believe God has a special relationship with humans. Muslims and Christians have a **(3)** _____ view of God as the creator to whom they submit in obedience. Islam and Christianity share a moral code based on a Covenant, or agreement, established by God. Both religions view Satan **(4)** _____, as an enemy of God and humanity. **(5)** _____, Muslims and Christians agree that humans have free will and are going to face a final judgment based on their actions in light of God's moral code. In a similar fashion, both believe in the return of Jesus Christ at the end of this age to defeat Satan and judge humanity.

Contrast

Contrast points out the ways in which two or more ideas are different. Sample signal words are *different*, *but*, and *yet*.

Words and Phrases of Contrast

although	conversely	different from	in spite of	on the other hand
as opposed to	despite	differently	instead	still
at the same time	differ	even though	nevertheless	to the contrary
but	difference	however	on the contrary	unlike
by contrast	different	in contrast	on the one hand	yet

Here are some examples:

Capitalism and socialism are two very **different** worldviews.

Women **differ** from men in their styles of communication.

Weather refers to the current atmospheric conditions, such as rain or sunshine. Climate, **on the other hand**, describes the general weather conditions in a particular place during a particular season or all year round.

Each of these sentences has two topics that differ from each other in some way. The difference is the author's main point. For example, the first sentence sets up a contrast between two points of view: capitalism and socialism. The contrast is introduced by the word *different*. The second sentence states that the communication styles of women *differ* from the communication styles of men. And the third sentence contrasts the definitions of *weather* and *climate*; the author connects the definitions with the signal phrase *on the other hand*.

When contrast is used to organize an entire paragraph, the pattern looks like this.

Contrast Pattern		
Idea 1		**Idea 2**
Idea 1	*differs from*	Idea 2
Idea 1	*differs from*	Idea 2
Idea 1	*differs from*	Idea 2

EXAMPLE Determine a logical order for the following five sentences. Write **1** by the sentence that should come first, **2** by the sentence that should come second, **3** by the sentence that should come third, and so on. Then use the information to fill in the chart.

_____ Even though Alec had rarely spoken to others in the hallways, he had often interrupted coworkers who were speaking during meetings.

_____ In contrast, after counseling, he listened politely to others as they spoke during meetings.

_____ Quiet and withdrawn before counseling, Alec rarely spoke, smiled, or made eye contact with his coworkers as he passed them in the hallways or at their desks.

_____ However, after counseling, he became more friendly and outgoing, taking time to make eye contact and speak with colleagues.

_____ Alec behaved very differently after attending a series of counseling sessions aimed at improving his communication skills.

Changes in Alec's Communication Skills	
Alec Before Counseling	**Alec After Counseling**
1. quiet and withdrawn in hallways	1. _____
2. interrupted others during meetings	2. _____
	_____

EXPLANATION Here are the sentences arranged in the proper order. The transition and signal words are in **bold** type.

[1]Alec behaved very **differently after** attending a series of counseling sessions aimed at improving his communication skills. [2]Quiet and withdrawn **before** counseling, Alec rarely spoke, smiled, or made eye contact with his coworkers as he passed them in the hallways or at their desks. [3]**However, after** counseling, he became more friendly and outgoing, taking time to make eye contact and speak with colleagues. [4]**Even though** Alec had rarely spoken to others in the hallways, he had often interrupted coworkers who were speaking during meetings. [5]**In contrast, after** counseling, he listened politely to others as they spoke during meetings.

The time signal words *before* and *after* provided important context clues for understanding the proper order of the ideas. You should have filled in the chart with the following information.

Alec Before Counseling	Alec After Counseling
1. quiet and withdrawn in hallways	1. friendly and outgoing
2. interrupted others during meetings	2. listened politely to others during meetings

PRACTICE 3

Complete the following sentences with a transition that shows contrast. Use each expression only once.

1. _____ his family is originally from Mexico, Juan does not speak Spanish.

2. Some people such as Oprah Winfrey choose to work _____ the fact that they no longer need the money.

3. Marie knows that she needs to take her allergy medicine every day; _____, she forgets unless she is reminded.

4. _____ of cramming for the test the night before, Jordan and his study group started studying two weeks before the scheduled exam date.

5. Every member of the study group performed well on the exam, _____ the students who waited and crammed.

PRACTICE 4

Read the following paragraph. Complete the ideas with transitions from the box that show contrasts. Use each word once.

contrast	difference	distinction	less	more
differ	differently	however	lower	than

Textbook
Skills

Global Discrimination against Women

In his textbook *Sociology: A Down-to-Earth Approach*, James Henslin points out four ways in which men and women are treated **(1)** _____ worldwide. The first **(2)** _____ is the global gap in education. Worldwide, more men **(3)** _____ women are literate. Almost 1 billion adults around the world cannot read; **(4)** _____, two-thirds are women (UNESCO 2006). The second **(5)** _____ between the treatment of men and women is the global gap in politics; around the world, men have **(6)** _____ access than women to national decision making. Except for Rwanda (at 49 percent), no national legislature of any country has as many women as men. A third way in which men and women **(7)** _____ is the global gap in pay. In every nation, women average **(8)** _____ pay than men. In the United States, full-time working women average only 70 percent of what men make. In some countries, the earnings of women are much **(9)** _____ than this. The fourth **(10)** _____ between men and women is related to violence. A global human rights issue is violence against women. Historical examples are foot binding in China, witch burning in Europe, and *suttee* (burning the living widow with the body of her dead husband) in India.

—Adapted from Henslin, *Sociology: A Down to Earth Approach*,
Text from p. 309 © 2008 James M. Henslin. Reproduced
by permission of Pearson Education, Inc.

Comparison and Contrast

The **comparison-and-contrast pattern** shows how two things are similar and also how they are different.

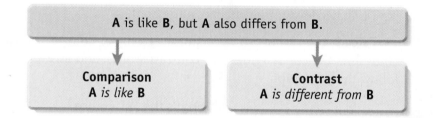

Yoga and Pilates: The Similarities and Differences

[1]Although yoga and Pilates share *similar* characteristics, an important *difference* exists. [2]*Both* yoga and Pilates are low-impact forms of exercise that improve posture, flexibility, and concentration. [3]*In addition, both* emphasize that a balance between body and mind is important. [4]*However*, the primary goal of Pilates is to strengthen the midsection and buttocks. [5]Pilates calls this area of the body the "powerhouse." [6]*On the other hand*, yoga does not focus on any one part of the body. [7]*Rather*, yoga works the opposing muscles of the entire body.

In the paragraph, two kinds of exercise are being compared and contrasted: yoga and Pilates. Remember, a topic sentence contains the topic and the author's controlling point about the topic. In this topic sentence, the author uses the words *similar* and *difference* to set up the points of comparison and contrast.

The author's supporting details are a list of similarities introduced by the word *both*. The second similarity is introduced with the addition transition phrase *in addition*. The shift in the paragraph from similarities to differences is introduced in sentence 4 with the word *however*. The supporting details that explain these differences are introduced with the expressions *on the other hand* and *rather*.

EXAMPLE Determine a logical order for the following four sentences. Write **1** by the sentence that should come first, **2** by the sentence that should come second, **3** by the sentence that should come third, and **4** by the sentence that should come fourth.

_____ Yet anorexia and bulimia are two different eating disorders.

_____ Although anorexia and bulimia share certain similarities, they are very different.

_____ Bulimia occurs when a person binges on large amounts of food and then induces vomiting; in contrast, anorexia occurs when a person refuses to eat much of anything.

_____ Both arise out of a perceived need to be thin and lose weight, and both have devastating effects on the body.

Read the following paragraph from a college education textbook. Underline the comparison-and-contrast words, and answer the questions that follow the paragraph.

Textbook
Skills

What's the Difference?

[1]Those with a disability and those with a handicap often face similar reactions from others. [2]They are often misunderstood. [3]And both are often given the same labels. [4]However, the two conditions have a distinct difference. [5]The distinction between the two is important. [6]A disability is an inability to do something specific, such as see or walk. [7]On the contrary, a handicap is a disadvantage only in certain situations. [8]Sometimes a disability leads to a handicap, but not always. [9]For example, being blind (a visual disability) is a handicap if you want to drive. [10]But blindness is not a handicap when you are creating music or talking on the telephone.

—Adapted from Woolfolk, *Educational Psychology*, 8th ed., pp. 107–108. Published by Allyn and Bacon, Boston, MA. Copyright (c) 2001 by Pearson Education Inc.

1. What two ideas are being compared and contrasted? _____

_____

2. List four different comparison-and-contrast words or phrases in the para-graph. _____

_____

EXPLANATION   Here are the four sentences about eating disorders arranged in the proper order. The transition words are in **bold** type.

> [1]**Although** anorexia and bulimia share certain **similarities,** they are very **different.** [2]**Both** arise out of a perceived need to be thin and lose weight, and **both** have devastating effects on the body. [3]Yet anorexia and bulimia are two **different** eating disorders. [4]Bulimia occurs when a person binges on large amounts of food and then induces vomiting; **in contrast,** anorexia occurs when a person refuses to eat much of anything.

Here are the answers to the questions about the paragraph from an education textbook: The paragraph compares and contrasts a disability and a handicap. You were correct to choose any four of the following comparison-and-contrast words: *similar, both, same, however, difference, distinction, on the contrary, but.*

PRACTICE 5

The following paragraph from a college psychology textbook uses comparison and contrast. Read the paragraph, and underline the comparison-and-contrast signal words. Then answer the questions that follow the paragraph.

Textbook
Skills

> [1]Parents have two distinctly different choices of punishment that can bring similar results. [2]On the one hand, positive punishment responds to the child's misbehavior with an action that improves the behavior. [3]For example, if Mom's frown in response to Pete's rude remark causes Pete to be less rude, then Mom's frown is a positive punishment. [4]On the other hand, negative punishment removes a freedom or privilege. [5]After grabbing and pulling his sister's hair, Raymond is punished by having to leave the table and go without dinner. [6]Just as Pete changed his behavior, Raymond no longer mistreats his sister.

—Adapted from Jaffe, Michael L. *Understanding Parenting*, 2nd ed., p. 194.
Published by Allyn and Bacon, Boston, MA. Copyright (c)
1997 by Pearson Education, Inc.

_____   **1.** What pattern is used in this passage?
  a. comparison   c. comparison and contrast
  b. contrast

2. What two ideas are being discussed? _____ and

_____

PRACTICE 6

Read the following paragraph. Complete the ideas with transitions from the box. Use each word once.

conversely	different	even though	in contrast	same
despite	differs	however	just as	similar

The similarities between high school and college are numerous and even obvious. Both levels teach many of the **(1)** _____ subject areas: English, history, algebra, physics, and so on. Often the physical environment is **(2)** _____, with the same kinds of classroom configurations, desks, chalkboards, and technology. **(3)** _____ high school students can participate in various extra-curricular activities such as student government, sports, and clubs, so too can college students. However, **(4)** _____ these apparent similarities, the college experience **(5)** _____ significantly from the high school experience. First, high school is required and free; **(6)** _____, college is voluntary and expensive. Second, high school students must obtain parental permission to participate in extracurricular activities; **(7)** _____, college students only have to volunteer to participate. Finally, high school students often expect to be reminded about deadlines or guided through assignments. **(8)** _____, college students are expected to take full responsibility and to think independently. Overall, **(9)** _____ high school and college seem to be similar experiences, they are very **(10)** _____ indeed.

The Cause-and-Effect Pattern

Sometimes an author talks about *why* something happened or *what* results came from an event. A **cause** states why something happens. An **effect** states a result or outcome. Sample signal words include *because* and *consequently*.

Cause-and-Effect Words			
accordingly	consequently	leads to	therefore
affect	due to	outcome	thus
as a result	if . . . then	results in	
because	impact	since	
because of	influence	so	

Here are some examples:

Because Selena memorized the algebra formulas and practiced using them, she did well on the chapter test.

Lance seeks out personal and sensitive details in a conversation; he often repeats this information to others. **As a result,** those who know Lance have come to distrust him.

Due to the amount of snow on the streets and highways, schools and businesses have shut down.

Each of these sentences has two topics: one topic causes or has an effect on the second topic. The cause or effect is the author's controlling point. For example, the two topics in the first sentence are memorizing formulas and doing well on the test. This main idea states that memorizing is the cause of doing well. The cause is introduced by the word *because*. The two topics of the second sentence are Lance's behavior and the effect of that behavior. The effect is introduced by the signal phrase *as a result*. And the two topics in the third sentence are the amount of snow and the closing of schools and businesses; the author focuses on the cause by using the signal phrase *due to*. Note that cause and effect has a strong connection to time, and many of the transitions for this thought pattern therefore have a time element. Although many of these transition words have similar meanings and may be interchangeable, authors carefully choose the transition that best fits the context.

The writer using cause and effect introduces an idea or event and then provides supporting details to show how that idea *results in* or *leads to* another idea. Many times, the second idea comes about because of the first idea. Thus the first idea is the cause, and the following ideas are the effects.

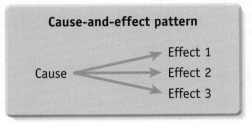

For example, read the following topic sentence:

> Over time, the eating disorder bulimia may damage the digestive system and the heart.

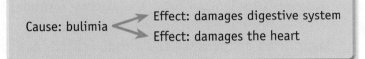

Often an author will begin with an effect and then give the causes.

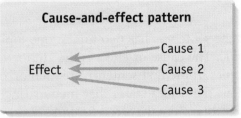

For example, read the following topic sentence:

> The eating disorder bulimia may be the result of poor self-esteem and cultural values.

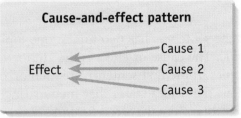

Sometimes the author may wish to emphasize a chain reaction.

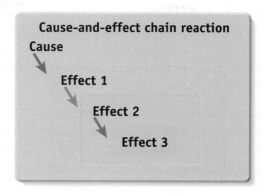

For example, read the following topic sentence.

> Low self-esteem leads to dissatisfaction with one's appearance, which leads to control issues and can ultimately result in bulimia.

Cause-and-effect chain reaction

Cause: low self-esteem → Effect: dissatisfaction with appearance →
Effect: control issues → Effect: bulimia

EXAMPLE Determine a logical order for the following three sentences. Write **1** by the sentence that should come first, **2** by the sentence that should come second, and **3** by the sentence that should come last.

_____ For example, a character may change due to an inner conflict such as the struggle between ambition and honor.

_____ In a piece of fiction, a change in a dynamic character is usually the result of conflict.

_____ In addition, a character may change because of a conflict with another person or group of people, such as a struggle between a father and a son or between a citizen and the government.

EXPLANATION Here are the sentences arranged in the proper order. The transition and signal words are in **bold** type.

What Causes a Character to Change?

[1]In a piece of fiction, a change in a dynamic character is usually the **result of** conflict. [2]**For example**, a character may change **due to** an inner conflict **such as** the struggle between ambition and honor. [3]**In addition**, a character may change **because of** a conflict with another person or group of people, **such as** a struggle between a father and a son or between a citizen and the government.

In this paragraph, two addition words combine with the cause-and-effect signal words. The cause-and-effect signal words are *result of*, *due to*, and *because of*. *For example* and *in addition* indicate the order of the cause-and-effect discussion. Also note that the addition phrase *such as* introduces examples of the kinds of conflict that cause change. This paragraph actually uses two patterns of organization to make the point—the listing pattern is used to add the cause-and-effect details. Even though two patterns are used, the cause-and-effect pattern is the primary pattern of organization.

PRACTICE 7

Complete each sentence with a cause-and-effect word or phrase from the box. Use each word only once.

consequently	if . . . then	leads to	results in	thereby

1. Reading magazines, newspapers, and books _____ a large vocabulary.

2. Over the summer, Molly grows to be several inches taller than all her peers. Her additional height _____ better performance and more playing time on the basketball court.

3. Maurice surfed the Internet and bought an essay for his history class. His teacher, who suspected that Maurice didn't write the essay he submitted, surfed the Internet and found the essay Maurice had bought. _____, Maurice received a failing grade for the assignment.

4. The American dream is based on the premise that _____ you work hard, _____ you will succeed.

5. On January 12, 2010 a 7.0 magnitude quake rocked Haiti, _____ killing thousands of people as it toppled both the presidential palace and hillside shanties and leaving the poor Caribbean nation appealing for international help.

VISUAL VOCABULARY

A technician at the French National Seism Survey Institute points at a map showing the **epicenter** of a major earthquake that hit Haiti.

The best meaning of epicenter is _____.

   a. focal point.
   b. large area.
   c. area of destruction.

PRACTICE 8

The following paragraph from a college science textbook uses the cause-and-effect pattern of organization. Read the paragraph, underline the cause-and-effect signal words in it, and complete the concept map that follows it.

Textbook Skills

An Evolutionary Arms Race

[1]Predators have a negative effect on the animals they consume, obviously. [2]As a result, in response, prey animals have evolved defenses against being consumed. [3]This change in the prey leads to the predator's developing more effective strategies. [4]There is an evolutionary arms race: predators change strategies, going one step farther, which causes prey to change strategies in the same general way. [5]As a result, both groups evolve at a fast pace. [6]As the predator becomes more successful, the pressure builds on the prey to improve defenses. [7]Conversely, the better the defense, the greater the need for the predator to develop its skills.

—Adapted from Maier, Richard. *Comparative Animal Behavior: An Evolutionary and Ecological Approach*, pp. 129–130. Published by Allyn and Bacon, Boston, MA. Copyright © 1998 by Pearson Education Inc.

Cause-and-effect chain reaction

Cause: _____ catches prey ➡ Effect: _____ develops new defenses ➡
Effect: _____ adjusts and becomes more effective ➡ Effect: evolutionary
_____

PRACTICE 9

Read the following paragraph. Complete the ideas with transitions from the box. Use each word once.

affects	consequence	effects	impacts	lead to
cause	due to	impact	influence	result

Alcohol's Damaging Effect on the Brain

Difficulty walking, blurred vision, slurred speech, slowed reaction times, impaired memory—clearly, alcohol **(1)** _____ the brain. Some of these **(2)** _____ are noticeable after only one or two drinks and quickly resolve when drinking stops. On the other hand, a person who drinks heavily over a long period of time may have brain deficits that persist well after he or she achieves sobriety. Exactly how alcohol affects the brain and the likelihood of reversing the **(3)** _____ of heavy drinking on the brain remain hot topics in alcohol research today. A number of factors **(4)** _____ how and to what extent alcohol **(5)** _____ the brain. For example, how much and how often a person drinks is one factor. Other factors include the age at which he or she first began drinking, and how long he or she has been drinking; the person's age, level of education, gender, genetic background, and family history of alcoholism; whether he or she is at risk **(6)** _____ prenatal alcohol exposure; and his or her general health status. Alcohol can **(7)** _____ obvious impairments in memory after only a few drinks and, as the amount of alcohol increases, so does the degree of impairment. Large quantities of alcohol, especially when consumed quickly and on an empty stomach, can **(8)** _____ a blackout, or an interval of time for which the intoxicated person cannot recall key details of events, or even entire events. People who have been drinking large amounts of alcohol for long periods of time risk the **(9)** _____ of serious and persistent changes in the brain. Damage may be a **(10)** _____ of the direct effects of alcohol on the brain or may result indirectly, from a poor general health status or from severe liver disease.

—Adapted from National Institute on Alcohol Abuse and Alcoholism, "Alcohol's Damaging Effect on the Brain." *Alcohol Alert.* Oct 2004. 14 Jan. 2010. http://pubs.niaaa.nih.gov/publications/aa63/aa63.htm.

 ## The Generalization-and-Example Pattern

> As technology evolves, it saves time; broadband Internet access cuts down on the time needed to access information on the World Wide Web.

Some people may read this sentence and think that the author's focus is on the topic of broadband Internet access. But evolving technology saves time in many other areas of our lives, such as in traveling, cooking, or cleaning. Adding an **example word** makes it clear that broadband Internet access is only one instance in which technology saves time.

Read the sentence about technology and the Internet again. Note how the use of the example word makes the relationship between ideas clear.

> As technology evolves, it saves time; *for example*, broadband Internet access cuts down on the time needed to access information on the World Wide Web.

In the generalization-and-example thought pattern, the author makes a general statement and then offers an example or a series of examples to clarify the generalization.

The Generalization-and-Example Pattern
Statement of a general idea
Example
Example

Example words signal that a writer is giving an instance of a general idea.

Words and Phrases That Introduce Examples			
an illustration	for instance	once	to illustrate
for example	including	such as	typically

EXAMPLE   Read each of the following items and fill in the blanks with an appropriate example word or phrase.   .

1. Food labels provide important information. _____, the label on Rich Harvest Sweet Dark Whole Grain bread states that one slice has 120 calories.

2. Fatigue can interfere with performance. _____, Carla was so tired after working straight through two shifts at the restaurant that she made careless mistakes on her math exam.

3. Tyler's intelligence and energy allows him to excel in a variety of areas _____ sports, academics, and community service.

EXPLANATION   Many words and phrases that introduce examples are easily interchanged. Notice that in the first two examples, the phrases *for example* and *for instance* are similar in meaning. In the third example, the use of the transition phrase *such as* signals a list. Even though transition words or phrases have similar meanings, authors carefully choose transitions based on style and meaning.

PRACTICE 10

Complete each selection with an example word. Fill in the blanks with words from the box.

1. Luis is a gracious host ready for an instant party; he always keeps his pantry stocked with items _____ soft drinks, bottled water, wine, and a variety of crackers, chips, and nuts.

2. Although Gene and Paula love each other deeply, they face significant problems in their relationship. _____, Paula wants to continue her education, yet Gene wants to have children right away.

3. Leigh seems to have a number of allergy symptoms, _____ extreme itching, scaly patches on her skin, watery eyes, and headaches.

4. Hunter will go to great lengths to have fun; _____ he drove for 22 hours round trip to attend a Saturday afternoon beach party with a group of friends.

5. Watching television can have a soothing effect. _____, when Jean has trouble falling asleep after a long, difficult day at the office, she turns the television volume down low, turns off all the lights, and lies down; the rhythm of the flickering images and low tones puts her right to sleep.

PRACTICE 11

Read the following passage. Complete the ideas with transitions from the box. Use each word once.

exemplifies	for instance	such as
for example	illustrated	

Textbook
Skills

Groups use different decision-making methods when deciding, **(1)** _____, which solution to accept. The method to be used should, naturally, be stated at the outset of the group discussion. The three main decision-making methods are as follows:

Decision by authority: Group members voice their feelings and opinions, but the leader, boss, or chief executive, **(2)** _____ the president of the company, makes the final decision. This method has the advantages of being efficient and of giving greater importance to the suggestions of more experienced members. The big disadvantage is that members may feel that their contributions have too little influence and therefore may not participate with real enthusiasm.

Majority rule: The group agrees to abide by the majority decision and may vote on various issues as the group searches to solve its problem. The United States Senate often **(3)** _____ majority rule. Like decision by authority, this method is efficient. A disadvantage is that it may lead the group to limit discussion by calling for a vote once a majority has agreed. Also, members not voting with the majority may feel disenfranchised and left out.

Consensus: In some situations, consensus means unanimous agreement; **(4)** _____, a criminal jury must reach a unanimous decision to convict or acquit a defendant. In most business groups, consensus means that members agree that they can live with the solution; they agree that they can do whatever the solution requires. Consensus is especially helpful when the group wants each member to be satisfied and committed to the decision and to the decision-making process as a whole. Consensus obviously takes the most time of any of the decision-making methods and can lead to a great deal of inefficiency, especially if members wish to prolong the discussion process needlessly or selfishly. Two groups that have historically **(5)** _____ decisions by consensus include the Iroquois Grand Council and the Quakers, a religious sect.

—Adapted from DeVito, *Essentials of Human Communication*, p. 199 © 2002.
Reproduced by permission of Pearson Education, Inc.

The Definition-and-Example Pattern

Textbooks are full of new words and special terms. Even if the word is common, it can take on a special meaning in a specific course. To help students understand the ideas, authors often include a definition of the new or special term. Then, to make sure the meaning of the word or concept is clear, the author also gives examples.

Textbook Skills

Emblems are body gestures that directly translate into words or phrases—for example, the OK sign, the thumbs-up for "good job," and the V for victory.

—Adapted from DeVito, *Messages: Building Interpersonal Communication Skills*, Text from p. 141. © 2004. Reproduced by permission of Pearson Education, Inc.

In this sentence, the term *emblem* is defined first. Then the author gives three examples to make the term clear to the reader.

The Definition Pattern

Term and definition
   Example
   Example

- The **definition** explains the meaning of new, difficult, or special terms. Definitions include words like *is, are,* and *means:* "Emblems *are* body gestures that directly translate into words or phrases . . ."
- The **examples** follow a definition to show how the word is used or applied in the content. Examples are signaled by words like *for example* and *such as:* "for example, the OK sign, the thumbs-up for 'good job,' and the V for victory."

EXAMPLES

A. Determine a logical order for the following three sentences. Write **1** by the sentence that should come first, **2** by the sentence that should come second, and **3** by the sentence that should come last. Then read the explanation.

_____ For example, a person may give up a high-paying job in the city to take a lower-paying job in a small town.

_____ Downshifting is a deliberate effort to reduce stress by choosing to live more simply.

_____ Some people who choose to downshift may also avoid the use of televisions, computers, and cell phones.

B. Read the following paragraph from a college communications textbook. Annotate the paragraph: Circle the term being defined, and underline the key words in the definition. Then answer the questions that follow it.

Textbook
Skills

Paralanguage

[1]**Paralanguage** is the meaning that is perceived along with the actual words used to deliver a message. [2]It is how we say something. [3]This is a broad category that includes a number of traits such as dialects, accents, pitch, rate, vocal qualities, pauses, and silence. [4]A pleasing voice, for example, will make people more likely to listen to us. [5]And a modulated voice indicates higher social status and educational levels.

—Adapted from Harris, Thomas E., and John C. Sherblom.
Small Groups and Team Communication, 2nd ed.,
p. 112. Published by Allyn and Bacon.

1. What are the two examples that illustrate the term being defined?

_____ and _____.

2. Which words signal each example? _____ and _____.

EXPLANATIONS

A. The sentences have been arranged in the proper order in the following paragraph. The definition, example, and transition words are in **bold** type.

Downshifting

Downshifting **is** a deliberate effort to reduce stress by choosing to live more simply. **For example**, a person may give up a high-paying job in the city to take a lower-paying job in a small town. Some people who choose to downshift may **also** avoid the use of televisions, computers, and cell phones.

This sequence of ideas begins by introducing the term _downshifting_. The term is linked to its definition with the verb _is_. The author provides two examples of behaviors common to people who downshift. The sentence that contains _for example_ would logically follow the definition. The example that contains the addition transition _also_ would come last.

B. By circling and underlining only key terms, you highlight the most important information for easy review. Compare your annotations to the following:

Textbook
Skills

Paralanguage

[1]Paralanguage is the meaning that is perceived along with the actual words used to deliver a message. [2]It is how we say something. [3]This is a broad category that includes a number of traits such as dialects, accents, pitch, rate, vocal qualities, pauses, and silence. [4]A pleasing voice, for example, will make people more likely to listen to us. [5]And a modulated voice indicates higher social status and educational levels.

—Adapted from Harris, Thomas E., and John C. Sherblom. _Small Groups and Team Communication_, 2nd ed., p. 112. Published by Allyn and Bacon.

1. The two examples are _a pleasing voice_ and _a modulated voice_.

2. The signal words that introduce the examples are _for example_ and _and_.

PRACTICE 12

Read the paragraph from a college science textbook. Finish the definition concept map that follows it by adding the missing details in the proper order.

What Are Fossils?

[1]**Fossils** are the remains or traces of prehistoric life found in sediment and sedimentary rocks. [2]Many types of fossils exist and are important basic tools for interpreting the geologic past. [3]One example is the petrified fossil. [4]*Petrified* literally means "turned into stone." [5]Another example of a fossil is the mold or cast fossil. [6]When a shell or other structure is buried in sediment and then dissolved by underground water, a *mold* of the organism's outer structure is created; if the hollow spaces of inside the organism are filled with mineral matter, then a *cast* is created. [7]Fossils are also made by *carbonization*. [8]In this case, fine sediment encases the remains of the organism. [9]As time passes, pressure squeezes out the liquid and gases and leaves behind a thin residue of carbon. [10]If the film of carbon is lost from a fossil preserved in fine-grained sediment, a replica on the surface, called an *impression*, may still show considerable detail. [11]Finally, delicate organisms, such as insects, have been preserved in *amber*, the hardened resin of trees. [12]After being trapped in the sticky resin, the remains of the organism are protected from damage by water and air.

—Adapted from Lutgens & Tarbuck, *Foundations of Earth Science*, 5th ed., pp. 230–234.

Term: _____

Definition: _____

Example: _____

Example: _____

Example: _____

Example: _____

VISUAL VOCABULARY

This collection of fossilized wood is an example of

_____ fossils.

a. amber
b. carbonized
c. petrified

PRACTICE 13

Read the following passage. Finish the definition concept map that follows it by adding the missing details in proper order.

What Is Child Abuse and Neglect?

[1]Each State provides its own definitions of child abuse and neglect based on minimum standards set by Federal law. [2]The Federal Child Abuse Prevention and Treatment Act (CAPTA) defines child abuse and neglect as the following:

- [3]Any recent act or failure to act on the part of a parent or caretaker which results in death, serious physical or emotional harm, sexual abuse or exploitation.
- [4]An act or failure to act which presents an imminent risk of serious harm.

[5]Four major types of **maltreatment** are recognized in most States: neglect, physical abuse, sexual abuse, and emotional abuse. [6]Although any of the forms of child maltreatment may be found separately, they often occur in combination. [7]The following examples are for general informational purposes only. [8]Not all States' definitions will include all of the examples listed below, and individual States' definitions may cover additional situations not mentioned here.

[9]Neglect is failure to provide for a child's basic needs. [10]Neglect may be:

- [11]Physical (failure to provide necessary food or shelter, or lack of appropriate supervision)
- [12]Medical (failure to provide necessary medical or mental health treatment)
- [13]Educational (failure to educate a child or attend to special education needs)
- [14]Emotional (inattention to a child's emotional needs, failure to provide psychological care, or permitting the child to use alcohol or other drugs)

—Adapted from Child Welfare Information Gateway, "What Is Child Abuse and Neglect?" U.S. Department of Health and Human Services April 2006 1 August 2007 http://www.childwelfare.gov/pubs/factsheets/whatiscan.pdf.

Terms: _____

Definition: Any recent act or failure to act on the part of a parent or caretaker which results in death, serious physical or emotional harm, sexual abuse or exploitation. An act or failure to act which presents an imminent risk of serious harm.

Term: _____

Definition: Neglect, physical abuse, sexual abuse, and emotional abuse.

Term: Neglect

Definition: _____

Examples: Failure to provide _____, _____, medical treatment, an education, emotional support. Permitting the child to use drugs.

Textbook
Skills

Thought Patterns and Textbooks

Textbook authors rely heavily on the use of transitions and thought patterns to make information clear and easier to understand.

EXAMPLES The following topic sentences have been taken from college textbooks. Identify the *primary* thought pattern that each sentence suggests.

_____ **1.** Issuing orders or making it clear that we have the power to control the behavior of others results in others' defensiveness.
   a. cause and effect   c. definition
   b. comparison and contrast

_____ **2.** Distress is stress that brings about negative mental or physical responses such as having trouble relaxing.
   a. cause and effect   c. definition
   b. comparison and contrast

_____ **3.** When stock prices fully reflect information that is available to investors, the stock market is efficient; in contrast, when stock prices do not reflect all information, the stock market is inefficient.
   a. cause and effect   c. definition
   b. comparison and contrast

EXPLANATION Topic sentence 1, from a psychology textbook, uses (a) cause and effect, signaled by the phrase *results in*. Topic sentence 2, from a health textbook, is organized according to (c) definition, using the verb *is* and the phrase *such as* to signal examples. Note that the sentence includes the phrase *brings about*, which suggests cause and effect; however, the sentence is set up in the form of a definition. Therefore, definition is the *primary* thought pattern. Topic sentence 3, from an economics textbook, uses (b) comparison and contrast as the primary thought pattern. Some readers may pick up on the author's use of time order, signaled by the word *when*. The use of time order can suggest cause and effect. However, in this sentence, *when* is used to describe two instances or events. The signal phrase *in contrast* joins these two events to point out the differences between them.

PRACTICE 14

Textbook
Skills

The following sentences are from college textbooks. Identify the thought pattern that each topic sentence suggests. (The type of textbook is identified after each topic sentence.)

_____ **1.** Creativity is the result of looking at things in a new way. (social science)
    a. cause and effect   c. generalization and example
    b. comparison and contrast

_____ **2.** The occasional drinker differs slightly from the social drinker. (health)
    a. cause and effect   c. generalization and example
    b. comparison and contrast

_____ **3.** Some pressed for war because they were suffering an agricultural depression. (history)
    a. cause and effect   c. definition and example
    b. comparison and contrast

_____ **4.** Several factors influence the way we relate to and use space in communicating. (communication)
    a. cause and effect   c. generalization and example
    b. comparison and contrast

_____ **5.** Analgesics, such as aspirin and ibuprofen, are pain relievers. (health)
    a. cause and effect   c. definition and example
    b. comparison and contrast

APPLICATIONS

Application 1: Using Example and Definition Patterns

A. The following paragraph lists a series of supporting details using the generalization-and-example thought pattern. Complete the outline that follows with the missing details of example.

Maxine excels at whatever she attempts. First, Maxine is a talented hostess. For example, she is able to create gourmet meals on short notice. She is also an avid competitor, excelling in sports such as tennis, golf, and swimming. In addition, Maxine is an award-winning student. For instance, she was awarded a full two-year scholarship at her local community college.

Main idea stated as a topic sentence: Maxine excels at whatever she attempts.

First major supporting detail: a talented hostess

Minor supporting detail of example: creates gourmet meals on short notice

1. **Second major supporting detail:** _____

Minor supporting detail of example: excels in tennis, golf, and swimming

2. **Third major supporting detail:** an award-winning student

Minor supporting detail of example: _____

_____

B. The following paragraph from a college science textbook contains a definition and three examples. In the spaces provided, write the term, the definition, and the missing example.

Textbook
Skills

Noise Pollution

[1]Noise pollution is the mix of sounds connected to working with machines. [2]This mix could include the following: car engines, radios, lawn mowers, garden blowers, factory machinery, office equipment, home appliances, televisions, and overhead jets. [3]Noise pollution is linked to urban cities such as New York City. [4]And noise pollution is more intense in some work settings. [5]For example, an automobile repair shop would have a high level of noise pollution.

—Adapted from McGuigan, *Encyclopedia of Stress*, p. 148.

3. Term: _____

4. Definition: _____

5. Example: car engines, radios, lawn mowers, garden blowers, factory machinery, office equipment, home appliances, televisions, and overhead jets

Example: _____

Example: an automobile repair shop

Application 2: Using the Contrast Pattern

The following paragraph uses the contrast thought pattern. Underline the main idea. Then complete the concept map that follows.

Textbook
Skills

Listening and Gender

[1]Deborah Tannen's bestselling book *You Just Don't Understand: Women and Men in Conversation* explores some of the differences in how men and women listen to one another. [2]Tannen shows that when men and women talk, men lecture while women listen. [3]The lecturer is set up as the superior, as the teacher, the expert; on the other hand, the listener is the inferior, the student, the nonexpert. [4]In addition, women use listening skills to build rapport and close relationships. [5]In contrast, men interrupt more and often change the topic to one they know more about or that is more factual, for example, sports or finance. [6]Finally, men, research shows, play up their expertise, using it to dominate the conversation. [7]However, women play down their expertise.

—Adapted from DeVito, *Messages: Building Interpersonal Communication Skills,* Text from p. 98. © 2004. Reproduced by permission of Pearson Education, Inc.

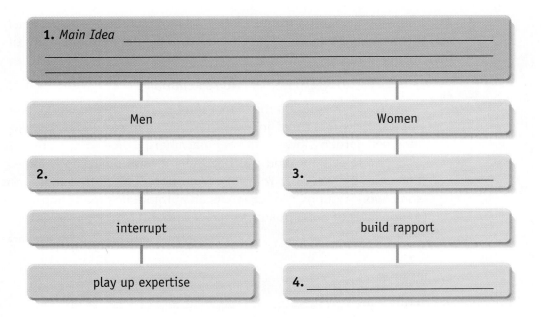

1. *Main Idea* _____

Men	Women
2. _____	**3.** _____
interrupt	build rapport
play up expertise	**4.** _____

Application 3: Using the Cause-and-Effect Pattern

The following series of sentences from a college psychology textbook uses the cause-and-effect thought pattern. Fill in each missing cause or effect.

1. Classical conditioning has an effect on deaths caused by drug overdose.

   Cause: _____

   Effect: deaths caused by drug overdose

2. A user who generally takes a drug in a particular place—the bathroom, say—develops a conditioned response to that place.

   Cause: generally taking a drug in a specific place

   Effect: _____

3. Because of classical conditioning, as soon as the user walks into the bathroom, his or her body begins to get ready for the influx of drugs that is about to come.

   Cause: classical conditioning

   Effect: _____

4. The conditioned response causes the body to counteract or dampen the effects of the drug.

   Cause: _____

   Effect: counteracts or dampens effects of drug

Textbook
Skills

Classically Conditioned Animal Training

◄ Dogs learn not to go beyond the boundary of an "invisible fence" because the fence delivers a mild shock through their collars.

—Adapted from Kosslyn, *Psychology: The Brain, The Person, The World*, Text Excerpt from p. 173 © 2001 Allyn and Bacon. Reproduced by permission of Pearson Education, Inc.

_____ 5. The primary thought pattern used in this figure is
   a. cause and effect.
   b. comparison and contrast.

REVIEW TEST 1   Score (number correct) _____ × 10 = _____%

Transition Words and Thought Patterns

A. Based on the thought pattern used to state each idea, fill in the blanks with the transition words from the box. Use each choice only once.

because	even though	for example	on the other hand	so

1. _____ Chloe is afraid of heights, she went bungee jumping to celebrate her birthday.

2. Distance education is learning that takes place when the student is in a location apart from the classroom, building, or site; _____, online courses and telecourses are distance learning courses.

3. As a student, Armando likes distance education _____ he works a full-time job, and online courses offer a more flexible schedule.

4. Isabella wanted to become a professional stage actress, _____ she moved to New York City.

5. A person who takes too much of a group's time may be poorly perceived; _____, a person in an influential position may be granted more leeway in bending expectations regarding the use of time.

B. Underline the signal words. Then identify the thought pattern used in each short passage, as follows:

a. cause and effect
b. comparison and contrast
c. generalization and example

_____ **6.** The purpose of a documentary is to give depth and context for important public issues. One memorable example is Harvest of Shame, which exposed the mistreatment of migrant workers.

_____ **7.** Assertive communicators speak calmly, directly, and clearly to those around them; in contrast, nonassertive communicators may speak too rapidly, use a tone too low to be heard easily, or fail to say directly what is on their minds.

_____ **8.** Research shows that low doses of aspirin are beneficial to heart patients due to the blood-thinning properties of the drug.

_____ **9.** Rebekah overeats when she is under stress. Rebekah is overeating; therefore, she must be experiencing stress.

_____ **10.** The eureka experience is a sudden rush of understanding. I can recall one early instance of a eureka experience when the meaning of the word frown suddenly dawned on me. In that moment, by understanding one simple word, I became aware of the value of words.

REVIEW TEST 2

Score (number correct) _____ × 10 = _____%

Thought Patterns

A. Arrange the following sentences from a college health textbook in their proper order. Write **1** by the sentence that should come first, write **2** by the sentence that should come second, and so on. Use the transitions to figure out the proper order.

Textbook Skills

_____ In contrast, Gilligan believes that men have an ethic based on justice.

_____ According to Harvard Professor Carol Gilligan, men and women make very different decisions when facing moral choices.

_____ Gilligan believes that women have an ethic based on care.

_____ For example, men are more interested in fair play and individual rights.

_____ For example, women value loyalty, self-sacrifice, and peacemaking.

—Adapted from Donatelle, *Access to Health,* 7th ed., p. 135.

_____ **6.** What is the primary thought pattern used here?
  a. generalization and example   c. comparison and contrast
  b. cause and effect

B. Identify the thought pattern used in the following paragraphs, as follows:
a. cause and effect
b. comparison and contrast
c. definition

Textbook Skills

_____ **7.** Parenting style is the blend of attitudes and behaviors toward a child that creates an emotional climate. For example, a parent's style includes the parent's tone, a parent's body language, and signs of affection or hostility toward the child.

—Adapted from Jaffe, *Understanding
Parenting*, 2nd ed., pp. 163–64.

_____ **8.**   Marijuana has several short-term effects. First, physically, it speeds up the heart and reddens the eyes. In addition, psychologically, it may cause feelings of giddiness and increased hunger or sexual desire.

_____ **9.**   Even though Gary and Tony are identical twins, their personalities differ greatly. On the one hand, Gary is outspoken, outgoing, and overcommitted. He serves on several service clubs, volunteers, and leads study sessions. On the other hand, Tony is shy and withdrawn and has few commitments. He enjoys reading, creating music, and drawing and prefers to study alone.

_____ **10.**   Cassie suffered several long-term effects from the constant teasing she endured during her childhood. Because her peers ridiculed her for being too heavy, Cassie felt embarrassed about her body even as an adult and became unrealistic about what her ideal weight should be. In addition, the teasing caused Cassie to fear rejection; as a result, she often gave in to her children's demands in order to win their affection. Another impact of the teasing showed in Cassie's inability to trust people; she always had a vague feeling that others were judging her or saying negative things about her behind her back.

REVIEW TEST 3   Score (number correct) _____ × 25 = _____%

Thought Patterns

Read the following passage from a college political science textbook. Then, answer the questions that follow.

Textbook
Skills

The Media's Influence on the Public

[1]There are many important questions concerning the media's influence on the public. [2]For instance, how much influence do the media actually have on public opinion? [3]Do the media have an obvious point of view

or bias, as some people suggest? [4]Are people able to resist information that challenges their preexisting beliefs?

[5]In most cases, the press has surprisingly little effect on what people believe. [6]To put it bluntly, people tend to see what they want to see. [7]That is, human beings will focus on parts of a report that reinforce their own attitudes. [8]And they ignore parts that challenge their core beliefs. [9]Most people also selectively tune out or ignore reports that contradict their preferences in politics and other fields. [10]Therefore, a committed Democrat will remember certain parts of a televised news program about a current campaign—primarily the parts that reinforce his or her own choice. [11]And an equally committed Republican will recall very different sections of the report or remember the material in a way that supports the GOP position. [12]In other words, most voters are not empty vessels into which the media can pour their own beliefs. [13]Indeed, many studies were done from the 1940s and 1950s. [14]This was an era when partisan identification was very strong. [15]These studies suggested that the media had no effect at all on public opinion. [16]During the last forty years, however, the decline in political identification has opened the door to greater media influence. [17]On the one hand, research had indicated for some time that the media have little effect on changing public opinion. [18]On the other hand, more recent studies show that the media have a definite effect on shaping public opinion, especially during elections.

[19]Some experts argue that the content of network television news accounts for a large portion of the volatility and change in policy preferences of Americans, when measured over relatively short periods of time. [20]These changes are called **media effects**. [21]Let's examine how these media-influenced changes might occur.

[22]First, reporting can sway people who have no strong opinion in the first place. [23]So, for example, the media have a greater influence on political independents than on strong partisans. [24]That said, the politically unmotivated individual who is subject to media effects may not vote in a given election. [25]In that case, the media influence may be of little particular consequence.

[26]Second, it is likely that the media have a greater impact on topics far removed from the lives and experiences of readers and viewers. [27]News reports can probably shape public opinion about events in foreign countries fairly easily. [28]Yet, what the media say about domestic issues such as rising prices, neighborhood crime, or child rearing may have relatively little effect, because most citizens have personal experience of and well-formed ideas about these subjects.

[29]Third, in a process often referred to as agenda setting, news organizations can help tell us what to think about, even if they cannot determine what we think. [30]Indeed, the press often sets the agenda for a campaign or for government action by focusing on certain issues or concerns. [31]For example, nationwide in 2003, the media reported the abduction and recovery of fifteen-year-old Utah resident Elizabeth Smart. [32]Many in the press and in the Utah government attributed the success in finding Smart to the use of the state's Amber alert. [33]Due to the Amber alert system, the law enforcement uses the media to notify the public of a kidnapping. [34]Soon after, there were calls for a national Amber alert system. [35]Thus, Congress quickly passed as law the Protection Act of 2003, and the president just as quickly signed. [36]Before the Smart story, child kidnapping had not been a national issue. [37]It was only after sustained media coverage put Smart and the Amber alert system in headlines that the problem received national attention.

[38]Fourth, the media influence public opinion through a subtle process referred to as framing. [39]*Framing* is the process by which a news organization defines a political issue and consequently affects opinion about the issue. [40]For example, an experiment conducted by one group of scholars found that if a news story about a Ku Klux Klan rally was framed as a civil rights story, then viewers were generally tolerant of the rally. [41]In this case, the story was about the right of a group to express their ideas, even if they are unpopular ideas. [42]However, the same story, if framed as a law and order issue, then public tolerance for the rally decreased. [43]In this case, the story was about how the actions of one group disrupted a community and threatened public safety. [44]In either case, the media exert subtle influence over the way people respond to the same information.

[45]Fifth, the media have the power to indirectly impact the way the public sees politicians and government. [46]For example, choices voters make in presidential elections are often related to their view of the economy. [47]In general, a healthy economy causes voters to reelect the sitting president. [48]In contrast, a weak economy causes voters to choose the challenger. [49]Hence, if the media paint a consistently dismal picture of the economy, then that picture may well hurt the sitting president seeking reelection. [50]In fact, one study convincingly proves this point. [51]The media's relentlessly negative coverage of the economy in 1992 shaped voters' view of the economy. [52]Thus, negative media helped lead to George Bush's defeat in the 1992 presidential election.

—Adapted from O'Connor & Sabato, *American Government: Continuity and Change*, 2008 ed., pp. 571–572.

_____ **1.** The overall thought pattern for the passage is
   a. comparison.
   b. contrast.
   c. definition and example.
   d. cause and effect.

_____ **2.** The relationship of ideas between sentences 9 and 10 is
   a. comparison.
   b. contrast.
   c. cause and effect.
   d. generalization and example.

_____ **3.** The relationship of ideas between sentences 17 and 18 is
   a. comparison.
   b. contrast.
   c. definition and example.
   d. cause and effect.

_____ **4.** The relationship of ideas between sentences 39 and 40 is
   a. comparison.
   b. contrast.
   c. definition and example
   d. cause and effect.

WHAT DO YOU THINK?

Do you think media influences the way people think or the choices they make? Do you think *framing* is a fair practice in the media? Assume you are a reporter for your college newspaper. The administration has just made two announcements. Tuition is going up by 10%, and the college is going to build a multimillion dollar sports complex. Write an article that frames the story to either favor or oppose the administration's decisions.

REVIEW TEST 4   Score (number correct) _____ × 10 = _____%

Transitions and Thought Patterns

Before you read the following essay from the college textbook *Encyclopedia of Stress,* skim the passage and answer the Before Reading questions. Read the essay. Then answer the After Reading questions.

Technostress

[1]The computer revolution has created a new form of stress that is threatening the physical and mental health of many workers. [2]"Technostress" is a modern disorder caused by an inability to cope in a healthy manner with the new computer technology.

[3]Technostress reveals itself in several distinct ways. [4]It can surface as a person struggles to learn how to use computers in the workplace, which often **provokes** anxiety. [5]Some people develop a **phobia** about modern technology and need professional help to deal with their fears.

[6]Technostress can also surface as overidentification with computers. [7]Some people develop a machinelike **mind-set** that reflects the traits of the computer itself. [8]Some who were once warm and sensitive people become cold, lose their friends, and have no patience for the easy give-and-take of conversation. [9]In addition, they watch television as their major or only leisure activity.

[10]Further, *technostress* is the term used for such physical stress reactions as computer-related eyestrain, headaches, neck and shoulder tension, and backache. [11]Also, many people who use computer keyboards often develop carpal tunnel syndrome.

[12]These various reactions to technostress arise from long-term use of computers. [13]If someone spends most of their working hours **interacting with** only a computer screen and a keyboard, then that person may develop a number of the following symptoms.

[14]Eyestrain is caused by focusing continuously on a screen at close range. [15]The person who focuses for a long time on one specific colored screen may see the **complementary** color when looking up at a blank wall or ceiling. [16]This color reversal is normal and quickly lessens. [17]Headaches, though sometimes caused by eyestrain, are most often due to tension involving muscles of the brow, temples, jaw, upper neck, and base of the skull. [18]These headaches can be affected by improper height of the chair and screen. [19]Even the lack of an armrest can contribute. [20]Lack of an armrest causes the arms to pull down on the shoulders, creating, in turn, tension at the shoulder tip and base of the skull and spasms radiating up into the head. [21]Carpal tunnel syndrome, a numbness, tingling, or burning sensation in the fingers or wrists, may be induced by **inflammation** of the ligaments and tendons in fingers and wrists.

—Adapted from McGuigan, *Encyclopedia of Stress*, pp. 237–238.

VISUAL VOCABULARY

The best meaning of **ergonomic**
is ——————.

   a. poorly designed.
   b. well designed.
   c. cheaply produced.

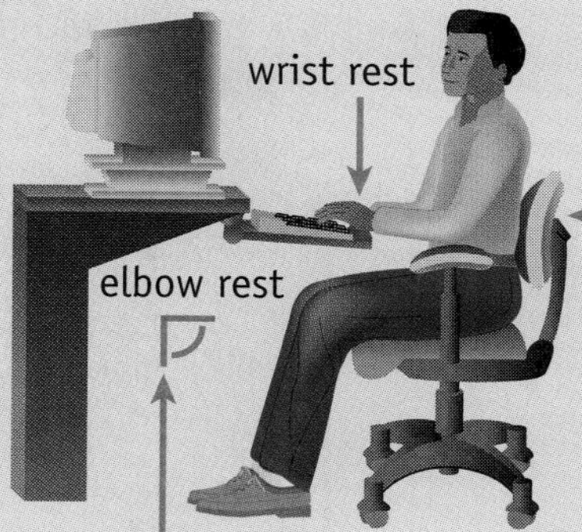

wrist rest

seat angle

elbow rest

knee angle

An ergonomic chair will provide appropriate support to the back, legs, buttocks, and arms. This support can reduce contact stress, overexertion, and fatigue. It will also promote proper circulation to the extremities.

"Ergonomic Solutions: Workstation Chair." Occupational Safety and Health Administration U. S. Department of Labor. Online 16 June 2003. http://www.osha.gov/SLTC/computerworkstations_ecat/chair.html

BEFORE READING
Vocabulary in Context

———— **1.** The term **mind-set** in sentence 7 means
   a. stubbornness.   c. attitude.
   b. decision.   d. opinion.

———— **2.** The best synonym for **complementary** in sentence 15 is
   a. beautiful.   c. praise.
   b. opposite.   d. similar.

AFTER READING
Concept Map

3–4. Finish the concept map by filling in the missing idea with information from the passage.

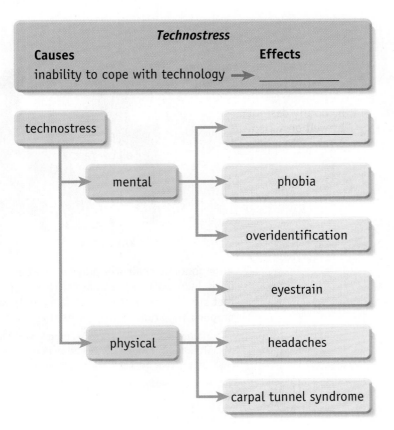

Central Idea and Main Idea

_____ **5.** Which sentence states the central idea of the passage?
  a. sentence 1   c. sentence 12
  b. sentence 2   d. sentence 13

Supporting Details

_____ **6.** Sentence 19 is a
  a. major supporting detail.   b. minor supporting detail.

Transitions

_____ **7.** The word **further** in sentence 10 is a signal word that shows
  a. comparison.   c. addition.
  b. cause.

_____ **8.** The word **though** in sentence 17 signals
   a. cause and effect.   c. addition.
   b. contrast.

Thought Patterns

_____ **9.** The primary thought pattern for the entire passage is
   a. cause and effect.   c. comparison and contrast.
   b. generalization and example.

_____ **10.** The thought pattern for the fourth paragraph (sentences 10–11) is
   a. cause and effect.   c. listing.
   b. generalization and example.

WHAT DO YOU THINK?

Do you or someone you know suffer from technostress? Although this selection discusses the negative effects of technology, what are some of the benefits of technology? Do the advantages outweigh the disadvantages? What other technology besides computers could lead to technostress? How could a person lessen the stress associated with technostress? Assume you are an office manager, and you are giving a presentation about technostress at a training session for new employees. Write a draft of your presentation. Warn new employees about the dangers of technostress and offer ways in which they can avoid or reduce technostress.

After Reading About More Thought Patterns

Before you move on to the Mastery Tests on thought patterns, take time to reflect on your learning and performance by answering the following questions. Write your answers in your notebook.

- How has my knowledge base or prior knowledge about thought pattenrs changed?

- Based on my studies, how do I think I will perform on the Mastery Test(s)? Why do I think my scores will be above average, average, or below average?

- Would I recommend this chapter to other students who want to learn more thought patterns? Why or why not?

Test your understanding of what you what have learned about thought patterns by completing the Chapter 8 Review Card in the insert near the end of the text.

CONNECT TO myreadinglab

To check your progress in meeting Chapter 8's learning outcomes, log in to www.myreadinglab.com, and try the following activities:

- The "Patterns of Organization" section of MyReadingLab gives additional information about transitions and patterns of organization. The section provides a model, practices, activities, and tests. To access this resource, click on the "Study Plan" tab. Then click on "Patterns of Organization." Then click on the following links as needed: "Overview," "Model," "Signal Words (Flash Animation)," "Other Patterns of Organization (Flash Animation)," "Practice," and "Tests."

- To measure your mastery of the content of this chapter, complete the tests in the "Patterns of Organization" section and click on Gradebook to find your result.

Name _____ Section _____

Date _____ Score (number correct) _____ × 5 = _____ %

A. Write the numbers **1** to **9** in the spaces provided to show the correct order of the ideas. Then answer the question that follows the list.

Textbook
Skills

Expected Effects of Cocaine

_____ The first effect the user can expect is a powerful burst of energy.

_____ However, if snorted through the nose, the effect begins in about three to five minutes; it peaks after fifteen to twenty minutes and wears off in sixty to ninety minutes.

_____ If the cocaine is injected through the veins, the effect is immediate and intense; it peaks in three to five minutes and wears off in thirty to forty minutes.

_____ Cocaine users can expect certain effects.

_____ The time it takes to feel the effects vary, based on whether the cocaine is injected or snorted.

_____ Users can also expect to experience a general sense of well-being.

_____ However, in some instances, cocaine may cause a panic attack.

_____ Finally, these uncomfortable aftereffects create a powerful craving for another dose.

_____ Once the cocaine wears off, the user becomes irritable and depressed.

—Adapted from Levinthal, Charles F. Drugs, *Behavior, and Modern Society*, 3rd ed., p. 81. Published by Allyn and Bacon, Boston, MA. Copyright © 2002 by Pearson Education.

_____ **10.** The primary thought pattern is
   a. generalization and example.
   b. comparison and contrast.
   c. cause and effect.

B. Fill in the blanks with the correct transition word or phrase from the box. Use each transition once.

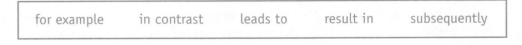

| for example | in contrast | leads to | result in | subsequently |

Rest Well

Adequate rest **(11)** _____ improved performance. **(12)** _____, sleep deprivation causes a host of problems. **(13)** _____, lack of rest may **(14)** _____ loss of concentration and loss of energy. **(15)** _____, poor concentration and lack of energy could lead to slow and flawed work.

C. Write the letter of the appropriate thought pattern before each item, as follows:

a. generalization and example
b. comparison and contrast
c. cause and effect

_____ **16.** Marcel began to practice yoga because of a shoulder injury.

_____ **17.** Marcel compared several types of yoga to determine which method was best for him.

_____ **18.** For example, he considered Iyengar yoga, a style of yoga emphasizing body placement and alignment.

_____ **19.** In addition, he thought about Ashtanga yoga, also known as power yoga, which focuses on high-energy, free-flowing movement.

_____ **20.** Marcel chose Ashtanga because he enjoys an intense workout.

Read the paragraphs from college textbooks. Then answer the questions and complete the concept maps.

Public Speaking Anxiety

[1]Fear of public speaking causes major anxiety for a number of Americans. [2]Understanding some of its causes and effects often helps relieve public speaking anxiety. [3]This anxiety is triggered by the anticipation of performing in front of an audience. [4]Many fear public speaking because they fear they will make a mistake and look foolish. [5]In some instances, lack of preparation contributes to the problem. [6]A few obvious physical effects are a quavering voice, stuttering, vomiting, cold and sweaty hands, dry mouth, and even fainting. [7]This fear can also have mental effects, such as blocked ideas or short-term memory loss.

—Adapted from McGuigan, *Encyclopedia of Stress*, p. 210.

_____ **1.** The relationship between sentence 4 and sentence 5 is
a. cause and effect.   c. comparison.
b. addition.

Causes and Effects of Public Speaking Anxiety

Main idea: Understanding some of its causes and effects often helps lessen the fear of speaking in public.

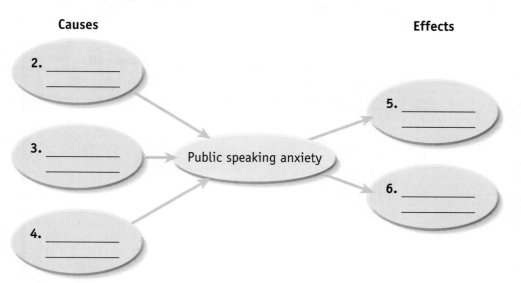

Causes

2. _____

3. _____

4. _____

Public speaking anxiety

Effects

5. _____

6. _____

Textbook
Skills

Different Perspectives

[1]The same event in a family has a different meaning for each of its family members, based on age and cognitive ability. [2]This difference in perspectives can be clearly seen in studies on the effects of parents' divorce on their children. [3]Children who are 5 years old when parents divorce respond in predictable ways that are different from the predictable ways that 11-year-olds respond. [4]Five-year-olds assume the divorce is a result of something they did, whereas 11-year-olds can reason and understand that the divorce may be caused by other factors.

—Adapted from Kosslyn, *Psychology: The Brain, The Person, The World,*
Text Excerpt from p. 378 © 2001 Allyn and Bacon. Reproduced
by permission of Pearson Education, Inc.

_____ **7.** The relationship between sentence 1 and sentence 2 is
    a. definition.
    b. comparison and contrast.
    c. cause and effect.

_____ **8.** The thought patterns used in the paragraph are comparison and contrast and
    a. generalization and example.
    b. time order.
    c. cause and effect.

> The same event in a family has a different meaning for each of its family members, based on age and cognitive ability.

9. 5-year-olds _____
_____
_____

10. 11-year-olds _____
_____
_____

A. Read the following paragraph from a college finance textbook. Then answer the question and complete the concept map.

Buying a Car Online Versus Buying a Car on a Lot

Textbook
Skills

[1]Buying a new car online is still not as efficient as buying a car off a dealer's lot. [2]The personal options of a car make online buying difficult. [3]First, at a dealership, a customer can actually see the difference in the design of the two models of a particular car. [4]It is not as easy to detect the differences on a Web site. [5]Second, unlike a Web site, a dealer can also anticipate your questions and arrange for a test drive. [6]It is also more difficult to communicate with an online service. [7]For example, it is difficult to force an online service to meet its delivery promise to you because you have limited access to them through email and phone messages. [8]However, you can place pressure on a local dealership to meet its promise by showing up at the dealership to express your concerns in person.

> —Adapted from Madura, *Personal Finance Update*, Text Excerpt from p. 235 © 2006 Pearson Education Inc. Reproduced by permission of Pearson Education, Inc.

_____ **1.** The thought patterns used in the paragraph are listing and
   a. definition.
   b. comparison and contrast.
   c. cause and effect.

Buying a Car Online Versus Buying a Car on a Lot

Main idea: Buying a new car online is still not as efficient as buying a car off a dealer's lot.

	Online	Dealership
First difference	Customer can't see differences in cars.	Customer can see differences in cars.
Second difference	(2) _____ _____	(3) _____ _____
Third difference	(4) _____ _____	(5) _____ _____

B. Read the following paragraph from a college psychology textbook. Then answer the question and complete the outline with the major supporting details.

Textbook
Skills

Effects of Sleep Deprivation

¹If you have ever stayed up late, say, studying or partying, and then awakened early the next morning, you have probably experienced sleep deprivation. ²In fact, you may be sleep-deprived right now. ³What happens as a result of sleep deprivation? ⁴Young adults who volunteered for a sleep deprivation study were allowed to sleep for only five hours each night, for a total of seven nights. ⁵After three nights of restricted sleep, volunteers complained of mental, emotional, and physical difficulties. ⁶Moreover, their abilities to perform visual motor tasks declined after only two nights. ⁷Hormones are also affected by sleep deprivation. ⁸For example, the loss of even one night's sleep can lead to increases in the next day's level of cortisol. ⁹Cortisol helps the body meet the demands imposed by stress. ¹⁰Finally, going without sleep for long stretches of time, such as 4 to 11 days, causes profound psychological effects. ¹¹Long-term sleep deprivation can lead to feelings of losing control and anxiety.

—Adapted from Kosslyn, *Psychology: The Brain, The Person, The World,*
Text Excerpt from p. 138 © 2001 Allyn and Bacon. Reproduced
by permission of Pearson Education, Inc.

_____ **6.** The thought patterns used in the paragraph are listing and
   a. generalization and example.
   b. comparison and contrast.
   c. cause and effect.

Effects of Sleep Deprivation

(7) _____

(8) _____

(9) _____

(10) _____

Name _____ Section _____

Date _____ Score (number correct) _____ × 10 = _____%

Formal versus Informal Organizational Systems

Textbook
Skills

[1]An organization's formal structure is its official arrangement of jobs and job relationships. [2]In reality, however, all organizations also have another aspect. [3]Informally, people do their jobs in different ways. [4]And they often do not follow formal lines of communication.

[5]The **formal organization** of a business is the part that can be seen and represented in chart form. [6]The structure of a company, however, is by no means limited to a chart and the formal levels of authority. [7]The **informal organization** is the everyday social interactions among employees. [8]And it often rises above formal jobs and job interrelationships. [9]The informal organization in effect alters a company's formal structure. [10]Indeed, this level of organization is sometimes just as powerful—if not more powerful—than the formal structure.

[11]On the negative side, the informal organization can strengthen office politics that put the interests of individuals ahead of those of the firm. [12]Likewise, a great deal of harm can be caused by distorted or wrong information shared without management input or review. [13]For example, the informal organization may share false information about possible layoffs. [14]Then, valuable employees may act quickly (and unnecessarily) to seek other jobs. [15]Among the more important elements of the informal organization are informal groups and the grapevine.

—Adapted from Griffin & Ebert, *Business*, 8th ed., p. 201.

_____ 1. The relationship of ideas between sentences 1 and 2 is
    a. comparison.   c. definition.
    b. contrast.   d. effect.

_____ 2. The relationship of ideas between sentences 4 and 5 is
    a. comparison.   c. definition.
    b. contrast.   d. generalization and example.

_____ 3. The relationship of ideas within sentence 10 is
    a. comparison.   c. definition.
    b. contrast.   d. effect.

_____ 4. The relationship of ideas between sentences 12 and 13 is
    a. comparison.   c. definition.
    b. contrast.   d. generalization and example.

_____   **5.** The title implies that the thought pattern of the passage is
     a. comparison.   c. definition.
     b. contrast.   d. generalization and example.

Read the passage and answer the questions that follow. Then complete the study notes with information from the passage.

Formal organization is (**6**) _____

_____. Informal organization is (**7**) _____

_____. Two negative aspects of informal

organization are the reinforcement of (**8**) _____ and the harm

done by (**9**) _____ or (**10**) _____ information.

Fact and Opinion

9

LEARNING OUTCOMES

After studying this chapter you should be able to do the following:

1. Define the following terms: *fact* and *opinion*.
2. Ask questions to identify facts.
3. Analyze biased words to identify opinions.
4. Analyze supposed "facts."
5. Distinguish between fact and opinion.
6. Evaluate the importance of facts and opinions.

Before Reading About Fact and Opinion

You are most likely already familiar with the commonly used words *fact* and *opinion*, and you probably already have an idea about what each one means. Take a moment to clarify your current understanding about fact and opinion by writing a definition for each one in the spaces below:

Fact: _____

_____

Opinion: _____

_____

_____

As you work through this chapter, compare what you already know about fact and opinion to new information that you learn about each one using the following method:

On a blank page in your notebook, draw a line down the middle of the page to form two columns. Label one side "Fact" and the other side "Opinion." Just below each heading, copy the definition you wrote for each one. As you work through the chapter, record new information you learn about facts and opinions in their corresponding column.

What Is the Difference Between Fact and Opinion?

Fact: Eva Longoria is known for her role as Gabrielle Solis on ABC's *Desperate Housewives*.

Opinion: Eva Longoria is one of the most influential Hispanics in Hollywood.

Effective readers must sort fact from opinion to properly understand and evaluate the information they are reading.

> A **fact** is a specific detail that is true based on objective proof. A fact is discovered.
> An **opinion** is an interpretation, value judgment, or belief that cannot be proved or disproved. An opinion is created.
> **Objective proof** can be physical evidence, an eyewitness account, or the result of an accepted scientific method.

Most people's points of view and beliefs are based on a blend of fact and opinion. Striving to remain objective, many authors rely mainly on facts. The main purpose of using facts is to inform. For example, textbooks, news articles, and medical research rely on facts. In contrast, editorials, advertisements, and fiction often mix fact and opinion. The main purpose of these types of writing is to persuade or entertain.

Separating fact from opinion requires you to think critically because opinion is often presented as fact. The following clues will help you separate fact from opinion.

Fact	Opinion
Is objective	Is subjective
Is discovered	Is created
States reality	Interprets reality
Can be verified	Cannot be verified
Is presented with unbiased words	Is presented with biased words
Example of a fact	*Example of an opinion*
Spinach is a source of iron.	Spinach tastes awful.

A fact is a specific, objective, and verifiable detail; in contrast, an opinion is a biased, personal view created from feelings and beliefs.

EXAMPLE Read the following statements, and mark each one **F** if it states a fact or **O** if it expresses an opinion.

_____ **1.** *Avatar* is a 3D science fiction movie written and directed by James Cameron.

_____ **2.** James Cameron's films are always too predictable, with worn-out stories and stereotypical characters.

_____ **3.** Within three weeks of its release, earning over $1 billion, *Avatar* became the second highest-grossing film of all time worldwide, exceeded only by Cameron's previous film, *Titanic*.

_____ **4.** *Avatar* takes us to a spectacular world beyond imagination.

EXPLANATION Sentences 1 and 3 state facts that can be verified through research. Sentences 2 and 4 express opinions, personal reactions to James Cameron's work as a filmmaker. Sentence 2 expresses a negative personal opinion; sentence 4 expresses a positive personal opinion.

PRACTICE 1

Read the following statements and mark each one **F** if it states a fact or **O** if it expresses an opinion.

_____ **1.** Michelangelo is the greatest painter of all time.

_____ **2.** The Sistine Chapel is the private chapel of the popes in Rome.

_____ **3.** Between 1508 and 1512, Michelangelo produced frescos for the chapel's ceiling; the murals depict scenes from the Book of Genesis, from the Creation to the Flood.

_____ **4.** One cannot really understand what a human is capable of producing until one sees Michelangelo's work in the Sistine Chapel.

Ask Questions to Identify Facts

To test whether a statement is a fact, ask these three questions:

- Can the statement be proved or demonstrated to be true?
- Can the statement be observed in practice or operation?
- Can the statement be verified by witnesses, manuscripts, or documents?

If the answer to any of these questions is no, the statement is not a fact. Instead, it is an opinion. Keep in mind, however, that many statements blend both fact and opinion.

EXAMPLE Read the following statements, and mark each one **F** if it states a fact or **O** if it expresses an opinion.

_____ **1.** Lady Gaga collapsed and passed out before a show in West Lafayette, Indiana.

_____ **2.** Lady Gaga wears outlandish costumes just to get attention.

_____ **3.** Lady Gaga combines music, fashion, art, and technology in her body of work.

_____ **4.** Lady Gaga's stage name is based on the song "Radio Ga Ga" by Freddie Mercury and his band Queen.

EXPLANATION

1. F: This statement can be easily verified in newspapers.

2. O: This is a statement of personal opinion. Some critics and fans may think her costumes are innovative and fun.

3. F: This statement can be verified through research and eyewitness experiences.

4. F: This statement can be easily verified through research.

PRACTICE 2

Read the following statements, and mark each one **F** if it states a fact or **O** if it expresses an opinion.

_____ **1.** In 2010, reality shows like *American Idol, Survivor,* and *America's Next Top Model* still appealed to the American television market.

_____ **2.** Small dogs make the best house pets.

_____ **3.** The chemicals in marijuana smoke can cause cancer.

_____ **4.** Florida, with its mild winters, is the ideal place to retire.

_____ **5.** The poet Emily Dickinson composed over 1,000 poems.

_____ **6.** Spanking of any kind is a form of child abuse.

_____ **7.** The Harry Potter books and films have stimulated many children's interest in reading.

_____ **8.** Television reduces the intelligence of viewers.

_____ **9.** Within the next decade, as the "baby boom" generation retires, a significant number of teachers will leave the work place.

_____ **10.** The mass production of the automobile changed the way people and goods moved from one place to another.

Note Biased Words to Identify Opinions

Be on the lookout for biased words. **Biased words** express opinions, value judgments, and interpretations. They are often loaded with emotion. The box below contains a small sample of these kinds of words.

Biased Words					
amazing	best	favorite	great	miserable	stupid
awful	better	frightful	greatest	more	ugly
bad	disgusting	fun	handsome	most	unbelievable
beautiful	exciting	good	horrible	smart	very

Realize that a sentence can include both facts and opinions. The part of the sentence that includes a biased word may be an opinion about another part of the sentence that is a fact.

EXAMPLE Read the following sentences. Underline the biased words.

1. Even though actor George Clooney is around 50 years old, he is still very handsome.

2. The grasslands of the American West were tragically plowed under for crops.

EXPLANATION
In the first sentence, "George Clooney is around 50 years old" is a fact that can be proved by research. However, the second part of the sentence, "he is still very handsome," is an opinion about his appearance. In the second sentence, the grasslands of the American West _were_ plowed under to make way for crops, but whether that fact is tragic is a matter of opinion.

PRACTICE 3

Read the following sentences. Underline the biased words.

1. Even though spinach is low in calories and rich in fiber, iron, folate, and vitamin A, its bitter taste makes it a less desirable food.

2. A Labrador retriever is a medium-sized dog with a distinctive double coat that requires brushing; loyal and friendly, this breed makes an excellent pet for a family.

 Note Qualifiers to Identify Opinions

Be on the lookout for words that qualify an idea. A qualifier may express an absolute, unwavering opinion using words such as *always* or *never*. Other times a qualifier expresses an opinion in the form of a command as in *must*, or the desirability of an action with a word such as *should*. Qualifiers may indicate different degrees of doubt with words such as *seems* or *might*. The box below contains a few examples of these kinds of words.

Words That Qualify Ideas					
all	could	likely	never	possibly, possible	sometimes
always	every	may	often	probably, probable	think
appear	has/have to	might	only	seem	usually
believe	it is believed	must	ought to	should	

Remember that a sentence can include both fact and opinion. Authors use qualifiers to express opinions about facts.

EXAMPLE Read the following sentences. Underline the qualifiers.

1. Every citizen who wants to be informed about current events should subscribe to at least two newspapers and never miss the nightly news.

2. Amber, fossilized tree resin, was one of the first substances used for decoration; it is believed to exert a healthful influence on the endocrine system, spleen, and heart.

EXPLANATION

1. The qualifiers in this sentence are *every*, *should*, and *never*. The fact is that newspapers and the nightly news do cover current events, but these qualifiers express a personal opinion about this fact.

2. The qualifier in this sentence is the phrase *it is believed*. The author has signaled that what follows is not a proven fact, only a belief.

PRACTICE 4

Read the following sentences. Underline the qualifiers.

1. While swimming, the woman suddenly disappeared from sight, possibly pulled underwater by an alligator.

2. You have to let me go to the annual New Year's Eve celebration in Times Square; everybody is going. I will be the only one who can't go.

Think Carefully About Supposed "Facts"

Beware of **false facts,** or statements presented as facts that are actually untrue. At times, an author may mislead the reader with a false impression of the facts. Political and commercial advertisements often present facts out of context, exaggerate the facts, or give only some of the facts. For example, a retailer publishes the following claim in a local newspaper: "Batteries for $.10 each." However, the batteries are sold in packets of one hundred; they are not sold individually. Even though the advertisement told a partial truth, it misled consumers by leaving out an important fact. A truthful advertisement of the same situation states, "Batteries for $.10 each, sold only in packages of 100 for $10.00 per package."

Sometimes an author deliberately presents false information. Janet Cooke, a reporter for the *Washington Post,* concocted a false story about a boy named Jimmy, whom she described as "8 years old and a third-generation heroin addict," and whose ambition was to be a heroin dealer when he grew up. After she won a Pulitzer Prize for this story, it was learned that she had never met Jimmy and most of the details were simply not true. The *Washington Post* also learned that she had falsified facts on her résumé. She was fired, and the *Washington Post* returned the Pulitzer Prize. Cooke's use of false facts ruined her career and embarrassed the prestigious newspaper.

Read the following two examples of false facts:

1. The earliest humans lived at the same time as the dinosaurs.

2. The virus that causes mononucleosis, also known as the kissing disease, can be spread through the air.

Fossil records and scientific research have proved that the first statement is a false fact. The second statement is a false fact because the virus that causes mononucleosis can be spread only through contact with saliva. Often some prior knowledge of the topic is needed to identify false facts. The more you read, the more effective you will become at evaluating facts as true or false.

False facts can be used to mislead, persuade, or entertain. For example, read the following headline and four sentences published in the *National Enquirer* on March 2, 1976:

Carol Burnett and Henry K. in Row

In a Washington restaurant, a boisterous Carol Burnett had a loud argument with another diner, Henry Kissinger. Then she traipsed around the place offering everyone a bite of her dessert. But Carol really raised eyebrows when she accidentally knocked a glass of wine over one diner and started giggling instead of apologizing. The guy wasn't amused and "accidentally" spilled a glass of water over Carol's dress.

—*Carol Burnett v. National Enquirer, Inc.*

As a result of this article, Carol Burnett sued and won a settlement against the tabloid for making false statements. Note the value words the author used to describe Burnett's behavior: *boisterous, loud, traipsed, raised eyebrows,* and *giggling.*

VISUAL VOCABULARY

A bull wapiti (elk) **traipses** into a residential neighborhood in Banff, Alberta, disrupting traffic.

The best synonym for traipses

is _____.

a. wanders.
b. runs.
c. stumbles.

In addition to thinking carefully about false facts, beware of opinions stated to sound like facts. Remember that facts are specific details that can be researched and verified as true. However, opinions may be introduced as facts with phrases like "in truth," "the truth of the matter," or "in fact." Read the following two statements:

1. In truth, computers make life miserable.

2. Computers make life miserable; in point of fact, on November 2, 1988, Robert Morris sent out a computer "worm" that caused many computers around the country to crash. Damages to each computer ranged from $200 to $53,000.

—United States v. Robert Morris

The first statement is a general opinion that uses the value word *miserable*. The second statement is a blend of fact and opinion. It begins with a biased statement, but then uses the phrase "in point of fact" to introduce factual details.

EXAMPLES Read the following statements, and mark each one as follows:

F if it states a fact

O if it expresses an opinion

F/O if it combines fact and opinion

_____ **1.** *30 Rock* is the American television comedy series created by Tina Fey; the name "30 Rock" refers to the address of the building where NBC Studios is located, 30 Rockefeller Plaza.

_____ **2.** *30 Rock* is America's favorite comedy, winning several major awards; for example, the show won the Emmy Awards for Outstanding Comedy Series in 2007, 2008, and 2009.

_____ **3.** So far, the show's highest ratings occurred during its third season, with 8.5 million viewers.

_____ **4.** In addition to writing for and acting on *30 Rock*, Tina Fey also performs a hilarious and insulting parody of Sarah Palin.

_____ **5.** Everyone should watch *30 Rock*.

EXPLANATIONS

Items 1 and 3 are facts that can be verified through research. Item 5 states an opinion by using the phrasing "Everyone should." Item 2 is a mixture of fact and opinion. Research verifies that *30 Rock* has won the listed awards, but the word "favorite" is a value word, and the use of "America" implies that everyone in America favors this show—an idea that cannot be verified. Item 4 also blends fact and opinion. The facts are that Tina Fey writes and acts for *30 Rock* and she does perform a parody of Sarah Palin. However, the words "hilarious" and "insulting" are statements of opinion about which people will disagree.

EXAMPLE   Study the following editorial cartoon. Then write one fact and one opinion based on the issue as expressed in the cartoon.

Fact: _____

_____

Opinion: _____

_____

EXPLANATIONS   Answers will vary. Compare your answers to the following:

Fact: Texting while driving distracts drivers and causes accidents.

Opinion: Texting while driving should be illegal.

PRACTICE 5

A. Read the following statements. Circle biased words and qualifiers as needed. Then, mark each one as follows:

F if it states a fact

O if it expresses an opinion

F/O if it combines fact and opinion

_____ **1.** Unhealthy diets and lack of exercise are serious national problems; in fact, 300,000 deaths each year are linked to these two problems.

_____ **2.** Tobacco use kills more Americans than motor vehicle crashes, AIDS, cocaine use, heroin use, homicide, and suicide combined.

_____ **3.** Tobacco products should be outlawed.

_____ **4.** Diets high in fruits, vegetables, and fiber lower the risk for some types of cancer.

_____ **5.** Public schools ought to serve fruits and vegetables instead of pizza and hamburgers.

_____ **6.** Exercise is the only sure way to lose weight.

_____ **7.** Executives of tobacco companies murder millions of people with their products.

_____ **8.** All cancers caused by cigarette smoking could be prevented.

_____ **9.** The sugar glider, which is a small opossum, is smaller than a gerbil, larger than a mouse, and more adorable than a teddy bear.

_____ **10.** Pot-bellied pigs make great pets.

B. Read the following short reviews of destinations, restaurants, movies, and plays. Circle biased words and qualifiers as needed. Then, mark each one as follows:

F if it states a fact

O if it expresses an opinion

F/O if it combines fact and opinion

_____ **11.** The Palms Casino Resort in Las Vegas is the absolute best tourist destination.

_____ **12.** Russell Crowe stars in the thrilling remake of *Robin Hood,* the legendary hero who heroically fought against injustice by robbing from the rich to give to the poor.

_____ **13.** The Nine Steakhouse, which serves prime aged steaks and imported spirits, is Chicago's most popular night spot.

_____ **14.** Set at the edge of Texas Hill Country on the Colorado River, Austin, the capital of Texas, offers many unexpected pleasures to the visitor.

_____ **15.** After pirates, hurricanes, and wars, Key West, Florida survives as a great tourist town, with superb sunsets, informal living, wonderful festivals, relaxing beaches, top fishing possibilities, and all the services that a visitor could want.

_____ **16.** Wake up and break out of your old routine with breakfast at Sonic. Our one-of-a-kind breakfast menu offers a variety of tempting items like Toaster Sandwiches, breakfast burritos, smoothies and other morning favorites—all with the same, friendly Carhop service!

—Sonic, "Breakfast."

_____ **17.** Peter Jackson's Oscar-winning film of the *Lord of the Rings* epic by J. R. R. Tolkien remains one of the greatest achievements in cinema history.

_____ **18.** *Phantom of the Opera* is the longest-running production in Broadway history.

_____ **19.** Half of the land on Sanibel Island, Florida, is designated as natural areas, with two preserves protecting the island ecosystem and wildlife.

_____ **20.** The *Internet Movie Database* remains the ultimate source for movie and movie star information.

 ## Read Critically: Evaluate Details as Fact or Opinion in Context

Because the printed word seems to give authority to an idea, many of us accept what we read as fact. Yet much of what is published is actually opinion.

Effective readers question what they read. Reading critically is noting the use of fact and opinion in the context of a paragraph or passage, the author, and the type of source in which the passage is printed.

Evaluate the Context of the Passage

Much of what you read in print and electronic media is a mixture of factual details and the author's opinion. Often, an author words an opinion as a fact in an effort to make a point more believable. One way to distinguish between fact and opinion is to evaluate the context. The language used by an author helps us to decide whether a statement can be backed up with evidence and proven in some way. Language also indicates whether the statement is someone's point of view, judgement or belief. You have already studied biased words and qualifiers that signal an opinion. Also consider the following examples of language that expresses facts and opinions.

Examples of Language Expressing Facts	Examples of Language Expressing Opinions
According to the results of the latest poll.	The prosecution **argues** that
The latest studies **confirm**	The defense **claims** that
The research has **demonstrated**	In the President's **view**
Researchers have recently **discovered**	Most experts in this field **suspect** that

In addition to the wording of an idea, relationships between ideas and thought patterns may also signal a fact or an opinion. For example, facts are often stated as examples or details that can be verified.

Examples of Thought Patterns for Facts	Examples of Thought Patterns for Opinions
Definition	Comparisons
Causes and Effects	Reasons (explanations and interpretations)
Examples	Quality, Traits, Attributes
Details	

Of course, some comparisons and traits are factual. And authors can present possible or probable causes and effects that haven't been proven. So an effective reader must analyze the context of each statement.

The mixture of fact and opinion occurs when an author interprets or evaluates a fact. Look at the following three statements in which the facts are highlighted in red and the opinions are highlighted in green.

Fact: **A constitution is a document establishing the structure, function, and limitations of a government.**

Opinion: The United States Constitution is far superior to other forms of government.

Fact and **Opinion:** **The fifty-five delegates who attended the Constitutional Convention** labored long and hard that hot **summer of 1787.**

The first statement is a definition, a fact that can be verified. The second statement begins like a definition but really only offers an opinion based on a comparison. The third statement offers factual historical details. However, the author has also characterized the work of the delegates with biased language that describes traits of the work and the environment. The phrase "labored long and hard" may have different meanings to different people. The questions "how hard and how long" remain unverified. Likewise, what is "hot" to one person may not be "hot" to another. Thus, the trait "hot" is a statement of opinion.

EXAMPLE Read the passage, and identify each sentence as follows:

F if it states a fact

O if it expresses an opinion

F/O if it combines fact and opinion

Alexander the Great

[1]Alexander III, more commonly known as Alexander the Great, was one of the greatest military leaders in world history. [2]He was born in Pella, Macedonia. [3]The exact date of his birth was probably July 20 or 26, 356 B.C. [4]Shortly before his 33rd birthday, Alexander the Great died. [5]The cause of his death remains unknown.

1. _____ 2. _____ 3. _____ 4. _____ 5. _____

EXPLANATION

1. **F/O:** His name and title are factual, but the value word *greatest* is an opinion with which some people may disagree.

2. **F:** This statement can be verified in historical records.

3. **O:** The word *probably* makes this a statement of opinion.

4. **F:** This statement can be checked and verified as true.

5. **F:** This is a factual statement that something isn't known.

PRACTICE 6

A. Read the passage, and identify each sentence as follows:

F if it states a fact

O if it expresses an opinion

F/O if it combines fact and opinion

Tough Little Robot

[1]The United States government sponsors research projects to advance traditional military roles and missions. [2]One such project is the Tactical Mobile Robot program and one advanced robot created under this program is called Packbot. [3]Packbot is a tough little robot developed by iRobot of Somerville, MA, for The Defense Advanced Research Projects Agency, or DARPA. [4]Small in size, but durable and versatile, Packbot was designed to venture into areas too dangerous for people. [5]The value of robots in real-world situations was demonstrated after the collapse of the World Trade Centers. [6]Drew Bennent of iRobot helped deploy Packbots supporting search and rescue operations. [7]Packbots went where it was just too dangerous for the human crews. [8]Right now the robot is equipped with a video camera and the operator can "see" on a computer screen what the robot sees. [9]Researchers working with a special response team are exploring its existing capabilities. [10]They are developing scenarios where Packbot could gather intelligence, create a diversion, or act as a force multiplier.

—Gatens, Kathy. "Science Fiction becomes Science Reality." *Robotics and Intelligence Systems.* Idaho National Laboratory, U. S. Department of Energy. https://inlportal.inl.gov/portal/server.pt?open=512&objID=455& PageID=6129&cached=true&mode=2&userID=3338.

1. _____   2. _____   3. _____   4. _____   5. _____

6. _____   7. _____   8. _____   9. _____   10. _____

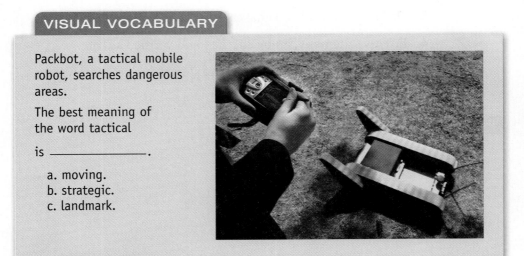

VISUAL VOCABULARY

Packbot, a tactical mobile robot, searches dangerous areas.

The best meaning of the word tactical

is —————————.

   a. moving.
   b. strategic.
   c. landmark.

Evaluate the Context of the Author

Even though opinions can't be proved true like facts can, many opinions are still sound and valuable. To judge the accuracy of the opinion, you must consider the source, the author of the opinion. Authors offer two types of valid opinions: informed opinions and expert opinions.

> An author develops an **informed opinion** by gathering and analyzing evidence.
> An author develops an **expert opinion** through much training and extensive knowledge in a given field.

EXAMPLE   Read the topic and study the list of authors who have written their opinions about the topic. Identify each person as **IO** if he or she is more likely to offer an informed opinion and **EO** if he or she is more likely to offer an expert opinion.

How to Parent a Teen

———— **1.** Dr. Lisa Boesky, a leading child psychologist, television guest expert, national speaker, and author of several books such as *When to Worry: How to Tell if Your Teen Needs Help—and What to Do About It*

———— **2.** An advice columnist such as Ann Landers or Dear Abby responding to a reader's question

_____ **3.** A pediatrician giving advice to the parents of one of his patients

_____ **4.** A high school science teacher who writes a lesson plan about disciplining children for a unit on human development in a health class

EXPLANATION

1. Dr. Boesky is considered to be an expert opinion in the field of child-rearing. One way to identify an expert opinion is to note if the person giving the opinion holds an advanced degree or title or has published articles or books about the topic being discussed. Boesky has both the education and the achievement of being a successful author about this topic.

2. Advice columnists offer informed opinions on a wide range of topics. They often cite experts in their advice.

3. A pediatrician is a medical doctor for children. A pediatrician has had extensive training in childhood development.

4. A health teacher offers an informed opinion based on research to prepare the lesson. The teacher's main field is not childhood development, but science.

Evaluate the Context of the Source

Often people turn to factual sources to find the factual details needed to form informed opinions and expert opinions. A medical dictionary, an English handbook, and a world atlas are a few excellent examples of factual sources.

EXAMPLE Read the passage, and then answer the questions that follow it.

Statement by the Secretary of the Norwegian Nobel Committee

[1]There are more than 300 peace prizes in the world. [2]None is in any way as well known and as highly respected as the Nobel Peace Prize. [3]The *Oxford Dictionary of Twentieth-Century World History*, to cite just one example, states that the Nobel Peace Prize is "the world's most prestigious prize awarded for the 'preservation of peace.'" [4]Personally, I think there are many reasons for this prestige: the long history of the Peace Prize; the fact that it belongs to a family of prizes, the Nobel family, where all the family members benefit from the relationship; the growing political

independence of the Norwegian Nobel Committee; and the monetary value of the prize, particularly in the early years and in the most recent years of its history. ⁵One important element of the history of the prize has been the committee's broad definition of peace.

—Adapted from Lundestad, "The Nobel Peace Prize, 1901–2000," p. 163.

_____ **1.** Sentence 1 is a
  a. fact.   b. opinion.

_____ **2.** The *Oxford Dictionary of Twentieth-Century World History* in sentence 3 serves as
  a. an informed opinion.   b. factual resource.

_____ **3.** Sentence 4 states
  a. a fact.   b. an expert opinion.

EXPLANATION

  1. Sentence 1 is a statement of fact.

  2. In sentence 3, the *Oxford Dictionary of Twentieth-Century World History* serves as a factual resource on which expert and informed opinions are based.

  3. Sentence 4 is the author's expert opinion backed up by facts. As the secretary of the Norwegian Nobel Committee, Lundestad offers a list of fact-based reasons to back up his personal, expert opinion.

PRACTICE 7

Read the passage, and then answer the questions that follow it.

¹Dreams, those mysterious worlds we enter once we fall asleep, have fascinated humankind for generations. ²According to the *Grolier Encyclopedia of Knowledge*, dream interpretation dates back to 2000 B.C. ³People in ancient Greece, Rome, Egypt, and China recorded and studied their dreams. ⁴Views on dreams have been as varied and as vivid as the cultures of the people who have studied them. ⁵Some believed dreams to be messages from God. ⁶Others thought them to be signs of indigestion. ⁷Neil Carlson and William Buskist, authors of the textbook *Psychology: The Science of Behavior,* state that people have long used dreams to wage war, predict the future, or detect the guilt or innocence of people accused of a crime. ⁸Sigmund Freud, noted psychiatrist, believed

that dreams are connected to our subconscious; he believed that our dreams are the result of emotions and desires we cannot express while awake. [9]Carl Jung, a widely published psychologist who studied under Freud, thought dreams were a way to work out problems we face in our waking lives. [10]No matter what the truth is, one-third of our life is spent dreaming, which adds up to a total of 27 years of our lifetime. [11]And everybody dreams!

_____ **1.** Sentence 1 is
     a. a fact.   b. an opinion.

_____ **2.** In sentence 2, the *Grolier Encyclopedia of Knowledge* offers
     a. a factual source.   b. an opinion.

_____ **3.** Sentence 2 is
     a. a fact.   b. an opinion.

_____ **4.** In sentence 8, Sigmund Freud's ideas are
     a. fact.   b. expert opinion.

_____ **5.** In sentence 9, Carl Jung's ideas are
     a. fact.   b. expert opinion.

VISUAL VOCABULARY

The names of Freud's and Jung's professions share a prefix and a suffix. What are they? The names also have word parts that differ. What are they?

What does each word part mean? Use your dictionary if necessary to complete the chart:

Shared Prefix: _____   Meaning: _____

Shared Suffix: _____   Meaning: _____

Other word parts: iatreia   Meaning: _____

                ology   Meaning: _____

A psychiatrist is one who heals the mind. A psychologist is one who studies the mind.

Fact and Opinion in Textbook Passages

Most textbook authors are careful to present only ideas based on observation, research, and expert opinion. Read the following passage from a college health textbook, and identify each sentence as follows:

F if it states a fact

O if it expresses an opinion

F/O if it combines fact and opinion

Textbook
Skills

EXAMPLE   **Safety Guidelines During Weight Training**

¹During a weight training program, the following guidelines should be followed. ²First, when you use free weights (like barbells), spotters or helpers should assist you as you perform an exercise. ³They help when you are unable to complete a lift. ⁴Second, tightening the collars on the end of the bars of free weights prevents the weights from falling off. ⁵Dropping weight plates on toes and feet results in serious injuries. ⁶Third, warming up before weightlifting protects muscles from injuries. ⁷Finally, using slow movements during weightlifting is a wise approach. ⁸Some experts argue that high-speed weightlifting is superior to slow-speed lifting in terms of strength gains. ⁹However, slow movements may reduce the risk of injury. ¹⁰And slow movement during weightlifting does increase muscle size and strength.

—Adapted from Powers & Dodd, *Total Fitness and Wellness,* 3rd ed., p. 111.

1. _____   2. _____   3. _____   4. _____   5. _____

6. _____   7. _____   8. _____   9. _____   10. _____

EXPLANATION Compare your answers to the ones below.

1. O: The word *should* indicates that this is an opinion or a suggestion. However, keep in mind that textbook authors offer information based on a great deal of research. This particular textbook lists the resources the authors used to form their opinions. This statement is therefore an expert opinion.

2. **O:** The word *should* indicates an opinion.

3. **F:** This is a statement of fact about what spotters can do.

4. **F:** This is a statement of fact that is supported by observation.

5. **F:** This is a statement of fact that can be verified by research and observation.

6. **F:** This is a statement of fact that can be verified through research. In fact, this textbook offers a list of expert and factual sources at the end of the chapter so that students can research the ideas for themselves.

7. **O:** This is an expert opinion based on research. The following sentences state facts to support this opinion.

8. **F:** This is a statement of fact. Experts do debate which method is best. This sentence does not favor one method over the other; it notes there is a debate and states both sides.

9. **F/O:** This is a statement that qualifies the facts. The facts can be verified through research and observation; however, the verb "may" indicates that results can vary.

10. **F:** This is a statement of fact that can be verified through research and observation.

PRACTICE 8

A. Read the following passage from a college history textbook. Then identify each sentence as follows:

> **F** if it states a fact
>
> **O** if it expresses an opinion
>
> **F/O** if it combines fact and opinion

Textbook
Skills

The TV President

¹John Fitzgerald Kennedy was made for television. ²His tall, lean body gave him the strong vertical line that cameras love, and his weather-beaten good looks appealed to women without intimidating men. ³He had a full head of hair, and even in the winter he maintained a tan. ⁴Complementing his appearance was his attitude. ⁵He was always "cool" in public. ⁶This too was tailor-made for the "cool medium," television. ⁷Wit, irony, and understatement, all delivered with a studied ease,

translate well on television. [8]Table-thumping, impassioned speech, and even earnest sincerity often just do not work on television.

[9]The first presidential debate was held in Chicago on September 26, 1960, only a little more than a month before the election. [10]Richard Nixon arrived looking ill and weak. [11]During the previous six weeks, he had banged his kneecap, which became infected, and he had spent several weeks in the hospital. [12]Then he caught a bad cold that left him hoarse and weak. [13]By the day of the debate, he looked like a nervous corpse. [14]He was pale, 20 pounds underweight, and haggard. [15]Makeup experts offered to hide his heavy beard and soften his jaw line, but Nixon accepted only a thin coat of Max Factor's "Lazy Shave," a pancake makeup base.

[16]Kennedy looked better, very much better. [17]He didn't need any makeup to appear healthy, nor did he need special lighting to hide a weak profile. [18]He did, however, change suits. [19]He believed that a dark blue suit rather than a gray suit would look better under the bright lights. [20]Kennedy was right, of course, as anyone who watches a nightly news program realizes.

[21]When the debate started, Kennedy spoke first. [22]Although he was nervous, he slowed down his delivery. [23]His face was controlled and smooth. [24]He smiled with his eyes and perhaps the corners of his mouth, and his laugh was a mere suggestion of a laugh. [25]His body language was perfect.

[26]Nixon fought back. [27]He perspired, scored debating points, gave memorized facts, and struggled to win. [28]But his efforts were "hot"—bad for television. [29]Viewers saw a nervous, uncertain man, one whose clothes did not fit and whose face looked pasty and white.

[30]After the debate, Kennedy inched ahead of Nixon in a Gallup poll. [31]Most of the people who were undecided before watching the debate ended up voting for Kennedy.

—Adapted from Martin et al., *America and Its Peoples: A Mosaic in the Making*, 3rd ed., pp. 1001–02.

———— **1.** His tall, lean body gave him the strong vertical line that cameras love, and his weather-beaten good looks appealed to women without intimidating men.

———— **2.** The first presidential debate was held in Chicago on September 26, 1960, only a little more than a month before the election.

———— **3.** During the previous six weeks, he had banged his kneecap, which became infected, and he had spent several weeks in the hospital.

_____ **4.** By the day of the debate, he looked like a nervous corpse.

_____ **5.** He was pale, 20 pounds underweight, and haggard.

_____ **6.** Kennedy looked better, very much better.

_____ **7.** He did, however, change suits.

B. Study the two pictures, and read the caption below them. Then identify each sentence based on the pictures as follows:

    F if it states a fact

    O if it expresses an opinion

    F/O if it combines fact and opinion

Tom Torlino, a Navajo Indian, photographed before and after his "assimilation." Torlino attended the Carlisle Indian School in Pennsylvania.

_____ **8.** Some Native Americans gave up their traditional dress to fit into white society.

_____ **9.** Native American men wore long hair and jewelry.

_____ **10.** Tom Torlino was more handsome dressed in his native attire than in white attire.

Application 1: Fact and Opinion

Textbook
Skills

The accompanying graph comes from a health textbook. Study the graph, and label each statement based on the graph as follows:

F if it states a fact

O if it expresses an opinion

F/O if it combines fact and opinion

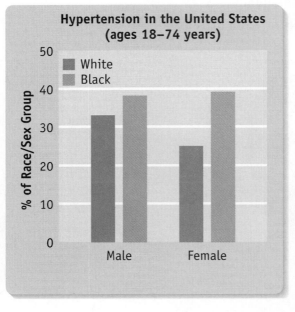

Hypertension in the United States (ages 18–74 years)

◄ The occurrence of hypertension (high blood pressure) in selected groups in the United States.

—Reprinted from Scott K. Powers and Stephen L. Dodd, *Total Fitness and Wellness,* 3rd ed. Figure 9.6. © Benjamin Cummings, 2003.

_____ **1.** The occurrence of hypertension in the United States is remarkably high.

_____ **2.** More white men suffer from hypertension than white women.

_____ **3.** More blacks suffer from hypertension than whites do.

_____ **4.** Because hypertension affects so many adults between the ages of 18 and 74, the federal government should fund research for prevention and treatment.

Textbook
Skills

Application 2: Opinions, Biased Words, and Qualifiers

Read the following paragraph from a college ecology textbook. Then complete the items about fact and opinion that follow.

Synthetic Chemicals Deplete Stratospheric Ozone

[1]Ozone in the troposphere is a pollutant that contributes to photochemical smog. [2]However, ozone in the stratosphere absorbs incoming ultraviolet radiation from the sun and shields life on Earth's surface. [3]In the 1960s, atmospheric scientists noticed that their measurements of stratospheric ozone were lower than they had predicted. [4]Researchers claim that chemicals must be depleting ozone. [5]Their research pinpoints a group of human-made compounds derived from simple hydrocarbons. [6]Some of these simple hydrocarbons were ethane and methane. [7]In these compounds, hydrogen atoms are replaced by chlorine, bromine, or fluorine. [8]One class of such compounds, chlorofluorocarbons (CFCs), was being mass-produced by industry at a rate of a million metric tons per year. [9]In 1985, scientists from the British Antarctic Survey announced that the stratospheric ozone levels over the Antarctica each autumn had declined by 40–60% in the previous decade. [10]This depletion left a thinned ozone concentration that was soon dubbed the *ozone hole*. [11]Research over a period of years confirmed the link between CFCs and the ozone loss in the Antarctic.

—Adapted from Withgott & Brennan,
Essential Environment, 3rd ed., p. 294.

_____ **1.** Sentence 1 is
    a. a fact.   c. a mixture of fact and opinion.
    b. an opinion.

_____ **2.** Sentence 4 is
    a. a fact.   c. a mixture of fact and opinion.
    b. an opinion.

_____ **3.** Sentence 11 is
    a. a fact.   c. a mixture of fact and opinion.
    b. an opinion.

_____ **4.** Overall, this paragraph relies on
    a. facts.   c. a mixture of fact and opinion.
    b. opinions.

VISUAL VOCABULARY

(1) The area in blue shows the ozone hole at its maximal recorded extent to date, according to the British Antarctic Survey. (2) An increase in skin cancers and other possible harmful effects may have occurred because of the depletion of the ozone due to CFCs.

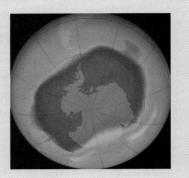

Sentence 1 states _____.

Sentence 2 states _____.

   a. a fact.
   b. an opinion.
   c. a mixture of fact and opinion.

Application 3: Informed and Expert Opinions

Following is a list of sources from which information can be obtained. Label each source as follows:

IO if it offers an informed opinion

EO if it offers an expert opinion

FS if it is a factual source

_____ **1.** *World Book Encyclopedia*

_____ **2.** A carefully researched and documented student essay about global warming

_____ **3.** *Webster's Dictionary*

_____ **4.** A statement about current fashion trends by a newly trained salesperson in the men's department at a major department store

_____ **5.** A family physician's recommendation for treatment of cancer

_____ **6.** An English teacher's advice about the best way to write an essay

_____ **7.** A college course catalog

_____ **8.** A financial advice column written by an economist

_____ **9.** A statement about football by Super Bowl–winning coach Sean Payton

_____ **10.** Botany.com, the Encyclopedia of Flowers and Plants, an online resource about gardening

REVIEW TEST 1   Score (number correct) _____ × 10 = _____%

Fact and Opinion

A. Read the following statements, and mark each one as follows:

F if it states a fact

O if it expresses an opinion

F/O if it combines fact and opinion

_____ **1.** Government should do more to help the poor and needy.

_____ **2.** Affirmative action programs give preference to qualified minorities.

_____ **3.** Denying welfare benefits to unwed mothers is not likely to affect the number of children born out of wedlock.

_____ **4.** In 2007, the percentage of births to unwed mothers was 39.5.

_____ **5.** By 2020, more than one in five children in the United States will be of Hispanic origin; Spanish should therefore be a required subject for all school children.

B. Study the graph and its accompanying text. Then read the statements that follow it, based on the given information. Mark each statement as follows:

F if it states a fact

O if it expresses an opinion

F/O if it combines fact and opinion

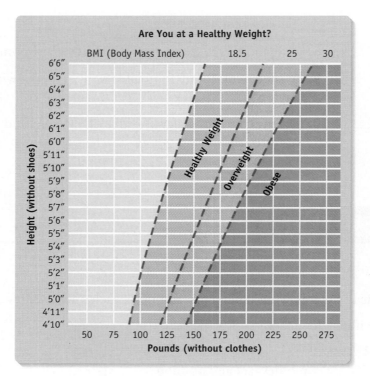

—Bren, Linda. "Losing Weight: Start By Counting Calories." *FDA Consumer* April 2004. 3 April 2007. U.S. Food and Drug Administration. http://www.cfsan.fda.gov/~dms/fdweigh3.html.

_____ **6.** The higher a person's BMI, the greater the risks for health problems.

_____ **7.** A 5′7″ person who weighs 175 lbs. is overweight.

_____ **8.** A 5′10″ person who weighs 225 lbs. is obese due to bad eating habits.

_____ **9.** Obesity is the result of moral choices.

_____ **10.** A BMI of 30 or above indicates obesity.

REVIEW TEST 2

Score (number correct) _____ × 20 = _____%

Fact and Opinion

Read the following passage from the *New York Times*. Complete the items that follow.

Forget Gum. Walking and Using Phone Is Risky.

By Matt Richtel

[1]On the day of the collision last month, visibility was good. [2]The sidewalk was not under repair. [3]As she walked, Tiffany Briggs, 25, was talking to her grandmother on her cellphone, lost in conversation.

[4]Very lost.

[5]"I ran into a truck," Ms. Briggs said.

[6]It was parked in a driveway.

[7]Distracted driving has gained much attention lately because of the inflated crash risk posed by drivers using cellphones to talk and text.

[8]But there is another growing problem caused by lower-stakes multi-tasking—distracted walking—which combines a pedestrian, an electronic device and an unseen crack in the sidewalk, the pole of a stop sign, a toy left on the living room floor or a parked (or sometimes moving) car.

[9]The era of the mobile gadget is making mobility that much more perilous, particularly on crowded streets and in downtown areas where multiple multitaskers veer and swerve and walk to the beat of their own devices.

[10]Most times, the mishaps for a distracted walker are minor, like the lightly dinged head and broken fingernail that Ms. Briggs suffered, a jammed digit or a sprained ankle, and, the befallen say, a nasty case of hurt pride. [11]Of course, the injuries can sometimes be serious—and they are on the rise.

[12]Slightly more than 1,000 pedestrians visited emergency rooms in 2008 because they got distracted and tripped, fell or ran into something while using a cellphone to talk or text. [13]That was twice the number from 2007, which had nearly doubled from 2006, according to a study conducted by Ohio State University, which says it is the first to estimate such accidents.

[14]"It's the tip of the iceberg," said Jack L. Nasar, a professor of city and regional planning at Ohio State, noting that the number of mishaps is probably much higher considering that most of the injuries are not severe enough to require a hospital visit. [15]What is more, he said, texting is rising sharply and devices like the iPhone have thousands of new, engaging applications to preoccupy phone users.

[16]Mr. Nasar supervised the statistical analysis, which was done by Derek Troyer, one of his graduate students. [17]He looked at records of emergency room visits compiled by the Consumer Product Safety Commission.

[18]Examples of such visits include a 16-year-old boy who walked into a telephone pole while texting and suffered a concussion; a 28-year-old

man who tripped and fractured a finger on the hand gripping his cell-phone; and a 68-year-old man who fell off the porch while talking on a cellphone, spraining a thumb and an ankle and causing dizziness.

[19]Young people injured themselves more often. [20]About half the visits Mr. Troyer studied were by people under 30, and a quarter were 16 to 20 years old. [21]But more than a quarter of those injured were 41 to 60 years old.

[22]Pedestrians, like drivers, have long been distracted by myriad tasks, like snacking or reading on the go. [23]But the constant interaction with electronic devices has made single-tasking seem boring or even unproductive.

[24]Cognitive psychologists, neurologists and other researchers are beginning to study the impact of constant multitasking, whether behind a desk or the wheel or on foot. [25]It might stand to reason that someone looking at a phone to read a message would misstep, but the researchers are finding that just talking on a phone takes its own considerable toll on cognition and awareness.

[26]Sometimes, pedestrians using their phones do not notice objects or people that are right in front of them—even a clown riding a unicycle. [27]That was the finding of a recent study at Western Washington University in Bellingham, Wash., by a psychology professor, Ira Hyman, and his students.

[28]One of the students dressed as a clown and unicycled around a central square on campus. [29]About half the people walking past by themselves said they had seen the clown, and the number was slightly higher for people walking in pairs. [30]But only 25 percent of people talking on a cellphone said they had, Mr. Hyman said.

[31]He said the term commonly applied to such preoccupation is "inattention blindness," meaning a person can be looking at an object but fail to register it or process what it is.

[32]Particularly fascinating, Mr. Hyman said, is that people walking in pairs were more than twice as likely to see the clown as were people talking on a cellphone, suggesting that the act of simply having a conversation is not the cause of inattention blindness.

[33]One possible explanation is that a cellphone conversation taxes not just auditory resources in the brain but also visual functions, said Adam Gazzaley, a neuroscientist at the University of California, San Francisco. [34]That combination, he said, prompts the listener to, for example, create visual imagery related to the conversation in a way that overrides or obscures the processing of real images.

35By comparison, walking and chewing gum (that age-old measure of pedestrian skill at multitasking) is a snap.

36"Walking and chewing are repetitive, well-practiced tasks that become automatic," Dr. Gazzaley said. **37**"They don't compete for resources like texting and walking."

38Further, he said, the cellphone gives people a constant opportunity to pursue goals that feel more important than walking down the street.

39"An animal would never walk into a pole," he said, noting survival instincts would trump other priorities.

40For Shalamar Jones, 19, the priority was keeping in touch with her boyfriend. **41**Last month while she was Christmas shopping in a mall near San Francisco, she was texting him when—bam!—she walked into the window of a New York & Company store, thinking it was a door.

42"I thought it was open," she said, noting that no harm was done. **43**"I just started laughing at myself."

44The worst part is the humiliation, said Christopher Black, 20, an art student at San Francisco State University who 18 months ago had his own pratfall.

45At the time, Mr. Black said, the sidewalks were packed with pedestrians. **46**So he decided he could move faster if he walked in the street, keeping close to the parked cars. **47**The trouble is he was also texting—with a woman he was flirting with.

48He unwittingly started to veer into the road, prompting an oncoming car to honk. **49**He said he instinctively jumped toward the sidewalk but, in the process, forgot about the line of parked cars.

50"I splayed against the side of the car, and the phone hit the ground," he said. **51**He and his phone were uninjured, except for his pride. **52**"It was pretty significantly embarrassing."

—Richtel, Matt, "Forget Gum. Walking and Using Phone Is Risky" from The New York Times, Business Section, January 17, 2010, (c) 2010 The New York Times. All rights reserved. Used by permission and protected by the Copyright Laws of the United States. The printing, copying, redistribution, or retransmission of the Material without express written permission is prohibited.

_____ **1.** Sentence 1 is
  a. a fact.
  b. an opinion.
  c. a mixture of fact and opinion.

_____ **2.** Sentence 2 is
  a. a fact.
  b. an opinion.
  c. a mixture of fact and opinion.

_____ **3.** Sentence 9 is
   a. a fact.   c. a mixture of fact and opinion.
   b. an opinion.

_____ **4.** In paragraph 9 (sentences 12–13), the details are
   a. facts   c. a mixture of fact and opinion.
   b. opinions.

_____ **5.** In paragraph 10 (sentences 14–15), Mr. Nasar's ideas are
   a. factual details   c. expert opinions.
   b. informed opinions.

REVIEW TEST 3

Score (number correct) _____ × 10 = _____%

Fact and Opinion

Textbook
Skills

Read the following passage from a college psychology textbook. Complete the items that follow.

Maslow's Hierarchy of Needs

[1]Humanist psychologist Abraham Maslow (1908–1970) formulated the theory that basic motives form a hierarchy of needs. [2]In Maslow's view, the needs at each level of the hierarchy must be satisfied—the needs are arranged in a sequence from primitive to advanced—before the next level can be achieved. [3]At the bottom of this hierarchy are the basic biological needs, such as hunger and thirst. [4]They must be met before any other needs can begin to operate. [5]When biological needs are pressing, other needs are put on hold and are unlikely to influence your actions. [6]When they are reasonably well satisfied, the needs at the next level—safety needs—motivate you. [7]When you are no longer concerned about danger, you become motivated by attachment needs—needs to belong, to affiliate with others, to love, and to be loved. [8]If you are well fed and safe and if you feel a sense of social belonging, you move up to esteem needs—to like oneself, to see oneself as competent and effective, and to do what is necessary to earn the esteem of others.

⁹At the top of the hierarchy are people who are nourished, safe, loved and loving, secure, thinking, and creating. ¹⁰These people have moved beyond basic human needs in the quest for the fullest development of their potentials, or self-actualization. ¹¹A self-actualizing person is self-aware, self-accepting, socially responsive, creative, spontaneous, and open to novelty and challenge, among other positive attributes.

¹²Maslow's theory is a particularly upbeat view of human motivation. ¹³At the core of the theory is the need for each individual to grow and actualize his or her highest potential. ¹⁴However, you know from your own experience that Maslow's strict hierarchy breaks down. ¹⁵You may, for example, have skipped a meal so that you could help out a friend. ¹⁶You may have endured the danger of a wilderness trek to boost your self-esteem. ¹⁷Even so, Maslow's scheme should enable you to bring some order to different aspects of your motivational experiences.

—Gerrig/Zimbardo, *Psychology and Life*, Text Excerpt from pp. 343–344 and Figure p. 435 © 2010 Pearson Education, Inc. Reproduced by permission of Pearson Education, Inc.

A. Complete the following items.

_____ **1.** Sentence 1 is
    a. a fact.
    b. an opinion.
    c. a mixture of fact and opinion.

_____ **2.** Sentence 2 is
    a. a fact.
    b. an opinion.
    c. a mixture of fact and opinion.

_____ **3.** Sentence 17 is
    a. a fact.
    b. an opinion.
    c. a mixture of fact and opinion.

_____ **4.** In this passage, Abraham Maslow ideas are
    a. factual details.
    b. informed opinions.
    c. expert opinions.

B. Complete the concept map with information from the passage.

5. _____
6. _____
_____

7. _____
Needs for confidence, sense of self worth,
confidence, self-esteem, and respect for others

8. _____
Needs to belong, to love and be loved

9. _____
Needs for security, comfort,
freedom from fear

10. _____
Needs for food, water, rest,
sexual expression, release from tension

Maslow's Hierarchy of Needs

WHAT DO YOU THINK?

Do you agree with Maslow's hierarchy of needs? Assume you are taking a college course in psychology, and you are preparing for a unit exam. Your professor has provided you with a list of study questions. Write a one-page response to the following question: What are the levels of human motivation in Maslow's hierarchy of needs? Identify and explain each level. Use examples from everyday life to illustrate each level.

REVIEW TEST 4   Score (number correct) _____ × 10 = _____%

Fact and Opinion

Textbook
Skills

Before you read the following passage from a psychology textbook, skim the passage and answer the Before Reading questions. Read the passage. Then answer the After Reading questions.

Vocabulary Preview

ritual (4): formal process or procedure

charismatic (6): appealing, fascinating

dictates (8): orders, commands

celibate (11): refraining from sex

omnipotence (19): state of being all-powerful

omniscience (19): state of being all-knowing

coercive (21): using force

litany (28): long list

Why Do People Join Cults?

¹Cults have no doubt forced themselves into your awareness in recent years. ²Their extreme, often bizarre behaviors are widely covered in the media. ³In the United States, 39 members of Heaven's Gate committed suicide in March 1997. ⁴They did so in an orderly **ritual** that was planned by their leader. ⁵Nearly 20 years earlier, more than 900 American citizens committed mass suicide-murder in a jungle compound in Guyana. ⁶They did so at the urging of their **charismatic** leader, Reverend Jim Jones. ⁷In France, Canada, and Switzerland, members of The Order of the Solar Temple also took their lives in **ritualized** cult deaths. ⁸Meanwhile, in Japan, members of Aum Shin Rikyo gased subway riders, and they had planned mass destruction to fulfill the **dictates** of their cult leader. ⁹Beyond these clearly dramatic examples, there are members of literally thousands of groups that qualify as cults. ¹⁰They give total loyalty to their groups and leaders. ¹¹Members obey every command: they marry a partner they have never met in mass ceremonies; beg, recruit, work long hours for no pay; give all their money and possessions to the group; or become **celibate.**

¹²Can you imagine doing such things? ¹³Are there any circumstances under which you would join a cult and become subject to the pressures that cults bring to bear on their members? ¹⁴Obviously, most of you would say, "No way!" ¹⁵But as psychologists, our task is to understand how such groups and leaders develop their coercive power and to recognize the conditions that make many people at risk to their persuasive message.

¹⁶So what exactly are cults? ¹⁷Cults vary widely in their activities, but they typically are nontraditional religious groups led by a strict, controlling leader who is the sole source of the group's thoughts, beliefs, and actions. ¹⁸This leader is often charismatic, filled with energy and intense dedication. ¹⁹And sometimes he or she claims special godlike powers of **omnipotence, omniscience,** and immortality. ²⁰Despite differences in the traits of particular cult groups, what is common are the recruiting promises. ²¹The group's **coercive** power undercuts the personal exercise of free will and critical thinking of its members.

²²Why, then, would people want to join a cult? ²³First of all, no one ever joins a *cult*, as such. ²⁴People join interesting groups to fulfill their pressing needs. ²⁵The groups are known as cults later on when they are seen as deceptive, dangerous, or opposing society's basic values. ²⁶Cults

become appealing when they promise to fulfill an individual's personal needs. [27]The need may be for instant friendship, an identity, or an organized daily agenda. [28]Cults also promise to make up for a **litany** of societal failures. [29]By eliminating people's feelings of isolation and alienation, cults make their slice of the world safe, healthy, caring, predictable, and controllable. [30]Cult leaders offer simple solutions to a complex world by offering a path to happiness, success, and salvation.

[31]Although the mass suicides of cult members make media headlines, most cults operate quietly to achieve their goals. [32]When they deliver on their promises, they can serve a valuable function for some people by helping fill voids in their lives. [33]But when they are deceptive, coercive, and distort basic values of freedom, independence, and critical thinking, they become dangerous to members and to society. [34]One question worth raising is, Can society provide what most cults promise so they need not become an alternate lifestyle for so many people throughout the world?

—Gerrig/Zimbardo, *Psychology and Life*, Text Excerpt from p. 588 © 2010 Pearson Education, Inc. Reproduced by permission of Pearson Education, Inc.

BEFORE READING
Vocabulary in Context

_____ **1.** What does the word **ritualized** mean in sentence 7?
   a. violent
   b. senseless
   c. organized
   d. dramatic

Topic

_____ **2.** The topic of this passage is
   a. the benefits of joining a cult.
   b. reasons to legally ban cults.
   c. cults, what they are and why people join.
   d. cults, freedom of religious expression.

AFTER READING
Central Idea

_____ **3.** The central idea of the article is stated in paragraph
   a. 1 (sentences 1–11).
   b. 2 (sentences 12–15).
   c. 4 (sentences 22–30).
   d. 5 (sentences 31–34).

Supporting Details

_____ **4.** According to the authors, people join cults when
a. they want to commit suicide.
b. they are in need.
c. they are deceptive.
d. they need to control others.

Transitions

_____ **5.** The relationship of ideas between sentence 27 and sentence 28 is one of
a. cause and effect.   c. contrast.
b. time order.   d. addition.

Thought Patterns

_____ **6.** The thought pattern for the first paragraph of the passage (sentences 1–11) is one of
a. cause and effect.   c. examples.
b. time order.   d. contrast.

Implied Main Ideas

_____ **7.** Which of the following best states the implied main idea of paragraph 4 (sentences 22–30)?
a. Cults offer security.
b. People join cults for a variety of reasons.
c. Loneliness is the major reason people join cults.
d. People who fail at life join cults.

Fact and Opinion

_____ **8.** Sentence 1 of the article is
a. fact.   c. a mixture of fact and opinion.
b. opinion.

_____ **9.** Sentence 5 is
a. fact.   c. a mixture of fact and opinion.
b. opinion.

_____ **10.** Sentence 23 is
a. fact.   c. a mixture of fact and opinion.
b. opinion.

WHAT DO YOU THINK?

Why do you think people seek out cults? Assume you are a peer counselor at your college. Several students have approached you about joining a cult. Write an article for your college newspaper that warns against the dangers of cults.

 ## After Reading About Fact and Opinion

Before you move on to the Mastery Tests on fact and opinion, take time to reflect on your learning and performance by answering the following questions. Write your answers in your notebook.

- How has my knowledge base or prior knowledge about fact and opinion changed?

- Based on my studies, how do I think I will perform on the Mastery Test(s)? Why do I think my scores will be above average, average, or below average?

- Would I recommend this chapter to other students who want to learn about fact and opinion? Why or why not?

Test your understanding of what you have learned about fact and opinion by completing the Chapter 9 Review Card in the insert near the end of your text.

CONNECT TO **myreadinglab**

To check your progress in meeting Chapter 9's learning outcomes, log in to **www.myreadinglab.com**, and try the following activities.

- The "Critical Thinking" section of MyReadingLab gives additional information about fact and opinion. The section provides a model, practices, activities, and tests. To access this resource, click on the "Study Plan" tab. Then click on "Critical Thinking." Then click on the following links as needed: "Overview," "Model," "Critical Thinking: Facts and Opinions (Flash Animation)," "Practice," and "Tests."

- To measure your mastery of the content in this chapter, complete the tests in the "Critical Thinking" section and click on Gradebook to find your results.

Name _____ Section _____

Date _____ Score (number correct) _____ × 5 = _____%

A. Read the following statements, and mark each one as follows:

F if it states a fact

O if it expresses an opinion

F/O if it combines fact and opinion

_____ **1.** Hydrogen is a perfect fuel and is undoubtedly the best that will be available for future use.

_____ **2.** In the United States, 39 states run lotteries to raise funds; this practice is immoral and should be stopped.

_____ **3.** Over 50 percent of Americans participate in state lotteries.

_____ **4.** State lotteries lure people who are poor and uneducated into playing by promising a quick way to get rich.

_____ **5.** Lotteries, which raise billions of dollars, are the only way for state governments to raise money for education and other services.

_____ **6.** Many of the people who play state lotteries have average to above-average levels of income and education.

_____ **7.** Road traffic is a growing source of pollution in Europe.

_____ **8.** Gas-guzzling cars account for half the oil consumed in the United States.

_____ **9.** Funding for electric cars should be supported by taxes.

_____ **10.** The drawbacks of automobiles far outweigh their benefits.

B. Read the following short reviews. Mark each one as follows:

F if it states only facts

O if it expresses opinions

F/O if it combines fact and opinion

_____ **11.** Three times the danger! Three times the drama! Three times the enjoyment! Fast-paced and action-packed, *Driving Dangerous* will air for the first time on television Thursday night at 9 P.M. and run for three nights in a row, same time, same channel.

_____ **12.** Outrageously fun and funny, don't miss *Blades of Glory* with Will Farrell and Jon Heder as two disgraced Olympic ice skaters who were banned from the sport but agree to perform together in the pairs figure skating category to get back into the competition.

_____ **13.** *Meet the Press* is the longest running United States television series.

_____ **14.** *American Idol* exploits people who have no talent for the sake of high ratings.

_____ **15.** Adam Lambert is the most talented and successful singer to have appeared on *American Idol*.

C. Study the advertisement for a lost dog prepared to run in a local newspaper and fliers. Then identify each item from the ad as follows:

F if it states a fact

O if it expresses an opinion

F/O if it combines fact and opinion

Our Dog, Brutus, is missing!

[16]Our dog, Brutus, is missing! [17]Brutus weighs four pounds and is a tan-colored Chihuahua. [18]Although he is a swift-moving little dog with a saucy personality, he has been well-trained. [19]Therefore, he should obey the command "come." [20]We are offering a $100 reward for his safe return.

_____ **16.** Our dog, Brutus, is missing!

_____ **17.** Brutus weighs four pounds and is a tan-colored Chihuahua.

_____ **18.** Although he is a swift-moving little dog with a saucy personality, he has been well-trained.

_____ **19.** Therefore, he should obey the command "come."

_____ **20.** We are offering a generous reward for his safe return.

Name _____ Section _____

Date _____ Score (number correct) _____ × 5 = _____%

A. Read the following statements, and mark each one **F** (states a fact); **O** (states an opinion); **F/O** (combines fact and opinion).

_____ **1.** Don't take Math 101 from Dr. Harvey; it is too hard.

_____ **2.** The college catalog states that two semesters of English and math are required.

_____ **3.** Small dogs such as toy poodles make annoying pets.

_____ **4.** Animals have improved the physical and emotional well-being of shut-ins such as the elderly in nursing homes.

_____ **5.** Hip-hop music is the voice of people oppressed by social injustice.

_____ **6.** Oprah Winfrey and Michelle Obama are the two most influential African American women of this generation.

_____ **7.** African American scientists have impacted society through their inventions and discoveries.

_____ **8.** It is not wise to get medical advice from online sources.

_____ **9.** Several types of cancer have been linked to diet.

_____ **10.** To be safe, airlines should weigh everyone who travels by air.

B. Read the following advertisements for used cars. Mark each one **F** (states a fact); **O** (states an opinion); **F/O** (combines fact and opinion).

_____ **11.** 2008 KIA Sedona LX. Red, V6 3.8 liter, automatic, grey interior, A/C, power windows, power locks, dual heated seats, cruise control, Bose sound system with CD, Premium wheels. Excellent condition. 32,000 miles. $18,900.

_____ **12.** Well kept SUV, Aztec Red. Mostly highway miles. Still has plastic under floor mats—A MUST SEE! 29,300 miles. $21,500.

_____ **13.** 2006 1500 Silverado. Truck is in excellent condition. Contains LS Decor package, 5300V8 engine with reclining bucket seats & armrest, all power locks, alarm system, includes towing special equip. package, CD player, aluminum alloy wheels, etc. Has sprayed bed

413

liner with fiberglass tonneau cover. Black and pewter color—very nice appearance with smooth ride. 21,000 miles. $20,995.

_____ **14.** 1994 Corvette. White with tan leather seats, automatic, A/C, 80,500 miles. $18,500.

_____ **15.** Lexus LS 430. Someone once said that perfection is a road, not a destination. If this is true, then the engineers and designers at Lexus probably have the route memorized. With no apparent fear of losing their way, the Lexus team has allowed their flagship sedan, the LS 430, to momentarily detour from its journey. For the time being, it is parked comfortably at the crossroads where science and art converge to create an extraordinary driving experience.

—*Kelley Blue Book.*

C. Following is a list of sources from which information can be obtained. Label each source **IO** (offers an informed opinion); **EO** (offers an expert opinion); **FS** (is a factual source).

_____ **16.** The National Aeronautics and Space Administration (NASA) at http://www.nasa.gov

_____ **17.** Nicholas D. Kristof, columnist on human rights for the New York Times, winner of the Pulitzer Prize for Commentary, the George Polk Award, and the Dayton Literary Peace Prize's 2009 Lifetime Achievement Award

_____ **18.** A news article on the front page of the *New York Times*

_____ **19.** *The Encyclopedia of Indians of the Americas*, Scholarly Publications, 1974

_____ **20.** A letter to the editor of a local paper from a concerned citizen

Read the following passage from a history textbook. Then identify each excerpt from the passage as follows:

F if it states a fact

O if it expresses an opinion

F/O if it combines fact and opinion

Textbook
Skills

A Nation Divided

1To the delight of the media, the race for the White House in 2000 proved to be close and exciting. **2**George Bush led in the polls until Al Gore moved ahead after the Democratic Convention in August. **3**Gore's running mate, Joe Lieberman, proved popular. **4**In contrast, Bush's choice of running mate, former defense secretary Dick Cheney, failed to excite the public. **5**But Gore's surprisingly uneven performance in three televised debates allowed Bush to regain a narrow lead in the polls in October. **6**Then, in the final week of the campaign, Gore began to draw even with Bush.

7The early returns on election night proved that the polls were right in stressing the closeness of the presidential race. **8**Gore seemed the likely winner when the networks mistakenly predicted a Democratic victory in Florida. **9**When the TV analysts put Florida back in the undecided column, Bush began to forge ahead, sweeping the rest of the South. **10**After midnight, when the networks again mistakenly called Florida, this time for Bush, Gore telephoned Bush to concede. **11**An hour later, however, he recanted when it became clear that the Bush margin in Florida was paper thin.

12For the next five weeks, all eyes were on the outcome in Florida. **13**Gore had a lead of more than 200,000 nationwide in the popular vote and 267 electoral votes. **14**Yet Bush, with 246 votes in the electoral college, could win the presidency with Florida's 25 electoral votes. **15**Both sides sent phalanxes of lawyers to Florida. **16**Bush's team sought to certify the results that showed him with a lead of 930 votes out of nearly six million cast. **17**Citing many voting problems disclosed by the media, Gore asked for a recount in three heavily Democratic counties in south Florida. **18**All three used old-fashioned punch card machines that resulted in some ballots not being clearly marked for any presidential candidate.

[19]The decision finally came in the courts. [20]Democrats appealed the first attempt to certify Bush as the victor to the Florida Supreme Court, where most of the judges had been appointed by Democrats. [21]The Florida court ordered recounts two times, but the Bush team appealed to the United States Supreme Court. [22]On December 12, five weeks after the election, the Supreme Court overturned the state's call for recounts. [23]The Supreme Court ruling was a 5–4 decision that reflected a long-standing divide in thought among the nine judges. [24]The next day, Gore gracefully conceded, and Bush finally became the president-elect. [25]Although the rule of law prevailed, neither the winner nor the loser could take much pride in his party's behavior.

—Adapted from Divine, Breen, Frederickson, & Williams,
The American Story, pp. 1116–17.

_____ **1.** To the delight of the media, the race for the White House in 2000 proved to be close and exciting.

_____ **2.** But Gore's surprisingly uneven performance in three televised debates allowed Bush to regain a narrow lead in the polls in October.

_____ **3.** In the final week of the campaign, Gore began to draw even with Bush.

_____ **4.** After midnight, when the networks again mistakenly called Florida, this time for Bush, Gore telephoned Bush to concede.

_____ **5.** An hour later, however, he recanted when it became clear that the Bush margin in Florida was paper thin.

_____ **6.** For the next five weeks, all eyes were on the outcome in Florida.

_____ **7.** Gore had a lead of more than 200,000 nationwide in the popular vote and 267 electoral votes.

_____ **8.** Bush's team sought to certify the results that showed him with a lead of 930 votes out of nearly six million cast.

_____ **9.** The next day, Gore gracefully conceded, and Bush finally became the president-elect.

_____ **10.** Although the rule of law prevailed, neither the winner nor the loser could take much pride in his party's behavior.

A. Read the following statements, and mark each one as follows:

F if it states a fact

O if it expresses an opinion

F/O if it combines fact and opinion

_____ **1.** The Super Bowl is the most watched show on television.

_____ **2.** The Super Bowl is America's favorite sporting event.

_____ **3.** In an open society such as the United States, secrecy in government is difficult to maintain, or should be.

_____ **4.** Hollywood exports movies to all parts of the world.

_____ **5.** Hollywood is to blame for the worldwide view that Americans are immoral and selfish.

_____ **6.** *Letter to My Mother* by Edith Bruck is an extraordinary incisive retelling of her life in wartime Auschwitz. It is one of the most important and impressive works of its kind. This book is a necessary and urgent read.

_____ **7.** In 1837, Michigan became the 26th state.

_____ **8.** The Hispanic population is one of the fastest-growing groups in America.

_____ **9.** Doctors fear that they will not be able to offer quality services due to the looming crisis caused by the rising costs of malpractice insurance.

_____ **10.** Doctors should not strike because of insurance malpractice issues.

B. Following is a list of sources from which information can be obtained. Label each source as follows:

IO if it offers an informed opinion

EO if it offers an expert opinion

FS if it is a factual source

_____ **11.** "Dr. Phil" McGraw. (2009) *Real Life: Preparing for the 7 Most Challenging Days of Your Life*, Free Press

_____ **12.** A college mathematics textbook

_____ **13.** A friend who has recently researched the best bargain for a flat-screen television

_____ **14.** Internal Revenue Service. (2009). *Your Federal Income Tax* (Publication 17). Washington, D.C.: U.S. Government Printing Office.

_____ **15.** A college history teacher with 25 years of experience

_____ **16.** The Modern Language Association's *Handbook for Writers of Research Papers*, 7th ed., 2009.

_____ **17.** A student research essay on the collapse of communism

_____ **18.** Randolph, J. (1992). "Recycling of Materials." In *The New Grolier Multimedia Encyclopedia*. [CD-ROM]. Danbury, Conn.: Grolier Electronic.

_____ **19.** A syllabus for a college course

_____ **20.** Roger Ebert, film critic for the *Chicago Sun-Times* and host of his own television show that reviews movies called *Ebert and Roeper at the Movies*

Tone and Purpose

LEARNING OUTCOMES

After studying this chapter you should be able to do the following:

1. Define the following terms: *tone* and *purpose*.
2. Understand how tone is established.
3. Identify subjective and objective tone words.
4. Determine the general purpose in the main idea.
5. Determine the primary purpose.
6. Evaluate a passage for the use of irony.
7. Apply tone and purpose to passages to improve comprehension.

Before Reading About Tone and Purpose

Study the learning outcomes and underline words that relate to ideas you have already studied. Did you underline the following terms: subjective, objective, and main idea? What you already know about these topics will help you learn about tone and purpose. Use the blanks that follow to write a short one- or two-sentence summary about each topic.

Subjective words: _____

_____.

Objective words: _____

_____.

Main idea: _____

_____.

Refer to the learning outcomes and draw upon your prior knowledge to create at least five questions that you can answer as you study about tone and purpose:

_____ ?

_____ ?

_____ ?

_____ ?

_____ ?

Compare the questions you created with the following questions. Then write the ones that seem the most helpful in your notebook, leaving enough space between each question to record the answers as you read and study the chapter.

What are tone and purpose? How is tone established? How will objective facts and subjective opinions help me identify tone? Will fact and opinion help me identify purpose? How will the main idea help me discover the general purpose? What is the primary purpose, and how do I figure it out? How is irony used for special effects?

 ## What Are Tone and Purpose?

Read the following two passages. As you read, think about the difference in the tone and purpose of each one.

What Is Distracted Driving?

There are three main types of distraction. The first type is visual—taking your eyes off the road. The second is manual—taking you hands off the wheel. The third is cognitive—taking your mind off what you're doing. Distracted driving is any non-driving activity a person engages in that has the potential to distract him or her from the primary task of driving and increase the risk of crashing. While all distractions can endanger drivers' safety, texting is the most alarming because it involves all three types of distraction. Other distracting activities include the following: using a cell phone, eating and drinking, talking to passengers, grooming, reading, including maps, using a PDA or navigation system, watching a video, or changing the radio station, CD, or Mp3 player.

Research on distracted driving reveals some surprising facts. Using a cell phone while driving, whether it's hand-held or hands-free, delays a driver's reactions as much as having a blood alcohol concentration at the legal limit of .08 percent. Driving while using a cell phone reduces the amount of brain activity associated with driving by 37 percent. 80 percent of all crashes and 65 percent of near crashes involve some type of distraction. Nearly 6,000 people died in 2008 in crashes involving a distracted or inattentive driver, and more than half a million were injured. The worst offenders are the youngest and least-experienced drivers: men and women under 20 years of age. Drivers who use hand-held devices are four times as likely to get into crashes serious enough to injure themselves.

—United States Department of Transportation. "Statistics and Facts about Distracted Driving." *Distraction.gov.* 20 Jan. 2010. http://www.distraction.gov/stats-and-facts.

Linda Doyle: Wife, Mother, Grandmother

On Sept. 3, 2008, after receiving a phone call offering food for the feral cats she rescued and nurtured, my mom left her home in Oklahoma City. She was driving through an intersection when a young man ran a red light and T-boned her car at 45–50 mph, which was the posted speed limit. Mom died within a couple of hours from blunt force trauma to the head, neck and chest.

The young man was a sober, churchgoing 20-year-old who had never even had a speeding ticket. Visibility on the day of the crash was excellent. The cause of the crash was a tiny device that fits in your pocket: a cell phone. He was on his phone for less than a minute. People don't realize it takes just seconds of not paying attention for a life to be taken away forever.

When the trooper asked the driver who caused the crash what color the traffic light had been, the distraught young man responded that he never saw it. The absence of skid marks at the scene indicates he never tried to stop.

Our lives will never be the same because of that crash and the loss of my mom. Losing someone and then finding out it was preventable, makes losing them even harder. I would like my mother's legacy to be that people hear her story and decide their call, email or text message is never as important as someone's life. If we do nothing, then it is no longer a matter of if this will happen to someone you love, it is a matter of when it happens to someone you love. I have two beautiful daughters to protect; I can't lose anyone else I love.

—Smith, Jennifer. "Who We Are: Jennifer Smith–President, Founding Board Member." *FocusDriven.org.* http://www.focusdriven.org/documents/jsmithbio.pdf. Reprinted with permission.

The differences in the tone and purpose of these two passages are obvious. The first passage was written and published by the government to inform the public about the dangers of distracted driving. The passage uses unbiased words and an objective, formal tone. The second passage approaches the same subject with a different purpose—to persuade people to avoid distracted driving. The second passage conveys a painful personal experience using biased words and a subjective, informal tone.

As the two passages demonstrate, tone and purpose work together to convey the author's meaning.

Every piece of information is created by an author who has a specific attitude toward the chosen topic and a specific reason for writing and sharing that attitude. The author's attitude is conveyed by the tone. **Tone** is the emotion or mood of the author's written voice. Understanding tone is closely related to understanding the author's reason for writing about the topic. This reason for writing is known as the author's **purpose.**

Tone and purpose are established with word choice. Effective readers read to understand the author's tone and purpose. To identify tone and purpose, you need to build on several skills you have already studied: vocabulary, fact and opinion, and main ideas.

> **Tone** is the author's attitude toward the topic.
> **Purpose** is the reason the author writes about a topic.

 ## Understand How Tone Is Established

The author's attitude is expressed by the tone of voice he or she assumes in the passage. An author chooses carefully the words that will make an impact on the reader. Sometimes an author wants to appeal to reason and just gives facts and factual explanations. At other times, an author wants to appeal to emotions and stir the reader to feel deeply.

For example, in an effort to share reliable information, textbooks strive for an objective tone. An objective tone includes facts and reasonable explanations. It is matter-of-fact and neutral. The details given in an objective tone are likely to be facts. In contrast, sharing an author's personal worldview through fiction and personal essays often calls for a subjective tone. A subjective tone uses words that describe feelings, judgments, or opinions. The details given in a subjective tone are likely to include experiences, senses, feelings, and thoughts. Study the following list of words that describe the characteristics of tone.

Characteristics of Tone Words	
Objective Tone impartial	**Subjective Tone** personal
unbiased	biased
neutral	emotional
formal	informal

An *unbiased* or *neutral* tone does not show any feelings for or against a topic. Instead, it focuses on facts. A *formal* tone chooses higher-level words and avoids using the pronouns *I* and *you,* thereby creating a sense of distance between the writer and the reader. An *objective* tone is thus impartial, unbiased, neutral, and most often formal. In contrast, a *biased* tone does show favor for or against a particular topic. A biased tone uses *emotional* words that focus on feelings. Finally, an *informal* tone uses the pronouns *I* and *you* to create a connection between the writer and the reader. A *subjective* tone is thus personal, biased, emotional, and often informal. In summary, to grasp the author's tone, you need to carefully note the author's choice of vocabulary and details.

EXAMPLES Look at the following list of statements. Based on word choice, choose the tone word that best describes each statement.

_____ **1.** In January of 2010, an earthquake devastated Port-au-Prince, Haiti.
    a. biased   b. unbiased

_____ **2.** The magnitude-7 quake killed an estimated 200,000, left 250,000 injured, and made 1.5 million homeless.
    a. objective   b. subjective

_____ **3.** Unless you saw it for yourself, you can't imagine the horror caused by the earthquake.
    a. formal   b. informal

_____ **4.** Reports of children crying for parents and parents digging with their fingers for children are heart-rending images of human suffering caused by the quake.
    a. neutral   b. emotional

_____ **5.** The United States government mobilized resources and manpower to aid in the relief effort.
    a. objective   b. subjective

EXPLANATION Compare your answers to the following: **1.** The word "devastated" may seem like a value judgment, but it is actually a factual description so the correct answer is (b) unbiased; **2.** This sentence states facts so the answer is (a) objective; **3.** The use of "you" is informal and is used to state an opinion so the answer is (b) informal; **4.** The sentence creates a vivid image that taps into human emotions so the answer is (b) emotional; **5.** The sentence states facts and does not evaluate or judge the government's effort, so the answer is (a).

PRACTICE 1

Read the followings statements from the online medical information site *WebMD*. Based on word choice, choose a tone word that best describes each statement.

_____ **1.** If you are reading this while sitting down, you might want to stand up for a moment.
      a. objective   b. subjective

_____ **2.** A new editorial published in the *British Journal of Sports Medicine* suggests that people who sit still for prolonged periods of time—such as desk workers—have a higher risk of disease than those who move a muscle every now and then in a non-exercise manner, such as walking up the stairs to grab a cup of coffee.
      a. objective   b. biased

_____ **3.** Coach potatoes are at risk, too.
      a. formal   b. informal

_____ **4.** Researchers say it appears that muscle movement and contractions may play a role in controlling important blood fats.
      a. neutral   b. emotional

—Adapted from Stacy, Kelli Miller. "Prolonged Sitting Boosts Bad Health: Daily Inactivity, Not Just Lack of Exercise, Could Be Making You Sick." 19 Jan. 2010 http://www.webmd.com/fitness-exercise/news/20100119/prolonged-sitting-boosts-bad-health.

Identify Subjective and Objective Tone Words

Recognizing tone and describing an author's attitude deepens your comprehension and helps you become a more effective reader. A small sample of words used to describe tone are listed here. Look up the meanings of any words you do not know. Developing your vocabulary helps you better understand an author's word choice to establish tone.

Subjective			Objective
admiring	disbelieving	persuasive	accurate
angry	discouraged	pleading	factual
annoyed	disdainful	poetic	impartial
anxious	dramatic	reverent	matter-of-fact
approving	earnest	rude	straightforward
arrogant	elated	sad	truthful
argumentative	entertaining	sarcastic	
assured	fearful	self-pitying	
belligerent	friendly	serious	
biting	funny	sincere	
bitter	gloomy	supportive	
bored	happy	suspenseful	
bubbly	hostile	sympathetic	
calm	humorous	tender	
candid	idealistic	tense	
cold	informal	thoughtful	
comic	informative	threatening	
complaining	irritated	timid	
confident	joking	urgent	
cynical	jovial	warning	
demanding	joyful	wistful	
direct	lively	wry	
disappointed	loving		

EXAMPLES   Read the following items. Choose a word that best describes the tone of each statement. Use each word once.

anxious	encouraging	persuasive
elated	gloomy	

1. "If you care about saving lives, you should vote for gun control."

   Tone: _____

2. "You can do anything if you put your mind to it. Come on! You can do it!"

   Tone: _____

3. "I hope I do all right on this test. Even though I studied all night, I might forget important information."

   Tone: _____

4. "I won! I won!" Snively shouted as he realized he held the winning lottery ticket.

   Tone: _____

5. Thick, heavy clouds hung low in the sky, like a soggy gray blanket. The trees were winter bare, and the ground was brown and wet. Though it was only 2 o'clock in the afternoon, a dusky shroud covered the neighborhood.

   Tone: _____

VISUAL VOCABULARY

The tone of the message in this photo and its caption is

_____.

  a. despairing.
  b. celebratory.
  c. neutral.

▶ We did it! We never gave up hope that she would be alive in the rubble even though it was 6 days after the earthquake.

EXPLANATIONS Compare your answers to these:

1. persuasive. As you learned when you studied fact and opinion, the words "should," "ought," and "must" are opinion words. They suggest a persuasive tone.

2. encouraging

3. anxious

4. elated

5. gloomy

PRACTICE 2

Read the following items. Based on word choice, choose a word from the box that best describes the tone of each statement. Use each word once.

| admiring | arrogant | factual | informative | warm |
| angry | bitter | happy | sad | wistful |

1. "It is with sorrow that I must submit my resignation."

   Tone: _____

2. "The best days were growing up on the farm before life became so fast-paced."

   Tone: _____

3. "It is so good to see you again after such a long time. How is your wonderful family?"

   Tone: _____

4. Manny shoots for the basket at an awkward angle. He hesitates. The ball is knocked out of his hands. The lost points may have just cost his team the win.

   Tone: _____

5. "Animals can be divided into three groups based on the way they maintain body temperature."

   Tone: _____

6. A quiet yet thrilling feeling of peace swept over her. Her children were healthy, she was successful in her job, and she was in love with her husband. It seemed she had all a person could want.

   Tone: _____

7. "It isn't enough to say you are sorry after years of doing wrong. You just can't say you are sorry! How dare you think you can! Don't expect forgiveness, either!"

   Tone: _____

8. "It is with pleasure and pride that I offer this recommendation on behalf of Kareem Smith. He is hardworking, intelligent, and honest."

   Tone: _____

9. "Who broke the vase in the foyer? When I find out who did it, that person is going to be so sorry. Do you know how much that vase cost?"

Tone: _____

10. "I am the best there is, and don't you forget it. There is no one who beats me."

Tone: _____

 ## Discover the General Purpose in the Main Idea

Many reasons can motivate a writer. These can range from the need to take a stand on a hotly debated issue to the desire to entertain an audience with an amusing story. Basically, an author writes to share a main idea about a topic. An author's main idea, whether stated or implied, and the author's purpose are directly related. One of the following three general purposes will drive a main idea: to inform, to entertain, and to persuade.

In Chapter 3, you learned that a main idea is made up of a topic and the author's controlling point. You identified the controlling point by looking for thought patterns and biased (tone) words. The next two sections will build on what you have learned. First, you will study the relationship between the three general purposes and the author's main idea. You will practice using the main idea to discover the general purpose. Then you will apply what you have learned to figure out an author's primary purpose.

- **To inform.** When a writer sets out to inform, he or she shares knowledge and information or offers instruction about a particular topic. A few of the tone words often used to describe this purpose include *objective, matter-of-fact,* and *straightforward.* Authors use facts to explain or describe the main idea to readers. Most textbook passages are written to inform. The following topic sentences reflect the writer's desire to inform.

    1. The main causes of road rage are stress and anxiety.
    2. A healthful diet includes several daily servings from each of the major food groups.

In sentence 1, the topic is *road rage*, and the words that reveal the controlling point are *main causes, stress,* and *anxiety.* The author uses a tone that is unbiased and objective, so the focus is on the information. In sentence 2, the topic is *diet*, and the words that reveal the controlling point are *healthful, several daily servings,* and *major food groups.* Again, the author chooses words that are matter-of-fact and that suggest factual details will follow. Both topic sentences indicate that the author's purpose is to provide helpful information.

- **To persuade.** A writer who sets out to persuade tries to bring the reader into agreement with his or her view on the topic. A few of the tone words often used to describe this purpose include *argumentative, persuasive, forceful, controversial, positive, supportive, negative,* and *critical.* Authors combine facts with emotional appeals to sway the reader to their point of view. Politicians and advertisers often write and speak to persuade. The following topic sentences reflect the writer's desire to persuade.

   3. Violence that arises from road rage must be harshly and swiftly punished.

   4. How to achieve should be a part of public school education from elementary through high school.

In sentence 3, the topic is *violence.* The words that reveal the author's controlling point include *arises from, must be, harshly,* and *swiftly punished.* This sentence deals with the same general topic as sentence 1. Notice the difference in the treatments of this topic. Sentence 3 refocuses the topic from the causes of road rage to the effect of road rage: the *violence* that *arises from* road rage. The author then introduces a forceful, biased viewpoint.

In sentence 4, the topic is *public school education.* The author uses the process thought pattern to limit the topic with the phrase *how to achieve.* Additional words that reveal the controlling point are *should be,* which are followed by a recommendation for action. The author is offering a controversial personal opinion about how children should be educated. In both of these sentences, the authors want to convince others to agree with them about taking a specific course of action.

- **To entertain.** A writer whose purpose is to entertain sets out to captivate or interest the audience. A few of the tone words often used to describe this purpose include *amusing, entertaining, lively, humorous,* and *suspenseful.* To entertain, authors frequently use expressive language and creative thinking. Most readers are entertained by material that stirs an emotional reaction such as laughter, sympathy, or fear. Thus, authors engage readers creatively through vivid images, strong feelings, or sensory details (such as sights, sounds, tastes, textures, and smells). Both fiction and nonfiction writers seek to entertain. The following topic sentences reflect the writer's desire to entertain.

5. Think of our highways as a place to study how operating a powerful machine can turn normal people into four types of maniacs: the bully, the loudmouth, the speed-demon, and the exterminator.

6. I am zealously committed to eating a balanced diet from the four basic food groups: low-calorie, low-carbohydrate, low-fat, and low-taste.

You may have found identifying the topic and controlling point a little more challenging in these two sentences. Often, when writers entertain, they imply the main idea. And when they use an implied main idea, they rely much more heavily on tone words. Sentence 5, like sentences 1 and 3, deals with the topic of the stresses of driving. In this sentence, the author focuses the topic on the drivers with the phrase *four types of maniacs*. The use of *maniacs* (a biased word) offers a strong clue that the author's purpose is to entertain. Other words that reveal tone include *powerful*, *normal*, *bully*, *loudmouth*, *speed-demon*, and *exterminator*. The author seeks to amuse the reader with the contrast between "normal people" and what they become behind the wheel of a vehicle.

Sentence 6, like sentence 2, deals with the topic of a *diet*. In this case, the words that reveal the author's controlling point are *balanced* (which suggests healthful) and *four basic food groups* (which indicates the classification thought pattern). However, the main idea is not really about a balanced diet. The point seems to be about dieting. Clearly, the author is trying to make us smile by setting up an unexpected contrast. In most cases, the words *four food groups* are followed by a very different list of details. Surprising contrasts often set up an ironic tone. And irony often amuses the reader. You will learn more about irony later in this chapter. Authors also use other methods to entertain such as exaggerations, vivid details, and dramatic descriptions.

These six sentences show that a topic can be approached in a variety of ways. The author chooses a topic and a purpose. The purpose shapes the focus of the main idea. The author carefully chooses tone words to express the main idea in light of the purpose. Each of these choices then controls the choices of supporting details and the thought pattern used to organize them.

EXAMPLES Read each of the following paragraphs. Annotate them for main idea and tone.

I = to inform   **P** = to persuade   **E** = to entertain

_____ **1.**   A young woman suffering from anxiety was constantly biting her nails. Worried about her habit of biting her fingernails down to the quick, she asked her doctor for some advice. To her surprise, her doctor advised her to take up yoga. She did, and soon her fingernails were growing normally. During her next scheduled appointment, her doctor noticed her healthy nails asked her if yoga had totally cured her nervousness. "No," she replied, "but now I can reach my toe-nails so I bite them instead."

_____ **2.**   Yoga exercises benefit a person in three ways. Yoga leads to physical balance, mental alertness, and fewer injuries. The practice of yoga uses slow, steady motions to enter and hold poses that stretch and strengthen the body's muscles. Because each pose is held for at least 10 seconds, the body learns to adjust and find its natural balance. To find this balance, the mind must be actively involved. And as the muscles are stretched and strengthened, injuries are less likely to occur.

_____ **3.**   Yoga is a much healthier practice than simple stretching. Stretching relies on a jerky movement that forces the body into a certain position. Often stretching is dynamic, using a bouncing motion, and the stretch is only held for a moment or two. Such stretching can lead to injuries. In contrast, yoga uses a static stretch that relies on inner balance to hold the pose for at least 10 to 15 seconds. To successfully enter and hold a yoga pose, the mind must focus on what the body needs to stay balanced. By holding a stretch, the body becomes strong and flexible, and the connection between the mind and body is strengthened more so than with simple stretching.

VISUAL VOCABULARY

The purpose of the lawyer is to

_____.

a. entertain.
b. inform.
c. persuade.

EXPLANATIONS

1. The topic of this paragraph is presented in the middle of the paragraph—yoga. The author uses the narrative thought pattern to set up a personal experience as the basis of a joke about yoga. Throughout the narrative, the author uses vivid details, descriptions, and a surprise ending—a punch line—(E) *to entertain* the reader.

2. This paragraph opens with the main idea stated in a topic sentence. The topic is yoga exercises, and the words that reveal the author's controlling points are *benefit* and *three ways*. The details consist of a list and explanations of these benefits. The author's purpose here is simply (I) *to inform* the reader about three benefits of yoga.

3. This paragraph also opens with the main idea stated in a topic sentence. Again, the topic is yoga, and the words that reveal the controlling point are *much healthier* (which is an opinion) and *than simple stretching* (which indicates the contrast thought pattern). The author clearly believes that yoga is better than simple stretching and gives details (P) *to persuade* the reader that this view is correct.

PRACTICE 3

Read the following topic sentences. Label each according to its purpose:

I = to inform   **P** = to persuade   **E** = to entertain

_____   **1.** Cloning human beings should be banned.

_____   **2.** The National Hurricane Center predicts a record number of hurricanes in the upcoming months.

_____   **3.** Friends don't let friends drive drunk.

_____   **4.** Bulimia and anorexia are two serious eating disorders.

_____   **5.** A celebrity is a person who works hard all his life to become well known, then wears dark glasses to avoid being recognized.

—James B. Simpson

_____   **6.** Spanking as a way to discipline a child has a long history in many cultures.

_____   **7.** Age is strictly a case of mind over matter. If you don't mind, it doesn't matter.

—Jack Benny

_____ **8.** Kwanzaa is an African American tradition that is based on the African celebration of the "first fruits" of the harvest.

_____ **9.** When I was a boy of fourteen, my father was so ignorant I could hardly stand to have the old man around. But when I got to be twenty-one, I was astonished at how much he had learned in seven years.
——Mark Twain

_____ **10.** Rely on Denta-Fresh toothpaste to stop bad breath just as millions of others have.

Figure Out the Primary Purpose

In addition to the three general purposes, authors often write to fulfill a more specific purpose. The following table offers several examples of specific purposes.

General and Specific Purposes		
To inform	**To entertain**	**To persuade**
to analyze	to amuse	to argue against
to clarify	to delight	to argue for
to discuss	to frighten	to convince
to establish		to criticize
to explain		to inspire (motivate a change)

Often a writer has two or more purposes in one piece of writing. Blending purposes adds interest and power to a piece of writing. Take, for example, the award-winning documentary _Fahrenheit 9/11_. This film attempts to inform and entertain, but its primary purpose is to argue. The film uses facts, personal bias, and humor to take a strong stand against President Bush. Comics like Jon Stewart and Jimmy Fallon use facts from daily events to entertain their audiences. In these cases, when an author has more than one purpose, only one purpose is in control overall. This controlling purpose is called the **primary purpose.**

You have studied several reading skills that will help you grasp the author's primary purpose. For example, the author's primary purpose is often suggested by the main idea, the thought pattern, and the tone of the passage. Read the following topic sentence. Identify the author's primary purpose by considering the main idea, thought pattern, and tone.

_____ Spanking must be avoided as a way to discipline due to its long-term negative effects on the child.

  a. to discuss the disadvantages of spanking
  b. to argue against spanking as a means of discipline
  c. to make fun of those who use spanking as a means of discipline

This topic sentence clearly states a main idea "against spanking" using the tone words *must* and *negative*. The details will be organized using the thought pattern *long-term effects*. Based on the topic sentence, the author's primary purpose is (b) to argue against spanking as a means of discipline. Even when the main idea is implied, tone and thought patterns point to the author's primary purpose.

You should also take into account titles, headings, and prior knowledge about the author. For example, it's easy to see that Jay Leno's primary purpose is to entertain us with his book *If Roast Beef Could Fly*. The title is funny, and we know Jay Leno is a comedian. An effective reader studies the general context of the passage to find out the author's primary purpose.

> **Primary purpose** is the author's main reason for writing the passage.

EXAMPLES Read the following paragraphs. Identify the primary purpose of each paragraph.

1.
On the Decay of the Art of Lying
by Mark Twain [Samuel Clemens]

Observe, I do not mean to suggest that the "custom" of lying has suffered any decay or interruption—no, for the Lie, as a Virtue, A Principle, is eternal; the Lie, as a recreation, a solace, a refuge in time of need, the fourth Grace, the tenth Muse, man's best and surest friend, is immortal, and cannot perish from the earth while this club remains. My complaint simply concerns the decay of the "art" of lying. No high-minded man, no man of right feeling, can contemplate the lumbering and slovenly lying of the present day without grieving to see a noble art so prostituted. . . . No fact is more firmly established than that lying is a necessity of our circumstances—the deduction that it is then a Virtue goes without saying. No virtue can reach its highest usefulness without careful and diligent cultivation—therefore, it goes without saying that this one ought to be taught in the public schools—even in the newspapers. What chance has the ignorant uncultivated liar against the educated expert? What chance have I against Mr. Per—against a lawyer?

—Excerpt from Mark Twain, "On the Decay of the Art of Lying." *Classic Literature Library.* http://mark-twain.classic-literature.co.uk/on-the-decay-of-the-art-of-lying/.

_____ The main purpose of this passage is to
a. explain the virtue of lying.
b. amuse the reader with by poking fun at the human act of lying.
c. convince the reader that lying is a virtue.

2.

Letter from Birmingham Jail
by Martin Luther King Jr.

We know through painful experience that freedom is never voluntarily given by the oppressor; it must be demanded by the oppressed. Frankly, I have yet to engage in a direct-action campaign that was "well timed" in the view of those who have not suffered unduly from the disease of segregation. For years now I have heard the word "Wait!" It rings in the ear of every Negro with piercing familiarity. This "Wait" has almost always meant "Never." We must come to see, with one of our distinguished jurists, that "justice too long delayed is justice denied."

—Martin Luther King Jr. "Letter from Birmingham Jail." Copyright 1963 Dr. Martin Luther King Jr., copyright renewed 1991 by Coretta Scott King.

_____ The main purpose of this paragraph is
a. to entertain the reader with details from the civil rights movement.
b. to convince the reader that the Negro deserves justice now.
c. to explain why the Negro has been treated unfairly.

3.

Long-Term Memory

Textbook
Skills

Think of long-term memory as a "data bank" or warehouse for all of your feelings and ideas. Information you heard hours, days, weeks, even years ago is stored in long-term memory. Long-term memory differs from short-term memory in several ways. Long-term memory can handle large amounts of information; short-term memory has less space for storage. Putting information in and getting it out again is a slow process in long-term memory. On the other hand, short-term memory is a rapid process.

—Adapted from Brownell, *Listening: Attitudes, Principles, and Skills*, p. 150 © 2002 by Pearson Education, Inc. Reproduced by permission of Pearson Education, Inc.

_____ The main purpose of this paragraph is
   a. to argue against poor memory skills.
   b. to amuse the reader with humorous details about long-term memory.
   c. to inform the reader about the differences between long-term and short-term memory.

EXPLANATIONS

1. Mark Twain, also known as Samuel Clemens, is a well-known American humorist. Thus, a reader can expect his primary purpose to be (b) to amuse the reader with by poking fun at the human act of lying. Notice how his use of tone words makes this piece amusing, as in calling lying an "art" and "grieving to see a noble art so prostituted." His unexpected praise of a dishonest behavior is meant to make us smile.

2. It is common knowledge that Dr. Martin Luther King, Jr. is a beloved martyr of the civil rights movement. He is famous for his stand against injustice. The title tells us that this piece was written from the Birmingham jail. He was jailed for his stand against segregation. His main purpose is (b) to convince the reader that the Negro deserves justice now.

3. Based on the source note, you know that this paragraph comes from a textbook, and the primary purpose of a textbook is to inform. In addition, the tone of the title and details is factual and objective. Its main purpose is (c) to inform the reader about the differences between long-term and short-term memory.

PRACTICE 4

Read each of the following paragraphs. Identify the primary purpose of each.

1.   **Different Words, Different Worlds**
                    by Deborah Tannen

Many years ago, I was married to a man who shouted at me, "I do not give you the right to raise your voice to me, because you are a woman and I am a man." This was frustrating because I knew it was unfair. But I also knew just what was going on. I ascribed his unfairness to his having grown up in a country where few people thought women and men have equal rights. Now I am married to a man who is a partner and friend. We come from similar backgrounds and share values and interests. It is a continual source of pleasure to talk to him. It is wonderful to have someone I can tell everything to, someone who understands. But he doesn't always see things as I do, doesn't always react to things as I expect him to. And I often don't understand why he says what he does.

—Tannen, *You Just Don't Understand*, p. 23.

_____ The main purpose of this paragraph is
   a. to entertain with amusing details about marriage.
   b. to explain that men and women often perceive things differently.
   c. to argue against the idea that men are superior to women.

Textbook Skills

2.   **Human Impact on Lakes**

Wakes created by motorboating disturb vegetation and the birds that nest in it. Motorboats discharge an oily mixture with gas exhausts beneath the surface of the water. This mixture escapes notice. One gallon of oil per million gallons of water imparts an odor to lake water. Eight gallons per million taints fish. These oily discharges can lower oxygen levels and hurt the growth and life span of fish.

—Adapted from Smith & Smith, *Elements of Ecology*, 4th ed., p. 462.

_____ The main purpose of this paragraph is
   a. to inform the reader about the impact of human motorboating activity on lakes.
   b. to argue against the use of boats in lakes.
   c. to entertain the reader with interesting details about boating.

Textbook Skills

3.   **The Metamorphosis**
                          by Franz Kafka

As Gregor Samsa awoke one morning from uneasy dreams he found himself transformed in his bed into a gigantic insect. He was lying on his hard, as it were armor-plated, back and when he lifted his head a little he could see his dome-like brown belly divided into stiff arched segments on top of which the bed quilt could hardly keep in position and was about to slide off completely. His numerous legs, which were pitifully thin compared to the rest of his bulk, waved helplessly before his eyes.

—Kennedy & Gioia, *Literature*, 8th ed., pp. 345–346.

_____ The main purpose of this paragraph is
   a. to explain to the reader that a human has turned into a bug.
   b. to convince the reader that a human has turned into a bug.
   c. to engage the reader with an absurd story.

VISUAL VOCABULARY

The purpose of this poster is to
_____.

a. inform.
b. entertain.
c. persuade.

Recognize Irony Used for Special Effects

Irony is a tone often used in both conversation and written text. An author uses **irony** when he or she says one thing but means something else. Irony is the contrast between what is stated and what is implied, or between actual events and expectations.

Irony is often used to entertain and enlighten. For example, in the novel *Huckleberry Finn* by Mark Twain, the boy Huckleberry Finn believes he has done something wrong when he helps his older friend Jim escape slavery. The ironic contrast lies between what Huckleberry Finn thinks is wrong and what really is wrong: slavery itself. Twain set up this ironic situation to reveal the shortcomings of society.

Irony is also used to persuade. In her essay "I Want a Wife," Judy Brady seems to be saying she wants a wife to take care of the children, do the household chores, and perform all the other countless duties expected of a wife in the mid-twentieth century. However, she doesn't really want a wife; she wants equality with men. As she describes the role of a wife as a submissive servant, she argues against the limitations that society placed on women.

Due to its powerful special effects, authors use irony in many types of writings. For example, you will come across irony in fiction, essays, poetry, comedy routines, and cartoons. When authors use irony, they imply their main ideas and rely heavily on tone. Thus you need to understand two common types of irony so that you can see and enjoy their effects: verbal irony and situational irony.

> **Verbal irony** occurs when the author's words state one thing but imply the opposite.

During a violent storm, your friend says, "Nice weather, eh?"

At the finish line of a marathon, a tired runner says, "Why, I'm ready to run another 26 miles."

A father reviews his son's straight A report card and says, "Well, you have certainly made a mess of things!"

> **Situational irony** occurs when the events of a situation differ from what is expected.

A high school dropout eventually becomes a medical doctor.

An Olympic swimmer drowns.

A multimillionaire clips grocery coupons.

EXAMPLES Read the items, and identify the type of irony used in each.

_____ **1.** Martha and Charlotte, who can't stand each other, show up at the prom wearing the exact same dress.
a. verbal irony
b. situational irony
c. no irony

_____ **2.** The burglar who had robbed the neighborhood garages of golf clubs and bicycles turned out to be a grandmother of six.
a. verbal irony
b. situational irony
c. no irony

_____ **3.** After getting stuck babysitting for her younger brothers and sisters, Kerry said, "This must be my lucky day."
a. verbal irony
b. situational irony
c. no irony

_____ **4.** Dark- or bright-colored foods are the healthiest because of their nutrients.
a. verbal irony
b. situational irony
c. no irony

EXPLANATIONS

1. (b) situational irony: The fact that people who can't stand each other have similar taste in fashion is unexpected.

2. (b) situational irony: Most would not suspect a grandmother to be a thief.

3. (a) verbal irony: The author provides a clue to the tone by using the phrase "getting stuck babysitting." These words let us know that Kerry is not pleased and doesn't mean what she is saying.

4. (c) no irony: The author provides facts without emotion.

PRACTICE 5

Read the items, and identify the type of irony used in each.

_____ **1.** Looking out the window at the gray skies and wind-blown trees, Robert said, "Great day for a picnic."
a. verbal irony   c. no irony
b. situational irony

_____ **2.** On opening night, the beautiful, talented, and famous actress stood frozen with stage fright as the curtain rose.
a. verbal irony   c. no irony
b. situational irony

_____ **3.** "Driving while under the influence of drugs or alcohol is really smart."
a. verbal irony   c. no irony
b. situational irony

_____ **4.** Kim stayed up all night typing the paper that was due the next day. Just as she was ready to print, her computer crashed, and she lost all her information. She had failed to save her work as she wrote. It was the best paper she had ever written.
a. verbal irony   c. no irony
b. situational irony

_____ **5.** Algebra is a challenging course for many college students.
a. verbal irony   c. no irony
b. situational irony

Textbook
Skills

Author's Tone and Purpose

Read the excerpt from the textbook *Messages: Building Interpersonal Communication Skills*. Then answer these questions about the author's purpose and tone.

264   PART 3: Messages in Context

How would you explain the cartoon to the right in terms of social exchange theory?

ACCOUNTANTS IN LOVE (SOME SAMPLE NOTES)

Intimacy

At the intimacy stage you commit yourself still further to the other person and, in fact, establish a kind of relationship in which this individual becomes your best or closest friend, lover, or companion. Usually the intimacy stage divides itself quite neatly into two phases: an *interpersonal commitment* phase in which you commit yourselves to each other in a kind of private way and a *social bonding* phase in which the commitment is made public—perhaps to family and friends, perhaps to the public at large through formal marriage. Here the two of you become a unit, a pair.

Commitment may take many forms; it may be an engagement or a marriage; it may be a commitment to help the person or to be with the person, or a commitment to reveal your deepest secrets. It may consist of living together or an agreement to become lovers. The type of commitment varies with the relationship and with the individuals. The important characteristic is that the commitment made is a special one; it's a commitment that you do not make lightly or to everyone. This intimacy stage is reserved for very few people at any given time—sometimes just one, sometimes two, three, or perhaps four. Rarely do people have more than four intimates, except in a family situation.

True love comes quietly, without banners or flashing lights. If you hear bells, get your ears checked.

—Erich Segal

Immature love says: "I love you because I need you."
Mature love says: "I need you because I love you."

—Erich Fromm

—DeVito, *Messages: Building Interpersonal Communication Skills,* Text and figure from p. 264. © 2004. Reproduced by permission of Pearson Education, Inc.

_____ **1.** The author's primary purpose for this section of the text is
    a. to inform.   c. to persuade.
    b. to entertain.

_____ **2.** The tone of the main text is
    a. biased.   b. objective.

_____ **3.** The purpose of the cartoon "Accountants in Love" is
    a. to inform.   c. to persuade.
    b. to entertain.

_____ **4.** The tone of the quote by Erich Segal is
    a. earnest.   c. irritated.
    b. loving.   d. sarcastic.

_____ **5.** The tone of the quote by Erich Fromm is
    a. biting.   c. poetic.
    b. cheerful.   d. insulting.

APPLICATIONS

Application 1: Tone

Read each of the following items. Choose the tone word from the box that best describes each item.

doubtful	sad	self-pitying	sympathetic
irritated	sarcastic	straightforward	threatening

_____ **1.** "Please note in your checkbook how much money you spent using your ATM card today."

_____ **2.** "Hey, lay off, you don't have to nag me. I was going to do it anyway!"

_____ **3.** "When are you going to take the garbage out? Sometime this year, maybe?"

_____ **4.** "You know how hard it's been. I have been working two jobs and going to school nights just to make ends meet and get ahead. I hardly have time to do any of the things I need to do, much less have any fun. No one else works as hard as I do."

_____ **5.** "I know it's been hard. And I appreciate all you are going through right now. If you will just put the receipts on the counter, I will take care of the paperwork for you."

Application 2: Author's Purpose

Read each item, and identify the author's purpose: to inform, to entertain, or to persuade.

1. Pain is a normal part of a physical process that lets us know something is wrong.

_____

2. The death penalty is deeply flawed and should be abolished.

_____

3. "Yes, I have gained weight. I weighed only 8 pounds when I was born."

_____

4. Each of our cozy, long-sleeved knit shirts is available in an array of colors. They're the perfect additions to your wardrobe for any season. Hurry! The marked-down sale price is good only through Saturday.

_____

5. The sound of glass shattering downstairs startled Kalein out of her sleep. She held her breath as she listened to the sound of footsteps coming closer to her bedroom. Frantically, she dialed 911. "Hurry," she whispered into the phone, "someone is in the house." She knew as soon as the words were out that help was too far away. Her eyes cast about the room in search of a weapon to use to defend herself.

_____

Application 3: Author's Primary Purpose

Identify the primary purpose of each passage.

1.
Sequoya and the Cherokee Alphabet

Sequoya was a brilliant and proud Cherokee. He was born in Tennessee around 1770 and lived in Georgia until 1843. He is best known for his amazing feat of creating the Cherokee alphabet. This remarkable man is thought to be the son of Nathaniel Gist, an English trader, and a part-Cherokee woman. He was also known by his English name, George Guess. In a heroic effort to save Cherokee culture, Sequoya created a system of writing for the Cherokees. He began this work around 1809, and by 1821, he had created an alphabet made up of over 80 symbols. With the alphabet, the Cherokees published newspapers and books in their own language. Thousands of Cherokees learned to read and write in the new written language. The giant sequoia trees and Sequoia National Park in California are named after him.

Purpose: _____
a. to inform
b. to entertain
c. to persuade

2.   **Justice Fulfilled or Justice Denied?**

On January 12, 2003, the governor of Illinois, George Ryan, commuted death penalties into life sentences for 167 inmates on death row. The debate about the death penalty usually focuses on the fear that an innocent person sits on death row. However, Governor Ryan spared the lives of many vicious killers. In his effort to combat the unfairness of the death penalty, he abused his power. And he hurt the chances of true and lasting reform of the death penalty.

Purpose: _____
a. to inform
b. to entertain
c. to persuade

3.   **The Reconstruction Period**
                                  by Booker T. Washington

The years from 1867 to 1878 I think may be called the period of Reconstruction. This included the time that I spent as a student at Hampton and as a teacher in West Virginia. During the whole of the Reconstruction period two ideas were constantly agitating the minds of the coloured people, or, at least, the minds of a large part of the race. One of these was the craze for Greek and Latin learning, and the other was a desire to hold office.

It could not have been expected that a people who had spent generations in slavery, and before that generations in the darkest heathenism, could at first form any proper conception of what an education meant. In every part of the South, during the Reconstruction period, schools, both day and night, were filled to overflowing with people of all ages and conditions, some being as far along in age as sixty and seventy years. The ambition to secure an education was most praiseworthy and encouraging. The idea, however, was too prevalent that, as soon as one secured a little education, in some unexplainable way he would be free from most of the hardships of the world, and, at any rate, could live without manual labour. There was a further feeling that a knowledge, however little, of the Greek and Latin languages would make one a very superior human being, something bordering almost on the supernatural. I remember that the first coloured man whom I saw who knew something about foreign languages impressed me at that time as being a man of all others to be envied.

— Booker T. Washington, *Up from Slavery: An Autobiography*.
New York: Doubleday, Page, 1901; Bartleby.com, 2000.
www.bartleby.com/1004/. 6 April 2007.

Purpose: _____
a. to inform   b. to entertain   c. to persuade

Application 4: Irony

Read each item, and identify the type of irony used, if any.

_____ **1.** Water, water, everywhere,

And all the boards did shrink

Water, water, everywhere,

Nor any drop to drink.

—*The Rime of the Ancient Mariner*, by Samuel Taylor Coleridge

a. verbal irony   c. no irony
b. situational irony

_____ **2.** In the short story "The Lottery" by Shirley Jackson, an entire town excitedly gathers to take part in a long-established lottery. Each year, the person who wins the lottery is stoned to death by the entire community.
a. verbal irony   c. no irony
b. situational irony

_____ **3.** On a beautiful sunny day, a young couple walk hand in hand.
a. verbal irony   c. no irony
b. situational irony

_____ **4.** "All animals are created equal, but some are more equal than others."

—*Animal Farm*, by George Orwell

a. verbal irony   c. no irony
b. situational irony

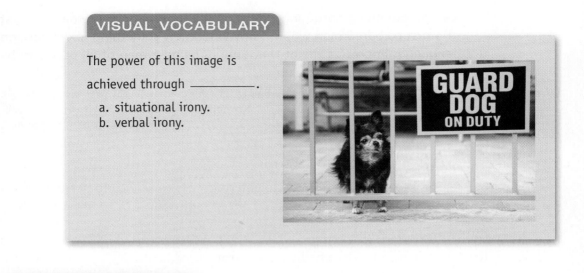

VISUAL VOCABULARY

The power of this image is achieved through ──────────.
   a. situational irony.
   b. verbal irony.

REVIEW TEST 1

Score (number correct) ──────── × 10 = ────────%

Tone

Read the following items, and choose a tone word from the box that best describes each.

angry	encouraging	pessimistic	sympathetic
confident	joking	pleading	timid
disbelieving	joyful	sarcastic	warning

──────────────── **1.** "Quitting smoking is easy; I quit two or three times a day."

──────────────── **2.** "Very funny, Joe, I can hardly stop laughing. I mean, risking cancer is just so funny."

──────────────── **3.** "I am not going to get cancer because I can kick the smoking habit any time I choose to."

──────────────── **4.** "You'd better think again, Joe. That's what my uncle thought, too."

──────────────── **5.** "Oh, yeah, I'm sorry, how is he doing? I know you must be worried."

_____ 6. "Not so good. The chemotherapy is making him really sick. I'm afraid he might not make it."

_____ 7. "Don't worry, Sue, the treatment is going to work. The doctors said he had an 80 percent chance of beating the cancer."

_____ 8. "Well, those odds don't mean anything when you act as stupidly as my uncle. He still smokes at least a pack a day!"

_____ 9. "You have to be kidding! Still smoking? That's hard to believe!"

_____ 10. "Please, Joe, don't end up like my uncle. Please, stop smoking now before it becomes impossible for you to quit, too."

REVIEW TEST 2   Score (number correct) _____ × 10 = _____%

Tone and Purpose

A. Read the following topic sentences. Label each according to its purpose:

I = to inform
P = to persuade
E = to entertain

_____ 1. The best way to survive babysitting a set of triplets is to come armed with plenty of energy, lots of patience, and a first-aid kit.

_____ 2. The Trail of Tears is the name of the journey that more than 70,000 Indians took when they were forced to give up their homes and move to Oklahoma.

_____ 3. According to fitness specialist Jack Tremagne, a long-term weightlifting program is the only effective method for losing and keeping off unhealthy body fat.

_____ 4. The northbound lane of State Road 17 will be shut down for several days this week due to road construction.

_____ **5.** The death penalty is unfair and cruel and should be abolished.

_____ **6.** The sound of a thousand motorcycles fills the night air as leather-clad, tough-looking, party-minded bikers roar into the sleepy coastal town for one wild, crazy, unforgettable week.

B. Read the following items, and identify the primary purpose of each.

Editorial Cartoon Published in a Newspaper

_____ **7.** The primary purpose of this cartoon is
    a. to inform the reader about the need to ban smoking.
    b. to entertain the reader with a funny situation about smoking bans.
    c. to persuade the reader to ban smoking outside.

Literary Passage Published in a Book

Fog

by Carl Sandburg

The fog comes
on little cat feet.
It sits looking
over harbor and city

on silent haunches
and then moves on.

—Sandburg, *Chicago Poems* (1916).

_____ **8.** The tone of this poem could best be described as
    a. mysterious.   c. ironic.
    b. humorous.   d. loving.

_____ **9.** The primary purpose of this passage is
    a. to inform the reader about the traits of fog.
    b. to entertain the reader with its poetic language and the similarities between the fog and a cat.
    c. to persuade the reader to see the fog as a threat to the city.

Paragraph from a Health Textbook

Smokeless Tobacco

**Textbook
Skills**

    Smokeless tobacco is used by approximately 5 million U.S. adults. Most users are teenage (20 percent of male high school students) and young adult males, who are often emulating a professional sports figure or family member. There are two types of smokeless tobacco—chewing tobacco and snuff. Chewing tobacco contains tobacco leaves treated with molasses and other flavorings. The user places a "quid" of tobacco in the mouth between the teeth and gums and then sucks or chews the quid to release the nicotine. Once the quid becomes ineffective, the user spits it out and inserts another. Dipping is another method of using chewing tobacco. The dipper takes a small amount of tobacco and places it between the lower lip and teeth to stimulate the flow of saliva and release the nicotine. Dipping rapidly releases the nicotine into the bloodstream.

    Snuff can come in either dry or moist powdered form or sachets (teabaglike pouches) of tobacco. The most common placement of snuff is inside the cheek. In European countries, inhaling dry snuff is more common than in the United States.

—Donatelle, *Access to Health*, 7th ed., p. 365.

_____ **10.** The primary purpose of this passage is
    a. to inform the reader about smokeless tobacco.
    b. to entertain the reader with graphic details about smokeless tobacco.
    c. to persuade the reader to avoid using smokeless tobacco.

REVIEW TEST 3

Score (number correct) _____ × 25 = _____%

Tone and Purpose

Read the following passage from a college sociology textbook. Answer the questions that follow.

Textbook
Skills

Is Big Brother Knocking on the Door? Civil Liberties and Homeland Security

[1]See if you can guess which country this is. [2]Government agents can break into your home while you are at work, copy the files on your computer, and leave a "bug" that records every keystroke from then on all this without a search warrant. [3]Government agents can also check with the local library and make a list of every book, record, or movie that you've ever checked out.

[4]Is this Russia? [5]Albania? [6]Maybe there, too, but this is now how it is in the United States.

[7]We have had fundamental changes since 9/11. [8]There is no question that we must have security. [9]Our nation cannot be at risk, and we cannot live in peril. [10]But does security have to come at the price of our civil liberties?

[11]Balancing security and civil liberties has always been a sensitive issue in U.S. history. [12]In times of war, the U.S. government has curtailed freedoms. [13]During the War Between the States, as the Civil War is called in the South, Abraham Lincoln even banned the right of habeas corpus (Neely 1992). [14]This took away people's right to appear in court and ask judges to determine whether they had been unlawfully arrested and imprisoned.

[15]After the terrorist attacks on New York City and Washington, D.C. in 2001, Congress authorized the formation of the Department of Homeland Security. [16]Other than beefed-up security at airports, few citizens noticed a difference. [17]People who were suspected of terrorism, however, felt a major impact. [18]They were imprisoned without charges being lodged against them in a court, and they were denied the right to consult lawyers or to have a hearing in court.

[19]People shrugged this off. [20]"Terrorists deserve whatever they get," they said. [21]What ordinary citizens didn't realize was that behind the scenes, their own liberties were being curtailed. [22]FBI agents placed Listening devices on cars, in buildings, and on streets. [23]They used Night Stalkers (aircraft outfitted with electronic surveillance equipment) to listen to conversations (Hentoff 2003). [24]No longer does the FBI need a judge's

order to search your e-mails, telephone records, travel records, or credit and bank transactions. [25]The FBI can simply demand that telephone and Internet access companies, colleges, libraries, banks, and credit companies produce them—and be punished as criminals if they reveal that the FBI has demanded these records ("FBI Director . . . " 2007).

[26]Then there is the "no-fly list" of the Transportation Security Agency. [27]Anyone who might have some kind of connection with some kind of terrorist is not allowed to board an airplane. [28]This agency has also developed CAPPS II (Computer Assisted Passenger Pre-Screening System). [29]Each traveler is labeled as a "green," "yellow," or "red" security risk. [30]Green means you're fine, and red is reserved for known terrorists.

[31]But what about the yellow code? [32]These people are "suspects." [33]The American Civil Liberties Union points out that anyone can get stamped yellow—with no way to know it or to change it. [34](For all I know, I could be coded yellow for criticizing Homeland Security in this essay.) [35]Agents in "government intelligence"—an oxymoron, if ever there was one—are known for being humorless, suspicious, and almost downright paranoid. [36]You could get stamped yellow simply for reading the wrong books—because agents of the Department of Homeland Security now have the right to track the books we buy or those we check out at libraries. [37]They can even record the Internet sites we visit at libraries. [38]This is all done in secret. [39]When librarians receive orders to reveal who has checked out certain books, they can be arrested if they even tell anyone that they received such an order (Lichtblau 2005).

[40]If such surveillance continues, our government will become like the former police state of East Germany and eventually keep secret files on almost all of us. [41]If you get coded yellow, that information could be shared with other government agencies. [42]This, in turn, could affect your chances of getting a job or even a college scholarship.

[43]Security we must have. [44]But at what cost? [45]Government watchdogs looking over our shoulders, writing down the names of our friends and associates, even the books and magazines we read? [46]Microphones planted to eavesdrop on our conversations? [47]Will they eventually install a computer chip in our right hand or in our forehead?

_____ **1.** The tone of sentence 20 is
   a. cynical.
   b. objective.
   c. hateful.
   d. resigned.

_____ **2.** The tone of sentence 47 is
       a. neutral.   c. sarcastic.
       b. timid.   d. supportive.

_____ **3.** The overall tone of the passage is
       a. objective.   b. biased.

_____ **4.** The main purpose of this essay is to
       a. explain the relationship between civil rights and homeland security.
       b. amuse the reader with details about civil rights and homeland security.
       c. warn the reader about the dangers posed to civil rights for the sake of homeland security.

VISUAL VOCABULARY

This humor in this cartoon relies on _____.

a. situational irony
b. verbal irony

"Look, you've got to accept some curtailment of your freedom in exchange for increased security."

WHAT DO YOU THINK

What civil liberties do you think we should give up to help our nation be secure from terrorists? Are you willing to have the government keep track of your everyday affairs in the name of homeland security? What is your opinion of the government keeping a list of the books you check out at the library? Listening to your conversations? Keeping track of the people you associate with? Write a letter to the editor of your local newspaper or to your senator. In your letter express your support for or against government surveillance for security.

REVIEW TEST 4

Score (number correct) _____ × 10 = _____%

Combined Skills Test

Read the following letter written by Conan O'Brien to the general public about the controversy surrounding the *Tonight Show* in 2010. Before you read, skim the passage and answer the Before Reading questions. Then, read the passage carefully and answer the After Reading questions that follow.

Open Letter from Conan O'Brien

Vocabulary Preview

predicament (4): difficult situation

lucrative (7): profitable

predecessor (8): previous holder of the job

accommodate (12): to adjust actions in response to the needs of another

[1]People of Earth:

[2]In the last few days, I've been getting a lot of sympathy calls, and I want to start by making it clear that no one should waste a second feeling sorry for me. [3]For 17 years, I've been getting paid to do what I love most and, in a world with real problems, I've been absurdly lucky.

[4]That said, I've been suddenly put in a very public **predicament** and my bosses are demanding an immediate decision.

[5]Six years ago, I signed a contract with NBC to take over *The Tonight Show* in June of 2009. [6]Like a lot of us, I grew up watching Johnny Carson every night and the chance to one day sit in that chair has meant everything to me. [7]I worked long and hard to get that opportunity, passed up far more **lucrative** offers, and since 2004 I have spent literally hundreds of hours thinking of ways to extend the **franchise** long into the future.

[8]It was my mistaken belief that, like my **predecessor,** I would have the benefit of some time and, just as important, some degree of ratings support from the prime-time schedule. [9]Building a lasting audience at 11:30 is impossible without both.

[10]But sadly, we were never given that chance. [11]After only seven months, with my *Tonight Show* in its infancy, NBC has decided to react to their terrible difficulties in prime-time by making a change in their long-established late night schedule.

[12]Last Thursday, NBC executives told me they intended to move the *Tonight Show* to 12:05 to accommodate the *Jay Leno Show* at 11:35. [13]For years the *Tonight Show* has aired immediately following the late local news. [14]I sincerely believe that delaying the *Tonight Show* into the next day to **accommodate** another comedy program will seriously damage what I consider to be the greatest franchise in the history of broadcasting.

¹⁵The *Tonight Show* at 12:05 simply isn't the *Tonight Show*. ¹⁶Also, if I accept this move I will be knocking the *Late Night* show, which I inherited from David Letterman and passed on to Jimmy Fallon, out of its long-held time slot. ¹⁷That would hurt the other NBC franchise that I love, and it would be unfair to Jimmy.

¹⁸So it has come to this: I cannot express in words how much I enjoy hosting this program and what an enormous personal disappointment it is for me to consider losing it. ¹⁹My staff and I have worked unbelievably hard and we are very proud of our contribution to the legacy of the *Tonight Show*. ²⁰But I cannot participate in what I honestly believe is its destruction.

²¹Some people will make the argument that with DVRs and the Internet a time slot doesn't matter. ²²But with the *Tonight Show*, I believe nothing could matter more.

²³There has been speculation about my going to another network but, to set the record straight, I currently have no other offer and honestly have no idea what happens next. ²⁴My hope is that NBC and I can resolve this quickly so that my staff, crew, and I can do a show we can be proud of, for a company that values our work.

²⁵Have a great day and, for the record, I am truly sorry about my hair; it's always been that way.

²⁶Yours, Conan

— Conan O'Brien. "Open Letter from Conan O'Brien." Los Angeles Daily News. 12 Jan. 2010. http://www.dailynews .com/news/ci_14173746. Reproduced with permission.

Before Reading

Vocabulary in Context

_____   **1.** What does the word **franchise** mean in sentence 7?
    a. right   c. authority
    b. business   d. profit

Purpose

_____   **2.** The primary purpose of Conan O'Brien's open letter was to
    a. inform the public about his views on the situation.
    b. entertain the public and increase his audience.
    c. persuade the network to retain him as host of the *Tonight Show*.

After Reading

Central Idea and Main Idea

_____ **3.** Which sentence best states the central idea of the passage?

    a. sentence 4   c. sentence 20

    b. sentence 14   d. sentence 22

Supporting Details

_____ **4.** Sentence 6 is a

    a. major supporting detail for the central idea

    b. minor supporting detail for the central idea.

Transitions

_____ **5.** The relationship between sentences 21 and 22 is

    a. cause and effect.   c. contrast.

    b. time order.   d. generalization and example.

Thought Patterns

_____ **6.** The overall thought pattern of the passage is

    a. cause and effect.   c. contrast.

    b. time order.   d. generalization and example.

Fact and Opinion

_____ **7.** Sentence 5 is a statement of

    a. fact.   c. fact and opinion.

    b. opinion.

_____ **8.** Sentence 22 is a statement of

    a. fact.   c. fact and opinion.

    b. opinion.

Tone

_____ **9.** Sentence 11 is an example of

    a. situational irony.   b. verbal irony.

_____ **10.** The tone of sentence 25 is

    a. bitter.   c. humorous.

    b. embarrassed.   d. humble.

Did you follow this story when it occurred? Are you a fan of late night comedy shows? Why do you think the Leno show failed in prime time? Should NBC have supported Jay Leno or Conan O'Brien as the host of the *Tonight Show*? Write an open letter to NBC in which you express an opinion about the *Tonight Show*. Have you disagreed with other decisions made by a network, such as the decision to air a particular show or take a show off the air? If so, write an open letter to a network that expresses your support or opposition to a decision that affected a program of your choice.

 ## After Reading About Tone and Purpose

Before you move on to the Mastery Tests on tone and purpose, take time to reflect on your learning and performance by answering the following questions. Write your answers in your notebook.

- How has my knowledge base or prior knowledge about tone and purpose changed?

- Based on my studies, how do I think I will perform on the Mastery Test(s)? Why do I think my scores will be above average, average, or below average?

- Would I recommend this chapter to other students who want to learn about tone and purpose? Why or why not?

Test your understanding of what you have learned about tone and purpose by completing the Chapter 10 Review Card in the insert near the end of your text.

CONNECT TO **myreadinglab**

To check your progress in meeting Chapter 10's learning outcomes, log in to **www.myreadinglab.com,** and try the following activities.

- The "Purpose and Tone" section of MyReadingLab provides an overview, model, practices, activities, and tests. To access this resource, click on the "Study Plan" tab. Then click on "Purpose and Tone." Then click on the following links as needed: "Overview," "Model," "Practice," and "Tests."

- To measure your mastery of the content in this chapter, complete the tests in the "Purpose and Tone" section and click on Gradebook to find your results.

A. Read the following items. Choose a tone word from the box that best describes each item.

a. amazed
b. argumentative
c. factual

d. logical
e. reflective

_____ **1.** Just imagine for a moment what life in this country might have been like if women had been properly represented in Congress. Would a Congress where women in all their diversity were represented tolerate the countless laws now on the books that discriminate against women in all phases of their lives? Would a Congress with adequate representation of women have allowed this country to reach the 1970s without a national health care system? Would it have permitted this country to rank fourteenth in infant mortality among the developed nations of the world? Would it have allowed the situation we now have in which thousands of kids grow up without decent care because their working mothers have no place to leave them? Would it allow fraudulent packaging and cheating of consumers in supermarkets, department stores and other retail outlets? Would it consent to the perverted sense of priorities that has dominated our government for decades, where billions have been appropriated for war while our human needs as a people have been neglected?—Bella Abzug

—*Bella!* "February 7" section (1972). *The Columbia World of Quotations.* New York: Columbia University Press, 1996. www.bartleby.com/66/. [6 April 2007].

_____ **2.** The sky was as full of motion and change as the desert beneath it was monotonous and still,—and there was so much sky, more than at sea, more than anywhere else in the world. The plain was there, under one's feet, but what one saw when one looked about was that brilliant blue world of stinging air and moving cloud. Even the mountains were mere ant-hills under it. Elsewhere the sky is the roof of the world; but here the earth was the floor of the sky. The landscape one longed for when one was away, the thing all about one, the world one actually lived in, was the sky, the sky!— Willa Cather, *Death Comes for the Archbishop.*

—*The Columbia World of Quotations.* New York: Columbia University Press, 1996. www.bartleby.com/66/. [6 April 2007].

_____ **3.** When things are investigated, then true knowledge is achieved; when true knowledge is achieved, then the will becomes sincere; when the will is sincere, then the heart is set right (or then the mind sees right); when the heart is set right, then the personal life is cultivated; when the personal life is cultivated, then the family life is regulated; when the family life is regulated, then the national life is orderly; and when the national life is orderly, then there is peace in this world.—Confucius

—Liki (*Record of Rites*), Chapter 42.—*The Wisdom of Confucius*, ed. and trans. Lin Yutang, Chapter 4, pp. 139–40 (1938). *Respectfully Quoted: A Dictionary of Quotations Requested from the Congressional Research Service.* Washington D.C.: Library of Congress, 1989; Bartleby.com, 2003. www.bartleby.com/73/. [6 April 2007].

_____ **4.** We are all citizens of one world; we are all of one blood. To hate a man because he was born in another country, because he speaks a different language, or because he takes a different view on this subject or that, is a great folly. Desist, I implore you, for we are all equally human. . . . Let us have but one end in view, the welfare of humanity.—John Amos Comenius

—Respectfully Quoted: A Dictionary of Quotations Requested from the Congressional Research Service. Washington D.C.: Library of Congress, 1989; Bartleby.com, 2003. www.bartleby.com/73/. [6 April 2007].

_____ **5.** The United Arab Emirates is a federation of sheikhdoms (1995 est. pop. 2,925,000), c.30,000 sq mi (77,700 sq km), SE Arabia, on the Persian Gulf and the Gulf of Oman. The federation, commonly known as the UAE, consists of seven sheikhdoms: Abu Dhabi (territorially the largest of the sheikhdoms), Ajman, Dubai, Fujairah, Ras al-Khaimah, Sharjah, and Umm al-Qaiwain. The city of Abu Dhabi (1991 est. pop. 798,000) in Abu Dhabi is the capital.—World Fact Book, 2003.

—The World Factbook. Washington, D.C.: Central Intelligence Agency, 2003; Bartleby.com, 2003. www.bartleby.com/151/. [7 April 2007].

B. Read the following topic sentences. Label each one according to its purpose:

I = to inform   **P** = to persuade   **E** = to entertain

_____ **6.** Florida offers a wide variety of fun vacation activities, from traditional tourist attractions to pristine natural retreats.

_____ **7.** Paris never sleeps; at night, the River Seine glistens as the City of Light comes alive.

_____ **8.** Explore the nature of Armada—with our all natural hair care products, offering the purest of ingredients designed to bring out the shine and body of healthy hair.

_____ **9.** The number of teenagers who are choosing to not have sex is growing for a variety of reasons.

_____ **10.** Congress must act quickly to head off the looming health care crisis.

Read each item; then answer the questions that follow it.

Poem

Richard Cory

by Edwin Arlington Robinson

Whenever Richard Cory went down town,
We people on the pavement looked at him:
He was a gentleman from sole to crown,
Clean favored, and imperially slim.

And he was always quietly arrayed,
And he was always human when he talked;
But still he fluttered pulses when he said,
"Good-morning," and he glittered when he walked.

And he was rich—yes, richer than a king—
And admirably schooled in every grace:
In fine, we thought he was everything
To make us wish that we were in his place.

So on we worked, and waited for the light,
And went without the meat, and cursed the bread;
And Richard Cory, one calm summer night,
Went home and put a bullet through his head.

_____ **1.** The primary purpose of this poem is to
    a. inform.   c. entertain.
    b. persuade.

_____ **2.** The overall tone of this poem can be described as
    a. ironic.   c. disbelieving.
    b. humorous.   d. excited.

Passage from a Health Textbook

Eating for Health

    Americans consume more calories per person than any other group
of people in the world. A *calorie* is a unit of measure that indicates the

Textbook
Skills

amount of energy we get from a particular food. Calories are eaten in the form of protein, fats, and carbohydrates. These are three basic nutrients needed for life. Three other nutrients—vitamins, minerals, and water—are necessary for bodily function but do not add any calories to our diets.

Taking in too many calories is a major factor in our tendency to be overweight. However, it is not the amount of food we eat that is likely to cause weight problems and related diseases. It is the relative amount of nutrients in our diets and lack of exercise. Most Americans get about 38 percent of their calories from fat, 15 percent from proteins, 22 percent from complex carbohydrates, and 24 percent from simple sugars. Experts recommend that complex carbohydrates be increased to make up 48 percent of our total calories. They also suggest that we reduce proteins to 12 percent, simple sugars to 10 percent, and fats to no more than 30 percent of our total diets.

—Adapted from Donatelle, *Access to Health*, 7th ed., p. 217.

_____ **3.** The primary purpose of this passage is to
    a. convince students to lose weight.
    b. condemn the typical American diet.
    c. share useful information that will lead to a healthy lifestyle.

_____ **4.** The overall tone of this passage can be described as
    a. critical.   c. cynical.
    b. bossy.   d. neutral.

VISUAL VOCABULARY

The power of this image relies on

_____.

    a. situational irony.
    b. verbal irony.

Read each passage; then answer the questions that follow it.

Paragraph from a Health Textbook

Textbook
Skills

Alcohol

Since the beginning of recorded history, there has always been a part of the world population that has problems with alcohol. The Old Testament of the Bible includes stories of the Jewish people dealing with problems related to drinking alcohol. Plato, the great Greek philosopher, noted problems linked to public drunkenness. Some of his recommendations for dealing with the problem serve as models for current laws in the United States. (Plato recommended no alcohol for those under eighteen years of age.) The Institute of Medicine in 1990 estimated that 25 percent of U.S. citizens consume large amounts of alcohol. According to their data, nearly 5 percent of the population are dependent on alcohol, and 5 to 15 percent are problem drinkers. Problem drinkers include those who struggle to control or limit their alcohol intake, those who drink despite growing health problems, and those who lose control over their behavior or mood while drinking.

—Adapted from Fishbein & Pease, *The Dynamics of Drug Abuse*, p. 103.

_____ **1.** The primary purpose of this paragraph is to
   a. encourage the reader to avoid alcohol.
   b. inform the reader about widespread alcohol use.
   c. delight the reader with interesting information about alcohol's history.

_____ **2.** The tone of this paragraph can be described as
   a. accusing.   c. objective.
   b. helpful.   d. depressing.

Passage from an American History Textbook

Textbook
Skills

The Question of Slavery

Early on the evening of January 21, 1850, Senator Henry Clay of Kentucky trudged through knee-deep snowdrifts to visit Senator Daniel

461

Webster of Massachusetts. Clay, 73 years old, was a sick man, wracked by a severe cough. But he braved the snowstorm. He feared for the Union's future.

For four years, Congress had bitterly debated the issue of the expansion of slavery in new territories. Ever since Daniel Wilmot had proposed that slavery be banned from any territory acquired from Mexico, those against slavery had argued that Congress had the right to ban slavery in all of the territories. Southerners who were for slavery strongly disagreed.

Politicians had been unable to work out a compromise. One simple proposal had been to extend the Missouri Compromise line to the Pacific Ocean. Thus slavery would have been outlawed north of 36'30" north latitude, but it would have been allowed south of that line. Moderate southerners supported this proposal, but few others agreed. Another proposal was known as "squatter sovereignty." It stated that the people who lived in a territory should decide whether or not to allow slavery.

Neither idea offered a solution to the whole range of issues dividing the North and the South. It was up to Henry Clay, who had just returned to Congress after a seven-year absence, to work out a solution. For an hour on the evening of January 21, Clay outlined the following plan to save the Union:

- California be admitted as a free state.
- Mexico and Utah have no restrictions on slavery.
- Texas give up land in exchange for unpaid debts.
- Congress enact a strict Fugitive Slave Law.
- Slave trade, but not slavery, be banned in the District of Columbia.

Clay's proposal set off an eight-month debate in Congress and led to threats of southern succession. Eventually parts of Clay's compromise were accepted. The compromise gave the false sense that the issue had been resolved. Hostility was defused, and calm returned. But as one southern editor correctly noted, it was "the calm of preparation, and not of peace."

—Adapted from Martin et al., *America and Its Peoples: A Mosaic in the Making,* 3rd ed., pp. 455–457.

_____ **3.** The primary purpose of this passage is to
    a. inform.   c. persuade.
    b. entertain.

_____ **4.** The overall tone of this passage can be described as
    a. argumentative.   c. bitter.
    b. factual.   d. stern.

Name _____ Section _____

Date _____ **Score** (number correct) _____ × 10 = _____%

Read the following items. Choose a tone word from the box below that best describes each.

admiring	factual	humble	ironic	pleading
cautionary	hopeful	humorous	persuasive	prayerful

_____ **1.** When you become senile, you won't know it.—Bill Cosby

—James B. Simpson, comp. *Simpson's Contemporary Quotations.* Boston: Houghton Mifflin, 1988. www.bartleby.com/63/. [6 April 2007].

_____ **2.** I believe that unarmed truth and unconditional love will have the final word in reality. This is why right, temporarily defeated, is stronger than evil triumphant.—Martin Luther King, Jr., accepting Nobel Peace Prize 10 Dec 64

—James B. Simpson, comp. *Simpson's Contemporary Quotations.* Boston: Houghton Mifflin, 1988. www.bartleby.com/63/. [6 April 2007].

_____ **3.** Tennis is a perfect combination of violent action taking place in an atmosphere of total tranquillity.—Billie Jean King, tennis player

— James B. Simpson, comp. *Simpson's Contemporary Quotations.* Boston: Houghton Mifflin, 1988. www.bartleby.com/63/. [6 April 2007].

_____ **4.** Let every nation know, whether it wishes us well or ill, that we shall pay any price, bear any burden, meet any hardship, support any friend, oppose any foe to assure the survival and the success of liberty.—John F Kennedy, 35th US President

—James B. Simpson, comp. *Simpson's Contemporary Quotations.* Boston: Houghton Mifflin, 1988. www.bartleby.com/63/. [6 April 2007].

_____ **5.** Tell him, if he doesn't mind, we'll shake hands.—John F Kennedy, 35th US President, On meeting Soviet Premier Nikita S Khrushchev

—James B. Simpson, comp. *Simpson's Contemporary Quotations.* Boston: Houghton Mifflin, 1988. www.bartleby.com/63/. [6 April 2007].

_____ **6.** Mama and Daddy King represent the best in manhood and womanhood, the best in a marriage, the kind of people we are trying to become.—Coretta Scott King

> —James B. Simpson, comp. *Simpson's Contemporary Quotations.* Boston: Houghton Mifflin, 1988. www.bartleby.com/63/. [6 April 2007].

_____ **7.** God give me the serenity to accept things which cannot be changed; Give me courage to change things which must be changed; And the wisdom to distinguish one from the other.

> —*Respectfully Quoted: A Dictionary of Quotations Requested from the Congressional Research Service.* Washington D.C.: Library of Congress, 1989; Bartleby.com, 2003. www.bartleby.com/73/. [6 April 2007].

_____ **8.** The term embryology, in its widest sense, is applied to the various changes which take place during the growth of an animal from the egg to the adult condition.

> —Henry Gray. *Anatomy of the Human Body.* Philadelphia: Lea & Febiger, 1918; Bartleby.com, 2000. www.bartleby.com/107/. [6 April 2007].

_____ **9.** A novel everyone should read is H. G. Well's *Invisible Man*, a tale of psychological terror. Wells created a gripping masterpiece on the destructive effects the invisibility has on the scientist and the insane and murderous chaos left in his malicious wake.

> —Bartleby.com, 2000. www.bartleby.com/1003/. [6 April 2007].

_____ **10.** "Yet, I implore you, pause! Yield to my advice, do not do this deed."—Jocaste, *Oedipus the King.*

Inferences

LEARNING OUTCOMES

After studying this chapter you should be able to do the following:

1. Define the term *inference*.
2. Distinguish between a valid and invalid inference.
3. Identify and apply the five steps for making a VALID inference.
4. Form valid inferences.
5. Define the following terms: *connotation, metaphor, personification, simile*, and *symbol*.
6. Infer meanings based on connotations, metaphors, personification, simile, and symbol.
7. Evaluate the importance of inferences.

Before Reading About Inferences

Predict what you need to learn based on the learning outcomes for this chapter by completing the following chart.

What I already know: _____

_____

_____

_____.

What I need to know: _____

_____

_____

_____

_____.

Now, skim the chapter to find three additional topics that you have already studied. List those topics.

_____

_____

Copy the following study outline in your notebook. Leave ample blank spaces between each topic. Use your own words to fill in the outline with information about each topic as you study about inferences.

Reading Skills Needed to Make VALID Inferences

   I. Verify facts.

  II. Assess prior knowledge.

 III. Learn from text.

      A. Context clues

      B. Thought patterns

      C. Implied main ideas

  IV. Investigate bias.

   V. Detect contradictions.

Inferences: Educated Guesses

Read the following passage.

> The air in the darkened movie theater felt chilly on Crystal's bare shoulders and arms. Her best friend, Julie, who had seen the movie three times already, had been smart to wear layered shirts, even if they were short-sleeved. Crystal placed the icy soft drink she had been holding in her chair's cup holder. Her right hand was freezing cold. She shivered as she watched the shark's fin, larger than life on the big screen, approaching the pretty young woman swimming in the ocean. As the music became faster and louder and the shark moved closer, a tingle ran up her spine. The shark struck. The victim screamed. At the same time, Crystal's right hand suddenly grabbed Julie's arm. Julie screamed too.

Which of the following statements might be true, based on the ideas in the passage?

_____ Crystal shivered because she was cold.

_____ Crystal shivered because she felt fear.

_____ Julie screamed because Crystal's cold hand surprised her.

_____ Julie screamed because she was afraid.

Did you choose the first three statements? Congratulations! You just made a set of educated guesses or **inferences**. An author suggests or **implies** an idea, and the reader comes to a conclusion and makes an inference about what the author means.

In the paragraph about Crystal and Julie, the first three statements are all firmly based on the information in the passage. However, the last statement is not backed by the supporting details. The facts point to Crystal's being cold and afraid, yet there is no hint of any fear on Julie's part. The only evidence given that could explain Julie's scream is Crystal's cold hand suddenly grabbing her.

What Is a Valid Inference?

People constantly draw conclusions about what they notice. We observe, gather information, and make inferences all the time.

For example, as we communicate with other people, we read their body language and facial expressions to determine their moods, their comprehension, or their acceptance of what is being said. In general, we assume a frown means that someone is unhappy or puzzled. And we assume a smile means someone is pleased. Of course, these inferences have to be confirmed with all the evidence in context.

> An **inference** or **conclusion** is an idea that is suggested by the facts or details in a passage.

Just as we rely on inferences to make sense of our everyday life, we also rely on inferences in our work and academic lives. For example, scientists make inferences based on clues they gather from photographs, fossils, artifacts, and their own prior knowledge. Study the following photo. Then, make inferences to fill in the blanks in the caption.

A **valid inference** is a rational judgment based on details and evidence. The ability to make a valid inference is a vital life skill. Making valid inferences

VISUAL VOCABULARY

Based on the skull and teeth of this animal, the traits of its mouth include

(**1**) _____

_____ .

Based on the traits of the mouth, this animal eats

(**2**) _____ . This is

the skull and teeth of a

(**3**) _____ .

aids us in our efforts to care for our families, succeed in our jobs, and even guard our health.

For example, doctors strive to make inferences about our health based on our symptoms. A red throat and swollen glands may lead a doctor to conclude that a patient has a strep infection. The doctor then orders a strep test to find out if her educated guess (a guess based on evidence) is correct. If it is correct, she prescribes an antibiotic to treat the infection.

> A **valid inference** is a logical conclusion based on evidence.

EXAMPLE   Read the following passage. Write **V** beside the three valid inferences. (Hint: valid inferences are firmly supported by the details in the passage.)

> ¹At 15 years old, José is the oldest child in a family of five brothers and one sister. ²His family came to the United States from Mexico when José was 6 years old. ³His parents are still unable to speak much English. ⁴The only work his father and mother have been able to find is picking crops. ⁵They are migrant workers. ⁶To earn a living, the family constantly moves to find new crops to help harvest. ⁷Because their pay is based on how much they pick, often the older children join their parents in the fields and work from dawn to dusk. ⁸Over the years, José and his siblings have attended more than a dozen different schools. ⁹All of the children receive low scores and are several grade levels behind other children their age. ¹⁰José has learned to speak English fairly well, and he reads whenever he can find discarded newspapers, magazines, or books. ¹¹His mother and father always take José with them when they buy food or clothes.

_____ **1.** José and his family work hard and sacrifice to make a living.

_____ **2.** José's parents don't care about their children's education.

_____ **3.** Migrant work does not provide a stable lifestyle.

_____ **4.** José is not very smart.

_____ **5.** José's ability to speak English is a help to his parents.

EXPLANATION Statements 1, 3, and 5 are valid inferences firmly based on the information in the passage. It is valid to infer that picking crops is hard work. It is also valid to infer that the family's need to move around to follow the work demands sacrificing friends and stability. Finally, it is valid to infer that José's parents take him shopping because he speaks English better than they do, so he is a help to them.

Statements 2 and 4 are not based on the information in the passage. It is invalid to assume that José's parents don't care about education. The facts only support the idea that the family's need to move interferes with the children's education. It is also wrong to infer that José is not smart. In fact, his desire to read is a sign of intelligence.

PRACTICE 1

Each of the following items contains a short passage and three inferences. In each item, only one inference is valid. In the space provided, write the letter of the inference that is clearly supported by each passage.

_____ **1.** Randall took great notes in class and from his textbooks. He studied every night for a week before the test. Of all the students in his class, Randall earned the highest grade on the test.
   a. Randall is smarter than his classmates.
   b. Randall is the teacher's favorite student.
   c. Randall worked hard for his grade.

_____ **2.** Sandra was 20 pounds overweight, so she decided to cut out all carbohydrates (such as cereal, rice, potatoes, and bread) from her diet. Instead, she ate a bowl of fruit every morning and extra helpings of meat, colorful vegetables, and salads for lunch and dinner. Sandra lost the 20 pounds in four months.
   a. Sandra did not look good before she changed her diet.
   b. Eating too many carbohydrates may cause weight gain.
   c. Sandra enjoyed her new diet.

_____ **3.** Mark takes charge of the TV's remote control every night. He watches three or four different sports events at the same time. During the commercials or when the sportscasters are talking, he switches to the other games. By doing this, Mark is able to follow racing, basketball, tennis, and golf.

    a. There is nothing else good on television, so Mark watches only sports.

    b. Mark is rude to his family.

    c. Mark is a dedicated sports fan.

Making VALID Inferences and Avoiding Invalid Conclusions

Two of the most common pitfalls of making inferences are ignoring the facts and relying too much on personal opinions and bias. Often we are tempted to read too much into a passage because of our own prior experiences or beliefs. Of course, to make a valid inference, we must use clues based on logic and our experience. However, the most important resource must be the written text. As effective readers, our main goal is to find out what the author is saying, stating, or implying. Sound inferences come from orderly thinking. Effective readers learn to use the VALID thinking process to make valid inferences. The VALID approach avoids drawing false inferences or coming to invalid conclusions.

> An **invalid conclusion** is a false inference that is not based on the details, or facts in the text, or on reasonable thinking.

The VALID approach is made up of 5 steps:

    Step 1: **V**erify and value the facts.

    Step 2: **A**ssess prior knowledge.

    Step 3: **L**earn from the text.

    Step 4: **I**nvestigate for bias.

    Step 5: **D**etect contradictions.

Step 1: Verify and Value the Facts

Develop a devotion to finding the facts. In Chapter 9, you learned to identify facts and to beware of false facts. You learned that authors may mix fact with opinion or use false information for their own purposes. Just as authors may make this kind of mistake, readers may, too. Readers may draw false inferences by mixing the author's facts with their own opinions or by misreading the facts. So it is important to find, verify, and stick to factual details. Once you have all the facts, only then can you begin to interpret the facts by making inferences.

EXAMPLE Read the following short passage. Then write **V** next to the two valid inferences firmly supported by the facts.

> [1]Korea has long been known as the "Eastern Land of Courtesy." [2]When happy, a Korean simply smiles or gently touches the one who brings the happiness. [3]When angry, a Korean simply stares directly at the person, and that person's humble smile is a powerful apology.

_____ **1.** Koreans are quiet and reserved people.

_____ **2.** Koreans show their emotions.

_____ **3.** Koreans are afraid of hurting the feelings of other people.

EXPLANATION The first two statements are correct inferences based on the facts. However, there is no hint or clue that Koreans are afraid of hurting anyone's feelings. In fact, directly staring at someone when angry is a bold act in this Asian culture. The third statement goes beyond the facts without any reason to do so. Effective readers draw conclusions that are supported by the facts.

VISUAL VOCABULARY

These protestors are members of _____.

   a. scientific research team.
   b. an animal rights group.
   c. a farmer's union.

Step 2: Assess Prior Knowledge

Once you are sure of the facts, the next step is to draw on your prior knowledge. What you have already learned and experienced can help you make accurate inferences.

EXAMPLE Read the following excerpt of an article posted on a government website. Identify the facts. Check those facts against your own experience and understanding. Write V next to the three inferences firmly supported by the facts in the passage.

Chronic Media Multi-tasking Makes It Harder to Focus

[1]You may think e-mailing, texting, talking on the phone and listening to music all at once is making you more efficient. [2]But new research suggests the opposite is true.

[3]Processing multiple streams of information from different sources of media is a challenge for the human brain, according to a recent study.

[4]New research shows that students who did the most multi-tasking were less able to focus and concentrate—even when they were trying to do only one task at a time.

[5]"The human mind is not really built for processing multiple streams of information," said study author Eyal Ophir. [6]Ophir is a researcher at Stanford University's Communication Between Humans and Interactive Media Lab. [7]"The ability to process a second stream of information is really limited."

[8]Researchers had 262 college students fill out a questionnaire about how often they multi-tasked. [9]Students then completed a series of tests that measured cognitive control. [10]Cognitive control is a mental process. [11]In this process, the brain directs attention, decides where to assign mental resources at a given moment, and determines what's important from the many bits of information being received.

[12]Students who were at the upper end of the media multi-tasking spectrum performed more poorly on all the tests than those who multi-tasked the least. [13]Interestingly, the students had similar overall intelligence and SAT scores.

[14]Computers are well-equipped to switch rapidly from one task to another. [15]But the human brain struggles with such demands.

—Adapted from Jennifer Thomas. "Chronic Media Multi-tasking
Makes It Harder to Focus." *HealthDay*. Healthfinder.gov.
http://www.healthfinder.gov/news/printnewsstory.aspx?docID=630268.

_____ **1.** Eyal Ophir offers an expert opinion.

_____ **2.** People with short attention spans tend to multi-task.

_____ **3.** The reasons for the decreased cognitive control are clear.

_____ **4.** Multi-tasking damages cognitive control.

_____ **5.** People should multi-task less and instead build periods of time to focus on one thing.

_____ **6.** Multi-tasking includes doing one or more activities at once, including e-mailing, surfing the Web, writing on a computer, watching TV, texting, playing video games, listening to music, or talking on the phone.

EXPLANATION Items 1, 5, and 6 are valid inferences based on the information in the passage. However, the article offers no evidence or discussion about items 2, 3, or 4. For example, the article does not give any data about short attention spans as a cause for multi-tasking. Likewise, the article only discusses the decrease in cognitive control. It does not explain the reasons for the decrease. Finally, the article asserts that cognitive control is decreased, not damaged. The term "damaged" has long-term implications not addressed in the article.

VISUAL VOCABULARY

Write a caption that states the cartoonist's message:

_____

_____

Step 3: Learn from the Text

When you value and verify facts, you are learning from the text. A valid inference is always based on what is stated or implied by the details in the text; in contrast, an invalid inference goes beyond the evidence. Thus, to make a valid inference, you must learn to rely on the information in the text. Many of the skills you have studied from previous chapters work together to enable you to learn from the text. For example, context clues unlock the meaning of an author's use of vocabulary. Becoming aware of thought patterns teaches you to look for the logical relationship between ideas. Learning about stated and implied main ideas trains you to examine supporting details. (In fact, you use inference skills to find the implied main idea.) In addition, tone and purpose reveal the author's bias and intent. (Again, you often use inference skills to grasp the author's tone and purpose.) As you apply these skills to your reading process, you are carefully listening to what the author has to say. You are learning from the text. Once you learn from the text, only then can you make a valid inference. The following examples show you how you learn from the text.

EXAMPLE Read the following paragraph from a psychology textbook. Answer the questions that follow.

Textbook
Skills

¹Motives can arise from something inside yourself, such as when you keep studying because you find the subject matter interesting. ²Such activities are pursued as ends in themselves, simply because they are enjoyable, not because any external reward is attached. ³This type of motivation is known as **intrinsic motivation**. ⁴Other motives originate from outside. ⁵Some external stimulus, or **incentive**, pulls or entices you to act. ⁶When the desire to get a good grade—or to avoid a bad grade—causes you to study, the grade is serving as this kind of external incentive. ⁷When we act so as to gain some external reward or to avoid some undesirable consequence, we are pulled by **extrinsic motivation**. ⁸According to B. F. Skinner, a **reinforcer** is a result that increases the frequency of a behavior. ⁹Once the link between a behavior and a reinforcer has been established, the prospect of receiving the reinforcer again serves as an incentive to perform the behavior. ¹⁰For example, the prospect of getting a generous tip serves as an incentive for restaurant servers to serve their customers promptly and courteously.

—Adapted from Wood, et al., *Mastering the World of Psychology,*
Text from p. 289 © 2008 Pearson Education, Inc. Reproduced
by permission of Pearson Education, Inc.

_____ **1.** The best synonym for the word *intrinsic* is
    a. enjoyable.   c. hidden.
    b. basic.   d. learned.

_____ **2.** The best synonym for the word *extrinsic* is
    a. profitable.
    b. accidental.
    c. inessential.
    d. essential.

_____ **3.** The overall thought pattern of the paragraph is
    a. listing.   c. definition and example.
    b. time order.   d. comparison and contrast.

_____ **4.** The author's tone is
    a. emotional.   b. neutral.

_____ **5.** The author's purpose is
    a. to inform the reader about the basic terms used to discuss motivation.
    b. to persuade the reader to analyze his or her own motivations.
    c. to entertain the reader with interesting details about motivation.

_____ **6.** Which of the following is a valid inference?
    a. An example of intrinsic motivation is a person donating money to college to build a library, provided the library bears the name of the donor.
    b. An example of extrinsic motivation is a child reading one book a week to avoid losing television privileges.
    c. An example of intrinsic motivation is a person secretly donating money to Haiti to help the survivors of the earthquake.

EXPLANATION Compare your answers to the following: **1.** Something that comes from within or "inside" is basic or inherent. It is the very nature of the being; thus the correct answer is (b) basic. **2.** Because the paragraph makes it clear that extrinsic is the opposite of intrinsic, we can infer that anything extrinsic is (c) inessential. **3.** The overall thought pattern is (c) definition and example as indicated by the bold print, the details, and the phrase "for example." **4.** The author's tone is (b) neutral. **5.** The author's purpose is (a) to inform. **6.** Based on the definitions and examples in the paragraph, (c) is the only valid inference.

A food treat is _____ that taps into a dog's _____ motivation to perform a trick.

    a. an incentive
    b. a reinforcer
    c. intrinsic
    d. extrinsic

Step 4: Investigate for Bias

One of the most important steps in making a valid inference is confronting your biases. Each of us possesses strong personal views that influence the way we process information. Often our personal views are based on prior experiences. For example, if we have had a negative prior experience with a used car salesperson, we may become suspicious and stereotype all used car salespeople as dishonest. Sometimes, our biases are based on the way in which we were raised. Some people register as Democrats or Republicans and vote for only Democratic or Republican candidates simply because their parents were members of either the Democratic or Republican party. To make a valid inference, we must investigate our responses for bias. Our bias can shape our reading of the author's meaning. To investigate for bias, note biased words and replace them with factual details as you form your conclusions.

EXAMPLE Read the following paragraph. Investigate the list of inferences that follow for bias. Underline biased words. Mark each item as follows: **V** if the inference is valid or **I** if the inference is invalid due to bias.

The Five Pillars of Islam

¹The guiding principles of the Islamic faith are known as the Five Pillars of Islam. ²Muslims, the believers of Islam, devote their lives to these principles. ³The first principle is called *shahadah* (shah-HAH-dah). ⁴*Shahadah* is the prayer of faith that says, "There is no God but Allah, and Muhammad is his messenger." ⁵The second rule is known as *salat* (sah-LAHT); *salat* is

the act of praying five times a day to Allah. [6]Prayer occurs at dawn, noon, afternoon, dusk, and night. [7]The third principle is *saum* (sah-OHM); *saum* is a fast from food or drink that lasts 30 days during the holy month of Ramadan. [8]The fourth pillar is called *zakat* (zeh-KAHT); this is the act of giving money to the poor and needy. [9]The final principle of Islam is *haj* (HAHDJ); this is the journey of pilgrimage that Muslims all over the world must make to the holy city of Mecca in Saudi Arabia at least once in their lifetime.

_____ **1.** The word *shahadah* is a word for a very specific prayer that is always worded the same way.

_____ **2.** Islam teaches one to seek God and to help others.

_____ **3.** Islam takes discipline to practice.

_____ **4.** Islam is a radical belief that teaches people to think selfishly of themselves first.

EXPLANATION Items 1, 2 and 3 are (**V**) valid inferences based on the details in the paragraph. Item 1 includes the qualifier *always* which usually indicates a bias. However, based on the fact that the paragraph gives the name and exact wording of the prayer, it is reasonable to infer that the exact wording is the unique trait of the prayer and always used. Item 4 is an (**I**) invalid inference. This sentence includes two biased words: *radical* and *selfishly*. This biased statement is not grounded in the details.

VISUAL VOCABULARY

A crowd of poor people in Bangladesh gather near the house of a rich man in anticipation. Muslims pay

_____ (two and a half percent of their savings) to the poor according to Islamic law.

  a. shahadah
  b. salat
  c. zakat
  d. haj

Step 5: Detect Contradictions

Have you ever misjudged a situation or had a wrong first impression? For example, have you ever assumed a person was conceited or rude, only to find out later that he or she was acutely shy? Many times, there may be a better explanation for a set of facts than the first one that comes to mind. The effective reader hunts for the most reasonable explanation. The best way to do this is to consider other explanations that could logically contradict your first impression.

EXAMPLE Read the following list of behaviors. Then, in the blank, write as many explanations for the behaviors as you can think of.

- Slurred words
- Poor balance
- Slow movement
- Uncontrolled shaking in limbs
- Rigid muscles and stooped posture
- Fatigue or tiredness
- Depression

_____

_____

EXPLANATION Some people may think the behaviors in this list describe an alcoholic or a drug addict. But the list is actually a list of symptoms for Parkinson's disease, a brain disease that affects body movement. Often, people with this disease, like actor Michael J. Fox, also suffer from depression. Alcoholics and drug addicts do share most of the listed symptoms, except for rigid muscles and stooped posture. Those who suffer from Parkinson's disease struggle with muscles that become stiff and even freeze into place.

A reader who does not think about other possible views can easily jump to a wrong conclusion. Effective readers consider all the facts and all the possible explanations for those facts. Effective readers look for contradictions.

Use the 5 VALID steps to think your way through to logical conclusions based on sound inferences: (1) verify and value the facts, (2) assess prior knowledge, (3) learn from the text, (4) investigate for bias, and (5) detect contradictions.

VISUAL VOCABULARY

Based on the details in the image, we can reasonably come to the conclusion that this is a photo of

_____.

a. sea fan coral.
b. a pigmy seahorse.
c. a tree in autumn.

PRACTICE 2

Read the following passage from a college textbook about nursing. Investigate the list of inferences that follow for bias. Underline biased words. Mark each inference as follows: **V** for a valid inference firmly supported by the facts, **I** for an invalid inference.

Textbook
Skills

Definitions of Nursing

[1]Florence Nightingale defined nursing nearly 150 years ago as "the act of utilizing the environment of the patient to assist him in his recovery." [2]Nightingale considered a clean, well-ventilated, and quiet environment essential for recovery. [3]Often considered the first nurse theorist, Nightingale raised the status of nursing through education. [4]Nurses were no longer untrained housekeepers. [5]Instead they were people educated in the care of the sick.

[6]Virginia Henderson was one of the first modern nurses to define nursing. [7]She wrote, "The unique function of the nurse is to assist the individual, sick or well, in the performance of those activities contributing to health or its recovery (or to peaceful death) that he would perform unaided if he had the necessary strength, will, or knowledge, and to do this

in such a way as to help him gain independence as rapidly as possible." [8]Like Nightingale, Henderson described nursing in relation to the client and the client's environment. [9]Unlike Nightingale, Henderson saw the nurse as concerned with both healthy and ill individuals. [10]She acknowledged that nurses interact with clients even when recovery may not be feasible. [11]She also mentioned the teaching and advocacy roles of the nurse.

[12]In the latter half of the 20th century, a number of nurse theorists developed their own theoretical definitions of nursing. [13]Theoretical definitions are important. [14]They go beyond simplistic common definitions. [15]They describe what nursing is and the interrelationship among nurses, nursing, the client, the environment, and the intended client outcome: health.

—Adapted from Berman, Snyder, Kozier, & Erb, *Kozier & Erb's Fundamentals of Nursing: Concepts, Process, and Practice*, 8th ed., p. 11.

_____ **1.** Florence Nightingale never focused on preventing illness, just treating illness.

_____ **2.** Nursing focuses only on the sick.

_____ **3.** Nursing should include assisted suicide for the terminally ill to promote a peaceful death.

_____ **4.** A theoretical definition of nursing serves as a mission statement for nurses.

_____ **5.** Nursing involves treating the whole person, not just the symptoms of an illness.

Inferences in Creative Expression

As you have learned, nonfiction writing, such as in textbooks and news articles, directly states the author's point. Everything is done to make sure that the meanings are clear and unambiguous (not open to different interpretations). However, in many other types of writing, both fiction and nonfiction, authors use creative expression to suggest layers of meaning. Creative expressions are also known as literary devices. The following chart is made up of a few common literary devices, their meanings, and an example of each.

Creative Expression: Literary Devices		
Connotations of words	The emotional meaning of words	Mother was never stingy with her advice.
Metaphor	A direct comparison	Lies are sinkholes.
Personification	Giving human traits to things that are not human	The sun woke slowly.
Simile	An indirect comparison	Lies are like sticky webs.
Symbol	Something that stands for or suggests something else	A skull and crossbones is a symbol for poison and death.

By using these devices, a writer creates a vivid mental picture in the reader's mind. When a creative expression is used, a reader must infer the point the writer is making from the effects of the image. The following paragraph is the introduction to an essay about alcoholism. Notice its use of literary devices. After you read, write a one-sentence statement of the author's main idea for this paragraph.

Trapped in the Darkness

[1]Jean squeezed her eyes tight against the painful light that poured into the room with daybreak. [2]She groaned, rolled over, and buried her head in her pillow. [3]Hiding was useless; her misery followed her. [4]As she lay there, fighting the jumping nausea, she tried to recall the night before, but the events seemed shrouded in a dense fog. [5]She lifted her fingers to press on her temples; she had her usual tequila headache. [6]Her stomach twisted with familiar shame. [7]I *am* going to quit, she promised herself—again. [8]She groaned and curled into the darkness of her blanket.

_____

_____

This paragraph uses several creative expressions. Darkness is often used as a symbol of death, pain and suffering, or denial. All of these meanings could apply to Jean's situation. Light is often used as a symbol for wisdom and truth. The use of contrast between dark and light suggests many meanings. The painful light (sentence 1) could represent Jean's inability to face the truth or act wisely. The phrase "jumping nausea" (sentence 4) is the use of personification. Live beings jump, so to give such an action to nausea is to give it lifelike qualities. The phrase "events seemed shrouded in a dense fog" (sentence 4) is a simile. Perhaps the author is comparing Jean's memory to a fog. Or maybe the author is referring to

Jean being drunk the night before. The phrase "tequila headache" (sentence 5) is a metaphor for a hangover. Based on all the details, it is valid to infer that Jean has a drinking problem. The author could have simply stated "Jean suffers from a serious drinking problem." But the creative expressions intensify the meaning. And they suggest many levels of meaning. Therefore, as an effective reader, carefully consider the shades and levels of meaning while reading examples of creative writing.

EXAMPLE   A fable is a short story that makes a pointed statement. Read the following short fable written by Aesop in the sixth century B.C.E. Then answer the questions that follow it.

The North Wind and the Sun

¹A dispute arose between the North Wind and the Sun, each claiming that he was stronger than the other. ²At last they agreed to try their powers on a traveler, to see which could strip him of his cloak the fastest. ³The North Wind had the first try; gathering up all his force for the attack, he came whirling furiously down upon the man and caught up the man's cloak as though he would **wrest** it from the man in a single effort. ⁴But the harder he blew, the more closely the man wrapped the cloak around himself. ⁵Then came the turn of the Sun. ⁶At first, he beamed gently upon the traveler, who soon unclasped his cloak and walked on with it hanging loosely about his shoulders. ⁷Then the Sun shone forth in full strength, and the man, before he had gone many steps, was glad to throw his cloak right off and complete his journey lightly clad.

1. Choose the three valid inferences that are firmly based on the information in the passage by writing a **V** next to each one.

_____ a. The North Wind and the Sun are given human traits.

_____ b. The traveler is not very smart.

_____ c. The North Wind uses force to try to make the man take off his cloak.

_____ d. The Sun uses heat to influence the man to take off his cloak.

_____ 2. Based on context clues, we can infer that the meaning of the word *wrest* in sentence 3 is
a. wrap.   b. rip.   c. give.

_____ **3.** Based on the details in the passage, we can conclude that the implied main idea of the passage is
   a. persuasion is better than force.
   b. the Sun is harsher than the North Wind.
   c. humans are easily controlled by nature.

EXPLANATION

1. The correct inferences are (a), (c), and (d). Often creative writers give human traits to things that are not human. In this fable, the wind and the sun, like some humans, are in competition with one another, each wanting to be the stronger one. The text clearly implies the North Wind's use of force in words such as *force, attack, whirling,* and *wrest.* However, the Sun's efforts are described with words such as *gently* and *shone forth.* There is nothing to suggest that the traveler is not smart. Instead, he acts very logically.

2. The words *force* and *attack* indicate that the best meaning of the word *wrest* is (b) "rip."

3. The main idea suggested by the details is (a) persuasion is better than force. To make logical inferences, we must use our common sense and life experiences. Based on our own experiences, we know that the wind and the sun are both strong, but they are harsh in different ways. Although humans are influenced by nature, that point is a supporting detail and not the main idea.

PRACTICE 3

Read the following poem written by Robert Herrick in 1648. Choose the inferences that are most logical, based on the details in the poem.

To the Virgins, to Make Much of Time

Gather ye rose-buds while ye may,
Old Time is still a-flying;
And this same flower that smiles today,
Tomorrow will be dying.

5   The glorious lamp of heaven, the sun,
The higher he's a-getting,
The sooner will his race be run,
And nearer he's to setting.

10

That age is best which is the first,
When youth and blood are warmer;
But being spent, the worse, and worst
Times still succeed the former.

Then be not coy, but use your time,
And while ye may, go marry;

15

For having lost but once your prime,
You may forever tarry.

> **Vocabulary Preview**
>
> *coy* (13): shy
> *tarry* (16): delay

_____   **1.** The poet is speaking to
　　　a. unmarried women.
　　　b. married men.
　　　c. married young people.

_____   **2.** In the first verse, the rosebuds represent
　　　a. time.
　　　b. death.
　　　c. love.

_____   **3.** In the second stanza (group of lines), the sun measures
　　　a. a person's life span.
　　　b. a foot race.
　　　c. the time span of one day.

_____   **4.** In the third stanza, the poet implies that
　　　a. the wisdom of old age is best.
　　　b. it is better to be young than to be old.
　　　c. the young are foolish.

_____   **5.** The main idea of the poem is to
　　　a. enjoy life now.
　　　b. wait for wisdom.
　　　c. get married.

Textbook Skills ## Inferences and Visual Aids

Textbook authors often use pictures, photos, and graphs to imply an idea. These visuals are used to reinforce the information in that section of the textbook.

EXAMPLE This "Dilbert" cartoon was reprinted in a textbook. Based on the cartoon, what was the topic of the textbook chapter?

▲ Dilbert @ 1997 Reprinted by permission of United Features Syndicate, Inc.

_____ marriage and communication in intimate relationships

_____ women and low self-esteem

_____ effects of nonverbal communication

EXPLANATION The woman in the cartoon is obviously self-confident and outspoken about what she wants, so the chapter is not about women and low self-esteem. In addition, the artist did not include any gestures in the cartoon, so the chapter is not about the effect of nonverbal communication. Indeed, the humor is based on the kind of communication the woman expects. The cartoon was in a chapter about marriage and communication in intimate relationships.

PRACTICE 4

Study the figure on page 486, taken from the textbook *Access to Health*. Then, answer the questions.

_____ **1.** What is the topic of the chapter?
a. benefits of exercise
b. overall health of a man
c. causes of cancer

2. Write a caption in a complete sentence that best states the implied main idea of the figure.

_____

◄ **Figure A**
Suspected Causes of Cancer

—Rebecca J. Donatelle. *Access to Health,* 7th ed., p. 432. Copyright © 2002
Pearson Education, publishing as Benjamin Cummings.

APPLICATIONS

Textbook
Skills

Application 1: Making Inferences from a List

Read the following list of details. Write **V** for valid by the three inferences that
are firmly based on the information.

Traits of a Successful Team Member

- Commits to the team's goals
- Has high standards for self and others
- States disagreements
- Accepts differing views as sources of information
- Listens carefully

- Shares information
- Attends all meetings
- Completes assignments
- Looks for solutions

—Adapted from Barker & Gaut, *Communication*, 8th ed., p. 151.

_____ Successful team members should always agree with one another.

_____ Successful team members challenge one another to do their best.

_____ Successful team members are responsible and dependable.

_____ Successful team members are problem solvers.

_____ Successful team members set personal goals as a top priority.

_____ Successful team members rarely offer differing views.

Application 2: Making Inferences from a Visual

Read the following comic strip in the series known as "Blondie," by Dean Young and Denis Lebrun. Write **V** for valid by the two inferences that are firmly based on the details.

Reprinted with Special Permission of King Features Syndicate.

_____ Dagwood is a distracted walker.

_____ Everyday life is always dangerous.

_____ Dagwood's dog remains calm during the walk.

_____ The humor in this strip relies on verbal irony.

_____ The humor in this strip relies on situational irony.

Application 3: Making Inferences from a Poem

Read the following poem, which was written by James Stephens in 1915. Write **V** for valid by the three inferences that are firmly based on the details.

The Wind
The wind stood up and gave a shout.
He whistled on his fingers and
Kicked the withered branches about
And thumped the branches with his hand
And said he'd kill and kill and kill,
And so he will and so he will.

_____ The poet is referring to a gentle breeze.

_____ The poet is referring to a gale or hurricane-force wind.

_____ The wind is given human traits.

_____ The wind acts like a gentleman.

_____ The wind is like a strong, wild man.

_____ The wind is not dangerous.

REVIEW TEST 1   Score (number correct) _____ × 10 = _____%

Making Inferences

A. Study the cartoon. Then answer the questions.

"Because my genetic programming <u>prevents</u> me from stopping to ask directions—<u>that's</u> why!"

_____ **1.** The cartoon is about
   a. communication.
   b. cars.
   c. differences between men and women.

2–4. Write **V** for valid by the three inferences that are firmly supported by the details in the cartoon.

_____ The couple is getting along well.

_____ The couple is lost in the country.

_____ The woman has asked the man why he doesn't ask for directions.

_____ The woman knows where they are.

_____ The cartoon suggests that most men do not ask for directions when they are lost.

B. Read the following textbook passage. Write **V** for valid by two inferences firmly supported by details in the passage.

5–6.   [1]Before AIDS, Botswana was known as an African success story. [2]Rich diamond mines were discovered within its borders after it gained independence from Britain in 1966. [3]But it avoided the warfare and corruption that followed the discovery of gemstones elsewhere in the region. [4]It evolved into a well-run democracy with a fast-growing economy. [5]It had the continent's strongest credit rating and lowest infant mortality rate.

[6]Now the nation spends its weekends at funerals. [7]More than one-third of Botswana's adults are HIV-positive. [8]Life expectancy has plunged from over 65 to under 40. [9]More than 65,000 children have lost their parents to AIDS, and that number is projected to double or triple by 2010. [10]If the United States had Botswana's rate of AIDS deaths, it would lose 15,000 citizens per day.

—Adapted from Grunwald, "A Small Nation's Big Effort Against AIDS," *Washington Post*, 2 Dec. 2002.

_____ AIDS has devastated the country of Botswana.

_____ The growing number of orphans in Botswana is a social crisis.

_____ Botswana loses 15,000 people a day to AIDS.

_____ Botswana is a poor country.

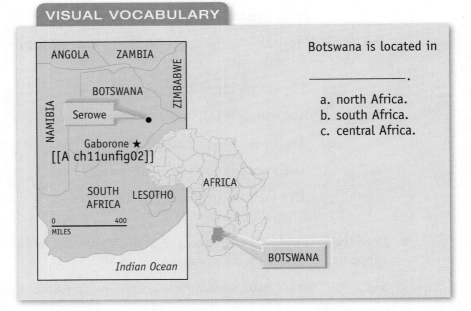

VISUAL VOCABULARY

Botswana is located in

_____.

a. north Africa.
b. south Africa.
c. central Africa.

—"A Small Nation's Big Effort Against AIDS" by Michael Grunwald, from *The Washington Post Foreign Service*, December 2, 2002. Copyright © 2002, The Washington Post. Reprinted with permission.

C. (7–10). Write **V** for valid by the four inferences that are firmly based on the information in the label that follows the paragraph.

Reading Nutritional Labels

[1]The first place to start when you look at the Nutrition Facts panel is the serving size and the number of servings in the package. [2]Serving sizes are given in familiar units, such as cups or pieces, followed by the metric amount, such as the number of grams. [3]Serving sizes are based on the amount of food people typically eat, which makes them realistic and easy to compare to similar foods. [4]Calories are a measure of how much energy you get from a serving of this food. [5]The nutrients listed first are the ones Americans generally eat in adequate amounts, or even too much. [6]Eating too much fat or too much sodium may increase your risk of certain chronic diseases, like heart disease, some cancers, or high blood pressure. [7]Eating too many calories is linked to being overweight and obesity. [8]Americans often don't get enough dietary fiber, vitamin A, vitamin C, calcium, and iron in their diets. [9]Eating enough of these nutrients can improve your health, and they help reduce the risk of some diseases. [10]For example, getting enough calcium can reduce the risk of osteoporosis. [11]This disease causes bones to become brittle and break as one ages. [12]The Percent Daily Value section of the Nutrition Facts panel tells you whether the nutrient (fat, sodium, fiber, etc.) in a serving of food adds a lot or a little to your total daily diet.

—"Guidance on How to Understand and Use the Nutrition Facts Panel on Food Labels," U.S. Food and Drug Administration: Center for Food Safety and Applied Nutrition, June 2000.

Sample Label for Macaroni and Cheese

Nutrition Facts

Serving Size 1 cup (228g)
Serving Per Container 2

Amount Per Serving	
Calories 250	Calories from Fat 110

	% Daily Value*
Total Fat 12g	**18%**
Saturated Fat 3g	**15%**
Cholesterol 30mg	**10%**
Sodium 470mg	**20%**
Total Carbohydrate 31g	**10%**
Dietary Fiber 0g	**0%**
Sugars 5g	
Protein 5g	

Vitamin A	**4%**
Vitamin C	**2%**
Calcium	**20%**
Iron	**4%**

*Percent Daily Values are based on a 2000 calorie diet. Your Daily Values may be higher or lower depending on your calorie needs:

	Calories:	2,000	2,500
Total Fat	Less than	65g	80g
Sat Fat	Less than	20g	25g
Cholesterol	Less than	300mg	300mg
Sodium	Less than	2,400mg	2,400mg
Total Carbohydrate		300g	375g
Dietary Fiber		25g	30g

_____ Food labels are designed to make it easier for you to use nutrition labels to make quick, informed food choices that contribute to a healthy diet.

_____ Macaroni & cheese is not a healthy food.

_____ An entire package of macaroni & cheese has a total fat of 24g.

_____ Macaroni & cheese does not contain enough iron to be of value in a healthy diet.

_____ Macaroni & cheese has 20% of the recommended daily amount of calcium for a healthy diet.

_____ Macaroni & cheese is a good food to eat to reduce the risk of osteoporosis.

_____ A person who eats macaroni & cheese runs the risk of becoming obese.

REVIEW TEST 2

Score (number correct) _____ × 20 = _____%

Making Inferences

Read the poem by Sylvia Plath. Then, answer the questions that follow it.

Metaphors

I'm a riddle in nine syllables,
An elephant, a ponderous house,
A melon strolling on two tendrils,
O red fruit, ivory, fine timbers!
This loaf's big with its yeasty rising,
Money's new-minted in this fat purse.
I'm a means, a stage, a cow in calf,
I've eaten a bag of green apples,
Boarded the train there's no getting off.

_____ **1.** The overall tone of the poem is one of
    a. pain.
    b. celebration.
    c. discomfort.

_____ **2.** The line "an elephant, a ponderous house" implies that the narrator feels
    a. strong.   c. intelligent.
    b. massive.

_____ **3.** The metaphor money in line 6 refers to
    a. the narrator.   c. an unborn child.
    b. wealth.

_____ **4.** The metaphor "I've eaten a bag of green apples" implies that the narrator feels
    a. sick.
    b. hungry.
    c. full.

_____ **5.** Based on the clues provided in the poem, the "I" (the narrator of the poem) is
  a. a pregnant woman.
  b. an unborn child.
  c. the author, Sylvia Plath.

REVIEW TEST 3

Score (number correct) _____ × 25 = _____%

Read the following editorial about the earthquake in Haiti published in the *Miami Herald.* Then, write **V** for valid by the four inferences that are firmly supported by the details in the passage.

Don't Let Haiti's Tragedy Fade Away

by Carl Hiaasen

[1]After the terrible earthquake, a man named Steve Driscoll went to Haiti with his search dog.

[2]Driscoll is a Palm Beach County firefighter, and his dog is a border collie named Blaze. [3]Last week they were working with a Miami-Dade search crew in Port-au-Prince when Blaze started barking and pawing at a concrete wall.

[4]Workers made a hole and pulled out a 2-year-old girl, covered in dust but still alive. [5]Six days she had survived in an air pocket beneath the rubble.

[6]Members of the rescue crew could hardly believe it, and there were tears. [7]Driscoll and Blaze got written up in his hometown newspaper, the *Palm Beach Post,* which is where I read about them.

[8]Many stories about the tragedy in Haiti don't have happy endings and, as the long days pass, more of us will turn away from the news. [9]This is human nature.

[9]Scenes of such total devastation and heartbreaking loss of life carry a weight that becomes difficult to bear, even from far away.

[10]The situation in Haiti is not incomprehensible, and it's not indescribable—just the opposite. [11]A graphic rendition of hell is what it is, a nightmare of nightmares.

[12]Officials still don't know how many people died in the earthquake, and they'll never know. [13]The current estimates range from 50,000 to 200,000, but it's all grim guesswork.

[14]Nobody is keeping count of all the bodies being trucked to mass gravesites. [15]Beneath the debris are thousands more, lost forever.

[16]Those who survived are in dire peril. [17]The healthy are desperate for food and water; the injured are desperate for medical care.

[18]Despite the huge international relief effort, some clinics are operating at primitive levels. [19]The *New York Times* reports that surgical instruments are being sterilized with vodka, and ordinary hacksaws are being used to perform emergency amputations.

[20]If the quake had struck a developed country, the destruction would have been crippling. But in a place of such wretched poverty as Haiti, with a government that barely functions in the best of times, the disaster is magnified to cataclysmic dimensions.

[21]Back here in the States, we all know friends and relatives who can't watch any more of it on television—and not because they don't care. [22]There's just too much misery to absorb. [23]They feel sad and sickened and helpless to do anything.

[24]Diversions are plentiful and, some might argue, therapeutic. [25]If you tuned in to other recent news, you would have learned that Simon Cowell is leaving *American Idol* and, for $32 million, Conan O'Brien is leaving *The Tonight Show*.

[26]Meanwhile, Tiger Woods is laying low at a clinic for sex addicts in Hattiesburg, Miss., of all places. [27]Or so says the *National Enquirer*.

[28]And, apparently inspired by home-run slugger Mark McGwire's overdue admission of being a steroid juicer, former Democratic presidential contender John Edwards finally confessed that he fathered a mistress's child.

[29]None of this stuff is very important, but it definitely gives a brain some down-time. [30]Those who are strong enough to stick with the Haiti story will find daily flashes of hope, like the amazing rescue that happened because of Steve Driscoll and his dog.

[31]In the earthquake zone, heroes are abundant and tireless. [32]Just as there's no way to count the dead, there's no way to know how many lives have been saved—or will be saved, as long as the rest of the world remains riveted.

[33]According to Partners in Health, which has provided medical care in Haiti for almost 25 years, the operating rooms at the General Hospital in Port-au-Prince have been ruled structurally safe and will start taking patients.

[34]Trauma surgery is being performed at seven other emergency operating tables on the property, and a helicopter pad has been opened to fly in the most seriously injured.

[35]The very images that are so painful for us to watch are fueling an astounding flow of donations to the many relief agencies on the

ground—UNICEF, the Red Cross, Partners in Health, Doctors Without Borders and others.

³⁶People on the outside passionately want to help, and giving money is the swiftest, most effective way. ³⁷How long it continues at this extraordinary pace will depend on the media's fluttery attention span, and on the public's endurance for what will be an arduous rebuilding.

³⁸In a 24/7 news cycle, the coverage of every natural calamity, from hurricanes to tsunamis, reaches a saturation point at which a sort of cauterizing numbness sets in. ³⁹Nothing would be worse for Haiti.

⁴⁰To glance away from its horrors is understandable, but to lose interest would be ruinous.

—Carl Hiaasen. "Don't Let Haiti's Tragedy Fade Away." *Miami Herald.* 24 Jan. 2010. http://www.miamiherald.com/news/columnists/carl-hiaasen/story/1441249.html.

_____ Before the earthquake, Haiti had a strong and vibrant government.

_____ Human nature is callous and uncaring.

_____ Human nature has a capacity for compassion.

_____ World-wide help for Haiti's earthquake victims is only temporary.

_____ The American public may be interested in the lives of celebrities to escape stress.

_____ The tone of sentence 27 is sarcastic.

VISUAL VOCABULARY

The best meaning of the word

seismicity is the _____.

a. location and frequency of earthquake events.
b. study of earthquakes around the world.

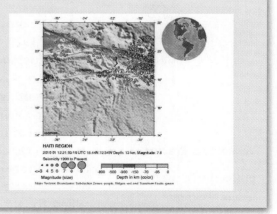

_____ The tone of sentence 27 is objective.

_____ The purpose of this editorial is to inform the public about the long-term needs of the Haitian people.

_____ The purpose of this editorial is to persuade people to make a long-term commitment to help the Haitian people.

WHAT DO YOU THINK?

Carl Hiaasen published this editorial just weeks after the earthquake devastated Haiti. Has the world looked away, or is the global community still concerned about the problems in Haiti? Search the Internet for information about the current conditions in Haiti and the latest efforts to rebuild the country. Write a letter to the editor of your local newspaper about the current conditions in Haiti and suggest some actions that should be taken, or acknowledge the good work that has been done on behalf of the people in Haiti.

REVIEW TEST 4   Score (number correct) _____ × 10 = _____%

Making Inferences

Before you read the following passage from a college history textbook, skim the passage. Answer the Before Reading questions. Then read the passage and answer the After Reading questions.

Textbook
Skills

The Great Depression

[1]The **prosperity** of the 1920s came to an abrupt halt in October 1929. [2]The stock market, which had boomed during the decade, suddenly faltered. [3]Investors who had borrowed heavily to take part in the buying **mania** that had swept Wall Street were suddenly forced to sell their securities to cover their loans. [4]The wave of selling triggered an avalanche of trading.

[5]On October 24, later known as Black Thursday, nearly 13 million shares were traded as **highfliers** such as RCA and Westinghouse lost nearly half their value. [6]The stock market rallied for the next two days, but on Tuesday, October 29,

Vocabulary Preview

prosperity (1): wealth
mania (3): craze

Vocabulary Preview

deprivation (15): lack
optimistic (20): hopeful
vagrants (32): homeless
persons

the downslide resumed. [7]Frightened sellers dumped more than 16 million shares, and the industrial stock price average fell by 43 points. [8]The panic ended in November, with stocks at 1927 levels. [9]For the next four years, there was a steady drift downward. [10]By 1932, prices were at only 20 percent of their 1920 highs.

[11]The Great Depression that followed the crash of 1929 was the most devastating economic blow ever suffered by the nation. [12]It lasted for more than ten years, and it dominated every aspect of American life during the 1930s. [13]Unemployment rose to 12 million by 1932. [14]Though it dipped midway through the decade, it still stood at 10 million by 1939. [15]Children grew up thinking that economic **deprivation** was the norm rather than the exception in America. [16]Year after year, people kept looking for a return to wealth. [17]But the outlook remained **dismal**. [18]The Depression loosened its grip on the nation only after the outbreak of World War II in 1939. [19]Even then, it left lasting mental and emotional scars. [20]The Americans who lived through it would never again be so **optimistic** about their economic future.

[21]It is difficult to measure the human cost of the Great Depression. [22]The material hardships were bad enough. [23]Men and women lived in lean-tos made of scrap wood and metal. [24]Families went without meat and fresh vegetables for months. [25]They existed on a diet of soup and beans. [26]The emotional burden was even greater: Americans suffered through year after year of grinding poverty with no relief in sight. [27]The unemployed stood in lines for hours waiting for relief checks. [28]Veterans sold apples or pencils on street corners.

[29]Many Americans sought escape in movement. [30]Men, boys, and some women rode the rails in search of jobs. [31]They hopped freight trains to move south in the winter or west in the summer. [32]One town in the Southwest hired special police to keep **vagrants** from leaving the boxcars. [33]Those who became tramps had to keep on the move, but they did find a sense of community in the hobo jungles that sprang up along the major railroad routes. [34]Here the unfortunate could find a place to eat and sleep and people with whom to share their misery. [35]Louis Banks told interviewer Studs Terkel what the informal camps were like:

[36]Black and white, it didn't make any difference who you were, 'cause everybody was poor. [37]All friendly, sleep in a jungle. [38]We used to take a big pot and cook food, cabbage, meat, and beans all together. [39]We all set together, we made a tent. [40]Twenty-five or thirty would be out on the side of the rail, white

and colored. **⁴¹**They didn't have no mothers or sisters, they didn't have no home, they were dirty, they had overalls on, they didn't have no food, they didn't have anything.

—Adapted from Divine, Breen, Fredrickson, & Williams,
The American Story, pp. 834–839.

Before Reading

Vocabulary in Context

_____ **1.** The word **highflier** in sentence 5 means
   a. stocks usually sold at a higher price than other stocks.
   b. stocks usually sold at a lower price than other stocks.
   c. stocks usually sold at the same price as most stocks.

Tone and Purpose

_____ **2.** Which of the following best describes the author's tone and purpose?
   a. to delight the reader with entertaining details
   b. to inform the reader with factual details
   c. to persuade the reader with emotional details

After Reading

Concept Maps
Finish the timeline with information from the passage.

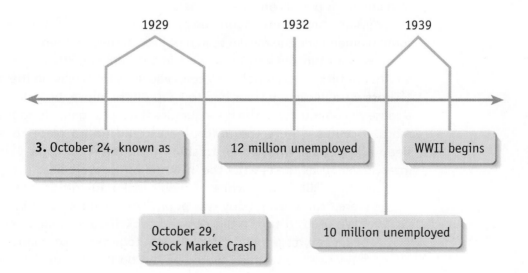

1929

1932

1939

3. October 24, known as
_____

12 million unemployed

WWII begins

October 29,
Stock Market Crash

10 million unemployed

Central Idea and Main Idea

_____ **4.** Choose the best statement of the central idea of the passage.
   a. The Great Depression was a devastating economic and emotional blow to the United States.
   b. The Great Depression put millions of people out of work.
   c. The Great Depression lasted for more than ten years.

Supporting Details

_____ **5.** Sentence 6, "The stock market rallied for the next two days, but on Tuesday, October 29, the downslide resumed," is a
   a. major supporting detail.   b. minor supporting detail.

Transitions

_____ **6.** "Year after year, people kept looking for a return to wealth. But the outlook remained dismal." (sentences 16–17)

The relationship between the ideas in these two sentences is one of
   a. cause and effect.   c. contrast.
   b. time order.

Thought Patterns

_____ **7.** The thought pattern used in the second paragraph (sentences 5–10) is
   a. cause and effect.   c. classification.
   b. time order.   d. definition.

Fact and Opinion

_____ **8.** Sentence 11 is a statement that expresses
   a. a fact.   c. a mixture of fact and opinion.
   b. an opinion.

Inferences

9–10. Write **V** for valid by the two inferences that are firmly based on the information in the passage.

_____ Fear was a factor in causing the stock market crash in October 1929.

_____ The outbreak of World War II created jobs for Americans.

_____ Many Americans made their fortunes during the Great Depression.

_____ Racial tensions between whites and blacks were common in the "hobo jungles."

WHAT DO YOU THINK?

Based on the details in the passage, what were the major causes and effects of the Great Depression? In 2008, the economy experienced another downturn that many have called the "Great Recession." Are there similarities between the Great Depression and the recession of 2008? In what ways does the 2008 recession differ from the Great Depression? Assume you are taking a college course in history, and your professor has asked you to make a connection between a recent event and an historic event. Write an essay that compares and contrasts the causes and effects of the Great Depression with the "Great Recession" of 2008.

 ## After Reading About Inferences

Before you move on to the Mastery Tests on inferences, take time to reflect on your learning and performance by answering the following questions. Write your answers in your notebook.

- How has my knowledge base or prior knowledge about inferences changed?

- Based on my studies, how do I think I will perform on the Mastery Test(s)? Why do I think my scores will be above average, average, or below average?

- Would I recommend this chapter to other students who want to learn more inferences? Why or why not?

Test your understanding of what you have learned about inferences by completing the Chapter 11 Review Card in the insert near the end of the text.

CONNECT TO myreadinglab

To check your progress in meeting Chapter 11's learning questions, log in to **www.myreadinglab.com** and try the following activities.

- The "Inference" section of MyReadingLab gives additional information about inferences. The section provides an overview, model, practices, and tests. To access this resource, click on the "Study Plan" tab. Then click on "Inference." Then click on the following links as needed: "Overview," "Model," "Practice," and "Test."

- To measure your mastery of the content in this chapter, complete the tests in the "Inference" section and click on "Gradebook" to find your results.

A. Read the passage. Then answer the questions that follow it.

Textbook
Skills

Diagnosing Alcoholism

[1]Alcoholism involves the development of certain harmful behaviors associated with long-term use of great amounts of alcohol. [2]It is a **chronic** illness with medical and social effects. [3]Alcoholism advances slowly as tolerance and dependence develop. [4]Although there is some disagreement about what alcoholism is, the following eight symptoms usually aid in its diagnosis:

1. Being drunk frequently in ways that are obvious and destructive
2. Failing in marriage and increasing absences from work
3. Being fired
4. Seeking medical treatment for drinking
5. Suffering physical injury
6. Being arrested for driving under the influence
7. Being arrested for drunkenness
8. Being hospitalized for cirrhosis of the liver or DTs [delirium tremens, or mental confusion that may include hallucinations]

—Adapted from Fishbein & Pease, *The Dynamics of Drug Abuse*, p. 116.

1. Write **V** for valid by the inference that is firmly supported by the passage.

_____ Alcoholism can be difficult to diagnose.

_____ Most people who drink become alcoholics.

_____ Alcoholism is not a life-threatening disease.

_____ **2.** The word **chronic** in sentence 2 implies
   a. short-term.
   b. curable.
   c. constant.

B. Read the following excerpt from a 2000 report based on research by Stanford University. Then answer the questions that follow it.

What Do Users Do on the Internet?

[1]We asked each of our 4,000 respondents to select among a list of 17 common Internet activities and tell us which they did or did not do. [2]This is what we found:

- [3]E-mail is by far the most common Internet activity. [4]Ninety percent of all Internet users claim to be e-mailers.
- [5]For the most part, the Internet today is a giant public library with a definite commercial tilt. [6]A widespread use of the Internet today is as a search tool for products (62 percent of users), travel (54 percent), hobbies (63 percent), and general information (77 percent). [7]Almost all users who were interviewed stated that they engaged in one or more of these activities.
- [8]A little over a third of all Internet users report using the Web to engage in entertainment such as computer games (online chess, role games, and the like). [9]Thus the Internet is also emerging as an entertainment utility.
- [10]Chat rooms are for the young and the anonymous. [11]While a quarter of Internet users claim to have used chat rooms, this activity largely decreases after age 25. [12]And the chatters report that the vast portion of their chat room time is spent with others whose identities remain unknown.
- [13]Consumer activity, such as buying, stock trading, online auctions, and e-banking, are engaged in by much smaller fractions of Internet users. [14]Only a quarter of those surveyed reported making purchases online, and less than 15 percent do any of the other activities. [15]Despite all the sound and fury, consumer commercial online transactions are in their earliest stages.

—Adapted from Nie, "What Do Users Do on the Internet?" *The Internet Study*, Institute for the Quantitative Study of Society, Stanford University.

3–5. Write V for valid by the three inferences that are firmly supported by details in the passage.

_____ More Internet users use the Internet to find travel information than to e-mail others.

_____ The Internet offers a wide variety of activities.

_____ Use of the Internet cuts down on time spent with family and friends.

_____ All information located on the Internet is reliable.

_____ People rarely use chat rooms to talk with friends and loved ones.

_____ Most Internet users do not use online banking services.

Read the passage. Then answer the questions that follow it.

Criticism

[1]Kay has been married less than a month. [2]But she's ready to give up on Don for his habit of dumping his clothes and belongings wherever he happens to be. [3]"When he left his muddy running shoes on top of my new microwave, I screamed at him like a fishwife," she says, "and asked him why his mother had brought up such a slob. [4]He immediately defended his mother and started to criticize mine. [5]Then we both got on the defensive and had a knock-down fight."

[6]Dr. Harriet Lefkowith, a Tenafly, N.J., human resource development specialist who leads workshops on communication throughout the country says, "Because criticism has such a negative **connotation,** we get into situations where the people we criticize invariably react defensively.

[7]"Before you know it, the act of criticism turns into an armed camp with two sides. [8]Nobody's thinking. [9]There's no problem solving. [10]Everyone's defending himself or herself."

[11]Since each of us has our own systems and standards, it's human to criticize. [12]But in order to do it in a manner that keeps personal and working relationships from landing on the rocks, it's important to understand how we can give it in a way that won't make temperatures rise.

[13]Depending on how you criticize, you can look for a variety of responses. [14]Jean, for instance, got a good response when she appeared to be taking responsibility for the situation. [15]In another case, Susan got the hoped-for results by getting to the point instead of beating around the bush. [16]Initially, she was critical of her husband Steve, in a general way. [17]But Steve never got the message—especially about visiting her mother.

[18]"In a situation such as this, it's not useful to say 'You hate my relatives and you never visit my mother,'" states Dr. Clifford Swenson, clinical psychologist of Purdue University. [19]"A **concrete** suggestion such as 'I think my mom would really like it if you could come along with me when I go down to visit her this Saturday' will always get a better reaction than 'You never want to come with me.'"

—Adapted from Roesch, "How to Take a Bite Out of Criticism,"
as appeared in *Relationships Today*, August 1988.

_____ **1.** The word **connotation** in sentence 6 means
    a. meaning.
    b. action.
    c. reaction.

_____ **2.** Kay's mistake in criticizing Don was
    a. expecting Don to be neat.
    b. telling him what she thought.
    c. attacking his mother.

_____ **3.** The word **concrete** in sentence 19 means
    a. helpful.
    b. specific.
    c. polite.

_____ **4.** Most people criticize others because of
    a. the desire to control.
    b. low self-esteem.
    c. a desire to hurt others.

_____ **5.** The best statement of the implied central idea of the passage is
    a. Criticism builds strong relationships.
    b. Criticism is unavoidable.
    c. Criticism can be harmful if not handled properly.

VISUAL VOCABULARY

A fishwife, a woman who sold fish, was known to be loud and foul-mouthed most likely

because she _____,

    a. was uneducated and crude.
    b. needed to sell her perishable goods quickly to make money.

Read the following information. Then use inference skills to label each movie review with a movie rating of G, PG, PG-13, R, or NC-17.

The Movie Rating System

The movie rating system is a voluntary system sponsored by the Motion Picture Association of America and the National Association of Theatre Owners. The purpose of the rating system is to provide parents with information about films, so that they can make judgments about what they want or do not want their children to see. The rating board considers various criteria to determine a movie rating, such as theme, language, violence, nudity, sex, and drug use. Here are descriptions used by the rating board for each rating.

G — General Audiences. All Ages Admitted.

A G-rated motion picture signifies that the film rated contains nothing most parents will consider offensive for even their youngest children to see or hear. Nudity, sex scenes, and scenes of drug use are absent; violence is minimal; snippets of dialogue may go beyond polite conversation but do not go beyond common everyday expressions.

PG — Parental Guidance Suggested. Some Material May Not Be Suitable for Children.

The PG rating indicates that parents may consider some material unsuitable for their children. A PG-rated motion picture may contain some profanity and some depictions of violence, sensuality or brief nudity. But, these elements are not deemed so intense as to require that parents be strongly cautioned beyond the suggestion of parental guidance. There is no drug use content in a PG-rated motion picture.

PG-13 — Parents Strongly Cautioned. Some Material May Be Inappropriate for Children Under 13.

A PG-13 motion picture may go beyond the PG rating in theme, violence, nudity, sensuality, language, adult activities or other elements, but does not reach the restricted R category. Any drug use; more than brief nudity, though not sexually oriented; some depictions of violence, though not both realistic and extreme or persistent violence; and the use of one of the harsher sexually-derived words, though only as an expletive, will initially require at least a PG-13 rating.

R — Restricted. Children Under 17 Require Accompanying Parent or Adult Guardian.

An R-rated motion picture may include depiction of adult themes, adult activity, hard language, intense or persistent violence, sexually-oriented nudity, drug abuse or other elements, so that parents are counseled to take this rating very seriously. Generally, it is not appropriate for parents to bring their young children with them to R-rated motion pictures.

NC-17 — No One 17 and Under Admitted.

An NC-17 rated motion picture is one that most parents would consider patently too adult for their children 17 and under. An NC-17 rating can be based on violence, sex, aberrational behavior, drug abuse or any other element that most parents would consider too strong and therefore off-limits for viewing by their children. The rating does not indicate that the motion picture is "obscene" or "pornographic" in the common or legal meaning of those words, and should not be construed as a negative judgment in any sense.

—"The Ratings Are Your Friend." *Filmratings.com.* The Classification and Rating Administration/
MPAA. Accessed 19 Sept. 2010. http://www.filmratings.com/filmRatings_Cara/
downloads/pdf/resources/brochure/cara_brochure.pdf.

_____ **1.** *The Blind Side*, released by Warner Bros. Pictures in November 2009, is the story of Michael Oher, a homeless and traumatized boy who became an All American football player and first round NFL draft pick with the help of a caring woman and her family. The film has one scene involving brief violence, drug and sexual references.

_____ **2.** *Alvin and The Chipmunks: The Squeakquel* released by Twentieth Century Fox Film Corp. in 2009, is an animated comedy. The world famous singing pre-teen chipmunk trio return to contend with the pressures of school, celebrity, and a rival female music group known as The Chipettes. This film has some mild rude humor.

_____ **3.** WALL-E, released in 2008 by Walt Disney Studios Motion Pictures, is an animated science fiction film about a small waste-collecting robot that inadvertently embarks on a space journey that will ultimately decide the fate of mankind. This family movie is an adventure set in the distant future.

_____ **4.** *100 Tears*, released in 2007 by Crytzer Enterprizes & Manic Entertainment & Pop Gun Pictures, is about two journalists who are on the trail of a demented serial killer who may be much closer than they think. The film contains extreme horror violence.

_____ **5.** *Resident Evil: Afterlife,* released in 2010 by Sony Pictures/Screen Gems, is the fourth installment of the popular *Resident Evil* franchise, based on the also popular video game series, and will this time be presented in 3-D. This time, our hero Alice journeys through a virus-infected world to find and save survivors. This film contains sequences of strong violence and language.

Read the following passage from a college psychology textbook. Then, choose the four inferences that are firmly supported by the details in the passage. Write **V** for valid by your choices.

Learning Styles: Different Strokes for Different Folks

[1]Life would be so much easier, if everyone learned new information in exactly the same way. **[2]**Teachers would know exactly how to present material so that all students would have an equal opportunity to learn. **[3]**Unfortunately, that just is not the way it works—people are different in many ways, and one of the ways they differ is in the style of learning that works best for each person.

[4]What exactly is a learning style? **[5]**In general, a learning style is the particular way in which a person takes in information (Dunn et al., 1989, 2001; Felder, 1993, 1996; Felder & Spurlin, 2005). **[6]**People take in information in several ways: through the eyes, by reading text or looking at charts, diagrams, and maps; through the ears, by listening, talking things out, and discussing things with others; and through the sense of touch and the movement of the body, by touching things, writing things down, drawing pictures and diagrams, and learning by doing (Barsch, 1996).

Types of Learning Styles

[7]Learning styles are often classified based on personality theories or theories of intelligence. **[8]**The number of different learning styles varies with the theory, but most theories of learning styles include visual learners, who learn best by seeing, reading, and looking at images; **auditory learners**, who learn best by hearing and saying things out loud; **tactile learners**, who need to touch things; **kinesthetic learners**, who prefer to learn by doing and being active; and **social learners**, who prefer to learn with other people or in groups (Dunn et al., 1989). **[9]**Most people will find that they have one dominant, or most powerful, learning style along with one or two secondary styles. **[10]**Notice that several of the learning styles described would work well together: Auditory learners and social learners, for example, work well together, as do tactile and kinesthetic learners, because they are both hands-on kinds of learners. **[11]**Many theories simply divide people into four basic styles of learning (Barsch, 1996; Dunn et al., 1989; Jester, 2000):

Visual/Verbal. **[12]**These people learn best when looking at material, particularly things that are written down. **[13]**Reading the textbook, using classroom notes, and having an instructor who uses overhead projections, writes on the board, or uses visual multimedia presentations are very helpful. **[14]**Visual/verbal learners, because they focus on reading and taking notes, tend to learn best when studying alone rather than in a group.

Visual/Nonverbal. [15]These visual learners learn best through the use of diagrams, pictures, charts, videos, and other image-oriented material rather than printed text. [16]This type of learner, like the visual/verbal learner, also prefers to study alone.

Auditory/Verbal. [17]Auditory/verbal learners take in information best by listening. [18]Group discussions and a lecture format in which the instructor talks about the subject are of the most benefit to this style of learning.

Tactile/Kinesthetic. [19]This style of learner needs a "hands-on" opportunity to learn. [20]Lab classes are very good ways for this type of learner to absorb material. [21]Instructors who do lots of demonstrations and use field experiences outside of the classroom are good for this style of learner. [22]Some kinesthetic learners benefit from writing notes during a lecture or from writing a summary of their lecture notes afterward.

—Ciccarelli/White, *Psychology: Exploration,* "Learning Styles: Different Strokes for Different Folks"
pp. 1–2, © 2010 Pearson Education, Inc. Reproduced by permission of Pearson Education, Inc.

_____ Knowing one's learning style guarantees higher grades.

_____ Most professors create lessons based on their students' learning styles.

_____ Visual learners are less likely to be social learners.

_____ Creating and studying flash cards only helps visual learners.

_____ Auditory learners most likely benefit from participation in study groups outside of class.

_____ Visiting museums and historical sites promotes learning for kinesthetic/tactile learners.

_____ All types of learners benefit from taking notes.

_____ All four of these learning styles make use of similar methods.

The Basics of Argument

12

LEARNING OUTCOMES

After studying this chapter you should be able to do the following:

1. Define the terms *argument, claim,* and *evidence.*
2. Identify the author's claim and evidence.
3. Determine whether evidence is relevant.
4. Determine whether evidence is adequate.
5. Analyze the argument for bias.
6. Apply inference skills to evaluate arguments for validity.
7. Evaluate the importance of the basics of argument.

Before Reading About the Basics of Argument

Many of the same skills you learned to make valid inferences will help you master the basics of argument. Take a moment to review the five steps in the VALID approach to making sound inferences. Fill in the following blanks with each of the steps.

Step 1: _____

Step 2: _____

Step 3: _____

Step 4: _____

Step 5: _____

Skim the chapter and list any other reading skills you have studied from prior chapters that seem to apply to the basics of argument: _____

_____

Use your prior knowledge about valid inferences, other reading skills, and the learning outcomes to create at least three questions that you can answer as you study:

1. _____
   _____?

2. _____
   _____?

3. _____
   _____?

Reading skills you have studied in prior chapters that will help you master the basics of arguments are main ideas, supporting details, fact and opinion, and tone and purpose (to persuade). Compare the questions you created based on your prior knowledge and the learning outcomes with the following questions. Then write the ones that seem the most helpful in your notebook, leaving enough space between questions to record your answers as you read and study the chapter.

How will verifying and valuing the facts help me decide if supports in an argument are relevant? How will learning from the text help me decide if supports in an argument are adequate? How does an argument use bias? What is the relationship between main ideas and the author's claim? How does opinion affect an argument? What is the connection between tone, purpose, and the basics of argument?

 ## What Is an Argument?

Have you noticed how many of us enjoy debating ideas and winning arguments? You can see this on television, where many shows thrive on conflict and debate. For example, the *Jerry Springer* show uses the conflicts between guests to amuse the audience. Programs such as *Meet the Press,* hosted by David Gregory, or *The O'Reilly Factor* with Bill O'Reilly debate political and social issues. Likewise, talk radio fills hours of air time with debate about issues related to culture and politics. Two examples are *The Rush Limbaugh Show* and *The Diane Rehm Show*.

Some people are so committed to their ideas that they become emotional, even angry. However, effective **argument** is reasoned: It is a process during which a claim is made and logical details are offered to support that claim.

> An **argument** is made up of two types of statements:
> 1. The author's claim—the main point of the argument
> 2. The supports—the evidence or reasons that support the author's claim

The purpose of an argument is to persuade the reader that the claim is valid. To decide if a claim is valid, you must analyze the argument in four basic steps.

1. Identify the author's claim and supports.

2. Decide whether the supports are relevant.

3. Decide whether the supports are adequate.

4. Check the argument for bias.

Step 1: Identify the Author's Claim and Supports

Read the following claim:

Avatar is a movie worth seeing.

The claim certainly states the speaker's point clearly. But it probably wouldn't inspire most of us to go see the movie. Instead, our first response to the claim is likely to be "why?" We need reasons before we can decide if we think a claim is valid. Notice that a claim, like any main idea, is made up of a topic and a controlling point. Here, *Avatar* is the topic, and the controlling point is "worth seeing." Notice that the details that follow answer a question about the controlling point: "Why is *Avatar* a movie worth seeing?"

1. *Avatar* has made more money than any film in history.

2. *Avatar* is a love story with a lesson about protecting the environment.

3. *Avatar's* special effects are stunning.

These three sentences offer the supports for the author's claim. We are now able to understand the basis of the argument, and we now have details about which we can agree or disagree.

Writers frequently make claims that they want us to accept as valid. To assess whether the claim is valid, an effective reader first identifies the claim and the supports. Identifying the author's claim and supports for that claim is the first step in analyzing an argument.

EXAMPLES

A. Read the following groups of ideas. Identify the claim and supports in each group. Write **C** if the sentence states the author's claim or **S** if the sentence offers support for the claim.

Group 1

[1]Dog bites pose a serious national problem. [2]Dogs bite an estimated 4.7 million people each year, with 800,000 individuals needing medical treatment.

_____   **1.** Sentence 1

_____   **2.** Sentence 2

Group 2

[1]They never wave or say hello. [2]Our neighbors are unfriendly people.

_____   **3.** Sentence 1

_____   **4.** Sentence 2

Group 3

[1]Popcorn contains only 15 calories per cup when it is air-popped. [2]Popcorn is a good snack. [3]Popcorn is a good source of fiber.

_____   **5.** Sentence 1

_____   **6.** Sentence 2

_____   **7.** Sentence 3

Group 4

[1]Mrs. Overby takes time to explain difficult ideas in class. [2]Mrs. Overby is always available for student conferences. [3]Mrs. Overby's students have a high passing rate. [4]Mrs. Overby is a good teacher.

_____   **8.** Sentence 1

_____   **9.** Sentence 2

_____   **10.** Sentence 3

_____   **11.** Sentence 4

B. Editorial cartoons offer arguments through the use of humor. The cartoonist has a claim to make and uses the situation, actions, and words in the cartoon as supporting details. Study the cartoon reprinted here. Then write a claim based on the supports in the cartoon.

—The Detroit News, Larry Wright © 2002

_____

_____

_____

EXPLANATIONS

A.

Group 1

1. Sentence 1 states the author's claim (C). **2.** Sentence 2 offers support for the claim (S).

Group 2

3. Sentence 1 offers support for the claim (S). **4.** Sentence 2 states the author's claim (C).

Group 3

5. Sentence 1 offers support for the claim (S). **6.** Sentence 2 states the author's claim (C). **7.** Sentence 3 offers support for the claim(s).

Group 4

8–10. Sentences 1, 2, and 3 offer support for the claim (S). **11.** Sentence 4 states the author's claim (C).

B. The note from school came from the school's administration. The horrible spelling is a sign that the people running the school do not have basic writing or thinking skills. Several claims can be suggested by the details in the cartoon. The following are a few possibilities.

> Students must not be receiving a good education.
>
> School administrators should not allow teachers to teach outside their fields.
>
> School administrators are the main problem in education.
>
> School administrators are not smart.
>
> School administrators must not care about education.

PRACTICE 1

Read the following groups of ideas. Identify the claim and supports in each group. Write **C** if the sentence states the author's claim or **S** if the sentence offers support for the claim.

Group 1

¹Everyone needs to wear sunglasses while outdoors. ²The sun contains UV rays that damage the eyes by causing cataracts, skin cancer on the eyelids, and macular degeneration.

_____ **1.** Sentence 1

_____ **2.** Sentence 2

Group 2

¹Spaying or neutering a pet reduces the animal's chance of suffering from diseases, and spaying or neutering reduces the pet's urge to roam or mark its territory. ²Spaying or neutering a pet is the action of a responsible pet owner.

_____ **3.** Sentence 1

_____ **4.** Sentence 2

Group 3

[1]In the past 60 years, researchers have conducted more than 21,000 studies on the effects of caffeine. [2]Caffeine has several benefits. [3]Caffeine produces feelings of well-being, improves memory, speeds the metabolism, and may reduce diseases such as cancer and Parkinson's disease.

_____ **5.** Sentence 1

_____ **6.** Sentence 2

_____ **7.** Sentence 3

Group 4

[1]Fish is a protein source rich in omega 3 fatty acids. [2]These healthy fats have amazing brain power: higher dietary omega 3 fatty acids are linked to lower dementia and stroke risks; slower mental decline. [3]Omega 3 fatty acids may also play a vital role in enhancing memory, especially as we get older. [4]For brain health, you should eat fish two times a week.

_____ **8.** Sentence 1

_____ **9.** Sentence 2

_____ **10.** Sentence 3

_____ **11.** Sentence 4

Group 5

[1]"Sexting" usually refers to teens sharing nude photos or sexually explicit messages via cellphone, but "sexting" also occurs through the use of other devices and the Web. [2]A recent survey said a third of young adults and 20% of teens had posted or sent nude or semi-nude photos or videos of themselves. [3]Sexting violates current child pornography laws and can lead to serious legal consequences. [4]Sexting is a disturbing trend among young people.

_____ **12.** Sentence 1

_____ **13.** Sentence 2

_____ **14.** Sentence 3

_____ **15.** Sentence 4

Group 6

[1]School vouchers are government cash grants or tax credits for parents, equal to all or part of the cost of educating their child at an elementary or secondary school of their choice. [2]School vouchers are not the best ways to improve education. [3]The greatest gains in student achievement have occurred in places where vouchers do not exist. [4]Private schools who receive money from school vouchers are not required to adopt the academic standards, hire highly qualified teachers, or administer the assessments required of public schools. [5]School vouchers require taxpayers to fund both public and private schools.

_____ **16.** Sentence 1

_____ **17.** Sentence 2

_____ **18.** Sentence 3

_____ **19.** Sentence 4

_____ **20.** Sentence 5

Step 2: Decide Whether the Supports Are Relevant

In Step 1, you learned to identify the author's claim and supports. The next step is to decide whether the supports are relevant to the claim. Remember, a claim, like any main idea, is made up of a topic and a controlling point. Irrelevant supports change the topic or ignore the controlling point. Relevant supports will answer the reporter's questions (*Who? What? When? Where? Why?* and *How?*). Use these questions to decide whether the supports for a claim are relevant.

For example, read the following argument a teenager makes about her curfew. Identify the support that is irrelevant to her claim.

[1]"I am mature enough to make my own decisions about my curfew. [2]When I work the closing shift at McDonald's, I am out until 2 A.M., and no matter where I am, I always make sure to stick with a group of people. [3]And I am not just out roaming the streets; I only want to stay out late for specific events like a concert or a late movie. [4]None of my friends even have curfews. [5]Just like always, I will tell you ahead of time where I will be and when I will be home, and I do have my cell

phone in case you get worried and want to call me. [6]Or I can call you if I need help."

By turning this teenager's claim into a question, she and her parents can test her ability to offer valid reasons: "How have I shown I am mature enough to make my own decisions about my curfew?" Sentences 2, 3, 5, and 6 offer relevant examples of her maturity. However, sentence 4 states an irrelevant support that changes the topic. The argument is about *her* curfew based on *her* maturity, not her friends' curfews.

When evaluating an argument, it is important to test each piece of supporting evidence to determine whether it is relevant.

EXAMPLES

A. Read the following lists of claims and supports. Mark each support **R** if it is relevant to the claim or **N** if it is not relevant to the claim.

1. Claim: Online shopping offers a lot of benefits.
Supports

_____ a. You can shop at any time of the day or night.

_____ b. You don't have to leave your house.

_____ c. You can't try on clothes to see if they fit.

_____ d. You may have to pay postage to return items.

_____ e. You can save money because comparison shopping takes less time.

2. Claim: Water supplies should have fluoride added to prevent tooth decay.
Supports

_____ a. Research shows that drinking fluoride from birth reduces tooth decay by as much as 65 percent.

_____ b. Fluoride is a safe, natural mineral that makes bones and teeth stronger.

_____ c. Drinking eight glasses of water every day promotes good health.

_____ d. Although fluoride is present in plants, animals, and water, the amount is too low to offer protection against tooth decay.

_____ e. Fluoride is tasteless and odorless.

3. Claim: Gun ownership by citizens reduces crime in the United States.

_____ a. Since 1991, the number of guns in the U.S. has risen by more than four million annually, to an all-time high.

_____ b. Since 1991, federal and state gun control laws have been eliminated or made less restrictive.

_____ c. Citizens of the United States own more than half of all guns owned worldwide.

_____ d. Most school shooters used guns taken from their homes.

_____ e. Nationwide, the rate of violent crime has decreased to about a 30-year low, and the murder rate has decreased to about a 40-year low.

B. Argument is also used in advertisements. It is important for you to be able to understand the claims and supports of ads. Many times advertisers appeal to emotions, make false claims, or give supports that are not relevant because their main aim is to persuade you to buy their product. Study the advertisement for milk put out by America's Dairy Farmers and Milk Processors. Mark each support **R** if it is relevant to the claim or **N** if it is not relevant to the claim.

4. Claim: Drinking milk is good for your health.

Supports

_____ a. Taylor Swift drinks milk.

_____ b. Exercise leads to physical fitness.

_____ c. Taylor Swift pours herself into her music.

_____ d. Taylor Swift is a popular entertainer.

_____ e. The protein and nutrients in low-fat milk builds muscles.

EXPLANATIONS

1. Items (a), (b), and (e) are relevant to the claim. Items (c) and (d) are not relevant because they point out drawbacks to online shopping instead of supporting the claim that online shopping offers a lot of benefits.

2. Items (a), (b), and (d) are relevant to the claim. Items (c) and (e) are not relevant. The benefits of drinking water are not the issue. The taste and odor of fluoride are not directly tied to its ability to prevent tooth decay.

3. Items (a), (b), and (e) are relevant to the claim. Items (c) and (d) are not relevant. The claim focuses on reducing crime in the United States, so any information about worldwide gun ownership is not relevant.

4. Only item (e) is relevant to the claim that drinking milk is good for your health. Advertisers often use celebrities as spokespeople, but personal remarks or information about Taylor Swift are not relevant to the healthfulness of milk. Item (b) states a fact, but this detail has nothing to do with the claim about milk.

PRACTICE 2

A. Read the following lists of claims and supports. Mark each support **R** if it is relevant to the claim or **N** if it is not relevant to the claim.

1. Claim: Use of steroids is harmful and should be avoided.

   Supports

   _____ a. Excessive use of steroids can cause rage.

   _____ b. One short-term effect of steroid use is acne.

   _____ c. One long-term effect of steroid use is stunted growth in teenagers.

   _____ d. Other long-term effects of steroid use may be liver damage, prostate cancer, and a higher risk of heart disease.

   _____ e. Drinking alcohol poses greater risks than using steroids.

2. Claim: Left-handed people face obstacles in the classroom and in school activities.

   Supports

   _____ a. In school sports, standard equipment (for example, hockey sticks and baseball gloves) is designed for right-handed players.

   _____ b. Musician Kurt Cobain, who dropped out of high school, was left-handed.

_____ c. The word *left* comes from an old Anglo-Saxon word that means "weak."

_____ d. In schools, colleges, and universities, the standard desk has a small top attached to the right side of the desk, which makes it difficult for left-handed students to write.

_____ e. School supplies such as scissors, three-ring binders, and keyboards are mostly made for right-handed writers.

3. Claim: Migrant farmworkers boost the economy.

Supports

_____ a. Most migrant farmworkers are legal residents or U.S. citizens.

_____ b. The efforts of migrant workers support the multibillion-dollar farming business.

_____ c. Most of the vegetables and fruits in this country are grown and picked with the aid of migrant workers.

_____ d. Without migrant workers, farmers would not be able to produce and harvest their crops.

_____ e. Farming is ranked as one of the three most dangerous jobs in the nation.

4. Claim: Easter Seals is a nonprofit organization worthy of support in terms of time and money.

Supports

_____ a. Easter Seals provides adult and senior service programs across the country.

_____ b. Easter Seals runs hundreds of camping and recreation programs nationwide for children and adults with disabilities.

_____ c. Easter Seals offers job training and employment programs.

_____ d. Dr Pepper/Seven Up is a corporate sponsor of Easter Seals.

_____ e. Easter Seals uses the lily as its official logo.

B. Study the mock advertisement that encourages viewers to consume a soy product. Read the claim, and then mark each support **R** if it is relevant to the claim or **N** if it is not relevant to the claim.

5. Claim: Soy-Sublime is a healthful food that you should buy.

Supports

_____ a. Soy reduces the risks of certain types of cancer.

_____ b. Soy alleviates symptoms of menopause.

_____ c. Soybeans grow abundantly and actually replenish the soil they grow in.

_____ d. Consuming 25 grams of soy protein per day, as part of a diet that is low in saturated fat and cholesterol, may reduce the risk of heart disease.

_____ e. Good cooks use soy.

Now that you have practiced identifying relevant supports in a list format, you are ready to isolate relevant supports in reading passages. In a paragraph, the topic sentence states the author's claim. Each of the supporting details must be evaluated as relevant or irrelevant supports for the topic sentence.

EXAMPLE Read the following paragraph.

[1]A culture of drug abuse permeates many of the college campuses in the United States of America. [2]This chronic problem must be immediately addressed by the proper authorities. [3]According to government statistics, nearly one fourth of full-time college students display the medical symptoms of substance dependence and abuse. [4]The government studies show that the number of college students who abuse drugs—nearly 2 million—is more than double the number of those who abuse drugs in the public as a whole. [5]Alcohol, illegal drugs, and prescription drugs are widely available, easy to get, and frequently abused by college students across the country. [6]First, the age-old problem of alcohol abuse has not abated. [7]Not only do around 70 percent of current students drink alcohol, but also many more than ever before are frequent drinkers and binge drinkers, drinking for the sole purpose of getting drunk. [8]While alcohol use has remained constant since the 1990s, according to experts, students' daily use of marijuana has risen to alarming levels. [9]Likewise in recent years, college students have turned to abuse of prescription drugs. [10]Adderall and Ritalin are taken to stay alert while studying while OxyContin is used to create an intense feeling of euphoria. [11]Parents, students, and educators must come together and take a firm stand against this plague. [12]Fortunately, more and more students are choosing to live in substance-free housing.

1. Underline the topic sentence (the sentence that states the author's claim).

_____   2. Which sentence is *not* relevant to the author's point?
a. sentence 2
b. sentence 5
c. sentence 11
d. sentence 12

EXPLANATION

1. Sentence 2 is the topic sentence that states the author's claim.

2. The sentence that is *not* relevant to the author's point is (d), sentence 12. The author's claim is that the chronic problem of drug abuse must be addressed by the proper authorities. The fact that more students are choosing to live in substance-free housing is good news. However, the fact does not support the author's claim.

PRACTICE 3

Read the following paragraphs.

"At Risk" with AD/HD

[1]Occasionally, we may all have difficulty sitting still, paying attention, or controlling impulsive behavior. [2]For some people, the problems are so severe that they interfere with their lives. [3]AD/HD is the common label for Attention-deficit/hyperactivity disorder. [4]This disorder is marked by developmentally inappropriate levels of behavior in three areas: inattention, impulsivity, and hyperactivity. [5]Until recently, experts believed that children outgrew AD/HD because hyperactivity diminishes during the teen years. [6]However, many symptoms continue into adulthood. [7]Individuals with AD/HD can be very successful. [8]Nevertheless, without proper treatment AD/HD may have serious long-term consequences. [9]Some consequences may include school failure, problems with relationships, substance abuse, risk for accidental injures, and job failure.

—Adapted from CHADD, "The Disorder Named AD/HD."

1. Underline the topic sentence (the sentence that states the author's claim).

_____ **2.** Which sentence is *not* relevant to the author's point?
   a. sentence 3   c. sentence 7
   b. sentence 4   d. sentence 9

Intimate Partner Violence

[1]Intimate partner violence (IPV) occurs between two people in a close relationship. [2]The term "intimate partner" includes current and former spouses and dating partners. [3]IPV exists as a range of behaviors—from a single episode of violence to ongoing battering. [4]IPV is a serious problem in the United States. [5]Each year, women experience about 4.8 million intimate partner related physical assaults and rapes. [6]Of course, rape is also committed by complete strangers. [7]Men are the victims of about 2.9 million intimate partner related physical assaults. [8]IPV resulted in 1,510 deaths in 2005. [9]Of these deaths, 78% were females and 22% were males. [10]The medical care, mental health services, and lost productivity (e.g., time away from work) cost of IPV was an estimated $5.8 billion in 1995. [11]Updated to today's dollars, that's more than $8.3 billion.

—Adapted from National Center for Injury Prevention and Control. "Understanding Intimate Partner Violence: Fact Sheet 2009." CDC 29 Jan. 2010 http://www.cdc.gov/ViolencePrevention/intimatepartnerviolence/index.html.

3. Underline the topic sentence (the sentence that states the author's claim).

_____   **4.** Which sentence is *not* relevant to the author's point?
a. sentence 3   c. sentence 6
b. sentence 4   d. sentence 7

Step 3: Decide Whether the Supports Are Adequate

In Step 1 you learned to identify the author's claim and supports. In Step 2 you learned to make sure the supports are relevant. In Step 3 you must decide whether the supports are adequate. A valid argument is based not only on a claim and relevant support but also on the amount and quality of the support given. That is, supports must give enough evidence for the author's claim to be convincing. Just as you use the reporter's questions to decide whether supports are relevant, you also can use them to test whether supports are adequate. Supporting details fully explain the author's controlling point about a topic. Remember, those questions are *Who? What? When? Where? Why?* and *How?*

For example, you may argue, "A vegetarian diet is a more healthful diet. I feel much better since I became a vegetarian." However, the reporter's question "Why?" reveals that the support is inadequate. The answer to "Why is a vegetarian diet a more healthful diet?" should include expert opinions and facts, not just personal opinion. Often in the quest to support a claim, people oversimplify their reasons. Thus, they do not offer enough information to prove the claim. Instead of logical details, they may offer false causes, false comparisons, or forced choices, or leave out facts that hurt the claim. You will learn more about inadequate argument in Chapter 13.

In Chapter 11, you studied how to avoid invalid conclusions and make valid inferences (see pages 470–480). The same thinking steps you use to make valid inferences help you identify valid claims: consider the facts, don't infer anything that is not there, and make sure nothing contradicts your conclusion.

EXAMPLE   Read the list of supports.

Supports

- One pound of muscle burns 50 calories a day.
- One pound of fat burns 2 calories a day.

- Two pounds of muscle can burn up 10 pounds of fat in one year.
- Lean muscle mass weighs more than fat.

Write **V** for valid by the claim that is adequately supported by the evidence in the list.

_____ a. Building muscles will help one lose weight.

_____ b. Muscles burn more calories than fat.

_____ c. It is hard to lose weight.

_____ d. Weight training is the best way to lose weight.

EXPLANATION Choices (a), (c), and (d) use the evidence to jump to false conclusions about losing weight. However, none of the evidence mentions weight loss. In fact, since muscle weighs more than fat, adding muscle can cause a weight gain. The only logical conclusion based on the evidence is (b), *muscles burn more calories than fat.*

PRACTICE 4

A. Read the list of supports.

1. Supports

- When a couple fights, name-calling creates distrust, anger, and a sense of helplessness.
- Assigning blame makes others defensive during a fight.
- When two people fight, words like *never* or *always* are usually not true and create more anger.
- Exaggerating or making up a complaint can keep the couple's real issues hidden during a fight.
- A couple bringing up gripes and hurt feelings stockpiled over time can lead to explosive anger in a fight.

Write **V** for valid by the claim that is adequately supported by the evidence.

_____ a. Fighting leads to violence.

_____ b. Using unfair methods during a fight makes the situation worse.

_____ c. Everyone uses unfair fighting methods.

_____ d. Fighting cannot be avoided.

B. Study the graph.

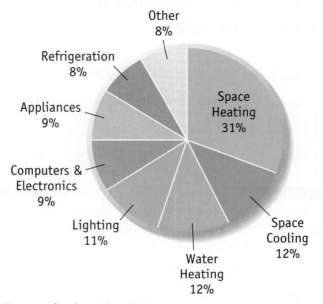

How We Use Energy in Our Homes

—*2007 Buildings Energy Data Book, Table 4.2.1., 2005 Energy Cost Data.* 29 Jan. 2010
https://www1.eere.energy.gov/consumer/tips/printable_versions/home_energy.html.

Write **V** for valid by the claim that is adequately supported by the evidence.

_____ a. Our homes are not energy efficient.

_____ b. We use too much energy.

_____ c. Our homes are energy efficient.

_____ d. Home heating systems use the most energy.

Step 4: Check the Argument for Bias

In Step 1, you learned to identify the author's claim and supports. In Step 2, you learned to make sure the supports are relevant to the claim. In Step 3, you learned to avoid false inferences and identify valid claims based on adequate supports. Again, the skills you use to make sound inferences help you determine whether an argument is valid. In Step 4, you must also check for the author's bias for or against the topic. Authors may use emotionally slanted language or biased words to present either a favorable or a negative view of the topic under debate. In addition, authors may include only the details that favor the stances they have taken. A valid argument relies on objective, factual details. As you evaluate the argument for the author's bias, ask the following questions:

- Does the author provide mostly positive or negative supports?
- Does the author provide mostly factual details or rely on biased language?
- Does the author include or omit opposing views?

EXAMPLE Read the following information that was posted on the website *Choose Responsibility*, a non-profit organization founded in 2007. *Choose Responsibility* addresses the impact of the 21-year old drinking age. The organization was started by President Emeritus John M. McCardell Jr., of Middlebury College. Answer the questions that follow.

The Failure of Legal Age 21

[1]It seems like a simple answer: "all we need to do to keep kids from drinking is enforce Legal Age 21." [2]But if it were possible, we would have brought an end to underage drinking long ago. [3]Legal Age 21 has been in place for over 20 years across the nation and there remains a complete lack of consistency in how it is carried out and enforced. [4]One study predicts that only two out of every 1,000 cases of underage drinking results in citation or arrest. [5]Such low rates of enforcement present inadequate deterrence to young people under 21 who choose to drink. [6]If the 21 year-old drinking age were enforceable, it is unbelievable that we would have the problem of reckless and irresponsible drinking by young people that we have in America today.

[7]Legal Age 21 has failed utterly at its goal of protecting young people from the dangers of excessive alcohol use. [8]To cite an alarming statistic from the Center on Alcohol Marketing and Youth: 96% of the alcohol drunk by 15–20 year-olds is consumed when the drinker is having five or more drinks at a time. [9]Science tells us that this has devastating consequences for developing brains. [10]Since Legal Age 21, less young people are drinking. [11]But those who choose to drink are drinking more. [12]Young peoples' drinking is moving to the extremes. [13]Between 1993 and 2001, 18–20 year-olds showed the largest increase in binge drinking episodes. [14]This trend should serve as a call to action for parents, educators, and lawmakers. [15]While moderate consumption represents little harm to young people and may even be psychologically beneficial, excessive

and abusive consumption—binge drinking—spells disastrous consequences for our nation's youth.

—Adapted from "Myths and Realities." *Choose Responsibility*.
1 Feb. 2010 http://www.chooseresponsibility.org
/myths_realities/. Reprinted by permission.

_____ **1.** Overall, the passage mostly relies on
   a. factual details.
   b. emotionally slanted language.

_____ **2.** Which of the following statements is true?
   a. Sentence 1 offers an opposing view.
   b. Sentence 8 offers an opposing view.
   c. Sentence 11 offers an opposing view.
   d. No opposing view is offered.

_____ **3.** In this passage, the author expresses a biased attitude
   a. in favor of lowering the drinking age.
   b. in favor of raising the drinking age.
   c. against the effectiveness of the current law Legal Age 21.
   d. against all teenage alcohol consumption.

EXPLANATION **1.** Although the passage contains some emotionally slanted language such as *unbelievable*, *failed utterly*, *alarming*, and *disastrous*, overall, the author relies on (a) factual details that can be verified through research. **2.** The author begins the passage by addressing a common opposing view in (a) Sentence 1. **3.** In the passage, the author expresses a biased attitude (c) against the effectiveness of the current law Legal Age 21. In fact, this biased attitude is the author's main idea.

PRACTICE 5

Read the following information that was posted on the website *Why21.org*, sponsored by Mothers Against Drunk Drivers (MADD). Answer the questions that follow.

Old Enough to Drink?

[1]A common argument to lower the legal drinking age is the statement "If I'm old enough to go to war, I should be old enough to drink." [2]However, many rights have different ages of initiation. [3]You can get a hunting license at age 12, drive at 16. [4]You can vote and serve in the military at 18. [5]You can serve in the U.S. House of Representatives at 25,

and serve as the U.S. President at 35. [6]Other regulated rights include the sale and use of tobacco, and legal consent for sexual intercourse and marriage. [7]Vendors, such as car rental facilities and hotels, also have set the minimum age for a person to use their services—25-years-old to rent a car and 21-years-old to rent a hotel room.

[8]And these minimum ages are set for a reason. [9]In the case of alcohol, 21 is the minimum age because a person's brain does not stop developing until his or her early to mid-20s. [10]Drinking alcohol while the brain is still developing can lead to long-lasting deficits in cognitive abilities, including learning and memory.

[11]Alcohol use by those under 21 is also related to numerous health problems including injuries and death resulting from alcohol poisoning, car crashes, suicide, homicide, assaults, drowning and recreational mishaps. [12]Not to mention that the early onset of drinking by youth significantly increases the risk of future health problems such as addiction.

—Adapted from "Myths and Facts." *Why21.org*. MADD 2007 1 Feb. 2010.
http://www.why21.org/myths/. Reproduced with permission.

_____ **1.** Overall, the passage relies on
   a. factual details.
   b. emotionally slanted language.

_____ **2.** Which of the following statements is true?
   a. Sentence 1 offers an opposing view.
   b. Sentence 7 offers an opposing view.
   c. Sentence 11 offers an opposing view.
   d. No opposing view is offered.

_____ **3.** In this passage, the author expresses a biased attitude
   a. in favor of lowering the drinking age.
   b. in favor of the law Legal Age 21.
   c. against minimum ages of initiation for various rights.
   d. against alcohol consumption.

Textbook
Skills # The Logic of Argument

Most of the subjects you will study in college rely on research by experts, and these experts may have differing views on the same topic. Often textbooks spell out these arguments. Sometimes textbook authors will give several experts' views. But sometimes only one view will be presented. In this case, be aware that there may be other sides to the story.

Textbook arguments are usually well developed with supports that are relevant and adequate. These supports may be studies, surveys, expert opinions, experiments, theories, examples, or reasons. Textbooks may also offer graphs, charts, and photos as supports. An effective reader tests passages in textbooks for the logic of the arguments they present. The exercises that follow are designed to give you practice evaluating the logic of arguments in textbooks.

PRACTICE 6

A. Read the following paragraph from a college psychology textbook, and study the figure that accompanies it. Mark each statement in the passage and the figure **C** if it is an author's claim or **S** if it provides support for the claim.

Textbook
Skills

Locus of Control

[1]Locus of control is the most important trait of a person's personality. [2]**Locus of control** is a person's belief about who or what controls the consequences of actions. [3]A person who expects to control his or her own fate has an *internal* locus of control. [4]This person thinks that rewards come through effort. [5]A person who sees his or her life as being controlled by forces outside himself or herself has an *external* locus of control. [6]This person thinks that his or her own behavior has no effect on outcomes.

—Carlson/Buskist, *Psychology: Science of Behavior,* Text Excerpt from pp. 460–461
© 1997. Reproduced by permission of Pearson Education, Inc.

_____ **1.** sentence 1   _____ **4.** sentence 4

_____ **2.** sentence 2   _____ **5.** sentence 5

_____ **3.** sentence 3   _____ **6.** sentence 6

    7. The person's will is the most powerful driving force in a person who has an internal locus of control.

    8. "It's my own fault. I should have spent more time studying."

    9. The environment is the most powerful driving force in a person who has an external locus of control.

    10. "Did I get lucky or what? The teacher must really have gone easy on the grading."

B. Read the following paragraph from a textbook on parenting.

Chinese Children

Textbook
Skills

[1]Some American experts believe that the good behavior of Chinese children is the result of the way Chinese parents and teachers treat their children and students. [2]Chinese children are quiet, quick to follow instructions, and rarely act selfishly. [3]Chinese children do not cry, whine, throw tantrums, or suck their thumbs. [4]American children are taught to be independent. [5]Chinese parents and the teachers in nurseries and kindergarten tend to be warm, kind, and attentive. [6]Chinese parents strive to promote intense closeness between themselves and their children. [7]They do not use physical punishment or harsh verbal rebukes.

—Adapted from Jaffe, Michael L. *Understanding Parenting*, 2nd ed., p. 150. Published by Allyn and Bacon, Boston, MA. Copyright (c) 1997 by Pearson Education, Inc.

11. Underline the topic sentence that states the claim of the author's argument.

    12. Which sentence is *not* relevant to the author's point?

      a. sentence 1   c. sentence 4

      b. sentence 5   d. sentence 7

C. The following information comes from a college health textbook. Read each list of supports. Choose the claim that is adequately supported by the evidence in the list.

13. Supports

- People who chronically skip breakfast burn an average of 150 fewer calories per day than regular breakfast eaters.

- Breakfast eaters awaken with a souped-up metabolism.

- Breakfast skippers greet each day cold and tired with the "metabolic furnace" set on low until lunch.

Write **V** for valid by the claim that is adequately supported by the evidence.

_____ a. People who skip breakfast lose more weight than people who eat breakfast.

_____ b. People who skip breakfast use less energy.

_____ c. Breakfast is the most important meal of the day.

_____ d. People who skip breakfast are more hungry than people who eat breakfast.

14. Supports

- Eat a juicy apple or a cup of soup instead of a dry granola bar or a bag of popcorn.
- Dehydration stimulates the appetite.
- Foods with high water content will make you feel even more full than drinking water to wash down dry foods with the same calorie count.

Write **V** for valid by the claim that is adequately supported by the evidence.

_____ a. Wet foods are healthier than dry foods.

_____ b. Dry foods are not appropriate diet foods.

_____ c. The water content of foods plays an important role in weight control.

_____ d. Water intake is the most important part of a diet aimed at weight control.

VISUAL VOCABULARY

The context given in the three supports, along with this photo, suggests that **dehydrated** means

_____. The word **dehydrated** is composed of three word parts: a prefix, a root, and a suffix. What is the root, and what does it mean?

Root: _____

Meaning: _____

▲ Dehydrated food

15. Supports

- A Tufts University study of women who took up moderate weightlifting found that they increased their strength by 35 to 75 percent.
- The women increased their balance by 14 percent.
- And they increased their bone density by 1 percent.
- The greater your muscle mass, the greater your metabolic rate and hence the more calories you burn.

Write **V** for valid by the claim that is adequately supported by the evidence.

_____ a. Women who lift moderate weights develop large muscle mass.

_____ b. Beginning a moderate weightlifting program demands time and dedication.

_____ c. Weightlifting is the best way to lose weight.

_____ d. A moderate weightlifting program has several health benefits in addition to burning calories.

—Adapted from Donatelle, *Health Basics,* 5th ed., p. 271.

APPLICATIONS

Application 1: Argument: Author's Claim and Supports

A. Read the following groups of ideas. Mark each statement **C** if it is an author's claim or **S** if it provides support for the claim.

1. _____ a. The television show *America's Most Wanted* has helped capture more than 700 criminals.

_____ b. *Sesame Street* has taught millions of preschoolers about the alphabet, arithmetic, and social values.

_____ c. Television can be a force for good.

_____ d. The Discovery Channel supports education by offering high-interest programs about history, science, and various cultures.

_____ e. News channels like CNN, MSNBC, and Fox News bring up-to-the-minute information to the audience.

B. Study the photograph of people protesting for legal reforms in the medical field. Then mark each statement that follows **C** if it is an author's claim or **S** if it provides support for the claim.

▲ Physicians, nurses and support staff of Flagler Hospital in St. Augustine gather in front of the hospital for a noon protest Wednesday to urge Florida lawmakers to pass medical malpractice law reform. Doctors are calling for a $250,000 cap on noneconomic malpractice awards, saying out-of-control jury awards are behind insurance increases.

2. _____ a. Protesters are calling for a cap on malpractice suits.

_____ b. Doctors, nurses, and support staff of Flagler Hospital in St. Augustine, Florida, are gathered in front of the hospital.

_____ c. Without a cap on malpractice suits, doctors may "pull up roots" by leaving Florida.

_____ d. Florida lawmakers should put a cap on malpractice insurance costs.

_____ e. Out-of-control jury awards are behind insurance increases.

Application 2: Argument: Relevant Supports

A. Read the following outline of a claim and its supports. Mark each support **R** if it is relevant to the claim or **N** if it is not relevant to the claim.

Claim: For senior citizens who live alone, owning a pet increases physical and mental well-being.

Supports

_____ **1.** Seniors who own a pet must be physically active in order to take care of the pet.

_____ **2.** Pets offer companionship and lessen loneliness.

_____ **3.** Pets cost money.

_____ **4.** Senior citizens may have to give their pets up when they move into assisted living homes.

_____ **5.** Caring for a pet can give a senior citizen a sense of purpose, a reason to get up each day.

B. Read the following paragraph.

Volusia County Had Most Shark Attacks In World

[1]In 2007, there were 71 shark attacks reported from around the world, according to the International Shark Attack File in its annual report on attacks and fatalities. [2]That number dipped to 59 in 2008. [3]ISAF director George Burgess said that's the fewest number since 2003's 57 attacks. [4]Of the 59 unprovoked shark attacks worldwide, 32 were in Florida and 22 were in Volusia County. [5]That's Volusia County's highest yearly total since 2001. [6]New Smyrna Beach accounted for 21 of those attacks. [7]There were four deadly shark attacks in 2008 compared to one in 2007. [8]"The fatalities were recorded in Mexico (2), Australia and Hawaii." [9]Florida, with its warm waters, has more sharks, including black tip sharks and spinner sharks, species not found in lower temperatures. [10]Florida even had a slow tourist season in 2008 due to the recession. [11]New Smyrna Beach has many more surfers than other portions of Florida. [12]As in past years, surfers accounted for most of the world's attacks: Surfers—57 percent, swimmers and waders—36 percent, and divers—8 percent. [13]Volusia county remains the shark-bite capital of the world.

—"ISAF 2008 Worldwide Shark Attack Summary." The Florida Museum of Natural History. 20 February 2009 http://www.flmnh.ufl.edu/ fish/sharks/statistics/2008attacksummary.htm. Reprinted with permission.

6. Underline the topic sentence (the sentence that states the claim).

_____ **7.** Which sentence is *not* relevant to the author's point?
a. sentence 2   c. sentence 10
b. sentence 6   d. sentence 13

Application 3: Argument: Adequate Supports and Author's Bias

1. The following paragraph consists only of supports. Choose the claim (topic sentence) that the evidence adequately supports.

They Can Get Away With It

[1]A person who uses your Social Security number, credit card numbers, checking account information, and birth date has committed identity theft. [2]As many as 1 in 20 Americans say that they have been the victim of identity theft during their lives. [3]The total loss so far due to identity theft may reach as high as $23 billion. [4]But in the year 2000, the FBI reported making only 922 arrests for identity theft. [5]"This is the fastest-growing crime today because the thieves know they can get away with it," said Linda Foley, director of the Identity Theft Resource Center. [6]"If you talk to law enforcement and ask them why they aren't prosecuting, they will say they have limited resources," said Barbara Span, vice president of Star Systems (the largest network of bank ATM machines). [7]"And they prosecute crimes that are easier to prove. [8]Also, violent crimes tend to take priority."

—Adapted from Sullivan, "ID Theft Victims Get Little Help."

_____ a. Identity theft happens every day and costs billions of dollars.

_____ b. Police don't care about identity theft crimes.

_____ c. Identity theft, a costly crime, is easy to get away with due to a lack of response from law enforcement.

_____ **2.** The details in the paragraph are mostly
a. negative.   b. positive.

3. Study the graph; then indicate which conclusion is *not* adequately supported by evidence.

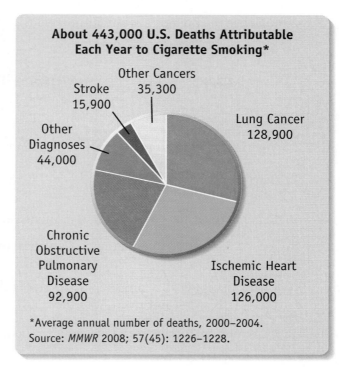

About 443,000 U.S. Deaths Attributable Each Year to Cigarette Smoking*

Other Cancers 35,300

Stroke 15,900

Other Diagnoses 44,000

Lung Cancer 128,900

Chronic Obstructive Pulmonary Disease 92,900

Ischemic Heart Disease 126,000

*Average annual number of deaths, 2000–2004.
Source: *MMWR* 2008; 57(45): 1226–1228.

_____ a. Cigarette smoking and exposure to tobacco smoke are associated with premature death from chronic diseases.

_____ b. The three leading specific causes of smoking-attributable death were lung cancer, ischemic heart disease, and chronic obstructive pulmonary disease (COPD).

_____ c. The number of people who smoke is increasing each year.

_____ d. Smoking tobacco contributes to preventable deaths.

REVIEW TEST 1   Score (number correct) _____ × 5 = _____%

Argument

A. Read the following groups of ideas. Mark each statement **C** if it is an author's claim or **S** if it provides support for the claim.

Group 1

_____ **1.** Julie has a high fever.

_____ **2.** Julie has the flu, not just a common cold.

_____ **3.** Julie's symptoms came on suddenly.

_____ **4.** Julie also has a cough, chills, and muscle aches.

Group 2

_____ **5.** Veterinary pet insurance is a good investment for a pet owner.

_____ **6.** A good insurance policy can cost as little as $15 a month for cats and $18 a month for dogs.

_____ **7.** Benefits cover the cost of tests, treatments, and medicine.

_____ **8.** After a $50 deductible, all the pet's medical bills are covered.

B. Read the following lists of claims and supports. Mark each support **R** if it is relevant to the claim or **N** if it is not relevant to the claim.

Claim: A negative outlook on life is a key barrier to success.
Supports

_____ **9.** Many people play a "tape" of negative messages in their heads, and these negative messages control their thoughts.

_____ **10.** Messages like "I can't do this" or "No one cares what I do" are often untrue statements that block positive action.

_____ **11.** Most actions begin as thoughts or beliefs.

_____ **12.** Success begins with the belief or thought that the goal is attainable.

_____ **13.** Everybody fails sometimes.

_____ **14.** Success leads to more success.

Claim: The study of mathematics is essential to becoming a well-educated person with a large number of career options.
Supports

_____ **15.** Knowledge of mathematics makes one a smarter, better-informed consumer.

_____ **16.** The study of mathematics is difficult for many people.

_____ **17.** Solving mathematical problems helps develop critical thinking skills.

_____ **18.** Mathematics has always been a part of a good education.

_____ **19.** Understanding mathematical concepts helps one understand and use technology better.

_____ **20.** Mathematical skills are the basis of hundreds of good-paying jobs in accounting, engineering, and computer programming.

REVIEW TEST 2

Score (number correct) _____ × 5 = _____%

Argument

A. Read the following groups of ideas. Mark each statement **C** if it is an author's claim or **S** if it provides support for the claim.

_____ **1.** In California, Senator Deborah Ortiz proposed a law that would ban soft drinks from all public schools in the state.

_____ **2.** In Maine, State Representative Sean Faircloth sponsored the "Maine Obesity Package"; this law would force fast-food chains to place nutritional information on menus.

_____ **3.** The obesity bill would also set aside dollars for walking trails, bike lanes, and cross-country ski trails in Maine.

_____ **4.** Lawmakers in several states believe that Americans should become more active and eat healthier fare.

—Adapted from Hellmich, "Legislators Try to Outlaw Soft Drinks, Sugary Snacks at Schools."

B. Study the following mock advertisement for gun locks. Read the claim and the list of supports. Mark each support **R** if it is relevant to the claim or **N** if it is not relevant to the claim.

Claim: Gun owners should use gun locks on their firearms to ensure safety.

An Unlocked Gun is an Open Door to Disaster

Most often, you do not leave home without locking your front door in order to ensure your personal safety. Locking the door just makes sense. Use common sense also when you own and use firearms. A gun lock ensures personal safety. When not in use, a gun should be kept unloaded, in a gun safe, and equipped with a gun lock.

Shut the door on disaster. Lock your firearms.

Supports

_____ **5.** Most often, you do not leave home without locking your front door in order to ensure your personal safety.

_____ **6.** Locking the door just makes sense.

_____ **7.** Use common sense also when you own and use firearms.

_____ **8.** A gun lock ensures personal safety.

_____ **9.** When not in use, a gun should be kept unloaded, in a gun safe, and equipped with a gun lock.

_____ **10.** Responsible gun ownership is just common sense.

C. Read the following lists of claims and supports. Mark each support **R** if it is relevant to the claim or **N** if it is not relevant to the claim.

Claim: Anger can be controlled.

Supports

_____ **11.** Relaxation skills such as deep breathing and slowly repeating words like *relax* can ease angry feelings.

_____ **12.** Avoiding situations that cause anger can help prevent anger; for example, a person who is angered by traffic should take less traveled roads when possible.

_____ **13.** Anger is healthy and normal.

_____ **14.** Some people are hotheads and just can't help themselves.

Claim: Some Web sites sell medicine that may not be safe to use and could put your health at risk.

_____ **15.** Some Web sites that sell medicine aren't U.S. state-licensed pharmacies or aren't pharmacies at all.

_____ **16.** Some Web sites may give a diagnosis that is not correct and sell medicine that is not right for you or your condition.

_____ **17.** Some medicines sold online are fake (counterfeit or "copycat" medicines); they are too strong or too weak, or they are made with dangerous ingredients.

_____ **18.** Identity theft is always a concern when buying from online sources.

D. Study the following table.

> **College Students' Top Ten Reasons for Cheating**
>
> 1. The instructor gave too much material.
> 2. The instructor left the room.
> 2.* A friend asked me to cheat, and I couldn't say no.
> 4. The instructor doesn't seem to care if I learn the material.
> 5. The course information is useless.
> 6. The course material is too hard.
> 6.* Everyone else seems to be cheating.
> 8. I'm in danger of losing a scholarship due to low grades.
> 9. I don't have time to study because I'm working to pay for school.
> 10. People sitting around me made no effort to protect their work.
>
> * = tied

—"College Cheating," *Research in Higher Education*, p. 52.

19–20. Choose the *two* claims that are *not* adequately supported by the evidence.

_____ a. Instructors are unfair in their expectations.

_____ b. Students blame their actions on teachers and other students.

_____ c. Students may cheat because of grades and time concerns.

_____ d. Most students take responsibility for their own cheating.

Read the following passage from a textbook for a college business course. Answer the questions that follow.

Textbook
Skills

High Seas Dumping

¹Cruising has become a very popular vacation.

²More than eight million passengers take an ocean voyage each year, cruising many areas of the world's oceans in search of pristine beaches and clear tropical waters. ³The Caribbean Sea, the Mediterranean Sea, and the coast of Alaska are among the most popular destinations. ⁴The coasts of Europe and Asia are also growing in popularity. ⁵While tourists and the giant ships that carry them are usually welcome for the revenues that they bring, unfortunately, the ships also bring something much less desirable—pollution.

⁶A modern cruise ship carries an average of 2,000 passengers and 1,000 crew members. ⁷This many people, of course, generate a lot of waste. ⁸On a typical day, a ship will produce seven tons of solid garbage, which is incinerated and then dumped; fifteen gallons of highly toxic chemical waste; 30,000 gallons of sewage; 7,000 gallons of bilge water containing oil; and 225,000 gallons of "gray" water from sinks and laundries. ⁹Cruise ships also pick up ballast water whenever and wherever it's needed and then discharge it later, releasing animals and pollution from other parts of the world. ¹⁰Multiply this problem by more than 167 ships worldwide, cruising 50 weeks per year, and the scope of the environmental damage is staggering.

¹¹Environmental groups see the top pollution-related problem as death of marine life, including extinction. ¹²Foreign animals bring parasites and diseases, and in some cases, replace native species entirely. ¹³Bacteria that are harmless to human beings can kill corals that provide food and habitat for many species. ¹⁴Oil and toxic chemicals are deadly to wildlife even in minute quantities.

¹⁵Turtles swallow plastic bags, thinking they are jellyfish, and starve. ¹⁶Seals and birds become entangled in the plastic rings that hold beverage cans and drown.

¹⁷Other problems include the habitat destruction or disease that affects U.S. industries, costing $137 billion each year. ¹⁸For example, cholera, picked up in ships' ballast water off the coast of Peru, caused a devastating loss to fish and shrimp harvesters in the Gulf of Mexico in the

1990s when infected catches had to be destroyed. [19]Heavy metal poisoning of fish is rising. [20]And concern is on the rise that the poisons are moving up the food chain from microscopic animals, to fish, and ultimately to humans. [21]Phosphorus, found in detergents, causes an overgrowth of algae, which then consume all the available oxygen in the water, making it incapable of supporting any flora or fauna. [22]One such "dead zone" occurs each summer in the Gulf of Mexico at the mouth of the Mississippi River. [23]The area, caused by pollution and warm water, is about the size of Massachusetts—8,000 square miles of lifelessness.

[24]Lack of regulation is the biggest obstacle to solving the problem. [25]By international law, countries may regulate oceans for three miles off their shores. [26]International treaties provide some additional regulation up to 25 miles offshore. [27]Beyond the 25-mile point, however, ships are allowed free rein. [28]Also, each country's laws and enforcement policies vary considerably. [29]And even when laws are strict, enforcement may be limited. [30]The U.S. Coast Guard enforces regulations off the U.S. coast, but it is spread thinly. [31]Only about 1 percent of the Coast Guard's annual budget is spent.

[32]While some polluting by cruise ships can be expected, intentional illegal dumping may also be growing in scope. [33]Over the last decade, for instance, as enforcement has tightened, 10 cruise lines have collectively paid $48.5 million in fines related to illegal dumping. [34]In the largest settlement to date, Royal Caribbean (www.royalcaribbean.com) paid $27 million for making illegal alterations to facilities, falsifying records, lying to the Coast Guard, and deliberately destroying evidence. [35]The fine may seem high, but it covers 30 different charges and 10 years of violations and seems small compared to the firm's 2001 profits of almost $1 billion. [36]Observers agree that Royal Caribbean's fine was less than what the firm would have paid to dispose of the waste properly over a decade. [37]In addition, a lawsuit is pending regarding the firing of a whistle-blower, the firm's former vice president for safety and environment. [38]"This [case] is like the Enron of the seas," says attorney William Arnlong, who represents the whistle-blower.

[39]Many feel that the fines haven't been steep enough. [40]Norwegian Cruise Lines (www.ncl.co.m) recently paid just $1 million for falsifying records in a case that included "some of the worst [violations] we've ever seen," according to Rick Langlois, an EPA investigator. [41]Langlois and others are outspoken against the cruise lines profiteering from an environment that they are destroying. [42]But the critics note that the companies won't stop as long as the profits continue. [43]Technology exists to make

the waste safe. [44]But industry experts estimate that dumping can save a firm millions of dollars annually. [45]From that perspective, Norwegian's actions were just a "brilliant business decision," says Langlois.

—Adapted from Griffin & Ebert, *Business*,
8th ed., pp. 57–58, 83.

_____ **1.** The main claim asserted by the author is stated in
    a. sentence 1.   c. sentence 10.
    b. sentence 5.   d. sentence 11.

_____ **2.** In paragraph 6, sentence 20 states
    a. a claim.
    b. evidence supporting a claim.

_____ **3.** In paragraph 7, sentence 27 states
    a. a claim.
    b. evidence supporting a claim.

_____ **3.** In paragraph 8, sentence 32 states
    a. a claim.
    b. evidence supporting a claim.

_____ **4.** The author expresses a bias
    a. in favor of the cruise lines' waste management systems.
    b. in favor of high fines against cruise lines for acts against the environment.
    c. against tourists who enjoy cruising.
    d. against regulations of cruise lines.

5–10. Complete the following outline with the series of claims asserted by the author in the passage.

Main claim: _____

_____

    I. _____

_____

    II. _____

_____

    III. _____

IV. _____

_____

V. _____

WHAT DO YOU THINK?

Is taking a cruise a vacation you would enjoy? Why or why not? What are the possible benefits of the cruise industry for individuals or society? Has reading this passage affected your views about cruising? Assume you are a representative of one side of this issue—either as an environmental activist or as a spokesperson for the cruising industry. Write a letter to the editor of your local newspaper in which you take a stand on this issue.

REVIEW TEST 4   Score (number correct) _____ × 10 = _____ %

Combined Skills Test

Read the following article published on the website of the non-profit organization Environmental Literacy Council. The Council offers free background information on common environmental science concepts. Before you read, skim the passage and answer the Before Reading questions. Then, read the passage carefully and answer the After Reading questions that follow.

Vocabulary Preview

efficiency (7): effectiveness, well done or without wasted energy

sustainably (10): able to be maintained

ingested (29): swallowing or absorbing food, liquid, or some other substance

Paper or Plastic?

[1]Shoppers have the opportunity to make a choice every time they make a trip to the grocery store: paper or plastic? [2]Many consumers may wonder which type of bag is better for the environment. [3]To compare the impacts of each material on the environment is not a simple matter. [4]It requires studying the inputs of matter and energy throughout each stage of the life cycle of each product.

[5]Plastics are produced from the waste products of oil refining. [6]An analysis of the life cycle of plastic bags includes thinking about the environmental impacts associated with the extraction of oil, the separation of products in the refining process, and

the manufacturing of plastics. [7]The total environmental impact depends upon the **efficiency** of operations at each stage and the effectiveness of their environmental protection measures. [8]Paper is produced from trees. [9]Environmental impacts include those associated with extracting timber and processing it for paper products. [10]Again, the environmental impacts depend on whether the timber was obtained from a **sustainably** managed forest—most industrial timber products in the U.S. come from plantations—and the environmental management of the paper processing plant. [11]Comparatively, plastic bags require less energy to produce.

[12]Both paper and plastic bags have to be transported to stores. [13]Transportation requires energy and creates emissions. [14]In this comparison, plastic is preferable because plastic bags are lighter in weight and more compact than paper bags. [15]It would take approximately seven trucks to transport the same number of paper bags as can be transported by a single truck full of plastic bags.

[16]The disposal of bags entails additional environmental impacts. [17]If landfilled, plastic bags are more environmentally **benign** than paper, as they require less space. [18]Paper occupies approximately half of overall landfill volume. [19]Plastics (not just bags) generate 14 to 28 percent of the volume of trash in general. [20]But because much of it can be compressed, plastics occupy only 9 to 12 percent of the volume of waste in landfills. [21]Although plastics do not biodegrade, modern landfills are designed in such a way that nothing biodegrades, because the waste is isolated from air and water in order to prevent groundwater contamination and air pollution. [22]As manufacturers have continued to make their plastic packaging thinner and lighter to save materials, the percentage of landfill volume taken up by plastics has remained steady since 1970 even as plastics have become more widely used.

[23]Not all trash ends up in landfills. [24]In the U.S. about 80 percent does. [25]Stray plastic bags are estimated to be at one to three percent of the hundreds of billions that are produced each year. [26]Stray plastic bags are now found almost everywhere on the planet. [27]Littering and trash laws in developing countries have significantly reduced the amount of improperly disposed trash. [28]However, many developing countries have fewer trash receptacles, landfills, and programs to handle the increasing amount of trash.

[29]Plastic bags pose a threat to marine life. [30]If **ingested**, the bags can block the stomach and cause starvation. [31]Sea turtles, for example, mistake plastic bags for jellyfish. [32]In 2002 a minke whale that washed up on a beach at Normandy was found to have 800 grams of plastic and other packaging in its stomach. [33]Stray plastic bags can also clog sewer pipes, leading to stagnant, standing water and associated health hazards. [34]In 2002, Bangladesh banned plastic bags after drains blocked by bags contributed to widespread

monsoon flooding in 1988 and 1998. [35]Ireland has decreased plastic bag consumption by placing a consumer tax on plastic bags. [36]Perhaps the most strict plastic bag regulations are found in the Indian province of Himachal Pradesh, where people caught with plastic bags are fined $2000.

—Adapted from "Paper or Plastic?" Environmental Literacy Council.
4 August 2008. http://www.enviroliteracy.org/article.php/1268.html.
Reprinted by permission The Environmental Literacy Council.

Before Reading

Vocabulary in Context

_____ **1.** What does the word **benign** mean in sentence 17?
  - a. beneficial
  - b. small
  - c. deadly
  - d. harmless

Tone and Purpose

_____ **2.** The overall tone of the passage is
  - a. objective.
  - b. biased.

_____ **3.** The primary purpose of the passage is
  - a. to inform.
  - b. to entertain.
  - c. to persuade.

After Reading

Central Idea and Main Idea

_____ **4.** Which sentence best states the central idea of the passage?
  - a. sentence 1
  - b. sentence 2
  - c. sentence 3
  - d. sentence 4

Supporting Details

_____ **5.** Sentence 16 is a
  - a. major supporting detail for the central idea.
  - b. minor supporting detail for the central idea.

Transitions

_____ **6.** The relationship between sentences 30 and 31 is
  - a. cause and effect.
  - b. time order.
  - c. generalization and example.
  - d. contrast.

Thought Patterns

_____ **7.** The overall thought pattern of the passage is
   a. cause and effect.
   b. time order.
   c. comparison and contrast.
   d. generalization and example.

Fact and Opinion

_____ **8.** Sentence 14 is a statement of
   a. fact.
   b. opinion.
   c. fact and opinion.

Inferences

_____ **9.** Based on the details in the passage, we can infer that
   a. plastic bags are more expensive to produce and transport than paper bags.
   b. paper bags are better for the environment.
   c. paper bags are more expensive to produce and transport than plastic bags.
   d. plastic bags are better for the environment.

Argument

_____ **10.** Which statement is not relevant to the following claim?

   Claim: Plastic bags are preferable to paper bags.

   a. Plastic bags require less energy to produce and transport.
   b. Paper bags do not biodegrade in landfills.
   c. Paper occupies approximately half of overall landfill volume.
   d. Plastic bags pose a threat to marine life.

WHAT DO YOU THINK?

Before reading this passage, which type of bag did you prefer—paper or plastic? Why? After reading this passage, has your view changed? Why or why not? Assume you are an assistant manager of a local grocery store, and the store management has been thinking about switching from paper to plastic bags. Write a memo in support of or in opposition to the switch from paper to plastic. State a clear claim and offer at least three pieces of evidence to back up your claim.

After Reading About the Basics of Argument

Before you move on to the Mastery Tests on the basics of argument, take time to reflect on your learning and performance by answering the following questions. Write your answers in your notebook.

- How has my knowledge base or prior knowledge about the basics of argument changed?

- Based on my studies, how do I think I will perform on the Mastery Test(s)? Why do I think my scores will be above average, average, or below average?

- Would I recommend this chapter to other students who want to learn more about the basics of argument? Why or why not?

Test your understanding of what you have learned about the basics of argument by completing the Chapter 12 Review Card near the end of the text.

CONNECT TO myreadinglab

To check your progress in meeting Chapter 12's learning outcomes, log in to www.myreadinglab.com, and try the following activities.

- The "Critical Thinking" section of MyReadingLab gives additional information about the basics of argument. The section provides an overview, model, practices, and tests. To access this resource, click on the "Study Plan" tab. Then click on "Critical Thinking." Then click on the following links as needed: "Overview," "Model," "Critical Thinking: Facts and Opinions (Flash Animation)," "Practice," and "Test."

- The "Study Skills Website" section of MyReadingLab also gives additional information about the basics of argument. To access these resources, go to the "Other Sources" box on the home page of MyReadingLab. Click on "Study Skills Website." Then scroll down the page to the heading "Life Skills" and click on "Critical Thinking." Explore each of the links on the bar on the left side of the page.

- To measure your mastery of the content of this chapter, complete the tests in the "Critical Thinking" section and click on Gradebook to find your results.

A. Read the following group of ideas. Mark each statement **C** if it is an author's claim or **S** if it provides support for the claim.

_____ **1.** On a Pennsylvania road on November 2, 1999, a driver using a cell phone ran a stop sign and broadsided Patricia N. Pena's family car, killing 1-year-old Morgan Lee.

_____ **2.** The harshest penalty the driver of the car could receive was a $50 fine and two traffic tickets.

_____ **3.** "My husband and I were outraged," Pena wrote later.

_____ **4.** Pena also believes the driver "would have gotten into more trouble if he had just threatened to kill my daughter; since he did kill her and blamed it on his cell phone, he walks away."

_____ **5.** Cell phones should be banned from use while driving.

—"Should Cell Phones Be Banned in Cars?"
CQ Researcher, p. 210.

B. Read the author's claim and the list of supports. Then mark each support **R** if it is relevant to the claim or **N** if it is not relevant to the claim.

Claim: Parents and teachers disagree about whether state testing has a negative effect on students' learning.

Supports

_____ **6.** A poll taken of parents showed that over 50 percent of the parents did not think testing was a problem.

_____ **7.** In the same poll, 18 percent of parents thought that teachers focused too much on "teaching to the test."

_____ **8.** In the same year, a poll taken of teachers showed that nearly 70 percent of teachers thought that state testing forced them to focus too much on teaching the information on the test.

_____ **9.** Many students may know the information but do not test well.

_____ **10.** Only 4 percent of teachers said they didn't know if state testing had negative effects, whereas 33 percent of the parents polled said they didn't know.

—"Is There Too Much Testing?" *CQ Researcher*, p. 327.

VISUAL VOCABULARY

A woman holds a sign during a protest to demand climate action in central Sydney.

The maps in this protest sign state _____.

   a. a claim.
   b. evidence for a claim.

A. Read the following groups of ideas. Each group contains the author's claim and supports for that claim. Identify the author's claim in each group.

_____ **1.** a. Reading short stories allows us to experience times and places other than our own.
   b. Reading short stories stimulates our imagination.
   c. Short stories should be read for a number of reasons.
   d. Reading short stories helps us connect with the experiences and feelings of others.

_____ **2.** a. Space tourism will someday be a money-making business.
   b. Businessman Dennis Tito was the first space tourist.
   c. Tito flew aboard a Russian rocket to the international space station on April 30, 2001.
   d. In a survey of over 1,000 households, 60 percent of those surveyed said they were interested in traveling to space for a vacation.

_____ **3.** a. Daytona Beach plays host to hundreds of thousands of race fans during the world-famous Daytona 500 NASCAR race every February.
   b. Year-round mild climate and beautiful beaches make Daytona a perfect family vacation spot.
   c. Every October and March, thousands of motorcycles thunder into Daytona Beach for Oktoberfest and Bike Week, respectively.
   d. Daytona Beach appeals to a wide array of tourists.

_____ **4.** a. Some computer users complain about the amount of time their service provider is down and inaccessible.
   b. Computers have some disadvantages.
   c. Many computer users are discouraged by the amount of e-mail they must deal with on a daily basis.
   d. A growing concern among parents is the access children have to unsuitable material on the Internet.

B. Read the following claim and its supports. Mark each support **R** if it is relevant to the claim or **N** if it is not relevant to the claim.

Claim: Animals become extinct mainly as a result of human action.

Supports

_____   **5.** Humans destroy the natural environment of a species by damming rivers, filling in swamps and marshes, and cutting down trees to build homes, roads, and other developments.

_____   **6.** Many species of fish and birds have been damaged by oil spills, acid rain, and water pollution created by industry.

_____   **7.** Many animals are hunted to extinction for their meat, furs, or other valuable parts.

_____   **8.** Some people have taken positive steps to protect endangered species.

_____   **9.** New species introduced into a habitat by humans can bring diseases that destroy the native species.

C. Read the following paragraph, which consists of supports.

[1]American poet Emily Dickinson lived from 1830 to 1886 in Amherst, Massachusetts, the small town in which she was born. [2]She was an unusual and gifted woman who in her later years dressed in white, rarely left her house, and composed over 1,000 poems. [3]Common themes that run throughout her works are death, immortality, love, and nature. [4]Her verses, known for their strong images and nontraditional form, won her wide acclaim after her death. [5]Only five poems were published during her lifetime. [6]The poems published after her death were marred by unskillful editing to make them conform to standard forms of rhyme and punctuation. [7]Both the life and poetry of Emily Dickinson defied traditional expectations. [8]But her reputation and influence have grown steadily over the years, and she is now considered one of America's greatest poets.

_____   **10.** In this paragraph, the author expresses a bias
   a. in favor of Emily Dickinson for achieving widespread fame during her lifetime.
   b. against Emily Dickinson as a woman writer.
   c. in favor of Emily Dickinson because she defied tradition to become one of America's greatest poets.
   d. against Emily Dickinson because she did not want to publish her work during her lifetime.

A. Read each list of supports. Choose the claim that is adequately supported by the evidence in each list.

Textbook
Skills

Supports

- The push to create public schools began in earnest in the 1820s.
- Many people saw public education as the answer to poverty.
- Others saw public education as a way to fight crime and help immigrants fit into society.
- At first, many thought Sunday schools were the way "to reclaim the vicious, to instruct the ignorant, and to raise the standard of morals among the lower classes of society."
- But soon these religious reformers called for public schools, too.

—Adapted from Martin et al., *America and Its Peoples: A Mosaic in the Making,* 3rd ed., p. 340.

_____ **1.** Which claim is adequately supported by the evidence?
   a. Public schools were created for the good of both the individual and the country.
   b. Public schools were created so that everyone in the country could have free education.
   c. Education is the only way a person can become successful.
   d. Education is a basic right owed to everyone.

Supports

Textbook
Skills

- Whole grains are packed with vitamins, minerals, and fiber that you just don't find in plain white bread, processed cereals, white rice, or even many healthful-looking enriched "multigrain" breads.
- Researchers have found disease-fighting properties in the nutrients in whole grains.
- In addition to being nutritious, whole grains are loaded with flavor and texture, adding interest to meals.

—Donatelle, *Health,* 5th ed., p. 231.

_____ **2.** Which claim is adequately supported by the evidence?
   a. Whole grains are the most healthful food available.
   b. Multigrain breads are not good for you.
   c. Whole-grain foods are hard to beat for nutrition, taste, and texture.
   d. The easiest way to get whole grain in the diet is by eating whole-wheat bread.

Supports

- Infant mortality rates are higher for boys, and women live an average of seven years longer than men.

Textbook
Skills

- Females have a more acute sense of smell and taste than males, and women's hearing is better and lasts longer than men's.
- While alcoholism is twice as common in men as in women, alcoholic women are at much greater risk for death from drinking.
- Women have a higher risk than men of developing diabetes, and a heart attack is more likely to be fatal for a woman than for a man.

—Adapted from Benokraitis, *Marriages and Families: Changes, Choices and Constraints*, text excerpt from p. 75, © 2002 Pearson Education, Inc. Reproduced by permission of Pearson Education, Inc.

_____ **3.** Which claim is adequately supported by the evidence?
   a. Women are stronger than men.
   b. Men are stronger than women.
   c. Women live longer than men.
   d. Men and women are different from each other.

B. Read the following paragraph. Then answer the questions that follow it.

Power Goes to the Less Interested

Textbook
Skills

¹If you can walk away from the rewards that your partner controls or can suffer the punishment your partner gives, then you control the relationship. ²If, on the other hand, you need the rewards that your partner controls or are unable or unwilling to suffer the punishments that your partner can give, then your partner has the power and controls the relationship. ³Power corrupts people. ⁴In a love relationship, for example, the person who maintains the greater power is the one who would find it easier to break up the relationship. ⁵The person who is unwilling or unable to break up has little power. ⁶This lack of power is due to the fact that he or she is dependent on the relationship and the rewards provided by the other person.

—Adapted from DeVito, *Messages: Building Interpersonal Communication Skills*, Text from p. 328. © 2004. Reproduced by permission of Pearson Education, Inc.

_____ **4.** Which sentence states the author's claim?
   a. In any interpersonal relationship, the person who holds the power is the one who is less interested in and less dependent on the other person.
   b. Some people like to be controlled by others.
   c. Some people like to control others.
   d. Powerful people do not make lasting commitments to others.

_____ **5.** Which sentence is *not* relevant to the argument?
   a. sentence 1   c. sentence 3
   b. sentence 2   d. sentence 6

Read the following passage from a college psychology textbook. Answer the questions that follow.

Textbook
Skills

Issues in Animal Research

[1]Should animals be used in psychological and medical research? [2]This question has often produced very polarized responses. [3]On one side are researchers who point to the very important breakthroughs research with animals has allowed in several areas of behavioral science. [4]The benefits of animal research have included discovery and testing of drugs that treat anxiety and mental illnesses. [5]Research with animals has also yielded important knowledge about drug addiction. [6]Animal research benefits animals as well. [7]For example, psychological researchers have shown how to ease the stresses of confinement experienced by zoo animals. [8]Their studies of animal learning and social organization have led to the improved design of enclosures. [9]Their research has brought about animal facilities that promote good health.

[10]For defenders of animal rights "ethical concerns about compromised animal welfare cannot be eased by human benefits alone." [11]Specialists in ethics encourage researchers to adhere to the 3 *Rs*: reduce, replace, and refine. [12]Researchers should use tests of their hypothesis that *reduce* the number of animals they require. [13]Or researchers should *replace* the use of animals altogether. [14]They should *refine* their tests to minimize pain and distress. [15]Each animal researcher must judge his or her work with heightened scrutiny. [16]The American Psychological Association provides firm ethical guidelines for researchers who use nonhuman animals in their research.

[17]Surveys of 1,188 psychology students and 3,982 American Psychological Association members on their attitudes toward animal research support a standard of heightened scrutiny.

[18]Roughly 80 percent of the people surveyed believed that animals should be observed in naturalistic settings. [19]Smaller numbers (30 to 70 percent) supported studies involving caging or confinement. [20]Support of caging depended in part on the type of animal (for example, rats, pigeons, dogs, or primates). [21]Both students and their professors disapproved of studies involving physical pain or death.

[22]A majority of both groups (roughly 60 percent) supported the use of animals in undergraduate psychology courses. [23]But only about a third of each group felt that laboratory work with animals should be a required part of an undergraduate psychology major.

—Adapted from Gerrig/Zimbardo, *Psychology and Life,* Text Excerpt from pp. 37, 58 © 2010 Pearson Education, Inc. Reproduced by permission of Pearson Education, Inc.

_____ **1.** The author expresses
  a. a bias for use of animals in testing.
  b. a bias against use of animals in testing.
  c. a balanced view of the issues in animal research.

_____ **2.** Sentence 6 states
  a. a claim.   b. evidence in support of a claim.

_____ **3.** The main claim of the passage is stated in
  a. sentence 1.   c. sentence 3.
  b. sentence 2.   d. sentence 16.

_____ **4.** Which statement is not relevant to the following claim?

  Claim: Use of animals in psychological and medical testing should be banned.
  a. Confined animals experience stress.
  b. Use of animals in research compromises animal welfare to benefit humans.
  c. Researchers should replace the use of animals in research altogether.
  d. Use of animals in research benefits animals as well.

VISUAL VOCABULARY

Sea lion in naturalistic habitat of Seward SeaLife Center, Seward, Alaska, USA. The best meaning of the word

naturalistic is _____.

a. real life.
b. safe.
c. ideal.

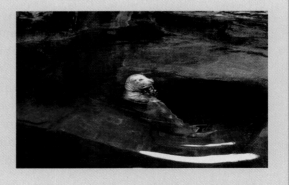

Advanced Argument: Persuasive Techniques

13

LEARNING OUTCOMES

After studying this chapter you should be able to do the following:

1. Define the terms *fallacy, propaganda, personal attack, straw man, begging the question, name-calling, testimonial, bandwagon, plain folks, either-or, false comparison, false cause, card stacking, transfer,* and *glittering generalities.*

2. Detect fallacies based on irrelevant arguments: *personal attack, straw man,* and *begging the question.*

3. Detect propaganda techniques based on irrelevant arguments: *name-calling, testimonials, bandwagon,* and *plain folks.*

4. Detect fallacies based on inadequate arguments: *either-or, false comparison,* and *false cause.*

5. Detect propaganda techniques based on inadequate arguments: *card stacking, transfer,* and *glittering generalities.*

6. Evaluate the importance of advanced arguments: persuasive techniques.

Before Reading About Advanced Argument: Persuasive Techniques

In this chapter, you will build on the concepts you studied about the basics of argument. Take a moment to review the four steps in analyzing an argument. Fill in the following blanks with each of the steps.

Step 1: _____

Step 2: _____

Step 3: _____

Step 4: _____

Based on the learning outcomes and what you learned about the basics of argument, complete the following idea:

A valid argument is made up of relevant and adequate supports.

Biased arguments that use logical fallacies and propaganda techniques are composed of _____ and _____ supports.

To help you master the material in the chapter, create a three-column chart in your notebook. In the left column write the headings from the learning outcomes, as in the example that follows. Leave enough room between each heading to fill in definitions and examples as you work through the chapter.

General definition: A fallacy is

Fallacy	**Definition**	**Example**
Personal attack		
Straw man		

General definition: Propaganda is

Propaganda technique	**Definition**	**Example**
Name-calling		
Testimonials		

 # Biased Arguments

Much of the information that we come in contact with on a daily basis is designed to influence our thoughts and behaviors. Advertisements, editorials, and political campaigns constantly offer one-sided, biased information to sway public opinion.

This biased information is based on two types of reasoning: the use of **fallacies** in logical thought and the use of **propaganda**. An effective reader identifies and understands the use of these persuasion techniques in biased arguments.

What Is a Fallacy in Logical Thought?

You have already studied logical thought in Chapter 12, "The Basics of Argument." Logical thought or argument is a process that includes an author's claim, relevant support, and a valid conclusion. A **fallacy** is an error in the process of logical thought. A fallacy leads to an invalid conclusion. You have also studied two general types of fallacies: irrelevant details and inadequate details. By its nature, a fallacy is not persuasive because it weakens an argument. However, fallacies are often used to convince readers to accept an author's claim. In fact, the word *fallacy* comes from a Latin word that means "to deceive" or "trick." You will learn more about irrelevant and inadequate arguments in the next two sections of this chapter.

Fallacies are not to be confused with false facts. A fact, true or false, is stated without bias, and facts can be proven true or false by objective evidence. In contrast, a fallacy is an invalid inference or biased opinion about a fact or set of facts. Sometimes the word *fallacy* is used to refer to a false belief or the reasons for a false belief.

A **fallacy** is an error in logical thought.

EXAMPLE Read the following sets of ideas. Mark each statement as follows:

UB for unbiased statements
B for biased arguments

_____ **1.** Thomas Edison invented the light bulb.

_____ **2.** Every time Ralph has worn his New York Mets t-shirt, he has passed his math exams; therefore, to pass the next exam he will wear it again.

_____ **3.** Lashonda trusts the news story because it's printed in the newspaper.

_____ **4.** Randall attended classes regularly, took detailed notes during classes and from his textbooks, reviewed his notes daily, asked questions during classes, and, as a result, earned a high grade point average.

_____ **5.** Even though sunlight travels approximately 93 million miles to reach earth, its ultraviolet rays cause premature aging of the skin, cataracts, and skin cancer.

EXPLANATION

1. This is an unbiased statement (UB); however, it is a false fact. Thomas Edison did not invent the light bulb. Research reveals that several men had produced various types of electrical lights before Edison. Edison improved upon a 50-year-old idea based on a patent he bought from inventors Henry Woodward and Matthew Evans. This idea is not a fallacy; it does not represent an error in thinking. The detail is simply incorrect information. Logical thinking begins with verifying the facts.

2. This is a biased argument (B) based on a fallacy in logical thought. Ralph has jumped to the wrong conclusion about why he did well on his math exams. By not considering other reasons for his success, he has identified a false cause and made an invalid inference. You will learn more about the fallacy of false cause later in this chapter.

3. This is also a biased argument (B) based on a fallacy in logical thought. Lashonda is arguing in a circle. She has a favorable bias toward words in print. She trusts the news because it is in the paper. Unfortunately, publication does not guarantee accuracy. You will learn more about the fallacy of circular reasoning later in this chapter.

4. This is an unbiased statement (UB). Every detail can be verified through testimony or eyewitness accounts of Randall's classmates, teachers, and transcripts.

5. This is an unbiased statement (UB). This statement is factual and can be proven with objective evidence, case histories, and expert opinions.

PRACTICE 1

Read the following sets of ideas. Mark each statement as follows:

> **UB** for unbiased statements
> **B** for biased arguments

_____ 1. Birds evolved from dinosaurs.

_____ 2. Teenager to his friend, "You are jealous because I have my own car."

_____ 3. People under the age of 18 should not be allowed to vote because they are too young.

_____ 4. British soldiers fired in self-defense on American colonists in the Boston Massacre.

What Is Propaganda?

Propaganda is a means by which an idea is widely spread. The word *propaganda*, first used by Pope Gregory XV, comes from a Latin term that means to "propagate" or "spread." In 1612, the Pope created a department within the church to spread the Christian faith throughout the world by missionary work.

Centuries later, President Woodrow Wilson used propaganda to sway the American people to enter World War I. **Propaganda** is a biased argument that advances or damages a cause. Propaganda is often used in politics and advertising.

Read the following two descriptions of a fictitious version of a common product used in daily life by millions. The first description is a mock advertisement. The second description includes withheld details about the fictitious product—information not included in the advertisement.

> **Mock Advertisement**: Sweet has changed the world of sweeteners by offering a healthy, no-calorie, sugar-based option. Sweet measures and pours just like sugar. Sweet is the brand name of glucralose. Glucralose comes from sugar, so Sweet tastes like sugar. For the natural taste of sugar without the guilt of added calories and carbohydrates, sweeten your life with Sweet. Made from sugar—tastes like sugar. Use Sweet instead of sugar in all your favorite recipes. Life is sweet with Sweet.

> **Withheld Details**: Glucralose is not a natural product. Instead, it is a chlorinated artificial sweetener. Glucralose is a chemical compound derived from sugar in a laboratory. A significant number of scientific tests reveal that glucralose may weaken the human immune system.

Notice how many times the mock advertisement repeats the word "sugar." This repetition creates a false comparison between the natural substance sugar and the synthetic compound glucralose. This direct comparison to sugar is misleading and may confuse consumers into thinking glucralose is as natural as sugar because it's "made from sugar and tastes like sugar." In addition to its misleading wording, the advertisement also may also be making a false claim by using the term "healthy." The advertisement withholds information about scientific tests that raise concerns about the harmful effects of glucralose on the human immune system. The mock advertisement offers only a positive view of the artificial sweetener. Thus, this advertisement is an example of **propaganda**.

> **Propaganda** is an act of persuasion that systematically spreads biased information that is designed to support or oppose a person, product, cause, or organization.

Propaganda uses a variety of techniques that are based on **emotional appeal**. If you are not aware of these techniques, you may be misled by the way information is presented and come to invalid conclusions. Understanding propaganda techniques will enable you to separate factual information from emotional appeals so that you can come to valid conclusions.

For example, the mock advertisement of the product Sweet uses emotional appeals with phrases such as *healthy*, *without guilt*, *favorite recipes*, and "Life is sweet with Sweet." Often advertisements like this one appeal to the readers' personal values; in contrast, the withheld details report only facts.

> **Emotional appeal** is the arousal of emotions to give a biased meaning or power to an idea.

EXAMPLE Read the following sets of ideas. Mark each statement as follows:

UB for unbiased statements
B for biased arguments

_____ **1.** A healthful diet includes a variety of foods including grain, fresh fruits and vegetables, fats, and protein.

_____ **2.** Use your vote to put Grace McKinney in the Senate because, like you and me, she comes from a hardworking, middle-class family and wants to give control of government back to the people.

_____ **3.** Spicy foods and stress cause stomach ulcers.

_____ **4.** Don't buy your insurance from DealState; that outfit is a bunch of crooks. Instead trust us, TruState, to meet your insurance needs.

_____ **5.** To avoid identity theft, do not give out personal information, periodically obtain a copy of your credit report, and keep detailed records of your banking and financial accounts.

EXPLANATION

1. This is an unbiased statement (UB). It is factual and can be proven with objective evidence, research studies, and expert opinions.

2. This is a biased argument (B) using the emotional appeal of propaganda. The statement uses the "plain folks" appeal. Grace McKinney is described as an everyday person with the same values of everyday people. You will learn more about this propaganda technique later in this chapter.

3. This is an unbiased statement (UB); however, it is a false fact. Research reveals that stomach ulcers are caused by an infection from a bacterium or by use of pain medications such as aspirin or ibuprofen. Cancer can also cause stomach ulcers. Stress and spicy food can aggravate an ulcer, but they do not cause one to occur.

4. This is a biased argument (B) using the emotional appeal of the propaganda technique of "name-calling." You will learn more about this propaganda technique later in this chapter.

5. This is an unbiased statement (UB). This statement offers factual advice, based on research, about how to respond to the crime of identity theft.

PRACTICE 2

Read the following sets of ideas. Mark each statement as follows:

> **UB** for unbiased statements
> **B** for biased arguments

_____ 1. Buy Gold Plus Jeans; they are made in America by Americans.

_____ 2. Advertisement: "This beautiful and famous actress wears Gold Plus Jeans."

_____ 3. Cortisol is a hormone triggered by stress that causes fat to collect in the abdomen.

_____ 4. Charles Darwin is respected by many in the scientific community for his theory of evolution.

Often the emotional appeal of propaganda is found in the supporting details, which are either irrelevant or inadequate (for more information on irrelevant and inadequate details, see Chapter 12, "The Basics of Argument"). The following sections of this chapter offer in-depth discussions and practices to help you identify irrelevant and inadequate arguments that use fallacies in logical thought and propaganda techniques.

Irrelevant Arguments: Fallacies

Writing based in logical thought offers an author's claim and relevant supporting details, and it arrives at a valid conclusion. Fallacies and propaganda offer irrelevant arguments based on irrelevant details. Irrelevant details draw attention away from logical thought by ignoring the issue or changing the subject.

Personal Attack

Personal attack is the use of abusive remarks in place of evidence for a point or argument. Also known as an *ad hominem* attack, a personal attack attempts to discredit the point by discrediting the person making the point.

For example, Sam, a convicted felon, takes a stand against smoking in public places and calls for a law to ban smoking in restaurants. Those who oppose the law focus attention on Sam's criminal record and ignore his reasons for being against smoking in restaurants with statements like "Now the law-breakers want to make the laws" or "Don't listen to a loser who can't stay out of jail." However, Sam's criminal past has nothing to do with smoking laws; making it a part of the argument is a personal attack.

EXAMPLE Read the following paragraph. Underline two uses of the logical fallacy of *personal attack*.

> [1]Teenager Tyrone is trying to persuade his father that he, Tyrone, should have a motorcycle. [2]Tyrone points out that he has held a steady part-time job for three years and has saved enough money to pay for the motorcycle. [3]Tyrone's father asks, "What about the cost of insurance?" [4]Tyrone replies that he has checked with several insurance companies and found a reasonable rate. [5]He added that he has enough money in his budget to cover the costs. [6]When his father still hesitates, Tyrone says, "You don't like this because it wasn't your idea; you would rather be the one in control." [7]His father retorts, "Well, it's hard to trust your judgment when you have a dozen piercings in your face."

EXPLANATION Tyrone is trying to assert that he is mature enough to handle the responsibility of owning a motorcycle. He begins with logical reasons to support this claim. He works, saves, and budgets his own money. In addition, he took the initiative to shop for the best price for insurance. These are impressive supports for his argument. However, when his father resists his logic, Tyrone falls into the use of personal attack in sentence 6. Tyrone accuses his father of selfishly trying to stay in control of his life. Tyrone's father responds in sentence 7 with his own personal attack on the way Tyrone looks. The issue of the motorcycle is no longer the focus of their discussion.

Straw Man

A **straw man** is a weak argument substituted for a stronger one to make the argument easier to challenge. A straw man fallacy distorts, misrepresents, or falsifies an opponent's position. The name of the fallacy comes from the idea that it is easier to knock down a straw man than a real man who will fight back. The purpose of this kind of attack is to shift attention away from a strong argument to a weaker one that can be more easily overcome. Study the following example:

> Governor Goodfeeling opposes drilling for oil in Alaska. But the United States is too dependent on foreign oil supplies, and the American economy would benefit from having an American supply of oil. Governor Goodfeeling is opposed to American-based oil drilling and wants to keep us dependent on foreign oil cartels.

This passage doesn't mention Governor Goodfeeling's reasons for opposing drilling for oil in Alaska. Instead, the writer restates the governor's position in ways that are easy to attack: continued dependence on foreign supplies and the implied economic hardships this might bring.

EXAMPLE Read the following paragraph. Underline the *straw man* fallacy in it.

> *Candidate Manual Cortez:* [1]"We must protect our natural environment. [2]Unique and irreplaceable habitats are being devoured by uncontrolled growth. [3]I propose that we set the area known as the Loop aside as a natural reserve. [4]The Loop is a 30-mile stretch of road that cuts through a section of the vanishing Florida forests and marshes. [5]Let us work together to halt McRay's Building Corporation's plans for a new housing development in the Loop once and for all."
>
> *Candidate Rory Smith:* [6]"New construction is a sign of healthy economic development." [7]Candidate Cortez is against economic development.

EXPLANATION Candidate Rory Smith uses the straw man fallacy when he accuses his opponent of being against economic development in sentence 7. Candidate Manual Cortez has not said he is against economic development. He is against this particular development in this one specific area known as the Loop. He is for protecting the environment.

Begging the Question

Begging the question restates the point of an argument as the support and conclusion. Also known as *circular reasoning*, begging the question assumes that an unproven or unsupported point is true. For example, the argument, "Spinach is an awful tasting food because it tastes bad" begs the question. The point "Spinach is an awful tasting food" is assumed to be true because it is restated in the phrase "tastes bad" without specific supports that give logical reasons or explanations. Compare the same idea stated without begging the question: "I never eat spinach because it has a bitter taste, and I don't like foods that taste bitter."

EXAMPLE Read the following paragraph. Underline the irrelevant argument of *begging the question*.

King Cameron

[1]*Avatar* reigns supreme at the box office worldwide. [2]In 2010, *Avatar*, directed by James Cameron, passed *Titanic*, also directed by Cameron, as the highest grossing film of all time. [3]*Avatar* made $1.859 billion globally—after only 37 days in theaters. [4]*Titanic*, released in 1997, held the previous record with $1.843 billion. [5]The public embraced *Avatar's* themes of "protecting the environment, respecting life, and yearning for a peaceful planet." [6]But the true power of *Avatar* comes from its visually stunning special effects. [7]Cameron created a fantastical and beautiful world on screen and became king of the movie world. [8]James Cameron is the best director of his generation because he is better than all the other directors.

EXPLANATION Sentence 8 begs the question. To say that James Cameron is *better than all the other directors* is simply restating the idea that he is *the best director of his generation* without giving any concrete evidence or reasons to back up the claim. If he is the best, then naturally he is better than the others. As an effective reader, you want to know the reasons that explain why he is the best director or better than other directors.

PRACTICE 3

Identify the fallacy in each of the following items. Write **A** if the statement begs the question, **B** if is constitutes a personal attack, or **C** if it is a straw man.

_____ **1.** Big Red chewing gum is my favorite gum because I like it.

_____ **2.** Don't re-elect the senator; she is a dishonest anti-American liberal posing as a patriot.

_____ **3.** Alfred Simmons should not hold a public office because he admitted to experimenting with drugs when he was a teenager.

_____ **4.** Biology is a difficult subject because the concepts are hard to understand.

_____ **5.** We should not fund the construction of more roads because more roads will increase driving for pleasure.

Irrelevant Arguments: Propaganda Techniques

Name-Calling

Name-calling uses negative labels for a product, idea, or cause. The labels are made up of emotionally loaded words and suggest false or irrelevant details that cannot be verified. Name-calling is an expression of personal opinion. For example, a bill for gun control may be labeled "anti-American" to stir up opposition to the bill. The "anti-American" label suggests that any restriction to the ownership of guns is against basic American values.

EXAMPLE Read the following paragraph. Underline the irrelevant details that use *name-calling*.

From Good Girl to Diva

¹Christina Singer has veered a long way from the bubblegum pop music and teeny-bop image that made her famous. ²In her newest album, *Taunt and Tease*, she has the air of a raunchy diva. ³Even though her voice delivers a decent mix of pop, rock, soul, and R&B, her vampire-in-leather costume and wicked-witch makeup makes her act scary to watch.

EXPLANATION The first sentence uses two labels to name the kind of appeal of this fictitious singer: *bubblegum pop* is a kind of music aimed at the preteen market, and *teeny-bop image* is usually linked to this market. Sentence 2 calls Christina Singer a *raunchy diva*. The word *raunchy* means "crude" or "vulgar," and the word *diva* suggests the large ego of a star. So saying she has the air of a raunchy diva is calling her rude and full of herself. Sentence 3 includes three negative labels: *vampire-in-leather costume, wicked-witch*, and *scary*. These names evoke images of the singer's evil and dark side.

Testimonials

Testimonials use irrelevant personal opinions to support a product, idea, or cause. Most often the testimonial is provided by a celebrity whose only qualification as a spokesperson is fame. For example, a famous actor promotes a certain brand of potato chips as his favorite, or a radio talk show host endorses a certain type of mattress.

EXAMPLE Read the following paragraph. Underline the irrelevant details that use a *testimonial*.

The Benefits of Milk

¹Milk and milk products are important dietary sources of calcium. ²Milk and milk products are also good sources of other vital nutrients, including high-quality protein for building and repairing body tissues and vitamin A for better eyesight and healthy skin. ³They are also rich in riboflavin, vitamin B_{12}, and phosphorus. ⁴Famous athlete Jerome High-Jumper says, "Drinking milk every day makes me the athlete I am."

EXPLANATION Sentences 1 through 3 offer factual details about milk and milk products. However, sentence 4 uses the testimonial of a famous athlete. Being a famous athlete doesn't make the spokesperson an expert about the nutritional value of milk. A doctor, nurse, or nutritionist could offer a relevant expert opinion.

PRACTICE 4

Identify the propaganda technique used in each of the following items. Write **A** if the sentence is an example of name-calling or **B** if it is a testimonial.

_____ **1.** I have used Dr. Smith as our pets' veterinarian for over 25 years. He is knowledgeable and compassionate. You should make an appointment with him when you adopt your puppy from the pound.

_____ **2.** Winfield Scott was "the Peacock of American politics, all fuss and feathers and fireworks."

_____ **3.** Marie Osmond and Dan Marino claim that Nutrisystem helped them lose weight because Nutrisystem is easy to follow and easy to stay on.

_____ **4.** Supreme Court Chief Justice John G. Roberts is a conservative judicial activist whose rulings are robbing citizens of basic freedoms.

_____ **5.** I write this letter to inform you about the impact of your gift on the lives of the children in Haiti. Your donation is supplying life-giving food, and we have seen amazing results. On average we have seen a weight increase of at least 10% in the first two to four weeks of placing the children on our food program. The food we provide due to your support is reversing the starvation process for hundreds of children. –Thank you on behalf of these children, Martha Dugall, CEO, Helping Hands for Children

Bandwagon

The **bandwagon** appeal uses or suggests the irrelevant detail that "everyone is doing it." This message plays on the natural desire of most individuals to conform to group norms for acceptance. The term *bandwagon* comes from the 19th-century use of a horse-drawn wagon that carried a musical band to lead circus parades and political rallies. To *jump on the bandwagon* meant to follow the crowd, usually out of excitement and emotion stirred up by the event rather than out of thoughtful reason or deep conviction.

EXAMPLE Read the following paragraph. Underline the irrelevant details that use the *bandwagon* appeal.

Prom Curfew

[1]Alissa, a sophomore, has been asked to the senior prom by a popular football player. [2]Her parents are protective and strict, so she has a curfew that will force her to come home long before the after-prom parties are over. [3]As she is talking over her plans with her parents, she offers to pay for her dress with her own money, and she reassures them that her date is trustworthy and comes from a family that her parents know and respect. [4]She also tells them that all her friends' parents are letting them stay out until 3 A.M. [5]She reminds them that she has a cell phone and can call if she needs to for any reason. [6]When her parents resist, she says, "I'm the only one who isn't allowed to stay out late on prom night."

EXPLANATION Alissa uses the bandwagon appeal in two sentences. In sentence 4, she implies that her parents should jump on the bandwagon and conform to what other parents are doing when she says all her friends' parents are letting them stay out until 3 A.M. She then follows this argument in sentence 6 with "I am the only one who isn't allowed," a statement that shows she has already jumped on the bandwagon and wants to do what everyone else is doing. Read the paragraph with the bandwagon details removed.

Prom Curfew

Alissa, a sophomore, has been asked to the senior prom by a popular football player. Her parents are protective and strict, so she has a curfew that will force her to come home long before the after-prom parties are over. As she is talking over her plans with her parents, she offers to pay for her dress with her own money, and she reassures them that her date is trustworthy and comes from a family that her parents know and respect. She reminds them that she has a cell phone and can call if she needs to for any reason.

Plain Folks

The **plain folks** appeal uses irrelevant details to build trust based on commonly shared values. Many people distrust the wealthy and powerful, such as politicians and the heads of large corporations. Many assume that the wealthy and powerful cannot relate to the everyday concerns of plain people. Therefore, the person or organization of power puts forth an image to which everyday people can more easily relate. For example, a candidate may dress in simple clothes, pose for pictures doing everyday chores like shopping for groceries, or talk about his or her own humble beginnings to make a connection with "plain folks." These details strongly suggest that "you can trust me because I am just like you." The appeal is to the simple, everyday experience, and often the emphasis is on a practical or no-nonsense approach to life.

EXAMPLE Read the following paragraph. Underline the irrelevant details that appeal to *plain folks*.

Cooking with Helen

[1]A woman dressed in everyday casual clothes, wearing a sleeveless blue-collared shirt and khaki slacks, is busy preparing food in a television studio that has been created to look like a cozy kitchen. [2]She says, "Hello, my name is Helen. [3]Welcome to my kitchen. [4]For the next hour, I will share with you a few of the family-secret, down-home cooking techniques that have put my book, *Helen's Favorite Southern Recipes,* on the national best-seller list for the past three years."

EXPLANATION The woman, Helen, is described as wearing clothes that many plain folks also wear: She is *dressed in everyday casual clothes, wearing a sleeveless blue-collared shirt and khaki slacks.* So plain folks can relate to the woman based on her style of clothing. The kitchen is described as *cozy,* which suggests basic or simple values common to many people. Helen sets a friendly tone with the use of her first name, and the word *my* in *my kitchen* suggests that she is inviting the audience into her home. She then taps into everyday family values with the phrases *family-secret* and *down-home.* All of these details suggest that this best-selling author and television spokesperson is just one of the "plain folks." Once you identify these irrelevant details, you can come to a conclusion based on the relevant details. Read the paragraph with the appeals to plain folks removed; the remaining details are facts that can be verified.

Cooking with Helen

A woman is busy preparing food in a television studio that has been created to look like a kitchen. She says, "Hello, my name is Helen. Welcome to this kitchen. For the next hour, I will share with you a few of the cooking techniques that have put my book, *Helen's Favorite Southern Recipes,* on the national best-seller list for the past three years."

PRACTICE 5

Label each of the following items according to the propaganda techniques they employ:

A. plain folks	C. testimonial
B. bandwagon	D. name-calling

_____ **1.** People who support health care reform are socialists who favor big government.

_____ **2.** The President of the United States, wearing a collar-less shirt and casual sports jacket, goes on late night talk shows such as *David Letterman* and *Jimmy Kimmel* to talk about his plans for education and jobs.

_____ **3.** Over three million people can't be wrong—buy Stay Trim now.

VISUAL VOCABULARY

This protestor uses the propaganda technique of

_____ during a protest organized by a group called "Moratorium Now" in front of the Bank of America building in downtown Detroit, Michigan.

a. bandwagon
b. plain folks
c. testimonial

_____ **4.** "I suffered with acne all through high school. It robbed me of any self-confidence and made it really hard for me to make friends. Then my college roommate told me about AcuClear. Within three months, my skin was smooth and healthy. If you suffer from acne, I recommend AcuClear," Melinda, college student.

_____ **5.** If you think government can reform health care and education, then you really are naïve.

Inadequate Arguments: Fallacies

In addition to offering relevant supporting details, logical thought relies on adequate supporting details. A valid conclusion must be based on adequate support. Fallacies and propaganda offer inadequate arguments that lack details. Inadequate arguments oversimplify the issue and do not give a person enough information to draw a proper conclusion.

Either-Or

Either-or assumes that only two sides of an issue exist. Also known as the *black-and-white fallacy*, either-or offers a false dilemma because more than two options are usually available. For example, the statement "If you don't give to the toy drive, you don't care about children" uses the either-or fallacy. The statement assumes there is only one reason for not giving to the toy drive—not caring about children. Yet it may be that a person doesn't have the money to buy a toy for the drive, or the person may help children in other ways. Either-or leaves no room for the middle ground or other options.

EXAMPLE   Read the following paragraph. Underline the *either-or* fallacy in it.

Peer Pressure

[1]Clay, Chad, Diego, and Stefan are spending the night together at Chad's house. [2]Around 3 A.M., Chad suggests that they sneak out, take his father's car, and go for a ride around town.

[3]Diego says, "I don't know. [4]What if we get caught?"

[5]"We won't," Chad says. [6]"Don't be such a wuss. [7]It will be fun."

[8]"Yeah," Clay chimes in. [9]"Everyone sneaks out at least once in their life—no big deal."

[10]"Listen, Diego," Chad says in a low, serious voice, "either you're with us or you're not. [11]What's it going to be?"

¹²Diego is still not sure and says, "I don't know, guys, we will be grounded for life if we get caught. ¹³Why can't we just stay here and watch movies like we planned?"

¹⁴"Fine," Stefan says, "you just stay home like a good little boy."

EXPLANATION Sentence 10 asserts the either-or fallacy "either you're with us or you're not." Chad makes it sound like Diego will be an enemy if he doesn't go along with the plans. Diego is actually looking out for their best interests. He reminds them of the punishment they will face if they are caught.

False Comparison

False comparison assumes that two things are similar when they are not. This fallacy is also known as a *false analogy*. An analogy is a point-by-point comparison that is used to explain an unfamiliar concept by comparing it to a more familiar one.

For example, an author may draw an analogy between a computer and the human anatomy. The computer's motherboard is like the human nervous system; the computer's processor is like the part of the human brain that tells the other parts of the body what to do. Just like a human brain, a computer's brain also has memory. However, the analogy breaks down when one considers all the differences between a computer and the human anatomy. The human body can repair itself, and the human brain can think creatively and critically. A false comparison occurs when the differences outweigh the similarities.

EXAMPLE Read the following paragraph. Underline the logical fallacy of *false comparison*.

¹A community college president is giving a speech at a local gathering of business professionals. ²He says, "The community college is just like your own business. ³We charge fees for our services. ⁴We worry about public relations. ⁵We have to pay for buildings, water, and electricity. ⁶We hire, train, and promote employees. ⁷And we both have the same bottom line."

EXPLANATION Sentences 1 through 6 state traits that community colleges do have in common with businesses. However, sentence 7 draws a false analogy. Businesses do not receive public funding from tax dollars. And the primary purpose of a community college is to educate the public, not make large profits. So in significant ways, a community college's bottom line is very different from the bottom line of a business.

False Cause

False cause, also known as **Post Hoc,** assumes that because events occurred around the same time, they have a cause-and-effect relationship. For example, Tyrell wears a blue baseball cap and hits a record number of homeruns. To continue hitting homeruns, he feels he must wear his blue baseball cap. Tyrell has made the mistake of believing that his blue baseball cap has something to do with his ability to hit a record number of homeruns. What are the other possible causes? The Post Hoc fallacy is the false assumption that because event B *follows* event A, event B *was caused by* event A. An effective reader does not assume a cause without thinking about other possible causes.

EXAMPLE Read the following paragraph. Underline the logical fallacy of *false cause.*

¹Haley's family moved from the small town in which she was born and had lived her entire 16 years to a large city. ²At first, the separation from her lifelong friends caused her to feel lonely and depressed. ³Eventually she made new friends. ⁴They were very different from any friends she had before. ⁵They wore body art in the form of tattoos and piercings, and they loved heavy metal music. ⁶Around the same time, her parents noticed that Haley was drinking alcohol frequently and heavily. ⁷Her parents blamed her new bad habits on her new friends and forbade Haley to see them anymore.

EXPLANATION Haley's parents jumped to a false conclusion based on a false cause in sentence 7. Because Haley made new friends around the same time they noticed her drinking habits, her parents blamed her new friends. Instead, they should consider other explanations. Perhaps Haley is still depressed and is using alcohol as a means of self-medication. Or maybe Haley began drinking long before they moved, but her parents just now noticed the behavior.

PRACTICE 6

Identify the fallacy in each of the following items. Write **A** if the sentence states a false cause, **B** if it makes a false comparison, or **C** if it employs the either-or fallacy.

_____ **1.** A true patriot serves in the military.

_____ **2.** Animals deserve the same legal rights as humans.

_____ **3.** I shouldn't have gone to bed with my hair wet; now I have a cold.

_____ **4.** If you don't vote, you have no right to complain.

_____ **5.** Corbin smoked marijuana before he became addicted to heroin. Marijuana use leads to addiction to hard drugs.

_____ **6.** Which logical fallacy does this World War II poster use?
a. false cause
b. false comparison
c. either-or

Inadequate Arguments: Propaganda Techniques

Card Stacking

Card stacking omits factual details in order to misrepresent a product, idea, or cause. Card stacking intentionally gives only part of the truth. For example, a commercial for a snack food labels the snack "low in fat," which suggests that it is healthier and lower in calories than a product that is not low in fat. However, the commercial does not mention that the snack is loaded with sugar and calories.

EXAMPLE Read the following paragraph and the list of details used to create the paragraph. Place a check beside the details that were omitted by *card stacking*.

BriteTeeth

[1]BriteTeeth will turn yellow teeth into a dazzling smile. [2]Recent research revealed that 9 out of 10 people who used BriteTeeth had noticeably

whiter teeth. ³Apply BriteTeeth to your teeth every night before you go to sleep. ⁴Then in the morning, brush your teeth as you normally do. ⁵Results should be apparent in two applications.

Omitted Details:

_____ BriteTeeth is made of a special mix of baking soda and carbamide peroxide.

_____ BriteTeeth has been used by more than 300,000 people.

_____ BriteTeeth has a temporary effect and must be used on a daily basis.

_____ BriteTeeth was linked in the research to softer teeth and higher rates of tooth decay.

EXPLANATION The detail that should not have been left out but was omitted as a method of card stacking is the last detail in the list: *BriteTeeth was linked in the research to softer teeth and higher rates of tooth decay.* Consumers who are truly concerned about their teeth will not want a product that is likely to cause softening and tooth decay.

Transfer

Transfer creates an association between a product, idea, or cause with a symbol or image that has positive or negative values. This technique carries the strong feelings we may have for something over to something else.

Symbols stir strong emotions, opinions, or loyalties. For example, a cross represents the Christian faith; a flag represents a nation; a white lab coat represents science and medicine; and a beautiful woman or a handsome man represents acceptance, success, or sex appeal. Politicians and advertisers use symbols like these to win our support. For example, a political candidate may end a speech with a prayer or the phrase "God bless America," to suggest that God approves of the speech. Another example of transfer is the television spokesperson who wears a white lab coat and quotes studies about the health product she is advertising.

Transfers can also be negative. For example, a skull and crossbones together serve as a symbol for death. Therefore, placing a skull and crossbones on a bottle transfers the dangers of death to the contents of the bottle.

EXAMPLE Read the following paragraph. Underline the irrelevant details that use *transfer*.

Governor Edith Public

1Governor Edith Public, who is appearing at a campaign rally in her bid for reelection, says, "Let me begin by saying thank you to the president of the United States for being here today. **2**Your support is deeply appreciated, particularly now that your numbers in the public opinion polls are soaring again." **3**The president, the governor, and the audience laugh good-naturedly. **4**"Good people," the governor continues, "examine my record. **5**Like the president, I have vetoed every bill that attempted to raise your taxes. **6**At the same time, I have carried out new legislation designed to lower the rising cost of living and still provide good health care."

EXPLANATION Governor Public opens her remarks with a statement that creates a strong link between the president of the United States and her campaign. The weight, authority, and grandeur of the presidency are carried in the physical presence of the president. Thus his mere appearance transforms any occasion into a powerful event. However, Governor Public's thank-you to the president lays claim to his personal and official support. The phrase "particularly now that your numbers in the public opinion polls are soaring again" combines band-wagon appeal with transfer by suggesting that many people in a poll support the president. If many support the president and the governor has the same values as the president, then many support the governor as well. Governor Public uses transfer again when she says, "Like the president," in sentence 5.

Glittering Generalities

Glittering generalities offer general positive statements that cannot be verified. A glittering generality is the opposite of name-calling. Often words of virtue and high ideals are used, and the details are inadequate to support the claim. For example, words like *truth, freedom, peace*, and *honor* suggest shining ideals and appeal to feelings of love, courage, and goodness.

EXAMPLE Read the following paragraph. Underline the irrelevant details that use *glittering generalities*.

A Vote for Education

1A candidate for political office has been asked about her views on education. **2**She responds, "Our democracy is based on the rights of all individuals to be educated. **3**The ability to read and write allows citizens to express their views to those who represent them in government. **4**A society that is uneducated is less likely to enjoy the right to pursue happiness and is less able to protect hard-won freedoms. [5]Research indicates that those with at least a two-year college education are better able to make a good living and pay taxes. [6]And I applaud those teachers who hold their students to standards of moral and academic excellence. [7]I propose that we raise the beginning salaries of teachers and limit class size."

EXPLANATION Most of the glittering generalities used by the candidate call to mind American virtues. Sentence 2 includes *democracy* and *rights.* Sentence 4 includes *right to pursue happiness,* which is a paraphrase from the U.S. Constitution, and *freedoms.* Sentence 6 includes *applaud* which is a glittering generality that expresses a feeling, not an action, and *standards of moral and academic excellence.* These are all noble ideals that few people would argue against; however, they do not add any substance to her ideas. Read the paragraph with the glittering generalities removed.

A Vote for Education

A candidate for political office has been asked about her views on education. She responds, "The ability to read and write allows citizens to express their views to those who represent them in government. Research indicates that those with at least a two-year college education are better able to make a living and pay taxes. I propose that we raise the beginning salaries of teachers and limit class size."

PRACTICE 7

For **1–4**, label each of the following items according to the propaganda techniques they employ:

    A. transfer   C. card stacking
    B. glittering generality

_____ **1.** A candidate campaigning to be a United States senator is photographed in front of an American flag with a group of decorated soldiers who served in Afghanistan.

_____ **2.** A new dawn is breaking in America. Fight for freedom. Cast your vote. A vote for me is a vote for liberty.

_____ **3.** Health care is a human right.

_____ **4.** A law firm looking for clients hires actors for a series of television commercials. The male and female actors dress and behave as middle class workers who are worried about what to do if they are injured in a car accident or on the job. In a typical commercial, the actor is driving a car and talking to the camera as if talking to a passenger in the car, using the following script: "An auto accident can change your life in an instant. Suddenly, you may find yourself disabled, in pain, and out of work. Get the help you need and deserve. Call today. We're on your side."

_____ **5.** Identify the detail from this list of details that was **omitted** from the paragraph for purposes of card stacking.

Clinical tests prove that AcuClear stops acne breakouts for 8 out of 10 women. Made with green tea oil and aloe to sooth irritated skin, AcuClear kills bacteria and soothes irritated skin.

    a. The clinical tests only included 40 women, and over 50% of these women complained of redness and skin peeling.

    b. AcuClear is made up of all natural products.

    c. AcuClear is carried in drugstores nationwide.

VISUAL VOCABULARY

The demonstrator uses the propaganda technique known as

_____.

  a. transfer.
  b. glittering generality.
  c. card stacking.

▶ An anti-war demonstrator protests in Buenos Aires, March 21, 2003.

Textbook Skills **Examining Biased Arguments**

Textbooks strive to present information in a factual, objective manner with relevant and adequate support, in keeping with their purpose to inform. However, textbook authors may choose to present biased arguments for your examination. As an effective reader, you are expected to evaluate the nature of the biased argument and the author's purpose for including the biased argument.

EXAMPLE The following passage appears in a college mass communication textbook. It serves as an introduction for the chapter "Radio." As you read the passage, underline biased information. After you read, answer the questions.

Textbook
Skills

Limbaugh Speaks: His Listeners Act

[1]His program is unabashedly biased. [2]He sneers at liberals as "dittoheads" and worse. [3]He calls other members of the media liars. [4]He brags about himself on the air.

[5]Millions of his fans love it. [6]They devour his liberal-bashing and accept his statements as political gospel.

[7]That is Rush Limbaugh, the glib commentator who has been called the "800 pound gorilla of talk radio." [8]He is heard on more than 600 radio stations.

[9]Limbaugh's influence on his listeners is enormous. [10]Claiming that the media were distorting the Republican plan in Congress to transfer the federal school lunch program to the states, he urged listeners to call their newspapers, the national networks, and the news magazines to protest.

[11]"All you say is, 'Stop lying about the school lunch program' and hang up," he told them.

[12]Thousands from coast to coast immediately did so, many using his exact words. [13]Typically, Cable News Network in Atlanta received more than 300 calls.

[14]Critics of Limbaugh's bombastic style recognize his power but contend that he is preaching to the converted. [15]William Rentschler observed in *Editor & Publisher:* "His program is largely a love feast of like-minded listeners massaging the giant ego of their hero."

—Agee, et al, *Introduction to Mass Communications,* p. 213 © 1997.
Reproduced by permission of Pearson Education, Inc.

_____ **1.** Overall, the tone of the passage is
   a. positive about Rush Limbaugh.
   b. negative about Rush Limbaugh.
   c. neutral toward Rush Limbaugh.

_____ **2.** The primary purpose of the passage is
   a. to encourage readers to condemn Rush Limbaugh.
   b. to inform the reader about the power of radio, using Rush Limbaugh as an example.
   c. to persuade readers to listen to Rush Limbaugh by giving entertaining details about his show.

_____ **3.** In sentence 2, Rush Limbaugh uses the propaganda technique
     a. name-calling.   c. bandwagon.
     b. testimonial.   d. false cause.

_____ **4.** The words "gospel," "preaching," and "converted" are examples of the fallacy
     a. begging the question.   c. false comparison.
     b. personal attacks.   d. straw man.

_____ **5.** Sentences 11–13 illustrate the effect of the propaganda technique
     a. card stacking.   c. plain folks.
     b. bandwagon.   d. testimonial.

EXPLANATION The biased information includes the following words: _unabashedly, sneers, liberals, "dittoheads," liars, brags, devour, liberal-bashing, gospel, glib, 800 pound gorilla, enormous, distorting, bombastic, preaching, converted, love feast,_ and _giant ego._

1. This list of biased words indicates the negative tone (b) used in the discussion about Rush Limbaugh.

2. The primary purpose of the passage is (b) to inform the reader about the power of radio by using Rush Limbaugh as an example. As a well-known and controversial radio talk show host, Rush Limbaugh is an excellent example with which to open a chapter about radio and its influence on society. The authors' purpose was not to condemn or endorse Rush Limbaugh, but to make a point about the power of radio. Radio is a medium of mass communication, and Rush Limbaugh uses propaganda and fallacies in logical thought successfully in his daily broadcast. The authors of this mass communication textbook highlight the powerful relationship between radio and persuasion by using Rush Limbaugh as an example.

3. In sentence 2, Rush Limbaugh uses the propaganda technique (a) name-calling.

4. The words "gospel," "preaching," and "converted" are examples of the fallacy (c) false comparison. These words compare Limbaugh and his listeners to a religious leader and followers.

5. Sentences 11–13 illustrate the effect of the propaganda technique (b) bandwagon. Rush Limbaugh has earned the loyalty of a large audience that he can get to jump on the bandwagon of his choice.

PRACTICE 8

The following passage appears in a college history textbook. As you read the passage, underline biased words. After you read, answer the questions.

Textbook Skills

"Uncle Tom's Cabin"

[1]Tremendously important in increasing sectional tensions and bringing home the evils of slavery to still more people in the North was Harriet Beecher Stowe's novel *Uncle Tom's Cabin* (1852). [2]Stowe was neither a professional writer nor an abolitionist, and she had almost no firsthand knowledge of slavery. [3]But her conscience had been roused by the Fugitive Slave Act. [4]In gathering material for the book, she depended heavily on abolitionist writers, many of whom she knew. [5]She dashed it off quickly; as she later recalled, it seemed to write itself. [6]Nevertheless, *Uncle Tom's Cabin* was an enormous success: 10,000 copies were sold in a week; 300,000 in a year. [7]It was translated into dozens of languages. [8]Dramatized versions were staged in countries throughout the world.

[9]Harriet Beecher Stowe was hardly a distinguished writer; it was her approach to the subject that explains the book's success. [10]Her tale of the pious, patient slave Uncle Tom, the saintly white child Eva, and the callous slave driver Simon Legree appealed to an audience far wider than that reached by the abolitionists. [11]She avoided the self-righteous, accusatory tone of most abolitionist tracts and did not seek to convert readers to belief in racial equality. [12]Many of her southern white characters were fine, sensitive people, while the cruel Simon Legree was a transplanted Connecticut Yankee. [13]There were many heart-rending scenes of pain, self-sacrifice, and heroism. [14]The story proved especially effective on the stage: The slave Eliza crossing the frozen Ohio River to freedom, the death of Little Eva, Eva and Tom ascending to Heaven—these scenes left audiences in tears.

[15]Southern critics pointed out, correctly enough, that Stowe's picture of plantation life was distorted, her slaves atypical. [16]They called her a "coarse, ugly, long-tongued woman" and accused her of trying to "awaken rancorous hatred and malignant jealousies" that would undermine national unity. [17]Most Northerners, having little basis on which to judge the accuracy of the book, tended to discount southern criticism as biased. [18]In any case, *Uncle Tom's Cabin* raised questions that transcended the issue of accuracy. [19]Did it matter if every slave was not as kindly as Uncle Tom, as determined as George Harris? [20]What if only one white master was as evil as Simon Legree? [21]No earlier white American writer had looked at slaves as people.

[22]*Uncle Tom's Cabin* touched the hearts of millions. [23]Some became abolitionists; others, still hesitating to step forward, asked themselves as they put the book down: Is slavery just?

> —Garraty/Carnes, *American Nation Single Volume Edition,*
> Text Excerpt from pp. 378–379 © 2000 Pearson Education,
> Inc. Reproduced by permission of Pearson Education, Inc.

_____ **1.** Overall the tone of the passage
   a. is positive about *Uncle Tom's Cabin.*
   b. is negative about *Uncle Tom's Cabin.*
   c. remains neutral toward *Uncle Tom's Cabin.*

_____ **2.** The author's purpose is
   a. to argue against the injustices of slavery.
   b. to inform the reader about the importance of *Uncle Tom's Cabin.*
   c. to delight the reader by sharing the success of a nineteenth-century woman writer.

_____ **3.** The "heart-rending scenes of pain, self-sacrifice, and heroism" included in *Uncle Tom's Cabin* were most likely examples of the propaganda technique
   a. bandwagon.   c. transfer.
   b. testimonials.   d. name-calling.

_____ **4.** In sentence 16, Stowe's critics use the propaganda technique
   a. bandwagon.   c. transfer.
   b. testimonials.   d. name-calling.

APPLICATIONS

Application 1

Read the following mock advertisement for a weight loss system. Label each sentence using one of the following letters (some answers may be used more than once):

a. unbiased statement   e. transfer

b. bandwagon   f. testimonial

c. plain folks   g. glittering generality

d. false cause   h. false comparison

The Beauty of LeanBody

[1]Join the 3.1 million people who are already using LeanBody. [2]In just seven days you can lose from four to fourteen inches guaranteed with

the LeanBody System. [3]You can have a body as beautiful as Jennifer Aniston, Halle Berry, or Jennifer Lopez. [4]LeanBody introduces a new technique known as power breathing. [5]LeanBody's specially designed power breathing supercharges your blood with fat-burning oxygen causing you to lose inches fast. [6]With power breathing, your body acts like a fat-burning furnace. [7]Whether you are a busy homemaker, on-the-go teenager, harried office worker, or retired senior citizen, LeanBody is for you. [8]The LeanBody workout takes only minutes a day and can be performed sitting down. [9]You can easily attain a healthy, toned body with LeanBody and still enjoy your favorite foods. [10]Just listen to what superstar Charlene Lovely has to say about LeanBody: "With LeanBody I lost 45 pounds and 3 dress sizes; LeanBody saved my career."

_____ **1.** Sentence 1   _____ **6.** Sentence 6

_____ **2.** Sentence 2   _____ **7.** Sentence 7

_____ **3.** Sentence 3   _____ **8.** Sentence 8

_____ **4.** Sentence 4   _____ **9.** Sentence 9

_____ **5.** Sentence 5   _____ **10.** Sentence 10

Application 2

Study the following tobacco advertisement from the nineteenth century.

_____ **1.** Which of the following propaganda techniques is used in the advertisement?
a. testimonial
b. plain folks
c. transfer

2. Write a caption for the advertisement that uses a propaganda technique.

_____

_____

_____

REVIEW TEST 1

Biased Arguments

Read the following sets of ideas. Write **UB** if the statement is unbiased, or **B** if the idea is a biased argument.

_____ **1.** Joe E. Jones, nationally known film critic, writes, "*UP in The Air*, starring George Clooney, is a must-see movie. Clearly Clooney's best performance of his career thus far."

_____ **2.** Orange juice contains potassium and vitamins A and C, and it lowers blood pressure.

_____ **3.** A study released by the National Academy on an Aging Society found that care for people with Alzheimer's Disease can be costly. The average cost for a person with Alzheimer's who is still living at home is $12,572 a year.

_____ **4.** Obviously a politician cannot wear his heart on his sleeve when he is working for the success of his country. Only hypocrites and innocent dreamers would demand that he speak openly about his plans. Just as a businessman does not divulge his secrets to his rival, so also in politics, with even greater justification, much must remain a secret.

> —Lehmann, Ernst Herbert. "How They Lie." ©1939 by Nibelungen-Verlag, GmbH., Berlin W9 Preliminary translation by Katherine Lynch. Final page copyright ©2000 by Randall L. Bytwerk. http://www.calvin.edu/academic/cas/gpa/lugen0.htm

_____ **5.** A college sophomore says to her parents, "I can't believe you won't let me go to Cancun for spring break. Everyone I know is going. Not only do their parents let them go, but their parents pay for the trip, too. At least I am willing to pay my own expenses."

REVIEW TEST 2

Biased Arguments: Fallacies in Logical Thought and Propaganda Techniques

Read the following article written by journalist Anna Quindlen for *Newsweek* magazine. Answer the questions that follow.

Follow the Leader

[1]By the time the current political cycle is over, the term "populist" will have become a buzzword so misused and abused that it will be leached of all real meaning. [2]The dictionary definitions refer to the agrarian political party of the late 19th century, then segue into the use of the term that modern politicians have learned to embrace: "a believer in the rights, wisdom, or virtues of the common people."

[3]But what those people might be trying to say is not always clear. [4]The explanations for the current "populist rage" are almost as various as those legendary blind men feeling different parts of an elephant: big government, big banks, unemployment, and a health-care plan that went (choose one) too far, too fast, not far enough, not fast enough. [5]In fact, the Senate election results in Massachusetts, in which a Republican seized the seat held by Ted Kennedy for almost half a century and threw the Democratic Party into a monumental tizzy, was a classic toss-the-bums-out event, neither specific nor illuminating.

[6]So at the moment the problem in Washington is us, not them, or at least how they try to figure us out. [7]Good luck with that. [8]One poll of former Obama supporters who abandoned the Democrats in Massachusetts showed that 41 percent of those who opposed the health-care plan weren't sure exactly why. [9]If elected officials are supposed to act based on the wisdom of ordinary people, they're going to need ordinary people to be wiser than that.

[10]Social issues are easy: you're either for or against the death penalty, abortion, gay marriage. [11]Economics are complex. [12]Over and over again some Americans say they want lower taxes and smaller government. [13]Yet somehow, in a recurrent bit of magical thinking, they also expect those things that taxes are used to pay for and that government delivers. [14]The result is contradictory: vote down the school-board budget, then complain that Johnny can't read.

[15]Another political buzzword, "productivity," has come to stand for the proposition that you can always do more with less. [16]There's little evidence that that's accurate. [17]And it's hard to believe that even the most zealous tea-party types would shrug philosophically if a bunch of kids died of *E. coli* because we hadn't hired enough food inspectors. [18]The old dictum stands: you get what you pay for.

[19]And, more important, you get what you won't pay for. [20]There's no question that this is a moment in which the United States is poised for one future or another—the end of the American century or a new era of dominance based not on military might but on innovation. [21]A global economy, a technological revolution, an ecosystem in crisis, radically changing

demographics: these are matters that are inextricably linked and that require the long view. [22]When Barack Obama ran on a platform of change, it was not a pledge to tinker day by day, but to transform over time. [23]Chess, not pinball.

[24]If his party's recent reversal of fortune has given the president a jolt that leads him to refocus on the suffering of ordinary people who have lost their jobs and homes, that would be a good thing. [25]But if his administration and Congress expend their energy on knee-jerk reactions to perceived or imagined public sentiment, that will be terrible. [26]Already there is talk of narrowing an all-too-narrow health-care bill. [27]Already Obama is embracing some of those paint-by-numbers policies that politicians trot out when they're doing the populist polka: instituting spending freezes, raising the income ceilings for some tax benefits. [28]Governing by inches.

[29]The Democrats are in danger of learning the wrong lessons from their Massachusetts defeat. [30]After all, they seem to have learned the wrong lessons from their electoral triumph just a little more than a year ago. [31]They are the majority, and they should act like it—boldly, decisively. [32]Let the Republicans filibuster, and be confident that the sight would irritate, then enrage, most of the American people. [33]The president was given a mandate, and he should act like it—boldly, decisively. [34]There is consensus building, and then there is trading away real progress in deference to people whose fondest wish is your own failure.

[35]The campaign that was so tech-savvy needs to discount the most conspicuous change technology has brought to the political arena: the mindless thumbs-up, thumbs-down approach that makes elected officials Christians in a coliseum full of lions. [36]On the blogs and talk TV, the margins are presented as mainstream: thus, the preposterous notion that the president was not born in the U.S.A. morphs into something that sounds far larger, more serious, and more credible called the birther movement. [37]The voice of the people often seems like the voice of he who speaks loudest, and with the most vitriol. [38]Like car horns blaring on a gridlocked street, those sounds should be ignored.

[39]Sometimes the message we send to our politicians is that they should follow us, sometimes that they should lead us, and sometimes that they should try the gymnastic feat of doing both at the same time. [40]Along the way we forget that most of the things that make America great—civil rights, the safety net, Social Security—were pushed through despite their unpopularity. [41]Do we want reaction or vision, someone looking over his shoulder or into the future? [42]Did we elect a change agent as president so that someday we could say, wow, he increased the income cap on the child-care credit?

[43]It may be that finger-to-the-wind politics is so entrenched that the great, or the good, will always be held hostage. [44]If the aftershocks of the Massachusetts election mean that we'll now see innovative plans to create jobs and help lift the financial load from working people, that's great. [45]But if the people who lead us become ever more afraid of their own shadows, afraid to make plans, to take chances, to legislate for the future as well as the present, it will surely mean the slow death of American ingenuity and influence. [46]We are in a transformative moment in history, when the acceptance of the status quo counts as cataclysmic failure. [47]A very smart man once said, "Telling the American people what we think they want to hear instead of telling the American people what they need to hear just won't do." [48]That man was Barack Obama, and that attitude is one reason he got elected. [49]He should stick to that position, and the American people should embrace it.

—Anna Quindlen. "Follow the Leader." *Newsweek*. 29 Jan. 2010. http://www.newsweek.com/id/232833.

_____ **1.** The phrase "a believer in the rights, wisdom, or virtues of the common people" in sentence 2 is an example of
  a. straw man.
  b. begging the question.
  c. false comparison.
  d. glittering generalities.

_____ **2.** The phrase "toss the bums out" in sentence 5 is an example of
  a. straw man.
  b. personal attack.
  c. either-or.
  d. bandwagon.

_____ **3.** Sentence 10 is an example of
  a. card stacking.
  b. personal attack.
  c. false comparison.
  d. bandwagon.

_____ **4.** Sentence 38 is an example of
  a. false comparison.
  b. personal attack.
  c. transfer.
  d. name-calling.

REVIEW TEST 3

Score (number correct) _____ × 25 = _____%

Biased Arguments: Propaganda

Nostalgia Merchants

[1]Why did Reuben Harley think that throwbacks—replicas of old sports jerseys—would catch on?

[2]Call it instinct, street smarts, observing the reactions of others, or whatever you will, he trusted his personal tastes. [3]While making a living doing odd jobs in his West Philly neighborhood, he saved money to buy classic jerseys of legendary players such as Julius Irving, Nolan Ryan, and Jackie Robinson, from century-old Mitchell & Ness's retail store. [4]When people would ask where he got the Hank Aaron jersey he was wearing, the 300-pound-plus Reuben wouldn't tell them. [5]He wanted them all as his own. [6]"But just seeing the cat's reaction, I knew this could really catch on," he says. [7]And so it began for this high school graduate who had even started his own catering business, getting up at 3:00 A.M. to cook chicken, lasagna, and desserts in his grandmother's kitchen before eventually teaming up with Peter Capolino. [8]Capolino was the then 58-year-old owner of Mitchell & Ness Nostalgia Company (M&N). [9]Harley went to Capolino and offered to help him sell 1950s baseball jerseys to inner-city youths. [10]Together, in just two years' time they changed M&N (www. mitchellandness.com) into the nation's best-known marketer of clothing for urban teen African-Americans. [11]Sales jumped from $2.8 million in 2000 to $25 million in 2002, then to an estimated $40 million in 2003. [12]And there's no doubting who the prime mover is for M&N's success: "I consider it a miracle that Reuben fell into my lap. [13]He deserves all the credit," says Capolino.

[14]Reuben started by focusing on celebrities—rappers and pro athletes—who could afford the $250 to $470 price tag for these intricately stitched designs with authentic team colors. [15]He began meeting them by going uninvited to their parties in New York and Philadelphia nightclubs. [16]He soon became a trusted acquaintance with his charming and unassuming personality. [17]When shown samples of M&N's jerseys, hip-hop great Sean (P. Diddy) Combs immediately bought them, as did rapper Fabulous, whose album *Street Dreams* contains a track named "Throwback," dedicated to M&N. [18]Building on these initial successes, Harley—now M&N's new marketing director—targeted major music and sporting events. [19]He also targeted the celebrity consumers performing at them. [20]During the NBA All-Star weekend, for example, Rap star Eve wore an oversized Michael Jordon Chicago Bulls Jersey. [21]Throughout Super Bowl week, then-Tampa Bay football star Warren Sapp wore M&N throwbacks, including a bright green 1980s Philadelphia Eagles model, in various public appearances. [22]Indiana Pacers basketball star Jermaine O'Neal, who owns 150 throwbacks, says, "Acquiring the hottest model is a competitive sport among teammates." [23]The jerseys are so popular you'll find entertainment stars wearing them most any day in action movies, on MTV, and Black Entertainment Television.

Why all the popularity?

[24]"The materials, the colors are just a little different, a little special," says rapper Fabulous. [25]"If I wear a Dr. J jersey at a show in Philly or a Jerry West at a joint in L.A., I know the crowd will go crazy." [26]Adds rap star Eve, "Reuben's just a cool guy, and he delivers what you need on time." [27]With so much brand visibility, then, it's little wonder that suburban kids and adults of all races are eagerly imitating what Reuben Harley and Peter Capolino started a few short years ago in inner city Philadelphia. [28]Mitchell & Ness was once the longtime maker of tennis and golf equipment. [29]It now has been turned into the industry's most imitated manufacturer and marketer of authentic old sports jerseys.

Is Nostalgia Just a Fad?

[30]Reuben Harley was 17 years old in 1991 when he bought his first throwback—a 1983 Andre Thornton Cleveland Indians jersey—at Mitchell & Ness (M&N), a tiny retail shop with few young black customers in city-center Philadelphia. [31]In 2001, while watching an Outcast music video, Big Rube realized he owned (bought over the years on layaway) the same throwback jerseys the performers were wearing. [32]Soon thereafter, an Oprah Winfrey TV show about "following your dreams" inspired him to pursue selling, not just buying, vintage jerseys. [33]In joining Peter Capolino at M&N, Reuben came on board for $500 a month and received one of every jersey in the M&N line. [34]Today, most of M&N's jerseys are wholesaled to some 220 retailers around the country.

[35]The potential market as seen by Reuben was worlds apart from Capolino's pre-2001 vision for M&N. [36]Reuben envisioned an urban, largely African-American youth segment that idolizes basketball players with baggy shorts and bigger brightly colored jerseys with striking patterns in double-knits and mesh. [37]Capolino, in contrast, was aiming for middle-aged collectors of sports items, mostly from its retro-baseball line with body-hugging gray flannels. [38]At an age in life when established businesspeople might take a safer path, Capolino made a gutsy call in deciding to go along with Reuben. [39]"It's an all-sport thing, but guys identify with basketball players more than anybody," says Harley. [40]Now basketball, instead of baseball, accounts for the largest share of M&N's business.

[41]Because it holds exclusive licenses from the NFL, Major League Baseball, the National Basketball Association, and the National Hockey League, M&N can reproduce authentic jerseys that have been out of circulation for at least five years. [42]The fabric, the stitching, and the lettering are all accurate duplicates of the originals the players wore years ago.

⁴³Therein, according to Reuben, lies the staying power of M&N's throw-backs. ⁴⁴"This isn't a fad. ⁴⁵These uniforms are the history of sports. ⁴⁶Styles come and go, but you can't change the '79 Magic Johnson jersey." ⁴⁷That's why they captured an enthusiastic audience, even at such hefty prices as $325 for a 1979 Willie Stargell Pirates, $450 for the 1963 Lance Alworth Chargers, $300 for the 1983–84 Sidney Moncrief Bucks, and $250 for the 1966–67 Dave Bing Pistons.

⁴⁸Today, Harley is vice president of marketing with a lofty salary and lots of size XXXXL jerseys. ⁴⁹His duties include everything from hitting the road as traveling salesman to serving as M&N's public face to clothes design-ers. ⁵⁰With many of his clients, the conversations aren't just about the latest in jerseys but also personal matters and plain talk. ⁵¹And he takes time to be there to help. ⁵²Backstage when P. Diddy hosted ABC's American Music Awards, Reuben took charge of the star's costume changes during commer-cial breaks. ⁵³Eleven different jerseys were worn throughout the perfor-mance, including a '73 George McGinnis Pacers and a '74 Hank Aaron Braves. ⁵⁴"Shaq called the next day; he wanted every piece that Puff wore," says Harley. ⁵⁵The success in his personal approach for marketing is aided by encouragement from the clients he serves. ⁵⁶In his album *Street Dreams*, Fabulous yells out a message to the duo at M&N: "Rube, tell Pete to keep it comin'."

—Adapted from Griffin & Ebert, *Business*,
8th ed., pp. 351–352, 375.

_____ **1.** Sentences 20 and 21 are examples of
    a. bandwagon.   c. testimonials.
    b. transfer.   d. glittering generalities.

_____ **2.** Sentences 24–26 are examples of
    a. bandwagon.   c. testimonials.
    b. transfer.   d. glittering generalities.

_____ **3.** The phrase "follow your dreams" in sentence 32 is an example of
    a. card stacking.   c. glittering generalities.
    b. bandwagon.   d. bandwagon.

_____ **4.** Sentence 39 is an example of
    a. transfer.   c. testimonial.
    b. glittering generalities.   d. bandwagon.

WHAT DO YOU THINK?

Have you ever thought about starting your own business or creating a product to sell? Assume you are an entrepreneur who is starting up your own business or product line. Also assume some investors are interested in your ideas and have asked you to write up a proposal for their consideration. Write a one-page description of your business or product. Use persuasion techniques to gain support for your ideas.

REVIEW TEST 4

Score (number correct) _____ × 10 = _____%

Advanced Argument

Before you read, skim the following speech given by Mrs. Corinne Roosevelt Robinson. The sister of President Theodore Roosevelt, she supported the Republican ticket of Senator Harding and Governor Coolidge in the 1920 presidential election. Answer the Before Reading questions. Then, read the passage and answer the After Reading questions.

Safeguard America!

Vocabulary Preview

efficiency (2): skill, competence

prestige (11): status, reputation

deplorable (11): dreadful, shameful

resolution (17): motion, decision

sentinel (18): guard, lookout

[1]I am behind Senator Harding and Governor Coolidge for President and Vice-President of the United States for two reasons. [2]First, because they are the nominees of the Republican party, and secondly because I believe them to be 100% American, of true patriotism, who have not failed to show marked **efficiency** and ability in public office. [3]I am one who believes that the Republican party and the Democratic party have different ideas. [4]And I believe that the issues of the two parties are not as blurred and as **indistinguishable** as is sometimes said to be the case. [5]The Republican party is the party of concrete nationalism, as opposed to the hazy internationalism of the Democratic party. [6]The Republican party preached preparedness. [7][And] the Democratic party, influenced by its President, mind you I say the President of the Democratic party and not of the whole United States, was keeping us out of war. [8]Keeping us out of war until he was re-elected President.

[9]We need the Republican party in office during the hard days to come, when there must be the [up-building] and rebuilding of our nation. [10]We need preparedness for days of peace and against the always possible

dangers of war. [11]Shall we choose again the party which blindly turns from the right, and in so doing, dragged down the **prestige** of America and brought on our nation unbearable criticism and **deplorable** confusion?

[12]Fellow citizens, we are at the turning of the ways. [13]Theodore Roosevelt said in October, 1916, "I demand at this election that each citizen shall think of America first." [14]Who now does not regret that the country did not respond to that demand? [15]Let us, the Republican party, again make this demand.

[16]Senator Harding stood for a League of Nations with strong, Americanizing reservations, as Theodore Roosevelt did. [17]He also stood with the Senate in passing the **resolution** which would have enabled Theodore Roosevelt to lead a division into France when the morale of France and of America was at a low ebb. [18]And Senator Harding, in making the memorial address on Theodore Roosevelt before the Ohio Joint Legislative Assembly in January, 1919, said, "Colonel Roosevelt was the great patriotic **sentinel**, pacing the parapets of the republic, alert to danger and every menace, and in love with duty and service, and always unafraid."

[19]Those words of our presidential nominee, in admiration of my great brother, are almost a promise of what his own attitude will be. [20]Let us stand behind him, looking forward and onward as Theodore Roosevelt would have done. [21]And let us try with might and main to put our beloved country in the safe keeping of Warren Harding and Calvin Coolidge.

> —Corinne Roosevelt Robinson. "Safeguard America." *American Leaders Speak: Recordings from World War I and the 1920 Election, 1918–1920.* American Memory. Library of Congress. 20 August 2004.

Before Reading

Vocabulary

_____ **1.** What is the best meaning of the word **indistinguishable** in sentence 4?

  a. alike   c. different
  b. vague   d. clear

Tone and Purpose

_____ **2.** The author's tone and purpose is
  a. to entertain with inspiring details.
  b. to inform with objective evidence.
  c. to persuade with praise and warnings.

After Reading

Central Idea

_____ **3.** Which sentence states the author's central idea?
a. sentence 1
c. sentence 3
b. sentence 8
d. sentence 20

Supporting Details

_____ **4.** Who said " . . . at this election . . . each citizen shall think of America first"?
a. Calvin Coolidge
c. the President of the Democratic party
b. Senator Harding
d. Theodore Roosevelt

Thought Patterns

_____ **5.** The relationship of ideas within sentence 5 is
a. time order.
c. contrast.
b. cause and effect.
d. generalization and example.

Fact and Opinion

_____ **6.** Overall this passage relies on
a. fact.
b. opinion.
c. fact and opinion.

Inferences

_____ **7.** Based on the details in the passage, which of the following is a valid inference?
a. Theodore Roosevelt is President of the United States at the time this speech is given.
b. Theodore Roosevelt supported Senator Harding and Governor Coolidge for President and Vice President of the United States.
c. Theodore Roosevelt died before January 1919.
d. Theodore Roosevelt was a popular president within both the Republican and Democratic parties.

Argument

_____ **8.** In sentences 6 and 7, the author uses the fallacy of
a. begging the question.
c. personal attack.
b. straw man.
d. false cause.

_____ **9.** Paragraph 5 (sentences 16–18) uses the propaganda technique of
  a. bandwagon.   c. testimonial.
  b. transfer.   d. glittering generalities.

_____ **10.** In his description of Theodore Roosevelt (sentence 18), Senator Harding uses
  a. glittering generalities. c. name-calling.
  b. plain folks.   d. bandwagon.

WHAT DO YOU THINK?

What do you think are the most important character traits a person should possess to be an effective President of the United States? Assume this is an election year for a new President of the United States. Write a letter to the editor of your local newspaper or for the "My Turn" column in *Newsweek* magazine. In your letter, write a description of the type of person you would like to see elected as President. Feel free to nominate a candidate for your reader's consideration, and explain how your nomination fits your description of an ideal president.

After Reading About Advanced Argument: Persuasive Techniques

Before you move on to the Mastery Tests on advanced argument, take time to reflect on your learning and performance by answering the following questions. Write your answers in your notebook.

- How has my knowledge base or prior knowledge about advanced argument, persuasive techniques changed?

- Based on my studies, how do I think I will perform on the Mastery Test(s)? Why do I think my scores will be above average, average, or below average?

- Would I recommend this chapter to other students who want to learn more about advanced argument and persuasive techniques? Why or why not?

Test your understanding of what you have learned about advanced argument: persuasive techniques by completing the Chapter 13 Review Card in the insert near the end of the text.

CONNECT TO PEARSON **myreadinglab**

To check your progress in meeting Chapter 13's learning outcomes, log in to **www.myreadinglab**, and try the following activities.

- The "Critical Thinking" section of MyReadingLab gives additional information about advanced argument and persuasive techniques. The section provides an overview, model, practices, and tests. To access this resource, click on the "Study Plan" tab. Then click on "Critical Thinking." Then click on the following links as needed: "Overview," "Model," "Critical Thinking: Facts and Opinions (Flash Animation)," "Practice," and "Test."

- The "Study Skills Website" section of MyReadingLab also gives additional information about advanced argument and persuasive techniques. To access these resources, go to the "Other Sources" box on the home page of MyReadingLab. Click on "Study Skills Website." Then scroll down the page to the heading "Life Skills" and click on "Critical Thinking." Explore each of the links on the bar on the left side of the page.

- To measure your mastery of the content in this chapter, complete the tests in the "Critical Thinking" section and click on Gradebook to find your results.

Write the letter of the fallacy used in each of the following items.

_____ **1.** Love America or leave it.
    a. begging the question   c. personal attack
    b. either-or   d. straw man

_____ **2.** The senator doesn't care about the environment because it doesn't win him any votes to care.
    a. false cause   c. begging the question
    b. either-or   d. personal attack

_____ **3.** Being in school is like being in a concentration camp.
    a. false comparison   c. begging the question
    b. straw man   d. false cause

_____ **4.** I have won the football lottery at work three times. Every time I won, my boyfriend and I had a fight the night before. I am going to pick a fight with him tonight because I want to win the lottery tomorrow.
    a. straw man   c. false cause
    b. either-or   d. personal attack

_____ **5.** The government should continue research in the area of human cloning. Just as space research has brought us useful byproducts such as Teflon, research in human cloning will lead to unexpected discoveries that will benefit humanity.
    a. false comparison   c. straw man
    b. begging the question   d. false cause

_____ **6.** The candidate for city commission says, "We need lower taxes because the current taxes are too high."
    a. straw man   c. begging the question
    b. personal attack   d. either-or

_____ **7.** I touched a toad. Now I have a wart.
    a. false cause   c. either-or
    b. straw man   d. personal attack

_____ **8.** Speaker 1: Our prisons are overcrowded, and we don't have the money to build additional prisons. We need to find other solutions. Many of those in prison for lesser, nonviolent crimes could be placed on house arrest and equipped with technology that tracks their whereabouts.

Speaker 2: My opponent wants to set prisoners free to live in the comfort of their own homes.

a. begging the question   c. personal attack
b. false comparison   d. straw man

_____ **9.** The charges against the police for brutality are untrue because police are officers of the law.

a. straw man   c. personal attack
b. begging the question   d. either-or

_____ **10.** I could never date Samantha; she looks like a horse.

a. personal attack   c. straw man
b. false cause   d. either-or

Summary of Key Concepts of a Reading System for Effective Readers

LEARNING OUTCOME
① ② ③ ⑤
⑧

Assess your comprehension of prior knowledge and the reading process.

- Comprehension is _____.
- Prior knowledge is, _____
  _____.
- Use prior knowledge to _____:
  - _____ by asking "What do I already know about this topic?"
  - Check _____ against your prior knowledge by asking, "Does this make sense based on what I know?"
  - Check for _____ in your knowledge base by asking, "What did I learn?"
- The reading process has three phases: _____
  _____.
- SQ3R, an acronym for a reading process, stands for _____
  _____. SQ3R activates prior knowledge and offers strategies for each phase of the reading process:
  - Before Reading, _____: Skim _____
    _____. Ask questions such as _____
    _____
  - During Reading, _____ key words and ideas. Repair confusion. Reread.
  - After Reading, Recite and Review: Recall _____. Summarize. Answer questions such as _____

Test Your Comprehension of a Reading System for Effective Readers

Respond to the following questions and prompts.

LEARNING
OUTCOME
1 **8**

In your own words, what is prior knowledge? _____

_____

LEARNING
OUTCOME
3

Create a graph or draw a picture to illustrate SQ3R.

LEARNING
OUTCOME
3 **4** **6** **7**
8

Describe your reading process. How did you read before your studied this chapter? Will you change your reading process? If so, how? If not, why not?_____

_____

_____

_____

_____

2 Chapter Review

Summary of Key Concepts of Vocabulary and Dictionary Skills

LEARNING
OUTCOME
① ② ④

Assess your comprehension of vocabulary and dictionary skills.

- **Vocabulary** is _____ .
- Four of the most common types of context clues are as follows:
    - A **synonym** is _____
      _____ .
    - An **antonym** is a _____ .
    - The **general context** clue requires you read _____
      _____ .
    - **Example** clues are often introduced with _____
      _____ .
- The three basic word parts are as follows:
    - The _____ , the main part of the word.
    - The _____ , the group of letters with a specific meaning
      added to the beginning of word to make a new word.
    - The _____ , the group of letters with a specific meaning
      added to the end of a word to make a new word.
- A dictionary contains the following information:
    - _____ at the top of the page
    - _____ indicating the sounds of consonants and vowels
      of a word
    - _____ indicating the function of a word
    - _____ indicating the history of the word
- Each subject matter has its own _____ .

2-1

Test Your Comprehension of Vocabulary and Dictionary Skills

Respond to the following questions and prompts.

LEARNING OUTCOME
1 **8**

In your own words, what is vocabulary? Identify the most helpful skill you have learned. _____

_____

_____

LEARNING OUTCOME
2 **3** **4**
6 **9**

Demonstrate your use of context clues. Use the headings below and create a chart based on the four types of context clues. Then, complete the chart with new words you have come across recently as you read for this class, another class, or any reading situation.

Type of Clue	New Word	Meaning of Word	Source Sentence of Word

LEARNING OUTCOME
3 **5** **6**
7 **9**

Go to the vocabulary preview in Review Test 4 on page 82. Choose a word or set of words to learn. Then, demonstrate your ability to decode the meaning of words using word parts. Use the model of a psychology word web below to create your own web of words linked by word parts. Use a family of words you have come across recently as you read for this class, another class, or any reading situation.

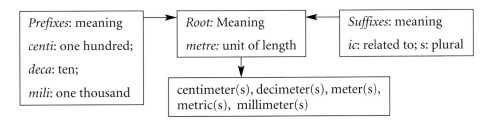

Prefixes: meaning
centi: one hundred;
deca: ten;
mili: one thousand

Root: Meaning
metre: unit of length

Suffixes: meaning
ic: related to; *s*: plural

centimeter(s), decimeter(s), meter(s), metric(s), millimeter(s)

LEARNING OUTCOME
3 **5** **6**
7 **9**

Demonstrate your use of the dictionary. Use the headings below and create a chart based on information found in a dictionary. Then, complete the chart with new words you have come across recently as you read for this class, another class, or any reading situation.

Word	Etymology	Part of Speech	Definition	Source Sentence of Word

3 Chapter Review

Summary of Key Concepts of Stated Main Ideas

LEARNING OUTCOME 1 3 5   Assess your comprehension of stated main ideas.

- The topic sentence states _____.
- A central idea is the _____
  _____.
- The thesis statement is a sentence that _____
  _____.
- The stated main idea of a reading selection can be located _____
  _____.
- Deductive thinking is based on the flow of ideas from _____ to
  _____.
- Inductive thinking is based on the flow of ideas from _____ to
  _____.

 ## Test Your Comprehension of Locating Stated Main Ideas

Respond to the following questions and prompts.

LEARNING OUTCOME 2 5   In your own words, what is the difference between deductive and inductive thinking? _____
_____
_____
_____

LEARNING OUTCOME 1 3   In your own words, what is the difference between a topic sentence and a thesis statement? _____

_____

_____

LEARNING
OUTCOME
2 4 5

Draw and label four graphs that show the possible locations of stated main ideas.

LEARNING
OUTCOME
5 6 7

Identify and discuss the two most important ideas in this chapter that will help you improve your reading comprehension.

_____

_____

_____

_____

4 Chapter Review

Summary of Key Concepts of Implied Main Ideas and Implied Central Ideas

LEARNING OUTCOME 1 Assess your comprehension of implied main ideas and implied central ideas.

- An implied main idea is a main idea that is _____ _____.

- To determine an implied main idea, ask three questions:
    - _____?
    - _____?
    - _____?

- Implied main ideas must be neither too _____ nor too _____.

- To determine a main idea, _____ or mark the _____ and the words that reveal the author's _____ and thought patterns or types of _____ used in the passage.

- When the idea of several paragraphs is implied, it is called the _____ _____.

 Test Your Comprehension of Implied Main Ideas

Respond to the following questions and prompts.

LEARNING OUTCOME 1 In your own words, what is an implied main idea? _____ _____ _____

LEARNING
OUTCOME
2 **3** **5**

Based on the instruction on pages 148 through 151, how can the skills you use to identify the stated main idea help you determine the implied main idea? _____

_____

_____

_____

_____

LEARNING
OUTCOME
7

Identify and discuss the two most important ideas in this chapter that will help you improve your reading comprehension. _____

_____

_____

_____

LEARNING
OUTCOME
3 **4** **6**

Study the following concept map. Then, write the implied main idea suggested by the details in the map.

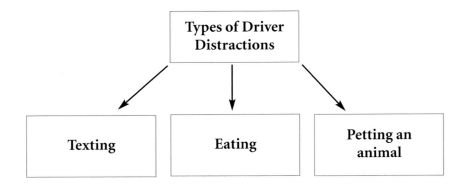

Implied main idea: _____

_____

5 Chapter Review

Summary of Key Concepts of Supporting Details

LEARNING
OUTCOME
① ③

Assess your comprehension of supporting details.

- To locate supporting details in a passage, an effective reader turns the _____ into a _____.

- A major supporting detail _____ _____.

- A minor supporting detail _____ _____.

- A _____ is a _____ _____.

- Often you will want to _____ or restate the ideas in your own words.

- _____ or marking your text _____ reading will help you create a _____ after you read.

- To create a summary for a passage with a stated main idea, _____ _____.

- To create a summary for a passage with an implied main idea, _____ _____.

 Test Your Comprehension of Supporting Details

Respond to the following questions and prompts.

LEARNING
OUTCOME
① ③

In your own words, how do major and minor supporting details differ? _____ _____ _____

_____

_____

LEARNING
OUTCOME
2 **4** **5**

In the space below, outline the steps for creating a summary for stated and implied main ideas. See pages 204–206.

LEARNING
OUTCOME
5 **6**

Summarize the two most important ideas in this chapter that will help you improve your reading comprehension. _____

_____

_____

6 Chapter Review

Summary of Key Concepts of Outlines and Concept Maps

LEARNING OUTCOME ❶ Assess your comprehension of concept maps and outlines.

- An outline shows _____
  _____.

- An author often uses _____ such as *a few causes, a number of reasons, several steps,* or *several kinds of* to introduce a _____.

- An author often uses signal words such as *first, second, furthermore, moreover, next,* or *finally* to introduce a _____.

- A formal outline uses _____ to indicate the _____, _____ to indicate the _____, and _____ to indicate the _____.

- A concept map is a _____
  _____.

Test Your Comprehension of Outlines and Concept Maps

Respond to the following questions and prompts.

LEARNING OUTCOME ❶ In your own words, what is an outline? _____
_____
_____
_____
_____
_____

LEARNING
OUTCOME
1

In your own words, what is a concept map? _____

_____

_____

_____

_____

_____

LEARNING
OUTCOME
2 3 5

In the space below, create an outline and a concept map for the following terms: Anxiety, Causes, Effects, Stress at work, Stress from school, Stress in personal life, Overwhelming fear, Shortness of breath, Chest pain.

Outline: Anxiety

    I. _____

       A. _____

       B. _____

       C. _____

    II. _____

       A. _____

       B. _____

       C. _____

Concept Map:

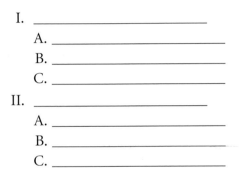

LEARNING
OUTCOME
4 5

Outline the three most important ideas in this chapter that will help you improve your reading comprehension.

    I. _____

    II. _____

    III. _____

7 Chapter Review

LEARNING OUTCOME 1 2 3 4   Assess your comprehension of transitions and thought patterns.

- Transitions are _____
  _____.

- A thought pattern is established by using _____ to show the logical relationship among ideas in a paragraph or passage.

- _____ and process are two uses of the _____ order thought pattern.

- In addition to showing a chain of events, the time order pattern is used to show _____, _____, or _____ that can be repeated at any time with similar results.

- The space order pattern allows authors to _____
  _____.

- Some of the words used to establish the space order pattern include *adjacent*, _____, and _____.

- Transitions of addition, such as _____, _____, and *furthermore*, are generally used to indicate a _____ pattern.

- Authors use the classification pattern to _____
  _____.

- Examples of classification signal words are _____, *second type*, or *another group*.

Test Your Comprehension of Transitions and Thought Patterns

Respond to the following questions and prompts.

LEARNING
OUTCOME
1
In your own words, what is a transition? _____

_____

LEARNING
OUTCOME
1
In your own words, what is a thought pattern? _____

_____

LEARNING
OUTCOME
2 3 5 7
In the space below organize the following ideas from a college earth science textbook into a logical thought pattern. Create an outline or concept map.

> The Earth can be thought of as having four major spheres. First, the hydrosphere is a dynamic mass of water that is always on the move, evaporating from the oceans to the atmosphere, precipitating to the land, and flowing back to the ocean again. Additionally, Earth is surrounded by a life-giving gaseous envelope called the atmosphere. This thin blanket of the atmosphere provides the air we breathe and protects us from the sun's rays. Next, lying beneath the atmosphere and the ocean is the solid Earth or the geosphere. The fourth sphere, the biosphere, includes all life on Earth.

—Adapted from Lutgens & Tarbuck. *Foundations of Earth Science,*
5th ed., pp. 4–6.

LEARNING
OUTCOME
6
Summarize the two most important ideas in this chapter that will help you improve your reading comprehension. _____

_____

_____

Summary of Key Concepts of More Thought Patterns

LEARNING OUTCOME ❶ ❷ ❸ ❹ Assess your comprehension of thought patterns.

- Comparison points out _____.
- Contrast points out _____.
- The words *like, similarly*, and *likewise* signal the _____ pattern.
- A cause states _____.
- An effect states _____.
- An author will often begin with the _____ and then give the effects.
- The phrases *as a result, leads to*, and *therefore* signal the _____ pattern.
- _____ words signal that a writer is giving an instance of a general idea to clarify a point.
- Definition explains the _____.
- Examples often follow a definition to show _____.

 ## Test Your Comprehension of More Thought Patterns

Respond to the following questions and prompts.

LEARNING OUTCOME ❶ ❷ ❸ In your own words, what is the difference between comparison and contrast? _____

_____

_____

LEARNING OUTCOME ❶ ❷ ❸

In your own words, what is the difference between a cause and an effect? _____

_____

_____

LEARNING OUTCOME ❶ ❷ ❸ ❹ ❻

In the space below create a concept map based on the information in the paragraph.

Carbon dioxide (CO$_2$) absorbs some of the radiation emitted by Earth and thus contributes to the greenhouse effect. Because CO$_2$ is a heat absorber, a change in CO$_2$ levels in Earth's atmosphere influences air temperature. Two main factors cause the increase of CO$_2$ and greenhouse warming. The use of coal and other fossil fuels is the most prominent means by which humans add CO$_2$ to the atmosphere, but it is not the only cause. The clearing of forests called deforestation also contributes substantially because CO$_2$ is released as vegetation is burned or decays.

—Adapted from Lutgens & Tarbuck, *Foundations of Earth Science*, 5th ed., pp. 309–310.

LEARNING OUTCOME ❺

Summarize the two most important ideas in this chapter that will help you improve your reading comprehension. _____

_____

_____

_____

Summary of Key Concepts of Fact and Opinion

LEARNING OUTCOME ❶ Assess your comprehension of identifying facts and opinions.

- A fact is _____ .
- An opinion is _____

  _____ .

- Objective proof can be _____

  _____ .

- An informed opinion is developed _____ .
- An expert opinion is developed _____

  _____ .

- A fact _____ reality and uses _____ words.
- An opinion _____ reality and uses _____ words.
- Biased words express _____ .
- A qualifier may express _____

  _____ .

 ## Test Your Comprehension of More Thought Patterns

Respond to the following questions and prompts.

LEARNING OUTCOME ❶ ❺ In your own words, what is the difference between a fact and an opinion? _____

_____

_____

LEARNING OUTCOME ② ③ ④   In your own words, what is the difference between an informed opinion and an expert opinion? _____

_____

_____

_____

_____

_____

LEARNING OUTCOME ① ② ③ ⑤   In your own words, describe how to distinguish between fact and opinion. _____

_____

_____

_____

_____

_____

LEARNING OUTCOME ⑥   Describe how you will use what you have learned about fact and opinion in your reading process to comprehend textbook material.

_____

_____

LEARNING OUTCOME ⑥   Summarize the two most important ideas in this chapter that will help you improve your reading comprehension. _____

_____

_____

10 Chapter Review

Summary of Key Concepts of Tone and Purpose

LEARNING
OUTCOME
❶ ❸

Assess your comprehension of tone and purpose.

- Tone is _____.
- Objective tone words _____.
- Subjective tone words _____.
- The author's purpose is _____.
- The primary purpose is _____.
- A writer whose purpose is _____ uses facts to teach or explain a main idea.
- A writer whose purpose is _____ sets out to amuse or interest the audience.
- A writer whose purpose is _____ combines facts with emotional appeals to sway readers to a particular point of view.
- Verbal irony occurs when _____
  _____.
- Situational irony occurs _____
  _____.

Test Your Comprehension of Tone and Purpose

Respond to the following questions and prompts.

LEARNING
OUTCOME
❶

In your own words, what is the relationship between tone and purpose?

_____

_____

_____

_____

_____

LEARNING
OUTCOME
②

In your own words, what is the difference between verbal and situational irony? _____

_____

LEARNING
OUTCOME
② ④ ⑤

In your own words, describe how to determine tone and purpose.

_____

_____

_____

_____

_____

LEARNING
OUTCOME
⑥ ⑦

Use a checklist to help determine the tone and purpose of passages.
Select a passage to analyze; then, complete the following checklist
with information from the passage.

Title of Passage:	Yes	No	Examples (words or phrases)/Explanations
Subjective Tone			
Objective Tone			
Irony			
Primary Purpose			
To Inform			
To Persuade			
To Entertain			

LEARNING
OUTCOME
⑦

Summarize the two most important ideas in this chapter that will
help you improve your reading comprehension. _____

_____

_____

_____

11 Chapter Review

Summary of Key Concepts about Inferences

LEARNING OUTCOME ① ③ ⑤ Assess your comprehension of inferences.

- An inference is an _____
  _____.

- An effective reader must sort _____ from _____
  to infer the author's meaning.

- Biased words express _____.

- A qualifier signals _____
  _____.

- A valid inference is _____.

- An invalid conclusion is _____
  _____.

- The VALID approach consists of 5 thinking steps to take to make a valid inference.
  - Step 1: Verify _____.
  - Step 2: Assess _____.
  - Step 3: Learn _____.
  - Step 4: Investigate _____.
  - Step 5: Detect _____.

🔖 Test Your Comprehension of Inferences

Respond to the following questions and prompts.

LEARNING
OUTCOME
1 2

In your own words, what is the difference between a valid and an invalid inference? _____

_____

_____

_____

_____

LEARNING
OUTCOME
4 5 6

Study the following examples of creative expressions. Identify the literary device each one represents.

Literary Device	**Example**
1. _____	"My love is like a red, red, rose."
2. _____	A gold cross on a necklace
3. _____	"… We can make the sun run."
4. _____	The Earth wept.
5. _____	home, shanty, palace

LEARNING
OUTCOME
7

Describe how you will use what you have learned about inferences in your reading process to comprehend textbook material. _____

_____

_____

_____

LEARNING
OUTCOME
7

Summarize the two most important ideas in this chapter that will help you improve your reading comprehension. _____

_____

_____

12 Chapter Review

Summary of Key Concepts about the Basics of Argument

LEARNING
OUTCOME
①   Assess your comprehension of the basics of argument.

- Effective argument is a _____
  _____.

- An argument is made up of two types of statements:
  - ▪ _____.
  - ▪ _____.

- An invalid conclusion is _____
  _____.

- The four steps to analyze an argument are as follows:
  - ▪ Step 1: _____.
  - ▪ Step 2: _____.
  - ▪ Step 3: _____.
  - ▪ Step 4: _____.

- An invalid conclusion is making a claim without _____
  _____.

 ## Test Your Comprehension of the Basics of Argument

Respond to the following questions and prompts.

LEARNING
OUTCOME
①   In your own words, explain the relationship between making an inference and analyzing an argument. _____
_____
_____
_____

_____

_____

_____

LEARNING
OUTCOME
2 **3** **4** **5**
6

Create a valid argument. Study the photograph. Then, based on the details in the photo, write a claim and two supports that clearly support the claim.

The Impact of Marine Debris

Claim: _____

Support 1: _____

Support 2: _____

LEARNING
OUTCOME
7

Summarize the two most important ideas in this chapter that will help you improve your reading comprehension.

_____

_____

_____

13 Chapter Review

Summary of Key Concepts about Advanced Argument: Persuasive Techniques

LEARNING OUTCOME ① ② ③ ④ ⑤

Assess your comprehension of advanced arguments and persuasive techniques.

- A fallacy is an _____.
- Irrelevant details draw attention away from logical thought by _____ _____.
- Inadequate details _____ the issue and do not _____ _____.
- Propaganda is an act of persuasion that systematically spreads _____ that is designed to _____ a person, product, cause, or organization.
- _____ is the arousal of emotions to give meaning or power to an idea.
- Supply the terms for the following definitions:
  - _____ is the use of abusive remarks in place of evidence for a point or argument.
  - _____ is a weak argument substituted for a stronger one to make the argument easier to challenge.
  - _____ restates the point of an argument as the support and conclusion.
  - _____ uses negative labels for a product, idea, or cause.
  - _____ use irrelevant personal opinions to support a product, idea, or cause.

13-1

- _____ uses or suggests the irrelevant detail that "everyone is doing it."

- _____ uses irrelevant details to build trust based on commonly shared values.

- _____ assumes that only two sides of an issue exist. Also known as the black-and-white fallacy that offers a false dilemma because more than two options are often available.

- _____ assumes that two things are similar when they are not. This fallacy is also known as a false analogy.

- _____, also known as _____, assumes that because events occurred around the same time, they have a cause-and-effect relationship.

- _____ omits factual details in order to misrepresent a product, idea, or cause.

- _____ creates an association between a product, idea, or cause with a symbol or image that has positive or negative values.

- _____ offer general positive statements that cannot be verified.

Test Your Comprehension of Advanced Argument: Persuasive Techniques

Respond to the following question.

LEARNING
OUTCOME
1 6

In your own words, explain the relationships among the following terms: *fallacy, irrelevant details, emotional appeal, inadequate details,* and *propaganda.* How will recognizing persuasive techniques help you improve your reading comprehension? _____

_____

_____

_____

_____

_____

A. Identify the propaganda technique used in each of the following items. Some techniques are used more than once.

a. plain folks   d. transfer
b. bandwagon   e. name-calling
c. testimonial   f. glittering generality

_____ **1.** A candidate promises, "Elect me, and I will serve the land of the free and the home of the brave with courage and humility."

_____ **2.** I would never listen to, much less buy, Fergie's music; she is an immoral person and a horrible role model.

_____ **3.** A commercial advertising ice cream shows a series of preschool children in settings that look like their homes reading the list of natural ingredients on the ice cream carton as they happily eat the ice cream.

_____ **4.** Michael Jordan, a famous basketball player, recommends Hanes T-shirts because they are comfortable.

_____ **5.** In a television commercial for a breath mint, a young woman is dripping with sweat. She pops a breath mint in her mouth; immediately a breeze begins to blow, she stops sweating, and she breathes out an icy cloud of air that turns the whole scene a refreshing blue color.

_____ **6.** Don't take classes with that professor; he's a tough grader and a boring lecturer.

_____ **7.** I am going to vote for gun control because all my friends and family are voting for gun control.

_____ **8.** If you want a good, old-fashioned home-cooked meal, come into Andy's. We make the meals mom used to make.

_____ **9.** Identify the propaganda technique used in this poster.
  a. plain folks
  b. bandwagon
  c. testimonial
  d. transfer
  e. name-calling
  f. glittering generality

B. Read the following fictitious advertisement. Identify the detail that was **omitted** from the advertisement for the purpose of card stacking.

_____ **10.** House for sale: Built in 2003, this four-bedroom, three-bath pool home with a total living space of 1,800 square feet is located close to shopping and in an excellent school district. All appliances are included.
  a. The house is underpriced for a quick move because the owner received a job transfer.
  b. The appliances are still under warranty.
  c. The house is sitting on a recently filled sinkhole.

A. Identify the propaganda technique used in each of the following items. Some techniques are used more than once.

a. plain folks
b. bandwagon
c. testimonial
d. transfer
e. name-calling
f. glittering generality

_____ **1.** In 1970, Lawton Chiles walked more than 1,000 miles across the state of Florida and won his bid for the U.S. Senate. One of his campaign buttons read, "I am walking with Lawton Chiles."

_____ **2.** In a 1964 political television advertisement, a little girl is counting the petals she is picking off a daisy. When she reaches the number 10, the audience hears another voice counting down, "ten . . . nine . . . eight." At the number zero, a deafening explosion is heard. The mushroom cloud of an atomic bomb is reflected in the little girl's eyes. Then the voice of Lyndon B. Johnson says, "These are the stakes—to make a world in which all God's children can live, or to go into the darkness. We must either love each other, or we must die." After this, another voice says, "Vote for Lyndon B. Johnson. The stakes are too high for you to stay home."

_____ **3.** My opponent is a weak-minded liberal.

_____ **4.** Valerie Bertinelli advertises how she lost weight using the Jenny Craig program.

_____ **5.** Everyone smokes marijuana, so it should be legalized.

_____ **6.** An advertisement for State Farm Insurance says, "Like a good neighbor, State Farm is there."

_____ **7.** The Internet is one of the greatest tools of democracy and should be cherished and protected as a basic American right to access information. Stop censorship of the Internet in public libraries.

_____ **8.** Identify the propaganda technique used in this advertisement.
  a. plain folks
  b. bandwagon
  c. testimonial
  d. transfer
  e. name-calling
  f. glittering generality

B. Read the following fictitious advertisements. Identify the detail from each list that was **omitted** from each advertisement for the purpose of card stacking.

_____ **9.** For sale: A 2006 white Malibu with low mileage. Maintenance work has been done on a regular basis. All new tires. AM/FM radio with CD player. Power steering. Only $6,000.
  a. The car has had only one owner, an elderly woman who didn't often drive.
  b. The car was recently in a wreck and has had major repairs.
  c. The car seats five people comfortably and has an adequate amount of trunk space.

_____ **10.** Be the gorgeous redhead you have always wanted to be. ColorLife Russet will turn your hair a luscious shade of auburn while leaving it soft and manageable. Turn heads your way with ColorLife Russet.
  a. ColorLife Russet is a temporary color that must be reapplied every two to three weeks.
  b. ColorLife Russet meets the Food and Drug Administration's recommended levels of lead acetate.
  c. ColorLife Hair Color comes in 26 other shades as well.

Name _____ Section _____

Date _____ Score _____ × 10= _____

A. Write the letter of the fallacy next to its definition.

a. begging the question   d. false cause
b. personal attack   e. false comparison
c. straw man   f. either-or

_____ **1.** In this fallacy, the original argument is replaced with a weaker version that is easier to challenge than the original argument.

_____ **2.** This fallacy assumes that two things are similar when they are not.

_____ **3.** This fallacy assumes that because events occurred around or near the same time, they have a cause-and-effect relationship.

_____ **4.** This fallacy assumes that only two sides of an issue exist.

_____ **5.** This fallacy restates the point of an argument as the support and conclusion.

_____ **6.** This fallacy uses abusive remarks in place of evidence for a point or argument.

B. Write the letter of the fallacy used in each of the following items.

_____ **7.** The truly patriotic citizen supports all elected officials.
a. straw man   c. false comparison
b. begging the question   d. either-or

_____ **8.** During the 2008 presidential campaign, Barack Obama used the slogans "Change we can believe in" and "Yes, we can!"
a. straw man   c. glittering generality
b. false comparison   d. false cause

_____ **9.** I knew I was going to see you today because my horoscope said that I was going to meet with someone special today.
a. either-or   c. begging the question
b. false cause   d. straw man

_____ **10.** I love going to the movies because watching movies is my favorite leisure time activity.
a. straw man   c. either-or
b. false cause   d. begging the question

Additional Readings

Textbook
Skills

Textbook
Skills

The Connection Between Reading and Writing

The link between reading and writing is vital and natural. Written language allows an exchange of ideas between a writer and a reader. Thus, writing and reading are two equal parts of the communication process. In fact, reading is a form of listening or receiving information. And writing is like speaking—the sending of information. So an effective reader makes every effort to understand and respond to the ideas of the writer. Likewise, an effective writer makes every effort to make ideas clear so the reader can understand and respond to those ideas. Most writers find that reading improves their writing. Reading builds prior knowledge and fuels ideas for writing.

Because of this close relationship between reading and writing, both share similar thinking steps in their processes. In Chapter 1, you learned that the reading process has three phases: Before Reading, During Reading, and After Reading. The writing process also has three phases that occur before, during, and after writing: Prewriting, Drafting, and Proofing. By coordinating these two sets of process, you can improve both your reading and your writing. For example, the following statements sum up one way to connect reading and writing:

Reading is a prewriting activity. Drafting is an after reading activity.

Once you think of reading as a prewriting activity, you become a responsive or active reader during the reading process. In fact, you can begin using your writing skills as you read by annotating the text.

Annotating a Text

The word *annotate* suggests that you "take notes" in your book. Writing notes in the margin of a page as you read keeps you focused and improves your comprehension. You can quickly note questions where they occur, move on in your reading, and later return to clarify answers. In addition, after reading, your annotations help you review and respond to the material. The following suggestions offer one way to annotate a text:

How to Annotate a Text

- Circle important terms.
- Underline definitions and meanings.
- Note key ideas with a star or a check.
- Place question marks above words that are unknown or confusing.
- Number the steps in a process or items in a list.
- Write summaries at the end of long sections.

- Write recall questions in the margin near its answer.

- Write key words and meanings in margin.

EXAMPLE The following passage from a college health textbook is marked up as an example of an annotated text. Read the passage. Study the annotations. Then work with a peer or in a small group and create a summary of the text based on the annotations. See page 610 to review how to write a summary.

The following passage from a college health textbook has been annotated for you as an illustration.

Textbook
Skills

Adapting to Stress

HEALTH SKILLS

Although there will always be some stress in your life, that does not mean you cannot do anything about it. In fact, the best medicine for stress appears to be learning how to adapt to or cope with stress.

Stress can be controlled!

Coping is adaptation to stress. In primitive times, coping with stress meant little more than exercising the basic fight-or-flight reaction to threatening situations. For example, if a tiger threatened a primitive man, he would either stand and fight (and do so with added strength and cunning brought about by the stress reactions described by the general adaptation syndrome) or run from the threat (also with the added strength and cunning brought about by the stress reaction).

What is "coping"? Describe "fight-or-flight." (F/F)

Today, we are not threatened by tigers. Threats come instead from difficult working situations, unexpected bills, and disappointing news. Although survival is still at issue, it is not as much the survival of an individual or the species as maintaining self-esteem in stressful situations. The fight-or-flight response still works well in some cases, as do defense mechanisms such as avoidance and denial. These responses, however, are usually effective only for the short term. In our complex society, more adaptive methods of coping are necessary for a long-term adaptation to stress. Fleeing or denying a stress situation might be very useful in diminishing the acute pain of an unhappy event, but it does not help you deal with the source of the stress over the long run.

What are two examples of defense mechanisms? (DM)

Summary: F/F and DM are 2 short-term ways to cope with stress.

Coping with Stress

There are several ways you can effectively minimize the negative effects of everyday stress, whether it is in school, on the job, or at home. One preventive action is to make sure that you take good care of your physical health. You do this by eating nutritiously, exercising, not smoking or using drugs, and getting an adequate amount of sleep. You will find tips on how to develop good health habits in the related chapters in this textbook. Being in good physical health can help your body fight the negative health effects that can accompany stress.

Healthy, long-term coping technique

Be Good to MYSELF!

—Reprinted from Pruitt, B.E. and Jane J. Stein. *Health Styles: Decisions for Living Well*, 2nd ed., Allyn & Bacon,1999, p. 85.

Writing a Summary

Writing a summary is an effective step in the reading and studying process.

> A **summary** is a brief, clear restatement of a longer passage.

A summary includes only the passage's most important points. Often a summary is made up of the main idea and major supporting details. The length of a summary should reflect your study needs and the kind of passage you are trying to understand. For example, a paragraph might be summarized in a sentence or two, an article might be summarized in a paragraph, and a textbook chapter might be summarized in a page or two.

You can discover how well you understand a passage by writing a summary of it as an after reading activity. Use the annotations you make during reading to create your summary.

For example, read the following summary of the "Adapting to Stress" section of a college health textbook. Underline the words and phrases that were annotated in the earlier section:

[1]By learning how to adapt to or cope with stress, stress can be controlled. [2]Two short-term ways to cope with stress are the fight-or-flight response and defense mechanisms. [3]During the primitive fight-or-flight response, a threat or stress creates a short-term burst of energy that allows a person to either stand and fight or turn and run with additional strength and skill. [4]Defense mechanisms include avoidance and denial. [5]However, healthy, long-term coping techniques for stress involve maintaining physical health. [6]To effectively cope with stress, eat a healthful diet, exercise, avoid use of tobacco and drugs, and get enough sleep.

This summary includes the author's main idea and the major supporting details. However, this summary also brings in a few minor supporting details. For example, sentence 3 explains the fight-or-flight reaction to stress. Including these details makes the summary longer than may be necessary. The following version includes only the main idea and the major supporting details.

[1]Two short-term methods of adapting to stress include the fight-or-flight response and defense mechanisms such as avoidance and denial. [2]Healthy, long-term ways to cope with stress involve maintaining physical

health by eating healthfully, exercising, avoiding use of tobacco and drugs, and getting enough sleep.

Remember, the length of the summary depends upon your study needs as well as the length of the passage you are summarizing.

A Reading-Writing Plan of Action

Can you see how annotating a text lays the ground upon which you can build a written response? The steps you take during reading feed into the process of writing a response after reading.

Remember, reading and writing is a conversation between the writer and the reader. One writes; the other reads. But the conversation often doesn't end there. A reader's response to a piece of writing keeps the dialogue going. When you write a summary, your response is to restate the author's ideas. It's like saying to the author, "If I understood you correctly, you said . . ." When you offer your own views about the author's ideas, you are answering the author's implied question, "What do you think?" In your reading and writing classes, your teacher often steps into the conversation. He or she stands in for the author and becomes the reader of your written response. In this case, your teacher evaluates both your reading and writing abilities. Your teacher checks your response for accuracy in comprehension of the author's message and development of your ability to write. The following chart illustrates this exchange of ideas.

The Conversation among Writers and Readers

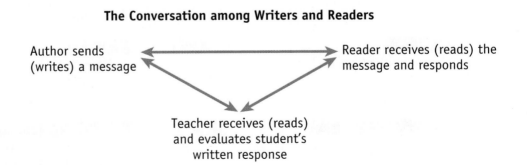

Author sends (writes) a message

Reader receives (reads) the message and responds

Teacher receives (reads) and evaluates student's written response

In each skill chapter of this textbook, the question "What Do You Think?" is posed after Review Tests 3 and 4. This question also appears after each reading selection in this section. The "What Do You Think?" writing assignments prompt you to respond to what you have read. This activity creates a writing situation and gives you a purpose for your written response. Just like a vocabulary word makes more sense in context than in a list, a writing assignment in context is more meaningful than an isolated topic or set of disconnected questions. The goal of "What Do You Think?" is to strengthen your connection between reading and writing. Because reading and writing are two distinct processes, it is helpful to have a guide that shows how to efficiently coordinate them. The following chart lays out a reading-writing plan of action. Note that the chart breaks the reading-writing process into a series of 6 steps. Keep in mind that any step can be repeated as needed. Also, you can move back and forth between steps as needed.

Study the 6-Step Reading-Writing Action Plan. Then work with a peer or small group of classmates and discuss the relationship between reading and writing, and how you will put this plan to use.

A 6-Step Reading-Writing Action Plan

Read		Write
1. Survey and Question	**BEFORE**	**4. Prewrite**
Call on Prior Knowledge		Build Prior Knowledge*
Identify Topic		Gather Information*
Identify Key or New Words		Read and Annotate*
Identify Patterns of Organization		Brainstorm ideas
Note Visual Aids		Choose Your Topic
Skim Introductions and		Generate Your Details
Conclusions		Create a Concept Map
		Outline Ideas
2. Read	**DURING**	**5. Draft**
Monitor Comprehension		Write Introduction, Body,
Fix Confusion		and Conclusion
Annotate Text		
3. Review and Recite	**AFTER**	**6. Revise and Proofread**
Recall Key Words and Ideas		Revise to Organize
Create Concept Maps		Revise for Exact Wording
Create Outlines		Correct Errors
Write a Summary		Fragments and Run-ons
Write a Response		Spelling
		Punctuation

* Prewriting steps accomplished during reading

READING 1

Some are Semi-sweet and Some are Semi-not

Bob Schwartz

Bob Schwartz is an author and freelance humor writer whose popular writings have appeared in over 150 magazines and numerous newspapers. The following essay appears in his book *Would Somebody Please Send ME to MY Room! A Hilarious Look at Family Life.* As you read this passage, consider the following questions: Are you just like your family? Do you and your parents agree on most things? Have you ever been surprised by the ways in which you differ from your family or friends?

Vocabulary Preview

stupefied (paragraph 3): bewildered, confused, amazed

aversion (paragraph 4): strong dislike, distaste

blasphemous (paragraph 4): expressing disrespect for God or sacred things, improper

monumental (paragraph 5): large, significant

rendezvous (paragraph 5): meeting

hallucinogenic (paragraph 5): mind altered, delusional

revulsion (paragraph 8): disgust, loathing

renegade (paragraph 8): rebel, traitor

1   With two small words from our two-year-old, my wife and I began to question the entire validity of genetics. Having been introduced to chocolate for the first time, our daughter exclaimed the most inconceivable reaction by any child born into our Willie Wonka Biosphere.

2   She truly shook the very fabric of our bon-bon world. Upon tasting a chocolate brownie, she provided a very **animated** facial expression, which seemed to indicate that she was chewing lukewarm and hot pepper flavored sawdust. She then quite matter-of-factly said, "No like."

3   My wife and I stared at each other **stupefied**. Her older brothers reacted with jaw dropping disbelief as their Ho-Ho's fell from their hands and landed in their Cocoa Puffs.

4   Now we certainly do monitor the nutritional intake of our children's food consumption, but the fact was that our daughter had been born into a family of chocoholics. It seemed beyond comprehension that given her present **aversion** we'd have to work on

her taste buds for a little choco-conversion. Otherwise, we ultimately might be required to integrate our dessert table with the **blasphemous** flavors of vanilla and dare I even say it, butterscotch.

5   A little background regarding my Hershey's history might be in order. My **confectionery** confession is that I really didn't give much thought to chocolate until I met my wife. Up to that point, I think my lack of full commitment stemmed from a **monumental** event I'd had as a nine-year-old. It was then that my stomach had a mind-altering **rendezvous** with a breakfast plate of chocolate chip pancakes, laden with chocolate syrup and doused with chocolate whipped cream. My grandfather had treated me to this **ambrosial** delicacy at 7:00 a.m. at the International House of Sugar Overload. I was pretty much in a hyperactive **hallucinogenic** state the remainder of that year. To this day, I have only an extremely vague recollection of fourth grade.

6   My wife, on the other hand, grew up on Rocky Road in Loompaland. I didn't initially realize her chocolate dependence, since I had no idea of the truffles she'd seen. I slowly learned that her idea of a balanced diet was equal amounts of dark and white chocolate. She followed the twelve-step chocoholic program, which required that a person be no more than twelve steps from chocolate at any given time.

She slowly introduced me to cocoa butter and the **decadent** underworld of dark-chocolate mousse. And now, one of our children was rebuking everything we believed in—the very framework of our bumpy cake home! The next thing we knew our daughter might actually do the unthinkable. That's right, request green Jell-O for dessert. 7

We looked on the bright side and figured this was simply a toddler stage that she'd grow out of. We had preferred she'd instead exhibit the more familiar two-year-old acts of temper tantrums or extreme defiance. We could handle that. But a chocolate **revulsion**? The little radical. Perhaps this was the beginning of **renegade** behavior. Were we destined for demands for nose rings by age three, and a pink Mohawk haircut by age four from our little double fudge dessert **dissenter**? 8

Maybe we could sneak some crushed Oreos into her applesauce or mix some pieces of 3 Musketeer candy bars into her Cheerios to have her satisfy our Recommended Daily Allowance of chocolate. 9

Then again, we knew the right thing was just to let her go in her own sugar direction. She obviously marched to the sound of her own candy wrapper. 10

Perhaps she'd ultimately convert us a little. But I'm not sure I could ever look those jovial M & M fellas in the eye if I defected over to strawberry licorice. 11

—Schwartz, Bob "Some Are Sweet and Some are Not" from SOMEBODY PLEASE SEND ME TO MY ROOM! A HILARIOUS LOOK AT FAMILY LIFE, © 2005. Reprinted by permission of Glenbridge Publishing Ltd. in Centennial, Colorado.

Fill in the blank in each sentence with a word from the Vocabulary Preview.

Vocabulary Preview

1. Chocoholics Anonymous is a support group for people who are _____ by their addiction to chocolate.

Vocabulary Preview

2. One group of Chocoholics Anonymous publically expressed their _____ to Tim Burton's film *Charlie and the Chocolate Factory* and demanded that the movie begin with a warning about the dangers of chocolate addiction.

Vocabulary Preview

3. Some claim that chocolate addiction is a _____ problem worse than addition to heroin or cocaine.

Vocabulary Preview

4. The real danger for a chocoholic is the ready availability of chocolate—no secret _____ is needed to get a fix—just a trip to the local grocery store.

Vocabulary Preview

5. Chocolate contains the chemical phenylethylamine; this compound has _____ properties similar to amphetamines.

For items 6 through 10, choose the best meaning of each word in *italics*. Use context clues to make your choice.

Vocabulary in Context

_____ **6.** "Upon tasting a chocolate brownie, she provided a very *animated* facial expression, which seems to indicate that she was chewing lukewarm and hot pepper flavored sawdust." (paragraph 2)
a. lifeless
b. lively
c. distasteful
d. eager

Vocabulary in Context

_____ **7.** "My *confectionery* confession is that I really didn't give much thought to chocolate until I met my wife." (paragraph 5)
a. baking
b. pastry
c. candy making
d. food candies

Vocabulary in Context

_____ **8.** "My grandfather had treated me to this *ambrosial* delicacy at 7:00 a.m. at the International House of Sugar Overload." (paragraph 5)
a. fruity
b. delightful
c. bland
d. offensive

Vocabulary in Context

_____ **9.** "She slowly introduced me to cocoa butter and the *decadent* underworld of dark-chocolate mousse." (paragraph 7)
a. self-indulgent
b. wild
c. corrupt
d. innocent

Vocabulary in Context

_____ **10.** "Were we destined for demands for nose rings by age three, and a pink Mohawk haircut by age four from our little double fudge dessert *dissenter*?" (paragraph 8)
a. follower
b. criminal
c. rebel
d. delinquent

Main Idea _____ **11.** Which of the following sentences states the central idea of the passage?
   a. "With two small words from our two-year-old, my wife and I began to question the entire validity of genetics." (paragraph 1)
   b. "She truly shook the fabric of our bon-bon world." (paragraph 2)
   c. "Upon tasting a chocolate brownie, she provided a very animated facial expression, which seemed to indicate that she was chewing lukewarm and hot pepper flavored sawdust." (paragraph 2)
   d. "Perhaps this was the beginning of renegade behavior." (paragraph 8)

Supporting Detail _____ **12.** The author's two-year-old said "No like" upon tasting
   a. Ho-Ho's.   c. Cocoa Puffs.
   b. Musketeer candy bars.   d. a chocolate brownie.

Supporting Detail _____ **13.** According to the author, his wife's idea of a balanced diet is
   a. truffles.
   b. chocolate mousse.
   c. equal amounts of dark and white chocolate.
   d. Cocoa Puffs and Cheerios.

Transitions _____ **14.** "Her older brothers reacted with jaw dropping disbelief as their Ho-Ho's fell from their hands and landed in their Cocoa Puffs." (paragraph 3)

   The relationship of ideas **within** this sentence is
   a. cause and effect.   c. comparison and contrast.
   b. time order.   d. generalization and example.

Transitions _____ **15.** "To this day, I have only an extremely vague recollection of fourth grade. My wife, on the other hand, grew up on Rocky Road in Loompaland." (paragraphs 5 and 6)

   The relationship of ideas **between** these sentences is
   a. cause and effect.   c. comparison and contrast.
   b. time order.   d. generalization and example.

Thought Patterns _____ **16.** The main thought pattern of the passage is
   a. time order.   c. comparison and contrast.
   b. classification.   d. definition and example.

Fact and Opinion _____ **17.** "My grandfather had treated me to this ambrosial delicacy at 7:00 a.m. at the International House of Sugar Overload." (paragraph 5)

   This sentence is a statement of
   a. fact.   c. fact and opinion.
   b. opinion.

Tone and
Patterns

_____ **18.** The overall tone and purpose of the author is
   a. to inform the reader about his struggles as a parent.
   b. to entertain the reader with an amusing personal story about parenting.
   c. to persuade the reader of the value of chocolate.

Inferences

_____ **19.** Based on the details in paragraph 3, we can infer that
   a. the author's two-year-old is an only child.
   b. the author's two-year-old is the youngest child.
   c. the author has only three children.
   d. the author's two-year-old is the only daughter in the family.

Argument

_____ **20.** The humor in paragraph 8 is based on the use of the persuasive technique
   a. false analogy.   c. transfer.
   b. bandwagon.   d. glittering generalities.

Mapping

Complete the following story web with information from the passage. Wording may vary.

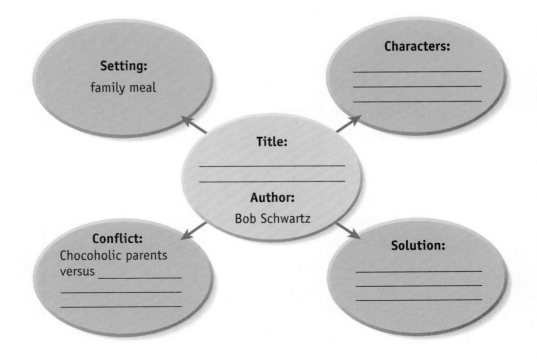

Setting:
family meal

Characters:
_____
_____
_____

Title:
_____
_____

Author:
Bob Schwartz

Conflict:
Chocoholic parents
versus _____
_____
_____

Solution:
_____
_____
_____

WHAT DO YOU THINK?

The humor of this essay comes from the author's use of irony—both verbal and situational. In what ways does the author use verbal irony? Give examples. In what ways is the situation described by the author ironic? Are you surprisingly different from your family? Or do you know someone who is ironically different from his or her family? Assume you are volunteering with troubled youth through a local branch of an organization such as the YMCA, Big Brothers, or Big Sisters. You have been asked to write an article of encouragement to post on the group's blog. Write an essay that relays a funny story about being different or about accepting someone else who is different.

EFFECTIVE READER Scorecard

"Some are Semi-sweet and Some are Semi-not"

Skill	Number Correct	Points		Total
Vocabulary				
Vocabulary Preview (5 items)	_____	× 10	=	_____
Vocabulary in Context (5 items)	_____	× 10	=	_____
		Vocabulary Score		_____
Comprehension				
Main Idea (1 item)	_____	× 8	=	_____
Supporting Details (2 items)	_____	× 8	=	_____
Transitions (2 items)	_____	× 8	=	_____
Thought Patterns (1 item)	_____	× 8	=	_____
Fact and Opinion (1 item)	_____	× 8	=	_____
Tone and Purpose (1 item)	_____	× 8	=	_____
Inferences (1 item)	_____	× 8	=	_____
Argument (1 item)	_____	× 8	=	_____
Mapping (4 items)	_____	× 5	=	_____
		Comprehension Score		_____

READING 2

Fifth Chinese Daughter

Jade Snow Wong

Jade Snow Wong, the daughter of Chinese immigrants who settled in San Francisco, became a renowned author and ceramic artist. In her two volumes of autobiography, *Fifth Chinese Daughter* and *No Chinese Stranger*, she chronicled her life growing up in California in the 1930s and 1940s. Wong describes her traditional Chinatown family and her struggle to succeed both as an American woman and as the daughter of an immigrant family. The following passage is an excerpt from *Fifth Chinese Daughter*. Have your parents ever forbid you to do something you thought important? How did you respond? Did you honor your parents' wishes or did you rebel and do as you wanted?

Vocabulary Preview

conventional (paragraph 2): traditional, typical

subsist (paragraph 2): live, survive

mediocrity (paragraph 2): ordinariness, weakness

incurred (paragraph 4): acquired, suffered, experienced

derived (paragraph 6): resulting

perpetual (paragraph 6): unending, ongoing

nepotism (paragraph 7): bias in favor of family or friends, particularly in granting power and position

revered (paragraph 12): respected, honored

innuendos (paragraph 14): an indirect remark or gesture that usually suggests something improper

devastated (paragraph 15): overwhelmed, distressed

perplexed (paragraph 16): puzzled, confused, baffled

1   By the time I was graduating from high school, my parents had done their best to produce an intelligent, obedient daughter, who would know more than the average Chinatown girl and should do better than average at a conventional job, her earnings brought home in repayment for their years of child support. Then, they hoped, she would marry a nice Chinese boy and make him a good wife, as well as an above-average mother for his children. Chinese custom used to decree that families should "introduce" chosen

partners to each other's children. The groom's family should pay handsomely to the bride's family for rearing a well-bred daughter. They should also pay all bills for a glorious wedding banquet for several hundred guests. Their daughter belonged to the groom's family and must henceforth seek permission from all persons in his home before returning to her parents for a visit.

2   But having been set upon a new path, I did not **oblige** my parents with the expected **conventional** ending. At fifteen, I had moved away from home to work for room and board and a salary of twenty dollars per month. Having found that I could **subsist** independently, I thought it regrettable to terminate my education. Upon graduating from high school at the age of sixteen, I asked my parents to assist me in college expenses. I pleaded with my father, for his years of encouraging me to be above **mediocrity** in both Chinese and American studies had made me wish for some undefined but brighter future.

3   My father was briefly **adamant**. He must conserve his resources for my oldest brother's medical training. Though I desired to continue on an above-average course, his material means were insufficient to support that ambition. He added that if I had the talent, I could provide for my own college education. When he had spoken, no discussion was expected. After this **edict**, no daughter questioned.

4   But this matter involved my whole future—it was not simply asking for permission to go to a night church meeting (forbidden also). Though for years I had accepted the authority of the one I honored most, his decision that night embittered me

as nothing ever had. My oldest brother had so many privileges, had **incurred** unusual expenses for luxuries which were taken for granted as his birthright, yet these were part of a system I had accepted. Now I suddenly wondered at my father's interpretation of the Christian code: was it intended to discriminate against a girl after all, or was it simply convenient for my father's economics and cultural prejudice? Did a daughter have any right to expect more than a fate of obedience, according to the old Chinese standard? As long as I could remember, I had been told that a female followed three men during her lifetime: as a girl, her father; as a wife, her husband; as an old woman, her son.

5   My indignation mounted against that tradition and I decided then that my past could not determine my future. I knew that more education would prepare me for a different expectation than my other female schoolmates, few of whom were to complete a college degree. I, too, had my father's unshakable faith in the justice of God, and I shared his unconcern with popular opinion.

6   So I decided to enter junior college, now San Francisco's City College, because the fees were lowest. I lived at home and supported myself with an after-school job which required long hours of housework and cooking but paid me twenty dollars per month, of which I saved as much as possible. The thrills **derived** from reading and learning, in ways ranging from chemistry experiments to English compositions, from considering new ideas of sociology to the logic of Latin, convinced me that I had made a correct choice. I was kept in a state of **perpetual** mental excitement by new

Western subjects and concepts and did not mind long hours of work and study. I also made new friends, which led to another painful incident with my parents, who had heretofore discouraged even girlhood friendships.

7   The college subject which had the most jolted me was sociology. The instructor fired my mind with his interpretation of family relationships. As he explained to our class, it used to be an economic asset for American farming families to be large, since children were useful to perform agricultural chores. But this situation no longer applied and children should be regarded as individuals with their own rights. Unquestioning obedience should be replaced with parental understanding. So at sixteen, discontented as I was with my parents' apparent indifference to me, those words of my sociology professor gave voice to my sentiments. How old-fashioned was the dead-end attitude of my parents! How ignorant they were of modern thought and progress! The family unit had been China's strength for centuries, but it had also been her weakness, for corruption, **nepotism**, and greed were all justified in the name of the family's welfare. My new ideas festered; I longed to release them.

8   One afternoon on a Saturday, which was normally occupied with my housework job, I was unexpectedly released by my employer, who was departing for a country weekend. It was a rare joy to have free time and I wanted to enjoy myself for a change. There had been a Chinese-American boy who shared some classes with me. Sometimes we had found each other walking to the same 8:00 A.M. class. He was not a special boyfriend, but I had enjoyed talking to him and had confided in him some of my problems. Impulsively, I telephoned him. I knew I must be breaking rules, and I felt shy and scared. At the same time, I was excited at this newly found forwardness, with nothing more purposeful than to suggest another walk together.

9   He understood my awkwardness and shared my anticipation. He asked me to "dress up" for my first movie date. My clothes were limited but I changed to look more graceful in silk stockings and found a bright ribbon for my long black hair. Daddy watched, catching my mood, observing the dashing preparations. He asked me where I was going without his permission and with whom.

10   I refused to answer him. I thought of my rights! I thought he surely would not try to understand. Thereupon Daddy thundered his displeasure and forbade my departure.

11   I found a new courage and I heard my voice announce calmly that I was no longer a child, and if I could work my way through college, I would choose my own friends. It was my right as a person.

12   My mother had heard the commotion and joined my father to face me; both appeared shocked and **incredulous**. Daddy at once demanded the source of this **unfilial**, non-Chinese theory. And when I quoted my college professor, reminding him that he had always felt teachers should be **revered**, my father denounced that professor as a foreigner who was disregarding the superiority of our Chinese culture, with its sound family strength. My father did not spare me; I was condemned as an ingrate for echoing dishonorable opinions which should

only be temporary whims, yet nonetheless inexcusable.

13   The scene was not yet over. I completed my proclamation to my father, who had never allowed me to learn how to dance, by adding that I was attending a movie, unchaperoned, with a boy I met at college.

14   My startled father was sure that my reputation would be subject to whispered **innuendos**. I must be bent on disgracing the family name; I was ruining my future, for surely I would yield to temptation. My mother underscored him by saying that I hadn't any notion of the problems endured by parents of a young girl.

I would not give in. I reminded them 15 that they and I were not in China, that I wasn't going out with just anybody but someone I trusted! Daddy gave a roar that no man could be trusted, but I **devastated** them in declaring that I wished the freedom to find my own answers.

Both parents were thoroughly an- 16 gered, scolded me for being shameless, and predicted that I would someday tell them I was wrong. But I dimly perceived that they were conceding defeat and were **perplexed** at this breakdown of their training. I was too old to beat and too bold to intimidate.

Fill in the blank in each sentence with a word from the Vocabulary Preview.

Vocabulary Preview
1. San Francisco's Chinese community is _____ as the oldest, largest, and most visually recognizable urban Chinese American district in the world.

Vocabulary Preview
2. Many early Chinese immigrants were able to _____ , as workers on farms, railroad construction crews, and in low-paying industrial jobs.

Vocabulary Preview
3. The Chinese brought with them _____ Chinese beliefs, values, and practices that defined their daily lives.

Vocabulary Preview
4. Early on, Chinese immigrants _____ the wrath of labor unions because the Chinese were willing to work hard and skillfully for low wages.

Vocabulary Preview
5. Despite hostility and discrimination, a _____ flow of Chinese immigrants poured into California to gain whatever opportunities awaited them in America.

For items 6 through 10, choose the best meaning of each word in *italics*. Use context clues to make your choice.

Vocabulary in Context
_____   **6.** "But having been set upon a new path, I did not *oblige* my parents with the expected conventional ending." (paragraph 2)
    a. accommodate   c. assist
    b. hinder   d. comfort

Vocabulary in Context _____ **7.** "My father was briefly *adamant*." (paragraph 3)
  a. agreeable   c. inflexible
  b. stingy   d. concerned

Vocabulary in Context _____ **8.** "After this *edict*, no daughter questioned." (paragraph 3)
  a. disappointment   c. suggestion
  b. command   d. reversal

Vocabulary in Context _____ **9.** "My mother had heard the commotion and joined my father to face me; both appeared shocked and *incredulous*." (paragraph 12)
  a. calm   c. convinced
  b. unquestioning   d. disbelieving

Vocabulary in Context _____ **10.** "Daddy at once demanded the source of this *unfilial*, non-Chinese theory." (paragraph 12)
  a. surprising   c. civil
  b. disrespectful   d. independent

Main Idea _____ **11.** Which of the following sentences states the central idea of the passage?
  a. "But having been set upon a new path, I did not oblige my parents with the expected conventional ending." (paragraph 2)
  b. "My indignation mounted against that tradition and I decided then that my past could not determine my future." (paragraph 5)
  c. "How old-fashioned was the dead-end attitude of my parents!" (paragraph 7)
  d. "I was too old to beat and too bold to intimidate." (paragraph 16)

Supporting Detail _____ **12.** Which college course had the greatest influence on the author's thinking and actions as described in the passage?
  a. chemistry   c. sociology
  b. Latin   d. English composition

Supporting Detail _____ **13.** According to the author's father, the superiority of Chinese culture was
  a. the strength of the family.   c. its loyalty to male children.
  b. its emphasis on education.   d. its devotion to religion.

Transitions _____ **14.** "Though I desired to continue on an above-average course, his material means were insufficient to support that ambition." (paragraph 3)

The relationship of ideas **within** this sentence is
  a. time order.   c. comparison and contrast.
  b. cause and effect.   d. generalization and example.

Transitions _____ **15.** "Both parents were thoroughly angered, scolded me for being shameless, and predicted that I would someday tell them I was wrong. But I dimly perceived that they were conceding defeat and were **perplexed** at this breakdown of their training." (paragraph 16)

The relationship of ideas **between** these sentences is
a. cause and effect.
b. time order.
c. comparison and contrast.
d. generalization and example.

Thought Patterns _____ **16.** The main thought pattern of the passage is
a. time order.
b. classification.
c. comparison and contrast.
d. definition and example.

Fact and Opinion _____ **17.** "So I decided to enter junior college, now San Francisco's City College, because the fees were lowest." (paragraph 6)

This sentence is a statement of
a. fact.
b. opinion.
c. fact and opinion.

Tone and Purpose _____ **18.** The overall tone and purpose of the author is
a. to inform the reader about her life growing up as a Chinese American female.
b. to entertain the reader with an amusing personal story about growing up as a Chinese American female.
c. to persuade the reader to challenge authority and become independent.

Inferences _____ **19.** Based on the details in the passage, we can infer that
a. the author's parents loved her brother more than they loved her.
b. the author's father thought his son more intelligent than his daughter.
c. educating a daughter was unwise since she is expected to leave the family once she marries.
d. the author disliked her parents.

Argument _____ **20.** "How old-fashioned was the dead-end attitude of my parents! How ignorant they were of modern thought and progress!" (paragraph 7)

Identify the logical fallacy used in these claims.
a. plain folks
b. straw man
c. transfer
d. personal attack

Mapping

Complete the following story web with information from the passage. Wording may vary.

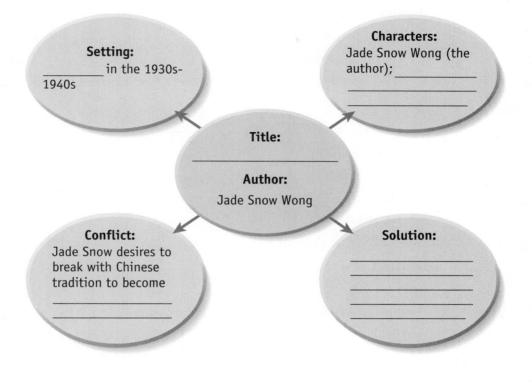

Setting:
_____ in the 1930s-1940s

Characters:
Jade Snow Wong (the author); _____
_____
_____

Title:
_____

Author:
Jade Snow Wong

Conflict:
Jade Snow desires to break with Chinese tradition to become _____
_____

Solution:
_____
_____
_____
_____

WHAT DO YOU THINK?

In this "coming of age" passage, Wong describes two powerful influences in her life: her family and education. How did what she learned in class affect her relationship with her parents? How did family and education help her come of age or initiate her into adulthood? Have you learned something in an academic class that changed your values or view of the world? Have you experienced a moment in your life when you felt you had to stand up for yourself as a responsible adult? Assume you are taking a sociology course, and you are studying how young people transition into adulthood. Write an essay on one of the following topics: "An important lesson I've learned from a class or an elder" or "The moment I knew I was an adult." If you prefer, you should feel free to write about someone else that you have observed.

EFFECTIVE READER Scorecard

"Fifth Chinese Daughter"

Skill	Number Correct	Points	Total
Vocabulary			
Vocabulary Preview (5 items)	_____ × 10 =		_____
Vocabulary in Context (5 items)	_____ × 10 =		_____
	Vocabulary Score =		_____
Comprehension			
Main Idea (1 item)	_____ × 8 =		_____
Supporting Details (2 items)	_____ × 8 =		_____
Transitions (2 items)	_____ × 8 =		_____
Thought Patterns (1 item)	_____ × 8 =		_____
Fact and Opinion (1 item)	_____ × 8 =		_____
Tone and Purpose (1 item)	_____ × 8 =		_____
Inferences (1 item)	_____ × 8 =		_____
Argument (1 item)	_____ × 8 =		_____
Mapping (5 items)	_____ × 4 =		_____
	Comprehension Score		_____

You DO Like Reading off a Computer Screen

(Originally published in Locus Magazine, March 2007)

Cory Doctorow

Cory Doctorow (craphound.com) is a science fiction author, activist, journalist and blogger—the co-editor of Boing Boing (boingboing.net) and the author of the bestselling Tor Teens/HarperCollins UK novel *Little Brother*. He is the former European director of the Electronic Frontier Foundation and co-founder of the UK Open Rights Group. Born in Toronto, Canada, he now lives in London. Do you like to read off a computer screen? Do you think e-books will eventually replace printed books?

Vocabulary Preview

cliché (paragraph 1): overused expression

Cthulhu (paragraph 1): a fictional high priest of elderly gods created by horror author H. P. Lovecraft; a symbol of horror or evil

RSS (paragraph 2): an acronym or short form that stands for "Really Simple Syndication"—a family of web feed formats used to publish frequently updated works

Don Quixote (paragraph 3): a novel written by Spanish author Miguel de Cervantes in the 1600s.

engendered (paragraph 4): produced, created

legend (paragraph 4): old stories passed down orally for generations before being recorded

advent (paragraph 6): arrival, introduction

apparatus (paragraph 8): equipment, device

protracted (paragraph 8): long-lasting, extended

Andrew Lloyd Webber (paragraph 10): a popular composer of Broadway musicals such as "The Phantom of the Opera" and "Cats"

shrine (paragraph 12): memorial, holy place

sig file (paragraph 14): a block of text automatically added to the bottom of an e-mail message, Usenet article, or forum post.

Sturgeon's 90th percentile (paragraph 16) a reference to a saying attributed to science fiction author Theodore Sturgeon: "90% of everything is crud."

---

1   "I don't like reading off a computer screen"—it's a **cliché** of the e-book world. It means "I don't read novels off of computer screens" (or phones, or PDAs, or dedicated e-book readers), and often as not the person who says it is someone who, in fact, spends every hour that **Cthulhu** sends reading off a computer screen. It's like watching someone shovel Mars Bars into his gob while telling you how much he hates chocolate.

2   But I know what you mean. You don't like reading long-form works off of a computer screen. I understand perfectly—in the ten minutes since I typed the first word in the paragraph above, I've checked my mail, deleted two spams, checked an image-sharing community I like, downloaded a YouTube clip of Stephen Colbert complaining about the iPhone (pausing my MP3 player first), cleared out my **RSS** reader, and then returned to write this paragraph.

3   This is not an ideal environment in which to concentrate on long-form narrative (sorry, one sec, gotta blog this guy who's made cardboard furniture) (wait, the Colbert clip's done, gotta start the music up) (19 more RSS items). But that's not to say that it's not an entertainment medium—indeed, practically everything I do on the computer entertains the hell out of me. It's nearly all text-based, too. Basically, what I do on the computer is pleasure-reading. But it's a fundamentally more scattered, splintered kind of pleasure. Computers have their own cognitive style, and it's not much like the cognitive style invented with the first modern novel (one sec, let me google that and confirm it), **Don Quixote**, some 400 years ago.

4   The novel is an invention, one that was **engendered** by technological changes in information display, reproduction, and distribution. The cognitive style of the novel is different from the cognitive style of the **legend**. The cognitive style of the computer is different from the cognitive style of the novel.

5   Computers want you to do lots of things with them. Networked computers doubly so — they (another RSS item) have a million ways of asking for your attention, and just as many ways of rewarding it.

6   There's a persistent fantasy/nightmare in the publishing world of the **advent** of very sharp, very portable computer screens. In the fantasy version, this creates an infinite new market for electronic books, and we all get to sell the rights to our work all over again. In the nightmare version, this leads to runaway piracy, and no one ever gets to sell a novel again.

7   I think they're both wrong. The infinitely divisible copyright ignores the "decision cost" borne by users who have to decide, over and over again, whether they want to spend a millionth of a cent on a millionth of a word—no one buys newspapers by the paragraph, even though most of us only read a slim fraction of any given paper. A supersharp, superportable screen would be used

to read all day long, but most of us won't spend most of our time reading anything recognizable as a book on them.

8   Take the record album. Everything about it is technologically pre-determined. The technology of the LP demanded artwork to differentiate one package from the next. The length was set by the groove density of the pressing plants and playback **apparatus**. The dynamic range likewise. These factors gave us the idea of the 40-to-60-minute package, split into two acts, with accompanying artwork. Musicians were encouraged to create works that would be enjoyed as a unitary whole for a **protracted** period—think of *Dark Side of the Moon,* or *Sgt. Pepper's.*

9   No one thinks about albums today. Music is now divisible to the single, as represented by an individual MP3, and then subdivisible into snippets like ringtones and samples. When recording artists demand that their works be considered as a whole—like when Radiohead insisted that the iTunes Music Store sell their whole album as a single, indivisible file that you would have to listen to all the way through—they sound like cranky throwbacks.

10   The idea of a 60-minute album is as weird in the Internet era as the idea of sitting through 15 hours of *Der Ring des Nibelungen* was 20 years ago. There are some **anachronisms** who love their long-form opera, but the real action is in the more fluid stuff that can slither around on hot wax—and now the superfluid droplets of MP3s and samples. Opera survives, but it is a tiny sliver of a much bigger, looser music market. The future composts the past: old operas get mounted for living anachronisms;

Andrew Lloyd Webber picks up the rest of the business.

Or look at digital video. We're watch- 11 ing more digital video, sooner, than anyone imagined. But we're watching it in three-minute chunks from YouTube. The video's got a pause button so you can stop it when the phone rings and a scrubber to go back and forth when you miss something while answering an IM.

And attention spans don't increase 12 when you move from the PC to a handheld device. These things have less capacity for multitasking than real PCs, and the network connections are slower and more expensive. But they are fundamentally multitasking devices—you can always stop reading an e-book to play a hand of solitaire that is interrupted by a phone call—and their social context is that they are used in public places, with a million distractions. It is socially acceptable to interrupt someone who is looking at a PDA screen. By contrast, the TV room—a whole room for TV!—is a **shrine** where none may speak until the commercial airs.

The problem, then, isn't that screens 13 aren't sharp enough to read novels off of. The problem is that novels aren't screeny enough to warrant protracted, regular reading on screens.

Electronic books are a wonderful 14 **adjunct** to print books. It's great to have a couple hundred novels in your pocket when the plane doesn't take off or the line is too long at the post office. It's cool to be able to search the text of a novel to find a beloved passage. It's excellent to use a novel socially, sending it to your friends, pasting it into your **sig file.**

15   But the numbers tell their own story—people who read off of screens all day long buy lots of print books and read them primarily on paper. There are some who prefer an all-electronic existence (I'd like to be able to get rid of the objects after my first reading, but keep the e-books around for reference), but they're in a tiny minority.

16   There's a generation of web writers who produce "pleasure reading" on the web. Some are funny. Some are touching. Some are enraging. Most dwell in **Sturgeon's 90th percentile** and below. They're not writing novels. If they were, they wouldn't be web writers.

17   Mostly, we can read just enough of a free e-book to decide whether to buy it in hardcopy—but not enough to substitute the e-book for the hardcopy. Like practically everything in marketing and promotion, the trick is to find the form of the work that serves as enticement, not replacement.

18   Sorry, got to go—eight more e-mails.

—Doctorow, Cory. "You DO Like Reading off a Computer Screen." Content: *Selected Essays on Technology, Creativity, Copyright, and the Future of the Future.* Tachyon Publications 2008 pp. 51–53.

VISUAL VOCABULARY

Complete the caption with a word from the Vocabulary Preview.

An e-reader is an _____ that makes an e-book portable.

Choose the best meaning of each word in *italics*. Use context clues to make your choice.

Vocabulary in Context   _____   **1.** "There are some *anachronisms* who love their long-form opera, but the real action is in the more fluid stuff that can slither around on hot wax—and now the superfluid droplets of MP3s and samples." (paragraph 10)

    a. holdovers   c. rebels

    b. relics   d. artists

Vocabulary in Context   _____ **2.** "Electronic books are a wonderful *adjunct* to print books." (paragraph 14)

    a. substitute   c. attachment

    b. advantage   d. addition

Implied Central Idea   _____ **3.** Which of the following sentences best states the implied central idea of the passage?

    a. No one likes to read novels off of computer screens.

    b. E-books are superior to hardcopy books.

    c. Hardcopy books are superior to e-books.

    d. Hardcopy books and e-books offer different but valuable reading experiences.

Main Idea   _____ **4.** Which of the following sentences states the main idea of paragraphs 4 and 5?

    a. "The novel is an invention, one that was engendered by technological changes in information display, reproduction, and distribution." (paragraph 4)

    b. "The cognitive style of the novel is different from the cognitive style of the legend." (paragraph 4)

    c. "The cognitive style of the computer is different from the cognitive style of the novel." (paragraph 4)

    d. "Computers want you to do lots of things with them." (paragraph 5)

Supporting Detail   _____ **5.** According to the author, which of the following was a factor in determining the length of a LP album?

    a. the playback apparatus   c. hot wax

    b. MP3 players   d. packaging

Supporting Detail   _____ **6.** *Der Ring des Nibelungen* is

    a. a popular LP.

    b. a compost.

    c. an opera.

    d. a musical by Andrew Lloyd Webber.

Transitions   _____ **7.** "'I don't like reading off a computer screen'—it's a cliché of the e-book world." (paragraph 1)

The relationship of ideas **within** this sentence is
a. time order.
b. cause and effect.
c. comparison and contrast.
d. definition and example.

Transitions _____ **8.** "It is socially acceptable to interrupt someone who is looking at a PDA screen. By contrast, the TV room—a whole room for TV!—is a shrine where none may speak until the commercial airs." (paragraph 12)

The relationship of ideas **between** these sentences is
a. cause and effect.
b. time order.
c. comparison and contrast.
d. generalization and example.

Thought Patterns _____ **9.** The thought pattern of paragraph 4
a. time order.
b. classification.
c. definition and example.
d. comparison and contrast.

Thought Patterns _____ **10.** The overall thought pattern of the passage is
a. time order.
b. classification.
c. comparison and contrast.
d. definition and example.

Fact and Opinion _____ **11.** "Music is now divisible to the single, as represented by an individual MP3, and then subdivisible into snippets like ringtones and samples." (paragraph 9)

This sentence is a statement of
a. fact.
b. opinion.
c. fact and opinion.

Fact and Opinion _____ **12.** "Electronic books are a wonderful adjunct to print books." (paragraph 14)

This sentence is a statement of
a. fact.
b. opinion.
c. fact and opinion.

Tone and Purpose _____ **13.** "It's like watching someone shovel Mars Bars into his gob while telling you how much he hates chocolate." (paragraph 1)

The tone of this sentence is
a. understanding.
b. sarcastic.
c. doubtful.
d. hateful.

Tone and Purpose _____ **14.** The tone of paragraph 2 is
a. belittling.
b. amused.
c. impatient.
d. neutral.

Tone and
Purpose

_____ **15.** The overall tone and purpose of the author is
   a. to inform the reader about the differences between reading an e-book and a print book.
   b. to entertain the reader with interesting details about reading e-books and print books.
   c. to persuade the reader that e-books will not replace print books.

Inferences

_____ **16.** Based on the details in the passage, we can infer that the author's main audience is
   a. youthful.
   b. highly educated.
   c. technology specialists.
   d. the general population familiar with technology.

Inferences

_____ **17.** Based on the details in the paragraphs 2 and 3, we can infer that the author
   a. has difficulty completing his tasks.
   b. enjoys multi-tasking.
   c. is overwhelmed by technology.
   d. doesn't like reading off a computer screen.

Inferences

_____ **18.** According to the author, the most pressing issue in the e-book versus the print book debate is
   a. piracy or theft of ideas.   c. pricing and marketing of ideas.
   b. free e-books.   d. cost of print books.

Argument

_____ **19.** The following items contain a claim and list of supports for that claim. Which sentence states the claim?
   a. Electronic books are a wonderful adjunct to print books.
   b. It's great to have a couple hundred novels in your pocket when the plane doesn't take off or the line is too long at the post office.
   c. It's cool to be able to search the text of a novel to find a beloved passage. It's excellent to use a novel socially, sending it to your friends, pasting it into your sig file.
   d. But the numbers tell their own story—people who read off of screens all day long buy lots of print books and read them primarily on paper.

Argument

_____ **20.** "Most dwell in **Sturgeon's 90th percentile** and below." (paragraph 16)

This statement asserts the logical fallacy

a. transfer.

b. personal attack.

c. name-calling.

d. glittering generality.

Outlining

Complete the following outline with information from the passage.

I. You don't like reading long-form works off of a computer screen.

II. The _____ of the computer is different from the _____ of the novel.

   A. The novel is an invention, one that was engendered by technological changes in information display, reproduction, and distribution.

   B. Computers want you to do lots of things with them.

III. The infinitely divisible copyright ignores the _____ borne by users.

   A. Take the _____.

   B. Or look at digital video.

IV. Electronic books are _____ to print books.

WHAT DO YOU THINK?

Do you surf the Internet for information? Do you like to read off of a computer screen? Do you think e-books will replace print books? Are some types of material easier to read using a computer? Assume the faculty at your college is considering switching to the use of e-books for all textbooks. Write a letter to the editor of your school's newspaper or to the community's local newspaper. In your letter, take a stand for or against the use of e-textbooks. Explain how your study habits differ when you are working with print and e-books.

EFFECTIVE READER Scorecard

"You DO Like Reading off a Computer Screen"

Skill	Number Correct	Points	Total
Vocabulary			
Vocabulary in Context (2 items)	_____	× 4 =	_____
Comprehension			
Implied Central Idea and Main Idea (2 items)	_____	× 4 =	_____
Supporting Details (2 items)	_____	× 4 =	_____
Transitions (2 items)	_____	× 4 =	_____
Thought Patterns (2 items)	_____	× 4 =	_____
Fact and Opinion (2 items)	_____	× 4 =	_____
Tone and Purpose (3 items)	_____	× 4 =	_____
Inferences (3 items)	_____	× 4 =	_____
Argument (2 items)	_____	× 4 =	_____
Outlining (5 items)	_____	× 4 =	_____
	Comprehension Score		_____

Brain Candy

Malcolm Gladwell

Malcolm Gladwell has been a staff writer with *The New Yorker* magazine since 1996. And in 2005, he was named one of *Time* magazine's 100 Most Influential People. He is the author of three books, *The Tipping Point: How Little Things Make a Big Difference* (2001), *Blink: The Power of Thinking Without Thinking* (2005), and *Outliers: The Story of Success* (2008), and *What the Dog Saw: And Other Adventures* (2009), all of which were number one *New York Times* bestsellers. The following article, a review of the book *Everything Bad Is Good for You*, by Steven Johnson, appeared in *The New Yorker* in 2005. Do you like to watch television and play video games? Do you think these activities are good for your mental development? Read the article to learn about some surprising benefits of pop culture.

Vocabulary Preview

recalibrate (paragraph 1): change, adjust

trajectory (paragraph 1): path, course, curve

eclecticism (paragraph 2): an approach that draws upon multiple styles or ideas

intricacies (paragraph 2): complexities, details

Nietzsche (paragraph 2): a German philosopher of the late 19th century who challenged traditional morality

excruciating (paragraph 3): extremely painful

intonation (paragraph 4): pitch of voice

cognitive (paragraph 5): relating to thought and acquiring of knowledge

denounce (paragraph 6): criticize, condemn

unambiguous (paragraph 7): clear, definite

hypotheses (paragraph 7): theories, assumptions

denigrating (paragraph 8): belittling, demeaning, criticizing

phenomena (paragraph 8): experiences, events

hierarchy (paragraph 8): formally ranked group, class, order

explicit (paragraph 11): clear and obvious

1

1   Twenty years ago, a political philosopher named James Flynn uncovered a curious fact. Americans—at least, as measured by I.Q. tests—were getting smarter. This fact had been obscured for years, because the people who give I.Q. tests continually **recalibrate** the scoring system to keep the

average at 100. But if you took out the recalibration, Flynn found, I.Q. scores showed a steady upward **trajectory**, rising by about three points per decade, which means that a person whose I.Q. placed him in the top ten per cent of the American population in 1920 would today fall in the bottom third. Some of that effect, no doubt, is a simple by-product of economic progress: in the surge of prosperity during the middle part of the last century, people in the West became better fed, better educated, and more familiar with things like I.Q. tests. But, even as that wave of change has subsided, test scores have continued to rise—not just in America but all over the developed world. What's more, the increases have not been confined to children who go to enriched day-care centers and private schools. The middle part of the curve—the people who have supposedly been suffering from a deteriorating public-school system and a steady diet of lowest-common-denominator television and mindless pop music—has increased just as much. What on earth is happening? In the wonderfully entertaining "Everything Bad Is Good for You" (Riverhead; $23.95), Steven Johnson proposes that what is making us smarter is precisely what we thought was making us dumber: popular culture.

2   Johnson is the former editor of the online magazine *Feed* and the author of a number of books on science and technology. There is a pleasing **eclecticism** to his thinking. He is as happy analyzing "Finding Nemo" as he is dissecting the **intricacies** of a piece of software, and he's perfectly capable of using **Nietzsche's** notion of eternal recurrence to discuss the new creative rules of television shows. Johnson wants to understand popular culture—not in the postmodern, academic sense of wondering what "The Dukes of Hazzard" tells us about Southern male alienation but in the very practical sense of wondering what watching something like "The Dukes of Hazzard" does to the way our minds work.

3   As Johnson points out, television is very different now from what it was thirty years ago. It's harder. A typical episode of "Starsky and Hutch," in the nineteen-seventies, followed an essentially linear path: two characters, engaged in a single story line, moving toward a decisive conclusion. To watch an episode of "Dallas" today is to be stunned by its glacial pace—by the arduous attempts to establish social relationships, by the **excruciating** simplicity of the plotline, by how *obvious* it was. A single episode of "The Sopranos," by contrast, might follow five narrative threads, involving a dozen characters who weave in and out of the plot. Modern television also requires the viewer to do a lot of what Johnson calls "filling in," as in a "Seinfeld" episode that subtly parodies the Kennedy assassination conspiracists, or a typical "Simpsons" episode, which may contain numerous allusions to politics or cinema or pop culture. The extraordinary amount of money now being made in the television aftermarket—DVD sales and syndication—means that the creators of television shows now have an incentive to make programming that can sustain two or three or four viewings. Even reality shows like "Survivor," Johnson argues, engage the viewer in a way that television rarely has in the past:

4   When we watch these shows, the part of our brain that monitors the emotional lives of the people around us—the part that tracks subtle shifts in **intonation** and gesture and facial expression—scrutinizes the action on the screen, looking for clues. . . . The phrase "Monday-morning quarterbacking" was coined to describe the engaged feeling spectators have in relation to games as opposed to stories. We absorb stories, but we second-guess games. Reality programming has brought that second-guessing to prime time, only the game in question revolves around social dexterity rather than the physical kind.

5   How can the greater **cognitive** demands that television makes on us now, he wonders, not *matter*?

6   Johnson develops the same argument about video games. Most of the people who **denounce** video games, he says, haven't actually played them—at least, not recently. Twenty years ago, games like Tetris or Pac-Man were simple exercises in motor coördination and pattern recognition. Today's games belong to another realm. Johnson points out that one of the "walk-throughs" for "Grand Theft Auto III"—that is, the informal guides that break down the games and help players navigate their complexities—is fifty-three thousand words long, about the length of his book. The contemporary video game involves a fully realized imaginary world, dense with detail and levels of complexity.

7   Indeed, video games are not games in the sense of those pastimes—like Monopoly or gin rummy or chess—which most of us grew up with. They don't have a set of **unambiguous** rules that have to be learned and then followed during the course of play. This is why many of us find modern video games baffling: we're not used to being in a situation where we have to figure out what to do. We think we only have to learn how to press the buttons faster. But these games withhold critical information from the player. Players have to explore and sort through **hypotheses** in order to make sense of the game's environment, which is why a modern video game can take forty hours to complete. Far from being engines of instant gratification, as they are often described, video games are actually, Johnson writes, "all about delayed gratification—sometimes so long delayed that you wonder if the gratification is ever going to show."

8   At the same time, players are required to manage a dizzying array of information and options. The game presents the player with a series of puzzles, and you can't succeed at the game simply by solving the puzzles one at a time. You have to craft a longer-term strategy, in order to juggle and coordinate competing interests. In **denigrating** the video game, Johnson argues, we have confused it with other **phenomena** in teen-age life, like multitasking—simultaneously e-mailing and listening to music and talking on the telephone and surfing the Internet. Playing a video game is, in fact, an exercise in "constructing the proper **hierarchy** of tasks and moving through the tasks in the correct sequence," he writes. "It's about finding order and meaning in the world, and making decisions that help create that order."

2

9   It doesn't seem right, of course, that watching "24" or playing a video game could be as important cognitively as reading a book. Isn't the extraordinary success of the "Harry Potter" novels better news for the culture than the equivalent success of "Grand Theft Auto III"? Johnson's response is to imagine what cultural critics might have said had video games been invented hundreds of years ago, and only recently had something called the book been marketed aggressively to children:

10   Reading books chronically understimulates the senses. Unlike the long-standing tradition of gameplaying—which engages the child in a vivid, three-dimensional world filled with moving images and musical soundscapes, navigated and controlled with complex muscular movements—books are simply a barren string of words on the page . . . Books are also tragically isolating. While games have for many years engaged the young in complex social relationships with their peers, building and exploring worlds together, books force the child to **sequester** him or herself in a quiet space, shut off from interaction with other children . . . But perhaps the most dangerous property of these books is the fact that they follow a fixed linear path. You can't control their narratives in any fashion—you simply sit back and have the story dictated to you . . . This risks instilling a general passivity in our children, making them feel as though they're powerless to change their circumstances.

Reading is not an active, **participatory** process; it's a submissive one.

He's joking, of course, but only in part. 11 The point is that books and video games represent two very different kinds of learning. When you read a biology textbook, the content of what you read is what matters. Reading is a form of **explicit** learning. When you play a video game, the value is in how it makes you think. Video games are an example of **collateral** learning, which is no less important.

Being "smart" involves facility in both 12 kinds of thinking—the kind of fluid problem solving that matters in things like video games and I.Q. tests, but also the kind of crystallized knowledge that comes from explicit learning. If Johnson's book has a flaw, it is that he sometimes speaks of our culture being "smarter" when he's really referring just to that fluid problem-solving facility. When it comes to the other kind of intelligence, it is not clear at all what kind of progress we are making, as anyone who has read, say, the Gettysburg Address alongside any Presidential speech from the past twenty years can attest. The real question is what the right balance of these two forms of intelligence might look like. "Everything Bad Is Good for You" doesn't answer that question. But Johnson does something nearly as important, which is to remind us that we shouldn't fall into the trap of thinking that explicit learning is the only kind of learning that matters.

In recent years, for example, a number 13 of elementary schools have phased out or reduced recess and replaced it with extra math or English instruction. This is the triumph of the explicit over the collateral.

After all, recess is "play" for a ten-year-old in precisely the sense that Johnson describes video games as play for an adolescent: an unstructured environment that requires the child actively to intervene, to look for the hidden logic, to find order and meaning in chaos.

14   One of the ongoing debates in the educational community, similarly, is over the value of homework. Meta-analysis of hundreds of studies done on the effects of homework shows that the evidence supporting the practice is, at best, modest. Homework seems to be most useful in high school and for subjects like math. At the elementary-school level, homework seems to be of marginal or no academic value. Its effect on discipline and personal responsibility is unproved. And the causal relation between high-school homework and achievement is unclear: it hasn't been firmly established whether spending more time on homework in high school makes you a better student or whether better students, finding homework more pleasurable, spend more time doing it. So why, as a society, are we so **enamored** of homework? Perhaps because we have so little faith in the value of the things that children would otherwise be doing with their time. They could go out for a walk, and get some exercise; they could spend time with their peers, and reap the rewards of friendship. Or, Johnson suggests, they could be playing a video game, and giving their minds a **rigorous** workout.

—Gladwell, Malcolm. "Brain Candy." *The New Yorker.* 16 May 2005. http://www.gladwell.com/2005/2005_05_16_a_brain.html.

Fill in the blank in each sentence with a word from the Vocabulary Preview.

Vocabulary Preview   **1.** Reality shows like *Survivor* and *American Idol* are television _____ that appeal to our spirit of competition.

Vocabulary Preview   **2.** Although critics may _____ reality shows, the public eagerly embraces the dramatic struggle to achieve a goal.

Vocabulary Preview   **3.** The contestants on reality shows are challenged on both emotional and _____ levels.

Vocabulary Preview   **4.** Contestants of reality shows are hoping that winning will change the _____ of their fortunes.

Vocabulary Preview   **5.** Those who are eliminated from these shows often must _____ their dreams to match the reality of losing.

For items 6 through 10, choose the best meaning of each word in *italics*. Use context clues to make your choice.

Vocabulary in Context _____ **6.** ". . . books force the child to *sequester* him or herself in a quiet space, shut off from interaction with other children . . ." (paragraph 10)
a. restore
b. enjoy
c. isolate
d. imprison

Vocabulary in Context _____ **7.** "Reading is not an active, *participatory* process; it's a submissive one." (paragraph 10)
a. pleasurable
b. involved
c. passive
d. simple

Vocabulary in Context _____ **8.** "Video games are an example of *collateral* learning, which is no less important." (paragraph 11)
a. indirect
b. accidental
c. direct
d. guaranteed

Vocabulary in Context _____ **9.** "So why, as a society, are we so *enamored of* homework?" (paragraph 14)
a. afraid of
b. spoiled by
c. addicted to
d. in love with

Vocabulary in Context _____ **10.** "Or, Johnson suggests, they could be playing a video game, and giving their minds a *rigorous* workout." (paragraph 14)
a. meaningless
b. amusing
c. demanding
d. mild

Main Idea _____ **11.** Which of the following sentences states the central idea of the passage?
a. "Americans—at least, as measured by I.Q. tests—were getting smarter." (paragraph 1)
b. "In the wonderfully entertaining 'Everything Bad Is Good for You' (Riverhead; $23.95), Steven Johnson proposes that what is making us smarter is precisely what we thought was making us dumber: popular culture." (paragraph 1)
c. "As Johnson points out, television is very different now from what it was thirty years ago." (paragraph 3)
d. "Reading is not an active participatory process; it's a submissive one." (paragraph 10)

Supporting Detail _____ **12.** Steven Johnson is
a. a political philosopher.
b. a film critic.
c. an author and former editor.
d. a video game designer.

Supporting
Detail
———— **13.** According to the passage, video games are an example of what type of learning?
  a. explicit
  b. collateral
  c. delayed gratification
  d. cognitive

Transitions
———— **14.** "We absorb stories, but we second-guess games." (paragraph 4)

The relationship of ideas **within** this sentence is
  a. cause and effect.
  b. time order.
  c. comparison and contrast.
  d. generalization and example.

Transitions
———— **15.** "We think we only have to learn how to press the buttons faster. But these games withhold critical information from the player." (paragraph 7)

The relationship of ideas **between** these sentences is
  a. cause and effect.
  b. time order.
  c. comparison and contrast.
  d. generalization and example.

Thought
Patterns
———— **16.** The main thought pattern of paragraph 11 is
  a. time order.
  b. classification.
  c. comparison and contrast.
  d. definition and example.

Fact and
Opinion
———— **17.** "Twenty years ago, a political philosopher named James Flynn uncovered a curious fact." (paragraph 1)

This sentence is a statement of
  a. fact
  b. opinion
  c. fact and opinion

Tone and
Purpose
———— **18.** The overall tone and purpose of the author is
  a. to inform the reader about the book *Everything Bad Is Good for You* by Steven Johnson.
  b. to entertain the reader with interesting details from Steven Johnson's book *Everything Bad Is Good for You.*
  c. to persuade the reader to consider the ideas raised by Steven Johnson in his book *Everything Bad Is Good for You.*

Inferences
———— **19.** Based on the details in paragraphs 9 and 10, we can infer that
  a. Steven Johnson's criticism against reading pokes fun at the criticism against gameplaying.
  b. Steven Johnson believes gameplaying is superior to reading.
  c. Steven Johnson's criticism against reading is sincere.
  d. Steven Johnson believes reading is a passive action.

Argument _____ **20.** Read the claim and supports taken from passage. Then identify the detail that does not support the claim.

> **Claim**: If Johnson's book has a flaw, it is that he sometimes speaks of our culture being "smarter" when he's really referring just to that fluid problem-solving facility.
>
> a. When it comes to the other kind of intelligence, it is not clear at all what kind of progress we are making, as anyone who has read, say, the Gettysburg Address alongside any Presidential speech from the past twenty years can attest.
> b. The real question is what the right balance of these two forms of intelligence might look like.
> c. "Everything Bad Is Good for You" doesn't answer that question.
> d. But Johnson does something nearly as important, which is to remind us that we shouldn't fall into the trap of thinking that explicit learning is the only kind of learning that matters.

Mapping

Complete the following comparison and contrast chart with information from the passage. Wording may vary.

Differences Between Contemporary Media and Media Twenty to Thirty Years Ago				
	Contemporary	**Examples**	**Twenty to Thirty Years Ago**	**Examples**
Television	Plots follow multiple _____; dozen of characters; viewer "filling in"	*The Sopranos; Seinfeld; Survivor; 24*	Plots follow _____; two characters; single story line; decisive conclusion	*Starsky and Hutch; Dallas*
Gaming	Involves fully realized imaginary worlds, dense with detail and levels of complexity; players explore, find order, and make decisions	_____ _____	Simple exercises in _____ _____ _____; unambiguous rules to be learned and followed	*Tetris; Pac Man; Monopoly; gin rummy; chess*

WHAT DO YOU THINK?

Do you agree with Stephen Johnson's claim that pop culture is making us smart? Why or why not? Would you rather read a book or see the movie? Why? Assume you are a reporter for the newspaper at your college or university. Write a review of a book, movie, or game that deepens understanding or enhances knowledge in some way.

EFFECTIVE READER Scorecard

"Brain Candy"			
Skill	**Number Correct**	**Points**	**Total**
Vocabulary			
Vocabulary Preview (5 items)	_____	× 10 =	_____
Vocabulary in Context (5 items)	_____	× 10 =	_____
	Vocabulary Score	=	_____
Comprehension			
Main Idea (1 item)	_____	× 8 =	_____
Supporting Details (2 items)	_____	× 8 =	_____
Transitions (2 items)	_____	× 8 =	_____
Thought Patterns (1 item)	_____	× 8 =	_____
Fact and Opinion (1 item)	_____	× 8 =	_____
Tone and Purpose (1 item)	_____	× 8 =	_____
Inferences (1 item)	_____	× 8 =	_____
Argument (1 item)	_____	× 8 =	_____
Mapping (4 items)	_____	× 5 =	_____
	Comprehension Score		_____

Curbing College Drinking Starts with a Change in Attitude

by Sara Fritz

College drinking is often seen as a harmless rite of passage into adulthood for American youth. Yet statistics reveal the seriousness of this behavior in the number of deaths, injuries, and assaults that occur each year in connection with college drinking. Sara Fritz, Washington Bureau Chief for the *St. Petersburg Times*, explores the problems of this long-standing dilemma and possible solutions for it.

Vocabulary Preview

trustee (paragraph 4): board member
intractable (paragraph 8): stubborn

1   Drinking by college students has long been seen as a relatively harmless rite of passage for young people. But we now have solid statistics that demonstrate the seriousness of the problem.

2   Each year, about 1,400 college students between ages 18 and 24 die of alcohol-related injuries, including auto accidents, alcohol poisoning and suicide. Another 500,000 sustain injuries under the influence of alcohol. More than 600,000 students are assaulted by a student who has been drinking, and about 70,000 of those are sexual assaults.

3   Of course, these statistics do not begin to portray the incredible loss that is felt on a campus or within families when young people with promising lives are killed while partying. These students are dying or killing themselves at the very moment when their lives are beginning to flourish. These are people who might otherwise find cures for disease, become our next political leaders or, at minimum, get married and raise children of their own.

4   As a college **trustee,** I have spent many long hours in discussions with students about this problem. Even though they frequently see fellow students being carried out of the dorm by paramedics after long bouts of excessive drinking, many of them still think the problem is being exaggerated.

5   "Our parents drank, did drugs and partied in college," they say, "so why are they trying to prevent us from doing the same thing?"

6   There are a couple of answers to this very good question. First, many of their parents have come to regret the excesses of their youth. Some have struggled with drug and

alcohol problems ever since. Second, because we now talk more openly about date rape and sexual assault, the real consequences of college drinking binges are better understood than they were two or three decades ago.

7   Nearly every college and university tries to do something to curb the problem, especially after a student dies. They appoint a counselor for students who get in trouble while abusing alcohol or they post signs or distribute brochures outlining the dangers of alcohol. Some campuses even establish chapters of Alcoholics Anonymous.

8   When these measures fail to curb reckless drinking, college administrators conclude it is an **insoluble** problem. "With each failed effort," says a new NIH report, "the image of college drinking as an **intractable** problem is reinforced, administrators are demoralized, and the likelihood that schools will devote resources to prevent programs decreases."

9   Now we have a group of social scientists who think their discipline can help solve the problem of college drinking. The group issued a report last week outlining a number of approaches that promise to change the drinking culture on college campuses.

10   What a concept! You'd think the nation's academics might have thought of using the tools of their trade on a problem in their own back yard long before now.

11   "We need not accept high-risk drinking on our campuses as inevitable," says Mark Goldman, a researcher at the University of South Florida and co-chairman of the NIH task force working on this problem. "If colleges and communities work together, they can change these harmful drinking patterns."

12   The key to solving the problem, according to Goldman's task force, is to attack the problem from three different angles. The approach must try to change the entire student population, the environment in which they exist and the specific at-risk drinkers. This means there is probably no college or university in the country that is doing enough. Goldman and the task force deserve thanks for their work, even though their findings seem somewhat self-evident. But my guess is their report will be lost in the blizzard of paper that arrives on college campuses from the government.

13   Before any such program can succeed, students must be convinced that binge drinking is not normal behavior. Parents and college administrators have to be convinced that it is possible for them to influence students' behavior.

Choose the best meaning of each word in *italics*. Use context clues to make your choice.

Vocabulary in Context _____ **1.** "When these measures fail to curb reckless drinking, college administrators conclude it is an *insoluble* problem." (paragraph 8)

    a. college   c. impossible to solve
    b. family   d. easily solved

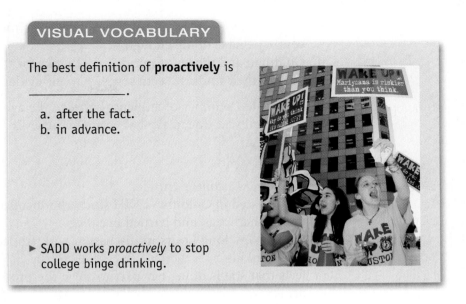

VISUAL VOCABULARY

The best definition of **proactively** is

_____.

a. after the fact.
b. in advance.

▶ SADD works *proactively* to stop college binge drinking.

Vocabulary in Context _____ **2.** " 'With each failed effort,' says a new NIH report, 'the image of college drinking as an intractable problem is reinforced, administrators are *demoralized*, and the likelihood that schools will devote resources to prevent programs decreases.'" (paragraph 8)
   a. right   c. inspired
   b. uninvolved   d. discouraged

Central Idea and Main Idea _____ **3.** Which sentence is the best statement of the implied central idea of the passage?
   a. Drinking by college students is a serious problem.
   b. A recent study suggests a program to address the serious and stubborn problems posed by college drinking.
   c. College drinking is an insoluble problem.
   d. Nearly every educational institution of higher learning is attempting to solve the problem of college drinking.

Central Idea and Main Idea _____ **4.** Which sentence is the best statement of the main idea of paragraph 12?
   a. The key to solving the problem, according to Goldman's task force, is to attack the problem from three different angles.
   b. The approach must try to change the entire student population, the environment in which they exist and the specific at-risk drinkers.

c. This means there is probably no college or university in the country that is doing enough.

d. Goldman and the task force deserve thanks for their work, even though their findings seem somewhat self-evident.

Supporting _____ **5.** The estimated number of students between the ages of 18 and 24
Details who die each year due to alcohol-related injuries is
a. 70,000.   c. 500.
b. 600,000.   d. 1,400.

Supporting _____ **6.** The author, as a college trustee,
Details a. participated in Goldman's NIH study about college drinking.
b. drank, did drugs, and partied in college.
c. spent many long hours in discussion with students about college drinking.
d. feels that she is doing her part to solve the problem of college drinking.

Thought _____ **7.** The main thought pattern for the overall passage is
Patterns a. comparing and contrasting drinking college students to non-drinking college students.
b. discussing the causes of college drinking.
c. listing and discussing the problems associated with college drinking and possible solutions.
d. a narrative account of college drinking.

Thought _____ **8.** The thought pattern for paragraph 6 is
Patterns a. comparison and contrast.   c. time order.
b. listing.

Transitions _____ **9.** "Each year, about 1,400 college students between ages 18 and 24 die of alcohol-related injuries, including auto accidents, alcohol poisoning and suicide. Another 500,000 sustain injuries under the influence of alcohol." (paragraph 2)

The relationship of ideas between these two sentences is
a. addition.   c. effect.
b. contrast.

Transitions _____ **10.** "Before any such program can succeed, students must be convinced that binge drinking is not normal behavior." (paragraph 13)

The relationship of ideas within this sentence is
a. time order.   c. cause and effect.
b. example.

Fact and Opinion _____ **11.** Overall, the ideas in this passage
   a. are based on research and statistics.
   b. are based on the personal experiences of the author.
   c. are based on a mix of statistics, research, and the personal experiences of the author.

Fact and Opinion _____ **12.** "These are people who might otherwise find cures for disease, become our next political leaders or, at minimum, get married and raise children of their own."

This sentence from paragraph 3 is a statement of
   a. fact.   c. fact and opinion.
   b. opinion.

Tone and Purpose _____ **13.** The overall tone of the passage is
   a. pessimistic.   c. angry.
   b. enthusiastic.   d. aloof.

Tone and Purpose _____ **14.** The tone of paragraph 10 is
   a. admiring.   c. ungrateful.
   b. sarcastic.   d. pleased.

Tone and Purpose _____ **15.** The tone of paragraph 13 is
   a. forceful.   c. bitter.
   b. unsure.   d. pleading.

Tone and Purpose _____ **16.** The author's main purpose in this article is
   a. to persuade students, parents, and educators to change the culture that leads to college binge drinking.
   b. to entertain readers with a personal reflection about a current issue.
   c. to inform the readers about the serious problem of college binge drinking.

Inferences _____ **17.** From paragraphs 5 and 6, we can conclude that
   a. some students who drink in college think that their parents' objections to college drinking are hypocritical.
   b. most parents don't mind if their college-aged students drink alcohol.
   c. all parents "drank, did drugs and partied in college."
   d. college students are spoiled and selfish.

Inferences _____ **18.** From the details in paragraph 2, we can conclude that
   a. college drinking is on the rise.
   b. college drinking is an isolated problem.

c. over a million students suffer serious problems as a result of college drinking each year.

d. the problem of college drinking cannot be solved.

Inferences _____ **19.** The article implies that

a. students are the only ones who can solve the problem of college drinking.

b. solving the problem of college drinking will require the efforts of students, parents, and educators.

c. the problem of college drinking cannot be solved.

d. the problem of college drinking is exaggerated.

Argument _____ **20. Claim:** Parents should share with their children their hard-won wisdom about college drinking.

Which statement does not support this claim?

a. Many parents have come to regret the excesses of their youth.

b. The real consequences of college drinking binges are better understood now than they were two or three decades ago.

c. No college or university in the country is doing enough to solve the problem of college binge drinking on their campuses.

d. Students who are at risk will not listen to their parents about college binge drinking.

Outlining

Complete the following study outline with information from the passage.

  I. The problem is very serious.

 II. _____ raise a question.

III. Colleges and universities respond to the problem.

IV. Social scientists study the problem.

    A. _____

    B. Attack problem from three angles

      1. Change the _____

      2. _____

      3. _____

  V. Students, parents, and college administrators must change attitudes and work together to solve the problem.

WHAT DO YOU THINK?

Is binge drinking a problem at the college you attend? How does the college respond to student drinking? Does binge drinking occur in places not related to college? How should one respond to a person or group involved in binge drinking? Assume you are a member of your college's Student Government Association. The administration is developing a policy about binge drinking and substance abuse. You have been asked to participate as a student representative on a college-wide committee. Write a report for the committee about the status of substance abuse by the student population. Recommend a plan of action.

EFFECTIVE READER Scorecard

"Curbing College Drinking Starts with a Change in Attitude"			
Skill	**Number Correct**	**Points**	**Total**
Vocabulary			
Vocabulary in Context (2 items)	_____	× 4 =	_____
Comprehension			
Central Idea and Main Idea (2 items)	_____	× 4 =	_____
Supporting Details (2 items)	_____	× 4 =	_____
Thought Patterns (2 items)	_____	× 4 =	_____
Transitions (2 items)	_____	× 4 =	_____
Fact and Opinion (2 items)	_____	× 4 =	_____
Tone and Purpose (4 items)	_____	× 4 =	_____
Inferences (3 items)	_____	× 4 =	_____
Argument (1 item)	_____	× 4 =	_____
Outlining (5 items)	_____	× 4 =	_____
	Comprehension Score		_____

Time to Look and Listen

Magdoline Asfahani

According to some experts, nearly 900,000 legal immigrants flow into the United States each year. These immigrants come from vastly different cultures and face tremendous challenges. In the following essay, published in *Newsweek* Magazine's "My Turn" column December 2, 1996, the author shares her love of America and the challenges of her multicultural upbringing.

Vocabulary Preview

conscious (paragraph 1): mindful, aware
incompatible (paragraph 2): mismatched, unable to coexist
heritage (paragraph 3): tradition, custom, birthright
monotheistic (paragraph 5): the belief in one god
nuances (paragraph 8): subtle degrees of meaning
collective (paragraph 11): group

---

1   I love my country as many who have been here for generations cannot. Perhaps that's because I'm the child of immigrants, raised with a **conscious** respect for America that many people take for granted. My parents chose this country because it offered them a new life, freedom and possibilities. But I learned at a young age that the country we loved so much did not feel the same way about us.

2   Discrimination is not unique to America. It occurs in any country that allows immigration. Anyone who is unlike the majority is looked at a little suspiciously, dealt with a little differently. I knew that I was an Arab and a Muslim. This meant nothing to me. At school I stood up to say the Pledge of Allegiance every day. These things did not seem **incompatible** at all. Then everything changed for me, suddenly and permanently, in 1985. I was only in seventh grade, but that was the beginning of my political education.

3   That year a TWA plane originating in Athens was diverted to Beirut. Two years earlier the U.S. Marine barracks in Beirut had been bombed. That seemed to start a chain of events that would forever link Arabs with terrorism. After the hijacking, I faced classmates who taunted me with cruel names, attacking my **heritage** and my religion. I became an outcast and had to apologize for myself constantly.

4   After a while, I tried to forget my heritage. No matter what race, religion or ethnicity, a child who is attacked often retreats. I was the only Arab I knew of in my class, so

I had no one in my peer group as an ally. No matter what my parents tried to tell me about my proud cultural history, I would ignore it. My classmates told me I came from an uncivilized, brutal place, that Arabs were by nature anti-American, and I believed them. They did not know the hours my parents spent studying, working, trying to preserve part of their old lives while embracing, willingly, the new.

5   I tried to forget the Arabic I knew, because if I didn't I'd be forever linked to murderers. I stopped inviting friends over for dinner, because I thought the food we ate was "weird." I lied about where my parents had come from. Their accents (although they spoke English perfectly) **humiliated** me. Though Islam is a major **monotheistic** religion with many similarities to Judaism and Christianity, there were no holidays near Chanukah or Christmas, nothing to tie me to the "Judeo-Christian" tradition. I felt more excluded. I slowly began to turn into someone without a past.

6   Civil war was raging in Lebanon, and all that Americans saw of that country was destruction and violence. Every other movie seemed to feature Arab terrorists. The most common questions I was asked were if I had ever ridden a camel or if my family lived in tents. I felt burdened with responsibility. Why should an adolescent be asked questions like "Is it true you hate Jews and you want Israel destroyed?" I didn't hate anybody. My parents had never said anything even alluding to such **sentiments**. I was confused and hurt.

7   As I grew older and began to form my own opinions, my embarrassment lessened and my anger grew. The turning point came in high school. My grandmother had become very ill, and it was necessary for me to leave school a few days before Christmas vacation. My chemistry teacher was very sympathetic until I said I was going to the Middle East. "Don't come back in a body bag," he said cheerfully. The class laughed. Suddenly, those years of watching movies that mocked me and listening to others who knew nothing about Arabs and Muslims except what they saw on television seemed like a bad dream. I knew then that I would never be silent again.

8   I've tried to reclaim those lost years. I realize now that I come from a culture that has a rich history. The Arab world is a medley of people of different religions; not every Arab is a Muslim, and vice versa. The Arabs brought tremendous advances in the sciences and mathematics, as well as creating a literary tradition that has never been surpassed. The language itself is flexible and beautiful, with **nuances** and shades of meaning unparalleled in any language. Though many find it hard to believe, Islam has made progress in women's rights. There is a specific provision in the Koran that permits women to own property and ensures that their inheritance is protected—although recent events have shown that interpretation of these laws can vary.

9   My youngest brother, who is 12, is now at the crossroads I faced. When initial reports of the Oklahoma City bombing pointed to "Arab-looking individuals" as the culprits, he came home from school crying. "Mom, why do Muslims kill people? Why are the Arabs so bad?" She was angry and brokenhearted, but tried to handle the situation in the best way possible through education.

She went to his class, armed with Arabic music, pictures, traditional dress and cookies. She brought a chapter of the social-studies book to life and the children asked intelligent, thoughtful questions, even after the class was over. Some even asked if she was coming back. When my brother came home, he was excited and proud instead of ashamed.

10   I only recently told my mother about my past experience. Maybe if I had told her then, I would have been better equipped to deal with the thoughtless teasing. But, fortunately, the world is changing. Although discrimination and stereotyping still exist, many people are trying to lessen and end it. Teachers, schools and the media are showing greater sensitivity to cultural issues. However, there is still much that needs to be done, not for the sake of any particular ethnic or cultural groups but for the sake of our country.

11   The America that I love is one that values freedom and the differences of its people. Education is the key to understanding. As Americans we need to take a little time to look and listen carefully to what is around us and not rush to judgment without knowing the facts. And we must never be ashamed of our pasts. It is our **collective** differences that unite and make us unique as a nation. It's what determines our present and our future.

Choose the best meaning of each word in *italics*. Use context clues to make your choice.

Vocabulary in Context _____ **1.** "Their accents (although they spoke English perfectly) *humiliated* me." (paragraph 5)
    a. provoked   c. embarrassed
    b. harmed   d. inspired

Vocabulary in Context _____ **2.** "My parents had never said anything even alluding to such *sentiments*." (paragraph 6)
    a. facts   c. ideals
    b. details   d. feelings

Central Idea and Main Idea _____ **3.** Which sentence best states the central idea of the passage?
    a. I love my country as many who have not been here for generations cannot.
    b. After the hijacking, I faced classmates who taunted me with cruel names, attacking my heritage and my religion.
    c. Although discrimination and stereotyping still exist, many people are trying to lessen and end it.
    d. As Americans we need to take a little time to look and listen carefully to what is around us and not rush to judgment without knowing the facts.

Central Idea
and Main Idea _____

4. Which sentence best states the main idea of paragraph 2?
a. Discrimination is not unique to America.
b. Anyone who is unlike the majority is looked at a little suspiciously, dealt with a little differently.
c. I knew that I was an Arab and a Muslim.
d. At school I stood up to say the Pledge of Allegiance every day.

Supporting
Details _____

5. What significant event occurred in 1985?
a. The author's family immigrated into the United States.
b. The U.S. Marine barracks in Beirut was bombed.
c. A TWA plane originating in Athens was hijacked to Beirut.
d. The author's younger brother faced cruelty at school.

Supporting
Details _____

6. What was the turning point in the author's acceptance of her heritage?
a. the hijacking of the TWA plane
b. the name calling by her peers
c. the chemistry teacher's response to her need to travel to the Middle East
d. her mother's visit to a classroom

Thought
Patterns _____

7. The main thought pattern for the entire passage is
a. a series of events of the author's struggles as an Arab-Muslim immigrant in the United States.
b. a list of causes for discrimination against Arab-Muslims.
c. a discussion of the differences between American and Arab cultures.
d. a list of reasons in an argument for legal immigration.

Thought
Patterns _____

8. The thought pattern for paragraph 6 is
a. listing.   c. definition.
b. comparison and contrast.

Transitions _____

9. "Civil War was raging in Lebanon, and all that Americans saw of that country was destruction and violence." (paragraph 6)

The relationship of ideas within this sentence is
a. cause and effect.   c. addition.
b. comparison and contrast.

Transitions _____

10. "Teachers, schools and the media are showing greater sensitivity to cultural issues. However, there is still much that needs to be done, not for the sake of any particular ethnic or cultural groups but for the sake of our country." (paragraph 10)

The relationship of ideas between these sentences is
a. cause and effect.   c. addition.
b. comparison and contrast.

Fact and Opinion _____ **11.** "I love my country as many who have been here for generations cannot."

This sentence from paragraph 1 is a statement of
a. fact.   c. fact and opinion.
b. opinion.

Fact and Opinion _____ **12.** "The Arabs brought tremendous advances in the sciences and mathematics, as well as creating a literary tradition that has never been surpassed."

This sentence from paragraph 8 is a statement of
a. fact.   c. fact and opinion.
b. opinion.

Tone and Purpose _____ **13.** The overall tone of the passage is
a. sincere.   c. angry.
b. sarcastic.   d. matter of fact.

Tone and Purpose _____ **14.** The tone of paragraph 8 is
a. embarrassed.   c. admiring.
b. humble.   d. neutral.

Tone and Purpose _____ **15.** The overall purpose of the passage is to
a. inform the reader about the strengths of the Arab-Muslim culture.
b. entertain the reader with a personal story.
c. persuade the reader to be more tolerant of different cultures.

Inferences _____ **16.** From the article, we can conclude that
a. discrimination can never be overcome.
b. all immigrants face prejudice and mistreatment.
c. prejudice can be overcome through education.
d. discrimination occurs more frequently in America than in other countries.

Inferences _____ **17.** From the details in paragraph 5, we can conclude that
a. the author was not well liked by her peers.
b. the author did not get along well with her family.
c. religious traditions can be a powerful force that unites or separates people.
d. separation of church and state is necessary.

Argument _____ **18. Claim:** Misconceptions about Arab-Muslim culture existed in America in the 1990s.

Which of the following statements does not support this claim?
a. Civil war was raging in Lebanon.
b. All that Americans saw of Lebanon was destruction and violence.
c. Every other movie seemed to feature Arab terrorists.
d. The author was often asked if she had ever ridden a camel or if her family lived in tents.

Argument _____ **19.** The following list of ideas contains a claim and supports for that claim. In the space, write the letter of the claim for the argument.
a. The Arab culture has a rich history.
b. Arabs brought tremendous advances in the sciences and mathematics, as well as creating a literary tradition that has never been surpassed.
c. The language itself is flexible and beautiful, with nuances and shades of meaning unparalleled in any language.
d. Islam has made progress in women's rights.

Argument _____ **20.** The following list of ideas contains a claim and supports for that claim. In the space, write the letter of the claim for the argument.
a. After a while, I tried to forget my heritage.
b. No matter what my parents tried to tell me about my proud cultural history, I would ignore it.
c. I tried to forget the Arabic I knew, because if I didn't I'd be forever linked to murderers.
d. I stopped inviting friends over for dinner, because I thought the food we ate was "weird."

Outlining

Add the ideas needed to complete this outline of "Time to Look and Listen."

I. Immigration and discrimination

  A. Author expresses love for America.

  B. Author experiences discrimination in school.

  C. World events link Arabs with terrorism.

    1. TWA hijacking

    2. _____

II. Rejection of Arab heritage

    A. _____

    B. Author feels humiliated by her family's traditions.

    C. Author becomes confused and hurt.

III. The turning point

    A. _____

    B. Teacher makes an insensitive remark.

    C. Classmates laugh.

IV. A rich history

    A. _____

       _____

    B. The Arabic language is flexible and beautiful.

    C. Islam has made progress in women's rights.

V. Education: the key

    A. Author's brother faces prejudice of peers.

    B. _____

    C. Author's brother feels pride in his heritage.

VI. America's need

    A. America is becoming somewhat more sensitive to cultural issues.

    B. Discrimination and stereotyping still exist.

    C. America's differences unite us and make us unique.

WHAT DO YOU THINK?

Have you experienced or witnessed someone else experience discrimination? What was its effect? The author ends her essay with the following statement: "It is our collective differences that unite and make us unique as a nation." What do you think she means? In what ways do our differences make us stronger as a country? Assume that Congress plans to pass a law that limits the number of legal immigrants allowed in the country. You have decided to take a public stand in favor of or in opposition to the proposed law. Write your position as a letter to your Congress representative.

EFFECTIVE READER Scorecard

"Time to Look and Listen"

Skill	Number Correct	Points		Total
Vocabulary				
Vocabulary in Context (2 items)	_____	× 4	=	_____
Comprehension				
Central Idea and Main Idea (2 items)	_____	× 4	=	_____
Supporting Details (2 items)	_____	× 4	=	_____
Thought Patterns (2 items)	_____	× 4	=	_____
Transitions (2 items)	_____	× 4	=	_____
Fact and Opinion (2 items)	_____	× 4	=	_____
Tone and Purpose (3 items)	_____	× 4	=	_____
Inferences (2 items)	_____	× 4	=	_____
Argument (3 items)	_____	× 4	=	_____
Outlining (5 items)	_____	× 4	=	_____
	Comprehension Score			_____

READING 7

The Quest for Peace and Justice
Nobel Lecture, December 11, 1964

Martin Luther King, Jr.

Dr. Martin Luther King, Jr. was awarded the Nobel Prize for Peace in 1964. At age 35, Dr. King was the youngest person to have received the Nobel Peace Prize. In the presentation of the award, Gunnar Jahn, Chairman of the Nobel Committee, offered the following praise of Dr. King. "Today we pay tribute to Martin Luther King, the man who has never abandoned his faith in the unarmed struggle he is waging, who has suffered for his faith, who has been imprisoned on many occasions, whose home has been subject to bomb attacks, whose life and the lives of his family have been threatened, and who nevertheless has never faltered." The following passage presents the introduction and the third major point of King's Nobel Lecture. To read his entire speech go to Nobelprize.org.

Vocabulary Preview

unfathomable (paragraph 1): impossible to measure, profound, unknowable

subjugates (paragraph 3): overpowers, overcomes, subdues

constitutes (paragraph 4): makes up, forms, composes

infantilism (paragraph 4): childishness, immaturity

inextricably (paragraph 4): inseparably, totally

annihilation (paragraph 5): total destruction, extinction

proneness (paragraph 6): tendency to do or be affected by something

inexorably (paragraph 6): unstoppable, unavoidably

inferno (paragraph 6): blaze, fire, hellhole

Dante (paragraph 6): a noted Italian poet of the Middle Ages

genocidal (paragraph 7): murderous

impotence (paragraph 8): powerlessness, inability, weakness

expulsion (paragraph 10): dismissed from a place of membership

cosmic (paragraph 11): vast, global, heavenly

elegy (paragraph 11): funeral song, mournful poem

ecumenical (paragraph 13): universal

Nietzsches (paragraph 14): followers of Fredrick Nietzsche, a German philosopher, poet, and critic, noted for his concept of the superman and his rejection of traditional Christian values

1   This evening I would like to use this lofty and historic platform to discuss what appears to me to be the most pressing problem confronting mankind today. Modern man has brought this whole world to an awe-inspiring threshold of the future. He has reached new and astonishing peaks of scientific success. He has produced machines that think and instruments that peer into the **unfathomable** ranges of interstellar space. He has built gigantic bridges to span the seas and **gargantuan** buildings to kiss the skies. His airplanes and spaceships have dwarfed distance, placed time in chains, and carved highways through the stratosphere. This is a dazzling picture of modern man's scientific and technological progress.

2   Yet, in spite of these spectacular strides in science and technology, and still unlimited ones to come, something basic is missing. There is a sort of poverty of the spirit which stands in glaring contrast to our scientific and technological abundance. The richer we have become materially, the poorer we have become morally and spiritually. We have learned to fly the air like birds and swim the sea like fish, but we have not learned the simple art of living together as brothers.

3   Every man lives in two realms, the internal and the external. The internal is that realm of spiritual ends expressed in art, literature, morals, and religion. The external is that complex of devices, techniques, mechanisms, and instrumentalities by means of which we live. Our problem today is that we have allowed the internal to become lost in the external. We have allowed the means by which we live to outdistance the ends for which we live. So much of modern life can be summarized in that arresting **dictum** of the poet Thoreau: "Improved means to an unimproved end." This is the serious **predicament**, the deep and haunting problem confronting modern man. If we are to survive today, our moral and spiritual "lag" must be eliminated. Enlarged material powers spell enlarged peril if there is not proportionate growth of the soul. When the "without" of man's nature **subjugates** the "within," dark storm clouds begin to form in the world.

4   This problem of spiritual and moral lag, which **constitutes** modern man's chief dilemma, expresses itself in three larger problems which grow out of man's ethical **infantilism**. Each of these problems, while appearing to be separate and isolated, is **inextricably** bound to the other. I refer to racial injustice, poverty, and war.

***

5   A third great evil confronting our world is that of war. Recent events have vividly reminded us that nations are not reducing but rather increasing their arsenals of weapons of mass destruction. The best brains in the highly developed nations of the world are devoted to military technology. The proliferation of nuclear weapons has not been halted, in spite of the Limited Test Ban Treaty. On the contrary, the detonation of an atomic device by the first nonwhite, non-Western, and

so-called underdeveloped power, namely the Chinese People's Republic, opens new vistas of exposure of vast multitudes, the whole of humanity, to **insidious** terrorization by the ever-present threat of **annihilation**. The fact that most of the time human beings put the truth about the nature and risks of the nuclear war out of their minds because it is too painful and therefore not "acceptable," does not alter the nature and risks of such war. The device of "rejection" may temporarily cover up anxiety, but it does not bestow peace of mind and emotional security.

6 So man's **proneness** to engage in war is still a fact. But wisdom born of experience should tell us that war is obsolete. There may have been a time when war served as a negative good by preventing the spread and growth of an evil force, but the destructive power of modern weapons eliminated even the possibility that war may serve as a negative good. If we assume that life is worth living and that man has a right to survive, then we must find an alternative to war. In a day when vehicles hurtle through outer space and guided ballistic missiles carve highways of death through the stratosphere, no nation can claim victory in war. A so-called limited war will leave little more than a calamitous legacy of human suffering, political turmoil, and spiritual disillusionment. A world war— God forbid!—will leave only smoldering ashes as a mute testimony of a human race whose folly led **inexorably** to ultimate death. So if modern man continues to flirt unhesitatingly with war, he will transform his earthly habitat into an **inferno** such as even the mind of **Dante** could not imagine.

7 Therefore, I venture to suggest to all of you and all who hear and may eventually read these words, that the philosophy and strategy of nonviolence become immediately a subject for study and for serious experimentation in every field of human conflict, by no means excluding the relations between nations. It is, after all, nation-states which make war, which have produced the weapons which threaten the survival of mankind, and which are both **genocidal** and suicidal in character.

8 Here also we have ancient habits to deal with, vast structures of power, indescribably complicated problems to solve. But unless we **abdicate** our humanity altogether and succumb to fear and **impotence** in the presence of the weapons we have ourselves created, it is as imperative and urgent to put an end to war and violence between nations as it is to put an end to racial injustice. Equality with whites will hardly solve the problems of either whites or Negroes if it means equality in a society under the spell of terror and a world doomed to extinction.

9 I do not wish to minimize the complexity of the problems that need to be faced in achieving disarmament and peace. But I think it is a fact that we shall not have the will, the courage, and the insight to deal with such matters unless in this field we are prepared to undergo a mental and spiritual reevaluation—a change of focus which will enable us to see that the things which seem most real and powerful are indeed now unreal and have come under the sentence of death. We need to make a supreme effort to generate the readiness, indeed the eagerness, to enter into the new world which is now possible, "the city which hath foundations, whose builder and maker is God."

10   We will not build a peaceful world by following a negative path. It is not enough to say "We must not wage war." It is necessary to love peace and sacrifice for it. We must concentrate not merely on the negative **expulsion** of war, but on the positive affirmation of peace. There is a fascinating little story that is preserved for us in Greek literature about Ulysses and the Sirens. The Sirens had the ability to sing so sweetly that sailors could not resist steering toward their island. Many ships were lured upon the rocks, and men forgot home, duty, and honor as they flung themselves into the sea to be embraced by arms that drew them down to death. Ulysses, determined not to be lured by the Sirens, first decided to tie himself tightly to the mast of his boat, and his crew stuffed their ears with wax. But finally he and his crew learned a better way to save themselves: they took on board the beautiful singer Orpheus whose melodies were sweeter than the music of the Sirens. When Orpheus sang, who bothered to listen to the Sirens?

11   So we must fix our vision not merely on the negative expulsion of war, but upon the positive affirmation of peace. We must see that peace represents a sweeter music, a **cosmic** melody that is far superior to the discords of war. Somehow we must transform the dynamics of the world power struggle from the negative nuclear arms race which no one can win to a positive contest to harness man's creative genius for the purpose of making peace and prosperity a reality for all of the nations of the world. In short, we must shift the arms race into a "peace race." If we have the will and determination to mount such a peace offensive, we will unlock hitherto tightly sealed doors of hope and transform our imminent cosmic **elegy** into a psalm of creative fulfillment.

12   All that I have said boils down to the point of affirming that mankind's survival is dependent upon man's ability to solve the problems of racial injustice, poverty, and war; the solution of these problems is in turn dependent upon man squaring his moral progress with his scientific progress, and learning the practical art of living in harmony. Some years ago a famous novelist died. Among his papers was found a list of suggested story plots for future stories, the most prominently underscored being this one: "A widely separated family inherits a house in which they have to live together." This is the great new problem of mankind. We have inherited a big house, a great "world house" in which we have to live together—black and white, Easterners and Westerners, Gentiles and Jews, Catholics and Protestants, Moslem and Hindu, a family unduly separated in ideas, culture, and interests who, because we can never again live without each other, must learn, somehow, in this one big world, to live with each other.

13   This means that more and more our loyalties must become **ecumenical** rather than sectional. We must now give an overriding loyalty to mankind as a whole in order to preserve the best in our individual societies.

14   This call for a worldwide fellowship that lifts neighborly concern beyond one's tribe, race, class, and nation is in reality a call for an all-embracing and unconditional love for all men. This oft misunderstood

and misinterpreted concept so readily dismissed by the **Nietzsches** of the world as a weak and cowardly force has now become an absolute necessity for the survival of man. When I speak of love I am not speaking of some sentimental and weak response which is little more than emotional bosh. I am speaking of that force which all of the great religions have seen as the supreme unifying principle of life. Love is somehow the key that unlocks the door which leads to ultimate reality. This Hindu-Moslem-Christian-Jewish-Buddhist belief about ultimate reality is beautifully summed up in the First Epistle of Saint John:

15   Let us love one another: for love is of
        God; and everyone
      that loveth is born of God, and
        knoweth God.
      He that loveth not knoweth not God;
        for God is love.
      If we love one another, God dwelleth
        in us, and His
      love is perfected in us.

16   Let us hope that this spirit will become the order of the day. As Arnold Toynbee says: "Love is the ultimate force that makes for the saving choice of life and good against the damning choice of death and evil. Therefore the first hope in our inventory must be the hope that love is going to have the last word." We can no longer afford to worship the God of hate or bow before the altar of retaliation. The oceans of history are made turbulent by the ever-rising tides of hate. History is cluttered with the wreckage of nations and individuals that pursued this self-defeating path of hate. Love is the key to the solution of the problems of the world.

17   Let me close by saying that I have the personal faith that mankind will somehow rise up to the occasion and give new directions to an age drifting rapidly to its doom. In spite of the tensions and uncertainties of this period something profoundly meaningful is taking place. Old systems of exploitation and oppression are passing away, and out of the womb of a frail world new systems of justice and equality are being born. Doors of opportunity are gradually being opened to those at the bottom of society. The shirtless and barefoot people of the land are developing a new sense of "some-bodiness" and carving a tunnel of hope through the dark mountain of despair. "The people who sat in darkness have seen a great light." Here and there an individual or group dares to love, and rises to the majestic heights of moral maturity. So in a real sense this is a great time to be alive. Therefore, I am not yet discouraged about the future. Granted that the easygoing optimism of yesterday is impossible. Granted that those who pioneer in the struggle for peace and freedom will still face uncomfortable jail terms, painful threats of death; they will still be battered by the storms of persecution, leading them to the nagging feeling that they can no longer bear such a heavy burden, and the temptation of wanting to retreat to a more quiet and serene life. Granted that we face a world crisis which leaves us standing so often amid the surging murmur of life's restless sea. But every crisis has both its dangers and its opportunities. It can spell either salvation or doom. In a dark confused world the kingdom of God may yet reign in the hearts of men.

Fill in the blank in each sentence with a word from the Vocabulary Preview.

Vocabulary Preview

1. Henry David Thoreau, Mahatma Gandhi, and Dr. Martin Luther King, Jr. believed in the _____ power of nonviolent resistance to oppression.

Vocabulary Preview

2. A tyrant _____ the values, way of life, and beliefs of the powerless.

Vocabulary Preview

3. Nonviolent resistance leads to the _____ of tyranny.

Vocabulary Preview

4. Non-cooperation, such as refusal to pay taxes, _____ one part of nonviolent resistance.

Vocabulary Preview

5. Gandhi also fought for the equality of women, an end to poverty, and the _____ of India's unfair social order based on classes or the caste system.

For items 6 through 10, choose the best meaning of each word in *italics*. Use context clues to make your choice.

Vocabulary in Context   _____

6. "He has built gigantic bridges to span the seas and *gargantuan* buildings to kiss the sky." (paragraph 1)
   a. huge   c. ugly
   b. gorgeous   d. many

Vocabulary in Context   _____

7. "So much of modern life can be summarized in that arresting *dictum* of the poet Thoreau: 'Improved means to an unimproved end.'" (paragraph 3)
   a. fact   c. plan
   b. saying   d. formula

Vocabulary in Context   _____

8. "This is the serious *predicament*, the deep and haunting problem confronting modern man." (paragraph 3)
   a. event   c. dilemma
   b. part   d. solution

Vocabulary in Context   _____

9. "On the contrary, the detonation of an atomic device by the first non-white, non-Western, and so-called underdeveloped power, namely the Chinese People's Republic, opens new vistas of exposure of vast multitudes, the whole of humanity, to *insidious* terrorization by the ever-present threat of annihilation." (paragraph 5)
   a. sinister   c. sincere
   b. obvious   d. harmless

Vocabulary in Context _____ **10.** "But unless we *abdicate* our humanity altogether and succumb to fear and impotence in the presence of the weapons we have ourselves created, it is as imperative and urgent to put an end to war ..." (paragraph 8)

    a. accept   c. secure

    b. understand   d. abandon

Main Idea _____ **11.** Which of the following sentences states the central idea of paragraphs 1 through 4?

    a. "This evening I would like to use this lofty and historic platform to discuss what appears to me to be the most pressing problem confronting mankind today." (paragraph 1)

    b. "Every man lives in two realms, the internal and the external." (paragraph 3)

    c. "If we are to survive today, our moral and spiritual 'lag' must be eliminated." (paragraph 3)

    d. "This problem of spiritual and moral lag, which constitutes modern man's chief dilemma, expresses itself in three larger problems which grow out of man's ethical infantilism." (paragraph 4)

Supporting Detail _____ **12.** According to Dr. King, what is the third great evil confronting our world?

    a. racial injustice   c. spiritual and moral lag

    b. war   d. poverty

Supporting Detail _____ **13.** According to Dr. King, man's internal realm includes

    a. morals.   c. devices.

    b. poverty.   d. progress.

Transitions _____ **14.** "We must concentrate not merely on the negative expulsion of war, but on the positive affirmation of peace." (paragraph 10)

The relationship of ideas **within** this sentence is

    a. cause and effect.   c. comparison and contrast.

    b. time order.   d. generalization and example.

Transitions _____ **15.** "This is a dazzling picture of modern man's scientific and technological progress. Yet, in spite of these spectacular strides in science and technology, and still unlimited ones yet to come, something basic is missing." (paragraphs 1 and 2)

The relationship of ideas **between** these sentences is

    a. cause and effect.   c. comparison and contrast.

    b. time order.   d. generalization and example.

Thought Patterns
_____ **16.** The main thought pattern of paragraph 10 is
  a. time order.
  b. classification.
  c. comparison and contrast.
  d. definition and example.

Fact and Opinion
_____ **17.** "If we assume that life is worth living and that man has a right to survive, then we must find an alternative to war." (paragraph 6)

  This sentence is a statement of
  a. fact.
  b. opinion.
  c. fact and opinion.

Tone and Purpose
_____ **18.** The overall tone and purpose of the author based on this passage is
  a. to inform the world community about the evils of war.
  b. to entertain the world community with lofty thoughts about war and peace.
  c. to persuade the world community to study and apply the strategies of nonviolence.

Inferences
_____ **19.** Based on the passage, we can infer that Dr. King
  a. accepts war as a means to ensure peace.
  b. opposes war as an option under any circumstance.
  c. holds little hope for the future of mankind.
  d. has great faith in the science and technology progress of mankind.

Argument
_____ **20.** The persuasive technique used in paragraph 1 is
  a. glittering generalities.
  b. transfer.
  c. a testimonial
  d. false cause.

Summary

Complete the following summary of the excerpts from the 1964 Nobel Lecture of Dr. Martin Luther King, Jr.

In his 1964 Nobel Lecture "The Quest for Peace and Justice," Dr. Martin Luther

King, Jr. asserts that mankind's chief moral dilemma is the _____

_____ that leads to racial injustice, poverty, and war. Dr. King further asserts that mankind's survival is dependent upon his ability to solve these problems.

Dr. King believes that man must align his _____ progress with his

_____ progress and learn to live in harmony. To avoid the annihilation made possible by nuclear arms, Dr. King suggests the study and application of _____ in conflicts between peoples and nations Finally, Dr. King calls for a worldwide fellowship based on the unifying principle of life: _____ .

WHAT DO YOU THINK?

In the introduction of his speech, Dr. King states, "The richer we have become materially, the poorer we have become morally and spiritually." Do you agree with this statement? Why or why not? Assume you are interested in public service, and you have decided to support a cause that will improve life in your local community. You also want to inspire others to join the cause as well. Identify a local cause such as homelessness, pollution, recycling, drug abuse, or graffiti removal. To gain public support for your cause, write an entry for the community blog sponsored by your local newspaper. In your posting, define the cause and call for specific action from your readers.

EFFECTIVE READER Scorecard

"The Quest for Peace and Justice"

Skill	Number Correct	Points	Total
Vocabulary			
Vocabulary Preview (5 items)	_____ × 10 =		_____
Vocabulary in Context (5 items)	_____ × 10 =		_____
		Vocabulary Score	_____
Comprehension			
Main Idea (1 item)	_____ × 8 =		_____
Supporting Details (2 items)	_____ × 8 =		_____
Transitions (2 items)	_____ × 8 =		_____
Thought Patterns (1 item)	_____ × 8 =		_____
Fact and Opinion (1 item)	_____ × 8 =		_____
Tone and Purpose (1 item)	_____ × 8 =		_____
Inferences (1 item)	_____ × 8 =		_____
Argument (1 item)	_____ × 8 =		_____
Summary (5 items)	_____ × 4 =		_____
		Comprehension Score	_____

A Just and Lasting Peace
Nobel Lecture, December 10, 2009

President Barack Obama

Barack Obama was awarded the Nobel Peace Prize just 9 months after he became President of the United States. In fact, nominations for the 2009 Nobel
Peace Prize closed only 11 days after he took office. Many wondered what he
had done so early in his presidency to deserve this highly esteemed award. In
selecting him, the Nobel Committee appears to be endorsing President
Obama's approach to solving the difficult world problems of conflict, nuclear weapons, and climate change. "It is now, today, that we have the opportunity to support President Obama's ideas. This year's prize is indeed a call
to action to all of us," stated the chairperson of the Nobel committee.
"Obama has the audacity to hope and the tenacity to make these hopes
come true." The following passage presents major portions of President
Obama's Nobel Lecture. To read his entire speech go to Nobelprize.org.

Vocabulary Preview

cynics (paragraph 3): doubters, skeptics

carnage (paragraph 8): bloodshed, massacre, slaughter

Third Reich (paragraph 8): The Nazi regime in Germany between 1933 and 1945

Axis (paragraph 8): alliance, partnership, bloc

vanquished (paragraph 9): beaten, defeated

genocide (paragraph 9): murder of all the people from a national, ethnic, or
   religious group

atrocities (paragraph 10): acts of extreme cruelty

sectarian (paragraph 12): relating to or involving relations between religious groups

secessionist (paragraph 12): belief in withdrawal from a nation, state, organization, or alliance

insurgencies (paragraph 12): rebellions, uprisings, riots, revolts

imperatives (paragraph 13): necessities, requirements, rules, obligations

eradicate (paragraph 14): eliminate, wipe out, destroy, remove

unilaterally (paragraph 22): decided by one party, accounting for one side only

mandate (paragraph 23): order, command, directive

intransigence (paragraph 25): inflexibility, stubbornness, narrow-mindedness

1   Your Majesties, Your Royal Highnesses, distinguished members of the Norwegian Nobel Committee, citizens of America, and citizens of the world:

2   I receive this honor with deep gratitude and great humility. It is an award that speaks to our highest **aspirations**—that for all the cruelty and hardship of our world, we are not mere prisoners of fate. Our actions matter, and can bend history in the direction of justice.

3   And yet I would be remiss if I did not acknowledge the considerable controversy that your generous decision has generated. In part, this is because I am at the beginning, and not the end, of my labors on the world stage. Compared to some of the giants of history who've received this prize—Schweitzer and King; Marshall and Mandela—my accomplishments are slight. And then there are the men and women around the world who have been jailed and beaten in the pursuit of justice; those who toil in humanitarian organizations to relieve suffering; the unrecognized millions whose quiet acts of courage and compassion inspire even the most hardened **cynics**. I cannot argue with those who find these men and women—some known, some obscure to all but those they help—to be far more deserving of this honor than I.

4   But perhaps the most profound issue surrounding my receipt of this prize is the fact that I am the Commander-in-Chief of the military of a nation in the midst of two wars. One of these wars is winding down. The other is a conflict that America did not seek; one in which we are joined by 42 other countries—including Norway—in an effort to defend ourselves and all nations from further attacks.

5   Still, we are at war, and I'm responsible for the deployment of thousands of young Americans to battle in a distant land. Some will kill, and some will be killed. And so I come here with an acute sense of the costs of armed conflict—filled with difficult questions about the relationship between war and peace, and our effort to replace one with the other.

6   Now these questions are not new. War, in one form or another, appeared with the first man. At the dawn of history, its morality was not questioned; it was simply a fact, like drought or disease—the manner in which tribes and then civilizations sought power and settled their differences.

7   And over time, as codes of law sought to control violence within groups, so did philosophers and clerics and statesmen seek to regulate the destructive power of war. The concept of a "just war" emerged, suggesting that war is justified only when certain conditions were met: if it is waged as a last resort or in self-defense; if the force used is proportional; and if, whenever possible, civilians are spared from violence.

8   Of course, we know that for most of history, this concept of "just war" was rarely observed. The capacity of human beings to think up new ways to kill one another proved inexhaustible, as did our capacity to exempt from mercy those who look different or pray to a different God. Wars between armies gave way to wars between nations—total wars in which the distinction between combatant and civilian became blurred. In the span of 30 years, such **carnage** would twice engulf this continent. And while it's hard to conceive of a cause more just than the defeat of the **Third Reich** and the **Axis**

powers, World War II was a conflict in which the total number of civilians who died exceeded the number of soldiers who perished.

9   In the wake of such destruction, and with the advent of the nuclear age, it became clear to victor and **vanquished** alike that the world needed institutions to prevent another world war. And so, a quarter century after the United States Senate rejected the League of Nations—an idea for which Woodrow Wilson received this prize—America led the world in constructing an architecture to keep the peace: a Marshall Plan and a United Nations, mechanisms to govern the waging of war, treaties to protect human rights, prevent **genocide**, restrict the most dangerous weapons.

10   In many ways, these efforts succeeded. Yes, terrible wars have been fought, and **atrocities** committed. But there has been no Third World War. The Cold War ended with jubilant crowds dismantling a wall. Commerce has stitched much of the world together. Billions have been lifted from poverty. The ideals of liberty and self-determination, equality and the rule of law have haltingly advanced. We are the heirs of the **fortitude** and foresight of generations past, and it is a legacy for which my own country is rightfully proud.

11   And yet, a decade into a new century, this old architecture is buckling under the weight of new threats. The world may no longer shudder at the prospect of war between two nuclear superpowers, but **proliferation** may increase the risk of catastrophe. Terrorism has long been a tactic, but modern technology allows a few small men with outsized rage to murder innocents on a horrific scale.

12   Moreover, wars between nations have increasingly given way to wars within nations. The resurgence of ethnic or **sectarian** conflicts; the growth of **secessionist** movements, **insurgencies**, and failed states—all these things have increasingly trapped civilians in unending chaos. In today's wars, many more civilians are killed than soldiers; the seeds of future conflict are sown, economies are wrecked, civil societies torn asunder, refugees amassed, children scarred.

13   I do not bring with me today a definitive solution to the problems of war. What I do know is that meeting these challenges will require the same vision, hard work, and persistence of those men and women who acted so boldly decades ago. And it will require us to think in new ways about the notions of just war and the **imperatives** of a just peace.

14   We must begin by acknowledging the hard truth: We will not **eradicate** violent conflict in our lifetimes. There will be times when nations—acting individually or in concert—will find the use of force not only necessary but morally justified.

15   I make this statement mindful of what Martin Luther King Jr. said in this same ceremony years ago: "Violence never brings permanent peace. It solves no social problem: it merely creates new and more complicated ones." As someone who stands here as a direct consequence of Dr. King's life work, I am living testimony to the moral force of non-violence. I know there's nothing weak—nothing passive—nothing naïve—in the creed and lives of Gandhi and King.

16   But as a head of state sworn to protect and defend my nation, I cannot be guided by their examples alone. I face the world as

it is, and cannot stand idle in the face of threats to the American people. For make no mistake: Evil does exist in the world. A non-violent movement could not have halted Hitler's armies. Negotiations cannot convince al Qaeda's leaders to lay down their arms. To say that force may sometimes be necessary is not a call to cynicism—it is a recognition of history; the imperfections of man and the limits of reason.

17   I raise this point, I begin with this point because in many countries there is a deep **ambivalence** about military action today, no matter what the cause. And at times, this is joined by a reflexive suspicion of America, the world's sole military superpower.

18   But the world must remember that it was not simply international institutions— not just treaties and declarations—that brought stability to a post-World War II world. Whatever mistakes we have made, the plain fact is this: The United States of America has helped underwrite global security for more than six decades with the blood of our citizens and the strength of our arms. The service and sacrifice of our men and women in uniform has promoted peace and prosperity from Germany to Korea, and enabled democracy to take hold in places like the Balkans. We have borne this burden not because we seek to impose our will. We have done so out of **enlightened** self-interest—because we seek a better future for our children and grandchildren, and we believe that their lives will be better if others' children and grandchildren can live in freedom and prosperity.

19   So yes, the instruments of war do have a role to play in preserving the peace. And yet this truth must coexist with another— that no matter how justified, war promises human tragedy. The soldier's courage and sacrifice is full of glory, expressing devotion to country, to cause, to comrades in arms. But war itself is never glorious, and we must never trumpet it as such.

20   So part of our challenge is reconciling these two seemingly irreconcilable truths— that war is sometimes necessary, and war at some level is an expression of human folly. Concretely, we must direct our effort to the task that President Kennedy called for long ago. "Let us focus," he said, "on a more practical, more attainable peace, based not on a sudden revolution in human nature but on a gradual evolution in human institutions." A gradual evolution of human institutions.

21   What might this evolution look like? What might these practical steps be?

22   To begin with, I believe that all nations—strong and weak alike—must adhere to standards that govern the use of force. I—like any head of state—reserve the right to act **unilaterally** if necessary to defend my nation. Nevertheless, I am convinced that adhering to standards, international standards, strengthens those who do, and isolates and weakens those who don't.

***

23   I believe that force can be justified on humanitarian grounds, as it was in the Balkans, or in other places that have been scarred by war. Inaction tears at our conscience and can lead to more costly intervention later. That's why all responsible nations must embrace the role that militaries with a clear **mandate** can play to keep the peace.

***

24   I have spoken at some length to the question that must weigh on our minds and our hearts as we choose to wage war. But let me now turn to our effort to avoid such tragic choices, and speak of three ways that we can build a just and lasting peace.

25   First, in dealing with those nations that break rules and laws, I believe that we must develop alternatives to violence that are tough enough to actually change behavior— for if we want a lasting peace, then the words of the international community must mean something. Those regimes that break the rules must be held accountable. Sanctions must exact a real price. **Intransigence** must be met with increased pressure—and such pressure exists only when the world stands together as one.

***

26   This brings me to a second point—the nature of the peace that we seek. For peace is not merely the absence of visible conflict. Only a just peace based on the inherent rights and dignity of every individual can truly be lasting.

27   It was this insight that drove drafters of the Universal Declaration of Human Rights after the Second World War. In the wake of devastation, they recognized that if human rights are not protected, peace is a hollow promise.

***

28   Third, a just peace includes not only civil and political rights—it must encompass economic security and opportunity. For true peace is not just freedom from fear, but freedom from want.

29   It is undoubtedly true that development rarely takes root without security; it is also true that security does not exist where human beings do not have access to enough food, or clean water, or the medicine and shelter they need to survive. It does not exist where children can't aspire to a decent education or a job that supports a family. The absence of hope can rot a society from within.

30   And that's why helping farmers feed their own people—or nations educate their children and care for the sick – is not mere charity. It's also why the world must come together to confront climate change. There is little scientific dispute that if we do nothing, we will face more drought, more famine, more mass displacement—all of which will fuel more conflict for decades. For this reason, it is not merely scientists and environmental activists who call for swift and forceful action—it's military leaders in my own country and others who understand our common security hangs in the balance.

31   Agreements among nations. Strong institutions. Support for human rights. Investments in development. All these are vital ingredients in bringing about the evolution that President Kennedy spoke about. And yet, I do not believe that we will have the will, the determination, the staying power, to complete this work without something more—and that's the continued expansion of our moral imagination; an insistence that there's something irreducible that we all share.

32   As the world grows smaller, you might think it would be easier for human beings to recognize how similar we are; to understand that we're all basically seeking the same things; that we all hope for the chance to live out our lives with some measure of

happiness and fulfillment for ourselves and our families.

33   And yet somehow, given the dizzying pace of globalization, the cultural leveling of modernity, it perhaps comes as no surprise that people fear the loss of what they cherish in their particular identities—their race, their tribe, and perhaps most powerfully their religion. In some places, this fear has led to conflict. At times, it even feels like we're moving backwards. We see it in the Middle East, as the conflict between Arabs and Jews seems to harden. We see it in nations that are torn asunder by tribal lines.

34   And most dangerously, we see it in the way that religion is used to justify the murder of innocents by those who have distorted and defiled the great religion of Islam, and who attacked my country from Afghanistan. These extremists are not the first to kill in the name of God; the cruelties of the Crusades are amply recorded. But they remind us that no Holy War can ever be a just war. For if you truly believe that you are carrying out divine will, then there is no need for restraint—no need to spare the pregnant mother, or the medic, or the Red Cross worker, or even a person of one's own faith. Such a warped view of religion is not just incompatible with the concept of peace, but I believe it's incompatible with the very purpose of faith—for the one rule that lies at the heart of every major religion is that we do unto others as we would have them do unto us.

35   Adhering to this law of love has always been the core struggle of human nature.

For we are fallible. We make mistakes, and fall victim to the temptations of pride, and power, and sometimes evil. Even those of us with the best of intentions will at times fail to right the wrongs before us.

36   But we do not have to think that human nature is perfect for us to still believe that the human condition can be perfected. We do not have to live in an idealized world to still reach for those ideals that will make it a better place. The nonviolence practiced by men like Gandhi and King may not have been practical or possible in every circumstance, but the love that they preached—their fundamental faith in human progress—that must always be the North Star that guides us on our journey.

37   For if we lose that faith—if we dismiss it as silly or naïve; if we divorce it from the decisions that we make on issues of war and peace—then we lose what's best about humanity. We lose our sense of possibility. We lose our moral compass.

38   Like generations have before us, we must reject that future. As Dr. King said at this occasion so many years ago, "I refuse to accept despair as the final response to the ambiguities of history. I refuse to accept the idea that the 'isness' of man's present condition makes him morally incapable of reaching up for the eternal 'oughtness' that forever confronts him."

39   Let us reach for the world that ought to be—that spark of the divine that still stirs within each of our souls.

—Barack Obama. "A Just and Lasting Peace." *Nobelprize.org* 10 Dec. 2009. http://nobelprize.org/nobel_prizes/peace/laureates/2009/obama-lecture.html.

Fill in the blank in each sentence with a word from the Vocabulary Preview.

Vocabulary
Preview

1. Native Americans faced _____ at the hands of European settlers in America who wanted to possess the land.

Vocabulary
Preview

2. Native Americans suffered _____ such as death marches, forced relocation to barren lands, destruction of their main food supply— the buffalo— and mass poisoning.

Vocabulary
Preview

3. Settlers brought diseases such as smallpox, measles, and mumps to which the Native Americans had no prior contact or resistance; the _____ from these diseases greatly reduced the number of Native American people.

Vocabulary
Preview

4. The "Reservation" system was created by the Federal Bureau of Indian Affairs to force _____ Native Americans to migrate to the West.

Vocabulary
Preview

5. Native Americans such as Red Cloud, Crazy Horse, Geronimo, and Sitting Bull led several _____ against the settlers and the United States government.

For items 6 through 10, choose the best meaning of each word in *italics*. Use context clues to make your choice.

Vocabulary
in Context

_____ **6.** "It is an award that speaks to our highest *aspirations*—that for all the cruelty and hardship of our world, we are not mere prisoners of fate." (paragraph 2)
   a. accomplishments   c. ambitions
   b. indifferences   d. satisfactions

Vocabulary
in Context

_____ **7.** "We are the heirs of the *fortitude* and foresight of generations past, and it is a legacy for which my own country is rightfully proud." (paragraph 10)
   a. force   c. resistance
   b. strength   d. resignation

Vocabulary
in Context

_____ **8.** "The world may no longer shudder at the prospect of war between two nuclear superpowers, but *proliferation* may increase the risk of catastrophe." (paragraph 11)
   a. use of nuclear arms   c. shortage of nuclear arms
   b. existence of nuclear arms   d. expansion of nuclear arms

Vocabulary in Context _____ **9.** "I raise this point, I begin with this point because in many countries there is a deep *ambivalence* about military action today, no matter what the cause." (paragraph 17)

    a. uncertainty   c. acceptance

    b. openness   d. fear

Vocabulary in Context _____ **10.** "We have done so out of *enlightened* self-interest—because we seek a better future for our children and grandchildren, and we believe that their lives will be better if others' children and grandchildren can live in freedom and prosperity." (paragraph 18)

    a. deluded   c. informed

    b. told   d. narrowed

Central Idea _____ **11.** Which of the following sentences states the central idea of the passage?

    a. "There will be times when nations—acting individually or in concert—will find the use of force not only necessary but morally justified." (paragraph 14)

    b. "I have spoken at some length to the question that must weigh on our minds and our hearts as we choose to wage war." (paragraph 24)

    c. "But let me now turn to our effort to avoid such tragic choices, and speak of three ways that we can build a just and lasting peace."(paragraph 24)

    d. "Only a just peace based on the inherent rights and dignity of every individual can truly be lasting." (paragraph 26)

Supporting Detail _____ **12.** According to President Obama, he stands as a direct consequence of the life work of

    a. President John Kennedy.   c. President Woodrow Wilson.

    b. Dr. Martin Luther King, Jr.   d. the American people.

Supporting Detail _____ **13.** According to President Obama, the Universal Declaration of Human Rights was drafted

    a. along with the U.S. Constitution.

    b. after World War I.

    c. after World War II.

    d. during the Iraq War.

Transitions _____ **14.** "So part of our challenge is reconciling these two seemingly inreconcilable truths—that war is sometimes necessary, and war at some level is an expression of human folly." (paragraph 20)

The relationship of ideas **within** this sentence is

    a. cause and effect.   c. comparison and contrast.

    b. classification.   d. definition and example.

Transitions _____ **15.** "The soldier's courage and sacrifice is full of glory, expressing devotion to country, to cause, to comrades in arms. But war itself is never glorious, and we must never trumpet it as such." (paragraph 19)

The relationship of ideas **between** these sentences is
a. cause and effect.   c. comparison and contrast.
b. listing.   d. time order.

Thought _____ **16.** The overall thought pattern for the passage is
Patterns
a. cause and effect.   c. comparison and contrast.
b. classification.   d. generalization and example.

Fact and _____ **17.** "And while it is hard to conceive of a cause more just than the defeat
Opinion
of the Third Reich and the Axis powers, World War II was a conflict in which the total number of civilians who died exceeded the number of soldiers who perished." (paragraph 8)

This sentence is a statement of
a. fact.   c. fact and opinion.
b. opinion.

Tone and _____ **18.** The overall tone and purpose of President Obama's speech is
Purpose
a. informative.   c. persuasive.
b. entertaining.

Inferences _____ **19.** Based on the details in the passage, we can infer that President Obama believes that
a. the war against terrorists in Afghanistan is a just war.
b. overall war is the best way to achieve peace.
c. war is never moral.
d. the war in Iraq was necessary.

Argument _____ **20.** The following list contains a claim and supports for the claim. Which item states the claim?
a. But perhaps the most profound issue surrounding my receipt of this prize is the fact that I am the Commander-in-Chief of the military of a nation in the midst of two wars.
b. One of these wars is winding down.
c. The other is a conflict that America did not seek; one in which we are joined by 42 other countries—including Norway—in an effort to defend ourselves and all nations from further attacks.
d. Still, we are at war, and I'm responsible for the deployment of thousands of young Americans to battle in a distant land.

Outlining

Complete the following outline with information from the speech "A Just and Lasting Peace."

   I. I would be remiss if I did not acknowledge the considerable controversy that your generous decision has generated.

     A. I am at the beginning, and not the end, of my labors on the world stage.

     B. I am the _____ of the military of a nation in the midst of two wars.

  II. I come here with an acute sense of the costs of armed conflict—filled with questions about the relationship between _____, and our effort to replace one with the other.

     A. War, in one form or another, appeared with the first man.

     B. The concept of a "just war" emerged.

     C. This concept of "just war" was rarely observed.

     D. There will be times when nations—acting individually or in concert—will find the use of force not only necessary but morally justified.

     E. Evil does exist in the world.

     F. The instruments of war do have a role to play in preserving the peace.

 III. But let me now turn to our effort to avoid such tragic choices, and speak of three ways that we can build a just and lasting peace.

     A. _____ must exact a real price.

     B. Only a peace based on the _____ can be truly lasting.

     C. A just peace includes not only civil and political rights—it must encompass _____.

WHAT DO YOU THINK?

What are your views about war? Do you agree with Dr. Martin Luther King, Jr. that war is never the answer? Or do you agree with President Obama that sometimes war is just and can lead to lasting peace? Assume you are taking a college class in political science, and your class is studying the relationship between war and peace. Your professor has required your class to read the

Nobel Prize lectures of Dr. Martin Luther King, Jr. and President Barack Obama and write an essay in response to the following prompt: "Compare and contrast President Obama's and Dr. King's views of war. With which view do you agree? Why?"

EFFECTIVE READER Scorecard

"A Just and Lasting Peace"

Skill	Number Correct	Points		Total
Vocabulary				
Vocabulary Preview (5 items)	_____	× 10	=	_____
Vocabulary in Context (5 items)	_____	× 10	=	_____
	Vocabulary Score			_____
Comprehension				
Central Idea (1 item)	_____	× 8	=	_____
Supporting Details (2 items)	_____	× 8	=	_____
Transitions (2 items)	_____	× 8	=	_____
Thought Patterns (1 item)	_____	× 8	=	_____
Fact and Opinion (1 item)	_____	× 8	=	_____
Tone and Purpose (1 item)	_____	× 8	=	_____
Inferences (1 item)	_____	× 8	=	_____
Argument (1 item)	_____	× 8	=	_____
Outlining (5 items)	_____	× 4	=	_____
	Comprehension Score			_____

Textbook
Skills

Encounters and Transformations: The Alphabet and Writing in Greece
An Excerpt from *The West: Encounters & Transformations, 2nd Atlas Ed.*

Levack, Muir, Veldman, and Maas

In the preface to this history textbook, the authors state "We wrote this text-book to answer questions about the identity of the civilization in which we live." To help answer that question, the authors provide a series of essays throughout the textbook in a recurring box called "Encounters and Transformations." Each essay gives a specific example of the ways in which contact among cultures changed the views and identity of Western civiliza-tion. The following passage is one of those essays. Have you taken time to consider the origin of writing or its impact on society? How would civiliza-tion be different without the ability to write?

Vocabulary Preview

derived (paragraph 1): came from
exploit (paragraph 2): take advantage
elite (paragraph 3): privileged minority
scribal (paragraph 3): of writing
aristocracy (paragraph 3): people of highest social class
arbitrarily (paragraph 3): random, subjectively
poleis (paragraph 3): ancient Greek city-state
Tragedians (paragraph 5): those who write tragedies

Encounters and Transformations: The Alphabet and Writing in Greece

1   Sometime around the middle of the eighth century B.C.E., Greek merchants brought the alphabet to Greece. They adopted this system of letters from seafaring Phoeni-cians whom they **encountered** while trading in the eastern Mediterranean. To write down their business transactions, Phoenicians used an alphabet of twenty-two letters. They **derived** this system from the one invented in the Bronze Age at Ugarit. Recognizing the potential of writing, the Greeks quickly adapted the Phoenician script to the Greek language and began to read and write. By 650 B.C.E., the Greek alphabet and the lit-eracy that went with it spread widely. This

spread of literacy followed trade routes throughout the Mediterranean world. The Greek alphabet reached Italy and eventually the Romans, whose adaptation of the alphabet is the one we use today.

2   The adoption of the alphabet deeply affected Greek society because it let information of all sorts be preserved in written form—and widely shared. The alphabet is easy to learn because each letter represents one sound, and therefore many people in the Greek world began to **exploit** the potential of reading and writing.

3   Unlike the cultures of Mesopotamia and Egypt, in which writing was the specialized expertise of an **elite scribal** class, the more open Greek culture never limited writing to a particular group. People of all sorts employed it. For example, government officials began to write down laws. For the first time laws became available for all members of the community to see. Having written laws posted in public helped to undercut the ancient privileges of the **aristocracy** to interpret the oral law, something they often did **arbitrarily** and unjustly. Thus written laws contributed to the development of fairer political institutions in the Greek **poleis**. Merchants kept track of shipments, payments, loans, and debts, thereby helping the economies of Greek communities to thrive and become more complex.

4   Perhaps the most significant development of all, however, was the beginning of written literature. The first works of literature to be rendered in writing were the *Iliad* and the *Odyssey* of Homer, the product of a long tradition of oral transmission combined with the particular genius of Homer, who gave them their final written form. These tales became central to Greek culture.

5   But soon writers were not just recording oral poetry, they were composing original poetry to be read and recited. **Tragedians** composed the intense dramas that explored fundamental questions of human psychology. Mythological tales were set down and considered critically, leading eventually to the development of scientific thought. As soon as historians could read the accounts of earlier historians, they began to criticize them in different ways, and the Western tradition of critical history took root.

6   Thus the adoption of the alphabet **transformed** Greek society. Reading and writing—which depend on the alphabet—helped shape the Greek intellectual legacy that we value so highly today. But the importance of the alphabet and of reading and writing in the West is still far more profound: Western civilization is based on the writing and interpretation of texts. Sacred books, legal codes, scientific inquiries, and the rich and varied traditions of literature are fundamental to who we are and how we experience the world. And they were made possible by the alphabet and the advent of reading and writing.

—Levack, Muir, Veldman, & Maas, *The West: Encounters & Transformations,* 2nd Atlas Ed., p. 68.

Choose the best meaning of each word in *italics*. Use context clues to make your choice.

Vocabulary
in Context _____ **1.** "They adopted this system of letters from seafaring Phoenicians whom they *encountered* while trading in the eastern Mediterranean." (paragraph 1)

    a. conquered   c. battled

    b. met   d. studied

Vocabulary
in Context _____ **2.** "Thus the adoption of the alphabet *transformed* Greek society." (paragraph 6)

    a. preserved   c. revolutionized

    b. devastated   d. reinforced

Central Idea _____ **3.** Which of the following sentences best states the central idea of the passage?

    a. "Sometime around the middle of the eighth century B.C.E., Greek merchants brought the alphabet to Greece." (paragraph 1)

    b. "The adoption of the alphabet deeply affected Greek society because it let information of all sorts be preserved in written form—and widely shared." (paragraph 2)

    c. "Thus, the adoption of the alphabet transformed Greek Society." (paragraph 6)

    d. "But the importance of the alphabet and of reading and writing in the West is still far more profound: Western civilization is based on the writing and interpretation of texts." (paragraph 6)

Main Idea _____ **4.** Which of the following sentences states the main idea of paragraphs 4 and 5?

    a. "Perhaps the most significant development of all, however, was the beginning of written literature." (paragraph 4)

    b. "These tales became central to Greek culture." (paragraph 4)

    c. "But soon writers were not just recording oral poetry, they were composing original poetry to be read and recited." (paragraph 5)

    d. "As soon as historians could read the accounts of earlier historians, they began to criticize them in different ways, and the Western tradition of critical history took root." (paragraph 5)

Supporting
Detail _____ **5.** According to the author, which civilization first developed an alphabet?

    a. Greeks   c. Phoenicians

    b. Egyptians   d. Mesopotamians

Supporting Detail _____ **6.** According to the author, who brought the alphabet to Greece?
a. the aristocracy   c. merchants
b. Phoenicians   d. government officials

Transitions _____ **7.** "The adoption of the alphabet deeply affected Greek society because it let information of all sorts be preserved in written form—and widely shared." (paragraph 2)

The relationship of ideas **within** this sentence is
a. time order.   c. comparison and contrast.
b. cause and effect.   d. definition and example.

Transitions _____ **8.** "Having written laws posted in public helped to undercut the ancient privileges of the aristocracy to interpret the oral law, something they often did arbitrarily and unjustly. Thus written laws contributed to the development of fairer political institutions in the Greek poleis." (paragraph 3)

The relationship of ideas **between** these sentences is
a. cause and effect.   c. comparison and contrast.
b. time order.   d. generalization and example.

Thought Patterns _____ **9.** The thought pattern of paragraph 1 is
a. time order.   c. definition and example.
b. cause and effect.   d. comparison and contrast.

Thought Patterns _____ **10.** The overall thought pattern of the passage is
a. time order.   c. comparison and contrast.
b. cause and effect.   d. definition and example.

Fact and Opinion _____ **11.** "By 650 B.C.E., the Greek alphabet and the literacy that went with it spread quickly." (paragraph 1)

This sentence is a statement of
a. fact.   c. fact and opinion.
b. opinion.

Fact and Opinion _____ **12.** "People of all sorts employed it." (paragraph 3)

This sentence is a statement of
a. fact.   c. fact and opinion.
b. opinion.

Tone and Purpose   _____ **13.** "To write down their business transactions, Phoenicians used an alphabet of twenty-two letters." (paragraph 1)

The tone of this sentence is
a. objective.
b. sarcastic
c. unbelieving.
d. biased.

Tone and Purpose   _____ **14.** The overall tone of the passage is
a. neutral.
b. appreciative.
c. argumentative.
d. sentimental.

Tone and Purpose   _____ **15.** The overall purpose of the author is
a. to inform the reader about the development and impact of the alphabet and writing in Western Civilization.
b. to entertain the reader with little known facts about the alphabet and writing in Greece.
c. to persuade the reader to value literacy.

Inferences   _____ **16.** Based on the details in paragraph 2, we can infer that
a. many people misused the ability to read and write.
b. many people benefited from reading and writing.
c. all Greek people were able to read and write.
d. information was not widely shared before writing and reading developed.

Inferences   _____ **17.** Based on the details in passage, we can infer that before the development of the alphabet and writing,
a. most information was shared orally.
b. only business transactions were recorded.
c. all civilizations were crude and unfair.
d. laws did not exist.

Inferences   _____ **18.** Based on the details in the passage, we can infer that
a. the development of civilization is affected as different cultures encounter each other.
b. Greek people were more intelligent than other people groups of their time.
c. greed led to the development of writing and reading.
d. writing did not exist until the Greek alphabet was developed.

Argument _____ **19.** The following items from paragraph 3 contain a claim and list of supports for that claim. Which sentence states the claim?
   a. "For example, government officials began to write down laws."
   b. "For the first time laws became available for all members of the community to see."
   c. "Having written laws posted in public helped to undercut the ancient privileges of the aristocracy to interpret the oral law, something they often did arbitrarily and unjustly."
   d. "Thus written laws contributed to the development of fairer political institutions in the Greek poleis."

Argument _____ **20.** The following items from paragraphs 5 and 6 contain a claim and list of supports for that claim. Which sentence states the claim?
   a. "Tragedians composed the intense dramas that explored fundamental questions of human psychology." (paragraph 5)
   b. "Mythological tales were set down and considered critically, leading eventually to the development of scientific thought." (paragraph 5)
   c. "As soon as historians could read the accounts of earlier historians, they began to criticize them in different ways, and the Western tradition of critical history took root." (paragraph 5)
   d. "Thus the adoption of the alphabet transformed Greek society." (paragraph 6)

Summary

Complete the following summary with information from the passage.

The adoption of the alphabet had a tremendous effect on Greek society and

_____. Reading and writing led to fairer _____, thriving

and complex _____, written _____, the development

of _____ thought, and the tradition of critical history.

WHAT DO YOU THINK?

How is current technology changing writing and reading? For example, does electronic messaging rely on the alphabet? Or has electronic messaging developed new symbols to use to share information? This essay describes the impact of the development of writing on society. What other developments have had a significant impact on society? Assume you are taking a college sociology course and your professor has asked for your written response to this article. You have been asked to choose one of the following topics and write an essay. Topic 1: What impact did the alphabet have on ancient Greek society, and what is its importance today? Topic 2: What invention or development has had a profound impact on society?

EFFECTIVE READER Scorecard

"Encounters and Transformations"			
Skill	**Number Correct**	**Points**	**Total**
Vocabulary			
Vocabulary in Context (2 items)	_____	× 4 =	_____
Comprehension			
Central Idea and Main Idea (2 items)	_____	× 4 =	_____
Supporting Details (2 items)	_____	× 4 =	_____
Transitions (2 items)	_____	× 4 =	_____
Thought Patterns (2 items)	_____	× 4 =	_____
Fact and Opinion (2 items)	_____	× 4 =	_____
Tone and Purpose (3 items)	_____	× 4 =	_____
Inferences (3 items)	_____	× 4 =	_____
Argument (2 items)	_____	× 4 =	_____
Summary (5 items)	_____	× 4 =	_____
	Comprehension Score		_____

Diversity in U.S. Families

Excerpt from *Sociology: A Down-to-Earth Approach, 9th Edition*

James M. Henslin

Do you like to watch people and try to figure out why they do what they do? Have you thought about how our society and the groups to which we belong affects us? If so, you think like a sociologist. Sociology is fundamentally the study of life in groups. In the preface to the book from which this passage is taken, James M. Henslin states the study of life in groups "pries open the doors of society so you can see what goes on behind them." Henslin believes that as we study life in groups, "we gain new insights into who we are and how we got that way." The following passage is a section of the chapter "Marriage and the Family."

Vocabulary Preview

machismo (paragraph 7): emphasis on traits usually regarded as male: physical strength, courage, aggressiveness, and lack of emotional response

acculturated (paragraph 8): adjusted into the culture of another group, learning and adapting the practices and customs of another culture

emigrated (paragraph 9): left to live in another country

Confucian (paragraph 10): related to the teachings of Confucius, emphasis on personal, social, and political order.

humanism (paragraph 10): belief in human-based moral codes, concern for people

collectivity (paragraph 10): state of being together, people or things work together to form a whole

permissive (paragraph 13): allowing freedom of behavior, lenient, tolerant

deferred (paragraph 14): postponed, delayed, overdue

conceptual (paragraph 24): theoretical, abstract, unapplied

Diversity in U.S. Families

1   It is important to note that there is no such thing as the American family. Rather, family life varies widely throughout the United States. The significance of social class, noted earlier, will continue to be evident as we examine diversity in U.S. families.

African American Families

2   Note that the heading reads African American families, not the African American family. There is no such thing as the African American family any more than there is the white family or the Latino family. The primary distinction is not between African Americans and other groups, but between social classes (Willie and Reddick 2003). Because African Americans who are members of the upper class follow the class interests reviewed in Chapter 10—preservation of privilege and family fortune—they are especially concerned about the family background of those whom their children marry (Gatewood 1990). To them, marriage is viewed as the merger of family lines. Children of this class marry later than children of other classes.

3   Middle-class African American families focus on achievement and respectability. Both husband and wife are likely to work outside the home. A central concern is that their children go to college, get good jobs, and marry well—that is, marry people like themselves, respectable and hardworking, who want to get ahead in school and pursue a successful career.

4   African American families in poverty face all the problems that cluster around poverty (Wilson 1987, 1996; Anderson 1990/2006; Venkatesh 2006). Because the men are likely to have few skills and to be unemployed, it is difficult for them to fulfill the cultural roles of husband and father. Consequently, these families are likely to be headed by a woman and to have a high rate of births to single women. Divorce and desertion are also more common than among other classes. Sharing scarce resources and "stretching kinship" are primary survival mechanisms. People who have helped out in hard times are considered brothers, sisters, or cousins to whom one owes obligations as though they were blood relatives; and men who are not the biological fathers of their children are given fatherhood status (Stack 1974; Fischer et al. 2005). Sociologists use the term **fictive kin** to refer to this stretching of kinship.

5   From Figure 1 you can see that, compared with other groups, African American families are the least likely to be headed by married couples and the most likely to be headed by women. Because African American women tend to go farther in school than African American men, they are more likely than women in other racial-ethnic groups to marry men who are less educated than themselves (South 1991; Eshleman 2000).

Latino Families

6   As Figure 1 shows, the proportion of Latino families headed by married couples and women falls in between that of whites and African Americans. The effects of social class on families, which I just sketched, also apply to Latinos. In addition, families differ by country of origin. Families from Mexico, for example, are more likely to be headed by a married couple than are families from Puerto Rico (Statistical Abstract 2007: Table 44). The longer that Latinos have lived in the United States, the more their families resemble those of middle-class Americans (Saenz 2004).

7   With such a wide variety, experts disagree on what is distinctive about Latino

Figure 1: Family Structure: The Percentage of U.S. Families Headed by Men, Women, and Married Couples

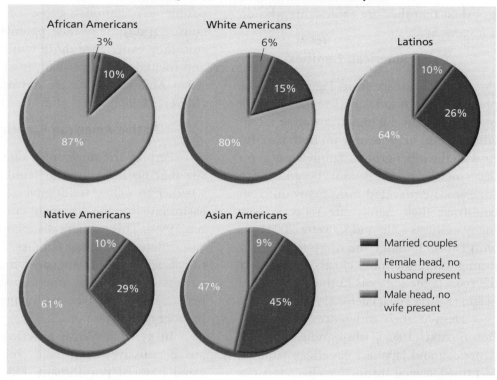

Source: By the author. For Native Americans, "American Community . . ." 2004. For other groups, *Statistical Abstract* 2007:Tables 41, 44, 62. Data for Asian Americans are for families with children under 18, while the other groups don't have this limitation. Totals may not equal 100 percent due to rounding.

families. Some point to the Spanish language, the Roman Catholic religion, and a strong family orientation coupled with a disapproval of divorce. Others add that Latinos emphasize loyalty to the extended family, with an obligation to support the extended family in times of need (Cauce and Domenech-Rodriguez 2002). Descriptions of Latino families used to include **machismo**—an emphasis on male strength, sexual vigor, and dominance—but current studies show that machismo now characterizes only a small proportion of Latino husband-fathers (Torres et al. 2002). Machismo apparently decreases with each generation in the United States (Hurtado et al. 1992; Wood 2001). Some researchers have found that the husband-father plays a stronger role than in either white or African American families (Vega 1990; Torres et al. 2002). Apparently, the wife-mother is usually more family-centered than her husband, displaying more warmth and affection for her children.

It is difficult to draw generalizations 8 because, as with other racial-ethnic groups, individual Latino families vary considerably

(Contreras et al. 2002). Some Latino families, for example, have **acculturated** to such an extent that they are Protestants who do not speak Spanish.

Asian American Families

9   As you can see from Figure 1 on the previous page, Asian American children are more likely than children in any other racial-ethnic group to grow up with both parents. As with the other groups, family life also reflects social class. In addition, because Asian Americans **emigrated** from many different countries, their family life reflects those many cultures (Xie and Goyette 2004). As with Latino families, the more recent their immigration, the more closely their family life reflects the patterns in their country of origin (Kibria 1993; Glenn 1994).

10   Despite such differences, sociologist Bob Suzuki (1985), who studied Chinese American and Japanese American families, identified several distinctive characteristics of Asian American families. Although Asian Americans have adopted the **nuclear** family structure, they have retained **Confucian** values that provide a framework for family life: **humanism**, **collectivity**, self-discipline, **hierarchy**, respect for the elderly, moderation, and obligation. Obligation means that each member of a family owes respect to other family members and is responsible never to bring shame on the family. Conversely, a child's success brings honor to the family (Zamiska 2004). To control their children, Asian American parents are more likely to use shame and guilt rather than physical punishment.

11   The ideal does not always translate into the real, however, and so it is here. The children born to Asian immigrants confront a bewildering world of incompatible expectations—those of the new culture and those of their parents. As a result, they experience more family conflict and mental problems than do children of Asian Americans who are not immigrants (Meyers 2006).

Native American Families

12   Perhaps the single most significant issue that Native American families face is whether to follow traditional values or to **assimilate** into the dominant culture (Garrett 1999). This primary distinction creates vast differences among families. The traditionals speak native languages and emphasize distinctive Native American values and beliefs. Those who have assimilated into the broader culture do not. . . .

13   In general, Native American parents are **permissive** with their children and avoid physical punishment. Elders play a much more active role in their children's families than they do in most U.S. families: Elders, especially grandparents, not only provide child care but also teach and discipline children. Like others, Native American families differ by social class.

14   From this brief review, you can see that race-ethnicity signifies little for understanding family life. Rather, social class and culture hold the keys. The more resources a family has, the more it assumes the characteristics of a middle-class nuclear family. Compared with the poor, middle-class families have fewer children and fewer unmarried mothers. They also place greater emphasis on educational achievement and **deferred gratification.**

One-Parent Families

15   Another indication of how extensively U.S. families are changing is the increase in one-parent families. From Figure 2, you can see that the percentage of U.S. children who live with two parents (not necessarily their biological parents) has dropped sharply. The concerns that are often expressed about one-parent families may have more to do with their poverty than with children being reared by one parent. Because women head most one-parent families, these families tend to be poor. Most divorced women earn less than their former husbands, yet about 85 percent of children of divorce live with their mothers ("Child Support" 1995; Aulette 2002).

To understand the typical one-parent 16 family, then, we need to view it through the lens of poverty, for that is its primary source of strain. The results are serious, not just for these parents and their children but also for society as a whole. Children from one parent families are more likely to drop out of school, to get arrested, to have emotional problems, and to get divorced (McLanahan and Sandefur 1994; Menaghan et al. 1997; McLanahan and Schwartz 2002; Amato and Cheadle 2005). If female, they are more likely to become sexually active at a younger age and to bear children while still unmarried teenagers.

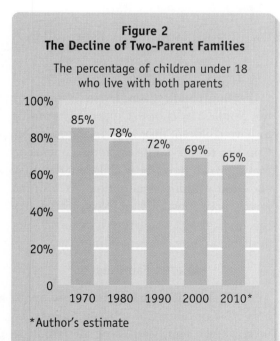

Figure 2
The Decline of Two-Parent Families

The percentage of children under 18 who live with both parents

*Author's estimate

Source: By the author: Based on *Statistical Abstract* 1995: Table 79;2007:Table 62.

Families Without Children

While most married women give 17 birth, about one of five (19 percent) do not (DeOilos and Kapinus 2003). The number of childless couples has doubled from what it was 20 years ago. As you can see from Figure 3, this percentage varies by racial-ethnic group, with whites and Latinas representing the extremes. Some couples are infertile, but most childless couples have made a choice to not have children. Why do they make this choice? Some women believe they would be stuck at home—bored, lonely, with dwindling career opportunities. Some couples perceive their marriage as too fragile to withstand the strains that a child would bring (Gerson 1985). A common reason is to attain a sense of freedom— to pursue a career, to be able to change jobs, to travel, and to have less stress (Lunneborg 1999; Letherby 2002).

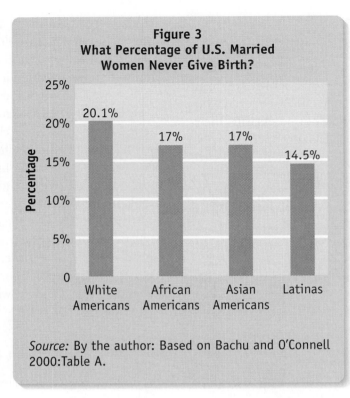

Figure 3
What Percentage of U.S. Married Women Never Give Birth?

Source: By the author: Based on Bachu and O'Connell 2000:Table A.

18   With trends firmly in place—more education and careers for women, advances in contraception, legal abortion, the high cost of rearing children, and an emphasis on possessing more material things—the proportion of women who never bear children is likely to increase. Consider this statement in a newsletter:

19   We are DINKS (Dual Incomes, No Kids). We are happily married. I am 43; my wife is 42. We have been married for almost twenty years . . . Our investment strategy has a lot to do with our personal philosophy: "You can have kids—or you can have everything else!"

20   Many childless couples, in contrast, are not childless by choice. Desperately wanting to have children, they keep trying to do so. Coming to the soul-searching conclusion that they can never bear children, the most common solution is adoption. As featured in the Sociology and the New Technology box on page 694, some turn to solutions not available to previous generations.

Blended Families

21   The blended family, one whose members were once part of other families, is an increasingly significant type of family in the United States. Two divorced people who marry and each bring their children

into a new family unit become a blended family. With divorce common, millions of children spend some of their childhood in blended families. One result is more complicated family relationships. Consider this description written by one of my students:

22   I live with my dad. I should say that I live with my dad, my brother (whose mother and father are also my mother and father), my half sister (whose father is my dad, but whose mother is my father's last wife), and two stepbrothers and stepsisters (children of my father's current wife). My father's wife (my current stepmother, not to be confused with his second wife who, I guess, is no longer my stepmother) is pregnant, and soon we all will have a new brother or sister. Or will it be a half brother or half sister?

23   If you can't figure this out, I don't blame you. I have trouble myself. It gets very complicated around Christmas. Should we all stay together? Split up and go to several other homes? Who do we buy gifts for, anyway?

Gay and Lesbian Families

24   In 1989, Denmark became the first country to legalize marriage between people of the same sex. Since then, several European countries have passed such laws. In 2004, Massachusetts became the first of the U.S. states to legalize same-sex marriages. Walking a fine **conceptual** tightrope, other states have passed laws that give legal rights to "registered domestic partnerships." This is an attempt to give legal status to same-sex unions and yet sidestep controversy by not calling them marriages.

25   At this point, most gay and lesbian couples lack both legal marriage and the legal protection of registered "partnerships." Although these couples live throughout the United States, about half are concentrated in just twenty cities. The greatest concentrations are in San Francisco, Los Angeles, Atlanta, New York City, and Washington, D.C. About one fifth of gay and lesbian couples were previously married to heterosexuals. Twenty-two percent of female couples and 5 percent of male couples have children from their earlier heterosexual marriages (Bianchi and Casper 2000).

26   What are same-sex relationships like? Like everything else in life, these couples cannot be painted with a single brush stroke. As with opposite-sex couples, social class is significant, and orientations to life differ according to education, occupation, and income. Sociologists Philip Blumstein and Pepper Schwartz (1985) interviewed same-sex couples and found their main struggles to be housework, money, careers, problems with relatives, and sexual adjustment—the same problems that face **heterosexual** couples. Some also confront discrimination at work, which can add stress to their relationship (Todosijevic et al. 2005). Same-sex couples are more likely to break up, and one argument for legalizing gay marriages is that the marriage contract will make these relationships more stable. If they were surrounded by laws, same-sex marriages would be like opposite-sex marriages—to break them would require negotiating around legal obstacles.

Sociology and the New Technology

The Brave New World of High-Tech Reproduction: Where Technology Outpaces Law and Sometimes Common-Sense

Jaycee has five parents—or none, depending on how you look at it. The story goes like this. Luanne and John Buzzanca were infertile. Although they spent more than $100,000 on treatments, nothing worked. Then a fertility clinic mixed a man's sperm with a woman's egg. Both the man and the woman remained anonymous. Pamela Snell agreed to be a surrogate mother, and a surgeon implanted the fertilized egg in Pamela, who gave birth to Jaycee (Davis 1998a; Foote 1998).

At Jaycee's birth, Pamela handed Jaycee over to Luanne, who was waiting at her bedside. Luanne's husband, John, decided not to be there. He had filed for divorce just a month before.

Luanne asked John for child support. John refused, and Luanne sued. The judge ruled that John didn't have to pay. He said that because Jaycee had been conceived in a petri dish with an egg and sperm from anonymous donors, John wasn't the baby's father. The judge added that Luanne wasn't the baby's mother either.

Five parents—or none? Welcome to the brave—and very real—new world of high-tech reproduction. Reproductive technologies have laid a trap for the unsuspecting, calling into question even what a mother is. Although Pamela Snell gave birth to Jaycee, she is not a mother. How about the donor of the egg? Biologically, yes, but legally, no. Is Luanne a mother? Fortunately, for Jaycee's sake, a higher court ruled that she is.

—Henslin, *Sociology: A Down to Earth Approach*, Text from pp. 470–480 © 2008
James M. Henslin. Reproduced by permission of Pearson Education, Inc.

Fill in the blank in each sentence with a word from the Vocabulary Preview.

Vocabulary Preview
1. The distinctly dressed Mormons are not _____ to current American society.

Vocabulary Preview
2. United Nations Ambassadors Angelina Jolie and Natalie Portman promote _____ in business; they call for commerce that raises the world's poorest people out of poverty.

Vocabulary Preview
3. Some view the 1960s in the United States as a time of rapid moral change that led to a more _____ society.

Vocabulary Preview
4. The cyborg as played by Arnold Schwarzenegger in *The Terminator* is _____ gone high-tech.

Vocabulary Preview
5. "We Are the World" is a song and charity single that celebrates the _____ of the human experience. Fans enjoy hearing racially

and musically diverse recording artists singing together on one track to raise money for those in dire need across the globe.

For items 6 through 10, choose the best meaning of each word in *italics*. Use context clues to make your choice.

Vocabulary in Context _____ **6.** "Sociologists use the term *fictive kin* to refer to this stretching of kinship." (paragraph 4)
   a. real
   b. desired
   c. invented
   d. true

Vocabulary in Context _____ **7.** "Although Asian Americans have adopted the *nuclear* family structure, they have retained Confucian values . . ." (paragraph 10)
   a. energized
   b. explosive
   c. secondary
   d. central

Vocabulary in Context _____ **8.** ". . . they have retained Confucian values that provide a framework for family life: humanism, collectivity, self-discipline, *hierarchy*, respect for the elderly, moderation, and obligation." (paragraph 10)
   a. authority
   b. individuality
   c. independence
   d. humiliation

Vocabulary in Context _____ **9.** "Perhaps the single most significant issue that Native American families face is whether to follow traditional values or to *assimilate* into the dominant culture." (paragraph 12)
   a. segregate
   b. integrate
   c. parrot
   d. impress

Vocabulary in Context _____ **10.** "They also place greater emphasis on educational achievement and deferred *gratification*." (paragraph 14)
   a. satisfaction
   b. repayment
   c. disappointment
   d. demands

Central Idea _____ **11.** Which of the following sentences states the central idea of the passage?
   a. "Rather, family life varies widely throughout the United States." (paragraph 1)
   b. "The primary distinction is not between African Americans and other groups, but between social classes." (paragraph 2)
   c. "From this brief review, you can see that race-ethnicity signifies little for understanding family life." (paragraph 14)
   d. "Another indication of how extensively U. S. families are changing is the increase in one-parent families." (paragraph 15)

Supporting Detail _____ **12.** According to Figure 1, "Family Structure," which family group has the largest percentage headed by married couples?

    a. White Americans   d. Asian Americans

    b. Native Americans   e. African Americans

    c. Latinos

Supporting Detail _____ **13.** According to Figure 3, "What Percentage of U. S. Married Women Never Give Birth?" which family group has the lowest percentage of women who never give birth?

    a. White Americans   c. Asian Americans

    b. African Americans   d. Latinos

Transitions _____ **14.** "Compared with the poor, middle-class families have fewer children and fewer unmarried mothers." (paragraph 14)

The relationship of ideas within this sentence is

    a. cause and effect.   c. comparison and contrast.

    b. classification.   d. generalization and example.

Transitions _____ **15.** "It is difficult to draw generalizations because, as with other racial-ethnic groups, individual Latino families vary considerably (Contreras et al. 2002). Some Latino families, for example, have acculturated to such an extent that they are Protestants who do not speak Spanish." (paragraph 8)

The relationship of ideas between these sentences is

    a. cause and effect.   c. comparison and contrast.

    b. classification.   d. generalization and example.

Thought Patterns _____ **16.** The overall thought pattern for the passage is

    a. cause and effect.   c. comparison and contrast.

    b. classification.   d. definition and example.

Fact and Opinion _____ **17.** "While most married women give birth, about one in five (19 percent) do not (DeOilos and Kapinus 2003)." (paragraph 17)

This sentence is a statement of

    a. fact.   c. fact and opinion.

    b. opinion.

Tone and Purpose _____ **18.** The overall tone and purpose of the author is

    a. to inform by offering a balanced overview of family groups based on expert opinions and factual detail.

    b. to please each family group with positive descriptions.

    c. to argue in favor of diversity in families.

Inferences _____ **19.** Based on the details in "The Brave New World of High-Tech Reproduction" in the *Sociology and the New Technology* box, we can infer that

    a. reproductive technology is harmful to families.

    b. reproductive technology has complicated the definition of *family*.

    c. reproductive technology should be banned.

    d. reproductive technology is a widespread method of conceiving children.

Argument _____ **20.** Read the claim and supports taken from "The Brave New World of High-Tech Reproduction" in the *Sociology and the New Technology* box. Then identify the detail that does not support the claim.

    Claim: "Reproductive technologies have laid a trap for the unsuspecting, calling into question even what a mother is."

    a. The judge added that Luanne wasn't the baby's mother.

    b. Although Pamela Snell gave birth to Jaycee, she is not the mother.

    c. How about the donor of the egg? Biologically yes, but legally no.

    d. Is Luanne the mother? Fortunately, for Jaycee's sake, a higher court ruled that she is.

Outlining

Complete the following outline with information from the passage "Diversity in U. S. Families."

Central Idea:

    I. African American Families

    II. _____

    III. _____

    IV. _____

    V. One-parent Families

    VI. _____

    VII. Blended Families

    VIII. _____

WHAT DO YOU THINK?

How did you respond to this passage? Do you agree with this classification of families? Why or why not? With artificial insemination becoming more common, many children are aware of the method of their conception and want to meet other children from the same sperm donor. To help locate their (half) brothers and sisters, they can consult a Web site, the Donor Sibling Registry. If your biological father were a sperm donor, would you want to meet him? How about your biological siblings? Why or why not? Assume your state is considering a law that requires open records for children of sperm donors. The law would require sperm donors to register and give a complete medical history. Write a letter to the editor of your local newspaper or to a state representative. In your letter, take a stand for or against a law for open records of sperm donors.

EFFECTIVE READER Scorecard

"Diversity in U.S. Families"			
Skill	**Number Correct**	**Points**	**Total**
Vocabulary			
Vocabulary Preview (5 items)	_____	× 10 =	_____
Vocabulary in Context (5 items)	_____	× 10 =	_____
		Vocabulary Score	_____
Comprehension			
Central Idea (1 item)	_____	× 8 =	_____
Supporting Details (2 items)	_____	× 8 =	_____
Transitions (2 items)	_____	× 8 =	_____
Thought Patterns (1 item)	_____	× 8 =	_____
Fact and Opinion (1 item)	_____	× 8 =	_____
Tone and Purpose (1 item)	_____	× 8 =	_____
Inferences (1 item)	_____	× 8 =	_____
Argument (1 item)	_____	× 8 =	_____
Outlining (5 items)	_____	× 4 =	_____
		Comprehension Score	_____

Combined-Skills Tests

Part Three contains 10 tests. The purpose of these tests is twofold: to track your growth as a reader and to prepare you for the formal tests you will face as you take college courses. Each test presents a reading passage and questions that cover some or all of the following skills: vocabulary in context, central ideas, supporting details, thought patterns, inferences, tone and purpose, fact and opinion, and argument.

TEST 1

Read the following passage, and then, answer the questions.

Against All Odds, Hope, Determination, and Generosity Win

by Sandra Offiah-Hawkins

[1]Life has its ways of attempting to deter one's hopes, dreams, and **aspirations;** however, my life illustrates the power of hope and determination. [2]My lesson begins in Picayune, a little southern town in Mississippi.

[3]You see, at the very young, easy-to-influence age of fifteen, I became pregnant while attending a church conference in Biloxi, Mississippi. [4]As an eleventh grade African American high school student in my hometown, my educational process would normally have been discontinued until after the birth of the child. [5]Therefore, I opted to keep my **predicament** a secret that I shared only with a close friend, Carolyn—to whom I offered many excuses about why I could not tell my parents; however, the most important one, I thought, was that they would kill me—I was determined to stay in school. [6]Although Carolyn did not disclose my secret, for she had been sworn to secrecy, each day she tried to convince me that honesty in this case was indeed the best policy and that sooner or later the truth would inevitably be revealed.

[7]During this time, I contemplated suicide. [8]My logic: I didn't want to "disappoint" my family. [9]If I had told the school counselor, who was a close family friend, he would have told my parents and suggested I remain out of school until the birth of the baby the following year.

[10]Finally, after a great deal of thought—and the fact that I was literally running out of time—I decided to tell my mother. [11]She was deeply saddened. [12]I shall never forget what she said to me on that day, "Baby, everyone makes mistakes; just don't make it a habit." [13]My mother told my father, who was crushed by the news; I had always been the closest to him of his five daughters. [14]Carolyn and I were both relieved when the pressure of secrecy ended. [15]My daughter, Daphne, was born, and my education had not been interrupted.

[16]I had never been an "A" student, but I was always an outgoing, witty, and determined "B" student. [17]During my senior year of high school, I longed to try out for the part of Mama in *A Raisin in the Sun* by

Lorraine Hansberry. [18]For a while I gave excuses why I could not take the part: the baby needed me, I had no time to study lines, and yes, I was pregnant with baby number two.

[19]Many people facing this new crisis would say to hell with the play, but I decided to take the lead role in *A Raisin in the Sun*. [20]Although I was six months pregnant and only days away from high school graduation, I played the part of Mama in what others told me was a "breathtaking performance," and I felt as though everyone in my African American community was there. [21]Today, people in Picayune still talk about my performance that evening, and during my graduation ceremony, I received a trophy for best actor.

[22]I had thought I might get a college scholarship. [23]Since seventh grade, I had been playing the trombone in Carver High School's marching and concert bands. [24]By the time I became a senior, my band director, Mr. Simmons, was convinced I would receive a full band scholarship to Jackson State University and become a member of the Sonic Boom of the South. [25]Because of my latest pregnancy, I knew that I would be unable to attend summer camp in preparation for the fall semester, so I had to inform the band director that I was unable to take advantage of the opportunity my talent and hard work had earned me.

[26]There didn't appear to be any hope of receiving a college education with one child and another on the way, especially given my family's financial situation. [27]Yet, I did hope. [28]I was determined to get an education.

[29]A few days after graduating from high school, I moved to Jackson, Mississippi, to live with my sister and her family in a cramped one-bedroom apartment. [30]A couple of months later, my parents generously offered to take care of my daughter, for it was almost time for the new baby.

[31]Two weeks after the birth of my son, I started college at Utica Junior College in Utica, Mississippi. [32]For the next two years, I commuted to college 45 miles on a 6:00 A.M. bus.

[33]My sister, who taught at the school, informed the band director of my musical abilities. [34]He offered to pay for my tuition and books if I would join the band. [35]Although I had planned to stop playing the instrument after the birth of my second child, I agreed to become captain of the trombone section in the marching and concert bands.

[36]Later, faced with the problem of finding a place for my son and me to live, I met an elderly woman, Ms. Woods, who ran a day care center

and rented rooms to 18 college girls. ³⁷Ms. Woods agreed to share her room with us until a bed became available. ³⁸We stayed in that room with her for more than a year. ³⁹For the first four years of his life, Ms. Woods's home was the only home my son ever knew.

⁴⁰Upon completion of my A.A. Degree, I transferred to Jackson State, which was located only two blocks from where we lived. ⁴¹The girls in the house would care for my son, Nick, while I worked and went to class. ⁴²By working two jobs to put myself through my last two years of college, I received a B.A. in English Literature. ⁴³I could not wait to finally have both my children living under the same roof, so I moved back home.

⁴⁴After returning home and teaching at East Side Elementary School for one year, I decided to uproot my small family and return to Jackson State to obtain certification in Reading and English. ⁴⁵A year and a half later, I received my M.A.T. in English and Reading.

⁴⁶I have taught English and Reading at two different colleges now for more than 23 years and am currently a professor and the Assistant Chair of the English Department. ⁴⁷I give thanks to God Almighty for all the many generous blessings He continues to bestow upon me—including hope and determination.

Vocabulary _____ **1.** The best meaning of the word **aspirations** as used in sentence 1 is
    a. barriers.
    b. ambitions.
    c. thoughts.
    d. differences.

Vocabulary _____ **2.** The best meaning of the word **predicament** as used in sentence 5 is
    a. position.
    b. dilemma.
    c. opportunity.
    d. contradiction.

Central Idea _____ **3.** Choose the sentence that best states the author's central idea.
    a. sentence 1
    b. sentence 2
    c. sentence 3
    d. sentence 47

Main Idea, Details _____ **4.** Sentence 9 is
    a. a main idea.
    b. a major supporting detail.
    c. a minor supporting detail.

Thought Patterns _____ **5.** Which thought pattern is suggested by the relationship between sentences 4 and 5?
    a. cause and effect
    b. classification
    c. contrast
    d. example

Transitions _____ **6.** What is the relationship of ideas within sentence 40?

      a. contrast   c. space order

      b. classification   d. example

Purpose _____ **7.** The author's purpose is

      a. to entertain readers with lively details from her life.

      b. to inspire readers by sharing personal experiences of overcoming life's challenges.

      c. to inform readers about the difficulties of life.

Argument _____ **8.** We can conclude that the author's driving goal was

      a. to become a mother.

      b. to receive a college education.

      c. to become a musical performer.

      d. to get off of welfare.

Tone _____ **9.** The tone of sentence 8 is

      a. matter-of-fact.   c. ironic.

      b. bitter.   d. reflective.

Fact and Opinion _____ **10.** Sentence 16 states

      a. fact.   c. fact and opinion.

      b. opinion.

TEST 2

Read the following article from *USA Today*. Then, answer the questions.

The Young Prefer Facebook to Blogging, Twitter

by Mary Brophy Marcus, USA TODAY

[1]A new report paints a picture of how teens and young adults are using social media these days.

[2]Teens are eating up Facebook but are not so keen on Twitter, and they are not blogging as much as they used to, according to the Pew Internet Project's report.

[3]"Out of all the data, we think in some ways it's most surprising to see a decline in blogging," says Pew researcher Amanda Lenhart, who

co-wrote the report, "Social Media and Mobile Internet Use Among Teens and Young Adults."

[4]The report highlights data gathered from two telephone surveys in September, one that focused on teens ages 12–17 and a second survey of adults 18 and older.

[5]Lenhart says blogging among teens and young adults has **plummeted** to half what it was in 2006. [6]In that year, 28% of teens ages 12–17 and adults ages 18–29 were bloggers. [7]By the fall of 2009, the numbers had dropped to 14% of teens and 15% of young adults. [8]During the same period, the percentage of online adults over 30 who were bloggers rose from 7% in 2006 to 11% in 2009.

[9]"What we think is really going on here—why young people aren't doing blogs anymore —is that there's been a move from MySpace, which put blogging front and center, to Facebook, which doesn't have that," Lenhart says.

[10]The report also indicates that wireless connectivity is high among adults under 30, and social networking continues to climb.

[11]But Twitter hasn't gained much ground with teens—only 8% of 12- to 17-year-olds who go online say they ever use it. [12]That's unusual, because teenagers have a history of being early adopters of nearly every online activity, Lenhart says.

[13]Lenhart says researchers asked some teens in focus groups about their Twitter perceptions.

[14]"Most had no idea what it was," Lenhart says. [15]"Some knew it as 'that thing Lance Armstrong and other celebrities do.' "

[16]She says there may be a perception with Twitter that you have to "feed the beast," and that may keep them away, Lenhart says.

[17]"To quote my 15 year-old-son, 'Twitter is lame,'" says Lee Aase, manager of social media at Mayo Clinic. [18]He says Facebook and texting may be satisfying teen chat needs.

[19]"They're so into text-messaging that that **niche** is already sort of filled for them," he says.

[20]Aase also says some teenagers may grow back into blogging as they hit adulthood: "Blogging has become a way to communicate with the world, about more meaningful issues, not just about communicating to friends."

—Brophy Marcus, Mary. "The Young Prefer
Facebook to Blogging, Twitter" in
USA TODAY, February 4, 2010.
Reprinted with permission.

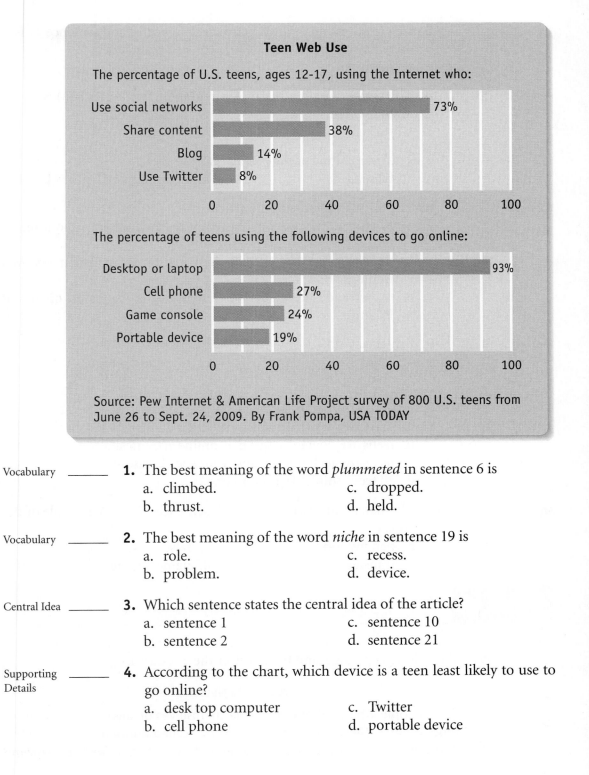

Teen Web Use

The percentage of U.S. teens, ages 12-17, using the Internet who:

Use social networks — 73%
Share content — 38%
Blog — 14%
Use Twitter — 8%

0   20   40   60   80   100

The percentage of teens using the following devices to go online:

Desktop or laptop — 93%
Cell phone — 27%
Game console — 24%
Portable device — 19%

0   20   40   60   80   100

Source: Pew Internet & American Life Project survey of 800 U.S. teens from June 26 to Sept. 24, 2009. By Frank Pompa, USA TODAY

Vocabulary _____ **1.** The best meaning of the word *plummeted* in sentence 6 is
    a. climbed.   c. dropped.
    b. thrust.   d. held.

Vocabulary _____ **2.** The best meaning of the word *niche* in sentence 19 is
    a. role.   c. recess.
    b. problem.   d. device.

Central Idea _____ **3.** Which sentence states the central idea of the article?
    a. sentence 1   c. sentence 10
    b. sentence 2   d. sentence 21

Supporting Details _____ **4.** According to the chart, which device is a teen least likely to use to go online?
    a. desk top computer   c. Twitter
    b. cell phone   d. portable device

Transitions _____ **5.** The relationship of ideas between sentence 10 and sentence 11 is
    a. time order.   c. cause and effect.
    b. addition.   d. contrast.

Thought Patterns _____ **6.** The main thought pattern of paragraph 5 (sentences 5–8) is
    a. time order.   c. cause and effect.
    b. listing.   d. contrast.

Tone _____ **7.** The overall tone of the passage is
    a. biased.   b. neutral.

Purpose _____ **8.** The overall purpose of the article is
    a. to inform the reader about recent research findings about media use.
    b. to amuse the reader with information from recent research findings about media use.
    c. to persuade the reader to change media use based on recent findings.

Fact and Opinion _____ **9.** Sentence 4 states
    a. a fact.   c. fact and opinion.
    b. an opinion.

Inference _____ **10.** Based on the details in the article, we can infer that
    a. Facebook is not popular with older adults.
    b. teens are slow to accept new online activities.
    c. teens use technology mostly for social reasons.
    d. all teens think "Twitter is lame."

Argument _____ **11.** The statement "Twitter is lame" (sentence 17) is an example of the fallacy
    a. bandwagon.   c. false cause.
    b. transfer.   d. name-calling.

TEST 3

Read the following passage, and then answer the questions.

Anorexia Nervosa

[1]People who deliberately starve themselves or severely restrict their food intake suffer from an eating disorder called **anorexia nervosa**. [2]The disorder usually begins around the time of puberty and leads to extreme

weight loss—at least 15 percent below normal body weight. ³Those who struggle with this problem also have an intense fear of becoming fat, even though they are underweight. ⁴Many people with the disorder look **emaciated**, yet they are convinced that they are overweight. ⁵Sometimes they must be hospitalized to prevent death by starvation. ⁶Still, they often continue to deny that they have a problem or face any health risk. ⁷Food and weight become obsessions. ⁸For some, the compulsiveness shows up in strange eating rituals or the refusal to eat in front of others. ⁹It is not uncommon for people with anorexia to collect recipes and prepare lavish gourmet feasts for family and friends but not partake in the meals themselves. ¹⁰They may adhere to strict exercise routines to keep off weight. ¹¹Ninety percent of all anorexics are women.

¹²The most important thing that family and friends can do to help individuals with anorexia is to love them unconditionally. ¹³Talk to physicians or counselors for help in determining the best way to approach and deal with the situation. ¹⁴People with anorexia will beg and lie to avoid eating and gaining weight; achieving a cure means giving up the illness and hence giving up the control. ¹⁵Family and friends should not give in to the pleadings of an anorexic patient but should not nag the person **incessantly** either. ¹⁶Anorexia is an illness that cannot be controlled by simple willpower; professional guidance is needed. ¹⁷Most important is to support the individual without supporting the person's actions.

—Adapted from National Women's Health Information
Center, "*Anorexia Nervosa.*"

Vocabulary _____ **1.** The best meaning of the word *emaciated* as used in sentence 4 is
  a. wasted.
  b. heavy.
  c. embarrassed.
  d. willful.

Vocabulary _____ **2.** The best meaning of the word *incessantly* as used in sentence 15 is
  a. endlessly, all the time.
  b. in silence.
  c. with violence.
  d. with good intentions.

Main Idea _____ **3.** Which sentence best states the main idea of the second paragraph?
  a. sentence 12
  b. sentence 13
  c. sentence 14
  d. sentence 15

Implied
Central Idea _____ **4.** What is the implied central idea of the passage?
  a. Many people suffer from the condition known as anorexia nervosa.
  b. Anorexia nervosa is an eating disorder that has horrible consequences.

    c. The person suffering from anorexia nervosa faces mental and physical problems and requires the support of others.

    d. Those who suffer from anorexia nervosa often deny that they have a life-threatening disorder.

Transitions _____ **5.** The relationship between sentences 5 and 6 is one of

    a. time order.   c. contrast.

    b. example.   d. cause.

Inferences _____ **6.** Choose the inference that is most soundly based on the information in the passage.

    a. Anorexia nervosa is not a serious problem.

    b. Anorexia nervosa is the result of childhood trauma.

    c. People who suffer from anorexia nervosa are seeking some sort of control over their lives.

    d. People who suffer from anorexia nervosa are selfish.

7–10. Complete the idea map based on the information in the passage.

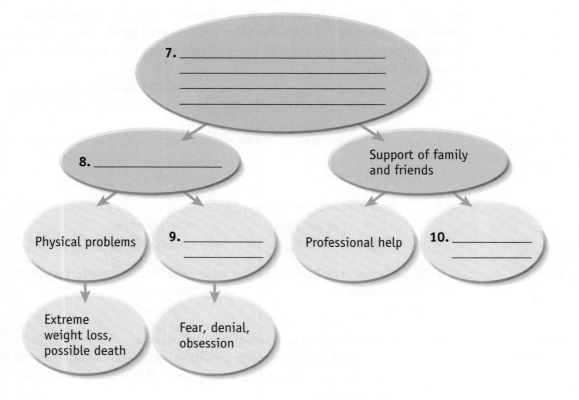

TEST 4

Read the following passage, and then, answer the questions.

The Health of Routines and Rituals

1Routines and rituals are alive and well in the United States—and keeping people well in the process. **2**That's the claim of a review of 50 years of research that appears in the December 2002 issue of the *Journal of Family Psychology*. **3**Many Americans take part in routines and rituals, and these practices help to improve their mental and physical health and sense of belonging, according to the researchers who did the analysis of 32 studies. **4**Routine events, such as evening dinners eaten together as a family, provide comfort simply by being predictable events people can count on, says study author Barbara Fiese, a psychologist at Syracuse University in New York.

5Routines are acts done regularly that need to be done, such as eating or preparing for bed, and take time but are seldom thought about afterward, she says. **6**"Having some predictability in life around routines is positive," Fiese says. **7**Children flourish when they can predict things in their life, such as family dinners or regular bedtimes, the study found. **8**Regular family dinners, even if only for 20 minutes a day, are the most common routine. **9**"If you look at dinner time, for example, it's not happening seven days a week but usually four or five times," Fiese says. **10**"Even that short period of time has a positive effect. **11**It's related to physical health in infants and children and academic performance in elementary children."

12Rituals, on the other hand, are symbolic practices people do or celebrate that help define who they are—and about which they often **reminisce**, she notes. **13**Every ritual stands for something, such as marriage, which is an entrance into a family. **14**The meaningful, symbolic parts of rituals seem to help emotional development and satisfaction with family relationships. **15**When rituals are continued during times of stress, such as a divorce, they lessen the negative impact. **16**"They have the potential to protect kids from risks associated with one-parent families," Fiese says. **17**"It seems that at points of transition, such as school or marriage, rituals can increase one's sense of security."

—Adapted from Deutsch, "A Slave to Routine?"

Vocabulary _____ **1.** The best meaning of the word *reminisce* as used in sentence 12 is
      a. guess.   c. remember.
      b. harp.   d. stare.

Central Idea _____ **2.** The sentence that best states the central idea of the passage is
      a. sentence 1.   c. sentence 5.
      b. sentence 2.   d. sentence 12.

Transitions _____ **3.** The relationship between sentences 11 and 12 is one of
      a. definition and example.
      b. cause and effect.
      c. time order.
      d. comparison and contrast.

Transitions _____ **4.** The relationship of the ideas within sentence 5 is
      a. definition and example.   c. time order.
      b. cause and effect.   d. comparison and contrast.

Thought Patterns _____ **5.** Which thought pattern does the passage use in addition to definition?
      a. comparison   c. time order
      b. effect

Supporting Details _____ **6.** Sentence 16 is a
      a. central idea.   c. minor supporting detail.
      b. major supporting detail.

Purpose _____ **7.** The author's main purpose in the passage is to
      a. inform.   c. persuade.
      b. entertain.

Tone _____ **8.** The tone of the passage is
      a. excited.   c. objective.
      b. bossy.   d. pessimistic.

9–10. Complete the study outline with information from the passage.

Central idea: _____

_____

    I. Routines

        A. Definition: acts done regularly that need to be done and take time but are seldom thought about afterward

B. Examples

    1. _____

    2. Preparing for bed

C. Effects

    1. Improve physical health in infants and children

    2. Improve academic performance in elementary children

II. Rituals

A. Definition: symbolic practices people do or celebrate that help define who they are—and about which they often reminisce

B. Example: Marriage

C. Effects

    1. Protect children from risks linked to one-parent families

    2. Increase sense of security

TEST 5

Read the following passage, and then answer the questions.

"Boyhood Days"

Taken from *Up from Slavery* by Booker T. Washington

[1]From the time that I can remember having any thoughts about anything, I recall that I had an intense longing to learn to read. [2]I determined, when quite a small child, that, if I accomplished nothing else in life, I would in some way get enough education to enable me to read common books and newspapers. [3]Soon after we got settled in some manner in our new cabin in West Virginia, I **induced** my mother to get hold of a book for me. [4]How or where she got it I do not know, but in some way she procured an old copy of Webster's "blue-back" spelling-book, which contained the alphabet, followed by such meaningless words as "ab," "ba," "ca," "da." [5]I began at once to devour this book, and I think that it was the first one I ever had in my hands. [6]I had learned from somebody

that the way to begin to read was to learn the alphabet, so I tried in all the ways I could think of to learn it,—all of course without a teacher, for I could find no one to teach me. [7]At that time there was not a single member of my race anywhere near us who could read, and I was too timid to approach any of the white people. [8]In some way, within a few weeks, I mastered the greater portion of the alphabet. [9]In all my efforts to learn to read my mother shared full my ambition, and sympathized with me and aided me in every way that she could. [10]Though she was totally ignorant, so far as mere book knowledge was concerned, she had high ambitions for her children, and a large fund of good hard, common sense which seemed to enable her to meet and master every situation. [11]If I have done anything in life worth attention, I feel sure that I inherited the **disposition** from my mother.

[12]In the midst of my struggles and longing for an education, a young coloured boy who had learned to read in the state of Ohio came to Malden. [13]As soon as the coloured people found out that he could read, a newspaper was secured, and at the close of nearly every day's work this young man would be surrounded by a group of men and women who were anxious to hear him read the news contained in the papers. [14]How I used to envy this man! [15]He seemed to me to be the one young man in all the world who ought to be satisfied with his attainments.

[16]About this time the question of having some kind of a school opened for the coloured children in the village began to be discussed by members of the race. [17]As it would be the first school for Negro children that had ever been opened in that part of Virginia, it was, of course, to be a great event, and the discussion excited the widest interest.

* * *

[18]This experience of a whole race beginning to go to school for the first time presents one of the most interesting studies that has ever occurred in connection with the development of any race. [19]Few people who were not right in the midst of the scenes can form any exact idea of the intense desire which the people of my race showed for an education. [20]As I have stated, it was a whole race trying to go to school. [21]Few were too young, and none too old, to make the attempt to learn. [22]As fast as any kind of teachers could be secured, not only were day-schools filled, but night-schools as well. [23]The great ambition of the older people was to try to learn to read the Bible before they died. [24]With this end in view, men and women who were fifty or seventy-five years old would often be found in the night-school. [25]Sunday-schools were formed soon after freedom, but the principal book studied in the Sunday-school was the

spelling-book. [26]Day-school, night-school, Sunday-school, were always crowded, and often many had to be turned away for want of room.

Booker T. Washington, *Up from Slavery: An Autobiography*.
New York: Doubleday, Page, 1901; Bartleby.com, 2000. www
.bartleby.com/1004/. 30 July 2007.

Vocabulary _____ **1.** The best meaning of the word *induced* in sentence 3 is
   a. offered.   c. persuaded.
   b. stopped.   d. allowed.

Vocabulary _____ **2.** The best meaning of the word *disposition* in sentence 11 is
   a. situation.   c. problem.
   b. character.   d. need.

Central Idea _____ **3.** Which sentence best states the central idea of this passage?
   a. sentence 1   c. sentence 9
   b. sentence 2   d. sentence 15

Transitions _____ **4.** The relationship between sentences 12 and 13 is one of
   a. time order.   c. contrast.
   b. effect.   d. example.

Main Ideas _____ **5.** Sentence 14 is a
Details
   a. main idea.   c. minor supporting detail.
   b. major supporting detail.

Fact and _____ **6.** Sentence 15 is a statement of
Opinion
   a. fact.   c. fact and opinion.
   b. opinion.

Inferences _____ **7.** Based on the information in the passage, we can infer that Booker T. Washington
   a. was a hardworking student.
   b. neglected work and chores to learn to read.
   c. was ashamed because he couldn't read.
   d. was one of many of his race who could read.

8–10. Complete the following time line with information from the passage.

I. Washington determines to learn to read

II. The influence of his (8) _____

III. His envy of a man who can (9) _____

IV. The opening of a (10) _____

V. The whole race learns to read

TEST 6

Read the following passage, and then, answer the questions.

Lincoln's Gettysburg Address 1863

[1]Fourscore and seven years ago our fathers brought forth on this continent a new nation, conceived in liberty, and dedicated to the **proposition** that all men are created equal.

[2]Now we are engaged in a great civil war, testing whether that nation, or any nation so conceived and so dedicated, can long endure. [3]We are met on a great battlefield of that war. [4]We have come to dedicate a portion of that field as a final resting-place for those who here gave their lives that the nation might live. [5]It is altogether fitting and proper that we should do this. [6]But, in a larger sense, we cannot dedicate, we cannot **consecrate**, we cannot hallow, this ground. [7]The brave men, living and dead, who struggled here have consecrated it, far above our poor power to add or detract. [8]The world will little note, nor long remember, what we say here, but it can never forget what they did here. [9]It is for us the living, rather, to be dedicated here to the unfinished work which they who fought here have thus far so nobly advanced. [10]It is rather for us to be here dedicated to the great task remaining before us—that from these honored dead we take increased devotion to that cause for which they gave the last full measure of devotion—that we here highly resolve that these dead shall not have died in vain—that this nation, under God, shall have a new birth of freedom and that government of the people, by the people, for the people, shall not perish from the earth.

—*American Historical Documents, 1000–1904*. Vol. XLIII. The Harvard Classics. New York: P.F. Collier & Son, 1909–14; Bartleby.com, 2001. www.bartleby.com/43/. 30 July 2007.

Vocabulary _____ **1.** A synonym of the word *proposition* in sentence 1 is
a. scheme.   c. conspiracy.
b. idea.   d. speech.

Vocabulary _____ **2.** The best meaning of the word *consecrate* in sentence 6 is
a. set apart.
c. destroy.
b. see.
d. own.

Thought _____ **3.** The main thought pattern used in the passage is
Patterns
a. cause and effect.
c. comparison and contrast.
b. time order.
d. definition and example.

Main Idea, _____ **4.** Sentence 1 is a
Details
a. main idea.
c. minor supporting detail.
b. major supporting detail.

Central Idea _____ **5.** The central idea of the passage is best stated in
a. sentence 1.
c. sentence 3.
b. sentence 2.
d. sentence 10.

Transitions _____ **6.** The relationship of ideas between sentence 5 and sentence 6 is
a. cause and effect.
c. time order.
b. addition.
d. comparison and contrast.

Purpose _____ **7.** The author's main purpose is
a. to inform the reader about the sacrifice of the soldiers.
b. to assert the ideal that all "are created equal."
c. to entertain the reader with a dramatic speech.

Tone _____ **8.** The overall tone of the passage is
a. unbiased.
c. reverent.
b. cautious.
d. sorrowful.

Fact and _____ **9.** Sentence 3 is a statement of
Opinion
a. fact.
c. fact and opinion.
b. opinion.

10. Complete the following summary with information from the passage.

In his famous Gettysburg Address, President Abraham Lincoln calls upon the principles set forth by the Declaration of Independence and defines the Civil War as a struggle for "a new birth of freedom" that offers true _____ to all of its citizens.

TEST 7

Read the following passage from the college history textbook *The American Story*, and then, answer the questions.

Textbook
Skills

The Enlightenment

¹European historians often refer to the eighteenth century as the Age of Reason. ²During this period, a body of new, often radical ideas swept the public meeting places and universities across Europe and America. ³These ideas changed the way that educated Europeans thought about God, nature, and society. ⁴This intellectual revolution was called the Enlightenment, and it involved the work of Europe's greatest minds, men such as Newton and Locke, Voltaire and Hume. ⁵In time, the writings of these thinkers reached the American colonies, where they received a mixed reception. ⁶On the one hand, the colonists welcomed new science; on the other hand, they defended the **tenets** of traditional Christianity.

⁷The thinkers in this new era replaced the idea of original sin with a much more positive view of human nature. ⁸They believed that a loving God set the universe in motion and gave human beings the power of reason. ⁹This ability to reason enabled them to understand the orderly workings of the created world. ¹⁰Everything, even human society, was based on **mechanical** rules or natural laws. ¹¹The responsibility of right-thinking men and women, therefore, was to make certain that society followed these natural laws. ¹²Some even believed that it was possible to achieve perfection in this world. ¹³In fact, human suffering had come about only because people had lost touch with the basic insights of reason.

—Adapted from Divine, Breen, Fredrickson, & Williams,
The American Story, pp. 117–118.

Vocabulary _____ **1.** The best meaning of the word *tenets* as used in sentence 6 is
  a. people.   c. tools.
  b. ideals.   d. ministers.

Vocabulary _____ **2.** The best meaning of the word *mechanical* as used in sentence 10 is
  a. handmade.   c. automatic.
  b. obvious.   d. flexible.

Central Idea _____ **3.** The sentence that best states the central idea of this passage is
  a. sentence 1.   c. sentence 3.
  b. sentence 2.   d. sentence 7.

Main Idea,   _____   **4.** Sentence 7 serves what purpose in the second paragraph?
Details
                  a. as a minor supporting detail
                  b. as a major supporting detail
                  c. as the main idea

Inferences   _____   **5.** Sentence 7 implies that
                  a. original sin does not offer a positive view of human nature.
                  b. the thinkers of the Enlightenment agreed with the idea of original sin.
                  c. human nature is evil.
                  d. life after death exists.

Transitions   _____   **6.** The relationship of ideas within sentence 6 is one of
                  a. listing.   c. cause and effect.
                  b. contrast.   d. time order.

Purpose   _____   **7.** The author's main purpose is to
                  a. inform.   c. persuade.
                  b. entertain.

Tone   _____   **8.** The tone of the passage is
                  a. objective.   b. emotional.

Fact and   _____   **9.** Sentence 4 is a statement of
Opinion
                  a. fact.   c. fact and opinion.
                  b. opinion.

Argument   _____   **10.** Which sentence is not relevant to the claim that the ideas of the Enlightenment caused a worldwide revolution in thought?
                  a. sentence 2   c. sentence 4
                  b. sentence 3   d. sentence 5

TEST 8

Read the following paragraph from the college textbook *Essentials of Human Communication*. Then, answer the questions.

Textbook
Skills

Territoriality

    [1]One aspect of communication having to do with space is **territoriality**, a term that comes to us from ethology (the study of animals in their natural habitat). [2]Territoriality refers to an ownership-like reaction

toward a particular space or object. ³Many animals mark their territory. ⁴Humans do too. ⁵We make use of three types of markers: central, boundary, and ear markers. ⁶Central markers signify that the territory is reserved. ⁷When you place a drink on a bar, books on your desk, or a sweater over your chair, you let others know that this territory belongs to you. ⁸Boundary markers distinguish your territory from that belonging to others. ⁹The divider in the supermarket checkout line, the armrests separating your theater seat from those on either side, the fence around your house, and the door to your apartment are examples. ¹⁰Ear markers identify your possessions. ¹¹Trademarks, nameplates, and initials on a shirt or attaché case specify that this particular object belongs to you.

—Adapted from DeVito, *Essentials of Human Communication*, p. 135
© 2002. Reproduced by permission of Pearson Education, Inc.

Vocabulary _____ **1.** The word *territoriality* in sentences 1 and 2 means
a. a study of animals.
b. a study of a natural habitat.
c. a study of animals in their natural habitat.
d. an ownership-like reaction.

Supporting Details _____ **2.** The divider in the supermarket checkout line is an example of a
a. central marker.   c. ear marker.
b. boundary marker.   d. none of the above.

Main Idea _____ **3.** The main idea of this paragraph is stated in
a. sentence 1.   c. sentence 3.
b. sentence 2.   d. sentence 5.

Inferences _____ **4.** Based on information in the paragraph, we can conclude that
a. humans can learn about themselves by studying other animals.
b. humans have evolved beyond the effects of territoriality.
c. animals use ear markers in their natural habitats.
d. other types of boundary markers exist.

Transitions _____ **5.** The relationship between sentences 10 and 11 is one of
a. cause and effect.   c. time order.
b. comparison and contrast.   d. definition and example.

Transitions _____ **6.** The relationship of ideas within sentence 5 is one of
a. listing.   c. cause and effect.
b. comparison.   d. time order.

Thought
Patterns
_____ **7.** The overall thought pattern used in the paragraph is
a. cause and effect.   c. comparison and contrast.
b. classification.   d. time order.

Purpose
_____ **8.** The author's main purpose is to
a. inform.   c. persuade.
b. entertain.

Tone
_____ **9.** The tone of the passage is
a. accusing.   c. comical.
b. objective.   d. controversial.

Fact and
Opinion
_____ **10.** The paragraph relies on details of
a. fact.   c. fact and opinion.
b. opinion.

TEST 9

Read the following passage from a college health textbook, and then, answer
the questions.

The Anger Urge

Textbook
Skills

[1]Although much has been said about how hotheaded, short-fused
people are at risk for health problems, recent research provides even
more **compelling** reasons for "chilling out." [2]A study of nearly 13,000
people found that anger, even in the absence of high blood pressure, can
increase a person's risk of heart attack by more than 2.5 times. [3]Stress
hormones released during anger may constrict blood vessels in the heart
or actually promote clot formation, which can cause a heart attack.

[4]Anger results when our wants, desires, and dreams differ from
what we actually get in life. [5]People who spend all their emotional energy in a **quest** for justice or grow frustrated over events that seem impossible to change can become driven by anger. [6]Because anger triggers
the fight-or-flight reaction, these people operate with the stress response
turned on long after it should have dissipated.

[7]Angry people usually display cynicism, which is a brooding, fault-
finding view of their world. [8]Like anger, cynicism keeps the fight-or-flight

reactions constantly flowing through their bodies. [9]Often thought of as "hostile," these constantly stressed folks may have weakened immune systems, and they may face an increased risk of disease.

—Adapted from Donatelle, *Health*,
5th ed., pp. 66–67.

Vocabulary _____ **1.** The best meaning of the word *compelling* as used in sentence 1 is
    a. forceful.   c. personal.
    b. obvious.   d. compiled.

Vocabulary _____ **2.** The best meaning of the word *quest* as used in sentence 5 is
    a. question.   c. search.
    b. denial.   d. thought.

Central Idea _____ **3.** The central idea of the passage is stated in
    a. sentence 1.   c. sentence 3.
    b. sentence 2.   d. sentence 4.

Transitions _____ **4.** The relationship between sentences 7 and 8 is
    a. example.   c. comparison.
    b. contrast.   d. time.

Transitions _____ **5.** The relationship of ideas within sentence 3 is one of
    a. listing.   c. cause and effect.
    b. comparison.   d. classification.

Purpose _____ **6.** The author's main purpose is to
    a. inform the reader about the dangers of anger.
    b. entertain the reader with details about anger management.
    c. persuade the reader to take specific steps against the anger urge.

Fact and Opinion _____ **7.** Sentence 6 is a statement of
    a. fact.   c. fact and opinion.
    b. opinion.

8–10. Complete the cause-and-effect flowchart with information from the passage.

    8. Central idea: _____

_____

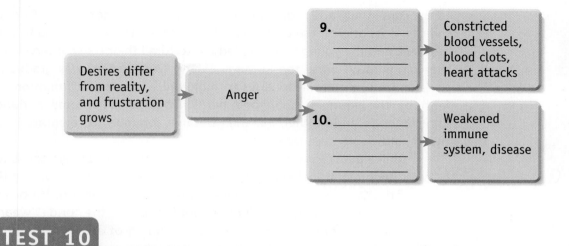

TEST 10

Read the following passage, and then, answer the questions.

Sweet Fifteen-La Quinceañera

[1]The need to recognize the transition between childhood and adulthood is universal. [2]Civilizations over the centuries have established rites of passage for both boys and girls. [3]For young women in the United States, that event is often marked at age sixteen with Sweet Sixteen parties or debuts. [4]This practice was promoted in the South in the nineteenth century with the **debutante** ball. [5]A similar event is the Jewish coming of age at thirteen with the bar mitzvah for boys and the bat mitzvah for girls.

[6]Coming-out parties were thought to have reached the New World during the French occupation of Mexico in the nineteenth century, but the *Quinceañera's* roots go much deeper than that. [7]In her book *Quinceañera*, author Michele Salcedo explains, "The beginnings [of the *Quinceañera*] go much further back, thousands of years back, to the indigenous people of our respective cultures. [8]The Tainos and Arawaks, the Quechua and Toltecs, the Aztecs and Mayas, to name but a few. [9]All had rites of passage to mark the point in a child's life when she was a child no longer, but ready to make her contribution to society as an adult."

[10]According to Mark Francis and Arturo J. Perez-Rodriguez in the book *Primero Dios: Hispanic Liturgical* Resource, both boys and girls initially participated in these rites of passage but only the celebration for girls has survived. [11]As part of the preparation, girls were separated at age fifteen from their playmates and instead instructed on their importance

to the community and their future roles as wives and mothers. [12]"During the rite in its origins, the gods were thanked for the lives of these future mothers, and the young women pledged to fulfill their roles of service to the community," write the authors. [13]"The *Quinceañera* was gradually Christianized by the missionaries to highlight a personal **affirmation** of faith by the young woman and her willingness to become a good Christian wife and mother. [14]It then became common to celebrate it in church, although apart from a Mass."

[15]Unlike many Latino traditions, however, the *Quinceañera* tends to be cross denominational and not exclusively Catholic. [16]The social significance of the *Quinceañera* may be what most attracts attention. [17]It bears a great similarity to many weddings, except in this case the "bride" wears pink. [18]The pink color symbolizes the girl's coming of age, but the preferred emphasis is on the girl's maturity rather than on her sexuality. [19]In many *Quinceañeras,* the event begins with a Mass, but this is not always the case. [20]Because of the event's great cost to the parents—an average of $10,000—some churches discourage their members from adopting the tradition. [21]To offset the costs, families sometimes enlist the support of *padrinos* (sponsors) to cover particular items, from the dress to the cost of a band for the reception. [22]This practice is also carried over to weddings.

[23]The *Quinceañera* chooses several of her friends to be her attendants, called the Court of Honor. [24]These girls—there are usually fourteen of them to represent the debutante's previous years—start the procession, accompanied by their escorts. [25]The parents usually enter the procession next, before their daughter. [26]The *Quinceañera* can have an escort, usually a brother, cousin, or friend, but some choose to have their parents as escorts instead.

[27]There are interesting twists to the celebration as well. [28]According to Salcedo, most Cuban families forgo the church service, while Mexican American, Dominican, and Colombian families will almost always include it. [29]The service can be a simple prayer or blessing from the priest, or a full Mass. [30]Puerto Ricans will also generally opt for the Mass, which culminates with the mother of the *Quinceañera* placing a tiara on her daughter's head and her father replacing her flats with high heels.

[31]Despite the ceremony's high cost, many parents see *Quinceañera* celebrations as a good investment. [32]It reinforces the fact that their daughter is expected to take on more responsibility, and that symbolism does not escape the *Quinceañera*. [33]"Not to brag, but my daughter is unique in a lot of ways," says Mary Mendez, the mother of Brandy, who celebrated her *Quinceañera* in 1994. [34]Brandy's *Quinceañera* was featured

in a June 15–21 article in the *New Times* of Phoenix, Arizona. [35]"I think it [the *Quinceañera*] is good. [36]Half of what's wrong with kids nowadays is they don't think about their future."

—Valerie Menard (2004), *The Latino Holiday Book*, pp. 88–90.

VISUAL VOCABULARY

Based on the passage a debutante is also known as a

_____.

▶ The debutante often dances her first dance of the ball with her father.

Vocabulary _____ **1.** The best meaning of the word *debutante* in sentence 4 is
- a. introduction.
- b. young person.
- c. young woman.
- d. finance.

Vocabulary _____ **2.** The best meaning of the word *affirmation* in sentence 13 is
- a. statement.
- b. denial.
- c. ceremony.
- d. marriage.

Implied Central Idea _____ **3.** Which sentence is the best statement of the implied central idea of the passage?
- a. La Quinceañera is a Hispanic debutante ball.
- b. La Quinceañera is a significant expense for the family.
- c. La Quinceañera reflects the religious beliefs of the Hispanic culture.
- d. La Quinceañera is a cultural event that recognizes the transition between childhood and adulthood for young Latino women.

Transitions _____ **4.** The relationship between sentences 15 and 16 is one of
- a. time order.
- b. contrast.
- c. effect.
- d. example.

Supporting   _____   **5.** Sentence 27 is a
Details   a. major supporting detail.   b. minor supporting detail.

Fact and   _____   **6.** Sentence 4 is a statement of
Opinion   a. fact.   c. fact and opinion.
                       b. opinion.

7–10. Complete the following summary with information from the passage.

A **(7)** _____ is a social event, similar to a debutante ball, recognizing the transition between childhood and adulthood of a young woman. The *Quinceañera's* roots go back thousands of years. Historically, girls were separated at age fifteen from their playmates and instructed on their importance to the community and their future roles as **(8)** _____ and **(9)** _____. Eventually, missionaries used this ritual to highlight a personal affirmation of **(10)** _____ faith. The Quinceañera reinforces the fact that the daughter is expected to take on more responsibility.

PART FOUR

Reading Enrichment

Appendix: Reading Graphics in Textbooks

Reading Graphics in Textbooks

Reading comprehension involves more than just reading words. Authors also use visual images such as photographs, cartoons, and graphics to relay ideas. Graphics are helpful for several reasons. First, graphics can simplify difficult ideas and make relationships among ideas easier to visualize. Second, graphics can sum up ideas so that they can be more quickly digested. Third, graphics can sway a reader by pointing out trends or gaps in information. An effective reader should know how to read different types of graphics. This chapter will discuss three basic types: tables, graphs, and diagrams. Although a variety of graphics exist, a few basic guidelines can be applied as a reading process for any graphic.

Basic Guidelines for Reading Graphics

Graphics give a great deal of information in a smaller space than it would take to write the ideas in the form of words. The following suggestions will help you understand the general format of a graphic. Apply the SQ3R strategies discussed in Chapter 1. Remember to survey, question, read, review, and recite the information.

1. **Read the Words Printed with the Graphic**
   A graphic has a main idea and supporting details, just as a paragraph does.

   - ***Read the title or caption.*** The title or caption is usually at the top of the graphic.

        The title or caption states the main idea of the graphic.

        Ask: What is this graphic about? What is being described?

   - ***Note the source.*** The source is usually at the bottom of the graphic. The source is the author or publisher of the ideas in the graphic.

        Ask: Who collected the information? Is the source a trusted authority?

        If the graphic reports the results of a survey, how many people took part? Who were they?

- *Read any footnotes.* The footnotes are also found at the bottom of a graphic. Footnotes can include important supporting details.

   Ask: Do the footnotes explain what any numbers or headings mean?

   How was the data collected?

- *Read the labels.* Many graphics use columns and rows. Other graphics use horizontal or vertical axes. Columns, rows, and axes are labeled. These labels give important supporting details for the graphic's main idea. Look up any words you do not know in a dictionary.

   Ask: Do the labels tell what the columns and rows represent?

   Are any symbols or abbreviations used? If so, what do they mean?

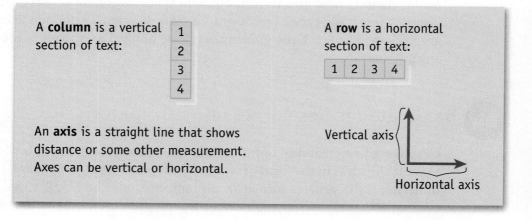

A **column** is a vertical section of text:

1
2
3
4

A **row** is a horizontal section of text:

1 2 3 4

An **axis** is a straight line that shows distance or some other measurement. Axes can be vertical or horizontal.

Vertical axis

Horizontal axis

2. Analyze the Graphic

- *Analyze the format.* Each type of chart has its own organization. For example, a table uses columns and rows. A pie chart is a circle divided into parts.

   Ask: How is the graphic organized?

   Why did the author use this type of graphic?

- *Analyze the unit of measurement.* Study the legend. A legend will list and explain symbols used as labels. Study the labels of rows, columns, and axes.

   Ask: Do the numbers represent hundreds? Thousands? Millions? Inches? Feet? Miles? Pounds? Ounces? Or are metric units used?

- *Analyze trends and patterns.* Trends and patterns suggest or imply important ideas that support the graphic's main idea.

> Ask: What are the extremes? How do the extremes compare to the total?
>
> What are the averages?
>
> What and how much are the increases? What and how much are the decreases?

Textbook Skills

EXAMPLE Study the accompanying graphic from the college textbook *Drugs, Behavior, and Modern Society*, 3rd ed. (Levinthal, p. 15). Answer the questions that follow with information from the graph.

Drug Use in the United States Across the Life Span

	Percentage by Age Group for Use in Past Year/Past Month				Estimated Total Number of Users Past Year/ Past Month
	12–17	18–25	26 and Older	Total Sample	
Any illicit drug	20/11	30/17	8/4	12/7	26,220,000/14,820,000
Marijuana	14/8	25/15	5/3	9/5	19,573,000/11,177,000
Cocaine	2/0.5	5/2	1/0.5	2/0.7	3,691,000/1,501,000
Crack cocaine	0.4/0.1	1/0.4	0.4/0.2	0.5/0.2	1,035,000/413,000
Heroin	0.3/0.02	0.5/0.2	0.1/0.1	0.2/0.1	403,000/208,000
Hallucinogens	4/1	7/2	0.2/0.1	1/0.4	3,169,000/907,000
Alcohol	35/19	75/58	64/49	63/47	138,346,000/104,603,000
Nicotine (any tobacco use)	27/17	54/45	34/30	36/30	79,778,000/66,766,000

Original source: Substance Abuse and Mental Health Services Administration (2000). *Summary of findings from the 1999 National Household Survey on drug abuse.* Rockville, MD: Office of Applied Studies, Substance Abuse and Mental Health Services Administration, Tables G.5–G.9, G.21–G.25.

1. What is the title of the table? _____

_____

2. What is the source of the table? _____

_____

_____

_____

_____

3. How many categories of drugs are listed in the table? _____

4. What time spans of drug use are tracked in the table? _____

_____

5. What are the three age groups the table uses? _____, _____,

   and _____

6. Which drug had the highest total number of users in the past year or past

   month? _____

7. Which drug had the lowest total number of users in the past year or past

   month? _____

8. Which age group had the highest level of marijuana use in the past year or

   past month? _____

9. Which drug has the highest level of use by the 12- to 17-year-old age group?

   _____

10. Based on the information in the table, which drug is most likely to have

    the greatest impact on the health of all age groups? _____

EXPLANATION

1. What is the title of the table? Drug Use in the United States Across the Life
   Span

2. What is the source of the table? Substance Abuse and Mental Health
   Services Administration (2000). _Summary of findings from the 1999
   National Household Survey on drug abuse._ Rockville, MD: Office of
   Applied Studies, Substance Abuse and Mental Health Services
   Administration, Tables G.5–G.9, G.21–G.25.

3. How many categories of drugs are listed in the table? _8_ The table lists five
   specific illicit (illegal) drugs: marijuana, cocaine, crack cocaine, heroin,
   and hallucinogens. The table also includes a more general label "any illicit
   drug"; this label includes many other drugs (such as Ecstasy) besides the

five types of illicit drugs already listed in the table. In addition, the table lists two types of legal drugs: alcohol and nicotine.

4. What time spans of drug use are tracked in the table? *past year and past month*

The time measurement is located in the subheading for the age groups and in the column heading for estimated total number of users. Note that the source indicates that the actual year during which the information was gathered was 1999.

5. What are the three age groups the table uses? *12–17, 18–25, and 26 and older*

6. Which drug had the highest total number of users in the past year or past month? *alcohol* More than 138 million people used alcohol in the past year, and more than 104 million did so in the past month.

7. Which drug had the lowest total number of users in the past year or past month? *heroin* In the past year there were 403,000 users; in the past month, there were 208,000.

8. Which age group had the highest level of marijuana use in the past year or past month? *18–25* Twenty-five percent of people aged 18–25 used marijuana in the past year, and 15 percent did so in the past month.

9. Which drug has the highest level of use by the 12- to 17-year-old age group? *alcohol* Of this age group, 35 percent used alcohol in the past year, and 19 percent used it in the past month.

10. Based on the information in the table, which drug is most likely to have the greatest impact on the health of all age groups? *alcohol* Note that the table does not describe the amount or frequency of use. Therefore, it is difficult to make a value judgment about the positive or negative health effects. However, common sense and general knowledge can lead to a reasonable inference that alcohol has a greater impact on the health of users based on the large numbers of total users.

 ## Three Basic Types of Graphics

Many magazines, newspapers, and textbooks use tables, graphs, and diagrams. These graphics call attention to key concepts. Thus an effective reader takes time to study the ideas within them.

Tables

Social science, health, and business textbooks often use tables. A **table** is a systematic ordering of facts in rows and columns for easy reference. The purpose of a table is to allow the reader to classify and compare the given facts. Often the facts are given as numbers or statistics. The basic guidelines for reading graphics apply to reading a table. In addition, some tables require that you study the places where columns and rows intersect.

Textbook
Skills

EXAMPLE   Study the accompanying table, taken from the college textbook *Politics in America,* 5th ed. (Dye, p. 192). Based on the data in the table, mark each of the statements that follow **T** if it is true, **F** if it is false, or **DK** if you don't know, based on the given data.

Sources of Political Campaign News in Presidential Election Years

Over time network news (ABC, CBS, NBC) has been declining as a major source of campaign news, while cable news (CNN, MSNBC, Fox) has been gaining. The Internet has also gained ground as a source of campaign news, yet it was cited by only 11 percent of Americans as their source of "most news."

News Sources	1992	1996	2000
Television	82%	72%	70%
Cable	29	21	36
Network	55	36	22
Local	29	23	21
Newspapers	57	60	39
Radio	12	19	15
Internet	—	3	11
Magazines	9	11	4

Note: Respondents were asked, "How did you get most of your news about the presidential election campaign? From television, from newspapers, from radio, from magazines, or from the Internet?" Television users were then asked, "Did you get most of your news about the presidential campaign from network TV news, from local TV news, or from cable news networks such as CNN or MSNBC?" Respondents could name two sources.

Original source: From "Campaign 2000 Highly Rated: Despite Uncertain Outcome", Nov. 16, 2000, Pew Research Center for the People and the Press. Copyright (c) 2000 Pew Research Center. Reprinted by permission.

_____ **1.** The source of this table is a reliable source.

_____ **2.** This table charts the voting patterns in presidential elections.

_____ **3.** This information was gathered by interviewing over 1,000 people by telephone.

_____ **4.** The percentage of people using the newspaper as a source of political campaign news declined from 1996 to 2000.

_____ **5.** The people who use cable television as a source of information are more likely to vote than people who use the Internet.

EXPLANATION Compare your answers to the ones given here.

1. T: This table is based on information gathered by the Pew Research Center for the People and the Press. This organization is well respected by serious journalists and news agencies. In addition, the table was published in a college government textbook.

2. F: The title of this table clearly states that it gives data concerning *sources* of political campaign news in presidential election years. The table has nothing to do with how people voted, only where they gathered information.

3. T: The source information at the bottom of the table states this.

4. T: You can check this way. First, begin in the row labeled "Newspapers"; follow that row over to the column for 1996. Note that 60 percent of people used newspapers in 1996. Continue to follow the newspaper row over to the 2000 column. Note that the data indicate that a smaller number, 39 percent, used newspapers in 2000. Subtracting 39 from 60, you can see that the percentage of people using newspapers as a source for political campaign news declined by 21 percent from 1996 to 2000.

5. DK: This table does not give us any information about how people vote, nor does it give any information about the relationship between where people gather information and their voting patterns.

PRACTICE 1

Textbook Skills

Study the following table, from the college textbook *Health Styles,* 2nd ed. (Pruitt & Stein, p. 154). Based on the data in the table, mark each numbered statement **T** if it is true, **F** if it is false, or **DK** if you don't know, based on the given data.

Who Likes to Run, Walk, or Swim: Exercise Participation by Sex and Age

Percentage of adults aged 18+ years reporting participation in selected common physical activities in the prior 2 weeks.

Activity Category	Males 18–29	Males All	Females 18–29	Females All	All ages and sexes
Walking for exercise	32.8	39.4	47.4	48.3	44.1
Gardening or yard work	22.2	34.2	15.4	25.1	29.4
Stretching exercises	32.1	25.0	32.5	26.0	25.5
Weight lifting or other exercise to increase muscle strength	33.6	20.0	14.5	8.8	14.1
Jogging or running	22.6	12.8	11.6	5.7	9.1
Aerobics or aerobic dance	3.4	2.8	19.3	11.1	7.1
Riding a bicycle or exercise bike	18.7	16.2	17.4	14.6	15.4
Stair climbing	10.5	9.9	14.6	11.6	10.8
Swimming for exercise	10.1	6.9	8.0	6.2	6.5
Tennis	5.7	3.5	3.1	2.0	2.7
Bowling	7.0	4.7	4.8	3.6	4.1
Golf	7.9	8.2	1.4	1.8	4.9
Baseball or softball	11.0	5.8	3.2	1.4	3.5
Handball, racquetball, or squash	5.2	2.7	1.0	0.5	1.6
Skiing	1.5	0.9	0.9	0.5	0.7
Cross-country skiing	0.1	0.4	0.3	0.4	0.4
Water skiing	1.5	0.7	0.7	0.4	0.5
Basketball	24.2	10.5	3.1	1.5	5.8
Volleyball	6.8	3.1	4.4	1.8	2.5
Soccer	3.3	1.4	0.9	0.4	0.9
Football	7.6	2.7	0.7	0.3	1.5
Other sports	8.6	7.3	4.5	4.1	5.7

Original source: *Physical Activity and Health: A Report of the Surgeon General,* 1996.

_____ **1.** Walking is the most frequently used form of exercise for all ages and sexes.

_____ **2.** Females do more stretching exercises than males do.

_____ **3.** Females do more strengthening activities, including weightlifting, than males do.

_____ **4.** This table tracks lifelong exercise behaviors.

_____ **5.** Soccer is the sport least liked by both males and females.

Graphs

Graphs show the relationship between two or more sets of ideas. The most common types of graphs you will come across in your reading are line graphs, bar graphs, and pie graphs.

Line Graphs

A line graph plots two or more sets of facts on vertical and horizontal axes. The vertical axis sets out a scale to measure one set of data, and the horizontal axis provides another scale to measure the other set of data. These features make a line graph ideal to show the curves, shifts, or trends in data. As the information varies, the line changes to show dips and surges. If the information does not change, the line remains steady. Remember to use the guidelines for reading graphs on pages 727–728, and pay special attention to the labels on the vertical and horizontal axes.

Textbook
Skills

EXAMPLE Study the following line graph, from the college textbook *Government in America: People, Politics, and Policy,* 5th ed. (Edwards et al., p. 341). Based on the data in the graph, mark each numbered statement **T** if it is true, **F** if it is false, or **DK** if you don't know, based on the given data.

Growth in Government Employees

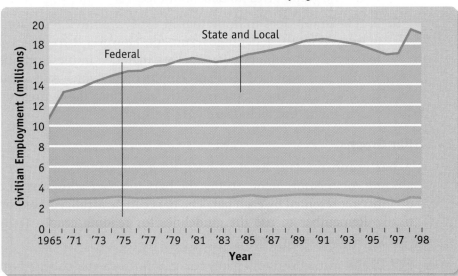

Note: The figures for federal employment do not include military personnel.

Original source: *Budget of the United States Government, Fiscal Year 2000: Historical Tables* (Washington, DC: U.S. Government Printing Office, 1999), Table 17-5.

_____ **1.** The horizontal axis plots the timeline of employment in ten-year periods.

_____ **2.** The vertical axis plots the number of civilian employees in millions.

_____ **3.** The number of people employed by state and local government nearly doubled from 1965 to 1998.

_____ **4.** Many state and local employees and programs are supported by the federal government through grants.

_____ **5.** In 1965, around 2.5 million people, including the military, were employed by the federal government.

EXPLANATION   Compare your answers to the ones given here.

1. F: The horizontal axis plots the timeline of employment in two-year periods, except at the first and last years given.

2. T: The vertical axis does plot the number of civilian employees in millions. The numbers are marked off in groups of 2 million.

3. T: The number of people employed by state and local government nearly doubled from 1965 to 1998. In 1965, a little over 10 million people were employed by state and local government. By 1998, that number had grown to nearly 20 million.

4. DK: The graph gives no data about federal grant programs.

5. F: The graph does indicate that in 1965, around 2.5 million people were employed by the federal government. However, two places on the graph tell us that no military personnel are included in these numbers. First, the vertical axis is labeled "civilian" employment, which excludes military, and the note below the graph explicitly states that "the figures for federal employment do not include military personnel."

Bar Graphs

A **bar graph** presents a set of bars. Each bar stands for a specific quantity, amount, or measurement. Seeing the bars together allows us to compare the quantity represented by each bar. The bars can be arranged horizontally or vertically. Remember to use the guidelines for reading graphs (pages 727–728) when you read bar graphs.

Textbook
Skills

EXAMPLE   Study the following bar graph, from the college health textbook *Total Fitness and Wellness*, 3rd ed. (Powers & Dodd, p. 200). Based on the data in the graph, mark each numbered statement **T** if it is true, **F** if it is false, or **DK** if you don't know, based on the given data.

Fat Loss from Different Areas of the Body in Women

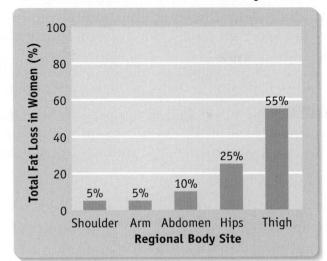

Note: Data based on study of obese women who completed a 14-week weight loss program that resulted in each participant losing approximately 20 pounds of fat.

Source: Data from King & Katch, Changes in Body Density, Fatfolds, and Girths at 2.3 kg Increments of Weight Loss *Human Biology 58*:709, 1986.

_____ **1.** The horizontal axis measures the fat loss in specific regions of the body.

_____ **2.** The vertical axis measures fat loss by percentages.

_____ **3.** Four regions of the body were measured for fat loss in this study.

_____ **4.** Each woman in the study lost approximately 20 percent of her body fat.

_____ **5.** The highest percentage of fat loss for women occurred in the thighs.

EXPLANATION

1. T: The horizontal axis measures the fat loss in specific regions of the body. The graph labels this axis "Regional Body Site."

2. T: The vertical axis measures fat loss by percentages. The numbers are marked off in 20 percent intervals.

3. F: Five regions of the body were measured for fat loss in this study: shoulder, arm, abdomen, hips, and thigh.

4. F: Each woman in the study lost approximately 20 pounds, not 20 percent of her body fat. This information is stated in the note below the graph.

5. T: The highest percentage of fat loss for women occurred in the thighs.

Pie Charts

Also known as a circle graph, a **pie chart** shows a whole group as a circle and divides the circle into smaller units that look like slices of a pie. Each smaller slice is a part, percentage, or fraction of the whole. Pie graphs are used to show proportions and the importance of each smaller unit in relation to the whole.

Textbook
Skills

EXAMPLE Study the following pie graph, from the college sociology textbook *Marriages and Families: Changes, Choices, and Constraints,* 4th ed. (Benokraitis, p. 195). Based on the data in the graph, mark each numbered statement **T** if it is true, **F** if it is false, or **DK** if you don't know, based on the given data.

Why We Marry

Fear of AIDS 2%   Dependence 3%
Money 5%
Habit or Convenience 5%
Love 36%
Happiness 9%
Desire for Children 12%
Companionship 14%

Source: Benokraitis, *Marriages and Families: Changes, Choices and Constraints,* "Why We Marry" p. 195, © 2002 Pearson Education, Inc. Reproduced by permission of Pearson Education, Inc. (Source: Patterson/Kim, The Day America Told the Truth © 1991 Prentice Hall Trade.)

_____ **1.** The pie chart is divided into eight parts.

_____ **2.** Fear of AIDS is a major reason for marrying.

_____ **3.** People marry for companionship as often as they marry for love.

_____ **4.** Over a third of the people in this sample said they married for love.

_____ **5.** The people in this sample said that an unplanned pregnancy is one of the reasons they married.

EXPLANATION Compare your answers to the ones given here.

1. T: The pie chart is divided into the following eight parts: love, companionship, desire for children, happiness, habit or convenience, money, dependence, and fear of AIDS.

2. F: At 2 percent, fear of AIDS does not rank as a major reason. The slice of the pie that represents fear of AIDS is the smallest section.

3. F: People do not marry for companionship as often as they marry for love. More than twice as many marry for love than for companionship.

4. T: Some 36 percent of the people in this sample said they married for love.

5. F: Unplanned pregnancies are not addressed in this pie chart.

PRACTICE 2

Textbook
Skills

A. Study the following graphic, from the college textbook, *The Interpersonal Communication Book*. Based on the data in the graph, mark each numbered statement **T** if it is true, **F** if it is false, or **DK** if you don't know, based on the given data.

Excuses in Romantic and Workplace Relationships

Here are the five intended messages along with some specific examples. As you read this table visualize a specific situation in which you recently made an excuse. Can what you said (or should have said) be organized into this five-step plan?

Intended Message	In Romantic Relationships	At Work
1. I see.	I should have asked you first; you have a right to be angry.	I understand that we lost the client because of this.
2. I did it.	I was totally responsible.	I should have acted differently.
3. I'm sorry.	I'm sorry that I didn't ask you first.	I'm sorry I didn't familiarize myself with the client's objections to our last offer.
4. Forgive me.	Forgive me?	I'd really like another chance.
5. I'll do better.	I'll never loan anyone money without first discussing it with you.	This will never happen again.

—DeVito, *Interpersonal Communication Book*, p. 230 © 2009 by Pearson Education, Inc. Reproduced by permission of Pearson Education, Inc.

_____ **1.** The graphic is a bar graph.

_____ **2.** The graphic presents a five-step process involved in making an excuse in a romantic relationship or at the workplace.

_____ **3.** Bad excuse makers rely on excuses too often.

_____ **4.** A good excuse takes responsibility for wrongdoing.

_____ **5.** The intended message of step 5 suggests that a good excuse is based on changing one's behavior.

B. Study the following graph, from the college sociology textbook. Based on the data in the graph, mark each numbered statement **T** if it is true, **F** if it is false, or **DK** if you don't know, based on the given data.

Textbook
Skills

Projections of Racial-Ethnic Makeup of the U.S. Population

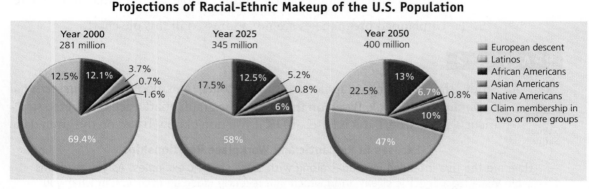

Sources: Henslin, *Sociology: A Down to Earth Approach,* Figure © 2008 James M. Henslin. Reproduced by permission of Pearson Education, Inc. Based on Bernstein and Bergman 2003; *Statistical Abstract* 2004:Table 16; 2005:Table 16. The projections I modified are the projections based on the new census category of membership in two or more groups and trends in interethnic marriage.

_____ **6.** This graph depicts ideas that are fact and opinion.

_____ **7.** Overall, the largest racial-ethnic population is of European descent.

_____ **8.** The population expected to grow the most in percentage are the African Americans.

_____ **9.** The racial-ethnic makeup of the U.S. population is expected to change.

_____ **10.** The percentage of Native Americans in 2050 is expected to have decreased from the percentage of Native Americans in 2000.

Diagrams

A **diagram** is a graphic that explains in detail the relationships between the parts of an idea to the whole idea. Diagrams include flowcharts, pictograms, and drawings.

Flowcharts

A **flowchart** is a diagram that shows a step-by-step process. Each step or phase of the process is typically shown in a box or circle, and the shapes are connected with lines and arrows to show the proper order or flow of the steps. Flowcharts are used in a number of subject areas including social sciences, science, history, and English.

Textbook Skills

EXAMPLE Study the following flowchart, from the college textbook *Psychology: The Brain, the Person, the World*. Based on the data in the diagram, mark each numbered statement **T** if it is true, **F** if it is false, or **DK** if you don't know, based on the given information.

Stages of Creative Thought

The four stages of creative thought proposed by Wallas (1926).

| **Preparation** The problem is understood and consciously thought through. | → | **Incubation** The unconscious works on the problem. | → | **Illumination** The solution filters up to consciousness. | → | **Verification** The solution is checked. |

Note: Creativity is defined as the ability to produce something original of high quality or to devise effective new ways of solving a problem.

Source: Kosslyn/Rosenberg, *Psychology: The Brain, the Person, the World*, "Stages of Creative Thought," © 2001 Allyn and Bacon. Reproduced by permission of Pearson Education, Inc.

_____ **1.** The flowchart illustrates four stages of creative thought.

_____ **2.** Creativity focuses only on the ability to produce something original.

_____ **3.** The creative process takes place mainly on a conscious level of thought.

_____ **4.** Incubation occurs before illumination.

_____ **5.** Creativity is a learned behavior.

EXPLANATION Compare your answers to the ones given here.

1. T: The flowchart illustrates four stages of creative thought.

2. F: Creativity does focus on the ability to produce something original. However, the definition in the footnote also states that creativity devises effective ways of solving a problem. Thus creativity includes both the ability to create a poem or painting and the practical ability to raise funds.

3. F: The flowchart explicitly states that during incubation, the creative process takes place mainly on an unconscious level of thought and filters into consciousness during the third stage, illumination.

4. T: According to this flowchart, incubation occurs before illumination.

5. DK: The flowchart reveals the creative process, but it does not address the question of whether or not creativity is a learned behavior.

Pictograms

A **pictogram** is a diagram that uses pictorial forms to represent data. Usually statistics are used in pictograms.

EXAMPLE Study the pictogram, from the website of the U.S. Department of the Interior, U.S. Geological Survey that depicts the devastating sequence of the eruption of Mount St. Helens. Based on the data in the pictogram, mark each numbered statement **T** if it is true, **F** it is false, or **DK** if you don't know based on the given information.

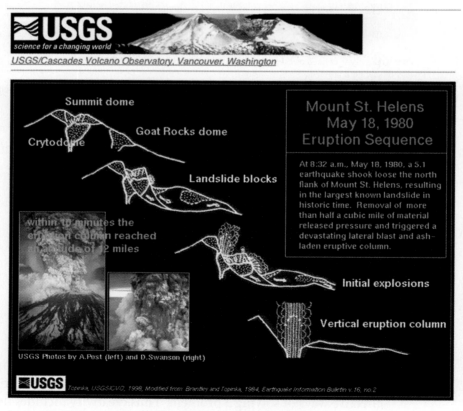

Source: http://vulcan.wr.usgs.gov/Photo/Pictograms/May18_sequence.html

_____ **1.** An earthquake caused the 1980 eruption of Mount St. Helens.

_____ **2.** The earthquake caused a landslide that released trapped pressure within Mount St. Helens.

_____ **3.** Within ten minutes Mount St. Helens was leveled to its base.

_____ **4.** A thick column of ash quickly rose to a height of twelve miles.

_____ **5.** Mount St. Helens will erupt again.

EXPLANATION

1. T: The caption beneath the pictogram's title states this fact.

2. T: The same caption states "removal of more than a cubic mile of material released pressure and triggered a devastating lateral blast." We can logically infer that the earthquake caused this removal of material.

3. F: Within ten minutes a column of tall ash developed. The pictogram clearly depicts that part of Mount St. Helens remains standing.

4. T: The pictogram clearly states that the column of ash rose to twelve miles.

5. DK: Though logic implies that Mount St. Helens will erupt again, this pictogram offers no evidence that it will do so. The purpose of this pictogram is to depict an historical event.

Drawing

A **drawing** is an artist's illustration of a process or idea. The drawing shows the relationships among all the details in the picture. Often these drawings are dependent on the accompanying text, and an effective reader must move back and forth between the drawing and text for full understanding.

EXAMPLE Study the following drawing, from the college textbook *Exercise Physiology*. Based on the data in the diagram, mark each numbered statement T if it is true, **F** if it is false, or **DK** if you don't know, based on the given information.

Textbook
Skills

_____ **1.** During an isometric exercise, the muscle does not lengthen or shorten.

_____ **2.** A concentric contraction shortens the muscle.

_____ **3.** During an eccentric contraction, the muscle does not move.

_____ **4.** Eccentric contractions occur when movement is in the same direction as gravity.

_____ **5.** During an isometric contraction, the joint does not move.

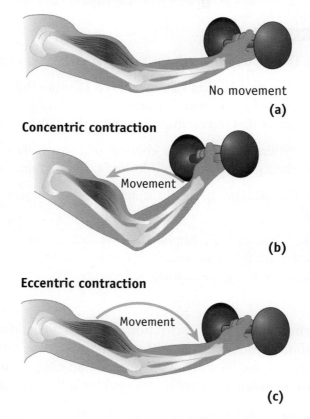

Isometric, Concentric, and Eccentric Muscle Actions
Isometric contraction
Muscle contracts but does not shorten

No movement
(a)

Concentric contraction

Movement

(b)

Eccentric contraction

Movement

(c)

Source: Powers, S., and E. Howley, *Exercise Physiology*. Copyright © 1997.
Published by Brown and Benchmark, Madison, WI. Reprinted by permission. The
McGraw-Hill Companies.

EXPLANATION

1. T: During an isometric exercise, the muscle does not lengthen or shorten.

2. T: A concentric contraction shortens the muscle.

3. F: During an eccentric contraction, the muscle lengthens.

4. T: Eccentric contractions occur when movement is in the same direction as gravity. The arrow points in a downward arc, representing downward motion, which is the same direction as gravity.

5. T: During an isometric contraction, the joint does not move.

PRACTICE 3

Based on the ideas in the following graphic, from the college textbook *Total Fitness and Wellness,* mark each numbered statement **T** if it is true, **F** if it is false, or **DK** if you don't know, based on the given information.

The Steps of the Cryokinetics Procedure for Rehabilitating Injuries

Cryokinetics is a fairly new rehabilitation technique that is applied after healing has been completed. It uses alternating periods of treatment using ice, exercise, and rest known as RICE, which stands for rest, ice, compression, elevation.

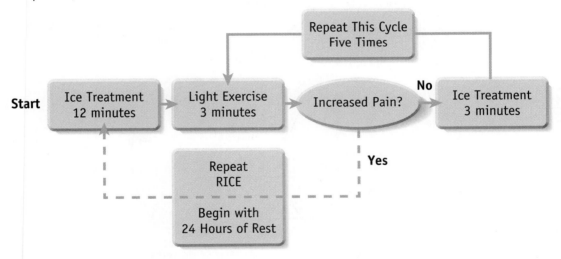

Source: Reprinted from Fig. 13.8, Scott K. Powers, *Total Fitness and Wellness,* 3rd ed., pp. 295, 296.

Textbook
Skills

_____ **1.** A synonym for *rehabilitation* is *treatment.*

_____ **2.** Exercise of the injured area during this treatment must be guided by the pain associated with its use.

_____ **3.** During a cryokinetics procedure, the injured area should be exercised for a total of 15 minutes if no pain occurs.

_____ **4.** RICE stands for the elements of a proper technique to promote healing.

_____ **5.** Ice is used during the procedure to reduce pain.

REVIEW TEST 1

A. Study the following graphic from the college textbook *Biology: Life on Earth*. Then mark each numbered statement **T** if it is true, **F** if it is false, or **DK** if you don't know, based on the given information.

Textbook
Skills

Seeds from (a) a gymnosperm and (b) an angiosperm. Both consist of an embryonic plant and stored food confined within a seed coat. Seeds exhibit diverse adaptations for dispersal, including the dandelion's tiny, tufted seeds that float in the air and the massive, armored seeds (protected inside the fruit) of the coconut palm, which can survive prolonged immersion in seawater as they traverse oceans.

QUESTION Can you think of some adaptations that help protect seeds from destruction by animal consumption?

—Adapted from Audesirk, Audesirk, & Byers.
Biology: Life on Earth, 8th ed., p. 413.

Seeds

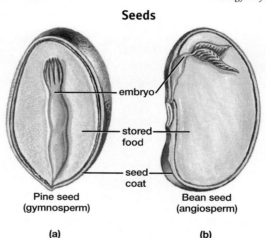

—Adapted from Audesirk, Audesirk, & Byers, *Biology: Life on Earth*, 8th ed., p. 413.

_____ **1.** The graphic is a pictogram.

_____ **2.** This graphic depicts two different types of seeds.

_____ **3.** This graphic depicts dandelion seeds that float in the air.

_____ **4.** Although both seeds have embryos, the embryos differ in size and shape.

_____ **5.** This graphic gives information about adaptations that protect seeds.

B. Based on the ideas in the following graphic from *Psychology and Life*, mark each numbered statement **T** if it is true, **F** if it is false, or **DK** if you don't know, based on the given information.

Textbook
Skills

Unstable

moody   touchy
anxious   restless
rigid   aggressive
sober   excitable
pessimistic   changeable
reserved   impulsive
unsociable   optimistic
quiet   Melancholic   Choleric   active

Introverted   **Extraverted**

passive   Phlegmatic   Sanguine   sociable
careful   outgoing
thoughtful   talkative
peaceful   responsive
controlled   easygoing
reliable   lively
even-tempered   carefree
calm   leadership

Stable

Source: Gerrig/Zimbardo, *Psychology and Life,* Figure © 2002. Reproduced by permission of Pearson Education, Inc.

_____   **6.** This graphic is a bar graph.

_____   **7.** The ideas in this graphic have been scientifically verified.

_____   **8.** A choleric personality type is restless and aggressive.

_____   **9.** A person with a choleric personality type is a less moral person than a person with a phlegmatic personality.

_____   **10.** Melancholic and phlegmatic types are withdrawn.

REVIEW TEST 2

A. Based on the ideas in the following graphic from the college textbook *Messages: Building Interpersonal Communication Skills,* 4th ed. (DeVito, p. 27), mark each numbered statement **T** if it is true, **F** if it is false, or **DK** if you don't know, based on the given information.

Textbook
Skills

Why You Engage in Interpersonal Communication

This figure illustrates three aspects of interpersonal communication: your purpose, your motivations, and the results you want to achieve. The innermost circle contains the general purposes, the middle circle the motivations, and the outer circle the results you might hope to achieve by engaging in interpersonal communication.

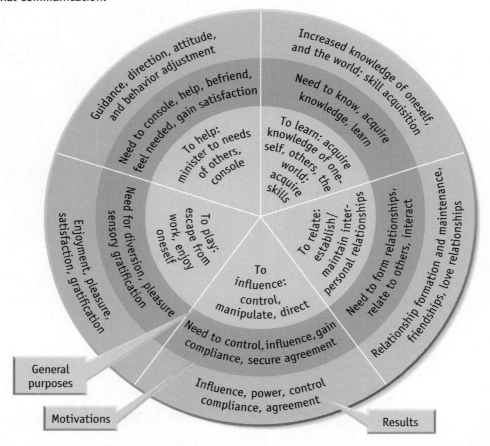

Source: DeVito, *Messages: Building Interpersonal Communication Skills,* Figure © 2004. Reproduced by permission of Pearson Education, Inc.

_____ **1.** This graphic is a flowchart.

_____ **2.** The figure illustrates five purposes for engaging in interpersonal communication.

_____ **3.** The general purpose "to influence" is motivated by the need to secure agreement and results in friendship.

_____ **4.** An attitude and behavior adjustment is the result of the need to minister to the needs of others.

_____ **5.** A person who determines to escape from work is often motivated by stress.

B. Based on the ideas in the following graphic, from the college textbook *Criminal Justice Today, 10th ed.* (Schmallege p. 601), mark each numbered statement **T** if it is true, **F** if it is false, or **DK** if you don't know, based on the given information.

Textbook
Skills

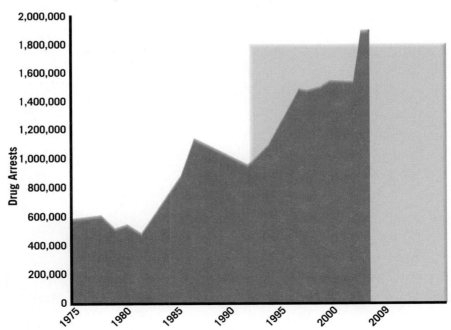

Drug Arrests in the United States, 1975–2006

Source: *Federal Bureau of Investigation, Crime in United States, various years.*

_____ **6.** The graphic is a line graph.

_____ **7.** The source of this information is reliable.

_____ **8.** Between the years 1980 and 1985, drug arrests increased very little.

_____ **9.** Between the years 1975 and 2006, drug arrests increased from almost 600,000 to over 2,000,000.

_____ **10.** Drug arrests are decreasing over time.

Text Credits

Adminstration on Aging. "Older Volunteers Leading the Way." U.S. Department of Health and Human Services, 2003.

Agee, et al. *Introduction to Mass Communications*. © 1997. Reproduced by permission of Pearson Education, Inc.

Asfahani, Magdoline. "Time to Look and Listen" from *Newsweek*, Dec. 2, 1996. All rights reserved. Reprinted by permission.

Audesirk, Teresa, Gerald Audesirk, and Bruce E. Byers. *Life on Earth*, 5th ed. © 2009. Printed and electronically reproduced by permission of Pearson Education, Inc., Upper Saddle River, New Jersey.

Barker, Larry L., and Deborah Roach Gaut. *Communication*, 8th ed. Copyright © 2002, 1996, 1993, 1990, 1987, 1984, 1981, 1978 by Pearson Education.

Benokraitis, Nijoke. *Marriages and Families: Changes, Choices and Constraints*. © 2002 Pearson Education, Inc. Reproduced by permission of Pearson Education, Inc.

Bergman, Edward, and William H. Renwick. *Introduction to Geography: People, Places and Environment*, 4th ed. © 2008. Printed and electronically reproduced by permission of Pearson Education, Inc., Upper Saddle River, New Jersey.

Berman, Audrey J., Shirlee Snyder, Barbara J. Kozier, and Glenora Erb. *Kozier and Erb's Fundamentals of Nursing*, 8th ed. © 2008. Printed and Electronically reproduced by permission of Pearson Education, Inc., Upper Saddle River, New Jersey.

Bittinger, Marvin L., and Judith A. Beecher, *Introductory and Intermediate Algebra: Combined Approach*, Text Excerpts from pp. 143, 12, 13, 143, 127, 805, 210, 387 and Figure p. 210 © 2003 Pearson Education, Inc. Reproduced by permission of Pearson Education, Inc.

Boen, Jennifer. "On-Q System a New Method of Pain Relief." *The News-Sentinel*, 24 April 2009.

Brownell, *Listening: Attitudes, Principles, and Skills*, pp. 88, 117–118, 150, 284 © 2002 by Pearson Education, Inc. Reproduced by permission of Pearson Education, Inc.

Bytwerk, Randall. "How They Lie: Must the Politician Lie?" © 2000 by Randall Bytwerk.

Carlson, Neil, and William Buskist. *Psychology: Science of Behavior*, Text Excerpts from pp. 449, 217, 191, 190, 189, and 460–461 © 1997. Reproduced by permission of Pearson Education, Inc.

CHADD. "At Risk with AD/HD" from What We Know Sheet #1. CHADD: Children and Adults with Attention-Deficit/ Hyperactivity Disorder, copyright 2004. http://www.help4 adhd.org. Reproduced with permission.

Ciccarelli, Saundra, and J. Noland White. *Psychology: Exploration*, "Learning Styles: Different Strokes for Different Folks" pp. 1–2 © 2010 Pearson Education, Inc. Reproduced by permission of Pearson Education, Inc.

Deckers, Lambert. *Motivation: Biological, Psychological, and Environmental*. Published by Allyn and Bacon, Boston, MA. Copyright © 2001 by Pearson Education.

Deutsch, Nancy. "A Slave to Routine? from *HealthDay News*. Copyright © 2002. Reprinted by permission of HealthDay.

DeVito, Joseph A. *Essentials of Human Communication*. © 2002. Reproduced by permission of Pearson Education, Inc.

DeVito, Joseph A. *Interpersonal Communication Book*. © 2009 by Pearson Education, Inc. Reproduced by permission of Pearson Education, Inc.

DeVito, Joseph A. *Messages: Building Interpersonal Communication Skills*. © 2004. Reproduced by permission of Pearson Education, Inc.

Divine, Robert A., T. H. H. Breen, George M. Frederickson, and R. Hal Williams. *The American Story*. © 2002. Printed and Electronically reproduced by permission of Pearson Education, Inc., Upper Saddle River, New Jersey.

DiYanni, Robert, and Pat C. Hoy II. *The Scribner Handbook for Writers*, 3rd ed. Copyright © 2001, 1998, 1995 by Allyn and Bacon. Reprinted by permission of Pearson Education, Inc.

Doctorow, Cory. *You Do Like Reading Off a Computer Screen* from LOCUS Magazine, March 2007, copyright © 2007. Reprinted by permission of the author and the author's agents, Scovil Galen Ghosh Literary Agency, Inc.

Donatelle, Rebecca J. *Health: The Basics*, 5th ed. © 2003. Printed and Electronically reproduced by permission of Pearson Education, Inc., Upper Saddle River, New Jersey.

Donatelle, Rebecca J., and Lorraine G. Davis. *Access to Health*, 7th ed. © 2002. Printed and Electronically reproduced by permission of Pearson Education, Inc., Upper Saddle River, New Jersey.

Dye, Thomas R. *Politics in America*, 5th ed. Copyright © 2003, 2001, 1999, 1997, 1994 by Pearson Education, Inc.

Edwards, III, George C., Martin P. Wattenberg, and Robert L. Lineberry. *Government in America: People, Politics, and Policy*, Brief version, 5th ed. Copyright © 2000 by Addison-Wesley Educational Publishers Inc.

Fishbein, Diana H., and Susan E. Pease. *The Dynamics of Drug Abuse*. Published by Allyn and Bacon, Boston, MA. Copyright © 1996 by Allyn and Bacon.

Folkerts, Jean, and Stephen Lacy. *The Media in Your Life: An Introduction to Mass Communication*, 2nd ed. Published by Allyn and Bacon, Boston, MA. Copyright © 2001, 1998 by Pearson Education, Inc.

Fritz, Sara. "Curbing College Drinking Starts with a Change in Attitude," from *St. Petersburg Times*, April 15, 2002. Copyright © 2002 St. Petersburg Times. Reprinted by permission.

Galvin, Kathleen M., and Bernard J. Brommel. *Family Communication: Cohesion and Change*, 5th ed. Published by Allyn and Bacon, Boston, MA. Copyright © 2000 by Pearson Education, Inc.

Gamble, Teri Kwal, and Michael W. Gamble. *The Gender Communication Connection*. Boston: Houghton Mifflin. Copyright © 2002.

Garraty, John A., and Mark C. Carnes. *American Nation Single Volume Edition*, Text Excerpts from pp. 130, 170, 130, 38 and 378–379 © 2000 Pearson Education, Inc. Reproduced by permission of Pearson Education, Inc.

Gerrig, Richard, and Philip Zimbardo. *Psychology and Life*, Text Excerpts from pp. 343–344 and 37–38 © 2010 Pearson Education, Inc. Reproduced by permission of Pearson Education, Inc.

Gladwell, Malcolm. "Brain Candy" as appeared in *The New Yorker*, May 16, 2005, © 2005 by Malcolm Gladwell. Reprinted by permission.

Griffin, Ricky W., and Ronald J. Ebert. *Business*, 8th ed. © 2006. Printed and Electronically reproduced by permission of Pearson Education, Inc., Upper Saddle River, New Jersey.

751

Grunwald, Michael. "A Small Nation's Big Effort Against AIDS" from *The Washington Post* Foreign Service, Dec. 2, 2002. Copyright © 2002, The Washington Post. Reprinted with permission.

Harris, Thomas E., and John C. Sherblom. *Small Groups and Team Communication*, 2nd ed. Published by Allyn and Bacon.

Hiaasen, Carl. "Don't let Haiti's Tragedy Fade Away" in *Miami Herald*, January 24, 2010. Reprinted by permission of Miami Herald and the author.

"Is There Too Much Testing?" from *CQ Researcher*, June 15, 2001, Vol. II, No. 23. Reprinted with permission.

Jaffe, Michael L. *Understanding Parenting*, 2nd ed. Published by Allyn and Bacon, Boston, MA. Copyright © 1997 by Pearson Education, Inc.

Kafka, Franz. *Metamorphosis*. New York, NY: Random House, 1946.

Kelley Blue Book. Excerpt from Reviews Luxury Sedans Lexus LS 430 in Kelley Blue Book's kbb.com, Feb. 2, 2003. Reprinted with permission.

Kelly, Marilyn. *Communication @ Work*. Published by Allyn and Bacon, Boston, MA. Copyright © 2006 by Pearson Education, Inc.

Kennedy, X. J., and Dana Gioia. *Literature: An Introduction to Fiction, Poetry, and Drama*, 8th ed., Interactive Edition. Copyright © 2002 by X. J. Kennedy and Dana Gioia. Reprinted by permission of Pearson Education, Inc.

Kennedy, X. J., and Dana Gioia. *Literature: An Introduction to Fiction, Poetry, and Drama*, 8th ed., Compact Edition. Copyright © 2003 by X. J. Kennedy and Dana Gioia.

King, Jr., Martin Luther. "The Quest for Peace and Justice" in Nobel Lecture, December 11, 1964. Reprinted with permission.

Kosslyn, Stephen. *Psychology: The Brain, the Person, the World*. Text Excerpts from pp. 52, 228–229, 206, 236, 173, 378 and 138 © 2001 Allyn and Bacon. Reproduced by permission of Pearson Education, Inc.

Levack, Brian, Edward Muir, Meredith Veldman, and Michael Maas. *West: The Encounters and Transformations, Atlas Edition, Combined Volume*, 2nd ed. © 2008. Printed and Electronically reproduced by permission of Pearson Education, Inc., Upper Saddle River, New Jersey.

Levinthal, Charles F. *Drugs, Behavior, and Modern Society*, 3rd ed. Published by Allyn and Bacon, Boston, MA. Copyright © 2002 by Pearson Education.

"Low Ground Waters Can Lead to Sinkholes" from *Streamlines*, Fall 2000. Used by permission of the St. Johns River Water Management District, State of Florida.

Lubar, Steven, and Kathleen Kendrick. "The Value of Artifacts" adapted from *Looking at Artifacts, Thinking about History* from Smithsonian Center for Education and Museum Studies. http://educate.si.edu/ap/essays/looking.htm. Reprinted with permission.

Lundestad, Geir. "The Nobel Peace Prize 1901–2000" from *The Nobel Prize, the First 100 Years* (eds. A. Wallin Levinovitz and N. Ringertz). Published by Imperial College Press and World Scientific Publishing. Reprinted by permission of the publisher.

Lutgens, Frederick K., Edward J. Tarbuck, and Dennis Tasa. *Foundations of Earth Science*, 5th ed. © 2008. Printed and Electronically reproduced by permission of Pearson Education, Inc., Upper Saddle River, New Jersey.

Madura, Jeff. *Personal Finance Update*, Text Excerpts from pp. 186–187, 160, 196, 40, 235 and Figure p. 187 © 2006 Pearson Education Inc. Reproduced by permission of Pearson Education.

Maier, Richard. *Comparative Animal Behavior: An Evolutionary and Ecological Approach*. Published by Allyn and Bacon, Boston, MA. Copyright © 1998 by Pearson Education.

Marieb, Elaine. *Essentials of Human Anatomy and Physiology*, 9th ed. © 2009 by Pearson Education, Inc. Reprinted by Pearson Education, Inc.

Martin, James Kirby, Randy J. Roberts, Steven Mintz, Linda O. McMurry, and James H. Jones. *America and Its People: Volume II: A Mosaic in the Making*, 3rd ed. © 1999. Printed and Electronically reproduced by permission of Pearson Education, Inc., Upper Saddle River, New Jersey.

McCafferty, Dennis. "How Long Will You Live?" Originally appeared in the March 2, 2007 issue of USA WEEKEND. Reprinted by permission.

McGuigan, F.J. *Encyclopedia of Stress*. ©1999. Printed and Electronically reproduced by permission of Pearson Education, Inc., Upper Saddle River, New Jersey.

Menard, Valerie, and Cheech Marin. *The Latino Holiday Book*. Copyright © 2004 Valerie Menard, Cheech Marin. Reprinted by permission of Da Capo Press, a member of the Perseus Group.

Nie, Norman, "What Do Users Do on the Internet?" from *The Internet Study*, Stanford Institute for the Quantitative Study of Society. Stanford University, CA. Reprinted by permission.

O'Connor, Karen, and Larry J. Sabato. *American Government: Continuity and Change*. Copyright © 2000 by Pearson Education, Inc.

Obama, Barak. "A Just and Lasting Peace" in Nobel Lecture, December 20, 2009. Reprinted with permission.

Parkay, Forrest W., and Beverly H. Stanford. *Becoming a Teacher*, p. 300 © 1995 by Pearson Education, Inc. Reproduced by permission of Pearson Education, Inc.

Plutchik, Robert, *Emotion* © 1980. Reprinted by permission.

Powers, Scott K., and Stephen L. Dodd. *Total Fitness and Wellness Student Textbook Component*, 3rd ed. © 2003. Printed and Electronically reproduced by permission of Pearson Education, Inc., Upper Saddle River, New Jersey.

Powers, S., and E. Howley. *Exercise Physiology*. Copyright © 1997. Published by Brown and Benchmark, Madison, WI. Reprinted by permission of The McGraw-Hill Companies, Inc.

Pruitt, B. E., and Jane J. Stein. *Healthstyles: Decisions for Living Well*, 2nd ed. © 1999. Printed and Electronically reproduced by permission of Pearson Education, Inc., Upper Saddle River, New Jersey.

Quindlen, Anna. "Follow the Leader." Reprinted by permission of Creative Management, Inc. Copyright © 2010.

The Ratings Are Your Friend brochure. Filmratings.com. The Classification and Ratings Administration/MPAA. Reproduced with permission.

Research in Higher Education, Vol. 25, Number 4. Copyright © 1986 Agathon Press, Inc. Reprinted with kind permission of Springer Science and Business Media.

Roesch, Roberta. "How to Take a Bite Out of Criticism" as appeared in *Relationships Today*, August 1988. Copyright © 1988 by Roberta Roesch. Reprinted by permission of the author.

Sanabria, Harry. *The Anthropology of Latin America and the Caribbean*, 4th ed. Published by Allyn and Bacon, Boston, MA. Copyright © 2007 by Pearson Education.

Sayre, Henry M. *Discovering the Humanities*. © 2010. Printed and Electronically reproduced by permission of Pearson Education, Inc., Upper Saddle River, New Jersey.

Schmalleger, Frank J. *Criminal Justice Today: An Introductory Text for the 21st Century*, 10th ed. © 2009. Printed and Electronically reproduced by permission of Pearson Education, Inc., Upper Saddle River, New Jersey.

Schwartz, Bob. "Some Are Semi-Sweet and Some Are Semi-Not" from *Somebody Please Send Me to My Room! A Hilarious Look at Family Life.* © 2005. Reprinted by permission of Glenbridge Publishing Ltd. in Centennial, Colorado.

"Should Cell Phones Be Banned in Cars?" from *CQ Researcher* Mar. 16, 2001, Vol. II, No. 10. Reprinted with permission.

Smith, Robert L., and Thomas M. Smith. *Elements of Ecology*, 4th ed. Copyright © 2000 by Addison Wesley Longman, Inc., publishing under the Benjamin Cummings imprint.

Sullivan, Bob. "ID Theft Victims Get Little Help" from MSNBC, on-line, Feb. 10, 2003. http://www.msnbc.com. Reproduced with permission of MSNBC Interactive, L.L.C.

Tannen, Deborah. "Different Words, Different Worlds" in *You Just Don't Understand: Women and Men in Conversation.* New York: Morrow, 1990, p. 23. Reproduced with permission.

Thomas, Jennifer, "Chronic Media Multi-Tasking Makes It Harder to Focus," Aug. 24, 2009 *Healthfinder.* Reprinted by permission of HealthDay.

Van Syckle, Barbara, and Brian Tietje. *Anybody's Business.* © 2010. Printed and Electronically reproduced by permission of Pearson Education, Inc., Upper Saddle River, New Jersey.

Walker, John R. *Introduction to Hospitality Management*, 2nd ed. © 2007. Printed and Electronically reproduced by permission of Pearson Education, Inc., Upper Saddle River, New Jersey.

Wilen, William, Richard Kindsvatter, and Margaret Ishler. *Dynamics of Effective Teaching*, 4th ed. Published by Allyn and Bacon, Boston, MA. Copyright © 2000 by Pearson Education.

Withgott, Jay H., and Scott R. Brennan. *Essential Environment: The Science Behind the Stories*, 3rd ed. © 2009. Printed and Electronically reproduced by permission of Pearson Education, Inc., Upper Saddle River, New Jersey.

Wollstadt, Loyd, MD. "Research Shows Potential Benefits, Risks of Wine" from *To Your Health*, May 6, 2003, University of Illinois College of Medicine at Rockford. Reprinted by permission of the author.

Wong, Jade Snow. *Fifth Chinese Daughter*, copyright © 1945, 1948, 1950, 1965, and 1989 by Jade Snow Wong. Originally published by Harper and Brothers. Reprinted by permission of Curtis Brown, Ltd.

Wood, et al., *Mastering the World of Psychology*, Text from pp. 39–40, 42, 78, 289 and 275 © 2008 Pearson Education, Inc. Reproduced by permission of Pearson Education, Inc.

Woolfolk, Anita. *Educational Psychology*, 8th ed. Published by Allyn and Bacon, Boston, MA. Copyright © 2001 by Pearson Education Inc.

Photo Credits

Index